In this book Valeriy Zamulin, the author of multiple Russian-language books on the Battle of Kursk including the award-winning *Destroying the Myth: The Tank Battle at Prokhorovka, Kursk, July 1943: An Operational Narrative* takes a fresh look at several controversial and neglected topics regarding the battle and its run-up.

He starts with a detailed look at the Soviet and Russian historiography on the battle, showing how initially promising research was swamped by Party dogma and censorship during the Brezhnev area, before being resumed with the collapse of the Soviet Union. Zamulin then transitions to discussions of how the southern shoulder of the Kursk bulge was formed, preparations for the battle on both sides, and the size and composition of Model's Ninth Army. He then examines such controversial topics as whether or not the II SS Panzer Corps was aware of the pending Soviet counterattack at Prokhorovka, and the effectiveness of the Soviet preemptive barrage that struck the German troops that were poised to attack. Zamulin also discusses whether or not General Vatutin, the Commander-in-Chief of Voronezh Front, erred when arranging his defenses. Zamulin also takes a look at how the myth of 1,500 tanks colliding on a narrow strip of farm fields became perpetuated in Soviet and foreign history books, when in fact it was impossible for the 5th Guards Tank Army's tanks to attack in massive wave after wave due to the constrictions of the terrain. Zamulin also reveals incidents of the battle that were long kept "behind the curtain" by Soviet censorship. For example, the 183rd Rifle Division defending the Prokhorovka axis was repeatedly struck by friendly aircraft, and a Soviet tank counterattack overran the positions of one of its battalions. Zamulin discusses other cases of fratricide in the Voronezh Front, including the death of one of the 1st Tank Army's foremost tank commanders in a friendly fire incident. In the process, he reveals that a wave of suicides swept through the junior command staff of the 5th Guards Tank Army immediately prior to the famous counteroffensive on 12 July 1943. All in all, with this collection of essays and articles, two of which have been reprinted from the *Journal of Slavic Military History*, Valeriy Zamulin makes a new contribution to our knowledge and understanding of this pivotal, epochal battle of the Second World War.

Valeriy Nikolaevich Zamulin, a PhD candidate, is a leading Russian scholar of the Battle of Kursk. Since 1996, he has been working intensively in the most important Russian and foreign archival institutes, including the Central Archive of Russia's Ministry of Defense and in the US National Archive, in order to gather and analyze documentary sources on the events in the Kursk bulge in the summer of 1943. In 2002, he was the first to describe the course of the famous Prokhorovka tank clash on a documentary basis, to publish previously unknown figures on the Red Army's armor losses in the tank battle of 12 July 1943, and to give his assessment of the results, which differed from that previously accepted in Russia. He is the author of more than 60 scholarly works, including six books, in both the Russian and English languages, which have attracted great interest among scholars and history buffs. His most well-known work is the award-winning *Demolishing the Myth: The Tank Battle at Prokhorovka, Kursk, July 1943: An Operational Narrative* (English edition published by Helion in 2011). The results of V.N. Zamulin's scholarly work are broadly used by military-historical authors, professors of state universities and Russia's military museums. Several documentary films and television programs have been made with his participation. In 2010-2011, he was the academic consultant during the creation of the new military history museum in the legendary village of Ponyri, which in the Battle of Kursk was the epicenter of the most savage and bloody fighting. At present, Zamulin is a member of the faculty of Kursk State University.

Stuart Britton is a freelance translator and editor residing in Cedar Rapids, Iowa. He has been responsible for making a growing number of Russian titles available to readers of the English language, consisting primarily of memoirs by Red Army veterans and recent historical research concerning the Eastern Front of the Second World War and Soviet air operations in the Korean War. Notable titles include *Boris Gorbachevsky's Through the Maelstrom: A Red Army Soldier's War on the Eastern Front 1942-45* (University Press of Kansas, 2008) and Yuri Sutiagin's and Igor Seidov's *MiG Menace Over Korea: The Story of Soviet Fighter Ace Nikolai Sutiagin* (Pen & Sword Aviation, 2009).

THE BATTLE OF KURSK

Controversial & Neglected Aspects

Valeriy Zamulin

Translated & edited by Stuart Britton

Helion & Company

Helion & Company Limited
Unit 8 Amherst Business Centre
Budbrooke Road
Warwick
CV34 5WE
England
Tel. 01926 499 619
Email: info@helion.co.uk
Website: www.helion.co.uk
Twitter: @helionbooks
Visit our blog http://blog.helion.co.uk/

Published by Helion & Company 2017. Reprinted in paperback 2022
Designed and typeset by Mach 3 Solutions Ltd (www.mach3solutions.co.uk)
Cover designed by Paul Hewitt, Battlefield Design (www.battlefield-design.co.uk)

Photographs in the book came from the following sources: the Russian State Archive of Film and Photo Documents (Krasnororsk, Russian Federation); the Central Archive of the Russian Federation Ministry of Defense (Podol'sk, Russian Federation); the Kursk Oblast Local History Museum (Kursk, Russian Federation); the Museum Diorama "Battle of Kursk. Belgorod direction" (Belgorod, Russian Federation); the US National Archives and Records Administration (Washington, D.C., United States of America); the FRG Bundesarchiv [Federal Military Archive] (Koblenz, Federal Republic of Germany); the Shebekino History and Art Museum (Shebekino, Russian Federation); private collections and the author's own personal collection.
Maps 2-8 drawn by and © Barbara Taylor 2011, maps 1 & 9 drawn by George Anderson © Helion & Company Limited 2017.

Part of the material included in the book was prepared within the framework of Academic Project No. 15-01-00150 with the support of the Russian Humanitarian Academic Foundation.

ISBN 978-1-915113-05-4

British Library Cataloguing-in-Publication Data.
A catalogue record for this book is available from the British Library.

Contents

List of Photographs

List of Maps

In Color Section

Tactical maps

Key to tactical maps

List of abbreviations and key to symbols used in maps.

German (blue) Symbols

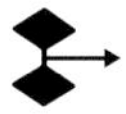 Panzer unit

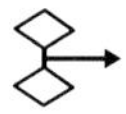 Panzergrenadier unit

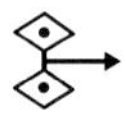 Self-propelled gun unit

 Artillery or anti-tank gun battery

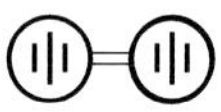 Anti-tank battalion or regiment

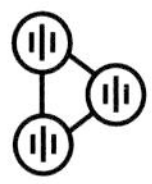 Three batteries, or an artillery battalion

 Werfer regiment

Abbreviation for map	Meaning
A	Army
AK	Army Corps
AR	Artillery Regiment
CO	combat outposts
GD	*Grossdeutschland*
ID	Infantry Division
KG	*Kampfgruppe*
PzD	Panzer Division
PzK	Panzer Corps
RBn	Reconnaissance Battalion
sPzAbt	Heavy Tank Battalion
SS DR	SS Panzergrenadier Division *Das Reich*
SSLAH	SS Panzergrenadier Division *LAH* (*Leibstandarte Adolf Hitler*)
SS PzGrR	SS Panzergrenadier Regiment
SS PzK	SS Panzer Corps
SS PzR	SS Panzer Regiment
SS TK	SS Panzergrenadier Division *Totenkopf*
WfrR	Werfer Regiment

Soviet (red) Symbols

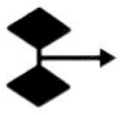 Tank unit

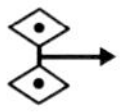 Self-propelled gun unit

 Artillery or anti-tank gun battery

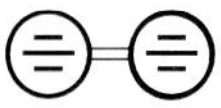 Anti-tank battalion or regiment

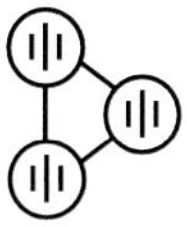 Three batteries, or an artillery battalion, normally of a rifle division's artillery regiment

 Mortar regiment

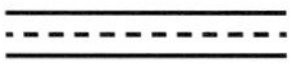 Anti-tank ditch

Abbreviation for map	Meaning
A	Army
ABn	Artillery Battalion
AC	Army Corps
AirAR	Airborne Artillery Regiment
AirD	Airborne Division
AirR	Airborne Regiment
AR	Artillery Regiment
ATBn	Destroyer Anti-tank Artillery Battalion (or simply Anti-tank Artillery Battalion)
ATR	Destroyer Anti-tank Artillery Regiment (or simply Anti-tank Artillery Regiment)
CO	combat outposts
CR	Composite Regiment
GAR	Gun Artillery Regiment
Gds	Guards
MB	Mechanized Brigade
MC	Mechanized Corps
MoRB	Motorized Rifle Brigade
MtrBn	Mortar Battalion
MtrR	Mortar Regiment
OG	Operational Group
OP	Observation Post
RD	Rifle Division
Rkt	Rocket Artillery
RR	Rifle Regiment
SATBn	Separate Destroyer Anti-Tank Artillery Battalion (or simply Separate Anti-tank Artillery Battalion)
SATB S	Separate Destroyer Anti-Tank Artillery Brigade (or simply Separate Anti-tank Artillery Brigade)
Bn	SeparateBattalion
SHAR	Separate Heavy Artillery Regiment
SMoB	Separate Motorized Brigade
SMtrB	Separate Mortar Brigade
SPCo	Separate Penal Company
STC	'Stalingrad' Tank Corps
STR	Separate Tank Regiment
TA	Tank Army
TB	Tank Brigade
TC	Tank Corps
TD	Tank Division
TR	Tank Regiment

List of Tables

Introduction

Over the past 70 years, three attempts have been made in our country to prepare a multi-volume academic work on the history of the Great Patriotic War and of the Second World War. In fact, unfortunately, they all ended in failure. The "Khrushchev" six-volume work[1] and the "Brezhnev" 12-volume work[2] from the outset didn't pretend to any objectivity or veracity. The world was in its "Cold War" phase and the events of the recent past played a noticeable role in it. The ideological bias was reinforced by the desire to note the special contribution made by leading members of the Soviet government to the attainment of victory in the Second World War. Thus it isn't surprising that even our leading military commanders, men who had to a certain degree formed the Soviet state and were themselves formed by it, recognized that the history presented in these multi-volume works was openly contrived, crudely re-worked to fit to the ideological mold, and far from the reality as it was.

The authors' collected work of the 12-volume *Velikaia Otechestvennaia voina 1941-1945* that recently came out also, in my view, unfortunately couldn't cope with that colossal task they had taken on when setting out to write it – at least with respect to the discussion of the events of the fundamental turning point in the war, the famous Battle of Kursk. There were two main reasons for this. First, there was no one to write it. The Soviet school of military historians, no matter how much we criticize it today for its dogmatism and myth-making, produced specialists with a rather high level of professional skill that rested upon their own life and combat experience (as a rule, at the front), which enabled them prepare rather good works on the history of large operations, battles, and military engagements even in the conditions of strict censorship and the deficit of sources, particularly documentary sources. By the early 1990s, the majority of the military officer-historians had retired from active work and together with them their unrealized plans and projects disappeared into oblivion. The generation of scholars that came up to replace this cohort has so far been unable to do so. There proved to be little demand for the practices and traditions of scholarly study in the "Time of Troubles" after the collapse of the Soviet Union, and they have virtually been lost by the start of the current century. Evidence of the woeful state of affairs in military history science is the books on this subject that are being published in our country today under the aegis of official military academic-research institutes, which with rare exception are wretched parodies of the work of the Soviet scholars.

Secondly, such major works of historical research are a compilation of many years of research by hundreds of scholars and academic groups. The past decades since the collapse of the Soviet Union, unfortunately, haven't even produced an academic environment for us, in which the genuine discussion of problems of history could take place, and ideas and projects might jell. Today, albeit very rarely, high-quality monographs are appearing on the shelves of bookstores, including ones written by military historians, and also individual articles in academic journals, which testify to the fact that deep academic research work is still going on along several directions of study of the Great Patriotic War in universities and independently by separate authors, including on problems of the history of the Battle of Kursk. However, in order to achieve high-quality results, these

1 *Istoriia Velikoi Otechestvennoi voiny Sovetskogo Soiuza 1941-1945*, in six volumes (Moscow: Voenizdat, 1960-1964).

2 *Istoriia Vtoroi mirovoi voiny 1939-1945*, in twelve volumes (Moscow: Voenizdat, 1973-1982).

scholars plainly lack "an independent review" – an interested discussion of the output of their work by a wide circle of professionals, well-intentioned advice, comradely assistance and the support of "brothers in trade". Academic conferences and seminars, as well as specialized periodicals, might have played a key role in resolving these problems, but so far one doesn't sense a positive influence from them. Each conference or seminar stands alone and goes its own way. Moreover, the editorial boards of some domestic academic journals that have adopted the mantle of "theoretical publications", consider the history of battles and clashes of the Great Patriotic War to be a second-rate subject, and decline to publish authors' exploratory studies, even while acknowledging their high academic standard of work. All this taken together, multiplied by the substantial decline in the general education and cultural level of the young generation, puts a brake on the development of the military history science, and diminishes the interest of graduate students and young scholars in this subject.

At the end of the 1990s I worked in the Prokhorovka Battlefield Park Museum, where I was lucky to have conversations and even be on friendly terms for a short while with several Soviet military "frontline-historians", who stood at the wellsprings of the history of the Battle of Kursk. Our contact, which unfortunately didn't last as long as I would have liked, turned out to be very substantive and useful. Thanks to their open, at times self-critical stories of the past, I was able not only to get a peek behind the curtain of the science of Soviet history of the 1940s to 1980s, but also became familiar with the "agenda in the smoking rooms", which is to say with the catalogue of topics, the analysis of which wasn't officially supported, but which were being actively discussed in academic circles, while some historians at their own risk and peril were even working on them independently ("for their own purposes"). The age of my conversation partners, as well as the oppressive situation in the country of those times, affected the contents of the subjects we discussed. Thus, the dialogue frequently was frequently carried through expressions like "the planned wasn't able to be realized" and "this needed to be done, had we had the ability". In such minutes, I involuntarily had the feeling that by sharing their own frustratons and unrealized plans, possibly reflexively they were handing me the baton of their work, and the main thing – responsibility for it. It is difficult to say whether these men, made wise by their experience, who'd given their whole life to their work, actually saw in this young museum staff member someone who was striving to learn about those terrible times and to carry on their work, or whether this was simply the fruit of my imagination. However, at the end of one of our last meetings, Colonel (ret.) Georgii Avtonomovich Koltunov, a leading Soviet specialist on the Battle of Kursk, when handing me part of his personal archive, told me:

> We, I and my comrades, have spent our entire lives "in the trenches". In the years of the Great Patriotic War – with a Mosin rifle in our hands, in the period of the Cold War – with a pen in our hands. I want to believe that you young Russian historians will be luckier. You will write the true history, without lies and braggadocio, of how our generation through colossal efforts and enormous blood broke the back of this ungodliness and saved everyone from extermination. May God grant you the strength and conscience to make this your own cause in life.

Even today I take his words not as a "baton" handed to me by a spokesperson of that heroic generation of our people, but first of all as an admonishment to work honestly, to get things right.

In your hands, reader, is a book by which I am striving to make my own modest contribution to changing the situation that has developed in our academic discipline of history. This is a collection of articles, in which I have attempted to answer some of the most actively discussed questions in domestic historiography about the history of the Battle of Kursk on the basis of recently de-classified documents of Russian archives, as well as captured German sources stored in the US National Archives. In addition, in the book I also touch upon a number of questions that have never officially been taken up by Soviet historians, even though they've long been actively discussed in veterans' circles and privately by scholars. The aim of this work is to share the results of my research over the past several years with specialists in the field of military history and all those who have an interest in the Great Patriotic War, and thereby give a nudge to the interest, first of all of young people, in the events at the Bulge of Fire [Ed. Note: another common Russian name given to the Kursk bulge and the fighting that took place around it] and to stimulate the discussion of little-known aspects of its history.

All of the articles are arranged in the chronological order of the described events, and according to their contents, they can tentatively be divided into two groups. The first, a review group, has been called upon to introduce the reader to the Battle of Kursk, which is to say, to review briefly the evolution of the literature on the battle in our country over the past 70 years and to give a general impression, based on new material, of separate large battles subsumed under the Battle of Kursk. I want to emphasize that one of the articles, "The Kastornoe Cauldron: The beginning of the process of forming the Kursk bulge" was prepared together with my son Viktor Zamulin, who is making his initital steps in the study of the events at Kursk. It was first published in one of the Russian academic journals and received a positive assessment by specialists.[3] The version included in this book has been substantially improved and expanded by us. I hope that it will be taken kindly by readers of this book. The second group of articles is dedicated not so much to major questions, but to something no less interesting: mainly controversial questions that have prompted lively debates to the present day. The book consists of these two types of articles.

As in my previous publications, together with traditional methods of research, when writing this collection of articles I used a comparative analysis of two bases of documents, kept in the TsAMO RF [Russian Federation Ministry of Defense's Central Archives] and the US NARA [National Archives and Records Administration], and supplemented them with information from open sources; this has proved to be very effective. This approach helps not only to present the analyzed question and its separate elements comprehensively, but also I hope to a certain extent reduces the level of subjectivity when assessing the events under examination. Significant attention is given in the book to the events that took place during the so-called "spring operational pause", connected with the opposing sides' planning and preparation for Operation Citadel and the Kursk defensive operation. When working on this topic, the captured papers of *Generaloberst* W. Model's Ninth Army for the period of March – June 1943, found in the US National Archives, were of particular value; in the course of Operation Citadel, this army attacked toward Kursk from the north. A significant number of them are being introduced into Russian academic circulation for the first time here. Documents from the files of the Steppe Military District found in the TsAMO RF also prompt no small interest, and are also being presented for the first time in these articles. Such a form for the concentration of the *Stavka* of the Supreme High Command's reserves, like a military district (subsequently a *front*) was being tested for the first time before the Battle of Kursk, and proved to be highly effective. The strategic reserves, equipped and trained over the three months prior to the start of the fighting, made an enormous contribution to our victory at the Bulge of Fire. However, up to now their formation and training has received very little study. I hope that the presented materials will contribute to resolution of this major problem.

The comparative analysis of the combat path of the two former tank army commanders M.E. Katukov and P.A. Rotmistrov occupies a substantial place in the book. Their names are firmly connected with the events at Kursk. I took up this subject for the first time while working on the

3 V.N. Zamulin and V.V. Zamulin, "Nachalo formirovaniia Kurskoi dugi" ["The beginning of the formation of the Kursk bulge"] *Nauchnye vedomisti Belgorodskogo gosudarstvennogo universiteta*, No. 7 (2011), pp. 214-222.

manuscript for my book *Kurskii izlom* [*Kursk turning point*],[4] in order to understand the role of each of them and their tank armies in the repulse of von Manstein's offensive on the Belgorod direction. Over recent time I've managed to gather an impressive amount of archival material, which allowed me to clarify a number of murky episodes related to their participation in the fighting not only in July 1943, but also during other periods of the Great Patriotic War. I want to believe that the documentary tale of these stellar generals, who passed through the heaviest trials of the past century together with our people, will not only help to plumb more deeply into the history of separate battles of the Battle of Kursk, but also expand the image of other important events in our history.

I consider it my duty to express my sincere gratitude to everyone who helped me in the course of my research, and first of all to the leadership of the Kursk State University. I felt special support on the part of its provost, a talented organizer of academic work, a man captivated by the history of Russia, Dr. Vitalii Alekseevich Kudinov. A splendid scholar, Doctor of Science and Professor Aleksei Borisovich Shevelev also gave me invaluable comradely assistance when processing the collected material. It is difficult to overestimate his contribution to this work.Thanks to his irrepressible energy, persistence and painstaking work, he managed to translate and process all of those captured German materials that I used in my work. I believe that it is thanks to these two remarkable men, the book came about. I express my sincere gratitude to them both.

Photo illustrations are an important part of this collection of articles; I gathered them from the files of a number of Russian and foreign archives, museums and private collections in the course of more than 20 years. Some of them are being published here for the first time. Employees of the reading room of the Russian State Archive of Film and Photo Documents in Krasnogorsk headed by Galina Viktorovna Koroleva gave me enormous practical assistance in the search for and analysis of photographic material. I want to thank them for their responsiveness to my requests and their selfless, diligent work.

I particularly want to stress that a significant amount of the material included in this book was gathered and prepared within the framework of Academic Project No. 15-01-00150 suppored by the Russian Government Academic Foundation.

An enormous THANK YOU to all!

Valeriy Zamulin, January 2016

4 V. Zamulin, *Kurskii izlom* [*Kursk turning point*] (Moscow: Iauza/EKSMO, 2007), pp. 960.

1

A review of the literature on the Battle of Kursk

"'Give them the black bread of truth.' Why on earth is this necessary, if it isn't advantageous to us?"[1]

If one doesn't conceal the truth, then history will remain as the authentic history, despite the various attempts to falsify it – primarily through the use of non-disclosures.

Konstantin Simonov[2]

The history of the Battle of Kursk, despite the more than 70 years that have passed since it took place, continues to attract the focused attention of scholars and the general public. The enormous bibliography, which has gathered around the battle over the past years, as well as the works of historians which continue to come out about the battle in many countries even today with enviable regularity, plainly testifies to this. However, in Russia ever since the battle, it has never yet been subjected to full, and most importantly, objective analysis. One of the Red Army's main strategic operations (and incidentally, of the entire Great Patriotic War) became an important piece of Communist propaganda, and myths and legends have densely shrouded its events. Some of them have not been conclusively dispelled even today.

Starting from the first days of July 1943, when this epic event began to unfold, all of the information on it was concentrated in two major centers: the General Staff of the Red Army (which collected more reliable and complete information, for the Army's needs), and the means of mass information (for propaganda work). As it was, civilian historians were distant from both of these channels of information. Thus, right up until the 1960s, Soviet Army historians acted as the "locomotive" in studying the Battle of Kursk. Even though the results of their work at the time remained classified, nevertheless, the main work to analyze the events at Kursk was conducted by officers of the General Staff, and their conclusions became the basis for the first publications in the Soviet Union and paved the way for future study by the civilian academic community and scholars.

In my view, the domestic historiography of the Battle of Kursk can be divided into four main stages. The first, initial stage, which extended from 1943 to 1956, featured primarily the generalization and conceptualization of those events (first of all by military men). The second stage (1957-1970) was more productive. Over these 14 years, scholars and war veterans, although with great difficulty, succeeded in laying down the basis for writing the history of the battle. The third stage (1971-1993), although the lengthiest over the time of the USSR's existence, proved to be

1 As discussed later in this chapter, this statement was made by General Epishev. The expression "black bread of truth" meant to talk about the war as it actually was, including both the good and the bad.

2 Lazarev, L.I., *Posledniaia rabota K.M. Siminova* [K.M. Simonov's final work] // Siminov, K.M., *Glazami cheloveka moego pokoleniia* [*Through the eyes of a man of my generation*] (Moscow: 1990), p. 13.

featureless and of little substance due to the "managed degradation" of military-historical research which had started, and the senseless and rampant wave of ideology that swept over this sphere of academic activity. The year 1993 can be considered the beginning of the fourth stage, which continues to the present day. This year marked the 50th Anniversary of the Battle of Kursk, and according to archival regulations, the process of declassifying the 1943 files of the Central Archive of the Russian Federation's Ministry of Defense began. Scholars gained access to a major source of information – the operational, reporting and captured documents of the acting army, without which an accurate and complete analysis of those events is impossible.

In the initial phase, the "military stage" of the historiography is clearly distinguishable, which continued from 1943 to 1947. Over these years, the study of the Battle of Kursk flowed up channels, from newspaper and journal publications to articles in digests of the General Staff dedicated to assimilating the war's experience and books on individual battles. This stage concluded with the completion of a two-volume monograph by military specialists, and although it was not approved for publication, it had a substantial influence on subsequent scholarly work.

Soviet military journalists should be considered the first historiographers of the Battle of Kursk. Already in the first half of July 1943, during the repulse of the German offensive according to the Citadel plan, large essays and articles on this subject appeared in the central newspapers. Their authors were primarily describing individual clashes and combats, the heroism of Soviet soldiers, and some of the articles even contained attempts to draw lessons from the experienced gained by the Red Army while conducting the successful operation that summer. After all, up to that moment the Soviet soldiers had never been able to achieve any significant results in the summertime. Then a journalist conceived the name "Kursk bulge", which subsequently became something of a "brand" name. Today this combination of words is applied to both the configuration of the front lines west of Kursk, which took shape by the end of March 1943, and the battle, which took place there that summer. It appeared for the first time in the open press in the title of an article written by B.A. Galin, a journalist for the Red Army's main newpaper *Kransaia Zvezda* [Red Star].[3] "Na kurskoi duge" ["At the Kursk bulge"] appeared on page 4 of the newspaper on 15 July 1943. Later it was picked up by other authors. Prior to its appearance, this area was called the "Orel – Kursk direction" or the "Belgorod axis" in the press. In the autumn of 1943, it appeared in journals for propagandists and special Army publications like "Bol'shevik", "Vestnik vozdushnogo flota" [Air Force Digest], "Zhurnal avtobronetankovykh voisk" [Journal of the Armored Forces] devoted to making known the events on the Kursk bulge.

It should be especially stressed that the articles in these publications (both newspaper and journal publications) were as a rule of a strictly propagandistic orientation and of a superficial, narrative nature, which distinguished all the open military publications of the Soviet Union of that era. In addition, it must be noted that their authors, journalists at all levels (army, *front* and central editions) were "fighters of the ideological front" (as they were called in documents of the Soviet Party organs), and not only because of censorship restrictions, but also at their own volition, they often distorted the facts and even made up entire military incidents and anecdotes out of whole cloth. This pernicious tendency arose in the very first days of the war, and already had already gathered such momentum after one and a half years of war that even certain clear-headed leaders of military-political work in the armed forces were compelled to note its extremely negative

3 Galin (real family name – Rogalin), Boris Abramovich (1904-1983), a Soviet novelist and journalist and prize winner of the Stalin Award (1948). From 1934 he worked for the *Pravda* newspaper; between 1941 and 1945 he was a special correspondent for the main army newspaper *Krasnaia Zvezda* on the Western, Southern, North Caucasus, Central and 1st Belorussian Fronts. For the courage and bravery he demonstrated while carrying out his professional duties, Galin was awarded the Order of the Red Star (1943), the Order of the Patriotic War, 2nd Degree, and many medals.

influence on the effectiveness of the propaganda, which is to say the level of trust shown to it on the part of the troops. A directive from a deputy People's Commissar of the Navy, chief of the Navy's Main Political Command Commissar Rogov No. 1 dated 22 January 1942 stated:

> Recently, all types of falsehoods and lies have a widespread circulation on ships and in units of the Fleet .... Cases of lying, all types of tales, at times incorrect and politically harmful fabrications of political workers are taking place in agitation-propaganda work and the fleet press. Certain political workers, instead of a decisive struggle with falsehoods and harmful ad-libbing in propaganda and agitation, themselves sometimes submit false reports and concocted facts in their speeches, statements and even in print.
>
> ...
>
> In the newspaper *Krasnyi Chernomorets* [Red Sailor of the Black Sea], it was stated in one of the articles that more than 1,000 bombs were dropped on the cruiser *Komintern*; two days later, in the same newspaper there was mention of "approximately 2,000 bombs". Both of these reports were false. Tale-telling and lying in propaganda, agitation and the press discredit Party-political work and the fleet press, and cause exceptional harm to the matter of a Bol'shevik upbringing of the masses.
>
> These shameful and harmful manifestations of deceit, in whatever forms they appear, cannot be tolerated on ships and in units of the Navy, and must be mercilessly rooted out.[4]

However, similar documents were unable to change the situation in a fundamental fashion. Legends and myths continued to occupy a significant place in Soviet periodical literature of the war years, and then a significant portion of them smoothly migrated into brochures, books and even dissertations dedicated to the history of the Great Patriotic War. There are several reasons for this; I will cite only the two most obvious, in my view. First, a significant share of the top leadership responsible for this branch of military-political work believed that such a method to a certain degree was fully allowable for the creation of "Potemkin villages", with which propaganda was primarily occupied.[5] Second, Soviet military journalism was experiencing an acute deficit of qualified workers, and indeed simply well-educated people. Therefore from the first days of the war, not only the flower of Soviet literature was directed into the acting army, but also a significant number of ordinary journalists from purely civilian newspapers and journals, who, naturally, were totally unfamiliar with army life, and indeed were not burning with a desire to learn it at the front among the troops, under the hum of bullets. Thus, articles with storybook, heroic subject matter, describing the "unparalleled feats" of the Red Army's men, were often born precisely in the quiet of offices.

However, let's return directly to the historiography of the events at Kursk. Studies using documentary material and the dissemination of the first results of this work to a relatively wide audience (the senior command staff) of the Red Army's General Staff began in the autumn of 1943. The initial, serious summarizing materials were published in the first issue (November 1943) of a new publication – the "Information Bulletin from the Department of Studying the War's Experience" and the "Collected Materials on Studying the War's Experience" [further referred to as the "*Sbornik*"], which came out at the end of 1943 and the beginning of 1944. The *Sbornik* was

4 Russkii arkhiv: Velikaia Otechestvennaia, T. 17-6 (1-2). T. 2 (Moscow: Terra, 1996), p. 42.

5 Ed. note: A "Potemkin village" in Russian is something that appears elaborate and impressive, but in reality lacks substance. It is based on the story that one of Catherine the Great's ministers, in order to impress her of his abilities to rebuild a devastated region, created fake village fronts along her river route to the Crimea. After she passed by each "village", it would be quickly disassembled and rebuilt overnight downstream. Modern scholars have largely come to the conclusion that this was a myth.

published from 1942 to 1948, and both its volume and range of the themes it touched upon were considerably superior to the "Bulletin", although there was only one audience for both publications – the Army's senior command staff and the instructors of military educational institutions. In issues No. 9-11 of the *Sbornik*, for the first time materials were published that were dedicated to the limited operations in the period of the spring operational pause (a description of the battle conducted by elements of the 13th Army's 148th Rifle Division to seize the Glazunovka strong point in May 1943), as well as to important episodes of the Battle of Kursk itself (the defensive engagements of the 2nd Tank Army's 19th Tank Corps from 7 to 10 July on the Samodurovka – Molotychi line, and the Voronezh Front's counterattack on 12 July 1943.)

Sbornik No. 11 was thematic, fully dedicated to the Battle of Kursk. Thanks to the summarization of significant combat experience on the basis of documentary material that was rich for those times, this was a major, deep work, consisting of 10 chapters and 27 diagrams with a total number of 216 pages. Initially its authors pursued only the practical purpose "to acquaint broad reading circles of generals and individuals of the officers' staff with certain materials and preliminary conclusions from this most important and extremely instructive operation."[6] However, in essence, it was the first attempt by General Staff officers to lay down a solid foundation for the further academic analysis of this pivotal event of the war. The studies in the *Sbornik* lay out the course of events and their interrelationship in considerable detail, and give an essentially correct assessment of the decisions taken by the Soviet command during the battle. The applied nature of the research to a significant degree spared the authors from bias and far-fetched arguments when describing the combat operations on all the sectors of the Kursk bulge, including those that would quickly become mythologized and included in the system of propagandizing the achievements of Soviet power. For example, when discussing the counterattack at Prokhorovka on 12 July 1943 on the Voronezh Front, the authors openly point to a number of genuine failures and miscalculations committed by the Soviet side. For example, the authors show that Lieutenant General P.A. Rotmistrov's 5th Guards Tank Army failed to carry out its assignment on this day. In addition, "at the decision of the commander, the 5th Guards Tank Army launched a frontal assault against crack German panzer divisions, not having a substantial superiority in force, which in the best case might lead only to pushing the enemy back."[7] Even though this decision was taken not by the army commander, but by the leadership of the Voronezh Front and the General Staff (it was they who decided the army's combat formation and place of deployment), and there was in fact a superiority in strength over the adversary (indeed, a significant one), which couldn't be exploited because of the restricted terrain conditions, nevertheless one of the main mistakes made in planning the preparation for the counterattack has been stated unambiguously in the *Sbornik*.

Thirdly, the authors remained silent about the already circulating opinion that a colossal tank clash took place at Prokhorovka, in which supposedly 1,500 tanks and self-propelled guns took part. They made no attempt to exaggerate the already large numbers, which were cited by the 5th Guards Tank Army's account, and honestly pointed out that the Germans over five days of fighting had lost approximately 300 tanks (and not just on 12 July 1943 alone, as P.A. Rotmistrov would later maintain) – though even these figures are plainly debatable.[8]

Fourthly, Issue No. 11 of the *Sbornik* also justly criticizes other decisions made by the Voronezh Front command, connected with the use of a major tank formation on the defense, and a large array of statistical material is brought to bear on the subject. Unfortunately, these and other objective

6 "Sbornik materialov po izucheniiu opyta voiny" ["Digest of materials on the study of the war's experience"], No. 11 (Moscow: Voenizdat, 1944], p. 5.
7 Ibid, p. 150.
8 Ibid., p. 153.

assessments didn't find their reflection in the post-war works of Soviet scholars, who would replace them with victorious rhetoric and inflated numbers.

At the same time, however, *Sbornik* Issue No. 11 became the source for a number of legends. For example, it gave rise to the notion that Germans used Ferdinand heavy tank destroyers in the Voronezh Front's sector, including at Prokhorovka, and that supposedly two brigades of Rotmistrov's tank army localized a German breakthrough of the 5th Guards Army in the bend of the Psel River on the evening of 12 July.[9] In addition, the study fudges on the issue of the reason for the 19th Tank Corps' failure to go on the counterattack at the proper time on 6 July 1943 in the Central Front's sector. In one place the authors note that the tank corps wasn't ready to carry out the assignment not only that morning, but also by noontime, because of a lack of maps of friendly minefields in the attack sector,[10] but a little below that text they state that the tank corps commander, having supposedly received information about the failure of the neighboring 16th Tank Corps' attack, decided to refrain from attacking.[11]

On the basis of the analyses included in *Sbornik* No. 11, which bore the seal "For official use",[12] in the middle of 1944 an officer of the General Staff Lieutenant Colonel I.V. Parot'kin[13] prepared and published the article "The Battle of Kursk", which came out in two issues of *Istoricheskii zhurnal* [*Historical journal*] and became the first academic article in the Soviet open press about this major event.[14] In it, Parot'kin reviewed the combat operations in considerable detail and made an attempt to offer a number of important operational-strategic conclusions. In addition, thanks to this publication, the name "Battle of Kursk" became firmly fixed to the fighting in the Kursk area in July 1943.

Between 1943 and 1945, military historians produced a number of small, soft-cover books, in essence brochures, on major operations of the Soviet Army and Navy, in order to make the successes of the Red Army known to a broad military and civilian audience. "The Battle of Kursk: A brief sketch" came out in 1945;[15] like all the publications in this series, it had a strictly propagandistic orientation. So although it in fact became the first individual work on the battle, it had

9 Ibid, p. 148; p. 157.

10 Ibid., p. 135.

11 Ibid., p. 136.

12 Not secret, but also meaning there was no free access to them.

13 Parot'kin, Ivan Vasil'evich (1909-1974), Major General (1966), Candidate of Military Science (for military history). In the Red Army from 1931. In 1937, he was a cadet, and then from 9 May 1940, a post-graduate at the M.V. Frunze Military Academy. He was a participant in the Soviet-Finnish Winter War. From 10 July 1941, Parot'kin was under the command of Deputy People's Commissar of Defense S.M. Budennyi. On 30 July 1941 he was appointed as the assistant chief of operations to the headquarters of the Southwestern Direction, and after it was disbanded, served in the same post with the headquarters of the Southwestern Front. From 4 May 1942, Parot'kin was the senior assistant chief of operations with the Southwestern Front headquarters, and then with the Don and Central Fronts. On 22 March 1943, Major I.V. Parot'kin was directed to the General Staff's Department for the Study of the War's Experience (headed by Major General P.P. Vechnyi), where he served until 1960. On 11 July 1943, Parot'kin became a research associate in this department. His first research in his new post, published by the General Staff, was the "Elets operation, 6-16 December 1941", and then in 1944, his article "The Battle of Kursk" came out. For his combat services in the war years, Parot'kin was awarded the Order of the Red Star, the Order of the Patriotic War, 1st Degree (13 June 1945) and Order of the Patriotic War, 2nd Degree (19 March 1943). Between 1952 and 1954, Parot'kin was a student at the K.E. Voroshilov Military Academy. From 1961 Colonel I.V. Parot'kin was a senior instructor, then a deputy department head at the General Staff Military Academy. On 11 March 1968, Parot'kin became the deputy head of the USSR Ministry of Defense's Institute of Military History.

14 I.V. Parot'kin, "Bitva pod Kurskom" ["Battle of Kursk"] *Istoricheskii zhurnal* (No. 7, 8; 1944).

15 *Bitva pod Kurskom. Iz opyta boev Otechestvennoi voiny* [*Battle of Kursk. From the experience of the battles of the Patriotic War*], Voenno-istoricheskii otdel General'nogo shtaba Krasnoi Armii (Moscow, 1945)

no noticeable influence on the understanding of this turning point in the Great Patriotic War by academics and society. It gave only a superficial treatment of the fighting and introduced a number of mistaken assessments, interpretations and facts, which unfortunately continue to circulate to the present day in the pages of books and periodicals. For example, its authors without any justification maintained that in the opinion of the German command, after the success of Operation Citadel "an advantageous basis for the further development of the German offensive into the depth of the Soviet Union – toward Moscow – would arise."[16] Yet Hitler in his well-known Operational Order No. 6 noted that if the situation would develop according to plan, the Wehrmacht should subsequently attack to the southeast, into the rear of the Southwestern Front (Operation Panther). It was also in this brochure that the myth about a colossal clash at Prokhorovka, in which "more than 1,500 from both sides simultaneously took part",[17] was presented to a wide audience for the first time. A new, important point in this publication was the fact that its authors for the first time in domestic literature gave stages to the Battle of Kursk: a defensive phase, which lasted from 5 to 23 July, and then a counteroffensive stage that lasted until 23 August, the aim of which was the destruction of the enemy's Orel and Belgorod-Khar'kov groupings. Nevertheless, despite the low quality and openly propagandistic nature, in the opinion of some Soviet scholars, the "Battle of Kursk: a brief sketch" had a "relatively prolonged influence on the elaboration of the history of the Kursk battle."[18]

In this same period, with the aim of spreading the successful experience with resolving concrete combat tasks by units and elements of all types of forces among the troops, various pamphlets with a description of tactical examples and successful combats, including during the Battle of Kursk as well, were printed in large numbers. Their orientation toward a military audience gave two important, special features to these materials. A positive characteristic was the fact that these pamphlets were prepared only on the basis of combat documents, which allowed their authors to describe events and draw conclusions with a great deal of accuracy. It was necessary to include in them both positive and negative examples of troop activity; the successful decisions of commanders with an accurate reference to terrain; and the complete names of villages and hills. In wartime conditions and with heightened security measures, this was uncommon. The information from these pamphlets was valuable for further study of the events at Kursk. Unfortunately, because of this detail, this literature was classified, and thus it was inaccessible to civilian historians, while those who received admittance to military libraries had to sign an oath of secrecy. Thus there could be no talk about any publications with reference to these sources, or about any exchange of information between scholars, which significantly complicated the start of any exhaustive analysis of the events of the summer of 1943 and postponed the academic analysis of the history of the Battle of Kursk. Nevertheless, the large amount of work done by military historians of the Red Army by the end of the war to gather and systematize the material had an important significance for the future study of the battle as a result of its direct connection with the combat activities of the troops. It was at this time that serious groundwork was also laid for the analysis of the history of the Great Patriotic War as a whole.

Even so, it is necessary to remark upon a number of negative factors, which at this time seriously affected both the quality and the scale of research done by military historians. First was the narrowness of the base of sources. Work went on primarily with accounts and reports that came in from the field immediately after operations. Second was the extremely limited number of military-historical organs; in essence, there was only one, which worked to produce tangible results – this

16 Ibid., p. 6.
17 Ibid., p. 20.
18 *Voenno-istoricheskii zhurnal,* No. 7 (1963), p. 98.

was the General Staff department, in which there were only 15 senior officers. The low level of qualification of the subordinate staff (the majority of them were ordinary line officers, who had a limited level of education and combat experience) and their lack of the necessary experience with processing the information about major (strategic) operations degraded the quality of the work. Documents of the first All-Army Conference of Employees of Military-History Departments, which took place in Moscow in the autumn of 1943, noted:

> The question of selecting and cultivating cadres is not being given sufficient attention everywhere. Often officers with weak operational-tactical training are being drawn into the study of the war's experience. Of course, in wartime conditions, the possibility of fully supplying the study of the war's experience with officers who are prepared for research work isn't possible. Thus, from the outset it is necessary to render daily practical assistance to the young officers who have been designated for this work. Incidentally, senior chiefs, unfortunately, don't do this everywhere.
>
> It is typical that the group to study and utilize the experiences of the war in *front* and army headquarters is understaffed with officers by up to 25%.
>
> The fact that enterprising, creative work of the "experience-officers"[19] doesn't always find proper evaluation and support on the part of senior chiefs also calls attention to itself.[20]

Third the closed nature of the military science made it impossible to recruit qualified civilian cadres for analyzing military subjects.

In addition, the cult of personality had an extremely negative influence. For example, the authors of the book *V boiakh za Orel* [*In the battles for Orel*] called the main and basic reason for the victory in the battle of Kursk "the deeply considered, extremely accurate and realistic plans of our Supreme Commander-in-Chief Marshal of the Soviet Union Comrade Stalin."[21] This thesis runs through practically all of the publications at the end of the 1940s and the early 1950s like a red thread. It deprived historians of the possibility of making legitimate assessments of the plans of the Soviet command not only on the strategic level, but also the operational level; of properly evaluating the results of the combat work of the Red Army in the course of the battle; and not to mention expressing any critical comments.

Wrote a leading Soviet specialist on the Kursk battle G.A. Koltunov, "For all the literature on the history of the Battle of Kursk that came out during the war years, characteristic was the fact that in it this battle was shown as one of the most important stages on the path to the complete destruction of the German-fascist aggressors. Events were viewed in most general outlines … in all the works, the correlation of forces and the content of combat orders were dropped from discussion. Little attention was given as well to questions of military art."[22]

Immediately after the defeat of Nazi Germany, the assimilation of the war's experience continued, but now on a higher level. The leadership of the USSR's Armed Forces considered it an important means to improve the forms and means of command. The number of military-historical departments in the headquarters of all types of troops grew noticeably. Military education institutes were actively included in this process. For example, in one of the leading military academies alone, the

19 That is how the officers of the departments and groups to study and utilize the war's experience were customarily called in the headquarters of the acting army.

20 *Informatsionnyi biulleten'. Otdel po ispol'zovaniiu opyta voiny General'nogo shtaba* [*Information bulletin. General Staff's Department for the Utilization of the War's Experience*] (No.1, 1943), pp. 6-7.

21 N.A. Talenskii [ed.], *V boiakh za Orel* [*In the battles for Orel*] (Moscow: Gospolitizdat, 1944), p. 29.

22 G.A. Koltunov, "Voenno-istoricheskaia literatura o bitve pod Kurskom." ["Military-historical literature on the Battle of Kursk"], *Voenno-istoricheskii zhurnal* (No. 7, 1963), pp. 97-98.

M.V. Frunze Academy, in the years 1947-1950 more than 550 academic hours was devoted to the subject "History of the military arts" in the program of instruction for line officers. For sake of comparison, in 2010, only 124 hours was given to this subject in the education plan of the Russian Federation's General Staff Academy.[23] Specifically for the preparation of military historians and increasing their level of qualification, a military history department was created in this academy, in which over the first 5-6 years after the war a number of frontline officers underwent training, which subsequently formed a small cohort of scholars, who would be fated to begin large-scale work to analyze the Battle of Kursk. Foremost among this group of military scholars were Major General I.V. Parot'kin and Colonels G.V. Koltunov, I.I. Markin, D.M. Palevich and B.G. Solov'ev.

As before, the General Staff remained as the central coordinating center of military-historical research. In the years 1946-1947, its military historians undertook a first attempt to prepare a fundamental academic work on the history of events at the Battle of Kursk. For this purpose, the preliminary work done by the General Staff's Department for Analyzing and Utilizing the War's Experience under the leadership of Major General P.P. Vechnyi between 1943 and 1945 was used. The manuscript of the future book was prepared on a broad documentary basis, distinguished by a great amount of detail on the combat operations down to the division and regiment level, and packed with statistical material. In it, for the first time several key moments of the battle, such as the tank clash at Prokhorovka, were divided into stages, which more accurately reflects the essence of what happened in the summer of 1943. However, the authors didn't use materials on the strategic planning (documents of the General Staff and the *Stavka* of the Supreme High Command) and made little use of captured documents. This prevented them from revealing the essence of the "Citadel" plan accurately and in detail; determining Berlin's subsequent plan in the event of the operation's success; giving an accurate estimate of the numerical strength and quality of the Wehrmacht's formations and units that were committed to the operation, or their losses, both in separate stages of the battle, or for the battle as a whole; or conducting a thorough strategic analysis of the decisions and actions of the opposing sides. However, the main defect in the study was that the authors failed to find an acceptable balance between descriptive material and material of an analytic nature.

The uncritical approach by the authors to the sources available to them (primarily the accounts of the corps, armies and *fronts*) led to the fact that a number of mistakes were made in the study; the forces of the two sides in certain clashes (for example, the one on 12 July 1943 at Prokhorovka) were exaggerated in size; certain aspects of important events in the battle received shallow treatment (for example, the actions of the 5th Guards Tank Army on 10 July 1943 were incorrectly described); and explicit conclusions and assessments on the results of on a number of key combat actions and important measures taken by the commands of the armies and *fronts* are absent. At the same time, as Colonel V.A. Savin justly noted during a discussion of this work at a conference held in the General Staff in May 1948, the authors attempted to gloss over negative aspects and the mistakes made by the Soviet side at every stage of this colossal event.[24]

This work became the first and, unfortunately, only fundamental research in our country on the given topic using documentary material over the entire post-war period, moreover one with few ideological strands. Initially it was assumed that it would serve as the basis of a multi-volume publication and the material, prepared by the author's collective, had every justification after follow-up revisions to qualify for this. However, the leadership of the General Staff and of the

23 Gareev, M.A., *Srazheniia na voenno-istoricheskikh frontax: Sbornik statei* [*Battle on military-historical fronts: A collection of articles*] (Moscow: INSAN, 2010), p. 22.

24 *Sbornik materialov voenno-istoricheskogo upravleniia General'nogo Shtaba* [*Collection of materials of the Military History Bureau of the General Staff*] 1st ed., (Moscow, 1949), p. 154.

Communist Party's Central Committee saw no sense in reworking the manuscript, because the authors didn't present the Battle of Kursk as a major military-historical event of the Second World War and of global military history, in which the Soviet Union played the key role, but as simply a successful combat operation by the Red Army. It was precisely this that prevented the realization of the initial idea. Although materials from it (conclusions, facts and statistical data) were widely used in the works of Soviet military historians right up to the beginning of the 1990s, due to reasons of secrecy, there could be no references to it in the open press.

The group's ceasing of activity and the turning over of the almost completed work to the archive negatively affected its development into a history of a turning stage of the war, just as it did the entire activity of Soviet scholars to study the Great Patriotic War. At this time the study of the Battle of Kursk was effectively closed to civilian historians and turned over to use by the propaganda organs, while the exploratory studies of the military historians were buried under a seal of secrecy. The general public received information about it only from scanty publications of dubious quality, in such publications as "Propagandist and agitator of the USSR Ministry of Defense", "Notepad of an agitator of the Soviet Army", "Red warrior" and so forth. Thus right up to the latter half of the 1950s, the given subject in our country wasn't open for sound academic research. All of the public literature on the battle carried a superficial character and was called upon to convey to the Soviet people only measured doses of strictly limited information as had been determined back in 1945 in the "Brief sketch".

There were several reasons for this, but the two main reasons, which had the most pernicious influence for the extent of the entire post-war period, were the ideological expedience and the personal biases of the USSR's top leaders and their own assessments of events of the past. Up until the beginning of 1953, study of the Great Patriotic War was in a frozen state; only military men were busy with analysis of several aspects of it for practical applications. Immediately after VE-Day I.V. Stalin banned the publication of any collections of remembrances or research on the war for a broad audience, arguing that little time had passed and that it was still impossible to evaluate such an epochal event objectively.[25] In reality the Leader wanted to forget as quickly as possible everything connected with the period 1941-1945, when he had personally made so many mistakes and miscalculations, and bury everything in the archives. I will remind the reader that it was at this time that 9 May ceased to be a national holiday. Nevertheless, toward the end of the Stalinist era, certain combat actions at Kursk nevertheless found their reflection in academic works by military historians. For example, at the end of 1952 Colonel D.Ia. Palevich[26] successfully defended his dissertation to secure the academic degree Candidate of Historical Science on the

25 A.M. Vasilevsky, *Delo vsei zhizni* [*Cause of an entire life*] (Moscow: Politizdat, 1988), p. 306.

26 Palevich, Dmitrii Iakovlevich, Candidate of Historical Sciences (1952), docent (1954). He was born on 8 November 1917 in Briansk. He served in the Red Army from 1936. After completing the Gor'kii Armored School in 1939, he commanded a tank platoon, before serving as an adjutant of a tank company and the chief of staff of a separate tank battalion. He was a participant in the Soviet-Finnish Winter War. On 12 September 1941 he was a student in the command school of the Military Academy of the Armored and Mechanized Forces. On 11 October 1941 Palevich became the assistant chief of staff for intelligence of the 25th Tank Regiment of the Western Front's 5th Army. On 26 October, he was severely wounded. After recovering, on 26 October 1942 he became a senior instructor of the Lenin Kuznetsk Machine-gun School of the Siberian Military District. On 6 May 1943 Palevich became the assistant chief of a department of the Bureau for the Development of Armored and Mechanized Forces. On 6 November 1943, Palevich was the 1460th Self-Propelled Artillery Regiment's chief of staff. On 2 March 1944, he became a teacher of military-political courses under the Red Army's Political Bureau. After the war, on 7 December 1946 Palevich enrolled in the Frunze Military Academy's military history department. Between 19 November 1948 and 7 December 1972, Palevich taught at the Lenin Military Academy. He retired on 7 December 1972.

subject "Counterattack of the 5th Guards Tank Army at Prokhorovka in July 1943". However, like all of the military analyses of this time, it carried the seal "For official use", and thus access to it was extremely limited and it could not appear in the open press. Ideological organs and unscrupulous authors took advantage of this for a long time, churning out, developing and polishing up all types of myths and legends about the events at the Battle of Kursk.

In the middle of the 1950s, the interest of our society in the recent past began to grow perceptibly. An important indicator of this was the appearance of memoir literature, and the sharp increase in its print runs in the following years. However, main attention was given by the government organs that had a connection to historical science and the propaganda of its results to the first stage of the war, to the battles of Moscow and especially Stalingrad. Both the colossal influence of those events on the outcome of the struggle with fascism and their tragic tint contributed to this, but the main factor for this was the fact that many of the major figures in the Soviet leadership and army back then had a direct connection to them, and considered their participation in them to be the pinnacle of their careers.

Completing our review of the initial phase of the historiography of the Battle of Kursk, it is impossible not to mention an important tendency that arose in the early 1950s. Immediately after I.V. Stalin's death, books written by the generals and field marshals of Nazi Germany began to be translated and printed in the Soviet Union. Moreover, the first to see light in the Soviet Union were the works of those who had lengthy service in the Wehrmacht and who had a connection to the Battle of Kursk. Thus, in 1954 the memoirs of the creator of the German panzer forces and a participant in the planning and preparations for Operation Citadel, Heinz Guderian's *Vospominaniia nemetskovo generala* [translated into English as *Panzer Leader*] were published; three years later, the Russian publisher *Voenizdat* simultaneously released two books by former German commanders: the former commander of Army Group South E. von Manstein's *Poteriannye pobedy* [*Lost victories*] and the chief of staff of the XXXXVIII Panzer Corps F. von Mellenthin's *Tankovye srazheniia 1939-1945* [*Panzer Battles 1939-1945*]. Despite the fact that these Russian translations of the books had the seal "For official use" their appearance played a positive role in expanding the perspective of Soviet scholars on the events of the summer of 1943. Thanks to them, for the first time the curtain was partially opened on the process of the preparation for Citadel, and also the opinions and assessments of key Wehrmacht figures on a number of important problems in planning and conducting the summer 1943 campaign became known. Assessments of the Red Army's level of preparation for the campaign, especially that of its command, and the strengths and weaknesses of the Soviet forces were also interesting to our former adversary. Even though Soviet historians at that time were obligated to look only for "specks in the enemy's eye", nevertheless this was valuable material, both for the academic analysis of everything connected with the Battle of Kursk, and for the constructive criticism of "ideological enemies". This positive tendency continued in later years, but between 1960 and 1980, our publishing houses unfortunately published only the memoirs of men who didn't take part in the Battle of Kursk. Even so, given the acute deficit of information about the military organization of Nazi Germany, these works became an important source for our scholars, including on the subject of our interest.

Summing up several results over the 14 years that followed the Battle of Kursk, two important diverging tendencies that arose at that time should be noted. First, unquestionably a large amount of work was done by military historians to assimilate the documentary material (including that of captured German documents) and to make an initial analysis of the events. The most substantial result of this, inarguably, was the two-volume work prepared by officers of the General Staff. The foundation that was created, even in conditions of strict ideological frameworks and the isolation of Soviet scholars from Western sources and the main bulk of captured German sources, allowed a shift to a new qualitative level – to the study of the subject on a broad strategic level and the preparation of fundamental academic work, not only in the interests of the Soviet Army, but for a broad circle of readers as well.

Second, in connection with the death of I.V. Stalin and the events that followed this, within the leadership of the Soviet Army the attitude toward military-historical science as a whole, and to work devoted to analysis of the Great Patriotic War in particular, changed. It was not considered a front and center matter. At the end of 1953 and in the first half of 1954, military-historical organizations and departments of history of the war and of military art in military education facilities underwent a substantial reduction. A significant number of qualified cadres were dismissed or sent into other spheres of activity. Considering that genuine academic research at that time was being conducted exclusively by military professionals, the study of the Battle of Kursk was also basically wrapped up, while the authors of books, which came out in print between 1954 and 1958 used the already available preliminary work. In this connection as an example, one can cite the activity of the Frunze Military Academy to publish a multi-volume work – *Kurs lektsii po voennomu iskusstvu* [*Course of lectures on the military art*], which also touched upon major questions of the Battle of Kursk. For example, its Sixth Volume (which was published in 1957) contained an analysis of the counterattack conducted by the Central Front's forces on 6 July 1943.

The new, second phase in the study of the Battle of Kursk began in 1957, and was connected with the XX Congress of the Communist Party of the Soviet Union, which augured a short, but dynamic and interesting page in the social life of the USSR, which received the name "the Khrushchev thaw".[27] In the historical science, this time was characterized by diverging tendencies in the study of both the war as a whole and of its separate battles and campaigns. On the one hand the scope and quality of military-historical research noticeably increased, and new approaches to the analysis of events of 1941-1945 began to form. The directions of work done by Soviet scholars expanded, the number of topics increased, and new documentary sources entered academic circulation, including captured sources, which contributed to the accumulation of a significant amount of knowledge about the turning stage in the war. An important feature of this period was a certain straying of domestic historians from a uniform treatment of the events; the analysis of combat operations in their development with the use of Western sources; and the study of problems and miscalculations when planning and conducting large-scale operations, both by the political leadership of the country and by the Red Army's command on every level. At the same time, a tendency to diverge from the principles worked out in the period of "the Khrushchev thaw" clearly marked the termination of this phase. Instead of exposing problems, the analysis of their causes, and how they were resolved (or not resolved), historians shifted to "smoothing rough edges" and applying a "victorious polish". These tendencies would find a reflection as well in the contradictory conclusions regarding major problems of the events of the summer of 1943 at Kursk.

Immediately following the XX Party Congress, changes in the life of the country, despite the broad resonance and rather substantial support in broad layers of society that its resolutions received, proceeded timidly, cautiously, under the strict, vigilant control of the Communist Party and its ideological organs. Just as before, all serious problems, including in the realm of social sciences, were resolved only by directives from above. Thus a key role in the activation of research on the Battle of Kursk was played by a speech given by the First Secretary of the Communist Party's Central Committee N.S. Khrushchev at a Party plenum in October 1957. In his speech at this commanding forum, where the head of state visibly showed his strength in the struggle for absolute power by sending the greatly esteemed Marshal of Soviet Union G.K. Zhukov into

27 This catch phrase became popular after the publication in 1954 of I. Ehrenburg's book *Ottepel'* [*Thaw*] and designated a short period of reform implemented by the First Secretary of the Communist Party Central Committee N.S. Khrushchev and his supporters.

retirement, he also touched upon problems in the study of history. Nikita Sergeevich, himself a war veteran who was present at the Battle of Kursk, then considered it necessary to express his opinion on how major questions of the history of the Great Patriotic War should be viewed; they still continued to be an important factor in the socio-political life of the USSR, which meant, in the Party's ideological work as well. Khrushchev stressed, "After Stalingrad an offensive by our forces began, and the battle to conclusively destroy the enemy went in a different manner. However, it seems to me that a decisive superiority and the turning point in the war were achieved in 1943 in the fighting for the Kursk bulge (emphasis the author's)."

If to compare N.S. Khrushchev with his successor L.I. Brezhnev, then Nikita Sergeevich was a relatively modest man: he didn't decorate himself with Orders of Victory, and when he retired to a deserved rest, he still had the same rank of lieutenant general that he had received in 1943. However, he also tended to his combat past and his role in the battles of the Great Patriotic War with great reverence. He jealously followed how it was treated in the press, even in classified pamphlets published in limited numbers. Indeed, if he believed his contribution to victory was underappreciated or diminished, he would arrange no-nonsense tongue lashings on the government level.[28] Knowing this trait, not only his "close circle", but also the entire bureaucratic system without any supplementary reminders actively began to work in the indicated direction after the 1957 October Plenum. Taking its cue from the First Secretary's opinion, the Party Central Committee quickly prepared a decree about publishing a six-volume history of the Great Patriotic War, in which the subject of the Battle of Kursk would be given the proper significance. In addition, the decision was made to publicize its events in the press, and to publish a number of academic and popular books on this subject, as well as collections of veterans' recollections of the fighting.

As concerns the development of military-historical science as a whole, then at that time, just as in the preceding years, it moved along two directions, within the military and in the civilian sphere, which rarely had any contact between each other. Military scholars, unquestionably, led the way, but the results of their work were inaccessible to broader society. Under the conditions of secrecy in the academic research institutes and education facilities that were subordinate to the USSR Ministry of Defense and served the needs of the army, the rich experience of the war was being analyzed and generalized, although not on such a scale as had been at the end of the 1940s. Given a rational approach to the matter, some of the military analyses might have been shared with civilian historians without any harm to the state's defense capabilities. This doubtlessly would have given a positive impetus for historical science as a whole. However, back in the war years, everything that concerned the acting army was kept classified, especially anything connected with the decisions of its high command. Cognizant of the scale of the catastrophe of the first phase of the Great Patriotic War and understanding its responsibility for the colossal losses, the higher political and military leadership of the USSR did everything to conceal the real events from the people. This tendency remained in effect right up to the collapse of the USSR, since the organizers and architects of failed operations and disastrous battles continued to hold important Party and state posts for many years after the victory. Total secrecy was considered to be a simple and reliable means to conceal the truth about the awkward past and to erase from the memory of the people entire decades, which failed to comply with the ideological conceptions of the authorities.

Realizing that the further development of the military-historical science in a closed regime was not very effective, striving to draw a broad circle of officers and generals into active, creative work on military subjects, and most importantly, in order to create an official (which means, controllable) conduit for the spread of military-historical knowledge, the Soviet leadership created (resurrected) a periodical publication – *Voenno-istoricheskii zhurnal* [*Military-history journal*]. Its first

28 RGANI, F. 5, Op. 30, D. 184, ll. 98-99.

issue came out in January 1959.[29] As several members of the editorial board recalled, they arrived at work with a great desire to create an interesting, genuinely scientific publication. Indeed, already in its first years it became a real leader in the struggle for an honest, comprehensive presentation of the history of the Great Patriotic War and the distribution of military-historical findings; its publication contributed to increasing the general methodological level of the Soviet historical science. It was precisely in this journal that articles began to be published for the first time, in which the authors presented the Battle of Kursk in a new way, using a broader base of sources than previously, in order to examine its key clashes and problems. Already in the sixth issue, the recollections of the former commander of the Central Front Marshal of the Soviet Union K.K. Rokossovsky about the fighting on the northern shoulder of the Kursk bulge were published. Its value consisted in the fact that a direct participant in those events divulged how the Soviet command worked out and adopted the plan to adopt a prepared defense, what factors affected this decision, and the objectives set by the *Stavka* of the Supreme High Command in the first phase of the battle.

Three years after the resumption of the journal's publication, the editorship, striving to get away from a unilateral presentation of the subject of the fundamental turning point and to introduce significant sources of the German Army into academic circulation, for the first time in the Soviet Union published the key document on Operation Citadel – Hitler's Operational Order No. 6 dated 15 April 1943. It was accompanied by the commentary of Colonel B.G. Solov'ev,[30] and laid out in detail the master plan of the offensive, the objectives and tasks of the forces of Army Group Center and Army Group South that were designated for the operation, and their possible alternative in the event of success.

This idea found a lively response from the readers and specialists, and thus received further development. In 1966 the journal printed the transcript of meeting in the Hitler Headquarters

29 The *Voenno-istoricheskii zhurnal* is a monthly publication of the Russian Federation's Ministry of Defense. The first issue came out on 29 August 1939. In the years 1939-1940, the journal was published by the USSR People's Commissariat of Defense, and between January and July 1941, by the Red Army's General Staff. With the start of the Great Patriotic War, publication of the journal was halted, and didn't resume until 1959. In the Soviet years the journal published historical articles, documents and materials devoted primarily to recent history, beginning with the Russian Civil War. It also published memoirs and recollections of public figures of the Russian Civil War and Great Patriotic War, as well as book reviews and research findings. Today it highlights topical problems in domestic and foreign military history, the Russian Federation's military policy at every stage of its formation and development, the history of military science and technology, and the activities of leading Russian and Soviet Army and Navy commanders.

30 Solov'ev, Boris Grigor'evich (1917 -- ?), Colonel (1951), and Candidate of Historical Sciences. In 1940 he graduated from the Saratov Pedagogical Institute with a degree in history. He was called up into the Red Army in 1941. He served at the fronts of the Great Patriotic War from February 1942, serving first as the adjutant of the 264th Separate Communications Battalion of the Kalinin Front's 4th Shock Army. In August 1942 he entered staff work, and rose from the assistant chief of staff of a separate battalion to the assistant chief of the 4th Shock Army's Operations Department. In January 1944 he became the assistant chief of the department responsible for studying the war's experience, and from January 1945, the chief of this same department within the 4th Shock Army's headquarters. He ended the war with the rank of major, and was awarded the Order of the Red Star and the Order of the Patriotic War 2nd Degree along with many medals. Subsequently for a short period of time he served in the headquarters of the Steppe Military District, before working in the General Staff's Military History Department between June 1946 and 30 October 1953. In 1953 he graduated from the Frunze Military Academy's Military History Department with distinction. On 31 December 1953 he became a research associate, then the chief of the editorial department of the journal *Voennaia mysl'* [*Military thought*]. On 5 July 1969 he was appointed deputy chief of the Third Department of the USSR Ministry of Defense's Institute of Military History. On 16 March 1971, Solov'ev became the chief editor and a leader of an authors' collective for a volume of the 5th Edition of the twelve-volume *Istoriia Vtoroi mirovoi voiny* [*History of the Second World War*]. On 22 April 1978 he retired due to age.

on 26 July 1943,[31] which plainly testified to the Wehrmacht's difficult situation after the failure of Operation Citadel. Two years later, it published another five documents, reprinted from a book by the West German scholar E. Klink,[32] which were directly related to the planning of the attack toward Kursk and included the commentary of Colonels G. Zastavenko and B. Solov'ev: "Army Group Center's plan for Operation Citadel, 12 April 1943;" "Evaluation of the situation for conducting Operation Zitadelle [Citadel] and its continuation" by the Fourth Panzer Army; orders for Operation Citadel for the Fourth Panzer Army and Army Detachment Kempf; and Hitler's address to the officers before the start of the offensive.[33]

All of the captured materials, which came out in the *Voenno-istoricheskii zhurnal* between 1961 and 1968 became a most valuable source for domestic historians, which noticeably expanded their insight into the real plans of the Nazi command. They enabled a re-thinking of a number of long-held beliefs, in particular regarding Berlin's plans in the event of a successful conclusion to the first phase of the offensive, and had a positive influence on the formulation of the history of the Battle of Kursk as a whole. It should be noted that even today, these materials haven't lost their significance.

The collection of articles *Sovershenno sekretno! Tol'ko dlia komandovaniia!: Strategiia fashistskoi Germanii v voine protiv SSSR; dokumenty i materialy* [*Totally secret! Only for the command!: Strategy of fascist Germany in the war against the USSR; documents and materials*], which was published in Moscow in 1967 by the publishing house *Nauka*, substantially supplemented this series of documents. All the previously revealed captured materials published in the USSR were published together in it, including those regarding the 1943 summer campaign; very important was the fact that they were given a detailed academic commentary. The article about the documentary sources on the Battle of Kursk contained an extremely deep, exhaustive analysis of the German command's plan for the summer of 1943 and the process of readying the troops for the attack toward Kursk, which for the first time was based upon a broad base of captured documents. Right up to the collapse of the Soviet Union, this work was the most complete and reliable book on the given subject. It had a serious influence on the further work of domestic historians.

The articles of a leading Soviet specialist on the Battle of Kursk Colonel G.A. Koltunov[34] that were published at this time in the *Voenno-istoricheskii zhurnal* were substantive and filled with

31 *Voenno-istoricheskii zhurnal*, (No. 6, 1966), p. 37.

32 E. Klink, *Das Gesetz des Handelns. Die Operation "Zitadelle" 1943* (Stuttgart, 1966).

33 *Voenno-istoricheskii zhurnal, (No. 8, 1968)*, pp. 67-76.

34 Koltunov, Georgii Avtonomovich, Colonel (1953), Candidate of Historical Sciences. He was born on 25 January 1916 in the village of Obukhov in the Kursk Guberniia. After graduating from the V.I. Lenin Moscow Pedagogical Institute's Department of History in 1939, he was called up into the Red Army. In March 1941 he completed the course for junior lieutenants. He received his combat baptism on 19 September 1941 on the Briansk Front in the vicinity of Glukhov as a platoon commander with the 744th Separate Signals Battalion of the 3rd Army's 283rd Rifle Division and remained as part of this division all the way to Berlin. On 4 February 1942 he became the commander of the 744th Separate Signals Battalion, in the post of which he took part in the Battle of Kursk On 2 September 1943 he became the chief of staff of the 109th Separate Signals Regiment, and from 5 May 1944 until the end of the war, he commanded a separate signals battalion of this regiment. Koltunov ended the war as a major, and was awarded the Order of the Patriotic War 1st and 2nd Degree, the Order of the Red Star and medals. In the years 1946-1947 he served as the chief of staff of a signals battalion in the Belorussian Military District, before taking command of the battalion. After graduating from the Frunze Military Academy's Department of Military History, he served in the military-historical department of the General Staff. On 6 April 1968, Koltunov was transferred to the USSR Ministry of Defense's Institute of Military History and assigned to lead a group of research associates. On 16 March 1971, he became the deputy chief editor and the leader of an author's collective for a volume of the 5th Edition of the 12-volume *Istoriia Vtoroi mirovoi voiny*. On 8 April 1978, he retired due to age. Koltunov was the author of a number of books and articles about the

new data. One of the characteristics of Koltunov's work was a critical approach to the discussed topics. For example, he was critical in his assessment of the level of the state of knowledge on the key problems of the summer of 1943. Thus, in his article "Voenno-istoricheskaia literature o bitve pod Kurskom" ["Military-historical literature on the Battle of Kursk"], he for the first time conducted a rather detailed analysis of the historiography of the Battle of Kursk from 1943 to the mid-1960s, and stressed a series of questions, which hadn't been resolved by domestic scholars by that time. The most significant of these problems were: the lack of a description of the Steppe Military District's line of defense, the planning of Operation Kutuzov and Operation Polkovodets Rumiantsev and their connection with the defensive phase of the Battle of Kursk, and an assessment of the deeply-echeloned Soviet defense and the application of the experience of its use by the Red Army's troops in the operations of 1944 and 1945. For example, he was the first of the Soviet scholars to express the important thought in the open press that the defense at Kursk was not typical for the Great Patriotic War:

> A major offensive grouping of Soviet forces was concentrated here. This was one of the rarest cases in history of military art, when the defending side had superiority in force and means ... All this doesn't give any basis to consider this defense, first of all the grouping of force and means, the engineered fortifications, etc. a model worthy of imitation.[35]

I especially want to dwell on G.A. Koltunov's article "Kurskaia bitva v tsifrakh (Period oborony)" ["Kursk battle in numbers (Defensive phase)"], which appeared in *Voenno-istoricheskii zhurnal* (No. 6, 1968). It became one of the most important publications on the given topic over the entire second stage of the historiography of the Battle of Kursk. This article introduced a large amount of statistical material on the numerical strength and the quantity of armaments and equipment of the Soviet (Central and Voronezh Fronts) and German forces that were deployed in the area of the Kursk bulge by the beginning of July 1943, which had never before been introduced into academic circulation. In addition, it presented summary data on the operational density of forces of the Central and Voronezh Fronts before the battle, gave the tactical density and correlation of force between the opposing sides in the breakthrough sectors of the Soviet defense, and also calculated the daily average rate of advance made by the German forces in the course of Operation Citadel. All of this information was contained in 14 tables and accompanied by commentary. This information at this moment had very important significance, although it immediately must be noted that the author also made a number of crude mistakes, first of all with respect to the enemy forces, since almost all of them were estimated and as is known today, far from reality. In addition, an attentive analysis of German data prompts the thought that the figures were contrives in order to conceal a mistake made by the Soviet side when preparing for the Kursk defensive operation. As is known, back then Moscow assembled significantly greater force in the Central Front's sector, where the opposing German grouping (the Ninth Army) was perceptibly weaker than that opposite the Voronezh Front. G.A. Koltunov's tables, however, speak to the opposite: supposedly the Ninth Army was numerically greater than its neighbors, Army Group South's Fourth Panzer Army and Army Detachment Kempf. It isn't clear on what basis he made this decision, but in his calculations Koltunov also used data for the German Second Army, which as is known today didn't take part in Operation Citadel. In addition, when calculating the operational density of troops in the sector of Army Detachment Kempf on 5 July 1943, Koltunov made another mistake:

Battle of Kursk, the best known being his work together with Colonel B.G. Solov'ev, *Kurskaia bitva* [*Battle of Kursk*] (1970).

35 *Voenno-istoricheskii zhurnal,* (No. 7, 1963), p. 105.

its two corps that took part in the operation (the III Panzer Corps and Korps Raus [XI Corps]) were deployed not in a sector of 170 kilometers, as he indicated, but in a sector of just 32 kilometers.[36] Today it is difficult to understand whether this was done intentionally (under the pressure of censors), or whether the author, because of a lack of information, was forced to use numbers that were prepared long before him on the basis of mistaken intelligence. However, in any case in this portion his article worked not in favor of a scientific approach to the subject, but to justify one of the myths formed by Soviet propaganda.

Nevertheless, this was the first time that such a significant quantity of statistical material on this event appeared in the open Soviet press. It unquestionably broadened the perspective of civilian historians and allowed the presentation of the real scale of the defensive phase of the Battle of Kursk and the assessment of the Red Army's forces and means that were deployed on the northern and southern shoulders of the Kursk bulge, not on the basis of words, as had been the case to a considerable degree previously, but on the basis of dry numbers. Unfortunately, this article became not only the first, but also the only one of its type in the Soviet historiography of the Battle of Kursk, and thus some Russian scholars use the data from it even today – often without any critical analysis.[37]

Nevertheless, even so the changes that occurred in the Soviet Union under Khrushchev didn't render any perceptible influence on fundamental research in history. The four-volume *Operatsiia sovetskikh Vooruzhennykh Sil v Velikoi Otechestvennoi voine 1941-1945* [*Operations of the Soviet Armed Forces in the Great Patriotic War 1941-1945*], prepared by officers of the General Staff and which started to come out in 1958, can serve as an example of this. It not only laid out previous, mistaken views and material on the battles and engagements (for example, it continued to say that 1,500 armored vehicles took part in the clash at Prokhorovka), but it also understated the actions of several armies in major operations and gave incorrect reasons for a number of the Red Army's failures. For example, its authors maintained that the failure of the 5th Guards Tank Army's counteroffensive on 12 July 1943 was connected with "the lack of adequate time to prepare the counterattack" and "the passivity of the 1st Tank and of the 5th, 6th and 7th Guards Armies, which took part in the counterattack", although neither statement is true.[38] Rotmistrov's forces began to assemble in the Prokhorovka area on the afternoon of 9 July 1943, and accordingly had two days in reserve in order to bring themselves back into order after the march and prepare for combat actions. According to frontline standards, this was fully adequate. As concerns the rebuke addressed to the other armies, which supposedly didn't take part in the counteroffensive, this assertion is also far from the historical truth. In the first place, it was the active operations of the 1st Tank Army's 10th Tank Corps on 12 July that prevented a pivoting of *Grossdeutschland* (one of the XXXXVIII Panzer Corps' strongest divisions) to go to the assistance of the II SS Panzer Corps at Prokhorovka. Secondly, Lieutenant General A.S. Zhadov's 5th Guards Army, which operated on the right of Rotmistrov's tank army, although it in fact did fail to counterattack, and its rifle divisions in the bend of the Psel River due to objective reasons were forced to retreat somewhat to the east, nevertheless prevented a breakthrough of its line of defense, while the SS *Totenkopf* Panzer Grenadier Division, as recognized by the Germans themselves, lost more armor here than did the SS forces on the axis of 5th Guards Tank Army's main attack.

An important feature of the military-historical publications of the early 1960s was the description of the overall course of combat actions in the sector of the Central Front in the summer of

36 NARA, t. 312, r. 54, f. 7569611.

37 For example: *Ognennaia duga* [*Fiery bulge*] (Moscow: Izdatel'skii dom "Zvonnitsa-MG", 2003), pp. 596-599.

38 *Operatsiia Sovetskikh Vooruzhennykh Sil v Velikoi Otechestvennoi voine 1941-1945* [*Operations of the Soviet Armed Forces in the Great Patriotic War 1941-1945*], Vol. 2 (Moscow: Voenizdat, 1959), p. 248.

1943 and separate battles of its forces without any particular slant or open exaggerations, as were observed with respect to the events on the southern shoulder of the Kursk bulge. For example, the defensive fighting at Ponyri Station, which in the 1970s began to be compared in scale with the Prokhorovka clash, is only assessed in the book *Operatsiia sovetskikh Vooruzhennykh sil v Velikoi Otechestvennoi voine 1941-1945* as "an instructive example of stubbornness on the defense" of the 307th Rifle Division, while the victory in the fighting was correctly ascribed to the high density of our forces, the correct use of units and formations of various types of forces and the skillfully established cooperation.

One of the substantial, negative features of the historiography of the Battle of Kursk of this period, and of later years, was the exaggeration of the merits of individual armies, corps and even divisions in the victory. This tendency first appeared back in 1943 and was connected with the desire of high-ranking generals of the Red Army to take part in the "awards marathon" and the discernible ossification in the work of military-historical teams of the General Staff. After the war it continued to develop, but now other factors were influencing it. First was the military-pedagogical and military-academic activity of P.A. Rotmistrov.[39] Second was N.S. Khrushchev's participation in the Battle of Kursk as a member of Voronezh Front's Military Council. The unrestrained praise of N.S. Khrushchev's actions in the years of the Great Patriotic War overflowed in practically every publication from the end of the 1950s and beginning of the 1960s. In order to accommodate the actively forming cult around the head of state, important events were distorted, entire pages in the chronicles of the war were wiped out, and the prolonged, painstaking, creative staff work in the army and *front* headquarters to plan and prepare for combat actions and battles was effaced. Striving to "keep up with the times", certain authors included entire paragraphs in their works that described how Nikita Sergeevich in fact carried out the functions of the army commander, without a direct order for this or at least the recommendation of the latter. The articles and brochures of P.A. Rotmistrov and the book by the former member of the 1st Guards Tank Army's Military Council N.K. Popel',[40] *Tanki povernuli na zapad* [*Tanks pivoted to the west*], which were published in this period, can serve as a clear example of such "creative interpretation of the past".[41]

39 Between 1948 and 1968, Rotmistrov headed a department in the K.E. Voroshilov Military Academy, the Armored Academy, and was an assistant of the USSR Minister of Defense responsible for training facilities.

40 Popel', Nikolai Kirillovich (1901-1980?), Lieutenant General, in the Red Army from 1920. From 1938, he was the military commissar of the 11th Motorized Brigade. In the period of repressions, he took part in writing "political testimonies" that contained damaging information regarding the command staff of the Red Army. At the start of the war, he was a Brigade Commissar and commissar of the 8th Mechanized Corps. He led the corps' mobile group, which was involved in heavy fighting at Dubno, after which a portion of the group withdrew from encirclement. Between 25 August and 8 December 1941, Popel' was a member of the 38th Army's Military Council. In September 1942, he was the military commissar of the 3rd Mechanized Corps. From 30 January 1943 until the end of the war, Popel' served as a member of the 1st Guards Tank Army's Military Council. In the period of preparing for and conducting the Battle of Kursk, he managed to forge good relations with N.S. Khrushchev, who highly valued his activities at this time. On 20 August 1943 for the participation in the Battle of Kursk of seven highly-posted political workers of the Voronezh Front, he was written up for high honors; three of them, including N.K. Popel', for the Order of Lenin, but Moscow rejected this recommendation. After the war he lived in Moscow and wrote books, including the following titles that were published: *V tiazhkuyu poru* [*At an arduous time*] (1959), *Tanki povernuli na zapad* [*Tanks pivoted to the west*] (1960), *Brigada "Revoliutsionnaia Mongoliia"* [*Brigade "Revolutionary Mongolia"*] (1977). He also wrote *Upravlenie voiskami v gody Velikoi Otechestvennoi voine* [*Command of troops in the years of the Great Patriotic War* (1974) together with V.P. Savel'ev and P.V. Shemansky. The literary critic E.V. Kardin worked on the transcript and editing of Popel's memoirs.

41 N.K. Popel', *Tanki povernuli na zapad* [*Tanks pivoted to the west*] (Moscow: Voenizdat, 1960).

In order to inflate the significance of N.S. Khrushchev's wartime activity, the ideological organs already at the beginning of the 1960s began to use the memoirs of former commanders as well, even though in their narrow circle Khrushchev, as a military specialist, to put it gently never had any authority. Nevertheless, ever more frequently panegyric odes about his sweeping and vigorous work began to appear in articles and recollections of the former *front* commanders, and then even of army commanders. For example, K.K. Rokossovsky in his collection of articles *Na Ognennoi duge. Vospominaniia i ocherki o Kurskoi bitve* [*On the Fiery bulge: Recollections and essays about the Kursk battle*] "related" how during the period of preparation for the summer fighting of 1943, Military Council member of the (neighboring!) Voronezh Front N.S. Khrushchev visited the headquarters of the Central Front, which Rokossovsky commanded, "in order to brief him on the situation that was facing the Soviet Union by that time".[42] As a rule, commanders and military chiefs were difficult characters. Thus in order to avoid scandals, which they might kick up, such insertions in the text absolutely had to be signed off by them. G.K. Zhukov, who for more than a year fought such "inclusions" in the manuscript of his own memoirs (not understanding how a marshal and Communist could so grovel and lie in this fashion), in a personal letter to K.K. Rokossovsky pointed to this specific episode very rudely:

> I attentively follow your appearances in the press. Indeed, I'm always waiting for a correct description of the history of the operations from you. But alas! You, Konstantin Konstantinovich, turn out to be not free of the desire to act coquettishly in front of the mirror of history, to embellish your personality and to distort the facts. I will remind you only of several. Describing the preparation of the troops of the Central Front for the Kursk battle, you wrote about the leading role of N.S. Khrushchev in this vital operation. You wrote that he visited you at the front and supposedly gave you wise advice "far exceeding the scale of the *fronts*." You presented him in the press as if Khrushchev played sort of some especially leading role in the war. This, as is known, wasn't the case, and you knew this. As you know, Khrushchev visited together with me. I'll remind you how it actually was: There was a good meal, over which Khrushchev and Bulganin drank way too much. A lot of jokes and stories were told by Khrushchev and Bulganin, and then Khrushchev drove off to the headquarters of the Voronezh Front, while I remained at the front entrusted to you, where we worked out questions of the forthcoming operation with a trip to visit the troops. I trust you haven't forgotten this?[43]

However, this noxious tendency showed even more visibly and on a larger scale in the six-volume *Istoriia Velikoi Otechestvennoi voiny 1941-1945* [*History of the Great Patriotic War 1941-1945*]. Here's how the former chief of the Red Army's General Staff Marshal of the Soviet Union A.M. Vasilevsky assessed this publication:

> You read the multi-volume *Istoriia Velikoi Otechestvennoi voiny 1941-1945* … and sometimes you're surprised. In the period of preparing for the Stalingrad operation and during the operation itself, including in the period of the most savage fighting with the Germans' Kotel'nikovo grouping, I drove from one army to the next, from some units to others literally all the time in the same vehicle with Khrushchev. He never climbed out of my vehicle, and was always located wherever I was. But look; you read this history, and in it is written: "Comrade

42 *Na Ognennoi duge. Vospominaniia i ocherki o Kurskoi bitve* [*On the Fiery bulge: Recollections and essays on the Kursk battle*] (Moscow: Voenizdat, 1963), p. 25.

43 RGVA, F. 41107, Op. 2, D. 13, l. 30.

> Khrushchev arrived somewhere," "Comrade Khrushchev arrived at the command post of some corps", "Comrade Khrushchev spoke somewhere and with someone" and so on and so on. As for where the Chief of the General Staff is, that remains unknown.
>
> In this *History*, the planning of the operation at Kursk has been described even more strangely. From this description one gets the impression that this operation was primarily planned on the Voronezh Front, when in actual fact I, Zhukov, and Rokossovsky came together to plan this operation; Vatutin and Khrushchev arrived there during this work. This is actually how it was, and not more than that.[44]

G.K. Zhukov seconded Vasilevsky's opinion: "... This is a varnished history. I believe in this respect that the description of the history given by German generals, although skewed, is nevertheless more honest; they write more truthfully. Yet this *Istoriia Velikoi Otechestvennoi voiny* is absolutely dishonest. This isn't history as it was, but history as has been written. It answers the spirit of the times. Who must be glorified, and who must be forgotten."[45]

In the words of a key figure of the Red Army, there is at a minimum a personal grievance about being forgotten. Actually, the publication was openly biased: it either overlooked or consigned to historical oblivion a number of important events, major personalities and essential factors, including those that had a genuine influence on the decisions of the Soviet and German command when planning the 1943 summer campaign.

For example, in the third volume when laying out the events in Ukraine in February-March 1943, emphasis was given to the thwarting of the enemy plans by Soviet forces. However, it remains silent about the defeat suffered by the Voronezh and Southwestern Fronts, their large losses in troops, and their abandonment of a significant area, 150 kilometers, of the territory they had liberated, including the yielding of the major industrial and administrative center of Khar'kov to the enemy. The authors "forgot" to mention the fact that a number of offensive operations by the Central and Briansk Fronts that were started at this time never made any progress. Not only these major failures in the area of the Kursk bulge were bypassed in silence, but what is most important, the reasons for these failures weren't fully identified. Nevertheless, as is known, correct conclusions drawn regarding already conducted large-scale operations, even unsuccessful ones, are highly productive, since not on a theoretical basis, but in actual practice the weakest places in the planning and readying of the troops can be revealed.

After all, already in the spring of 1943 the *Stavka* of the Supreme High Command and the General Staff analyzed both the results of the three-month counteroffensive in the south of the Soviet-German front, and the situation that developed after retreat of the two *fronts* from Ukraine. The conclusions were discomforting: the results of the combat operations after Stalingrad might have been more impressive. At the very least, given a proper reckoning of their strength, a sober assessment of the enemy and the emerging situation, there was a real possibility to hold the already liberated Khar'kov and Belgorod. At the same time, von Manstein's counterattack demonstrated that Germany's armed forces still retained a high degree of combat potential. In the course of those battles, the Red Army not only lost a significant portion of its manpower, armaments and equipment, but a blow had been inflicted to its prestige, which at that moment had not unimportant significance for the USSR's image in the world. This tragic experience in the spring of 1943 plainly affected the mood of the political and military leadership of the Soviet Union. It began to assess

44 K.M. Simonov, *Glazami cheloveka moego pokoleniia* [*Through the eyes of a man of my generation*] (Moscow: APN, 1988), pp. 464-465.

45 Nikoronov, A.B., Zvonov, V.I., Karpov, V.V., and Svetlishin, V.V., *Marshal Sovetskogo Soiuza G.K. Zhukov: Khronika zhizni* [*Marshal of the Soviet Union G.K. Zhukov: Chronicle of life*] (Moscow: Russkaia kniga, 1998), p. 323.

its own possibilities and the enemy's potential more cautiously and prudently. The process of planning the defense at Kursk demonstrated this particularly clearly. Owning a numerical superiority in every type of troops and having accumulated significant operational and strategic reserves, Moscow deliberately yielded the initiative to the enemy, so as to exhaust him through defensive fighting and only then go over to decisive actions to liberate the country fully from its occupiers. Hitler, on the other hand, didn't draw the necessary lessons from the tragedy on the Volga and the lengthy retreat that followed it. Von Manstein's success to a certain degree defused the "Stalingrad catastrophe", thanks to which, despite the serious risk, he ultimate resolved upon the conducting of the dubious, in essence, Operation Citadel.

One more substantive lesson, which the Soviet command drew from the failure of the spring 1943 offensive, concerned the forms and means of countering the enemy's armor. As before, tanks determined the success when conducting a defense or an offense. Operations Gallop, Star and especially the defensive fighting in March 1943 at Khar'kov and Belgorod clearly demonstrated that the Wehrmacht's armored formations retained a high combat capability. Thus during the period of the strategic pause, Moscow directed enormous efforts to create new types of weapons, to improve the organizational forms of the artillery, to liquidate the "tank fright" in the personnel of the acting army, and to teach it ways to counter the latest German tanks. Indeed the main point was that the entire defense at Kursk was constructed as an anti-tank defense and organized to the entire depth of each army's defensive sector. This was one of the decisive factors of the success in the summer of 1943, particularly on the Voronezh Front.

Unfortunately, the *Istoriia Velikoi Otechestvennoi voiny* didn't touch upon any of this. In addition, the six-volume work failed to illuminate in the proper fashion important, but inconvenient for the Soviet side, problems that arose already in the course of the Battle of Kursk. For example, it failed to discuss the reasons for the German breakthrough of an army-level belt of the Central Front already on 5 July 1943, even though at that moment its 13th Army possessed colossal forces; the failure to carry out the objectives of the counterattack on 12 July 1943 on the Voronezh Front; the mistakes in using the tank armies of homogenous composition on the Oboian' and Prokhorovka directions; and the low pace of advance by forces of the Central and Briansk Fronts in the Orel offensive operation. In addition, *Istoriia Velikoi Otechestvennoi voiny 1941-1945* failed to reveal and analyze the difficulties that arose in the first days of the defensive operation with the command and control over the troops in the 2nd Tank Army, which was operating on the axis of Army Group South's main attack.

The authors of this fundamental work also made a number of factual errors. For example, they maintained that the command of Army Group South by 10 July 1943 had rejected an offensive through Oboian' and had begun to assemble the majority of the Fourth Panzer Army's formations at Prokhorovka Station, thanks to which a never before seen density of armor – 100 tanks and self-propelled guns per 1 kilometer of front – had been created here by 11 July 1943.[46] In reality, the leadership of von Manstein's Army Group South had already rejected the idea of an offensive out of the Belgorod area directly to the north back in May 1943, and at the indicated time it wasn't conducting any regrouping whatsoever to the Prokhorovka area. Only the panzer grenadier divisions of the II SS Panzer Corps were as before continuing to operate on the distant approaches to Prokhorovka Station, and they weren't the main forces of Hoth's Fourth Panzer Army, while the authors plainly exaggerated their numerical strength. Thus the indicated density of armor in the Prokhorovka area doesn't correspond to reality.

46 *Istoriia Velikoi Otechestvennoi voiny 1941-1945* [*History of the Great Patriotic War 1941-1945*] (Moscow: Voenizdat, 1961), p. 272.

The six-volume work also unjustifiably maintained that when conducting the counterattack on 12 July 1943, the 1st Tank Army and the 6th, 7th and 5th Guards Armies were unable to take part in it "to the same extent that the Voronezh Front command had previously intended", and thus, supposedly, "the main burden of the fighting fell upon the 5th Guards Tank Army."[47] This not only distorts the essence of one of the most significant defensive measures taken by the Voronezh Front command when repelling the attack by Army Group South toward Kursk, but also plays down the role played by the troops of the other five armies that were activated for the counterattack. The book's editorial board plainly came under the influence of P.A. Rotmistrov, who advanced this thesis that is so far from historical reality back in 1960 in his first work on Prokhorovka. It is difficult to explain the coincidence between the point of view laid out in his memoirs and that of the editorial board. Pavel Alekseevich wrote:

> During the preparation of the Soviet forces for the counterattack, the enemy unexpectedly launched a powerful tank and air attack against these armies and shoved the 1st Guards Tank and 6th Guards Armies back in the direction of Oboian', while a portion of the left-flank formations of the 5th Guards Army were hurled back toward Prokhorovka. As a result, these armies didn't have time to prepare to conduct the counterattack on 12 July and took no part in it on this day. The enemy didn't fail to take advantage of this.[48]

This open fabrication is repeated again after several pages, which testifies to the fact that the former tank army commander wasn't simply mistaken, but was deliberately diminishing the role played by the neighbors in the counterattack. Such assertions, which one often encounters in other publications by P.A. Rotmistrov as well, became the reason for a sharp dispute that erupted in the mid-1960s among the veterans of the Battle of Kursk. The open disregard for the achievement of the hundreds of thousands of soldiers of these armies and the extravagant inflation of their own merits for a long time put not only Pavel Alekseevich, but also the 5th Guards Tank Army's Council of Veterans, at odds with their comrades in arms – the veteran's organization of the 1st Guards Tank Army. Subsequently, in works published at the beginning of the 1970s, Marshal Rotmistrov attempted to correct the point of view about the participation of the 5th Guards Army in the counterattack.

Unfortunately, the six-volume *Istoriia Velikoi Otechestvennoi voiny* also didn't avoid mistakes when laying out the course of combat operations on the northern shoulder of the Kursk bulge. It maintained that the 18th Guards Rifle Corps by 5 July 1943 was located in the Central Front's reserve.[49] In reality, it had been transferred to the command of the 13th Army back on 29 March, and by the start of the fighting comprised its second echelon.[50] Such mistakes are unquestionably annoying, although excusable for monographs or new research papers, but not for such fundamental publications as the *Istoriia*, which the country's best academic scholars worked on at that time.

One more substantial, negative feature of this work was the masking of the individuality (personal traits, style of work, command patterns, etc.) of all the more or less prominent and significant figures of the past war. As the American journalist A. Werth, who worked in the Soviet Union between 1941 and 1945, accurately noted, "The publication suffers from that shortcoming, common for many, but not all Soviet books on the Second World War – it shows essentially all

47 Ibid., p. 273.
48 P.A. Rotmistrov, *Tankovoe srazhenie pod Prokhorovkoi* [*Tank battle at Prokhorovka*] (Moscow: Voenizdat, 1960), p. 69.
49 *Istoriia Velikoi Otechestvennoi voiny*, p. 249.
50 TSAMO RF, F. 62, Op. 321, D. 5, l. 150, 151.

Russians to be virtually identical to one another."[51] Such an approach testified not only to the collected authors' failure to grasp the significance of personalities of the individuals who were part of the system of strategic and operational planning of combat operations and the command and control of forces, but mostly showed the desire of the Soviet leadership back then to assign a special role to the Communist Party and Soviet system by any and all means, and to deprive the individual (the Soviet soldier, commander or worker in a defense plant) of the right to act independently, to accomplish a feat or a conspicuous deed in defense of the Fatherland by his or her own will.

Subjected to just criticism immediately after separate volumes of *Istoriia* came out in print, the editorial board was forced to update it urgently. For example, an amended third volume came out in 1964. However, the government system, arranged under "one man", was incapable of transforming itself. Thus there were no principle changes in the reprinted books; only clerical errors were removed and several sections of the volumes were expanded. The chapter on the events of the Battle of Kursk also underwent only cosmetic changes.

It should be emphasized that in the first half of the 1960s, the subject of the Battle of Kursk was one of the most highly discussed in the Soviet mass media. The reason for this was not only contained in the personal interest of N.S. Khrushchev and his closest circle, although unquestionably this had substantial influence. However, in my view the ideological factor was nevertheless decisive. The point is that in the period of the Khrushchev "Thaw", for the first time the Soviet people heard about the tragic events of 1941 and 1942, albeit in a very abridged form. Nevertheless, for the majority of the public, the effect was stunning. The aim of this was the desire of N.S. Khrushchev's circle to reinforce the process of dismantling the cult of Stalin's personality, to fortify the thesis in the public conscience that I.V. Stalin commanded the forces by using a globe, and thereby enhance their own power and influence. Once this result was achieved, then an "anti-dote" was necessary – a powerful counterweight to the first phase of the war, so that the negative consequences of the released wave of information, directed at the former Supreme Commander-in-Chief, wouldn't be shifted in the public mind to the Communist Party of the Soviet Union and the government as a whole. The Battle of Kursk suited this purpose perfectly. Firstly, it was grand in scale and victorious. Secondly, it occurred in the summer, which in 1941 and 1942 had been an unsuccessful time of year for the Red Army to conduct combat operations. Thirdly, many of its participants (generals, major political workers and Party functionaries) were not only "in the ranks" back then, but they were also occupying prominent posts in the Red Army and government. Thus, to the leadership there appeared the possibility of resolving the ideological task, while also not forgetting about themselves. As a result, the three months before the beginning of July and the 49 fiery days of July and August 1943 became a "standby" topic not only on the eve of anniversaries, but in one or another form were present on the pages of Soviet newspapers and in the radio waves for years.

It is impossible not to recognize that in addition to the Soviet leadership's lack of interest in a deep academic analysis of the Great Patriotic War, a number of other objective factors affected the quality of historical research at that time. First was the inadequate knowledge of Soviet historians about the Soviet Union's military strategy in the war years and their unpreparedness to work on the given subject. Secondly, the base of accessible archival sources was extremely narrow. As in the previous years, all of the operational and most of the reports of the armies and *fronts* for the years 1941-1945 were as before classified and were not accessible to scholars. In addition, many of the archival files from the war were in disarray; the documents hadn't been systematized and were scattered across various military departments and offices. A.M. Vasilevsky testified:

51 A. Werth, *Rossiia v voine 1941-1945* [*Russia at war, 1941-1945*] (Moscow, 1966), p. 302.

> It is a surprising matter, how we make little use of documents. Twenty years have passed since the end of the war, people remember and argue, but argue often without documents, without verification, which could easily be done. Quite recently, while searching for several documents, I discovered an enormous quantity of documents in one of the departments of the General Staff. They included reports and conversations on the most important operations of the war, which with absolute accuracy testify to how things went in reality. But since the war itself and to the present day, these documents have been resting just as they were lying. No one has even glanced at them.[52]

One more important factor that concerns historians should be mentioned. A former member of the editorial board of *Voenno-istoricheskii zhurnal* Colonel V.M. Kulish wrote:

> The *Stavka* of the Supreme High Command and the State Defense Committee left behind few documents in the realm of strategic command over the forces. I.V. Stalin, preoccupied with the observation of secrecy, and perhaps due to other reasons banned participants of conferences to keep notes without his prompting. They, as Zhukov, Vasilevsky and others recalled, had to memorize the adopted decisions and instructions, and having returned to their offices, had to write them down in secret notebooks from memory. In addition, such notebooks, according to the regulations about classified document management, were periodically destroyed by a special commission. So this batch of documents disappeared, while other important operational documents were simply lost.[53]

The difficulties with documentary sources of a strategic nature were known not only to military historians, but also to the leadership of the Communist Party Central Committee and the USSR Ministry of Defense, because they created a substantial problem in their work. Thus, in the mid-1960s, the decision was made to publish a special multi-volume work, *Sbornik dokumentov Verkhovnogo Glavnokomandovaniia za period Velikoi Otechestvennoi voiny* [*Collection of documents of the Supreme High Command over the period of the Great Patriotic war*][54] Such a step, unquestionably, might have increased the level of knowledge of scholars and have had a beneficial effect on the quality of their research. However, this didn't happen; the first books began to be published when the arrow of the barometer of the social and political life of the country shifted away from "Thaw" and distinctly pointed at "Frosts", ushering in the third stage in the historiography of the Battle of Kursk and the war as a whole. Genuine academic historical works were not only of no interest to the authorities; they considered them harmful. However, the third volume of this *Sbornik dokumentov*, which came out in 1969, covered among other things the Battle of Kursk, and nevertheless plays a positive role. Exactly 30 years later, the materials gathered in it would enter a thematic collection of materials, be published by the TERRA publishing house in 1999, and become an event in the academic life of our country.

Despite the aforementioned problems, when reviewing the achievements of Soviet historical science in the entire postwar period, especially as they relate to the events of the summer of 1943, as well incidentally to the war as a whole, it must be recognized that the 1960s were the most productive. The rather large and fruitful volume of work done by military and civilian historians unquestionably contributed to the cultivation of a spirit of dedication among the Soviet people,

52 Simonov, *Glazami cheloveka*, p. 465.

53 *Voenno-istoricheskii zhurnal*, No. 8, 2009, p. 66.

54 A.N. Grylev (ed.), *Sbornik dokumentov Verkhovnogo Glavnokomandovaniia za period Velikoi Otechestvennoi voiny* [*Collection of documents of the Supreme High Command over the period of the Great Patriotic War*]; in 4 volumes (Moscow: Voenizdat, 1968-1969).

not so much to the Communist Party of the Soviet Union, but to the Motherland and the nation. At the same time, the best representatives of the academic community not without justification believed that the generalized experience of the past was not only important for the defense of the state, the combat capabilities of its military and the forming of ideology. A.G. Grylev wrote, "Knowledge of history, including military history as well, spiritually enriches the man, expands his perspective, and contributes to the breadth of thinking."[55] One can assert with confidence that a number of the works published at this time fully corresponded to these aims. Some of them even today haven't lost their relevance, because their authors treated the famous deeds of the military generation of the Soviet people with great respect, as far as this was possible, striving not to replace them with demagogy and empty praises, but to analyze the achievements and blunders conscientiously, painstakingly accumulating invaluable experience and knowledge about our country's past.

The memoir literature also developed actively in these years. Of all the memoir authors, the most open in describing and assessing the events at Kursk (considering the historical realities of that time) and the most consistent in defending his views on separate key moments of the Battle of Kursk was Marshal of the Soviet Union G.K. Zhukov. In his book *Vospominaniia i razmyshleniia* [*Reminiscences and Reflections*], published in 1969, distinctly discernible is the desire to sweep under the rug the unsuccessful operations, in which he acted as a key figure, like Operation Mars and Operation Polar Star. As concerns the 1943 summer campaign, then there Georgii Konstantinovich writes as openly as it was possible back then, and with considerable difficulty worked out an agreement with the ruling establishment regarding the publication of his memoirs.[56] Firstly, he openly acknowledged that when planning the defense at Kursk, the *Stavka* of the Supreme High Command (and he himself personally) committed a serious blunder in determining the axis of the Wehrmacht's main attack. They expected that the German command would hurl its main forces (Army Group Center) against the Central Front, whereas in reality the Wehrmacht's most powerful grouping (Army Group South) was concentrated opposite the Voronezh Front. This error had a substantially negative influence on the course of the first stage of the battle. In essence, everything that Vatutin's *front* and the *Stavka* did in the first two weeks of July 1943 was aimed at correcting this error.

Secondly, the Marshal quite self-critically remarked that the counter-artillery preparation, which was conducted on the evening of 4 July and the night of 4-5 July 1943, which had been officially recognized as successful,[57] didn't in fact bring the expected result. He also criticized the attempts by the air forces of the Voronezh and Southwestern Fronts to strike German airfields at dawn on 5 July, noting that "they fully failed to achieve their goal."[58]

Thirdly, G.K. Zhukov openly spoke out against P.A. Rotmistrov's self-aggrandizement and the myth he created, which purported that his tank army at Prokhorovka played the decisive role in collapsing the offensive of the entire Army Group South. However, the reader found out about this only in 1990, when the now uncensored Tenth Edition of his memoirs came out.[59]

55 A.G. Grylev, "Sovetskaia voennaia istoriografiia v gody Velikoi Otechestvennoi voiny i poslevoennyi period" ["Soviet military historiography in the years of the Great Patriotic War and the postwar period] *Voenno-istoricheskii zhurnal* (No. 3, 1968), p. 86.

56 See, for example, A.D. Mirkin, *Ne skloniv golovy; Marshal Zhukov: polkovodets i chelovek* [*Head unbowed; Marshal Zhukov: the commander and the man*] (Moscow: APN, 1988), pp. 47-78.

57 See, for example, *Istoriia Velikoi Otechestvennoi voiny Sovetskogo Soiuza 1941-1945* [*History of the Soviet Union's Great Patriotic War 1941-1945*] (Moscow: Voenizdat, 1964), p. 257, 263.

58 G.K. Zhukov, *Vospominaniia i razmyshleniia* [*Reminiscences and reflections*] 1st Ed. (Moscow: Novosti, 1969), p. 483.

59 Zhukov, *Vospominaniia i razmyshleniia*, 10th Ed. (Moscow: Novosti, 1990), p. 57.

Fourthly, Zhukhov objectively evaluated the results of the defensive phase of the Battle of Kursk in Voronezh Front's sector and brushed aside the unfounded assertion that his leadership incorrectly planned the defense and the actions of its forces, so the Germans were able to penetrate Voronezh Front's line to a depth of almost 35 kilometers, while Army Group Center's forces became stuck in Central Front's defenses after progressing just 12-15 kilometers.[60] The Marshal first expressed this point of view in an article published in the September 1967 issue of *Voenno-istoricheskii zhurnal*,[61] and subsequently developed it in his memoirs.

With the emergence of a new leadership in socio-political life of the USSR in October 1964, the retreat from the principles, which the leading Soviet scholars attempted to implement in research during the years of Khrushchev's "Thaw" began. The Brezhnev leadership adopted a course toward curtailing the relatively free discussion of important topics of the history of the war that had arisen in academic circles and in the press (on the pages of the "thick" journals, like *Voenno-istoricheskii zhurnal*). Already on 9 August 1967, even the laureate of six Stalin Awards, the well-known Soviet prose writer K. Simonov emphasized in a letter to the head of the Central Committee's Department of Culture V.F. Shauro that censorship in the country was "inordinately expanding" and its activity had taken on "unprecedented scope" recently.[62]

In fact, the year 1967 became the turning point in this respect. In the Central Committee decree issued on 14 August 1967 "O merakh po dal'neishemu razvitiiu obshchestvennykh nauk i povysheniiu ikh roli v kommunisticheskoi stroitel'stve" ["On the measures for the further development of social sciences and increasing their role in Communist construction"], Soviet historians were given their main task: to concentrate efforts on the analysis of problems that would reveal the decisive role of the CPSU and the popular masses in defeating Nazism in the years of the Great Patriotic War.[63] In order to achieve this aim, Party and government organs adopted yet more decrees, which curtailed Soviet historians' further activity. In the first stage the main efforts were directed at eliminating the process of de-Stalinization, which had started at the XX Party Congress. The ruling elite were striving to preserve fully the government system of control, created by I.V. Stalin. Thus, they weren't interested in Stalin's crimes of that period, the colossal human and material losses of the Red Army, or the mistakes made by the political and military leadership of the USSR, which had become publicly known. On the contrary, the name of the Supreme Commander-in-Chief began to emerge more frequently from out of historical oblivion, while everything connected with tragic pages in history was either suppressed or actively "glossed over". What moods were dominating in the country's leadership with respect to this important problem were clearly expressed in a statement made by the USSR Minister of Defense D.F. Ustinov[64] at a session of the Politburo on 12 July 1984, when the former peers of N.S. Khrushchev took an unprecedented step by restoring Party membership to V.M. Molotov, one of the main organizers of political repressions in the country. Declared D.F. Ustinov, "Not a single foe has inflicted as much

60 Zhukov, *Vospominaniia i razmyshleniia*, 1st Ed. (Moscow: Novosti, 1969), pp. 490-491.

61 *Voenno-istoricheskii zhurnal* (No. 9, 1967), p. 88.

62 A. Simonov, "Mne s kazhdym dnem vse tiazhelee zhit' i rabotat'" ["With each day it is harder for me to live and work"] *Rodina* (No. 11, 2015), p. 51.

63 A.P. Kosytsin, A.L. Nedavny, T.A. Pomynaeva, *Osnovnye zakonodatelnye akty po gosurdarstvennomu stroitel'stvu i pravu* [*Basic legal acts regarding government construction and law*] Vol. 1 (Moscow: Mysl', 1972), pp. 75-76.

64 D.F. Ustinov (1908-1984), Marshal of the Soviet Union (1976). From 1941 to 1953, he was a People's Commissar and the USSR Minister of Armaments, and from 1953 to 1957, the USSR Minister of the Defense Industry. Between 1957 and 1965, Ustinov was a deputy, then the first deputy chairman of the USSR Council of Ministers. In 1965 he became a secretary of the CPSU Central Committee, and from 1976 to 1984, served as the USRR Minister of Defense. Between 1966 and 1976, he was a candidate member of the Central Committee's Politburo, and from 1976 to 1984 a Politburo member.

damage as Khrushchev has brought upon us with his policy regarding the past of our Party and state, as well as with respect to Stalin."[65]

The ideological and censorship organs were given an instruction: strengthen the means of mass information, publishing houses and editorial boards to focus on revealing the leading role of the Communist Party in organizing a repulse of the Nazi aggressors and mass heroism of the Soviet people in the war years; and the description of the Red Army's victorious operations. It was "recommended" for groups of scholars in the social sciences, using the method of historical materialism and the principle of Party discipline in historical science, to put an emphasis on revealing the leading nature of Soviet military science, the prominent organizing role of the Communist Party in the struggle for victory, and so forth and so on. A former frontline veteran, the author of biting recollections of the Great Patriotic War Professor N.N. Nikulin, asked in his book:

> From where now, in the 1960s, did this myth arise once again that we won only thanks to Stalin, in the name of Stalin? I have no doubts on this account. Those, who won the war either fell on the battlefield or drank themselves to death, depressed by postwar hardships. After all, not only the war, but the country's resurrection came at their expense. Those of them that who are still alive are silent, broken down. Others stayed in power and held true – those who drove people into camps; those who in the war drove the soldiers into senseless, bloody attacks. They acted in the name of Stalin, and even now they are shouting about this. "For Stalin!" wasn't at the front. The commissars tried to pound this into our heads, but the commissars didn't take part in the attacks. This is all scum ....[66]

The decision taken back in the period when Khruschchev was in power also exacerbated the situation with the study of the events of 1941-1945. At the beginning of the 1960s, the point of view that a future war, if it erupted, would be a duel of nuclear rockets, gripped the leadership of the USSR. Thus the traditional structure of the country's military organization with a reliance on conventional types of weapons would supposedly gradually come to an end. Accordingly, the experience of past wars (primarily the Great Patriotic War), which was being studied by military historians and embodied in statutes, guidelines and other regulating documents, should remain in the past. After the new military doctrine was announced in 1963, the General Staff showed a tendency to curtail academic, military-historical research on the Great Patriotic War, and the turnover of this function to civilian scholars began to increase. Its culmination became the creation in August 1966 of the Institute of Military History, which was to become the chief academic research facility in the field of military history in the country. According to form it was a military institute (it was under the jurisdiction of the USSR Ministry of Defense), but according to the substance of its work it became an appendage of the Soviet Army's Main Political Command, which should be read as the Communist Party's Central Committee. Whereas previously for military historians the main standard for assessing their output was new knowledge gained from the study of both victories and defeats, primarily useful experience that would help commanders to work out methods of rational analysis, make correct decisions in the difficult conditions of battle and so forth, priority was now given to political expedience. The theme "History is primarily a powerful tool in the political struggle, and in past decades it has been underestimated" became actively embodied in academic life. Thus the Institute of Military History became the primary

---

65 A. Artizov and Iu. Sigachev, "Reabilitatsiia" ["Rehabilitation"] *Rodina* (No. 2, 2003), p. 48.

66 N.N. Nikulin, *Vospominaniia o voine* [*Recollections on the war*] (Saint Petersburg: Izdatel'stvo Gosudartsvennogo Ermitazha, 2008), p. 46.

instrument for bringing "proper order to this branch of propaganda work that had been neglected during Khrushchev's reign in power."

Many of the significant articles and publications on the military subject that came out when Khrushchev was in power were branded with the charge of "subjectivism". Thus in 1966 the CPSU Central Committee issued a decree regarding the publication of a new, 12-volume *Istoriia Vtoroi mirovoi voiny* [*History of the Second World War*]. Parallel with this, a special group for editing manuscripts and exerting control over publishable military-historical literature, primarily the memoirs of top commanders of the Great Patriotic War, was formed in the Main Political Command of the Soviet Army. Entire paragraphs and even sections, which didn't fit with modern notions, began to be excised from memoirs that were being prepared for publication, replaced by new ones that were far from true historically, but "necessary" for propaganda work.

However, the activity of the Brezhnev leadership to rewrite the history of the war immediately incurred the sharp resentment of former veterans of the war that were still in active service, including generals and marshals. Far from all of them, but many properly evaluated these steps by the authorities not as a return to historical truth, but as an attempt to create "a new history under the new General Secretary of the CPSU Central Committee." In a letter, sent in 1967 to the head of the Institute of Military History Major General P.A. Zhilin,[67] Marshal of Artillery N.D. Iakovlev wrote:

> Personally it seems to me that experienced readers expect from scholars of history not just a description of the course of combat operations on our part. Already a lot of them have been published and are being published. Unfortunately, the majority of them, which is to say articles, discussions, recollections and memoirs, are somehow similar to each other. In many instances they carry a touch of a rather cloying fawning toward a number of military commanders, the description of feats performed by individual soldiers, political workers, commanders and partisans ... *After all, not only panegyric reports are necessary, but also intensive research on the little, in which a lot of the big is hidden and where an academic approach is evident.*[68]

Several military commanders expressed their unwillingness to accommodate themselves with the expanding process of myth creation by attempts to write and publish honest memoirs. However, in those circumstances it proved practically impossible to do this. The majority of veterans, who had something to say about that war, now no longer believed in the possibility of passing along the truth to the Soviet citizen through the printed word. A veteran of the Battle of Kursk Lieutenant Colonel E.I. Shapiro[69] wrote in 1969 to the director of the Museum of the Battle of Kursk at the Kursk Home of Officers M.P. Bel'diev:

67 Zhilin, Pavel Andreevich (1913-1987), Lieutenant General (1968), Doctor of History (1956), professor (1961), member-correspondent of the USSR Academy of Science (1968), laureate of the USSR State Award (1952), and military historian. Zhilin was a veteran of the Great Patriotic War. Between 1946 and 1958, he did military research in the General Staff. Between 1958 and 1964, Zhilin was the deputy chief editor of the *Voenno-istoricheskii zhurnal*. From 1964 to 1966, Zhilin was a provost in the CPSU Central Committee's Academy of Social Science. In 1966 he was a founder and the first chief of the USSR Ministry of Defense's Institute of Military History. Zhilin was the deputy chairman of the main editorial board for the *Istoriia vtoroi mirovoi voiny 1939-1945*. He is the author of a number of monographs on the military history of Russia at the start of the 19th Century and the initial period of the Great Patriotic War.

68 N.D. Iakovlev, "Sovetskie vooruzhennye sily znachitel'no prevoskhodili vermakht po boevomu obespecheniiu" [The Soviet Army Forces were significantly superior to the Wehrmacht in combat logistics"] *Voenno-istoricheskii zhurnal* (No. 5, 2012), p. 19, 21.

69 From the middle of July 1943, Shapiro was the commander of the 507th Rifle Regiment of the 13th

Major K.I. Bukovsky (on the right), a correspondent of the *Krasnaia Zvezda* newspaper, at the command post of the 17th Guards Rifle Corps of the Central Front's 13th Army; September 1943 (RGAKFD).

Krasnaia Zvezda newspaper correspondents Lieutenant Colonel V.S. Grossman (on the left) and Major P. Olender (in the center) in a discussion with the newspaper's chief editor Corps Commissar D.I. Ortenberg in the area of the Kursk bulge before a trip to spend time with the troops; summer of 1943 (Photo by O.B. Knorring, RGAKFD).

A photograph of a knocked-out Ferdinand heavy self-propelled gun that was displayed at the first postwar exhibition of the Kursk Oblast Regional Museum. The caption reads, "Knocked-out Ferdinand self-propelled guns (they are also Panthers), Orel – Kursk axis, 28.7.43". (Kursk Oblast Regional Museum)

The famous *Krasnaia Zvezda* correspondent and author K. Simonov (in the center) strikes a pose together with the commander of the 13th Army's 75th Guards Rifle Division Major General A.A. Gorishnyi (left) and his political deputy Colonel I.V. Vlasenko; summer of 1943 (RGAKFD).

Major General I.V. Parot'kin, a military historian who made a weighty contribution to the study of the Battle of Kursk (a 1970 photograph; TsAMO).

Lieutenant Colonel I.I. Markin, the author of the first book about the Battle of Kursk that was published in the USSR for a wide audience and large circulation; a 1950 photograph (TsAMO).

A photograph of the cover of the 1958 2nd edition of I.I. Markin's book *Kurskaia bitva* [*Battle of Kursk*]

The Commander-in-Chief of the Main Political Directorate of the Soviet Army and Navy General of the Army A.A. Epishev (second from the right) and the First Deputy of the USSR Ministry of Defense A.A. Grechko during a 1963 meeting with family members of wartime partisans (RGAKFD).

The former Commander-in-Chief of the Central Front Marshal of the Soviet Union K.K. Rokossovsky addressing the crowd gathered in a stadium of the city of Kursk to mark the 20th Anniversary of the Battle of Kursk. 1963 (RGAKFD).

Маршал Советского Союза
И.С. КОНЕВ,
Дважды Герой Советского Союза

ВЕЛИКАЯ БИТВА ПОД КУРСКОМ И ЕЕ
ИСТОРИЧЕСКОЕ ЗНАЧЕНИЕ

Битва под Курском, которую мы вправе назвать великой битвой, характерна огромным размахом, исключительной напряженностью и ожесточенностью борьбы. Она охватила огромную территорию ныне Орловской, Брянской, Курской, Белгородской, Сумской, Харьковской и Полтавской областей. Пятьдесят дней шли упорные и напряженные бои на земле и в воздухе. За это время обеими сторонами было последовательно введено в сражения свыше 4 млн. человек, более 69 тыс. орудий и минометов, I3,2 тыс. танков и самоходных орудий и свыше II тыс. боевых самолетов. Развернувшиеся в ходе битвы танковые сражения не имели себе равных в военной истории. Это была величайшая танковая битва второй мировой войны.

В гигантских сражениях на Курской дуге была сорвана последняя попытка гитлеровского вермахта снова захватить стратегическую инициативу, потерянную под Сталинградом, и повернуть ход войны в свою пользу. Враг вынужден был перейти к стратегической обороне на всем советско-германском фронте - главном и решающем фронте второй мировой войны.

Иван Степанович Конев в период Курской битвы был командующим войсками Степного фронта.

The first page of the former Commander-in-Chief of the Steppe Front Marshal of the Soviet Union I.S. Konev's report to an academic conference dedicated to the 25th Anniversary of the victory at the Battle of Kursk, which was prepared for publication in the Major-General I.V. Parot'kin's edited book *Kurskaia bitva* after the inclusion of corrections. The handwriting in the upper left corner reads "With corrections. I. Konev, 17.1.69" (Author's personal archive).

Chief Marshal of the USSR's Armored Forces P.A. Rotmistrov before addressing the academic research conference dedicated to the 25th Anniversary of the Battle of Kursk. In the background is the Voronezh Front's former chief-of-staff General of the Army S.P. Ivanov; Moscow, August 1968 IAuthor's personal archive).

Chief of the USSR Ministry of Defense's Institute of Military History Lieutenant General P.A. Zhilin addresses a council of war veterans in Moscow, May 1985 (RGAKFD).

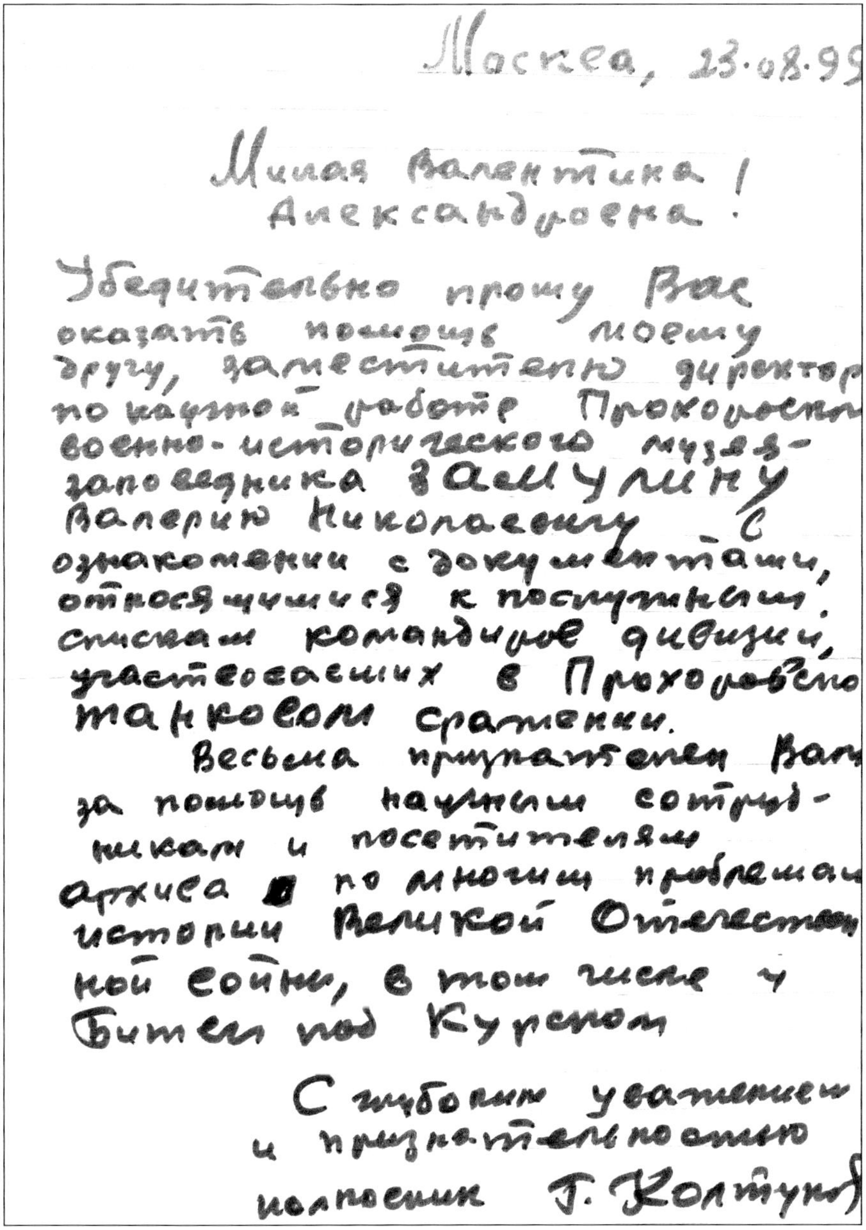
Москва, 23.08.99

Милая Валентина Александровна!

Убедительно прошу Вас оказать помощь моему другу, заместителю директора по научной работе Прохоровского военно-исторического музея-заповедника Замулину Валерию Николаевичу в ознакомлении с документами, относящимися к послужным спискам командиров дивизий, участвовавших в Прохоровском танковом сражении.

Весьма признателен Вам за помощь научным сотрудникам и посетителям архива по многим проблемам истории Великой Отечественной войны, в том числе и Битвы под Курском.

С глубоким уважением и признательностью

полковник Г. Колтунов

Colonel G. Koltunov's letter of recommendation to the director of the USSR Ministry of Defense's Central Archives reading hall. It reads,

Moscow, 23 August 1999

Dear Valentina Aleksandrovna!

I am earnestly asking you to give assistance to my friend, the deputy director for research work of the Prokhorovka Battlefield Park Museum Valeriy Nikolaevich Zamulin, in familiarizing him with the documents that relate to the service records of the division commanders that took part in the Prokhorovka tank battle. I'm fully indebted to you for the assistance given to academic colleagues and visitors of the archive regarding the many problems of the history of the Great Patriotic War, including the Battle of Kursk. With deep respect and gratitude, G. Koltunov

(Author's personal archive).

> I personally extremely doubt that it is possible to resurrect the true course of events [of the Kursk battle]. The process of the falsification of historical events has reached such frightening dimensions that it isn't possible through the efforts of one person, nor of any circle (Author's note: Shapiro has in mind here the military history community that existed in Kursk at that time) to restore the real course of events, with whatever good intentions it would be filled. A large number of people are interested in distorting the historical events, and thus I don't believe that your good intentions will be crowned with any serious success.[70]

Unfortunately, the opinion of this man, who passed through the furnace of the Great Patriotic War, accurately reflected the situation that had developed in the Soviet Union by that time. A former member of the editorial board of the *Voenno-istoricheskii zhurnal* V.M. Kulish, who through a lengthy period of service had to receive instructions from the people who were guiding the policy of the CPSU in the Soviet Army, also testified to this. The former journalist wrote:

> In a conversation with General N.G. Pavlenko [the journal's chief editor] and me, the chief of the Soviet Army's Main Political Command General A.A. Epishev himself translated the principle of Party discipline in a more accessible language. He said, "There, in *Novyi mir*[71] they say: 'Give them the black bread of truth.' Why on earth is this necessary if it isn't advantageous for us?" The idea of dividing historical truth into "advantageous" and "disadvantageous" found widespread circulation in the Party-propaganda and historical literature. The interpretation of Party discipline in science thus boiled down to the fact that the principle of academic rigor in research began to collide with the principle of political utility.[72]

To A.A. Epishev belongs another "immortal" point, which determined the objective of the authorities back then and essentially blocked the path to the progressive development of Soviet military history. Here's how it sounded in the words of the chief of the Soviet Army's Main Political Command in the course of a conversation with generals and marshals on 17 January 1966: "We cannot allow military chiefs to be criticized in the open press."[73]

Even so, nevertheless, at this time several military historians still attempted to get their message across to the intellectual element of the Party and society. Recognizing that the generation of victors was passing, while important problems of the war were not only being shunned in the works of domestic scholars, but that an active process of curtailing academic analysis had started, the authors of a collection of materials of a practical military conference under the editorship of Major General I.V. Parot'kin, dedicated to the 25th Anniversary of the victory at Kursk, expressed a bold and also urgent plea for that time:

> When studying the Kursk battle, it is necessary to pay attention not only to the positive, but also the negative experience, since the latter is no less valuable for the study of practical problems ... In research ... it is extremely desirable to subject the issue of losses to special examination, while in the process contrasting the losses with the achieved results. The comprehensive disclosure of this important question would allow the comparison of the contribution made

Army's 148th Rifle Division under the Central Front.

70 Author's personal archive.

71 *Novyi mir* is the oldest monthly literary journal of a liberal orientation, which came out against the hushing up of the crimes of the Stalin era, and which propagandized the ideas of democratic socialism.

72 V.M. Kulish, "Voenno-istoricheskii zhurnal v 1959-1967 gg." [Military-historical journal in the years 1959-1967" *Voenno-istoricheskii zhurnal* (No. 8, 2009), p. 69.

73 "My naprasno seichas deremsia" ["We are bickering in vain now"] *Rodina* (No. 5, 2005), p. 97.

> by *fronts* and armies to the common cause of defeating the foe at Kursk, and would give the opportunity to evaluate more objectively the role of individual formations and commanders in achieving victory in the Kursk battle.[74]

Unfortunately, this appeal made by the historians and frontline veterans remained unrealized right up to the end of the last century.

In addition to official censorship, another important factor had a substantial influence on the veracity, informational content and amount of detail about events in the books of high-ranking participants of the war, including about the Battle of Kursk, one which is rarely mentioned by historians. This is self-censorship, which is to say the "unwillingness to air one's dirty linen in public." This personal quality of many of the authors was formed not only under the influence of the public atmosphere, but also by the harsh conditions of long years of service in the army. General of the Army G.I. Obaturov recalls:

> In 1986 I had an opportunity to discuss this subject [Author's note: the unsuccessful combat operations at Nikopol in 1944] with D.D. Leliushenko.
>
> "Why, Dmitrii Danilovich, did you write so negligibly and little about the fierce fighting of the 3rd Guards Army on the Nikopol axis?" – I asked him.
>
> "And who is interested in writing about unsuccessful battles? When describing failures, I would have to say how they were attributed to the sins of neighbors and higher chiefs."
>
> "Failures often teach more than successes, which in fact is needed by our young officers," I persisted.
>
> "If you, Obaturov, like to dig into crap, then you go ahead and write; I have no intention to busy myself with this."

It is a pity that in many recollections, the description of lost battles and operations is ignored.[75]

The discussion that developed after the XX Party Congress, the publication of diverse military-historical and memoir literature in large print runs, the publication of genuine documents, and the release of the third volume of *Istoriia Velikoi Otechestvennoi voiny* not only expanded the knowledge of our society about the events in the fundamental turning point in the struggle against fascism, but also laid the foundation for the appearance in 1970 of the most well-known book by military historians G.A. Koltunov and B.G. Solov'ev, *Kurskaia bitva* [*Kursk battle*], which has been widely used by both scholars and publicists for many years.[76] It was written on the basis of accounts by officers of the General Staff with the headquarters of *fronts* and armies, which had never before been used in the open press. In a conversation with me, G.A. Koltunov recalled that the book had been initially planned as a simplified version of the research done by officers of the General Staff back at the end of the 1940s, designed for a wider audience and to assist both civilian historians and ideological workers. It was this circumstance that in fact determined the direction it would take. Together with a rather detailed look at a number of problems when planning the Kursk defensive operation and the summer campaign as a whole, the preparation of the troops, the construction of lines and the course of combat operations, the authors paid significant attention to the critique of Western studies and memoir literature, as well as Party-political work among the troops.

74 I.V. Parot'kin [ed.], *Kurskaia bitva* [Kursk battle] (Moscow: Nauka, 1970), p. 456.
75 G.I. Obaturov, *Dorogi ratnye krutye* [*Military roads are steep*] (1995), p. 240.
76 G.A. Koltunov and B.G. Solov'ev, *Kurskaia bitva* [*Kursk battle*] (Moscow: Voenizdat, 1970).

At the same time, however, in *Kurskaia bitva* the authors attempted to substantiate a number of myths about events at Kursk that were already persistent in the public conscience and historiography. In particular, the authors scrutinized the amount of armor that took part in the battle on 12 July 1943 at Prokhorovka, and analyzed how the enormous number of 1,500 tanks and self-propelled guns came about. In addition, Koltunov's and Solov'ev's book repeated the legend that formed back in 1943 in the account by Voronezh Front's Military Council, which purported that there had been no encirclement of the 5th Guards "Stalingrad" Tank Corps, which had moved out to the Prokhorovka axis on the night of 5-6 July. Moreover, their work included another batch of insignificant, but as time showed very tenacious myths. For example, the one about the flaming tank ramming, which was supposedly performed by the commander of a platoon of medium tanks of the 1st Tank Army's 1st Guards Tank Brigade Lieutenant V.S. Shalandin. We read in the book:

> The crew of the Komsomol member and Muscovite Guards Lieutenant V.S. Shalandin, consisting of driver-mechanic Guards Senior Sergeant V.G. Kustov, loader Guards Sergeant P.E. Zelenin, and radio operator-gunner Guards Senior Sergeant V.F. Lekomtsev, fought heroically. The crew knocked out two German Tiger tanks and one medium tank. Soon, our tankers' machine took a second direct hit and burst into flames. Choking in the smoke, Shalandin made another attempt to fire over open sights, but the damaged cannon poorly responded to the wounded commander. Then he decided to ram a hostile Tiger. Flaming, the T-34 went into motion and struck the Tiger's flank with full force. The enemy tank caught fire and its fuel tanks exploded. Enveloped in flames, the Guards crewmen were killed. By a decree of the USSR Presidium of the Supreme Soviet, V.S. Shandalin was posthumously awarded the title Hero of the Soviet Union.[77]

In the 1970s, the act of Shalandin's crew was turned by Soviet propaganda into a symbol of the resolve of our soldiers in the Battle of Kursk. Essays were published, films were made, and poems were composed about it. Here is just one example, the widely known lines from the work of a Belgorod poet V. Tat'ianin, "Posle boia" ["After the battle"]: "... *Here Shalandin in the menacing Thirty Four/steered his tank, burning, toward the foe .../You ask – and even children will tell you/what the Kursk bulge was like.*"[78] However, if we turn to documents, for example to V.S. Shalandin's commendation, which was signed by his direct superior, the commander of the 1st Guards Tank Brigade's 2nd Tank Battalion Major S.I. Vovchenko (when writing such commendations, the commanders never missed the opportunity to offer a colorful and dramatic description of the commendee's exploit), then we should really see an example of the tankers' genuine heroism and resolve when giving up their lives in the struggle against the foe. However, in the commendation there is not even a mention of the ramming episode. The document states: "Despite the enemy's constant bombing and artillery fire, Comrade Shalandin heroically fought for 10 hours. Comrade Shalandin burned to death in the tank on the very spot where his platoon had been ordered to hold the defense."[79]

77 Ibid., pp. 148-149.

78 *Tret'e pole. Krest'ianskoe delo* [*Third battlefield. Peasants' cause*] (Belgorod, 1998), p. 110. The title refers to the field at Prokhorovka. Two preceding, decisive battles in Old Russian history (the battle on the field of Kulikovo against the Mongols in 1380 and the battle on the field of Borodino in 1812 against Napoleon) have taken on the names "First Field" and "Second Field". So the field near Prokhorovka where the famous tank clash occurred on 12 July 1943 has been called "Third Field". I want to thank historian and author Boris Kavalerchik for this explanation of the title.

79 TsAMO RF, F. 33, Op. 793756, D. 54, l. 42.

If to follow the logic of the authors of *Kurskaia bitva*, then to be killed in a tank, having carried out one's orders to the very end is still not a worthy act, but to be killed while ramming an enemy tank – this is now an example for future generations. Such an approach to heroic feats, in essence, devalued the soldiers' heavy daily burden. Thus after the war, former frontline soldiers had unkind words for such types of fabrications and their creators, the political workers. More than once I was a witness to this.

Despite this, it is nevertheless impossible not to agree with Professor K.V. Iatsenko, who emphasized that "the appearance of this book (Koltunov's and Solov'ev's) marked an important milestone in the development of research on the history of the Battle of Kursk."[80] Together with the collection of articles published under the editorship of I.V. Parot'kin, it was a real success by Soviet scholars, which gave an impetus to the development of our military historical science. These publications became a solid foundation; to a great extent they determined the vector for the development of research on the Kursk battle right up to the beginning of the 1990s. Despite the significant ideological strand and the mistaken treatment of separate events, their authors already in a new socio-political reality clearly managed to enhance the level of academic knowledge on the given subject that had been achieved by that time. In effect, the Brezhnev leadership had placed a certain obstacle on the path to rewriting the history of the war starting in the mid-1960s.

In the final 20 years of the Soviet Union's existence, the academic approach to the study of the Battle of Kursk was almost fully repressed. As V.A. Zolotarev accurately noted, the historiography of the war "... was continually under the control of the CPSU Central Committee and to a great extent became a branch of Party propaganda."[81] At this time the Institute of Military History conclusively became the head organization in the study of the country's military history. In essence, it had a monopoly over the preparation of all significant publications about the Great Patriotic War. In the plan of work of its "Academic Council to Coordinate Research in the Field of Military History", 211 topics were registered in the years 1976-1980 (including in the form of 47 monographs, 26 doctoral dissertations, and 138 candidate dissertations). Of these, more than 100 topics were supposed to be "dedicated to researching the experience of the Party's ideological and political work in the army and fleet, its military organizational activity at the front and in the rear, as well as on land temporarily occupied by the enemy", and 54 were connected with research in military theory and practice (operational arts and tactics), including 26 on the Red Army's military art in the years of the Great Patriotic War.[82] The then head of the institute Lieutenant General P.A. Zhilin provided an explanation for such an approach in 1975. He announced that "the factual and historical part of our Great Patriotic War has been studied and for the most part described ... Now in the USSR the main direction of historical science is research of the Second World War. A deep Marxist analysis of this subject has important significance for academics, politics and ideology."[83] That's it, no more and no less! Thus Soviet scholars had to analyze more deeply the role of the Party in developing military capabilities and to struggle against the falsification of history in the West. Meanwhile, we would lease our own history to trustworthy writers and film makers, so that they could depict examples of the unity of the Party and the people in that harsh period of war more colorfully. This is an exaggerated, but in essence accurate assessment of the Party's approach to the study of the war's history, which dominated the 1970s and 1980s.

80 K.V. Iastsenko, *Kurskaia oblast' v period Velikoi Otechestvennoi voiny: istoriografiia* [*Kursk Oblast in the period of the Great Patriotic War: a historiography*] (Kursk, 2006), p. 20.

81 V.A. Zolotarev, "Problemy izucheniia istorii Velikoi Otechestvennoi voiny" ["Problems in the study of the history of the Great Patriotic War] *Novaia i noveishaia istoriia* (No. 2, 2000), p. 3.

82 *Voenno-istoricheskii zhurnal* (No. 6, 1975), p. 108.

83 P.A. Zhilin, "Voennaia istoriia i sovremennost'" ["Military history and modernity"] *Voenno-istoricheskii zhurnal* (No. 5, 1975), p. 76.

During this period, any publication was viewed from the point of view of its ideological utility, and nothing else. In all major academic and academic-popular publications, the tendency was clearly discernible of a shift from the analysis of "facts and numbers" to a superficial treatment of the events, the concentration of attention not on the essence of problems and their causes but on the military-political components of the victory, and the "inflation" of the role of individual battles and exploits, which were often "touched up" or simply fabricated from the beginning to the end.

Academic publications became shallow and non-substantive, while important directions of research were moved to the back burner. In the works of the overwhelming majority of authors on the subject of the Battle of Kursk, the level of preparation of the Soviet forces, the professional qualities of the Soviet generals, and the tenacity and courage of the Red Army troops when describing any, even tragic episodes for the Red Army, absolutely had to be higher or better than the Germans. Not only did they halt the printing of monographs by military scholars; even those that had already been published, whenever they were reprinted, the censors and ideological organs strove to eviscerate totally, not stopping before cutting their number of pages several times over. A new edition of G.A. Koltunov's and B.S. Solovev's book *Kurskaia bitva*, which came out in 1983, can serve as a clear example of this process. It noticeably differed from the preceding edition, published in 1970, being both substantially smaller in size (127 pages instead of the original 400 pages) and in layout. From an academic work, it was converted into a popular booklet. Yet all of this took place against the backdrop of the empty rhetoric of highly-posted military and political actors of the USSR about the fact that "the combat experience acquired by the Soviet Armed Forces in this hard and lengthy war [the Great Patriotic War] is our precious achievement, our pride, and one of the sources of the further development of Soviet military science."[84]

The 12-volume *Istoriia vtoroi mirovoi voiny 1939-1945* [*History of the Second World War 1939-1945* (Moscow: Voenizdat, 1976) and *Velikaia Otechestvennaia voina. Kratkii nauchno populiarnyi ocherk* [*Great Patriotic War. Short academic popular sketch*], edited by P.A. Zhilin and published by Politizdat in 1973 became the main publications of this period, in which a new official history, including that of the events at Kursk, was presented. The chief editor of the multi-volume work, USSR Minister of Defense and Marshal of the Soviet Union A.A. Grechko wrote, "This is a fundamental summation of the Second World War from the position of Marxism-Leninism not only in Soviet, but also world historiography. The preparation of a major work on the history of the Second World War – this is not only a sample of collective creativity, but also a test of analyzing the most important questions of the [Second] World War through the unified conception of Soviet historical science." In reality, though, except for the styling and excerpts from L.I. Brezhnev's speeches, the publications didn't introduce anything fundamentally new, nor was that their goal. Interesting in this respect are the already cited recollections of Colonel V.M. Kulish, who was personally acquainted with many of the work's authors:

> The new 12-volume history of the Second World War was assigned to the Institute of Military History, which had been created for this purpose. However, work on it dragged on; there were insufficient suitable sources and materials. In order to make faster progress, they found nothing better than to use the memoirs of G.K. Zhukov, A.M. Vasilevsky, A.A. Grechko, I.S. Konev, K.A. Meretskov, K.K. Rokossovsky and others, which had already been published or were being prepared for publication. But since they were published soon after the XX Party Congress, their contents weren't entirely suitable as a source for the new publication, so they

84 A.A. Grechko, "Nauka i isskustvo pobezhdat'" [Science and art of winning"] *Pravda*, 19 February 1975.

> created a special group within the Main Political Command of the Soviet Army and Navy. It was given the task of making conforming adaptations and edits to the selected works.[85]

In other words, first they re-wrote the sources, as was required "from above" (or to put it more simply, they falsified the pool of sources), and then on their basis, they prepared the 12-volume work. That's how this "fundamental work" and in general the entire history of the Great Patriotic War, was created.

However, the process of "creating the history" of the Great Patriotic War didn't end with this. After all, many veterans were still alive and engaged with literary work. Therefore these falsified academic publications were turned into a measuring stick by which to judge all military-historical works and memoirs on the Great Patriotic War. Recalls a former employee of the Russian Federation Ministry of Defense's Institute of Military History V.O. Daines:

> At the direction of the CPSU Central Committee, all memoirs underwent strict checking on how well they conformed to the 12-volume *Istoriia Vtoroi Mirovoi voiny* and 8-volume *Sovetskaia voennaia entsiklopediia* [*Soviet military encyclopedia*]. A Department of Military-Memoir Literature was created in the Institute, which made alterations to the recollections of the war's participants. The author of the given book [Author's note: V.O. Daines] also had to engage in this. Such were the times ....[86]

On the basis of his own memoirs, Marshal of the Soviet Union A.M. Vasilevsky talked about how this ideological filter functioned and how it affected the quality of publications even by well-known and respected authors:

> When my book went to the Politizdat [Political publisher], it immediately, of course, was taken under control. It was directed to the Institute of Marxism-Leninism for a review. I, of course, gave it the manuscript: If you will, fine, check it .... Minosian, a member of the Institute, read it. He checked everything and called me. He said, "Aleksandr Mikhailovich, everything, everything is correct. I will return the manuscript to you." But instead he went and sent it (as was later explained to me, "as directed by the authorities") to the Institute of Military History to Political Officer Makhalov. He was offended and raised a fuss: "Why hadn't the manuscript been sent immediately to our institute?" Here they began to "pickle" the manuscript and nit-pick it. Later I had a conversation on this matter with the chief of the Institute of Military History General Zhilin. He told me, "Aleksandr Mikhailovich, our institute's regard for you is super, we bow before you" and so on. But I saw that these words are not always supported by deeds. To put it briefly, after all these inspections and verifications, certain places in the manuscript and later even in the page proofs of my book were literally eradicated under the pretext of "undesirability" or some "secrecy".[87]

In this period, not only was there little honest military memoir literature, there wasn't even a call for it. The necessary conditions for its acceptance were lacking. The system of social sciences in the 1970s and 1980s became totally ossified, and it was simply impossible to conduct, not imitate, academic work. The ordinary reader in order to understand and conceptualize major military operations had to have training and a certain amount of real knowledge on the subject, and it is

85 *Voenno-istoricheskii zhurnal* (No. 8, 2009), p. 68.
86 V.O. Daines, *Vasilevskii* [*Vasilevsky*] (Moscow: Veche, 2012), p. 440.
87 Ibid., pp. 439-440.

precisely this that the organs of censorship sought to prevent. This is because the understanding of the real course of the war, the internal interrelationship of events, and the reasons for victories and defeats would inevitably give rise to questions connected with government policy and the competence of key figures in the country's leadership. Yet in the conditions of a closed society, like the USSR was, only myths and legends flowered in riotous colors, like the epic clash of tanks and self-propelled guns at Prokhorovka.

P.A. Rotmistrov continued to be the main "historiographer" of this battle in the 1970s. His articles and books came out in the press with enviable regularity. For example, in 1972 his work *Vremia i tanki* [*Time and tanks*] was published, which not only repeated the customary praises of the 5th Guards Tank Army and the sagacity of its command, but Pavel Alekseevich also attempted to develop the thesis he had raised in 1964 in a conversation with Colonel F.D. Sverdlov, which argued that on 12 July 1943 his tank army had allegedly resolved the strategic task for the entire Voronezh Front.[88] The absurdity of this assertion was obvious even to non-specialists. Here is how the well-known Belgorod local historian and war veteran A.S. Stetsenko recalled about Rotmistrov's work in a letter to Colonel G.A. Koltunov:

> Recently I came across P.A. Rotmistrov's book. Up to the point of the Kursk battle, I was reading the book with pleasure. But as soon as Prokhorovka appeared on the pages of the narrative, there's Rotmistrov on a steed with an unsheathed sabre. When showing the role of the 5th Guards Tank Army in the Prokhorovka counterstroke, the author remarks that using this success [of the 5th Guards Tank Army], the forces of the Briansk Front and the left wing of the Western Front went on the offensive.[89] M. Popov [the commander of Briansk Front] and A. Sokolovsky [the commander of Western Front], don't you see, were waiting on the results of the Prokhorovka battle and only then went on the offensive. It turns out that the forces of two *fronts* were introduced into the fighting in dependence on Rotmistrov's success. This just doesn't hold water. All interest in the author's narrative vanishes.[90]

However, judging from everything, the opinion of compatriots didn't particularly trouble Pavel Alekseevich, so he even subsequently continued to generate such notions.

By the start of the 1980, two important factors were clearly present in the historiography of the Battle of Kursk. First, the legend about Prokhorovka acquired unprecedented, even one can say larger than life dimensions. Such a significant number of authors of various works addressed it, that it almost totally obscured the other fighting in the Kursk battle on the southern shoulder of the bulge. As a result a surprising metamorphosis took place; individual researchers and memoirists, giving no particular consideration of the essence of the matter, began to use the term "Prokhorovka staging area" from the arsenal of wartime propaganda to refer to the entire territory, where forces of the Voronezh Front conducted defensive fighting in July 1943, with no reference to Prokhorovka Station. Episodes of the battle that not only occurred on the Prokhorovka axis, but also on the Oboian' axis [the XXXXVIII Panzer Corps' sector of attack] and east of Belgorod [Army Detachment Kempf's sector of attack] were included in this "staging area".

Secondly, the academic-historical literature on the combat operations at this small station began to degenerate into military-artistic literature, leaving the former behind. If prior to this moment as a rule historians or veterans of the battle wrote books about it, and in them the main attention

88 F.D. Sverdlov, *Neizvestnoe o sovetskikh polkovodtsev* [*Unknown about Soviet military leaders*] (Moscow: Biograficheskii klub, 1995), p. 56.

89 See P.A. Rotmistrov, *Vremia i tanki* [*Time and tanks*] (Moscow: Voenizdat, 1972), p. 156.

90 Author's personal archive

was given to major questions regarding the battle, then now the situation changed fundamentally. Instead of studying the battle, the overwhelming majority of authors began to popularize it, and as a rule these were people who were remote from military history and the army, but who had a great creative spark. Ever more frequently there began to appear publications, where instead of analysis of the battle on a wide archival base of sources, there was a superficial, schematic treatment of the events, making no attempts to connect them, intermingled with quotations from poetry, gazette publications and propaganda leaflets.[91] The depiction of the climactic events of the battles in such works was identical to the flights of thought of authors of epic artistic productions. Here, for example, is how V.I. Kardashov presents the start of the 5th Guards Tank Army's counterattack in his book *5 iulia 1943* [*5 July 1943*]:

> At 0830 on the morning of 12 July, the counterattack began. Approximately at this same time, the fascist tanks went on the attack. A meeting battle broke out! Let the reader on a fair weather day go out onto an expansive collective farm field. Whether it is spring, summer or fall, almost certainly a tractor or combine will be working in a field nearby or in the distance, and the sound of the motor will be clearly audible even at a distance of 2-3 kilometers, especially if the wind is blowing from that direction. If the tractor or combine approaches, then the sound of their motors will become rather loud. Let the reader imagine that on an ordinary field with a length of 15 kilometers and a width of just several kilometers, not just one or two machines come together and not even 10, but 1,200! And their motors are not running evenly, like is presumed in daily peacetime work, but in fits and starts: now revving up, now slowing down, before again revving up.
>
> Let the reader imagine that these machines are not simply moving to meet each other, but are also conducting a feverish fire, not sparing the shells. In addition to the tanks, anti-tank artillery is firing, and also from hundreds of barrels. Thousands of shells are constantly exploding, and if they strike a target, then afterward there is often an explosion of the machine's on-board ammunition, and then the multi-ton turrets of the tank soar into the sky and are blown dozens of meters away!
>
> Let the reader imagine that after just an hour or two, this entire field will be covered with hundreds of burning and exploding machines, and the smoke from them, suffocating and caustic, intermingles with the dust thrown up by tracks, and the blasted, mutilated earth like a dense shroud veils everything around and rises like an enormous column into the sky. And there, in this sky, dozens and hundreds of fighters and bombers are coming together in deadly clashes, and downed aircraft are also falling and exploding on this same field …
>
> Let the reader try to imagine all of this, and then he or she will recall and realize all of what our Soviet warrior had to endure and experience, endure and fight, fight to the end … This unfolded on the Prokhorovka field
>
> > A deadly battle not for the sake of glory,
> > But for the sake of life on earth! …[92]

There is not even a smidgen of truth (with the exception of the date) in the excerpt cited above – but neither the author nor the publishers were perturbed by this as a matter of principle. Such heroic odes were composed supposedly in order to make the presentation of the heroic past more

91 See, for example, M. Demin's *Rodina zovet* [*Motherland calls*] or R. Mazurkevich's *Splav muzhestva i stali* [Alloy of courage and steel]

92 V. Kardashov, *5 iulia 1943* [*5 July 1943*] (Moscow: Molodaia gvardiia, 1983), p. 151.

approachable for the young generation. In reality the goal was different: to veil those events with a denser smoke screen, in order to conceal more securely everything that the common Soviet individual wasn't supposed to know about the war.

As is known, history has not only a more educational value. It is an inexhaustible fount of the people's practical life experience, acquired through heavy labor, blood and suffering, which doesn't lose its significance and importance with the passing years, especially in a moral – ethical sense. The use of this experience in contemporary relationships helps resolve the daily problems in our life more effectively. Building a bridge between the past and the present, we preserve a tight connection between the generations, which is also a cementing foundation of any healthy society. Books like Kardashov's cause enormous harm. Substituting the genuine events of history with fabrications, they undermine this foundation, devalue the experience of past generations, which means the belief of the youth in the moral values laid down by our ancestors, and undermine our respect for them. Indeed, something extremely important, they destroy young people's desire to learn about the real, unadorned life of ancestors and their genuine accomplishments and exploits. Moreover, these "delayed-action mines" remain active for decades, like a gradually dispersing dangerous chemical, which upon entering the soil, kills everything living around it.

I'm deeply convinced that whatever the motives that were guiding the people, who distorted the events of the war, they caused irreparable damage not only to history as a science. Through their efforts, a false perception of the past of our Motherland formed among the younger generation, and the young were nurtured on contrived images of heroes, and a distorted image of the deeds of the Soviet people of that terrible and heroic time formed in them.

Starting approximately in the mid-1970s, an attempt was undertaken to create "Prokhorovka – 2" on the northern shoulder of the Kursk bulge, which is to say to "elevate" the fighting in the vicinity of Ponyri Station to the level of the Prokhorovka battle. However, this project wasn't crowned with success. This idea rose among local authorities under the influence of veterans organizations, who often conducted reunions on the sites of past battles in the Kursk and Orel Oblasts. Moscow saw no need in this, while the resources in the oblasts (material, cadre and access to the government system of propaganda) were inadequate to realize this idea. Thus everything boiled down to publishing articles in newspapers and to the release of small brochures from the series "Aid for the agitator" with simple text that stated that the fate of the German offensive toward Kursk in the summer of 1943 was decided by two battles – in the south at Prokhorovka, and in the north at Ponyri Station.

Just as with the fighting at Prokhorovka, the broad society of our country first found out about the battle for Ponyri from military reporters. In the beginning of July 1943, the famous novelist and journalist Lieutenant Colonel K.M. Simonov, being on assignment with the Central Front, spent several of the most intense days of the Kursk battle among the troops of the 13th Army, the defensive sector of which included Ponyri Station. Several articles, published by Simonov in *Krasnaia Zvezda* [Red Star], became the result of these trips.[93] Their main heroes were troops of Colonel N.V. Petrushin's 129th Separate Tank Brigade, which played an important role in the repulse of the enemy attack in this sector. However, unfortunately, the name of the station wasn't mentioned in any of the articles due to military censorship. Because of this, the fact that the events described by K.M. Simonov occurred at Ponyri became known only later. Nevertheless, his articles are interesting material, detailed and mainly written from the words of eyewitnesses and participants in the fighting, which for the scholar even today have definite significance. This station was mentioned for the first time in the open press in connection with the Battle of Kursk in the poem

93 The articles were titled "Nemets s Ferdinanda" [German from a Ferdinand] (14 July), "Okhotnik za panterami" ["Hunter for Panthers"] (16 July) and "Vtoroi variant" ["Second option"] (22 July).

"Ponyri", which was printed in *Komsomol'skaia Pravda* [*Komsomol Truth*] on 20 August 1943.[94] Its author was the well-known poet Major E.A. Dolmatovsky, who at the time worked for the Central Front's newspaper *Krasnaia Armiia* [*Red Army*] and was an eyewitness of the battle. In his work he brilliantly described the heroism of the Soviet soldiers, shown in the fighting for this tiny piece of Russian ground. Naturally, the poem didn't have any relationship to academic research of the battle, but it became the first major poetic work on the events of the Kursk bulge and a genuine monument to the defenders of its northern shoulder. In 1946 it was re-published as a separate brochure, and unfortunately, together with K.M. Simonov's articles, for a prolonged period of time was the only accessible, written source of information for broader society about the fighting at Ponyri Station in the summer of 1943.

Incidentally, there is an interesting detail: one of those July articles written by K.M. Simonov, "Okhotnik za 'panterami'" ["Hunter of Panthers"] was the basis for one of the Soviet myths purporting that the German Ferdinand tank destroyers and Panther tanks were one and the same, and accordingly, this equipment was used on both the northern and southern shoulders of the Kursk bulge. The point is that even immediately after the termination of Operation Citadel, the troops of the Red Army still didn't know that the Ferdinand and Panther were names of different types of armored vehicles. K.M. Simonov, though, dedicating his article to the combat deeds of Lieutenant A.V. Erokhin, a tank commander in the 129th Separate Tank Brigade, who with his crew supposedly knocked out 6 Ferdinands, called his article "Hunter a Panthers".[95] In addition, in the mouth of his hero Simonov also inserted the same words, saying at the front the Ferdinands were called Panthers. A short time later in this same *Krasnaia Zvezda* there was an article by special correspondent L. Vysokostrovsky with a story about Ferdinands and Tigers, and details of their use by the enemy, but with not a word about Panthers.[96] Given the absence of any other information, the article by a famous author, coming out in one of the most widely-circulated Soviet newspapers, together with the publications in army newspaper by his colleagues of the pen, played its role – the opinion that the Ferdinand and the Panther were one and the same type of armored vehicle gradually consolidated in the public conscience, historical literature and even in museums. The caption to a photograph, which was displayed in one of the first postwar expositions of the Kursk Local History Museum, dedicated to the events of July 1943, clearly shows this. It plainly states: "Knocked out Ferdinand self-propelled guns /also known as the Panther/ Orel – Kursk axis, 28 July 1943."[97]

Right up to the collapse of the Soviet Union, the defense of Ponyri Station received no particular significance in academic literature. Not a single individual work on this topic was prepared by civilian or military scholars. The means of mass information also didn't pay much attention to the battle. The first official version of the events at Ponyri Station was published only in 1953 in the *Bol'shaia Sovetskaia Entsiklopediia* [*Great Soviet Encyclopedia*]. It correctly notes that "on the morning of 5 July 1943 … two panzer corps of the German Ninth Army directed their attacks toward Ol'khovatka and Ponyri, striving to break through to Kursk on most direct axis. Auxiliary attacks were launched by an infantry corps northeast of Ponyri at 0530 and by a panzer corps northwest of Ol'khovatka at 0730."[98]

94 *Komsomol'skaia Pravda* [*Komsomol Truth*] 20 August 1943, p. 4.

95 The commander of the 129th Separate Tank Brigade's 2nd Tank Battalion, in which Lieutenant A.V. Erokhin served, wrote him up for the Order of the Patriotic War, 2nd Degree for the fighting at Ponyri, noting that he and his crew between 5 and 7 July 1943 knocked out not 6 Ferdinands, but 3 Pz-VI Tiger tanks.

96 *Krasnaia Zvezda*, 24 July 1943, p. 3.

97 The photograph was found in the files of the Kursk State Local History Museum.

98 *Bol'shoi Sovetskoi entsiklopediia* [*Great Soviet encyclopedia*], Vol 24 (Moscow, 1953), p. 116.

However, already at the beginning of the 1960s, the approach to presenting the events changed, and the start of the battle began to be described differently: the Germans launched the main attack only toward Ol'khovatka, but having run encountered stubborn resistance here, after several days of little progress supposedly turned their main forces toward Ponyri (which actually wasn't the case). However, this enemy maneuver also had no success, owing to the tenacity and courage of the Soviet troops. Such a treatment, for example, is given in the *Sovetskaia Istoricheskaia Entsiklopediia* [*Soviet Historical Encyclopedia*], which came out in 1965, in the *Bol'shaia Sovetskaia Entsiklopediia* [*Great Soviet Encylopedia*] (1973), and in other fundamental publications of the 1970s and 1980s.[99] Along with this, the main plaudits in repelling the Wehrmacht attack in the vicinity of the Ponyri Station supposedly belonged only to the 307th Rifle Division. So, unsurprisingly, starting in the 1960s, the source of information on the fighting at Ponyri became publications and memoirs of its commander during the battle, Major General M.A. Enshin.[100] They were small in size, but extremely biased, filled with eulogistic praise for his division. Colorfully describing the unquestionably worthy combat performance of his subordinates, the general didn't even utter a word about his neighbors, two powerful formations: Major General M.D. Sinenko's 3rd Tank Corps and Major General I.M. Afanas'ev's 18th Guards Rifle Corps, which just like the 307th Rifle Division, played a key role in the defense of this hard nut of resistance. Thus for a lengthy period of time, the participation of their soldiers and officers in one of the key clashes of the Battle of Kursk remained in the shadows.

Marshal of the Soviet Union K.K. Rokossovsky also made a large contribution to the consolidation of this mistaken image about the overall course of the German offensive on the Ponyri axis. In his memoir, he also asserted that "having achieved no success on 6 July against the center and left flank of our 13th Army, the enemy on the morning of 7 July shifted his main efforts to Ponyri."[101] It isn't clear what was connected with this sharp turn in the treatment of those events. Possibly, it was the desire of the ideological organs responsible for the interpretation of those events to show that the Soviet defense at Kursk was insurmountable for the foe on every axis. There is a basis to assume that it was precisely the point of view of K.K. Rokossovsky, who had great authority in society and the army, which he first expressed in his publications at the end of the 1950s, was in fact taken as the basis for the new interpretation of the events, without critical analysis and deep study of the documents.

Unquestionably, the fighting for this small railroad station was extremely bitter, bloody and went on for several days. Here is just one piece of evidence that testifies to the extreme intensity of the combat operations in this area. On the night of 9-10 July 1943, the command of Army Group Center was compelled to replace the 292nd Infantry Division, which had been attacking toward the station, with the 10th Motorized Division. Nowhere was there a similar case anywhere else in the area of the Kursk bulge over the entire period of Operation Citadel. Ponyri was not just one of the many "sore points" for the Germans in the battle. The possession of this strongpoint by the Soviet forces had important significance for the disruption of Berlin's plans. Nevertheless, it is incorrect to compare the fighting at Ponyri with the events at Prokhorovka, because their magnitude was completely different. Two panzer corps of the Wehrmacht (the II SS Panzer Corps and III Panzer Corps), each comparable in strength to a Soviet combined-arms Guards army,

99 For example, *Velikaia Otechestvennaia voina 1941-1945* [*Great Patriotic War 1941-1945*] (Moscow, 1985), p. 394.

100 See, for example, *Kurskaia bitva: Vospominaniia uchastnikov* [*Kursk battle: Recollections of participants*] (Voronezh, 1968), pp. 141-148; *Kurskaia bitva: Vospominaniia, stat'i* [*Kursk battle: Recollections, articles*] (Voronezh, 1973), pp. 241-247; A. Kochetkov, *Ogenennyi iul'. Dokumental'nye rasskazy, ocherki* [*Fiery july. Documentary stories, essays*] (Voronezh, 1984), pp. 52-59.

101 K.K. Rokossovsky, *Soldatskii dolg* [*Soldier's duty*] (Moscow: Voenizdat, 1997), p. 271.

and three Soviet armies (69th, 5th Guards and 6th Guards) plus the 5th Guards Tank Army fought for Prokhorovka, while just one German panzer corps (the XXXXI Panzer Corps) and two Soviet corps (3rd Tank Corps and 18th Guards Rifle Corps) clashed at Ponyri. Thus, the numerical strength of the opposing groupings, which dueled for these stations, differed by many times. Accordingly, the tasks that they were attempting to resolve were substantially different in both significance and size.

One important factor which tipped the scales in the direction of ceasing attempts to mythologize the battle for Ponyri was the absence of a serious basis for this. The legend about Prokhorovka began deliberately to form within just several weeks of the battle with a deeply practical purpose – to cover the miscalculation and high losses with a smoke screen – and it acquired its final form through the efforts of the entire Soviet propaganda machine only 30 years after its origin, whereas initially there was practically no need to create a myth about Ponyri, if you disregard the understandable desire of the local authorities to erect a worthy monument to its defenders at the expense of the national budget. This battle basically unfolded according to the plan adopted by the Central Front command, which proved to be fully successful. Given those forces and means that the Soviet command concentrated here, it could not have gone any other way. It is an extremely difficult and thankless task to "sculpt" a legend without a historical basis virtually from out of the blue after the passage of decades. Thus the scheme in fact failed.

Thus, up until the collapse of the Soviet Union, the work to study the Battle of Kursk continued with varying degrees of activity. However, the Soviet historians had no real possibility to study it deeply and exhaustively, to assess it objectively, or to bring the results of their research to a broader audience. Virtually all of the literature on this topic was substantially "lacquered over" by the censors, mistakes and omissions were "retouched", documentary sources were classified, and individual unsuccessful battles were depicted as conspicuous victories by Soviet arms. Moreover, in the 1970s and 1980s, this situation particularly deteriorated.

Firstly, the publication of academic books and articles dwindled, while at the same time the desire of censors increased to eviscerate open publications to the maximum, giving them a superficial, descriptive nature. The memoirs of military leaders and top commanders were "cleansed" and amended, in order to purge from the manuscript any personal judgements and generalizations, which might prompt doubts in the readers or mistrust in the official treatment of the Battle of Kursk.

Secondly, the pressure of official organs on authors and creative collectives increased, with the aim of preventing the appearance of "ideologically harmful" works, which meant the deep, thorough analysis of the events and relevant conclusions. Therefore, free access to the military and government archives, as before, was closed to scholars, even though at this time in the West a significant portion of the documents on the war had already been de-classified. All this led to the fact that in the USSR over the entire postwar period, not a single academic work was published in which the period of preparations for the summer 1943 campaign or the course of the Battle of Kursk as a whole were deeply analyzed with the use of available Soviet and captured documents. The single book by G.A. Koltunov and B.S. Solov'ev *Kurskaia bitva*, which came out in 1970s, was never updated to account for new findings and sources, but on the contrary was reprinted only once, in 1983, after being abridged to the size of a booklet.

Thirdly, the results of the work of historians and the opinion of veterans of the battle, published in the 1960s, were openly ignored. The scale of mythologizing the events at Kursk, especially the Prokhorovka battle, substantially expanded, and film studios, televisions and museums began to be drawn into this process more actively and broadly to replace the military-historical and memoir literature.

Fourthly, the tenuous tradition of issuing collections of documents on the history of the Great Patriotic War for specialists (instructors at academies and military historians) and publishing honest materials on the Battle of Kursk passed into oblivion. The effect of those archival materials, which were nevertheless published in the anniversary year of 1983 in *Voenno-istoricheskii zhurnal*, was comparable with the effect of a drop of water, falling on parched soil. For by this time, academic analysis of the history of the Battle of Kursk had practically come to an end.

In a word, a "holiday postcard" was made out of the dramatic events (49 days of the heaviest trials for our entire country) that glorified the wisdom of the Communist Party, under the keen leadership of which an unyielding force had been created by the summer of 1943, upon which the fascist aggressors were smashed. The monopoly of the CPSU on the interpretation of the past, the classified nature of the military archives, and the presence of twin censors (military and civilian) made any attempts by scholars to avoid highly-biased assessments and "pageantry", to elaborate a new, sober view of this epic event of the Second World War, impossible. All of this had an extremely negative influence on the development of historical science in the USSR and for an extended time undermined public trust in publications on the subject of the Battle of Kursk, and in official military-historical and memoir literature in general. For example, according to the data of an all-Union sociological research, conducted in 1987-1988 by the Department of Ideological Work in the Academy of Social Sciences under the CPSU Central Committee, only 3% of those questioned read the journal *Istoriia SSSR* [*History of the USSR*], which at that time was considered one of the most authoritative academic publications.[102] A similar picture formed for other history journals as well, even though at this time there was an unprecedented upsurge of public interest in the country's past and in printed publications that concerned this topic.

The beginning of the 1990s marked qualitative changes in the approach to the study of the Russian and Soviet history as a whole, and of the Great Patriotic War in particular, despite the fact that this was a difficult time for Russia that saw the collapse of the existing socio-economic order in the country. Even so, it was characterized by a wide variety of opinions and the search for new forms and methods in the work of researchers. The majority of existing assessments and conclusions were subjected to serious re-examination, and new views on the Battle of Kursk and on the role of key figures in it began to form. The year 1993 became a turning point for its study on a new basis, when three important events took place that in essence launched the beginning of an objective, deep and exhaustive study of the battles around the Kursk bulge.

First in the Russian Federations Central Archive of the Ministry of Defense [TsAMO], the seal of secrecy was removed from the Red Army's combat documents for the year 1943 (up to the *front*-level inclusively), including those of the military formations that took part in the defeat of the Wehrmacht's summer offensive toward Kursk. This allowed civilian scholars the possibility to work with archival materials and led to a broad discussion in the open press, initially regarding the battle's most contentious event – the 12 July 1943 counterattack at Prokhorovka – and then on the entire complex of problems connected with the battle on the basis of a new foundation of resources.

In 1993, the collection of articles *Grif sekretnost' sniat* [*Seal of secrecy has been removed*] under the editorship of G.F. Krivoshein came out, in which previously secret statistical data on the manpower losses of the Red Army in operations of the war years were presented. Even though this work was at the time subjected to just criticism for its political bias and inaccuracies (in particular, with respect to the Voronezh Front's manpower losses in the Kursk defensive operation), it became a unique reference point in the work of historians.

102 G.T. Zhuravlev, V.I. Merkushin and Iu.K. Fomichev, "Istoricheskoe soznanie: opyt sociologicheskogo issledovaniya" [Historical conscience: results of a sociological research"] *Voprosy istorii* (No. 6, 1989), p. 127.

Secondly, Soviet censorship passed into oblivion together with the Soviet Union, and historians had the real possibility to draw conclusions and make assessments, based now not on their political expedience, but on the factual results of their academic work. Thirdly, an academic conference was held in Moscow that was dedicated to the 50th anniversary of the Battle of Kursk, with the participation of foreign scholars. During the conference, domestic historians were able to communicate directly with colleagues, exchange opinions, and discuss and debate a number of important problems and events of the summer of 1943. In a conversation with me, Colonel F.D. Sverdlov observed, "The conference's main outcome became the establishment of direct and strong ties with American scholars, which offered the possibility of obtaining captured German sources out of the American National Archives, where Wehrmacht documents, including those of its forces that took part in the Battle of Kursk, were stored and had already been available for study."

The next important milestone on this path was the publication in 1997-1999 by the TERRA publishing house of documents of the USSR People's Commissariat of Defense, the General Staff, the *Stavka* of the Supreme High Command and of the *fronts* for the year 1943. One important detail: by this time only approximately 200 genuine domestic documentary materials related to the events of the Kursk bulge had ever been published in the open Soviet press since the end of the war. The majority of them, approximately 60, were primarily documents of the *Stavka* of the Supreme High Command and of the *fronts,* which had been published in journals.[103] Approximately 40, primarily of an operational or tactical character, were included in several publications of the *Sbornik boevykh domumentov Velikoi Otechestvennoi voiny* [*Collected combat documents of the Great Patriotic War*]. More than 40 were embedded in three volumes of the classified publication *Sbornik dokumentov Verkhovnogo Glavnokomandovaniia za period Velikoi Otechestvennoi voiny* [*Collected documents of the Supreme High Command over the period of the Great Patriotic War*] (Moscow: Voenizdat, 1968). In addition, approximately 20 documents that concerned major questions of strategic planning and the course of separate battles, were published in the memoirs of Soviet military chiefs and commanders like G.K. Zhukov, A.M. Vasilevsky and K.S. Moskalenko. A significant quantity of archival materials, primarily on the economic activity of the troops [like helping with harvests, etc.] and their daily life had been printed in collections of materials by oblast-level publishers.[104] Such a miserly number of genuine documents, compared to the scale of the battle, naturally made no contribution to its thorough study. In addition, each of the mentioned collection of documents was as a rule prepared under a previously elaborated and often tendentious conception, called upon to support not an academic task, but an ideological one. As a result of these reasons, among these documents naturally there could not have been any that would have revealed the mistakes and miscalculations of the Soviet command, the Red Army's high losses in manpower, the reasons for them, and so forth. Thus although at the time these materials in fact gave a certain discernible impetus to progress in understanding the history of the war, they couldn't form a coherent, correct image of the events of the fundamental turning point in the war.

103 *Voenno-istoricheskii zhurnal* (No. 5, 1983); *Sovetskie arkhivy* [*Soviet archives*] (No. 4, 1978); *Kommunist* (Nos. 4 and 10, 1983); and *Molodoi kommunist* [*Young communist*] (No. 8, 1978).

104 *Kurskaia oblast' v gody Velikoi Otechestvennoi voiny Sovetskogo Soiuza, 1941-1945: Sbornik dokumentov i materialov* [*Kursk Oblast in the years of the Soviet Union's Great Patriotic War, 1941-1945: Collected documents and materials*], in two volumes (Kursk, 1960-1962); *Orlovskaia oblast' v gody Velikoi Otechestvennoi voiny Sovetskogo Soiuza, 1941-1945: Sbornik dokumentov i materialov* [*Orel Oblast in the years of the Soviet Union's Great Patriotic War, 1941-1945: Collected documents and materials*] (Orel, 1960); *Trudiashchiesia Khar'kovskoi oblast' v gody Velikoi Otechestvennoi voiny Sovetskogo Soiuza, 1941-1945: Sbornik dokumentov i materialov* [*Workers of Khar'kov Oblast' in the years of the Soviet Union's Great Patriotic War, 1941-1945: Collected documents and materials*] (Khar'kov, 1953 and 1960); *Voronezhskaia oblast' v gody Velikoi Otechestvennoi voiny Sovetskogo Soiuza: Sbornik dokumentov i materialov* [*Voronezh Oblast in the years of the Soviet Union's Great Patriotic War: Collected documents and materials*] (Voronezh, 1948).

There were significantly more documents included in the multi-volume TERRA series, they encompassed significantly wider array of issues, and even more importantly, they weren't subjected to preliminary severe censorship. In the fifteenth thematic volume alone, dedicated to the Battle of Kursk, there were 358 documents, including captured German documents.[105] Several dozen more documents were included in Volumes 13, 16 and 23.[106] They disclosed the enormous, complex and also creative work to plan, prepare and conduct three major operations on the Soviet side: the Kursk defensive operation, Operation Kutuzov and Operation Polkovodets Rumiantsev. This mass of documents offered a unique opportunity to take a look at the turning point in the war from a strategic height, and to follow in detail the *Stavka* of the Supreme High Command's plan for the summer of 1943 as it unfolded, from the forming of main objectives to their implementation by the committed forces. Incidentally I will note that some of these documents were known to Soviet historians, because they'd already been published previously, in 1969 and 1975, in collections of materials that had the seal "For official use". Now, however, they were not only accessible to a broad circle of scholars, but there also appeared the possibility to use the information from them without restriction in monographs and academic publications.[107]

However, already during the first 2-3 years after access to the combat documents in the Russian Federastion's TsAMO became relatively free, the optimism of the majority of domestic scholars fell. Even though the historian's hand had never touched the overwhelming majority of the files from the moment of their arrival in the archive from the acting army, and there had never been any global "cleansing" in the archive, it proved extremely difficult to obtain a detailed, and more importantly, objective picture of the combat operations on their basis, even the course of major operations – at the very least without the use of other sources. There were several reasons for this.

First was the low work standards and administrative discipline of officers of the acting army, even at the level of the *front*. An order from the commander of Briansk Front on 26 June 1942 "O vedenii voenno-istoricheskoi raboty v chastiakh i soedineniiakh fronta" ["On the conducting of military-historical work in the units and formations of the Front"] stated:

> Experience has demonstrated that alongside the fine execution of military-historical work and the established standard practice for preparation of the documents, a number of mistakes and shortcomings still show up in certain units and formations:
>
> 1. Journals of combat operations are being implemented formally; daily entries are brief, dry, and fail to give the full picture of the combat day: frequently they don't even include standout performances ...; sometimes entries are given in pencil, illegibly and sloppily; the title page or first page doesn't indicate who is personally keeping the "Journal"; copies of the "Journal of Combat Operations" required by the *front* headquarters for the past

105 *Russkii arkhiv: Velikaia Otechestvennaia: Kurskaia bitva. Dokumenty i materialy 27 marta-23 avgusta 1943* [*Russian archive: Great Patriotic: Kursk battle. Documents and materials of 27 March to 23 August 1943*], Vol. 15 (4-4) (Moscow: TERRA, 1997).

106 *Russkii arkhiv: Velikaia Otechestvennaia: Prikazy Narodnogo komissara oborony SSSR (1943-1945)* [*Russian archive: Great Patriotic: Orders of the USSSR People's Commissar of Defense (1943-1945)*, Vol, 13 [2-3] (Moscow: TERRA, 1999; *Russkii arkhiv: Velikaia Otechestvennaia: Stavka Verkhovnogo Glavnokomandovaniia: Dokumenty i materialy, 1943* [*Russian archive: Great Patriotic: Stavka of the Supreme High Command: Documents and materials, 1943*], Vol. 16 [5-3] (Moscow: TERRA, 1999); and *Russkii arkhiv: Velikaia Otechestvennaia. Genera'nyi shtab v gody Velikoi Otechestvennoi voiny: Dokumenty i materialy, 1943* [*Russian archive: Great Patriotic: General staff in the years of the Great Patriotic War: Documents and materials, 1943*], Vol. 23 [12-3] (Moscow: TERRA, 1999).

107 The seal "For official use" didn't fully classify a document, but applied definite, serious restrictions for the publication of information from documents that bore this seal.

> month are not being submitted by all headquarters; necessary maps – on the course of combat operations; summaries – reports on the combat and numerical strength of their forces and enemy forces; and information on losses and captured enemy material are not being included.
>
> 2. Required "Accounts" on conducted combat operations are not being timely submitted.
> 3. Current maps of the operational and intelligence departments are not being carried out systematically. The drawers of the maps sometimes "forget" to give a date or to supply necessary captions, which verify the maps as a report document.
> 4. Photo/illustrative/ documents are not being collected, and the necessary photographic images aren't being made. In the units, as a rule, photographic albums are not present.
> 5. Many telephone conversations of the army commanders, chiefs of staff, corps commanders and division commanders, which have enormous historical interest, are not being transcribed.
>
> ...
>
> 9. So far adequate storage of the documents hasn't been provided, especially when transporting them in the conditions of combat operations ...[108]

Such problems did not only exist in the Briansk Front. A similar situation was observable to the entire acting army practically to the end of the war, although in the latter half of 1944, it gradually began to improve.

Second were the routine rules of record keeping in the field headquarters, which demanded at the end of a certain period of combat operations that the accumulated documentation be sorted "according to degree of historical significance", and that one portion be sent to the archive, while the other be destroyed for their lack of utility. For an example I will cite an excerpt from the 70th Army's Order No. 1/0254483 to the troops dated 21 July 1943:

> The commander has ordered: to execute the order of the Commander-in-Chief of Central Front No. 024 from 10 July 1943, with the aims of unburdening the army's commands, services and departments of archival matters for the first half of 1943 and of the files for other periods that have been designated as useless, to create for each command, service and department of the army a commission at the direction of its chief (!), upon which place:
>
> 1. The examination and selection of files and materials for the Central Archive, which have practical use or historical value, while files having no historical value and which have lost practical utility are to be destroyed by burning upon the execution of the established order.[109]

The sorting of the accumulated documents was done by an officer, who as a rule didn't have higher education,[110] the requisite training to evaluate the worth of this pile of sources, and moreover the willingness particularly to delve into the fine points of historical science. In addition, the files in every formation underwent checking according to the outcomes of operations, and where there were major breakdowns or serious setbacks (high combat losses and so forth), the original documents were removed by way of application to the commissions' charge, and later they, as a

108 TsAMO RF, F. 48 (Briansk Front), Op. 5, D. 218, l. 2.

109 TsAMO RF, F. 427, Op. 11103, D.8, l. 24.

110 For example, of the entire headquarters staff of the famous 5th Guards Tank Army, there was only one senior officer – the chief of the Operations Department Colonel F.M. Belozorov – who had by the start of the Battle of Kursk graduated from the I.V. Stalin Academy of Motorized and Mechanized Forces.

rule, were never returned to their former headquarters, but destroyed or "passed up the ladder." Thus even now it is extremely difficult to analyze many key events, for example, the battles at the Kursk bulge.

At the same time, it is impossible not to note that in the 1990s, along with the broad possibilities that had opened up, the attention given by academic research institutions to the analysis of the Great Patriotic War dropped substantially. Several factors were responsible for this. A crisis was raging in the country, as it was undergoing the breakdown of the existing socio-political system and the formation of a new one. The subject of the war, which previously had been one of the main ones in the ideological work of the Communist Party of the Soviet Union, was now considered no longer pressing, while those who attempted to make sense of it on a serious academic level in the best case took heat from reactionaries and conservatives.

In addition, at this time a disruption took place, which inflicted serious damage to the domestic historical science. The cohort of Soviet military historians, who were former veterans of the war, for natural reasons retired from active academic work. Meanwhile the youth, who were going to replace them, had only started their path in the profession, but unfortunately, there was no longer anyone to instruct them in the right way. Thus, the number of qualified and experienced specialists on the subject of the military began to fall. Moreover, back then there were few who wanted to become history scholars. A wave of negative information about our past, including about our Great Patriotic War, which was sweeping through society, and the sharp arguments about the tragic pages in the history of the Soviet Union, forced young people who planned to dedicate their lives to scholarly work to ponder the possibility of realizing this in the realm of history. The military subject had become particularly politicized and unattractive, not prestigious. Thus, even having chosen the profession of historian, a significant portion of the graduate students and young scholars sought to busy themselves with "safe" topics of the Old World, the Middle Ages, and in the extreme case with pre-revolutionary Russia, which guaranteed them against the negative influence of ideological currents, accusations of "besmirching our Holy past", etc. Thus, even though the possibility to raise history, including that of the Battle of Kursk, to a qualitatively new level had expanded, the academic study of the Second World War and particularly of the Great Patriotic War was neglected and farmed out to dilettantes, "ideological weathervanes" and commercial interests. As a result, primitive assessments, the absence of deep analysis, a non-critical approach to sources being used and the open distortion of facts, which all fall under the definition of "historical dilettantism", became a characteristic of a significant portion of the Russian military-historical literature that came out at this time. It is hard not to agree with the scholar A. Chubar'ian, who rightly noted:

> Very many of the books coming out in our time under the title "historical pulp fiction", bear the impression precisely of that danger for society, dilettantism. Putting it very delicately and gently, one can observe that such works are based upon an extremely poor knowledge of historical facts and processes and a particularly far-reaching attraction to various myths and open speculation. In particular this relates to the treatment of events of the 20th Century, when unproven conjecture, unsupported by facts, pass from book to book, even certain text books.[111]

A clear example of this is the fact that even today in textbooks on the history of Russia for the 11th grade, the formulations and numbers contrived by the headquarters of the 5th Guards Tank Army back in July 1943 continue to figure: "On 12 July Soviet forces launched a meeting counterattack.

111 A. Chubar'ian, "Navstrechu novomu uchebniku" ["Toward a new textbook"] *Rodina* (No. 7, 2013), p. 57.

In the vicinity of the village of Prokhorovka there occurred the largest tank battle of the Second World War: There were more than 1,200 tanks and self-propelled guns on the field of battle simultaneously."[112] The same sort of rubbish is repeated in study guides for students of institutes of higher education.[113]

Against this backdrop, both within Russia and abroad, attempts were undertaken to falsify the history of the 20th Century, to replace old myths with new ones, and to use the multiplicity of treatments of separate events, including the Battle of Kursk, as an instrument of political struggle and influence on the younger generation.

Nevertheless, the fundamental changes in socio-political life gave rise to a boisterous interest of society in the past. Thanks to the sweeping changes that occurred, already at the end of the 1990s the first promising results began to appear. In the first few years of the new century, a real process of re-thinking the history of the Battle of Kursk began both among domestic scholars and our society as a whole, thus bringing about the fifth stage in historiography of the Battle of Kursk. The first decade of the 21st Century became the most fruitful for the historiography of this epic event. The active academic research and publishing activity that emerged at this time in both its scale and results were not only comparable with the work of Soviet scholars in the 1960s, but in a certain sense noticeably surpassed it. The military-historical works that came out at this time had their own characteristic feature. In the first place the appearance of studies, genuinely free from ideological blinders and with a solid base of documentary sources, dedicated to the battle for Prokhorovka, should be noted.

The first of these books, *Prokhorovka – vzgliad cherez desiatiletiia* [*Prokhorovka – view through the decades*], was published in 2002.[114] In the essay "Prokhorovskoe srazhenie" ["Prokhorovka battle"] included in this collected volume, for the first time the plans of the opposing sides and the course of combat operations in the area of Prokhorovka Station between 10 and 16 July 1943 were revealed in detail, based upon the comparison and analysis of a significant base of de-classified documents out of the Russian Federation TsAMO, the previously unpublished recollections of veterans of the battle, and captured German documents. Through the rich factual material it was proven that contradictory to the official point of view, there was no epic meeting tank clash on the first day of the counterattack by the Voronezh Front's forces in the area,. The command of the II SS Panzer Corps, fearing the encirclement of a *kampfgruppe* of the SS Panzer Grenadier Division *Liebstandarte Adolf Hitler*, back on 11 July 1943 had issued an order for its units to go over to a temporary defense. As a result, the SS troops greeted the main forces of the 5th Guards Tank Army with dense fire from place and inflicted very heavy damage to them. The Guardsmen not only failed to carry out their order for the day, but also in several sectors yielded their positions under enemy pressure. In addition, for the first time, the essay described in detail the encirclement on 14-15 July 1943 of a portion of the 69th Army's forces in the area between the Lipovyi and Northern Donets Rivers (south of Prokhorovka), which had been ignored by Soviet historians throughout the entire postwar period, and analyzed its origins and consequences. In addition, data on the losses of the 48th Rifle Corps' rifle divisions in the course of fighting in this area and when

112 A.A. Danilov and A.V. Filippov [eds.], *Istoriia Rossii 1900-1945: Uchebnik dlia obshcheobrazovatel'nykh uchrezhdenii* [*History of Russia 1900-1945: Textbook for general education institutions*], 2nd printing (Moscow: Prosveshchenie, 2012), p. 357.

113 *Istoriia Rossii s drevneishikh vremen do kontsa XX veka: Uchebnoe posobie dlia studentov vuzov* [*History of Russia from the most ancient times to the end of the 20th Century: Study guide for university students*], updated and amended 3rd Ed. (Moscow: Drofa, 2011), p. 487.

114 *Prokhorovka – vzgliad cherez stoletiia. Kniga Pamiati pogibshikh v Prokhorovskom srazhenii* [*Prokhorovka – view through the decades. Book of Remembrance of the fallen in the Prokhorovka battle*] (Moscow: Fond "Narodnaia pamiat', 2002).

coming out of the pocket were presented.[115] Important statistical data on the 5th Guards Tank Army were also published in this book for the first time: its numerical strength on the evening of 11 July 1943, its losses in armor and men for 12 July, broken down by divisions and units, taken from documentary files for all its brigades and regiments stored in the TsAMO RF.[116]

L.V. Lopukhovsky's book *Prokhorovka bez grifa sekretnosti* [*Prokhorovka without the seal of secrecy*], which came out in 2005, also belongs to this group of books. In it, the author conducts a complex analysis of the fighting on the Prokhorovka axis. New sources introduced into academic circulation allowed the author to offer his own substantiated view on a number of issues. In particular, he examined in a totally new way that important and extremely difficult to research question of the Voronezh Front's personnel losses in the course of repelling Army Group South's offensive within the framework of Operation Citadel. Relying on genuine documents, the author studied and demonstrated the forms and methods, which its command used, in order to conceal the high losses in manpower suffered during the Kursk defensive operation.

While noting Lopukhovsky's high quality of research and the freshness and depth of his analysis of key issues, it is impossible not to note that it is difficult to agree with a number of his judgements. In particular, the overall tone of his assessments of the combat work of the senior and higher command staff of the Voronezh Front and its results appear to be excessively harsh and not always justified. This is clearly discernible especially with respect to the actions of General of the Army N.F. Vatutin and the active defense he conducted in the first stage of the Battle of Kursk. For example, L.N. Lopukhovsky, without sufficient analysis of the respective strengths of the Central and Voronezh Fronts asserts that in the course of the counterattack on 6 July 1943 K.K. Rokossovsky, who ran into a superior enemy armored force, began supposedly to operate more cautiously and prudently than N.F. Vatutin.[117] Having received information about the heavy losses in the brigades of the 16th Tank Corps, which was supporting the infantry of the 13th Army, already during the initial attack, the Commander-in-Chief of the Central Front ordered "Fortify the infantry's combat formations with tanks and dig them into the ground in order to conduct fire from fixed positions. The use of tanks for counterattacks is permitted only against infantry, as well as enemy light tanks. Even then, only once have the Hiterites' combat formations been disorganized by fire."[118]

Inarguably, K.K. Rokossovsky's decision in that situation was correct and prudent. However, it shouldn't be forgotten that he had all the capabilities for its realization. He had considerably more artillery and mortars than his neighbor N.F. Vatutin. Moreover, each of the commanders was holding a defense only with the forces and means that the *Stavka* had allocated to them and not necessarily those that were necessary for this. As concerns the concrete example of the 16th Tank Corps, then the documents make clear: having received the order against conducting further tank counterattacks, the commander of the 13th Army Lieutenant General N.I. Pukhov gave the commander of the 17th Guards Rifle Corps the 1st Guards Artillery Division, the 378th Destroyer Anti-tank Artillery Regiment and the 237th Tank Regiment of direct infantry support. Having such a powerful "fire" shield, the corps commander was able to hold the line even without the active support of armored vehicles.

It is also hard to agree with L.N. Lopukhovsky's criticism of N.V. Vatutin's decision regarding the employment of the tank corps on 8 July 1943 on the Prokhorovka axis. As he asserts, "The counterattack conducted on 8 July 1943 with the forces of five tank corps, not including the rifle

115 V. Zamulin, "Prokhorovskoe srazhenie" ["Prokhorovka battle"], in *ibid.*, pp. 283-292.

116 Ibid., p. 219.

117 L.N. Lopukhovsky, *Prokhorovka bez grifa sekretnosti* [*Prokhorovka without the seal of secrecy*] (Moscow, 2005), pp. 141-142.

118 Koltunov and Solov'ev, *Kurskaia bitva*, p. 118.

divisions, on a front of up to 50 kilometers did not achieve its objective, even though in four of the tank corps alone (the 2nd Guards, 5th Guards, 2nd and 10th Tank Corps) there were approximately 600 combat-ready tanks and self-propelled guns."[119]

Actually, if one looks at the fulfillment of the given orders formally, then the counterattacks launched by Vatutin were unsuccessful. The armored wedge of Army Group South (the shock forces of the Fourth Panzer Army) was not destroyed and General H. Hoth did not remove a single unit, not to mention entire divisions, from the Oboian' axis in order to strengthen the Prokhorovka axis, which in fact the Soviet command sought. However, this was only a portion of the tasks. In the situation when the Germans still had the initiative and the forces for containing them within the system of the second army-level defensive belt were insufficient, the counterattack on 8 July proved to be the only way to counter the Fourth Panzer Army simultaneously on two directions. N.F. Vatutin's counterattack on 8 July managed to achieve its main aim – Hoth's attempt to break through to the Psel River and to encircle forces of the 1st Tank Army and 6th Guards Army on the adjacent flanks of the XXXXVIII Panzer Corps and II SS Panzer Corps came to naught. The enemy not only failed to overrun the 1st Tank Army's 31st Tank Corps, but owing to the stubborn defense, in which the counterattacks became an important element, the II SS Panzer Corps was forced to abandon the settlements of Veselyi, Ryl'skii, Malye Maiachki and Greznoe (Griaznoe), which it already occupied, and to fall back to former positions. Meanwhile, the XXXXVIII Panzer Corps was also unable to eliminate the threat out of the bend in the Pena River on its deep left flank.

In addition, as captured documents testify, the attacks by the Soviet tank corps west of Prokhorovka had even more significant consequences. It was only after the Soviet side threw fresh mobile reserves into battle here on 8 July that H. Hoth and E. von Manstein took a more serious look at the situation on the flanks of the Fourth Panzer Army. It was decided on 10 July to halt the offensive to the north and northeast and to pivot the XXXXVIII Panzer Corps to the west and southwest (toward the bend in the Pena River), while the II SS Panzer Corps was fully directed to seize Prokhorovka and the territory (hills) adjacent to it.[120] Can it be considered an unsuccessful counterattack, if the adversary was not only unable to conduct the planned encirclement of Voronezh Front forces, but also abandoned already occupied ground, and moreover fundamentally changed plans, directing his forces not toward a further breakthrough, but to carry out separate tactical assignments: the elimination of a threat to the flank? The answer is obvious: of course not.

Considering that I was fortunate to take part in the appearance of L.N. Lopukhovsky's book, I'll briefly dwell upon the pre-history of its creation. After the book *Prokhorovka – vzgliad cherez desiatiletiia* came out, during the preparation of which L.N. Lopukhovsky acted both as a military consultant and editor, while I was the author of the article "Prokhorovskoe srazheniia" and of informational tables in the book, we decided to continue joint work. Indeed, we published an edited version of my article in the *Voenno-istoricheskii arkhiv* [*Military History archive*], and then set to work on a new book as co-authors. It was assumed that my article from *Prokhorovka – vzgliad cherez desiatiletiia* would serve as the basis for the new book, and would be supplemented with a brief description of the overall course of the fighting on the Oboian' axis from 5 to 16 July 1943 and an analysis of the Soviet losses in the course of the defensive phase of the Battle of Kursk.

However, having started the work, we found that the subject of Prokhorovka as an independent battle was already exhausted by the material that had already been prepared. In order to make further progress, to take a detailed look at the plans of the opposing sides for the summer of 1943,

119 Lophukovsky, *Prokhorovka bez grifa sekretnosti*, p. 137.

120 V. Zamulin, *Zasekrechennaia Kurskaia bitva. Neizvestnye dokumenty svidetel'svuiut* [*Classified Kursk battle: Unknown documents testify*] (Moscow: Iauza/EKSMO, 2007), pp. 776-777.

and most importantly, thoroughly assess the process of their realization and the achieved results, I saw that it would be necessary to lay out and analyze the course of fighting on the Oboaian' and Korocha directions in just as much detail. In the future, research would be needed on the battles in Central Front's sector as well. This would require significant time, energy and, of course, no distraction by other projects. The decisions came of their own accord: I abandoned work on a joint publication with L.N. Lopukovsky, and continued to analyze the subject of the Battle of Kursk according to my own plan. As a result, between 2005 and 2009, four of my books were published, in which the plan of detailed research of the repulse of Army Group South toward Kursk by the forces of Voronezh Front was fully realized.[121]

I managed to carry out what my former co-author had planned. His work on Prokhorovka was not only an example of high-quality academic literature, but also a worthy contribution to the matter of preserving the memory of the key role of the Soviet people in the defeat of fascism. I'm glad that, as Lev Nikolaevich noted in the introduction to his book, during work on it he had made broad use of my preliminary work as well. I think that it is comforting for every scholar of the Battle of Kursk to realize that the results of his work have a call for not only a broad audience of readers, but also history colleagues.

An important feature of domestic historiography in the first decade of the new century was the continuation of the publication of archival combat documents. In this connection, the two-volume work of an authors' collective under the leadership of V.A. Zhilin, *Kurskaia bitva. Khronika, fakty, liudi* [*Kursk battle. Chronicle, facts, people*], which in addition to other reference material included operational summaries of the Red Army's General Staff and intelligence summaries of Army Group South (excerpted from these documents) from 5 July to 23 August 1943.[122] This was the first voluminous quantity of captured documents that was published in the open press of our country since 1967. In addition, it should be particularly emphasized that whereas the book of collected materials *Sovershenno sekretno! Tol'ko dlia komandovaniia* [*Totally secret! Only for the command*] included materials that concerned that planning of Operation Citadel, the two-volume *Kurskaia bitva: Khronika, fakty, liudy* firstly contained significantly more documents, and secondly presented the materials of one of the Wehrmacht's two army groups, Army Group Center, which took direct part in Operation Citadel's implementation, and later led the defensive fighting in the Orel bulge. The value of these documents consists in the fact that the Russian reader, first of all scholars, can see those events through the eyes of the German command, become acquainted with its assessments of the general course of the offensive as well as separate clashes and combat actions, understand their nature, and identify the causes of our successes and the Wehrmacht's failures on separate directions.

Other materials in this collected work, related to the second phase of the Battle of Kursk, are of no little interest, in particular "Boevoi otchet komandovaniia 2-i tankovoi i 9-i armii vermakhta o boiiakh na Kurskoi duge za period s 5 iulia po 18 avgusta 1943" ["Combat account of the command of the Wehrmacht's Second Panzer and Ninth Armies on the fighting at the Kursk bulge from 5 July to 18 August 1943"].[123] It contains not only a broad overview of the combat

121 V. Zamulin, *Prokhorovka. Neizvestnoe srazhenie Velikoi voiny* [*Prokhorovka: Unknown battle of the Great war*] (Moscow: *AST-Tranzit*, 2005); *Kurskii izlom. Reshaiushchaia bitva Otechestvennoi voiny* [*Kursk breaking point. Decisive battle of the Patriotic war*] (Moscow: EKSMO, 2007); *Zasekrechennaia Kurskaia bitva* (Moscow: Iauza/EKSMO, 2007); and *Zasekrechennaia Kurskaia bitva* [*Classified Kursk battle*] (Moscow: Iauza/EKSMO, 2009).

122 V.A. Zhilin, V.A. Grezhdev, A.A. Kol'tiukov, O.V. Saksonov, V. Iu. Chernogor and V.L. Shirokov, *Kurskaia bitva: Khronika, fakty, liudi* [*Kursk battle: Chronicle, facts, people*], in two volumes (Moscow: OLMA-PRESS, 2003).

123 Ibid., pp. 326-337.

operations within the framework of Operation Citadel, but also a significantly detailed look at the events of the enemy's Orel defensive operation, and the decisions and motivations of its command in this period. Another unquestionably interesting document in this book deserves attention: "Obzor politiko-moral'nogo sostoianie nemetskogo-fashistskikh voisk, deistvovavshikh pered frontom 5 gv. TA v period avgustovskikh boev 1943" ["Review of the political-morale condition of the German fascist troops that operated opposite the 5th Guards Tank Army in the period of the August 1943 fighting"].[124] Significant in size, highly informative, with a large number of citations from combat and captured documents, it plainly demonstrates the critical condition of the Wehrmacht's forces after the failed offensive, and reveals the forms and methods, which in particular the command of Army Group South used in order to hide the deterioration of the troops' morale. The appearance of this publication became an important step on the path of the further study of those events.

Recently de-classified captured and Soviet documents were also being published in separate issues of *Voenno-istoricheskii zhurnal*. The most interesting and important for scholars of the Battle of Kursk was the publication of the German 19th Panzer Division's account regarding its participation in Operation Citadel,[125] and N.S. Khrushchev's report to I.V. Stalin about the fighting on 12 July 1943 near Prokhorovka.[126] Similar materials continued to be published in this journal in the future, at the start of the second decade of the current century. Foremost among these are the works of S.A. Kuziaeva, "Bezobrazie, a ne nastuplenie. Prikazyvaiut mne gnat' pekhotu na tanki protivnika. Ia uzhe poterial tselyi polk" ["A mess, not an offensive. They're ordering me to drive infantry toward enemy tanks. I've already lost an entire regiment"][127] and Iu.A. Bakhurin's " 'Nakoval'nia' Glavnogo bronetakovogo upravleniia Krasnoi Armii" ["'Anvil' of the Red Army's Main Armored Command"].[128]

Meanwhile, at this time there began to appear literature of a new type for our country. These were collections of materials and reference publications, which were based around the presentation of data from closed files of the TsAMO RF on the personal matters of the Red Army's command staff,[129] de-classified documents of the Headquarters of the Red Army's Armored and Mechanized Forces,[130] and materials from the departments and bureaus of the *SMERSH* counterintelligence agency in the *fronts* and armies of the Battle of Kursk period, preserved in the Central Archive of the Russian Federal Security Service [formerly known as the KGB, or Committee of State Security].[131] They not only substantially expanded the base of sources and provided the opportunity to clarify a number of important details, especially relating to tragic moments in the Battle of Kursk for our side, but even more importantly, allowed the start of analysis of entire sub-branches in the history

124 Ibid., pp. 339-360.

125 "19-ia tankovaia diviziia vermakhta na Kurskoi duge (iiul' 1943)" ["The Wehrmacht's 19th Panzer Division at the Kursk bulge (July 1943)"] *Voenno-istoricheskii zhurnal* (No. 1, 2009), pp. 24-29.

126 "Donesenie I.V. Stalinu o boiakh pod Prokhorovkoi" ["Report to I.V. Stalin about the fighting near Prokhorovka"] *Voenno-istoricheskii zhurnal* (No. 9, 2007), pp. 21.

127 Published in *Voenno-istoricheskii zhurnal* (No. 7, 2013), pp. 24-35.

128 Published in *Voenno-istoricheskii zhurnal* (No. 8, 2014), pp. 30-35.

129 *Velikaia Otechestvennaia voina: Komandarmy. Voennyi biograficheskii slovar'* [*Great Patriotic War: Army commanders. Military biographical dictionary*] (Zhukovskii: Kuchkovo pole, 2005); *Velikaia Otechestvennaia voina: Komkory. Voennyi biograficheskii slovar'* (Zhukovskii: Kuchkovo pole, 2006), in two volumes.

130 *Glavnoe avtobronetankovoe upravlenie. Liudy, sobytiia, fakty v dokumentakh – 1943-1945* [*Main Armored Command: People, events and facts in documents – 1943-1945*], Book Three (Moscow: GABTU, 2006).

131 A.T. Zhadobin, V.V. Markovich and V.S. Khristoforov, *Ogennaia duga Kurska. Kurskaia bitva glazami Liubianki* [Kursk's *bulge of fire. Kursk battle through the eyes of the Lubianka*] (Moscow: AO Moskovskie uchebniki, 2003). Editor's note: the Lubianka is the popular name for the NKVD's and KGB's headquarters and affiliated prison on Liubianka Square in Moscow.

of events at Kursk, which illuminate the level of professionalism and combat activity of the senior and higher command levels of the Red Army. For such type of research, V. Zhilin's book *Tankisty-Geroi 1943-1945* [*Tanker-Heroes 1943-1945*], which came out in 2008, was also valuable. In it, the combat path of a number of tank army commanders and mobile corps commanders, which actively took part in the Battle of Kursk (such as S.I. Bogdanov, M.E. Katukov, P.S. Rybalko, A.G. Kravchenko and a number of others) is described in detail and relatively openly, based upon new documentary material.

However, it must be recognized that at this time, there was not direct correlation between the quality and quantity of appearing publications and the number of published new archival materials. If in the 1960s citations from new documents and commentary upon those that had just been introduced into academic circulation could be encountered in books and articles by Soviet historians within six months of their release, and sometimes even sooner, then at the end of the 1990s and beginning of the 2000s, such expeditiousness could only be envied. This testifies to the lack of readiness of our contemporaries for intensive analytic work with archival materials and the underappreciation of the modern generation of domestic historians of the importance of studying genuine documentary sources on the history of the Great Patriotic War.

It should be noted that at present, a great deal of productive work on the study of the Battle of Kursk is being conducted locally. The quality of this work relative to that of previous years has risen substantially. I especially want to note the active work of Kursk scholar-historians.[132] For example, the main directions of activity of the organs of power in the Central – Black Earth region to organize armed struggle against the Germans, render assistance to the Red Army to build defensive fortifications in the spring of 1943, and secure the rear areas of the *fronts* that were defending the Kursk salient were subjected to detailed study in the doctoral dissertation and publications of K.V. Iatsenko.[133] In the research projects of Doctor of Historical Science V.V. Korovin, the organization of resistance in the temporarily-occupied Central Black Earth region has been thoroughly analyzed, and considerable attention has been given to the steps taken to prepare partisan resistance in Kursk Oblast on the eve of and during the battle.

At the same time on the regional level, however, just as before attempts to mythologize separate battles and clashes of the summer of 1943 are not ceasing. The two-volume history by Doctor of Historical Science E.E. Shchekotikhin, *Orlovskaia bitva – dva goda: fakty, statistika, analiz* [*Orel battle – two years: facts, statistics, analysis*], can serve as a clear example. Alongside the desire to pay tribute to the fallen and to investigate what really happened in the war years on the territory of Orel Oblast, the author set before himself, putting it gently, an unmanageable task from the point of view of historical science, which is given by the title of the book itself. He attempted to show that the combat operations in Orel Oblast and neighboring oblasts in the first two years of the war, were not a chain of independent operations, called upon to resolve operational-tactical and strategic tasks, which had arisen by the time of their conducting, but a "unified, continuous action – the Orel battle, which included within itself a cohesive, concerted action of both a defensive and offensive nature."[134] Those who are familiar with the course of fighting on the central sector of the Soviet-German front, including in the period of the Battle of Kursk, know full well that this opinion is quite debatable. In addition, the book offers one more paradoxical conclusion: "The

132 For more detail on them and their work, see *Rodina* (No. 12, 2013), pp. 154-156.

133 K.V. Iatsenko, *Frontovoi region: Tsentral'noe Chernozem'e Rossii v sisteme voenno-organizatorskoi deiatel'nosti mestnykh vlastnykh struktur v gody Velikoi Otechestvennoi voiny* [*Russia's Central Black Earth region in the system of military-organizational activy of the local authority structures in the years of the Great Patriotic War*] (Moscow, 2006).

134 E.E. Shchekotikhin, *Orel bitva – dva goda: fakty, statistika, analiz* [*Orel battle – two years: facts, statistics, analysis*] (Orel, 2006), p. 3.

Great Patriotic War, like the Second World War, reached its culmination not simply in the battles of the Orel – Kursk bulge, but in the Orel strategic Operation Kutuzov operation."[135] Just so! As if there'd never been the 49 days and nights of the heaviest and most bloody fighting near Belgorod and Khar'kov. Elsewhere with several lines the author emphasizes the efforts and sacrifices of three *fronts* simultaneously – the Voronezh, Steppe and Southwestern Fronts – in the struggle with the strongest enemy grouping (Army Group South), only two of which fought within the Kursk bulge. It is difficult to connect such assessments with historical fact.

The open exaggerations and forced arguments in E.E. Shchekotikhin's work don't end with this. For example, attempting to give the scale of combat operations on the Borilovo axis at the end of July 1943, when the 4th Guards Tank Army and two tank corps were introduced into the fighting, doesn't simply place them on the same rank as the events near Prokhorovka, which were even greater in their significance and the size of committed forces; he also demonstrates astonishing ignorance about what really took place near Prokhorovka Station for a scholar of the Battle of Kursk. E.E. Shchekotikhin asserts, "In distinction from the Prokhorovka battle, which lasted just a single day (12 July) and on three directions, the Borilovo battle took place on one axis [and continued for several days with two stages on a sector of front with a width of 15 kilometers."[136] Comparing these two events, the author examined the historiography on Prokhorovka insufficiently deeply. That is why his conclusions seem unconvincing. As the archival sources of the opposing sides show, the fighting near Prokhorovka lasted seven days and on three directions and directly near the railroad station on a sector of approximate of approximately 35 kilometers (according to the tracing of the frontlines). In it, three Soviet armies, one a tank army, and two separate tank corps took part. In total, more than 100,000 men and approximately 1,000 tanks and self-propelled guns took part on our side. Moreover, the main armor forces, four tank corps, on 12 July were deployed on a narrow sector that extended just 16 kilometers.

The significant amount of collected material and the title of Doctor of History don't allow one to call E.E. Shchekotikhin's assertions an error of omission. His later works, for example, his book *Krupneishee tankovoe srazhenie Velikoi Otechestvennoi voiny* [*Largest tank battle of the Great Patriotic War*], which asserts that the battle for Orel was the decisive battle of the summer of 1943, testifies to this.[137] So does his activity to inculcate a new myth in the public consciousness about "the Battle of Soborovskoe Field" [a large field near the village of Soborovka, which lies about 60 kilometers south of Orel], which supposedly unfolded in Orel Oblast within the framework of the very same Battle of Kursk.[138] Even for a non-professional this is difficult to understand: How can a Battle exist within a Battle? The perception arises that the author isn't engaged with academic research of the issue, but is attempting to reanimate the longstanding argument between regional historians about where in fact the turning point in the Battle of Kursk occurred – near Orel or near Belgorod? This isn't an analysis of the matter in essence, but an attempt to "dress up" what occurred on one or another territory by giving it particular scale and significance without regard for historical realities.

It is hard not to agree with E.E. Shchekotikhin when he writes: "Even today there are political forces in society, for which legends and myths are more important than the established truth."[139] However, his personal position prompts a mixed feeling. In the introduction to his book, we read:

135 Ibid.
136 Ibid., p. 217.
137 Published in Moscow by Iauza/EKSMO in 2009. The quote is taken from page 5.
138 See, for example, D. Peredel'sky's article, "Soborovskom perelom" ["Soborov turning point"] in *Rosiiskaia gazeta*, 3 May, 2012.
139 Shchekotikhin, *Orel bitva – dva goda*, p. 6.

> In front of me stood the task to handle carefully the genuine facts of the war's realities, not myths; to answer fully and clearly the questions set for the research; and make it known to the progeny. This resolution is possible in those instances when reasoning and will are governed by a sober, open-minded assessment of the indisputable, established historical facts.[140]

Unquestionably, the desire to adhere to his declared principles is discernible, but at the same time an unequivocal attempt to create new legends is going on. I've had the occasion to meet with Egor Egor'evich more than once and I've asked him to explain his position on the problems with his work indicated above, but never once I have I received a clear and sound reply. I've deliberately given so much attention to examining E.E. Shchekotikhin's publications. Unfortunately it isn't evidence of their academic significance and the author's large contribution to studying the history of the Kursk battle. It is only because I believe in the foreseeable future we will become witnesses to the fact the myths expressed by Egor Egor'evich will become accepted as realities, because many in our country today mistakenly assume that myth-making with respect to the past is precisely that method by which to consolidate society, and help inculcate patriotic feelings in the young population.

Summing up certain result of the contemporary stage of historiography, I will note its main aspects. First, at the present time the study of the events of the summer of 1943 at Kursk, and especially the fighting in the Voronezh Front sector, is going on actively, and on the basis of a broad foundation of sources from both domestic and foreign archives. Already, the combat actions in the area of Belgorod within the framework of the Kursk defensive operation have primarily been reconstructed.

Second, thanks to the de-classified documentary files of the Voronezh and Steppe Fronts in the TsAMO RF, a number of myths have been dispelled by domestic scholars (including the largest ones about the events at Prokhorovka), the losses of the Voronezh and Steppe Fronts in the first stage of the Battle of Kursk have been determined, and the mechanism by which their Military Councils covered up this data has been revealed. The results of this work have found their reflection in a number of monographs, published in the Russian and English languages.[141]

Third, the combat operations on previously "forgotten" directions (for example, the Korocha axis, Army Detachment Kempf's offensive sector), have been elucidated in rather sufficient detail. Moreover, new interesting publications have already appeared about the antecedents and preparation of the Kursk battle,[142] as well as about its results.

---

140 Ibid., p. 5.

141 For example, Valeriy Zamulin, *Demolishing the Myth. The Tank Battle at Prokhorovka, Kursk, July 1943: An Operational Narrative* (Solihull, UK: 2011).

142 V.N. Zamulin, "K predystorii Kurskoi bitvy: byli li u Germanii shansy na uspekh v mae-iiune 1943 goda? ["The pre-history of the Kursk battle: Did Germany have a chance for success in May-June 1943"] *Novaia i noveishaia istoriia* [*New and latest history*] (No. 1, 2014), pp. 224-230; ibid., "Severnaia udarnaia gruppirovka vermakhta pod Kurskom nakanune operatsii "Tsitadel'" ["The Wehrmacht's northern shock grouping at Kursk on the eve of Operation Citadel"] *Novaia i Noveishaia istoriia* (No. 3, 2015), pp. 65-81; ibid., "Byla li dopushchena oshibka pri planirovanii oborony Voronezhskogo fronta v xode podgotovki k Kurskoi bitve?" ["Was there a mistake made when planning the defense of the Voronezh Front in the course of preparing for the Battle of Kursk?"] *KLIO* (No. 7, 2015); ibid., "K voprosu o roli sovetskoi razvedki v period podgotovki Krasnoi Armii k boiiam v raione Kurskoi dugi" ["On the question of the role of Soviet intelligence in the period of the Red Army's preparation for the fighting in the area of the Kursk bulge"] *Nauchnye vedomosti KGU* [*Academic bulletin of Kursk State University*] (No. 3, 2015) (an on-line journal). Editor's note: A couple of these articles ["Did Germany have a chance?" and "Was a mistake made when planning ...?" have previously been translated and published in the *Journal of Slavic Military History*. Updated versions of these articles, and the other articles mentioned in this footnote, make up chapters in this book.]

Fourth, research work has started in a new direction in the history of the Battle of Kursk. This research illuminates the level of professional training and the activities of the Red Army's higher command staff in command of the troops in the course of the summer fighting of 1943.

Fifth, the serious changes that have occurred over the past 20 years in the field of studying the Battle of Kursk (the de-classification of archives, the appearance of primary monographs, etc.), as well as the publication of works by Russian scholars abroad on the given subject, judging from reviews in the press, have started to have a positive influence on the Western audience of all those who are interested in the problems of the Second World War. Writes the American scholar D. Showalter:

> Kursk generated accounts of memory and explanation. Two master narratives emerged. The German version depicted a heroic struggle, wearing down massively superior Soviet defenders, climaxing with the SS Panzer Corps's destruction of the Fifth Guards Tank Army at Prokhorovka – only to have their victory thwarted by Hitler's micromanaging and indecision. The Soviet counterpart depicted a German attack first ground down by a scientifically created, dauntlessly defended fortification system, then defeated by the intrepid attack of the Fifth Guards Tank Army at Prokhorovka.
>
> Addressing the contradictions between the two memes has been complicated until recently by a virtual German monopoly of Eastern Front narratives. The USSR's determination to control the story of the Great Patriotic War was complemented by a discouraging of memory and memoir at every rank from private to marshal of the Soviet Union. The improved post-Soviet access to archives, memories and battlefields has combined with post-reunification developments in German military historiography to revitalize, indeed revolutionize, the academic and general-audience writing on Kursk and its matrices.

Sixth, at this time there still exists an imbalance in the study of the Central Front's plan of repulsing the German offensive within the framework of Operation Citadel and its eventual realization. There has been no fitting research of the heavy fighting for Ponyri and on the Ol'khovatka axis.

In conclusion, along with the previously negative tendencies, today there are unfortunately a host of new ones, which are quickly developing. Over the past years in Russia, not a single fundamental work has been completed, which would illuminate the entire period of the Battle of Kursk, factoring in the new approaches and possibilities of the present. At the same time, approximately around 2010, a process of curtailing academic research with the use of archival sources on the given subject became clearly discernible. In mass historical literature on the given topic, the tendency is growing to lower the qualitative level of the work, and a substantial growth in groundless assertions and phony issues is noticeable. The books printed by oblast and republic publishers particularly sin in this respect. The cause is not only the absence of necessary sources, which is in fact the case. The main explanation is something else: it is difficult, labor-intensive and tedious to work in the military archives, and not everyone wants to take this on. Therefore domestic authors, unfortunately, frequently prefer to travel a well-worn path, and discuss already published facts without adequate study of the situation at the fronts and of the available material. As a result, already new legends and myths regarding the Battle of Kursk are being created.

2

The Kastornoe Cauldron: The beginning of the process of forming the Kursk bulge

At the end of January and beginning of February 1943, a major offensive operation that became known as the Kastornoe – Voronezh operation, unfolded on the land of several oblasts of the Central Black Earth region practically without any preparation. In Soviet historiography, it is usually treated as a seamless continuation of the destruction of Paulus's Sixth Army at Stalingrad. However, this operation had a direct connection as well to another epic battle in the Kursk area. Having smashed Army Group B in the snow-covered fields around Kastornoe and Gorschechnoe, the command of the Voronezh Front and Briansk Front managed to make full use of this victory. Over the next two weeks, their troops exploited the success without an operational pause, and pursuing the retreating foe, liberated Khar'kov and emerged on the approaches to Sevsk, thereby creating an enormous salient in the center of the Eastern Front, which entered history as the Kursk bulge. It was here, after not quite five months had passed from these events, that the final hopes of the Nazis for revenge and global supremacy were conclusively buried.

For an understanding of the events of the summer of 1943, this operation is interesting also because of the fact that the forces (*fronts*, armies and divisions) and command staff that conducted it, even those of the generals who weren't at the top of their games, would later take direct part in the Battle of Kursk. Thus, the analysis of the mistakes, miscalculations and successful decisions in the course of the winter campaign can yield a distinct image of their professional training and abilities in planning for major operations on the eve of this epochal event.

The new year of 1943 began with a powerful Red Army offensive along the entire Eastern Front. The victory on the Volga became the catalyst of this offensive. The Wehrmacht's unprecedented losses forced its high command to withdraw its forces hastily from the lines that they occupied almost along the entire front from Lake Ladoga in the north to the Northern Caucasus in the south. On 18 January the Leningrad and Volkhov Fronts broke through the German blockade of Leningrad. The forces of the Transcaucasian and Southern Fronts at the beginning of January 1943 launched a major operation to destroy the German forces in the Northern Caucasus. The Don Front went on the offensive against Paulus's encircled army on 10 January. Parallel with this, in the southern and southwestern parts of the Soviet – German front, the Red Army undertook an offensive, striving to shatter Army Groups B, Don and A, the main forces of which were positioned on the Voronezh axis, and in the eastern Donbass and Khar'kov. By 20 January 1943, the divisions of Southwestern Front's right flank on the Voroshilovgrad axis reached the line of the Aidar River.

In the middle of January, the most large-scale events began to unfold at first on the Voronezh direction, and then on the Belgorod and Kursk directions. On 13 January the Voronezh Front with its center and left wing formations launched the Ostrogozhsk – Rossosh offensive operation, while simultaneously continuing to hold the Kozinka – Ozerki – Ol'khovatka – Podgornoe

– Voronezh line, and with its right wing further along the Voronezh River to its mouth. As a result of the 40th Army's arrival on the Semidesiatkoe – Kazachek line, the southern face of a salient in the German lines, the so-called Voronezh salient, was formed, in the middle of which were the Kastornoe and Gorshechnoe railroad stations. It was being held by the obviously battered divisions of Army Group B's Second Army and Second Hungarian Army. Briansk Front, occupying the line Bol'shie Golubochki – Novosil' – Gremiachaia – (excl.) Kozinka with its left-flank 13th Army (which was stretched from Sidorovki to Kozinka), and the Voronezh Front's right-flank 38th Army (which was holding the Kozinka – Podgornoe sector), were looming over this German grouping, and presenting the threat of an attack into its flank and rear from the north. The salient's base ran along the Kshen' and Oskol Rivers and had a width of 130 kilometers, while the salient's tip extended to Voronezh, 100 kilometers to the east.

The forces of the German Army Group B had fortified the northern and eastern faces of the Voronezh salient back in July 1942, more than six months ago. The defense in these sectors rested primarily upon a system of strong points and focal points of resistance, linked by two to three lines of trenches with a large number of earth and timber firing positions, bunkers, dugouts and other types of field works. The depth of the main belt of resistance amounted to 4-8 kilometers. The hilly terrain, cut by ravines, descended in the direction of the Soviet forces, thereby giving the enemy a fine field of view and the possibility of placing fire on all the approaches to their positions. Sectors lying in front of the forward edge of defense and on the most important directions in the depth of the German defenses had been mined and reinforced with 2-3 bands of barbed wire entanglements.

The southern face of the salient (from Rudkino to Gorodishche), which had been created as a result of the enemy's hasty retreat in the middle of January 1943, wasn't fortified. Here, remnants of the Second Hungarian Army's III Corps were defending. Its command had only had time to adapt settlements, individual hills, patches of woods and road hubs for defense and to organize a system of fire. In the depth of the defense, the German command had prepared two intermediary lines. Increased attention had been focused on positions along the Olym River, further along the Kastornoe – Gorshechnoe – Staryi Oskol railroad and along the western banks of the Tim and Oskol Rivers.

The northern and eastern sectors of the Voronezh salient, from the Livny – Marmyzhi railroad to the mouth of the Voronezh River were being held by the VII and XIII Corps of *Generaloberst* H. von Salmuth's Second Army, which possessed, according to information from Soviet intelligence organs, approximately eight divisions.

The most weakly fortified southern sector was being held by Group Siebert, which consisted of two divisions of the Hungarian III Corps and several German units and elements, which had been shifted from Voronezh in the course of the Soviet offensive during the Ostrogozhsk – Rossosh operation. Altogether, according to Soviet intelligence, approximately three enemy divisions were operating here. The enemy didn't have any operational reserves on the Voronezh – Kursk axis in the latter half of January 1943, so back in December 1942 and the beginning of January 1943, some of the divisions of von Salmuth's Second Army had been sent against the attacking forces of the Southwestern Front and to Ostrogozhsk. German units (up to an infantry regiment each) were garrisoning the cities of Orel, Kursk, Oboian', Shchigry, and Staryi Oskol that were distant from Voronezh and Kastornoe, though Kastornoe had its own garrison.

Thus, the enemy grouping defending the Voronezh salient numbered approximately 12 divisions. According to Soviet intelligence information, their total numerical strength approached 125,000 soldiers and officers. The enemy had more than 4,500 machine guns, approximately 1,000 mortars (with a caliber of 81mm or higher), 1,100 field guns (including 500 anti-tank guns) and 65 tanks. The Luftwaffe operating on the Voronezh – Kursk axis had 300 aircraft.[1]

1 V.P. Morozov, *Zapadnee Voronezha* [*West of Voronezh*] (Moscow: Voenizdat, 1956), p. 93.

Despite the considerably significant strength of the grouping of the two enemy armies, our forces in this area had a number of advantages. The enemy's operational situation was extremely unfavorable. The forces of two Soviet *fronts* were deeply enveloping his grouping from the north and south. After the completion of the Ostrogozhsk – Rossosh operation, a 200-kilometer wide gap had been torn into the German lines between Oskino and Svatovoe, which the command of Army Group B didn't have the strength to close. The Second Army's supply line, running through Kastornoe, was under threat. The configuration of the front lines offered the Soviet side a favorable opportunity not only to encircle two enemy armies, but also to keep the initiative and to continue the offensive to the west. Indeed, the Soviet command didn't miss the opportunity to take advantage of this.

On the evening of 17-18 January 1943, the Voronezh Front was still in the process of mopping up to the remnants of the Ostrogozhsk – Rossosh grouping, and the Chief of the General Staff General of the Army A.M. Vasilevsky, who was located at the Front headquarters, having discussed the emerging favorable operational situation with its command staff, sent his observations regarding the conducting of a new offensive operation, the Kastornoe – Voronezh operation, to the *Stavka* of the Supreme High Command. Already on 20 January, Moscow granted its approval. Vasilevsky's plan foresaw meeting attacks from the north and south by three army groupings of the two *fronts* to encircle and destroy the German and Hungarian Second Armies at Voronezh and to seize the Elets – Valuiki railroad. This would not only permit the capture of an important operational area west of Voronezh, but also create the prerequisites for developing a further offensive toward Kursk and into Ukraine. It was planned that by the end of the operation, the enemy would be thrown back to the Sovetskii – Efrosinovka – Iastrebovka – Aleksandrovna – Russkaia Kholan' – Ol'khovatka line. Consequently, it should set the stage for the final destruction of the entire German Army Group B.

The offensive was planned according to the classical scheme of "pincers" with the forces of four armies from two Soviet *fronts*. From the left flank of Briansk Front, Lieutenant General M.A. Reiter's 13th Army would go on the attack, joined by three armies (the 38th, 60th and 40th Armies) from the right flank of Colonel General F.I. Golikov's Voronezh Front. Altogether, the plan proposed to activate 27 rifle divisions, a tank corps, and 7 rifle and 8 tank brigades for the offensive. Formations of the Voronezh Front's 2nd Air Army and Briansk Front's 15th Air Army were to cover them from the air. Altogether, approximately 250,000 men, more than 4,000 guns and mortars, more than 700 tanks and 527 aircraft were to be committed into the operation.[2]

The Soviet side would launch the main attack with two armies at the base of the Voronezh salient with converging attacks toward Kastornoe: from the north (out of the area southeast of Livny) with General N.P. Pukhov's 13th Army and from the south (out of the Rogovato – Pogoreloe area) with Major General K.S. Moskalenko's 40th Army. They were to create not only an outer, but also an inner ring of encirclement by pushing their second echelons to the line of the Tim River. Properly considering that the southern face of the Voronezh salient was the enemy's weakest sector of defense, the Soviet command allocated the leading role in the operation to Moskalenko's army.

In order to divert enemy forces from the axis of the main attack and complicate the enemy's maneuvering with reserves, in addition to 40th Army's main attack, Lieutenant General N.E. Chibisov's 38th Army (out of the Terbuny area) and Major General I.D. Cherniakhovsky's 60th Army (out of the Iablochnoe area) were preparing to launch secondary attacks in the general direction of Nizhniaia Veduga. Thus, if all four armies successfully carried out the designated plan, the Voronezh salient would be split into several pieces and at least three pockets would be created: the

2 *Velikaia Otechestvennaia voina 1941-1945, Kniga 2: Perelom* [*Great Patriotic War 1941-1945, Book 2: Turning point*] (Moscow: Nauka, 1998), p. 161.

first – between the 13th Army's left flank and the 38th Army's right flank (primarily using the forces of the 13th Army); the second – Group Siebert, squeezed between the 40th Army's right wing and the 60th Army's left wing, as well as by the 38th Army's shock forces; and finally, the third pocket would be formed in the Voronezh – Terbuny – Iablochnoe triangular area, after the forces of the 38th Army and 60th Army linked up at Nizhniaia Veduga.

Preparation for the operation didn't go smoothly. Since no reserves had been assigned, General Golikov and Reiter had to form shock groupings at the expense of their own forces and means by conducting an internal regrouping in difficult winter conditions. It was first necessary for 60th Army to obtain a necessary line for active operations, and also, considering that the 40th Army had to resolve the most difficult tasks relative to its neighbors and was going to have to cover a greater distance before linking up with the 13th Army at Kastornoe, it needed considerable reinforcement. Yet all this had to be done within a very short period before the deadline for the attack – just 3-4 days. In order to meet the scheduled deadline, F.I. Golikov transferred a 22-kilometer sector along the right bank of the Don River from Kostenka to Semidesiatskii together with its troops (the 141st, 252nd and 322 Rifle Divisions, the 150th Tank Brigade and the 10th Artillery Division) from Moskalenko's 40th Army to Cherniakhovsky's 60th Army, and sent the 4th Tank Corps, 183rd and 309th Rifle Divisions and the 129th Rifle Brigade out of Voronezh Front's reserve to the 40th Army.[3] However, these calculations, made on the fly without any deep analysis, proved to be not quite correct. When laying out the defenses, the enemy had exerted his main efforts to creating powerful strongpoints in the villages, the approaches to which were densely mined, while the intervals between the villages and hamlets were swept by fire. Because of the frequent snowfalls, there could be no reliance on airpower, and thus it was possible to destroy the German strongpoints effectively only with artillery means. Before the operation it was readily apparent that Moskalenko plainly didn't have enough artillery, which is why it was planned to compensate it with the forces of the 4th Tank Corps and 192nd Tank Brigade. However, these hopes proved to be extremely exaggerated. Unquestionably, armor would play an important role in the offensive, but there proved to be too little of it, on average just 8.2 tanks per kilometer of front, and thus in the difficult winter conditions, the tanks alone would be unable to shoulder the entire burden of the operation. This would become evident in the first days of the offensive, and the Front command would be compelled hastily to return the 10th Artillery Division from the 60th Army back to the axis of the main attack.

Secondly, the *Stavka* believed that both *fronts* had the necessary minimum amount of supplies necessary to support the troops. Thus on 21 January it issued an order to complete the preparations within 48 hours, and to launch the offensive already on 24 January. In reality the *fronts* did have the minimum amount of supplies, plus captured German and Hungarian stockpiles. However, it was necessary to deliver the supply loads from the railroad stations and stockpiles to the troops and to the designated positions for the operation along snow-covered roads, primarily by horse, and wherever this was impossible to do, first the roads had to be cleared from the meter-deep snow by the troops themselves while continuing to conduct the offensive. A special message from the 13th Army's Special Department of the NKVD stated:

> In the course of 23.01.1943, the army's artillery, mortar and tank units as before were continuing to assemble on the line of departure for the attack. By 0600, the 12th and 5th Artillery Divisions, the 16th Anti-aircraft Division and the 43rd Separate Tank Regiment hadn't yet arrived in their jumping-off positions. The main reason for delays in assembling remains the

3 K.S. Moskalenko, *Na iugo-zapadnom napravlenii* [*On the southwestern direction*] (Moscow: Nauka, 1969), p. 404.

> lack of fuel, particularly in the artillery units, which is explained primarily by interruptions in the delivery of fuel to the army's bases and the artillery units' shortage of motorized transport (5th and 12th Artillery Divisions and others). The main shortcoming in the preparation of the units for combat operations is the lack of communications between the artillery headquarters and the formations and units, as well as the absence of contact between separate units. For example: to the present day the artillery headquarters has had no contact with the 5th and 12th Artillery Divisions, the 5th Guards Mortar [rocket launching] Division, the 16th Anti-aircraft Division or with separate artillery regiments, and there is also intermittent communications within the divisions themselves. Only radio communications work out for the best. As a result of breakdowns and accidents of motorized transport, for the 5th Artillery Division alone 27 guns are still en route, of which 9 belong to the 16th Light Artillery Regiment and 18 to the 9th Howitzer Brigade. Of this latter number in the 293rd Howitzer Regiment, six 152mm howitzers have been left behind in the former position due to a lack of prime movers, which are undergoing repair in Tambov, and six 122mm howitzers have become stuck en route because the prime movers have either broken down or run out of fuel. The same situation exists in the 12th Artillery Division and 16th Anti-aircraft Division. The situation with the artillery division's supply of shells remains very bad; some have a supply level that varies from 0.4 to 1.0 standard combat load.[4]

A similar situation with ammunition supplies was also present in the rifle units of the 13th Army. For example, on 21 January 1943, the 307th Rifle Division had a 0.9 combat load of rifle cartridges, a 0.5 combat load of hand grenades, a 0.6 combat load of 50mm mortar shells, a 1.0 combat load of 81mm mortar shells, and a 0.9 combat load of 122mm artillery shells. Indeed, these deficits wouldn't even be eliminated by the end of the operation.

There was one more important factor, which both helped the Briansk Front leadership (by imparting organization, focusing attention and concentrating efforts) and also made it nervous. The point is that this would be Colonel General M.A. Reiter's first offensive operation in the post of *front* commander-in-chief, and moreover, he would have to conduct it in such difficult conditions. Thus he was working flat out and placing increased demands on his subordinates; even so, it was extremely difficult to take account of all the details over such a short period of time. Briansk Front's chief of staff Major General L.M. Sandalov recalled:

> The 13th Army was designated as Briansk Front's main assault force in the operation. Almost all of the Front's own tank and artillery units, as well as its air force, were assigned to support it. Back at the beginning of 1943, the Front's command post had been set up in the sector of General Reiter's 13th Army. The command post of the Front's air force was located nearby. The winter of that year was snowy. In order to select a breakthrough sector, Reiter drove up to the positions in an aerosled, and from the sled he would make his way to the front on skis after donning a knee-length camouflage smock. As soon as a breakthrough sector was chosen, they immediately began preparing the troops and headquarters for the operation.
>
> … On the night of 25-26 January the troops of Briansk Front's left wing took up their jumping-off positions and the air force was ready to launch airstrikes. Before dawn a fatigued, but satisfied Maks Andreevich returned to the Front's command post from the troops.

4 V.S. Khristoforov, *Velikaia Otechestvennaia voina, 1943: Issledovaniia, Dokumenty, Komentariia* [*Great Patriotic War, 1943: Research, Documents, Commentary* (Moscow: Glavnoe arkhivnoe upravleniia goroda Moskvy, 2013, p. 378.

> "I've visited all the divisions that stand ready for the attack," he said. "They understand their tasks pretty well, and have reliable communications with the supporting tanks, artillery and aviation. Whereas we trounced the Germans in the summer at Sychevka, we surely won't get the best of them in the same way now, in winter!"
>
> In these words there was both confidence and concern, which was fully understandable in that situation.[5]

The Voronezh Front command was also facing very difficult conditions. The majority of its troops of the Front's center and left wing were continuing to carry out the Ostrogozhsk – Rossosh operation. Recalled the 40th Army commander, "In the course of the regrouping, which went on simultaneously with actions to eliminate the pocketed enemy troops in the Alekseevka area, the divisions had to pivot 90° from the south and southwest directions to the north and northwest."[6] Considering that it was Moskalenko's 40th Army which was to play the main role in the forthcoming operation, this sudden regrouping had to tell on the quality of the combat preparation by its formations. However, when discussing the operation's plan, Moscow didn't focus the main attention on these problems, but on the enemy's discomfiture and the low morale of his troops after Stalingrad, which unquestionably were evident, but nevertheless gave no aid to the resolution of critical problems that were facing both *fronts*.

Despite the fact that 72% of the rifle divisions, 90% of the artillery and all of the tank formations[7] had been concentrated in the sector of the attacking armies of both *fronts*, and each of the first-echelon divisions had been assigned normal breakthrough sectors (4.5 kilometers in the 13th Army, 6 kilometers in the 40th Army), in the opinion of the former chief of staff of Voronezh Front Lieutenant General M.I. Kazakhov, "From the operation's outset, the combat operations became strained."[8]

The first five days were particularly hard. With the aim of throwing the enemy into confusion, the armies that took part in the operation were to go on the offensive in staggered fashion: the 40th Army – on 24 January, the 60th Army – on 25 January, and the 13th and 38th Armies – on 26 January.

K.S. Moskalenko deployed four rifle divisions and one brigade in his first echelon. In the center of the combat formation (on the axis of the main attack) was Major General P.M. Men'shikov's 309th Rifle Division; on its left was Colonel P.M. Bezhko's 107th Rifle Division, and on its right – Major General P.M. Shaferevich's 25th Guards Rifle Division. Further beyond the latter was Major General A.S. Kostitsyn's 183rd Rifle Division and Colonel I.I. Ladygin's 129th Rifle Brigade. Major General A.G. Kravchenko's 4th Tank Corps was to launch its attack in the sector of the 309th and 107th Rifle Division, which were to create the outer ring of encirclement. It received a very important task: after the infantry broke through the defenses, with a rapid advance in cooperation with the 25th Guards Rifle Division, it was to seize the major road hub of Gorshechnoe Station. It was assumed that the enemy's defense would collapse from a decisive blow by a major mobile formation like the 4th Tank Corps. As a result, first the conditions would be created for a rapid advance by the 40th Army's main forces to the town of Kastornoe in order to link up with the 13th Army, and second, this would hasten the formation of the inner ring of encirclement by the units of Kostitsyn's 183rd Rifle Division and Ladygin's 129th Rifle Brigade, which with the aim of preventing the enemy's withdrawal from the planned pocket, had been previously

5 General Sandalov, *Sbornik dokumentov I materialov* (Moscow, 2011), pp. 274-275.
6 Moskalenko, *Na iugo-zapadnom napravlenii*, p. 405.
7 *Velikaia Otechestvennaia voina 1941-1945. Kniga 2: Perelom* (Moscow: Nauka, 1998), p. 161.
8 M.I. Kazakov, *Nad kartoi bylykh srazhenii* [*Over the map of former battles*] (Moscow: Voenizdat, 1971), p. 156.

reinforced with the powerful means respectively of the 16th Destroyer Anti-tank Artillery Brigade and the 192nd Tank Brigade. In the second echelon were the 305th and 340th Rifle Divisions, as well as three ski brigades – the 4th, 6th and 8th, which on the second day of the operation were to attack toward the city of Staryi Oskol.[9]

On the first day of the operation, the 40th Army command decided to launch its attack simultaneously in the entire 50-kilometer sector between Semidesiatkoe and Gorodishche that had had been designated for the offensive. Dawn on 24 January found its troops that were assigned for the operation in their jumping-off positions, but in the morning the weather sharply deteriorated and the temperature dropped to -20 C. [-4 F.]. P.M. Shafarenko recalled:

> Snow developed and the roads became snow-covered. The artillery preparation was postponed several times, but it was nevertheless conducted at 1230 under conditions of poor visibility, and of course with little effectiveness. We realized this as soon as the infantry and tanks went on the attack. The Hitlerites opened up with a strong return fire at the attackers and resisted bitterly.[10]

The fighting took on a protracted character. Defending, the enemy in several sectors launched counterattacks. The situation in the army's sector began to change slowly in the Soviets' favor only after the 4th Tank Corps' introduction into combat.[11] Because of the heavy snowfall, its commander A.G. Kravchenko was compelled to alter the initial plan of actions. The tank brigades shifted to roads in the 25th Guards Rifle Division's sector, which enabled the infantry to advance more actively. Despite the fact that the deep snow deprived the tankers of the ability to maneuver, and forced them to move only along roads and to attack the enemy strongpoints in villages head-on, over the first two hours of combat the tank corps penetrated the enemy defense to a depth of 6-8 kilometers and by 1500 reached the Lebiazh'e area. By the onset of darkness, it seized the settlements of Novo- and Staro-Melovoe jointly with Major A.S. Belov's 73rd Guards Rifle Regiment, which meant a penetration of 16 kilometers. Nonetheless, this advance was less than half of that which had been planned on the first day. The remaining divisions were making no headway. The enemy opposite the 183rd Rifle Division was defending with particular stubbornness. In the village of Sinie Lipiagi, the German 57th Infantry Division's 196th Infantry Regiment had created a well-fortified strongpoint, which the 183rd Rifle Division had been unable to take from the march, and further progress of its units ground to a halt here for a long time. Thus, on the first day of the operation, 40th Army had been unable to carry out its assigned task. The reasons for this, in addition to the unfavorable weather conditions and the enemy's stubborn resistance, were the poorly-organized artillery support for the attack, as well as the poor cooperation between the infantry and the tanks.

The command of Army Group B correctly determined the intention of the Soviet side and its possibilities. Believing that the encirclement of the Second Army would only be a matter of several days, *Generaloberst* (from 1 February 1943 *Generalfeldmarschall*) M. Weichs began to withdraw VII Army Corps's divisions from Voronezh and across the Don River already on the afternoon of 24 January. That evening, reconnaissance probes by the 60th Army determined that the Germans were hastily retreating, leaving behind a rear guard of up to one-and-a-half regiments. Showing initiative, army commander I.D. Cherniakhovsky issued an order to go in pursuit of the enemy,

9 K.S. Moskalenko, *Na iugo-zapadnom napravlenii*, p. 407.

10 P.M. Shafarenko, *Na raznykh frontakh. Zapiski komandira divizii* [*On various fronts. Notes of a division commander*] (Moscow: Voenizdat, 1978), p. 123.

11 On 7 February 1943, the 4th Tank Corps would become the 5th Guards "Stalingrad" Tank Corps.

before reporting about this to F.I. Golikov, who approved his decision. By dawn on 25 January, Voronezh had been completely cleared of the Germans.

The morning of 25 January turned out to be fair and sunny, and the Voronezh Front command was able to initiate an artillery preparation according to plan. Simultaneously, units of the 2nd and 15th Air Armies took to the sky. After the artillery barrage, the shock groupings of the 40th Army stepped off on the attack. Major P.K. Kazakevich's 81st Guards Rifle Regiment of the 25th Guards Rifle Division and the Major General V.G. Lebedev's 96th Separate Tank Brigade that was attached to the division, breaking the German resistance, seized the villages of Boloto and Nizhnye Borki, and thereby opened a path to Gorshechnoe, which A.G. Kravchenko didn't tarry to use. With a decisive lunge, his tankers and Kazakevich's escorting rifle battalions overran enemy blocking detachments, and having broken into Gorshechnoe Station, fully mopped it up of its German occupiers.

However, this success was unable to have any cardinal effect on the situation in the sector of the entire 40th Army. Even so, despite the most difficult conditions, the rifle divisions made an advance of 10-18 kilometers through the enemy's main belt of defenses over the day; the Germans and their allies were continuing to cling stubbornly to every village and building. The adversary was using any and every opportunity to halt our offensive. For example, the 183rd Rifle Division was still involved in heavy fighting in the area of Sinie Lipiagi, and was thus unable to cover the left-flank of the rapidly advancing 25th Guards Rifle Division. As a result, at dawn on 25 January, its 78th Guards Rifle Regiment, having taken the villages of Berezov and Petrovka, was counterattacked in the flank and forced to abandon them again.

The 4th Tank Corps was also unable to exploit the success. It was consuming all of its fuel reserves, and the dispatched fuel trucks became stuck in the snow. Not only troops were engaged with clearing the roads, but also the local population. With the onset of twilight, aircraft were called upon to deliver fuel. The crews of Po-2 light bombers, several times a night, touched down on cleared roads, bringing barrels of fuel and lubricants.[12] However, in order to meet the tank corps' minimum needs, it was necessary to double the amount of fuel that was being delivered, but there was no way to do this. Because of this, the grand opportunity for a rapid advance to Kastornoe was missed, and the tankers spent several days stuck in Gorshechnoe.

The offensive launched by the 60th Army that day out of the Iablonochnoe area in the direction of Nizhniaia Veduga was also developing very slowly. Enemy firing positions had not been fully knocked out or suppressed by the artillery preparation, and thus the enemy met the attackers with intense machine-gun and artillery fire. In the course of the day, combat operations primarily went on to take strongpoints in the forward edge of the enemy's defense. The Germans were resisting bitterly. In the afternoon, some of the villages (Pereryvni, Parnishyi, Kochatovka) were liberated, but heavy fighting was going on for Khmelevoi Les and Semidesiatkoe. By the evening, on its entire front the 60th Army had only advanced by 2-3 kilometers.

On the morning of 25 January, trying to make use of the favorable situation – the German withdrawal from Voronezh, M.A. Reiter issued an order to the 38th Army to step off a day earlier with its forward detachments toward Cherniakhovsky's army, in order to link up with it in Nizhniaia Veduga. However, this didn't bring about the expected results. Going on the attack only at 1630, that is, just before twilight, Chibisov's troops were unable to make any penetration in the German defenses.

Thus, by the end of the second day of the operation, despite the fact that essentially the three shock groupings of both *fronts* had been put into motion, the offensive was having a hard time making progress. Only the 40th Army had achieved a certain success. The reasons for this are

12 TsAMO RF, F. 203, op. 353678, d. 1, l. 14.

several, including the poor prognosis of enemy actions by the headquarters of the Voronezh Front. According to information from our scouts and the testimony of prisoners, the enemy in the course of 25 January had withdrawn significant forces from Voronezh to Kastornoe. The German Second Army command had withdrawn one infantry regiment each of two divisions to the right bank of the Don River and had sent them along the Voronezh – Nizhnedevitsk road in order to hurl them against Moskalenko's attacking units. Meanwhile the enemy's main forces that were defending the eastern sector of the Voronezh salient were preparing to withdraw to the Semiluki – Golosnovka line (40 kilometers west of Voronezh). Taking this into account, F.I. Golikov should have exploited the 40th Army's success more actively, and in order to develop the offensive first introduce its second echelon into the breakthrough sector, and secondly, attempt to regroup a portion of the 60th Army's force to that breach. However, this wasn't done.

In addition, the inability of the headquarters of Voronezh Front's divisions to organize reliable communications and to exert intelligible control over their units was negatively affecting the course of the offensive. These problems proved to be so serious, that Voronezh Front's Military Council was eventually forced to send a special directive to the troops.[13] Substantial shortcomings in command at the tactical level were also exposed. As military historian V.P. Morozov notes, "This was a result of the poorly-organized collaboration between the infantry and tanks; the poor artillery preparation of the attack; the overestimation of the enemy's strength; and the absence of appropriate maneuver by the units and formations on the battlefield in order to develop the offensive into the depth."[14]

Unfortunately, threatening directives, strict orders and "tongue lashings" over the situation with respect to the command, control and cooperation in battles fundamentally didn't change anything. An incident cited in P.M Shafarenko's book can serve as an example:

> The 78th Rifle Regiment ... toward evening on 28 January on the approach to Gorshechnoe came under an attack by friendly aircraft. As a result, 20 men were wounded, including the deputy commander of the training battalion Captain I.M. Solomin. At that time we were conducting mobile fighting. There was no continuous front line in a number of sectors, and the situation was changing rapidly. The mistake by our aircraft wasn't coincidental. As became clear later, neither the infantry nor the pilots were using recognition signals.[15]

Let's return, though, to the course of the operation. Striving to conserve the shock grouping and to increase the pace of the operation, the leadership of the Briansk and Voronezh Fronts sent an order to all subordinate formation commanders: Cease frontal attacks against fortified villages, isolate German strongpoints, and continue a headlong thrust into the depth of the German defenses. However, to issue an order didn't automatically mean a corresponding shift in the thinking of the formation commanders.

On 26 January the *Stavka* committed all of the forces that had been planned for the operation into the battle – Briansk Front's 13th Army went on the offensive. Eight of its rifle divisions were deployed into two echelons on a sector of front that extended 47 kilometers. Army commander N.P. Pukhov decided to penetrate the defense with the forces of four divisions – the 8th, 307th, 148th and 132nd Rifle Divisions of the first echelon in a "corridor" between the Kshen' and Olym Rivers, which had a width of 18 kilometers. In total, of the 13th Army's 72 rifle battalions, 69 had

13 Direktiva shtaba Voronezhskogo fronta No. 0326 from 3 fevralia 1943 [Directive No. 0326 of the Voronezh Front headquarters from 3 February 1943] (TsAMO RF, F. 417, op. 6924ss, d. 14, l. 6.]

14 V.P. Morozov, *Zapadnee Voronezha* (Moscow: Voenizdat, 1956), p. 100.

15 Shafarenko, *Na raznykh frontakh*, p. 127.

been concentrated here, and 95% of the artillery.[16] Only the first three aforementioned rifle divisions were to advance in the direction of Kastornoe; the fourth, the 132nd Rifle Division, was to cover the shock grouping's right flank and expand the breakthrough to the west, thereby gradually forming an outer ring of encirclement. According to the calculations by the 13th Army headquarters, by the end of the day its forces should have advanced by 30-35 kilometers and reached the Dolgaia Station – Marmyzhi line. This was plainly a task beyond the reach of the attacking divisions; with great difficulty, they would be able to breakthrough to this area only on the fourth day of the offensive.

The artillery preparation began at 0815, and approximately an hour later all four divisions of the 13th Army's first echelon moved out on the advance. At the spearhead of the attack, frontal, flanking and dummy smokescreens had been placed that extended for a total of 6 kilometers. In various sectors, this smokescreen was maintained for anywhere between 15 minutes and 2 hours and 15 minutes. This was the first time that Pukhov's troops used smoke so extensively, but this approach demonstrated its effectiveness.[17]

The main efforts were concentrated in the center of the shock wedge, although in the first hours it was also extremely important to take the well-fortified villages on the flanks of the attacking grouping – Lomigory and Borki. Control over these villages was an important factor for the successful development of the breakthrough. However, just as on the preceding two days, the artillery preparation was unable to suppress the enemy's system of fire. In addition, Major General A.A. Mishchenko, the commander of the right-flanking 148th Rifle Division, which was operating in the direction of Lomigory and Mishino, ignored the directive from the Briansk Front command and continued throughout the morning to launch frontal attacks. In the course of these attacks, his division suffered heavy, unjustified losses and made no headway. Only after a second categorical order, now given personally by the 13th Army commander did the division commander report that he had begun to prepare to bypass Mishino on the east, although the frontal attacks didn't cease. This and a number of other mistakes by its commander cost the 148th Rifle Division dearly (it had been bled white already by the end of January), but it also noticeably complicated the start of the 13th Army's offensive already in the first hours, and indeed, in the future it would continue to unfold not very successfully.

Another circumstance was aggravating the situation: the left-flank 8th Rifle Division with the attached 43rd Tank Regiment was also unable to drive the Germans out of Borki from the march. Heavy fighting also erupted here. Success was noted only in the center, in the sector of Colonel G.S. Laz'ko's 307th Rifle Division. Lieutenant Colonel L.K. Bregvadze's 118th Tank Brigade (48 tanks), which was attached to the division served as the "locomotive" here. Having breached the German defenses between Lomigory and Borki, its tank companies surged ahead. The division commander immediately introduced his reserves – a ski battalion and motorized infantry – into the breakthrough with the task to reach the powerful enemy strongpoint of Volovo Station as quickly as possible. However, the stubborn resistance by the 82nd and 383rd Infantry Divisions in the villages on the flanks, the attackers' weak artillery support, as well as the poorly implemented cooperation between the rifle formations and the artillery units and tank companies, which already in the first hours affected the combat effectiveness of the 118th Tank Brigade, hampered progress. As the 13th Army's Special Department reported, "When penetrating the line of defense the [tank] brigade immediately lost 5 KV tanks and other machines knocked out. This is explained by the fact that passages for the tanks, at the fault of the chief of engineer services, had

16 *Sbornik materialov po izucheniiu opyta voiny* [*Collection of materials for studying the war's* experience] No. 10 (January-February 1944) (Moscow: Voenizdat, 1944), p. 64.
17 Ibid., p. 68.

been poorly cleared of mines, and a sapper company hadn't been attached to the brigade, so there was no one to clear the enemy minefields."[18]

The officer of the General Staff with the Briansk Front headquarters reported to Moscow on 28 January 1943:

> I'm reporting on the course of the 13th Army's operation.
>
> 1. The situation with ammunition supplies in the acting divisions continues to be difficult; by the end of 27 January there was ¼ of a combat load.
> 2. The artillery is lagging behind the combat formations as a consequence of the lack of prime movers ...
> 3. During the artillery preparation on 26 January, the supporting 28th Guards Mortar Regiment with its second salvo blanketed the 3rd Battalion of the 132nd Rifle Division's 712th Rifle Regiment; with the exception of single individual men, two platoons of the 7th Company and their command staff were wiped out. The third salvo fell on the 712th Rifle Regiment's reconnaissance platoon (of which only 4 men remain) and part of the 712th Rifle Regiment's 1st Battalion. Also the reinforcing artillery – the 5th Artillery Division dropped several shells on the 712th Rifle Regiment's observation post; the regiment's chief of staff Major Bulgakov and 3 Red Army soldiers were killed.
> 4. The infantry is fighting with great élan. On the battlefield there are the bodies of both our soldiers and the Germans. The overwhelming majority of them have machine-gun wounds.
> 5. During my examination of the enemy fortifications, I discovered: they hadn't suffered from the artillery fire; there were rounds both short and long of the target area.
> 6. Losses are insignificant, with the exception of the 148th Rifle Division, which took the settlement of Lomigory with a head-on attack.[19]

Problems also arose with arranging cooperation between the ground forces and aviation. The 132nd Rifle Division, going on the offensive 25 minutes ahead of the established schedule, seized the first enemy positions from the march. However, its forward companies didn't lay out recognition panels right away. As a result, a group of *Shturmoviki* [Il-2 ground attack aircraft] struck them.[20]

N.P. Pukhov reinforced the attack toward Borki, hurling two rifle regiments of the left-flank 8th Rifle Division and the ski battalion from Major General A.N. Slyshkin's 15th Rifle Division into the battle at 1300. Their commitment into the battle was supported by the 49th Armored Train Battalion, three engineer battalions, a light artillery regiment and the 65th Guards Mortar Regiment.[21] In addition, during the attack against this heavily-fortified strongpoint, a smoke screen was successfully emplaced, which totally blinded the defenders. All these steps played an important role. On the night of 26-27 January, the garrison in the village was crushed. By the end of the first day of the offensive, the 13th Army's divisions had reached the following line: the 148th Rifle Division was fighting for Lomigory; the 307th Rifle Division had driven the enemy out of Alekseevka and was continuing to advance toward Volovo; the 8th Rifle Division had

18 V.S. Khristoforov [ed.], *Velikaia Otechestvennaia voina 1943*, p. 391.
19 *Russkii arkhiv: Velikaia Otechestvennaia: Preliudiia Kurskoi bitve* [*Russian archive: Great Patriotic War: Prelude to the Battle of Kursk*] Vol. 15 (4-3) (Moscow: TERRA, 1997), pp. 148-149.
20 *Sbornik materialov po izucheniiu opyta voiny* [*Collection of materials for studying the war's experience*] No. 10 (January-February 1944), p. 68.
21 M.K. Sekirin, I.M. Belkin, and V.M. Doroshenko, *Cherez vsiu voinu: Ocherk o voinakh 13-I armii* [*Through the entire war: A study on the warriors of the 13th Army* (Moscow: Nauka, 1991), p. 75.

The Commander-in-Chief of Briansk Front Lieutenant M.A. Reiter (second from the left) ponders the operational situation in the Kastornoe area on a map. On the left is the Front's chief of staff Major General L.M. Sandalov. Second from the right is Military Council member Major General I.Z. Susaikov and on the right is the chief of the Political Department Major General A.P. Pigurnov; end of January 1943 (Archive of E.V. Iurinaia).

Commander-in-Chief of Voronezh Front Lieutenant General F.I. Golikov, January 1943 (TsAMO RF)

A squad of submachine gunners of one of the rifle divisions of the 40th Army attacking a village in Kursk Oblast, January 1943 (RGAGKFD)

Red Army infantry with the support of T-34 tanks attacking the enemy east of Kursk, February 1943 (RGAKFD)

Troops of the 40th Army examine German dead and knocked-out trucks on a street of the liberated Kastornoe, February 1943. (RGAKFD)

Another shot of destroyed German vehicles and wagons in Kastornoe, February 1943 (RGAKFD)

The German military cemetery in the center of Staryi Oskol, which was liberated in the course of the Voronezh – Kastornoe operation. The frozen body of a dead German soldier awaits its own burial, likely in an unmarked fraternal grave.

A column of a German artillery unit on the retreat; the Kursk axis, February 1943 (RGAKFD)

A forward group of the German combat units that are breaking out of encirclement in Kastornoe enters a village; February 1943. A captured German photograph (RGAKFD)

Soldiers of the 60th Army's 248th Rifle Brigade Senior Sergeant P.N. Pantalov (on the left) and Private N.F. Nikutin converse with residents of a liberated village west of Kursk; February 1943 (Photography by S. Fridliand, RGAKFD).

The commander of the 38th Army Colonel General N.E. Chibisov; a 1945 photograph. (TsAMO RF)

A marching column of troops moves along a road behind the attacking forward units of the Voronezh Front. In the foreground is the crew of an anti-tank rifle mounted on an improvised sled; February 1943 (RGAKFD)

The crew of a Pe-2 light bomber, navigator Lieutenant I.D. Shlakman, senior radio operator I.M. Nikolaenko and pilot A.N. Skopin discuss their upcoming mission by their aircraft; Voronezh Front, February 1943 (RGAKFD)

seized Gremuchil and was fighting for Aleksandrovka; the 132nd Rifle Division was assaulting Zakharkino; and the 15th Rifle Division with one regiment was continuing to defend the Afrosimovka – Soldatskoe line, while two of its regiments were assembled in Sapron.[22] Thus, while the 13th Army shock grouping's advance between Lomigory and the Olym River didn't exceed 6-8 kilometers, the size of the breach torn into the enemy lines grew to 22 kilometers, which provided the opportunity to introduce significant forces into the battle.

The 38th Army's combat against the German units that were covering the withdrawal of their divisions from the Don River's right bank was just as intense. By the evening its troops had battled their way forward to about the same distance as the 13th Army, having reached the Nikol'skoe – Golosnovka – Gremiachee line. Thus, Pukhov's and Chibisov's armies that were attacking toward Kastornoe and Nizhniaia Veduga from the north, although they'd been able to break through the Second Army's defense to a depth of 8 kilometers, were unable to exploit this tactical success.

The offensive on the axis of Voronezh Front's main attack was also not going so well. The troops of 40th Army's right flank were still unsuccessfully assaulting the enemy strongpoint in Sinie Lipiagi. Simultaneously, units of Major General A.S. Kostitsyn's 183rd Rifle Division were forced to repulse fierce counterattacks launched by *Gruppe* Siebert. Kravchenko's 4th Tank Corps was still idle in Gorshechnoe, waiting for fuel, while the 25th Guards Rifle Division and the 96th Separate Tank Brigade, which had started to expand the "corridor" toward Gorshechnoe created by the 4th

22 *Sbornik materialov po izucheniiu opyt voiny*, No. 10 (January-February 1944), pp. 57-58.

Tank Corps' advance, upon the approach to Nizhne-Gniloe were counterattacked by two enemy infantry regiments that had been shifted from the right bank of the Don River to the Viaziovatki area. Under their pressure, Shafarenko's Guardsmen and Lebedev's tankers were even forced to fall back somewhat. In the evening, they nevertheless managed to defeat the enemy battalion of the 68th Infantry Regiment that was defending this village, but darkness prevented any further advance. So, by the end of the day the 40th Army with great difficulty had only managed to reach the Zelenaia Poliana – Staroe-Melovoe – Zales'e line.

A similar situation had also developed in the sector of the neighboring 60th Army. Its divisions had become bogged down in positional fighting for the villages of Ivanovka, Prokudinskoe, Parnishnoe, Kochetovka and Semidesiatkoe. Because of the lack of cleared roads, the infantry was forced to attack the enemy fortifications head-on. As a result, over this day only Colonel A.P. Krutikhin's 253rd Rifle Brigade, which had conducted an outflanking maneuver, managed by evening to take the major strongpoint of Semidesiatkoe.

The ski battalions that the *front* possessed might have played an important role to develop a success. Offering stubborn resistance to the forces of Moskalenko's right wing and Cherniakhovsky's left wing with the forces of *Gruppe* Siebert, the German Second Army command had no significant forces opposite 40th Army's left flank, even though here the city and railroad of Staryi Oskol were located. Bypassing the enemy strongpoints in the northwest direction, these ski battalions might have increased the pace of the offensive. However, unfortunately a significant number of these ski battalions been thrown together hastily, and many of the soldiers and officers not only lacked the necessary skills to conduct fighting on skis, but also simply didn't even know yet how to ski. Therefore the Soviet command had to use them as regular infantry.

Thus, even on the third day of the operation, the Soviet command had not been able to achieve a turning point. The troops of Briansk Front, attacking from the north toward Kastornoe and Nizhniaia Veduga, had only fought their way forward for 8 kilometers, while Voronezh Front's shock grouping attacking from the south had only advanced 10 kilometers. Its 60th Army, which was also attacking toward Nizhniaia Veduga, but from the south, had made even less progress. It had eliminated only several enemy strongpoints and on individual directions had advanced by 5-8 kilometers. In addition to the objective problems that were hampering the offensive, substantial subjective problems had arisen in the attacking armies. The 60th Army commander had been appointed to his post a half year before, in July 1942, and this was his first major offensive operation, which moreover was being conducted under difficult winter conditions.

Recalled A.M. Vasilevsky about the events of the latter half of January 1943:

> I.D. Cherniakhovsky was a fully-trained military commander, with refined military prowess; commanding a division, he had given a favorable taste of his capabilities. However, an army is an army, and the demands on its commander are immeasurably higher than those on a division commander. Having driven to the army's command post, to my surprise I found him in an unusual condition … somehow sitting distractedly behind a table over a map … He rejoiced when he caught sight of me, quickly rose and came forward to meet me with the words:
>
> "Comrade General of the Army! It is you who are responsible for everything. I have nothing going well here. Return me to a division!"
>
> I.D. Cherniakhovsky didn't have the experience to lead the troops of such a major formation as an army, and at first he was a bit lost. I had to spend some time with him, to give him some practical assistance; he calmed down, gained confidence, and his actions showed resolve and firmness.[23]

23 Vasilevsky, *Delo vsei zhizni*, Vol. 1, p.307.

Skipping somewhat ahead of the events, I will note that it was precisely because of his discomfiture in the first days of the Voronezh – Kastornoe operation that Ivan Danilovich was deemed worthy of only the Order of the Red Banner on 4 February 1943, while his neighboring army commanders received higher commander honors.[24] Even so, already on 8 February 1943, his army with an impetuous attack would drive the enemy out of Kursk, and on that same day he would be decorated with the Order of Suvorov 1st Degree, and on 14 February become a lieutenant general.

On the evening of 26 January, the distance between Reiter's and Golikov's forward units was still rather impressive, approximately 60 kilometers, and the enemy still had the opportunity to withdraw a significant amount of forces out of the intended "pocket" to the west. However, it was already impossible to save the Second Army – the decision to withdraw it from the Voronezh salient was obviously made too late. At this moment the VII Army Corps was tied up in fighting in the Voronezh area, and the redeployment of it in wintry conditions under the pressure of attacking Soviet forces was an extremely complex matter, even though the command of Army Group B exerted every effort for this: both railroad and automotive transport was activated for this purpose. In addition, as Soviet reconnaissance reported, by the morning of 27 January, up to three infantry regiments, a ski battalion and several specialized elements had been shifted from the Voronezh area to the Kastornoe area in order to hold it.

In general, the *Stavka* of the Supreme High Command was accurately assessing the situation at the junction of the two *fronts*, believing the enemy's situation to be critical. At the same time, at this moment hastiness began to appear in its actions. Already by the end of 26 January, it considered the destruction of the enemy grouping in the Kastornoe area a settled matter. Recalled A.M. Vasilevsky:

> On the evening of 26 January, in the next telephone conversation with the Supreme Commander-in-Chief, in connection with the successful development of the operation the decision was taken regarding the course of the offensive after the capture of Kastornoe, according to which the left wing of Briansk Front with an attack towards Kolpny, Malo-Arkhangel'sk and further on to Fatezh was to prevent the enemy from digging in on the Tim River and thereby secure from the north the successful carrying out of tasks by the Voronezh Front. The right wing of the Voronezh Front after taking Kastornoe was to develop an offensive toward Kursk.[25]

Prognosticating the development of the operational situation and advance planning are a direct responsibility of military chiefs and a most important task in the course of an operation. However, striving to make fuller use of the initiative that was seized after Stalingrad, and to hurl the enemy back as far as possible by doggedly nipping at the heels of the retreating enemy, the Soviet side gradually began to lose a sense of reality. The first serious manifestation of this became precisely the Voronezh – Kastornoe operation. At a moment when its main task had not yet been resolved, at a time when the offensive was progressing with great difficulty, instead of reinforcing the axis of the main attack for the most rapid breakthrough of the defense to its entire depth and to create both a compact ring around the enemy's large grouping and the conditions to prevent it from being freed, Moscow was already busy with plans for a further offensive to the west. Moreover, this would be without any serious reserves and with those same combat formations that had already been engaged in hard combat for a month and which with their last ounce of strength were fighting for Gorshechnoe, Nizhiaia Veduga and Volovo. These overly ambitious plans, compounded by the

24 K.S. Moskalenko, N.P. Pukhov and N.E. Chibisov were awarded Orders of Suvorov 1st Degree.
25 Vasilevsky, *Delo vsei zhizni*, p. 307.

poor work of intelligence, at first prevented the complete liquidation of the "pocket" at Kastornoe, and then led to the destruction of our forces (including those of the Voronezh Front as well) in Ukraine in March 1943.

However, let's return to the course of the operation. Striving to increase the pressure of our forces against the enemy defenses, the *Stavka* of the Supreme High Command persistently demanded greater organization, flexibility in command of the troops, and decisiveness on the part of *front* commands. Therefore M.A. Reiter that same evening, on 26 January, issued an order to the 13th Army to continue the offensive throughout the night, in order to prevent the enemy from consolidating on the previously prepared Volovchik – Volovo – Lipovchik line. Meanwhile, F.I. Golikov exerted every effort to deliver fuel to the 4th Tank Corps. Indeed, all these efforts yielded a definite effect already on the following day.

The tank formations of both *fronts*, which their commands massed on the directions of the main attack, played the main role on 27 January. N.P. Pukhov before dawn introduced an operational mobile group under the command of his deputy Major General Glukhov[26] into the breakthrough in order to develop the success: Colonel N.V. Petrushin's 129th Separate Tank Brigade (48 tanks), an anti-tank artillery regiment, two aerosled battalions and two "Katiusha" rocket launching battalions. Passing through the combat formations of the 307th Rifle Division, it headed toward Volovo, which the same 82nd Infantry Division was defending. However, a blizzard that had started prevented it from closing upon the village until dawn. M.I. Glukhov divided his force into two parts and launched a simultaneous concentric attack against the village. At the peak of the fighting, units of the 307th Rifle Division began to arrive. In addition, the army commander assigned the 13th Army's 4th Ski Detachment under Major A.P. Zav'ialov to reinforce the group. As a result, by noon on 27 January, this final major German strongpoint on the path to Kastornoe was taken.

However, the situation in the sector of the 13th Army still remained complicated. The 148th Rifle Division was continuing to assault Lomigory without success, while the gap between its left-flank regiment and the other attacking formations of the first echelon increased to 15 kilometers. At this time, reconnaissance established that the Germans were bringing up fresh forces out of the Tim River area. A threat to the shock grouping's right flank was appearing. Therefore N.I. Pukhov decided to halt the movement of the army's second echelon (the 280th, 211th, 74th and 81st Rifle Divisions) to the south, and having pivoted it to the west, ordered it to fill in the line between Sovetskii and Marmiazhi, thereby creating an outer front of encirclement. Meanwhile, he gave the assignment to take Kastornoe to Glukhov's mobile group. In order to reinforce it further, he attached the 118th Tank Brigade to it, and in order to consolidate the success, he planned to use the 307th Rifle Division.

As General Staff officers who analyzed the combat operations in the sector of the 13th Army later observed in 1944:

> This task could only be resolved through an outflanking maneuver of Lomigory from the east. However, the commander of the 148th Rifle Division was still continuing to launch frontal attacks, and only after pressure from above did he decide to outflank Lomigory from the east with two battalions. The flank attack was crowned with success – by 2400 on 27 January, Lomigory fell. As a result of the needless stubbornness and inability to grasp the situation, the 148th Rifle Division lost more than 1,800 killed and wounded in the course of 26 and 27 January in frontal attacks.[27]

26 In documents, this formation would be called both an operational group and a mobile group.
27 *Sbornik materialov po izucheniiu opyta voiny*, No. 10 (January-February 1944), p. 58.

By the end of the day, the formations of 13th Army's first echelon were occupying a well-fortified line: Volovchik, Volovo, Lipovchik, which covered the direction toward Kastornoe, while the 129th and 118th Separate Tank Brigades took Bol'shoe and exploited the successful offensive toward Kulikovka, which was located 15 kilometers from Kastornoe. Thus, having covered approximately 25 kilometers over the course of two days and having overcome the German main and rear line of defenses, the troops of Briansk Front by the end of 27 January were already approaching the operation's main objective. Their dispositions were as follows: the 148th Rifle Division was occupying Lomigory; Glukhov's mobile group, having taken Volovo, was attacking toward Kastornoe; the 132nd Rifle Division had liberated Lipovchik and Novopavlovka, having a forward detachment in Vasil'evka (from this line it became part of Glukhov's mobile group); the 8th Rifle Division had driven the enemy out of Bol'shovka; the 15th Rifle Division with its main forces was occupying Borki; the 211th and 81st Rifle Divisions were on the march; and the 74th Rifle Division was mopping up the enemy on the eastern bank of the Kshen' River.[28]

Taking advantage of the success by the 13th Army, under the pressure of which the enemy had begun to withdraw to the southwest, Voronezh Front's 38th Army went in more active pursuit of the retreating enemy. As has already been noted, initially Chibisov's forces were supposed to split the encircled enemy grouping with an attack toward Nizhiaia Veduga, but this part of the plan couldn't be realized. Therefore F.I. Golikov ordered the 38th Army to redirect its main forces toward Kastornoe in order to increase the pressure on the enemy defending there. This gave a good impetus to the offensive's development, for on 27 January its forces made a 15-kilometer advance into the depth of the enemy defenses.

Owing to the decisive actions of Kravchenko's tankers, substantial success also attended the forces of Voronezh Front's main shock grouping. After the 4th Tank Corps received fuel, K.S. Moskalenko formed a composite detachment out of part of the corps' forces and infantry, which was headed by the commander of the 45th Tank Brigade Lieutenant Colonel P.K. Zhidkov. At dawn the detachment moved out of Gorshechnoe to the north and by the end of the day burst into Kastornaia Novaia Station, and also reached the southern approaches to Kastornoe. At this time the bulk of the tank corps was approaching the village of Bychek. Having reached this area, Kravchenko's tank corps was blocking the enemy's path of retreat to the southwest. Even though the infantry of the 40th Army on its right flank was still trying to take Sinie Lipiagi, and on its left flank, had just become tied up in fighting for Staryi Oskol, by the end of the day the operational situation had fundamentally changed: the encirclement of the German and Hungarian forces in the Voronezh salient had entered its final stage.

Together with the stubborn resistance, a number of problems that arose with command and control at the divisional level were negatively affecting the operation's progress. For example, a certain indecisiveness and inertia of thinking was observed on the Voronezh Front among division commanders of the 60th Army. The majority of them was unable to devise effective tactics in order to breach the enemy's defense under difficult conditions, and instead continued to launch frontal assaults with infantry against enemy knots of resistance. As a result, the command of the German Second Army with very insignificant forces (a portion of *Gruppe* Siebert), having pinned down the 60th Army's main grouping, continued stubbornly to hold the defenses in the sector of the neighboring 40th Army and to withdraw troops from out of the closing pocket.

On the Briansk Front, other problems, but also connected with command and control in the divisions, were hindering successful combat work. Order No. 05/op from the commander of the 13th Army on 28 January 1943 criticized a number of aspects:

28 Ibid., p. 59.

> The course of offensive operations shows that command over the troops in a number of formations remains on an impermissibly low level. To the number of shortcomings, which are sharply and negatively influencing the successful development of combat actions, I will assign:
>
> 1. The disregard of radio communications by several divisional chiefs of staff; this particularly relates to the chiefs of staff of the 132nd and 8th Rifle Divisions. The headquarters of the 129th Tank Brigade doesn't respond to radio calls from the army headquarters at all.
>
> ...
>
> 3. The headquarters of the divisions are not setting up communications at new command posts ahead of time. When relocating, they are losing contact with the army headquarters and are taking no steps to restore it on their part; this especially relates to the chiefs of staff of the 211th, 132nd and 81st Rifle Divisions. Such chiefs of staff don't understand the most elementary requirements for command and control over the troops.
> 4. Division commanders, heading to the front and located with one of their regiments, lost control over the remaining regiments, and are not ensuring control and communications with their own headquarters; as a result the headquarters, not knowing the commander's decisions, are incapable of controlling and organizing the implementation of the division commander's decision, so the troops remain uncontrolled. All of this disrupts methodical combat work, slows the pace of advance, and leads to needless losses and a wasteful loss of time.[29]

At this time too, problems with command and control in Glukhov's constantly growing mobile group of the 13th Army, which hadn't been considered during its hasty formation, began to render significantly negative influence. M.I Glukhov didn't receive a headquarters, or even a more or less efficient operational group for controlling the troops, even though already by the middle of the operation he was in essence commanding a corps. The necessary communication means were lacking; he'd been assigned only one car and one adjutant, who carried out the functions of a signals officer. A hierarchy of command within the group hadn't been established, as a result of which it had a lax and loose structure.[30] Thus the possibilities of the mobile group commander in the hard wintry conditions (blizzards, subzero temperatures) were limited. He was unable to resolve promptly any problems that arose, and accordingly, could not influence the situation in the sector of the offensive as the circumstances required.

A decisive turning point arrived only on the fifth day of the operation. Although with varying rates of advance, the troops of the 13th and 40th Armies' main shock groupings continued persistently to drive toward Kastornoe. At the same time, other units not part of the shock groupings were already operating to the west with the aim of creating the outer ring of encirclement. On the morning of 28 January, Glukhov's mobile group became tied up in fighting for Kastornoe. The 129th Separate Tank Brigade and the skiers of Zav'ialov's detachment were moving toward it from the south and west, while the 118th Tank Brigade entered its northwestern outskirts. The defenders were putting up fierce resistance. Soon, 40th Army's composite detachment came up from the south. At 1430 after heavy fighting, the tanks and motorized infantry of Bregvadze's 118th Tank Brigade were the first to break into the built-up area. Its 1st Tank Battalion under the command of Captain I.I. Volkov, having come upon a train that was departing the train station, knocked out the steam engine and prevented the evacuation of the enemy troops and equipment from the station. The encircled foe was clinging to every building, and the attackers didn't have

29 TsAMO RF, F. 417, op. 6924ss, d. 14, l. 6.

30 *Sbornik materialov po izucheniiu opyta voiny* (January-February 1944), p. 66.

enough strength, particularly infantry, while the 307th Rifle Division was still too far away to help. At this time with its main forces it had become engaged in fighting southwest of Kulikovka with a detachment of the 82nd Infantry Division numbering around 1,500 men, which was trying to break out of encirclement. Meanwhile, some of its elements, which had arrived that morning in the area of the 118th Tank Brigade's jumping-off area, were performing sluggishly and not giving the necessary assistance to Lieutenant Colonel Bregvadze's assault group. Reported the deputy chief of the 13th Army's Special Department Security Captain M.P. Aleksandrov: "During the attack on 28 January 1943, tankers with tank riders broke into the city; however, units of the 307th Rifle Division didn't enter the city behind them, but remained on the outskirts until 30 January 1943, until it had been mopped up of the enemy, and because of this the brigade lost several tanks, which were set ablaze by Molotov cocktails tossed from buildings."[31]

For the same reason, the lack of infantry, the 129th Separate Tank Brigade suffered even more significant losses in the fighting for possession of Kastornoe. According to a special message from the NKVD Special Department of the 13th Army, 17 combat machines in its battalions were knocked out, including 3 that were burned out, while the rest required light overhauls or factory repair.[32]

In order to assist the tankers, N.P. Pukhov sent the 8th Rifle Division, which on the afternoon of 28 January 1943 launched an attack along the railroad and reached the northern outskirts of the city. However, even though by the end of the day elements of three armies (the 13th, 38th and 40th Armies) had fully surrounded Kastornoe and were even occupying the city's center, they were unable to mop up the enemy from the blocks of buildings completely, because of weak cooperation between the units of separate formations and the lack of tight command and control within them. In isolated cases, because of the poorly-arranged communications by the headquarters, the situation reached the level of the absurd and combat clashes between their own elements. Reported the NKVD Special Department of the 13th Army:

> On 27 January the 8th Rifle Division's headquarters for 10-12 hours had no contact with the 229th and 310th Rifle Regiments and didn't know the direction in which they were operating. On 28 January at 2000, a mobile detachment took Kastornoe, but the division's regiments didn't know this. The 8th Rifle Division's 151st Rifle Regiment at 0500 on 29 January 1943 assembled its battalions at a distance of 1 kilometer from Kastornoe Station and waited for the signal to attack. Before the signal came from headquarters, the command of the 151st Rifle Regiment made the independent decision to launch the attack. At 0541, a report arrived at the headquarters of the 151st Rifle Regiment that its battalions had taken Kastornoe without meeting enemy resistance, not knowing that Kastornoe had been taken at 2000 on 28 January.
>
> On 27 January 1943, the headquarters of the 8th Rifle Division's 229th Rifle Regiment throughout the day had no contact with two battalions and didn't know where they were. Its training battalion during the attack against Kastornoe, remaining on its outskirts, at 1700 encountered a reconnaissance patrol sent out by the 310th Rifle Regiment. The patrol, taking the training battalion as the enemy, opened fire, as a result of which there were casualties. Despite the fact that the 8th Rifle Division had arranged for mounted and dismounted couriers, a report arrived from the regiments to the division headquarters after 72 hours, because the regiments didn't know where the division's command post was located, and vice versa. The same situation held in the 148th Rifle Division as well, when the division headquarters on 29

31 V.S. Khristoforov, *Velikaia Otechestvennaia voina, 1943*, p. 391.
32 Ibid.

> January had no actual communications with the regiments and effectively did not direct the fighting, while contact with the 507th Rifle Regiment wasn't established until 30 January.[33]

The situation in the 148th Rifle Division became the final straw for the Briansk Front command, which had exhausted its patience. On 30 January the division's commander A.A. Mishchenko was relieved of his post and the commander of the 654th Rifle Regiment Colonel N.P. Konoplev took his place, but not for long. Already by mid-February, Konoplev was transferred to the post of deputy commander, while A.A. Mishchenko resumed command of the 148th Rifle Division.[34]

However, let's return to the events at Kastornoe. On 27 January, with the onset of twilight, the 307th Rifle division managed to defeat the enemy detachment. More than 500 soldiers and officers surrendered; the rest of the detachment was killed or scattered piecemeal. Among the German dead was the commander of the 82nd Infantry Division *Generalleutnant* A. Bäntsch. The Germans plainly didn't expect such an impetuous dash by the Soviet troops in the conditions of hard freezes and snow. The captured chief of intelligence of the 82nd Infantry Division *Oberleutnant* Müller openly recognized:

> We never anticipated that the offensive would be so thoroughly prepared and would have such success. In the headquarters we were struck by its force and couldn't even collect our wits before the Russians broke through our line of defense and swiftly kept advancing. The division commander fled in a vehicle and I never saw him again. … On the third day of combat, there were less than 1,000 soldiers left in the division.[35]

However, the breakthrough to Kastornoe by Glukhov's mobile group and the composite detachment of Moskalenko's 40th Army, as well as the 40th Army's rifle divisions' arrival at the Gorshechnoe – Bykovo – Efrosinovka line were unable to close entirely the path of retreat left open to the troops of the two enemy armies. Between Kastornoe and Bykovo, which means between the tank formations of both Briansk and Voronezh Fronts, which were located in the Kastornoe – Lachinovo area, and the rifle units of the 40th Army, which were operating on the Prostornoe – Bykovo line, there was still a 25-kilometer-wide gap that wasn't fully controlled by Soviet forces. A similar gap formed between Gorshechnoe and Staryi Oskol after the 4th Tank Corps reached Gorshechnoe. K.S. Moskalenko was unable to close it in time, because he lacked adequate strength to do so. According to intelligence information, the main forces of the encircled Germans and Hungarians were located in just this area, southeast of Kastornoe, in the Verkhnee Turovo – Nizhnedevisk – Viaznovatka triangle, and were able to use both "corridors" in order to

33 Ibid., p. 395.

34 A special message from the NKVD Special Department of the 13th Army on 4 February 1943 reveals: "On the day of assuming command of the division, Konopalev summoned all the regiment commanders in order to give them their combat assignment. However, being drunk, he made a hash of the assignment between the regiments, and in essence the chief of staff had to give it. On 31 January 1943, Konoplev was sick and his political deputy Colonel Garanin assumed command of the division, but not having adequate knowledge in this field, he couldn't lead it. On the next day Konoplev again got drunk, and the division's deputy commander Romazan assumed the leadership post. Thus, in reality the division didn't have a leader, and Konoplev, being all the while in a non-sober condition, was unable to make a single healthy decision. The Army's Military Council has been informed about this in order to take corresponding measures." [V.S. Khristoforov, *Velikaia Otechestvennaia voina 1943*, p. 392.]

35 *V srazheniiakh za pobedu. Boevoi put' 38-i armii v gody Velikoi Otechestvennoi voiny, 1941-1945* [*In the battles for victory. The combat path of the 38th Army in the years of the Great Patriotic War, 1941-1945*] (Moscow: Voenizdat, 1988), p. 309.

break out. Meanwhile, the 38th and 60th Armies, which had been assigned to dismember this enemy grouping, demonstrated poor performance.

Neither the *Stavka* nor the Voronezh Front command fully took into account these factors, nor did they anticipate the enemy's strength and tenacity. Striving to exploit the favorable operational situation, even before completing the main phase of the Voronezh – Kastornoe operation, Moscow demanded the Briansk and Voronezh Front commands to develop an offensive toward Kursk and Khar'kov. Back on 21 January 1943, in the midst of the destruction of the enemy's Ostrogozhsk – Rossosh grouping, A.M. Vasilevsky and F.I. Golikov had ideas about a plan for the Voronezh Front's further actions once the Voronezh – Kastornoe operation concluded. According to the document, by 30 January they planned to deploy the Front's main forces along the line of the Oskol River (from Staryi Oskol to Urazovo), and launch three converging attacks with them in the direction of Khar'kov. This idea was confirmed by I.V. Stalin on the evening of 26 January. Stemming from Stalin's directions, on 28 January, which is to say at the most dramatic moment of the Voronezh – Kastornoe operation, Voronezh Front Commander-in-Chief F.I. Golikov, while issuing orders to destroy the still semi-encircled enemy grouping southeast of Kastornoe, simultaneously directed the formations of the Front's right wing to move up to the line of the Tim and Oskol Rivers on 1-2 February 1943 for an offensive in the Khar'kov and Kursk directions. The 38th Army was to launch an attack toward Oboian', the 60th Army – toward Kursk, and the 40th Army – toward Belgorod and further on toward Khar'kov.[36] Thus, the completion of the still unfolding Voronezh – Kastornoe operation was set on the side burner.

F.I. Golikov underestimated the encircled enemy grouping's potential; in his plan for subsequent actions, there wasn't even a hint of the possibility of it breaking out of the pocket. Consequently, no steps to oppose it were envisioned.[37] The destruction of the supposedly fully demoralized 35,000-man grouping was assigned to Chibisov's single 38th Army alone, for which it was given only two to three days, even though it numbered only 27,500 men.[38] This was a plain miscalculation regarding both the strength of the enemy still located in the pocket and one's own capabilities, which in fact led to a breakout from encirclement by part of the enemy force. Analyzing this problem after the war, officers of the General Staff wrote:

> It should be noted that the adversary managed to withdraw some of the Voronezh grouping primarily because the 13th Army of Briansk Front and the 40th Army of Voronezh Front, which had attacked toward Lachinovo Station from various directions, didn't complete the encirclement. The subsequent course of combat operations demonstrated that it was necessary to use 13th Army's main forces in order to create a compact ring of encirclement and to establish a shoulder-to-shoulder connection with units of Voronezh Front. For the operational support of the encirclement in these conditions, only a portion of the 13th Army's forces should have been moved out to the line of the Tim River. In addition, for this same purpose it was possible to use *front* reserves and a portion of the 48th Army's strength.[39]

The difficult situation that faced the 40th Army's attacking forces is shown by the following fact: The command of the 25th Guards Rifle Division, which on its right flank was virtually alone

36 TsAMO RF, F. 203, op. 2843, d. 360, l. 4.

37 *Velikaia Otechestvennaia voina 1941-1945: Voenno-istoricheskie ocherki. Kniga 2, Perelom* [*Great Patriotic War 1941-1945: Military-historical studies. Book 2: Turning point*], p. 168.

38 TsAMO RF, F. 203, op. 2777, d. 66, l. 25; F. 393, op. 2005, d. 107, l. 32.

39 *Sbornik materialov po izucheniiu opyta voiny,* No. 10 (January-February 1944), p. 65.

holding the inner ring of encirclement, because of heavy casualties and the lack of replacements at this time was forced to form two rifle battalions in each regiment instead of the standard three.[40]

The command of Army Group B, although it understood that its forces were very much exhausted and had suffered substantial losses, and were experiencing difficulties with supplies, transport and fuel, had no intention to surrender. It is impossible not to agree with Colonel V.P. Morozov, who observed: "Instead of securely closing the gaps and dismembering the enemy grouping, the main forces, in essence, were directed to eject the German-fascist troops. All of this, in the final result, led to the fact the struggle with the Voronezh – Kastornoe grouping became protracted and tied up considerably more forces than the Front command had contemplated."[41]

The hard, wintry conditions substantially complicated the destruction of the encircled enemy. Snow, which lasted for several days, was clogging routes and making advances difficult. The artillery and rear services were lagging behind by dozens of kilometers, and there wasn't enough ammunition, fuel and food. The armored vehicles became stuck in 1.5-meter snowdrifts, while the 2nd Air Army was practically grounded.

The Wehrmacht command was actively searching for a way out of the crisis. On 3 February 1943, there was a change in command of the Second Army; *Generalleutnant* H. von Salmuth was relieved of his post, and *General der Infanterie* W. Weiss arrived to replace him. The change in command was prompted by Berlin's dissatisfaction with the actions of the former commander and lack of confidence that he could turn the situation around. Simultaneously, active work was underway in the headquarters of the Second Army itself to find a solution to bring the encircled forces out of the incomplete pocket, and the main step in this, in its opinion, must be the recapture of the major road hub of Gorshechnoe Station.

Between 29 January and 1 February, the divisions of Voronezh Front's right wing were continuing to battle to destroy the Voronezh – Kastornoe grouping and simultaneously preparing for a new operation. According to K.S. Moskalenko's directive, the division commander of the 25th Guards Rifle Division entrusted the task of defending Gorshechnoe to Colonel A.S. Belov's 73rd Guards Rifle Regiment, having reinforced it with the training battalion and a machine-gun battalion, plus the 29th Separate Destroyer Anti-tank Artillery Battalion. However, these forces were incapable of holding back the enemy. On 31 January, a sizeable German detachment, which had kept its heavy weapons and armor, after a hard, bitter fight regained possession of Gorshechnoe Station. As P.M. Shafarenko recalled, "Disregarding the losses, the Hitlerites advanced in a solid wall behind the tanks, firing on the move from submachine guns. Plainly, the ghost of Stalingrad was driving them forward: their only aim was to break out of the pocket at whatever the cost."[42] Even after the Guards division commander issued an order to counterattack the enemy with the remaining two regiments, the situation couldn't be restored. Only on the night of 4-5 February, with the forces of now two divisions – the 25th Guards Rifle Division and the 206th Rifle Division, was the enemy driven back out of Gorshechnoe Station, but it was too late. Despite the enemy's obvious numerical superiority and the tenacity of the Guardsmen, 40th Army's Military Council placed the responsibility for giving up the station on Lieutenant Colonel A.S. Belov and dismissed him from his post.[43]

> After the capture of Gorshechnoe Station, the Second Army command quickly formed three groups for the subsequent breakout to the west:

40 P.M. Shafarenko, *Na raznykh frontov: Zapiski komandira divizii*, p. 128.
41 V.P. Morozov, *Zapadnee Voronezha*, p. 108.
42 P.M. Shafarenko, *Na raznykh frontov: Zapiski komandira divizii*, p. 129.
43 Subsequently this decision was overturned and A.S. Belov was re-appointed with a promotion to the post of deputy division commander.

- *Gruppe* Beckemann, which had up to 10,000 men (the remnants of the 75th, 340th and 377th Infantry Divisions, as well as those of two Hungarian divisions, the 6th and 9th).
- *Gruppe* Siebert, which had approximately 8,000 men (units of the 57th, 68th and 323rd Infantry Divisions
- *Gruppe* Gollwitzer, which consisted of the remnants of two infantry divisions, the 26th and 88th Infantry Divisions.

The corridor opened by the recapture of Gorshechnoe Station was one of the most important. *Gruppe* Siebert and *Gruppe* Gollwitzer emerged from the pocket through it, and between 12 and 15 February fully came out of encirclement together with disorganized groups that had joined up with them. However, *Gruppe* Beckemann was cut off and destroyed by Soviet forces.

Thus, there was no success in completing the reduction of the pocket as had been planned on 1 February. The Nazis defended fiercely, tying up the forces of Chibisov's entire army and a significant portion of Moskalenko's army. On 3 February, only the 60th Army and elements of the 40th Army went on the offensive toward Kursk and Khar'kov, and thus these armies were simultaneously participating in two operations: wrapping up the Voronezh – Kastornoe operation and launching (together with the 69th Army and 3rd Tank Army) the Khar'kov operation.

The absence of a unified center of command over the forces that were concluding the encirclement and destruction of the enemy grouping had a negative influence on the course of the events. The lack of coordination in the actions of the two *fronts* at Kastornoe also complicated the Khar'kov offensive operation. Moskalenko's troops, tied up with fighting around Gorshechnoe, were unable to launch an attack in the direction of Belgorod on 2 February simultaneously with the formations of Voronezh Front's left wing, and went on the offensive only on 3 February and at that not even fully. A large portion of the army was actively participating in mopping up the pocket until 7 February.

However, even after all the 38th Army's forces were re-united under the command of Lieutenant General N.E. Chibisov in the Kastornoe area, he now made some substantial mistakes. The 38th Army commander didn't show the proper initiative and administrative ability. Strong blocking forces weren't positioned on the enemy's paths of retreat to the west, his troops acted passively, and not once was the withdrawing enemy attacked by the army's main forces. As a result, of the approximately 125,000 Germans and Hungarians that fell into "encirclement", a significant number, from 25,000 to 30,000 men managed to break out of it. Although later some Soviet researchers would assert that up to 7,000 men made their way to Oboian' without their heavy weapons and equipment, these numbers have been plainly understated.[44] In addition, when it already became clear that a large group of enemy forces had slipped out of the pocket, two of our rifle divisions that were located in the area of the Tim River and which hadn't been tied up in the fighting were not directed to block the enemy's path of retreat to Oboian'.

In the Soviet historical literature one comes across the assertion that the operation at Kastornoe and Gorshechnoe concluded on 2 February 1943 (with the start of Voronezh Front's offensive toward Kursk and Khar'kov), but in fact the Voronezh Front's combat operations to eliminate the pocket concluded only on 17 February after its troops reached the Oboian' area. Marshal of the Soviet Union A.M. Vasilevsky also confirms this: "… Because of the unbelievably hard winter conditions, the conclusion of the Voronezh – Kastornoe operation became somewhat protracted. Soviet troops, pursuing and destroying the remnants of the hostile Group Siebert over 15 days of offensive made an advance of 130 kilometers with fighting."[45]

44 V.P. Morozov, *Zapadnee Voronezha*, p. 110.
45 A.M. Vasilevsky, *Delo vsei zhizni*, p. 309.

Thus, ultimately the operation created not only the requisite conditions for liberating the territory west of the Malo-Arkhangel'sk – Kursk – Shebekino line, but also already in the course of its dénouement, the so-called Kursk salient began to form, which became in July 1943 the epicenter of the epochal battle at the Bulge of Fire. The encirclement (though not a total one) of the main forces of Army Group B at Kastornoe and the swift lunge made by Soviet troops toward Kursk and Belgorod that followed forced Hitler to agree with the proposal made by the commander-in-chief of Army Group Center about the withdrawal of General Model's Ninth Army from the Rzhev salient, which he expressed during a personal meeting back on 26 January 1943. By 5 February 1943, the 13th Army reached the Shalimovo – Gnilaia Plota – Gorodishche – Telegino – Svoboda – Shchigry line, having cut the Orel – Kursk railroad and thereby having created a threat to the left flank of the Wehrmacht's Orel grouping. In order to cover it, the German command initiated the rapid withdrawal of Model's army to here. Already in April 1943, it would be assembled north of Kursk and on its basis Berlin began to form one of the two shock groupings in order to conduct the famous *Zitadelle* plan to encircle two Soviet *fronts* in the Kursk bulge. Incidentally, at dawn on 6 February 1943, a forward detachment of the 183rd Rifle Division under the command of Captain A.I. Tkachev with a decisive attack liberated the Prokhorovka railroad station, which would enter history as the epicenter of one of the largest clashes in the summer of 1943.

The Voronezh – Kastornoe operation entered the history of the Great Patriotic War as one of the Red Army's successes. Initially conceived as a more limited operation, it grew into a strategic operation. In the course of it, the Red Army made an advance to the west of 240 kilometers, having swept the Voronezh Oblast and a significant portion of Kursk Oblast clean of the occupiers. Several dozens of populated places were liberated, including three cities: Voronezh, Kastornoe and Staryi Oskol. Eight German and two Hungarian divisions were smashed. In total according to Soviet data, the Germans and Hungarians lost more than 83,000 soldiers and officers,[46] including three division commanders: *Generalleutnant* A. Bäntsch of the 82nd Infantry Division (mortally wounded), *Oberst* A. Neubauer of the 323rd Infantry Division, and *Generalmajor* A. Lechner of the 377th Infantry Division (both killed). Later, the former Wehrmacht general P. von Butler would write: "The Second Army was badly battered. Moreover during the breakout it had lost the bulk of its equipment."[47] However, the German allies suffered particularly heavy losses. As noted in the OKW's [*Oberkommando der Wehrmacht*, or Supreme Command of the Armed Forces] journal of combat operations: "The course of events in the Second Hungarian Army's sector over the past several days has led to its complete disintegration."[48] After the war, the former Wehrmacht general and military historian K. von Tippelskirch wrote: "The losses of the German Second Army were very large, but the Second Hungarian Army had to be written off. The German army corps introduced in its sector withdrew with fighting back beyond the Oka River. The remnants of the Alpine corps and of the XXIV Panzer Corps were also no longer able to conduct combat operations."[49]

The Voronezh – Kastornoe and Ostrogozhsk – Rossosh became the first operations after the victory at Stalingrad which ended with the encirclement of significant enemy groupings. In this respect, it is necessary to give proper credit to General of the Army[50] A.M. Vasilevsky and Lieutenant General F.I. Golikov, to whom by right the leading role in the planning and conducting

46 TsAMO RF, F. 203, op. 2874, d. 41, l. 14.

47 *Mirovaia voina, 1939-1945. S6: statei* [*World war, 1939-1945. S6: articles*] (Moscow: Voenizdat, 1957), p. 206.

48 *Velikaia Otechestvennaia voina, 1941-1945*, Book 2: Turning point, p. 166.

49 K. Tippelskirch, *Istoriia Vtoroi mirovoi voiny* [*History of the Second World War* – the Russian translation of his book *Geschichte des Zweiten Weltkriegs*] (Moscow: AST, 2001), p. 362.

50 A.M. Vasilevsky was awarded the title Marshal of the Soviet Union on 16 February 1943.

of these operations belongs. The *Stavka* highly evaluated the contribution of the commanders to this victory. On 28 January 1943, they were both awarded the Order of Suvorov 1st Degree. It is impossible also not to speak of the high cost that the Soviet soldiers and officers paid for this success. According to data of the Voronezh Front, in the first stage of the operation alone between 24 January and 1 February 1943, it lost more than 33,000 men killed, missing-in-action or wounded, and a third of this total, more than 11,500 casualties, belonged to the 40th Army.[51]

The powerful blows launched in the course of the Voronezh – Kastornoe operation against the German Army Group B, which was holding a significant portion of the southwestern direction of the Soviet-German front, placed this Wehrmacht army group on the precipice of a catastrophe. The *Stavka* of the Supreme High Command quickly took advantage of this by launching decisive attacks by three *fronts* simultaneously – the Briansk, Voronezh and Southwestern Fronts – in the direction of the Ukraine at the beginning of February 1943.

51 TsAMO RF, F. 203, op. 8695, d. 45, l. 18.

3

Stopping von Manstein's "Backhand Blow", 13-21 March 1943

In the history of the Battle of Kursk (during the period of the formation of the Kursk bulge), there are a number of important events that remain in the shadow of larger-scale clashes. The combat actions in the second stage of the Khar'kov defensive operation of the Soviet forces between 13 and 21 March 1943, which led to the completion of the forming of the Kursk bulge's southern face and the stabilization of the front here, belong to such overshadowed events. One of the primary reasons for the generally neglected study of this period was the paucity of primary sources. In the early 1990s, a number of files of the Russian Ministry of Defense's Central Archive were de-classified, including those for the year 1943. A significant amount of previously unknown materials began to enter academic circulation. They allow us not only to understand the course of combat operations and to assess the plans and decisions by the commands of the opposing sides, but also to determine the level of troop training and the amount of influence that separate formations and armies had on the results of a number of battles, the conception of which is already deeply-rooted in the academic world and society. The dramatic pages of the records of the accounts regarding the defense of the Belgorod area in March 1943 by the headquarters of two formations – the 3rd Guards "Kotel'nikovo" and 2nd Guards "Tatsinskaia" Tank Corps – are just such documents.

After the introduction into combat in the latter half of February 1943 of the SS panzer grenadier divisions that had transferred from France, the operational situation in the sector of the Voronezh Front became more acute with each passing day. Between 27 February and 3 March 1943, the armies of the right wing of General of the Army N.F. Vatutin's Southwestern Front, which had abandoned up to 120 kilometers of territory that had been liberated during the winter offensive, fell back behind the Northern Donets River [today known as the Severskii Donets River] and took up a defense along the Zmiev – Izium – Krasnyi Liman line. The adversary had not only inflicted heavy damage to their forces, but had also fully restored Army Group South's line of communications and created favorable conditions for launching a counterattack against Voronezh Front's left flank. However, its commander-in-chief Colonel General F.I. Golikov, just like its neighbor, failed to appreciate this threat in time. His armies continued to press toward Poltava even at the moment when the right flank of Vatutin's Southwestern Front had been fully crushed by the enemy. F.I. Golikov issued the order to go over to the defense only on 1 March, with the caveat that on his Front's right wing, its forces were to take Sumy and Sudzha. Moreover, this decision was approved by the *Stavka* of the Supreme High Command on 2 March. Under the pressure of Army Group South, the epicenter of the fighting began to shift toward Khar'kov and beyond, to the Borisovka – Tomarovka – Belgorod area.

The combat actions in March 1943 in the Belgorod area have received little study. The authors of a number of studies published in recent years on this subject usually conclude with the story about the German re-capture of Khar'kov and the withdrawal of General P.S. Rybalko's 3rd Tank Army and its attached units from the city on 16 March. However, even before the moment when the SS corps began its assault on the city on 11 March, the *Stavka* of the Supreme High Command, forecasting the enemy's desire to break through to Kursk, hastily began to assemble a major grouping of forces at Belgorod. On 9 March 1943, the Voronezh Front command was informed that the 2nd Guards Tatsinskaia Tank Corps, the 3rd Guards Kotel'nikovo Tank Corps and the 18th Tank Corps were being transferred to its operational control. In addition, trains carrying the troops of two Guards armies were already beginning to arrive its sector. However, the operational situation was growing more complex with each passing hour. The Germans took Staryi Liubotin, the western portion of Liubotin, the village of Ol'shany and Maksimovka Station (15 kilometers southeast of Bogodukhov). Thus, the enemy's intention to outflank Khar'kov from the north, through Dergachi, was plainly discernible.

Colonel General F.I. Golikov decided to concentrate the approaching mobile formations between Belgorod and Khar'kov in the Mikoianovka, Kazach'ia Lopan', Zolochev, Muravlevka area, in order to launch attacks to the southwest into the flank and rear of the enemy's combat groups. In this way, he was planning to throw the enemy advance toward Khar'kov from the west and southwest off stride and smash the forward German combat groups. However, he was unable to implement this idea. Major General B.M. Badanov's 2nd Guards Tatsinskaia Tank Corps had already assembled on Southwestern Front's right flank by 6 March 1943. But at Vatutin's insistence, it was left under his control and sent instead to Zmiev, and then to Taranovka and Novaia Vodolaga with the aim of launching at attack into the flank of the enemy that was attacking toward Khar'kov from the south out of the Novaia Vodolaga – Valki area. However, this plan also remained unrealized. As a result of the corps' repeated maneuvering, valuable time had been lost – a minimum of three days, and it arrived in Belgorod only by the evening of 10 March worn out and exhausted, having just 80 serviceable tanks. The corps commander received an order: with an attack in the direction of Dergachi, to destroy the enemy on the northern outskirts of the town and to take the Dergachi – Cherkasskaia Lozovaia area. However, it was unable to carry out the assignment. This made the situation facing the Soviet forces extremely difficult. By the end of 11 March the Germans seized Shevchenki (northeast of Khar'kov) and emerged on the Belgorod highway. At this time, the Voronezh Front's second echelon, Major General M.I. Kazakov's 69th Army, still hadn't taken up a defense in this area as planned. Thus, the path to Belgorod was effectively open.

Considering the configuration of the front lines, F.I. Golikov then shifted Badanov's 2nd Guards Tank Corps to the flank of the enemy combat groups that were advancing toward Khar'kov from the north (to the Kazach'ia Lopan' – Zhuravlevka area), giving it the assignment first to screen the Belgorod direction, and second, to secure the approach and deployment of the 3rd Guards Kotel'nikovo Tank Corps and 18th Tank Corps.

Major General I.A. Vovchenko's 3rd Guards Tank Corps, still having not completed its assembly on the night of 12-13 March, was sent from Volchansk through Belgorod to Mikoianovka. From that place it was quickly deployed to the Borisovka area to face the shock group of the *Grossdeutschland* Panzer Grenadier Division, which on 13 March had taken Borisovka and created a threat to Belgorod from the west. Vovchenko's tank corps played a very important role in this area: lacking motorized infantry, with only the tank brigades without their rear services and artillery support and while taking punishment from the German Luftwaffe, it detained the enemy units for eight days, even though it was unable to operate as a single, compact group together with the 2nd Guards Tank Corps.

Major General B.S. Bakharov's 18th Tank Corps arrived in the sector of the front only on 13 March at Rogan' (south), having only 20 operational tanks (8 T-34 and 12 T-70), at the moment when the SS Corps, bypassing Khar'kov to the northeast and north, seized Sorokovka (17 kilometers east of Khar'kov) and Rogan' (north of Khar'kov). Bakharov's tank corps was immediately

A German *kampfgruppe* enters a village on the Khar'kov axis, March 1943 (A captured German photograph, RGAKFD)

Next to a burning home in a village on the Khar'kov axis, an assault gun of one of the SS divisions fires at Soviet troops; March 1943 (A captured German photograph, RGAKFD)

Anti-tank rifle teams fighting to repulse an enemy attack in the Belgorod area, March 1943 (RGAKFD)

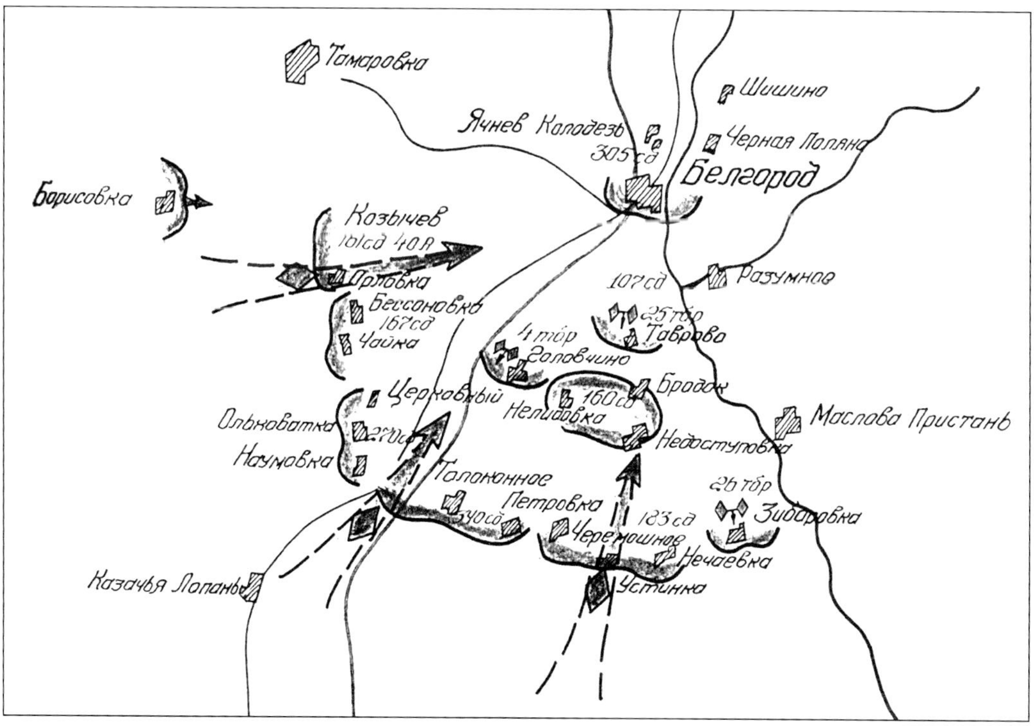

A map of the combat operations in the Belgorod area in March 1943 taken from the account of the Voronezh Front's command (TsAMO RF)

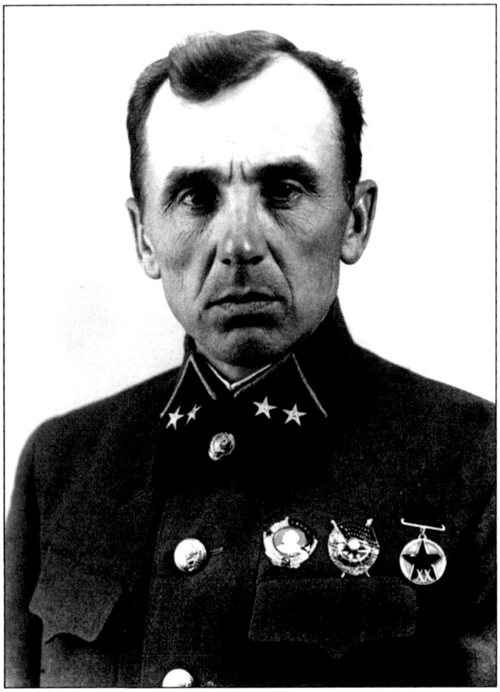

The commander of Voronezh Front's 40th Army Major General K.S. Moskalenko, January 1943 (TsAMO RF)

Major General I.A. Vovchenko, the commander of the 3rd Guards "Kotel'nikovo" Tank Corps, which successfully defended the Oboian' direction in March 1943 (TsAMO RF)

Major General V.M. Badanov, commander of the 2nd Guards "Tatsinskaia" Tank Corps that distinguished itself in the fighting near Belgorod in March 1943 (RGAKFD)

Soldiers and commanders of an anti-aircraft battery of the 64th Army's 27th Guards Tank Brigade en route from Stalingrad to the Belgorod area, March 1943 (Photograph by A. Zamsky, ShIXM)

Soviet tanks in their jumping-off positions prior to an attack; March 1943 (RGAKFD)

A grenadier of one of the SS divisions observes the battlefield from behind a knocked-out Soviet T-34 tank (A captured German photograph, RGAKFD)

A semi-demolished residence in the center of Belgorod, March 1943 (A captured German photograph, RGAKFD)

A funeral ceremony in the city of Novyi Oskol of Kursk (present-day Belgorod) Oblast for troops of the 3rd Guards Tank Corps' 3rd Guards Tank Brigade who were killed in the course of the fighting at Belgorod. (Photograph by S. Fridliand, RGAKFD)

made subordinate to General P.S. Rybalko for the struggle against the German units that had reached the Nepokrytoe – Kammenaia Iaruga area from the north. By the morning of the following day, Bakharov's tank corps had only four operational tanks left. Thus, the plan to create an armored grouping of three tank corps within the Voronezh Front was not realized, primarily due to objective circumstances.[1]

Nevertheless, the Soviet command had succeeded in taking control of the situation with the use of the mobile formations. It had finally halted Army Group South's advance, and quickly sealed the gap that had been created at the boundary between the 40th and 69th Armies, which was one of the most important building blocks of the success. As a result, by 27 March 1943 the front had become stabilized along the Northern Donets River, thereby completing the formation of the Kursk bulge's southern shoulder.

Unfortunately, although Badanov's and Vovchenko's tank corps fully managed the task that had been given to them by tying up the enemy's shock groups with combat and preventing a German breakthrough across the Northern Donets River, the foe was stopped at a very high cost. Of the 201 tanks that the 2nd Guards Tatsinskaia Tank Corps had operational on 9 March 1943, at the moment when it was withdrawn into the reserve (on the evening of 24 March), it had only 12 operational tanks, and 10 that had damaged running gear and were being used as immobile firing points.[2] The tank corps' irrecoverable losses over this period amounted to 128 combat machines.[3]

1 TsAMO RF, F. 3415, op. 1, d. 117, l. 174.
2 TsAMO RF, F. 3400, op. 1, d. 34, l. 36 obr.
3 TsAMO RF, F. 3400, op. 1, d. 22, l. 76.

The 3rd Guards Kotel'nikovo Tank Corps was in even worse shape. The situation in it was laid out in detail in an account produced by its command (see Document 1).

Together with the objective factors (the qualitative superiority of the enemy's armored vehicles, the Voronezh Front command's lack of reserves, the onset of the muddy season, and so forth), subjective factors also contributed to the high losses. At the beginning of March after the most arduous offensive as part of the Southwestern and Southern Fronts, both tank corps were undergoing re-formation. In fact, by the time of their transfer to Belgorod, this process hadn't been completed. The sorry condition of the tank corps before their arrival at Belgorod has been laid out without exaggeration in Documents 1 and 3. The corps had not been provided with the minimum means and time necessary in order to carry out their assigned tasks: the brigades were very short of personnel and armor, the crews hadn't been prepared for fighting, evacuation vehicles were lacking, and reinforcements hadn't yet arrived in the corps.

Moreover, having concentrated a large number of tanks on a narrow sector of the front, the Soviet side was unable to provide them with reliable air cover or get the proper command and control over the troops and cooperation with the rifle divisions of the 40th and 69th Armies up and running. As a result, despite the fact that the Guardsmen in the fighting demonstrated incomparable courage and heroism in the struggle with superior enemy forces, both of the tank corps, which had become famous during the Stalingrad operation, were essentially destroyed within a matter of days and ceased to be major tank formations.

The effectiveness of the tankers' combat performance and the high loss of armor were both substantially affected by the ill-judged, hasty decisions of key figures in the leadership of Voronezh Front and the 40th and 69th Armies, to which the tank corps were attached, as well as often their inability to handle the combat operations of such large troop formations. The report of a senior officer of the General Staff Colonel V. Chernov vividly testifies to this (see Document 2). Already on 15 March, F.I. Golikov would demand of the commander of 69th Army Major General M.I. Kazakov "to regard the use of tanks more sparingly, and not expend them to resolve local tasks."[4] However, this didn't have the proper effect. The armored vehicles were often used in penny-packets, not as a unified shock group, and in the role of infantry support tanks. The brigades were given tasks far beyond their capabilities, and when they were unable to carry them out, the tankers were accused of disobedience, negligence and even cowardice. For example, on the morning of 19 March, after the 69th Army had fallen back behind the Northern Donets River with its main forces and the *kampfgruppen* of two SS panzer grenadier divisions had taken Belgorod, the commander of the 40th Army Major General K.S. Moskalenko blamed the commander of the 3rd Guards Kotel'nikovo Tank Corps Major General A.I. Vovchenko for the fall of the city, even though his tank brigades were operating elsewhere on a different axis, at Borisovka. Moskalenko declared, "The actions of your corps on 18.3.43 were unsatisfactory, indecisive and cowardly. … If you continue to act in the same way, then the question will be posed about dismissing you from your post."[5]

At the end of March and beginning of April 1943, a deep review of Voronezh Front's combat operations during the two Khar'kov operations was conducted, which resulted in major changes in the leadership of a number of formations and armies; however, the commanders of the 3rd Guards Kotel'nikovo Tank Corps and 2nd Guards Tatsinskaia Tank Corps kept their posts, and in June 1943, Major General B.M. Badanov was appointed commander of the 4th Guards Tank Army. With this decision, the *Stavka* clearly made it known what an important role these tank corps had played at that critical moment. It should be noted that in the future as well, the tankers of the 2nd

4 TsAMO RF, F. 203, op. 2843, d. 301, l. 131.
5 TsAMO RF, F. 203, op. 2843, d. 319, l. 196.

Guards and 3rd Guards Tank Corps would more than once demonstrate high professional skill and tenacity in the fighting against the German fascist aggressors.

The documents presented below are interesting not only with their rich and diverse information about one of the major battles of the Great Patriotic War and the experience of using major mobile formations in combat operations against a superior foe, but are also a compelling example of the courage and resolve of the Soviet tankers.

Document 1

A brief account of the combat actions of the 3rd Guards Kotel'nikovo Tank Corps between 11 and 21 March 1943[6]

The corps in the course of December 1942, and in January and February 1943 took part in ceaseless fighting as part of the Stalingrad Front, and then the Southern Front; conducted a raid toward Rostov and Bataisk, and in the first days of March 1943 was withdrawn to the Glubokoe area for re-formation.

On 2-3.03.1943, the units of the corps with their own main elements were concentrated in the Glubokoe area. On 3.03 the corps began the process of switching to the new tables of organization, while at the same time the 5th Guards Tank Army began to form at the corps' expense; the entire transport pool of the corps command, as well as a significant number of important commanders of the corps were transferred to the tank army, including the corps' chief of staff, operations chief and communications chief.

On 4-5.03.1943, the materiel arrived – T-34 and T-70 tanks. On 5.03 an order was received to load up and move to a new assembly area for equipping and breaking-in [the new men and equipment]. On 6.03 the first trains carrying the tanks departed from Glubokoe Station, while at the same time replacements, weapons, ammunition and supplies for the corps unloaded at various points, and in separate trains moved on to the place of assembly.

While en route by rail, the original decision about assembling the corps in the Starobel'sk area was changed, and the trains were sent instead to Volchansk Station,[7] where the first trains arrived on 10.03.1943. The tank corps was given no time at all for forming up, reinforcement and breaking-in the units and formations; even the opportunity to take in replacements, weapons, and transport and allocate them to its units was excluded.

The unloading of the corps' trains in the Volchansk area began on 10.03 and continues to the present.[8] Up to the present time, the train carrying 2,500 replacements and the train with weapons (20 railcars) haven't arrived. By the beginning of 11.03, 3 trains of tanks were unloaded at Volchansk Station; the rest are en route via railroad. At this time [10-11 March], the 1436th Artillery Regiment, the self-propelled artillery, the 266th Mortar Regiment, the 388th Signals Battalion, the 153rd Engineer Battalion and the 73rd Motorcycle Battalion have been unloaded at railroad stations between Valuiki and Volchansk. However, up to the present time, the artillery regiment, the signals battalion and the engineer battalion have not yet joined up with the corps, while the motorcycle battalion arrived only on 23.03.1943.

6 TsAMO RF, F. 3401, op. 1, d. 15, ll. 3-9. Typescript

7 The town and associated railroad of Volchansk is located in Khar'kov Oblast (Ukraine) on the eastern bank of the Severskii Donets River.

8 The date of the document's composition isn't given on the document; possibly, it was generated in the early days of April 1943. Two notes on the first page of the document indicate this: "Arrival No. 526s 11.4.43. Secretariat of the 1st Deputy People's Commissar of Defense" and "Arrival No. 751s 13 April 1943. Department for studying the war's experience, Red Army General Staff."

Thus, on 10.03 the corps had only begun the process of assembling in its new area. On 11.03, I received an order – to assemble the corps in the Mikoianovka area by the end of the day 13.03.43, to wait for the arrival of the rest of the units.

In accordance with the order, without waiting for the unloading and assembly of the corps' remaining units in the Volchansk area, the corps with three tank brigades moved out in turn (without rear services, motorized rifle battalions and one tank battalion of the 19th Guards Tank Brigade) that evening along the route: Volchansk, Belgorod, Mikoianovka, while the remaining units were still en route along the railroad.

While the corps was on the march, an order was received at 0300 12.03.1943 – to pivot the corps to a new axis – Tomarovka,[9] Borisovka.[10] At this same time, I received the combat assignment – to attack Borisovka immediately and take possession of it.

The corps conducted its march to Borisovka along two roads: the 18th Guards Tank Brigade along the right-hand route – Belgorod, Tomarovka, Borisovka; the 3rd Guards Tank Brigade followed by the 19th Guards Tank Brigade (minus one tank battalion) along the left-hand route: Belgorod, Blizhnii, Borisovka.

The 3rd Guards Tank Brigade on the march in the Stanovoi area ran into an enemy grouping consisting of up to 60 tanks, 20 self-propelled guns, and up to a battalion of infantry, engaged it, drove the enemy out of Stanovoi and seized the village.

The 18th Guards Tank Brigade by this time reached the Striguny area, where it was carrying out the next combat assignments to seize Borisovka.[11]

Between 13-21.03.1943 the corps' five tank battalions without artillery or motorized infantry in constant fighting on the Borisovka – Tomarovka – Kalinina – Kozychev – Blizhnii line kept in check the stubbornly attacking enemy that was trying to take Belgorod from the west.

Meanwhile, the skeleton 2nd Guards Motorized Rifle Brigade with one battalion of the 19th Guards Tank Brigade and a mortar regiment received an assignment from Voronezh Front's deputy commander[12] to defend initially a line west of Volchansk, and subsequently Staryi Gorod and Mikhailovka,[13] where they are situated at the present time, now subordinate to the commanders of the 69th and 64th Armies.

On 17.03.1943 the enemy, operating from the southwest, reached the Khar'kov – Belgorod road, having crushed units of the 69th Army and 2nd Guards Tank Corps, and on 18.03 – took Belgorod. This placed the corps' tank battalions in very difficult combat conditions, since the roads to their rear services in the Belgorod area and west of there had been severed; supply to the tank battalions, and repair and overhaul of the combat machines were in essence prevented; however, the tank battalions fought on stubbornly, refusing to yield their occupied lines to the enemy. So only at 1330 on 19.03.1943 did they fall back while suffering large losses to new lines pursuant to an order from the commander of the 40th Army.[14]

In the course of six days of uninterrupted tank fighting, the corps' tankers for the first time encountered the massed use of enemy dive bombers, equipped with cannons and rockets.

9 A large village and district center 25 kilometers northwest of Belgorod.

10 A large village and district center 37 kilometers west of Belgorod.

11 On 14 March 1943, after bitter combat, the large village of Borisovka that was being defended by the 40th Army's 309th Rifle Division had been seized by forces of General W. Kempf's Army Detachment (Korps Raus).

12 Lieutenant General (from 1943) Dmitrii Timofeevich Kozlov (4 November 1896 – 6 December 1967)

13 Both of these places were located on the eastern bank of the Nothern Donets River next to Belgorod, and were connected with its eastern outskirts by bridges.

14 Lieutenant General K.S. Moskalenko (11 November 1902 – 21 February 1978).

With their actions, the enemy dive bombers inflicted unprecedented losses to the tank brigades, as for example:

> On 19.03.1943 an attack by enemy aircraft upon the combat formations of the 18th Guards Tank Brigade knocked out or set ablaze 26 tanks, including 19 T-34.
>
> In the area of the 3rd Guards Tank Brigade's operations, the enemy bombed and strafed the tank combat formations for entire days. Dive bombers dove upon some tanks up to 10 times.

The enemy was using a group of tanks of a new type, the Tiger, against our tanks. The enemy always had self-propelled artillery in its combat formations of tanks, and very skillfully organized cooperation between its artillery and infantry. At the same time, he was obtaining completely accurate information about our combat formations and directions of movement from aerial reconnaissance. It should be noted that on the very first day of battle, the enemy air force knocked out all the radio means of communication in the brigades and corps.

In the fighting from 13-21.03.1943, the corps suffered [the following] losses in personnel and equipment: killed and wounded – 903 men; 110 T-34 tanks, 46 T-70 tanks, 45 various types of vehicles, 8 mortars and 6 heavy machine guns.

Conclusions:

1. Despite the heavy losses, which the corps' tank battalions suffered in the fighting on the approaches to Belgorod from the west, the 3rd Guards Kotel'nikovo Tank Corps kept the enemy in check, preventing him from entering Belgorod until the enemy committed a major mechanized group from the south from the direction of Khar'kov.
2. The corps at that time and during the fighting wasn't ready to carry out offensive operations, because the absence of infantry, artillery, command and control means, signaling means, and the lack of rear services prevented the possibility of successfully developing offensive actions.
3. The corps, being incomplete and disaggregated in the period of combat actions was in fact split into two pieces: the tank battalions were engaged in battle, while the rest of the units were in the Volchansk area or still en route.
4. The corps' brigades were not up to establishment strength, lacking anti-tank batteries and motorized rifle and machine-gun battalions, and with a very limited number of motor transport vehicles.
5. The corps' command – the headquarters wasn't fully equipped, lacking communications equipment and motorized transport. The signals battalion as the main means of directing the troops still hasn't arrived at the present time.
6. The 250 motor vehicles earmarked from the Southern Front still haven't fully arrived at the present time. Only 170 vehicles have arrived, of which 100 are not running.
7. During the combat actions, the corps was left completely without air cover, was unsupported by artillery, and cooperation with the infantry was completely absent.

[Signed] Commander of the 3rd Guards Kotel'nikovo Tank Corps
Guards Major General of Tank Forces Vovchenko

Document 2

A short comment[15]

Only the indolent now don't swear by the need for cooperation among all types of troops, however, facts of a crying shame in this respect continue to multiply; in a complicated situation, they can be considered characteristic. All of this happens indeed because those commanders, who've been entrusted to coordinate the forces of such major formations as a tank corps, air division, artillery division and so forth, bear no personal responsibility for the isolated and ineffective use of one or another type of troops.

The complexity of the situation – that's the objective factor, which vindicates such chiefs not only formally and factually, but also fully relieves [them of] pangs of conscience for the blood spilled in vain by our soldiers and commanders, and for the needless losses in materiel.

A tank corps hastens to arrive piece by piece with its fighting body at a dangerous axis and engages in combat with superior enemy forces, but aviation? "There's nothing to say" about it! And anti-aircraft artillery – it's also absent. So the tankers must take on the enemy artillery, tanks, aviation and infantry by themselves! Junst think what can happen in that case, and the one that leads the way will say: "Enemy aircraft were brazen, diving down to turret level, shooting up the tanks with cannons and demolishing them with bombs, while out defenseless tankers curse both their commanders and the fate that made them tankers, and they fall as victims to the incompetent leadership of high-ranking officers." As a result 156 tanks were knocked out or set ablaze over 8 days of combat and maneuver.

It is possible to avoid such a disgrace not only with training based on the experience of the war, but also with a tough sentence for all the Red Army to hear for those chiefs guilty of such leadership. Shoot one "disastrous chief" and the notice to all the army's command staff will remind other commanders to study the war's best practices. Thus far, for poor organization of cooperation, the most that can happen is removal from a post, and this doesn't always become known to the command staff.

28 May 1943 [Signed] Colonel V. Chernov

Document 3

Conclusions from the "Account on the 2nd Guards Tatsinskaia Tank Corps's actions over the period from 25 February to 26 March 1943"[16]

I. On 9.03.1943 the corps was introduced into the fighting in the Zmiev area, having the assignment to prevent the enemy from reaching Khar'kov. At this time, the corps wasn't fully equipped with combat materiel and personnel. The 4th Guards Motorized Rifle Brigade and the motorized rifle – machine gun battalions of the tank brigades lacked weapons, and the men were without footgear, in view of which the 4th Guards Motorized Rifle Brigade took no part in the execution of the corps' combat tasks throughout the period discussed.

15 This document was attached to the first page of the account written by the command of the 3rd Guards Kotel'nikovo Tank Corps and judging by its contents, is a response to it (TsAMO RF, F. 3401, op. 1, d. 16, l. 2)

16 TsAMO RF, F. 3400, op. 1, d. 22, ll. 81-83.

The corps set out to carry out its combat assignment not in top shape, since there was absolutely no time for this. Primarily it had been replenished with personnel who in their majority had not seen any combat and who hadn't even gone through the introductory exercise of basic gunnery.

The Guards corps' personnel went through no sort of screening process. The driver-mechanics had 4-5 hours of experience each driving tanks. The tank commanders had little experience and the majority had never seen combat; were poor at getting their bearings via observation from within the tank; were untrained; could not work with target optical sights; and fired inaccurately from the tank's main gun. Of the men who arrived to replenish the motorized rifle – machine gun battalions, 75% had never seen combat and approximately 15% had never gone through the introductory exercise of basic riflery, and had not been instructed on how to mount and dismount from a tank.

The tanks came from two factories: the Cheliabinsk Tank Factory and the Sormovo Factory No. 112, both of which are inferior in quality to the [Nizhnyi] Tagil Factory. Defects were present in the bearings of the roller wheels and the bearings of the idler sprocket; adaptor couplings, water pumps, and head gaskets malfunctioned; screws in the roller pins of the drive wheel became severed; and the rims of the roller wheels became warped.

II. The corps set out to carry out assignments in response to an alarm, and subsequently was shifted to other sectors also unexpectedly, having no time to prepare for the march or to scout the routes and prepare the roads and bridges. Marches were conducted for the most part along routes that had not been scouted beforehand, as a result of which there were incidents when tanks needlessly dropped out of the column for some reason: they became stuck in swamps, toppled into ravines, or they fell through bridges. There was no time for maintenance or light repairs, despite the fact that long marches were conducted and constant battles were fought (on average each machine covered up to 500 kilometers and expended 250 motor hours).

The lack of evacuation means and the insufficient quantity of repair means in the brigades led to the excessive loss of tanks due to mechanical problems.

At the moment of setting out, the corps had only 50% of its authorized wheeled vehicles, of which 50% required major or light overhauls; subsequently large losses were suffered from enemy aviation, which as a result told on the resupply of the units. The lack of motorized transport in the motorized rifle – machine-gun battalions of the tank brigades and in the 4th Guards Motorized Rifle Brigade prevented the possibility of using the men as a concentrated force of infantry, since they had to maneuver on foot or partially as tank riders.

III. As a result of the circumstances, throughout the extent of the fighting over the month of March, the corps was used in combat in defiance of People's Commissar of Defense's Order No. 325.[17] Tanks were thrown into battle directly from the march without advance scouting of the terrain or of the enemy's forward edge of defense, without artillery preparation or its accompaniment, almost without infantry and absolutely without air cover.

17 People's Commissar of Defense Order No. 325 was issued on 16 November 1942 and was an accumulation of the practical experience of using the Red Army's tank forces over the previous year of the war. Until a combat manual for the tank forces was introduced in 1944, it was the main document for using tanks, both on the defense and when conducting offensive operations.

Our air force throughout the entire extent of the fighting was virtually absent, particularly at the time of our units' withdrawal to the eastern bank of the Northern Donets River. There are no anti-aircraft weapons in the corps, which resulted in excessive losses of combat materiel. The enemy air force operated with impunity, since other units also had no anti-aircraft weapons, which might have covered the corps' units against air attacks.

The tanks were used in very difficult terrain, where there were large snowdrifts and mud in places, which also led to the partial loss of tanks.

Our infantry, as a rule, only went into battle behind the tanks, as a result of which many tanks were knocked out, having triggered mines; the infantry, as a rule, didn't study the sector of attack, had no information on the enemy, and operated blindly there, wherever the tanks led.

At the time when our units' withdrew to the eastern bank of the Northern Donets, the corps was nothing like a shock fist, but had been scattered across 60-70 kilometers in order to cover the rifle units. The infantry of the 160th, 183rd, 107th and 340th Rifle Divisions was uncontrollable, and retreated without offering sufficient resistance to the enemy and without alerting our tanks of the enemy's appearance. As a result the corps' tanks remained alone, fought without air cover or ground cover, being attacked by superior enemy forces.

IV. The enemy had a numerical superiority in tanks, self-propelled artillery and motorized infantry. Throughout the entire period of the offensive, the enemy was covering his actions with ceaseless massed attacks by bombers and ground assault aircraft against our combat formations and our lines of communication.

The ground attack aircraft (obviously, tank hunters) used a 37mm automatic anti-tank cannon, a direct hit from which knocked out several T-34. The enemy uses tanks with great caution in cooperation with self-propelled artillery, motorized infantry and aviation. Tanks are not being used in heavily broken terrain.

In his motorized units there are a large quantity of transports and armored vehicles. Infantry are all seated in motorized transports. The activity of tanks and self-propelled artillery is always preceded by the appearance of vehicles and halftracks with submachine gunners, who, when certain of the absence of anti-tank weapons and mine fields, give a signal for the advance of the tank columns. Enemy aerial reconnaissance that accompanies the columns significantly cooperates with it in this, which on our side is not at all practiced.

Commander of the 2nd Guards Tatsinskaia Tank Corps
[Signed] Guards Lieutenant General of Tank Forces Badanov

4

Could Germany have won the Battle of Kursk if it had started in late May or the beginning of June 1943?

This chapter is an expanded version of an article which first appeared under the same title in The Journal of Slavic Military Studies, Volume 27, Issue 4 (October 2014). *It includes recently uncovered data for the Soviet Steppe Front in the period prior to the Battle of Kursk.*

This question is not at all a rhetorical one. There exists a persistent opinion (which is especially prevalent in Western historiography), according to which the multiple postponements of the start date of the Kursk offensive in May-June 1943 substantially brought about the defeat of the German forces in the summer of 1943. I will remind the reader that Operation Citadel was first postponed on 20 April due to fully objective reasons: *Generaloberst* W. Model's Ninth Army was not ready for the operation (it hadn't even had time to assemble fully for an attack). In principle, everyone was in agreement with this. However, the next postponement of the offensive's date to 12 June, at first raised by Hitler as a topic for discussion at a 4 May conference and later confirmed by him in an order on 6 May, generated Assaulty arguments among the Wehrmacht's high command. Hitler based his May decision on the fact that the main trump card for the summer campaign wasn't yet ready – the Tiger and Panther tanks. However, this delay didn't turn out to be the final one. Neither in May 1943 nor in the first 10 days of June 1943 had the German industry fulfilled the production plan for these armored vehicles, so Hitler again postponed the offensive, at first to 21 June, and then to 3 July; finally, on 25 June he set the final date for the start of Operation Citadel – 5 July 1943. This date indeed entered history as the beginning of one of the largest battles of the Second World War.

German military commanders first proffered this point of view – that the repeated postponements results in the offensive's failure – immediately after the war's conclusion. For example, former *Feldmarschall* E. von Kliest in 1951 maintained that the Germans were late in starting the Battle of Kursk by four weeks, "and such was our opinion before the start of the battle."[1] *Feldmarschall* E. von Manstein, the commander of Army Group South, which in July 1943 had launched the attack from the south out of the Belgorod area against Voronezh Front's defenses, expressed a similar opinion in his memoirs, which were published in Germany in 1955. He wrote

1 Khristoforov, V., Makarov, V., and Khavkin, B., "Fel'dmarshal fon Kliest na Liubianke" ["Field Marshal von Kleist in the Lubianka prison] *Rodina,* No. 6 (2010), p. 94.

that Citadel might have been successful, had it started no later than the end of May – beginning of June.[2] The main point of this line of reasoning was that prior to this time, the Russians were operating with divisions and corps that had been battered by the winter fighting and were weak in strength, but the pause in June gave Moscow the opportunity to bring them back to full strength.

Among scholars, the American historian S. Newton most fully elaborated this position in his book *Kursk: The German View* on the basis of *Generaloberst* W. Model's Ninth Army, which attacked from the north toward Kursk in Central Front's sector.[3] However, the figures cited in it, in particular with respect to the strength of the Soviet formations and armies, are not always accurate, which gives rise to large doubts about his conclusions. We'll try to look more deeply into this question, using the recently declassified wartime documents of the Red Army from that period in the Russian Federation's Central Archive of the Ministry of Defense (TsAMO RF).

There are several reasons that contributed to the success of the Soviet forces in the battle for the Kursk Bulge, but there are three main factors. Firstly was the high degree of readiness of the forces that were defending the Kursk salient. Secondly was the presence of the large reserves of the *Stavka* of the Supreme High Command. Finally, there were the powerful field defenses that had been constructed in this area in the period between April and June 1943.

The assertion of the German military commanders and their supporters among Western historians about the Soviet forces' supposed lack of readiness for combat in May 1943 in the Kursk area is based on the lack of knowledge about the details of the *Stavka*'s plans for the summer campaign and the scale of work conducted in the period of the spring operational pause. On 12 April 1943, in the course of a conference in the Kremlin involving I.V. Stalin, the deputy commander in chief Marshal of the Soviet Union G.K. Zhukov, the chief of the General Staff Marshal of the Soviet Union A.M. Vasilevsky and his deputy Colonel General A.I. Antonov, the conclusion was reached that the Werhmacht would launch an offensive with the aim of eliminating the Kursk salient immediately after the ground hardened following the spring thaw (approximately the beginning of May). Thus, a preliminary decision was adopted to go over to a strategic defense; it was planned to bring the forces of the Central and Voronezh Fronts that were defending the Kursk bulge back up to full strength by the end of May, while their military councils were in close cooperation with the General Staff were to work out plans for the defensive operation. On 25 and 28 April the command of both *fronts* reported that they were essentially finished with their given assignments. The *Stavka* confirmed the overall plan presented by them for conducting the Kursk strategic defensive operation,[4] and issued an order for the troops fully to be ready to repel an enemy attack by 10 May, and also set a date for when the Germans might go on the offensive – no later than 1 June 1943.[5]

It was precisely thanks to the fulfillment of the far-reaching decisions of 12 April 1943 that already by the first ten days of May, the Soviet side was basically ready to conduct successful defensive combat at Kursk against those forces that the Wehrmacht was fielding in this area at that moment. By the beginning of June, the numerical strength of the Central and Voronezh Fronts would already reach the level they would have in July, before the battle of Kursk. The following figures plainly testify to the fact that it was precisely because that the *Stavka*'s directive was carried out in a timely fashion.

For example, on 30 March 1943, the Central Front under Colonel General K.K. Rokossovsky had a total of 304,464 officers and soldiers, but by 5 May its strength had grown by 61,167 men

2 Manstein, E., *Uteriannye pobedy* [*Lost victories*] (Smolensk, Rusich, 2003), p. 543.
3 Newton, S., *Kurskaia bitva nemetskii vgliad* [*Kursk: the German View*] (Moscow: Iauza, EKSMO, 2006), pp. 463-476.
4 This is how the Battle of Kursk entered Russian historiography.
5 TsAMO RF, F.16-A, Op.321, D.138.

to 365,641,[6] which amounted to 78 percent of its numerical strength at the start of the Battle of Kursk. At the same time, the strength of its 13th Army under the command of Lieutenant General N.P. Pukhov, which would receive the main attack of Model's Ninth Army, over this same period of time rose by 42,552 men to 114,456, or 86% of its numerical strength on 5 July. This increase in manpower primarily came through the transfer of three rifle divisions to it, although the average strength of its inherent divisions also grew noticeably, by 18 percent (from 6,378 to 7,527). For Pukhov's army, April 1943 was the period when it took in the greatest number of replacements over the entire time of preparations for the summer fighting. By 29 May, another 14,701 men came under its command, and thereby its total strength grew to 129,157 officers and men, or 97 percent of those available on 5 July. Meanwhile, the overall manpower of the Central Front at the end of May amounted to 451,179 men, or 97 percent of the total number of officers and men it would have at the start of Operation Citadel.[7]

The rebuilding of the forces of General of the Army N.F. Vatutin's Voronezh Front went just as rapidly. On 5 April it had 208,391 men, but by 5 May, this number had grown by 143,068 to 351,459, or 84 percent of the planned level for 5 July.[8] Over this period of time between 5 April and 5 May, 30,262 replacements were directed to Lieutenant General I.M. Chistiakov's 6th Guards Army, which was positioned on the likely axis of the main attack, and its numerical strength rose to 72,836 officers and soldiers (the average manpower of its rifle divisions grew by 28 percent, from 5,982 to 7,666), while 9,407 replacements went to Lieutenant General M.S. Shumilov's 7th Guards Army (which was defending a sector where the enemy was possibly planning a secondary attack), and as a result its numerical strength grew to 67,231 men; the average strength of its rifle divisions grew by 27 percent, from 5,965 to 7,600). By 30 May, the total numerical strength of Vatutin's Front had grown to 409,975 (or 98 percent of the men on its roster on 5 July), while the armies of Chistiakov and Shumilov by 5 June had grown to 79,937 (approximately 100 percent of the 5 July figure) and 71,332 (approximately 93 percent of the 5 July figure) officers and soldiers respectively.

A similar pattern developed with respect to artillery. By 6 May, both the Central Front and its subordinate 13th Army had received 80 percent of the guns and mortars (not including the Guards mortars, or rocket artillery) of that number, which they would have on 5 July 1943. On 29 May the entire Central Front had 4,544 field and anti-tank guns and 7,161 mortars, or 85 percent and 89 percent respectively of the amount it would have by 5 July; 13th Army had 1,361 guns and 1,943 mortars, or 87 percent and 89 percent of the amount it would have by 5 July. The 70th Army, which was defending on the 13th Army's left, and would also take on a powerful enemy attack, had 796 guns (93 percent of the 5 July figure) and 1,280 mortars (98 percent of the 5 July figure).

The replenishment of Rokossovsky's and Vatutin's forces with tanks didn't go so smoothly or swiftly. On 3 May the Central Front had 674 tanks and 38 self-propelled artillery vehicles,[9] of 40 percent of their availability on 5 July, while the 13th Army had 137 tanks,[10] or 64 percent of the number it had by the start of the battle. However, the situation with armor on the southern shoulder of the Kursk bulge at this time was significantly better.

The point is that the mobile formations that had been operating in winter and at the beginning of spring 1943 on the Voronezh and Southwestern Fronts had suffered very large losses. In some tank corps, the total number of tanks didn't exceed the number of tanks of a full-strength

6 TsAMO RF, F.62, Op.1720, D.14,L.23.
7 TsAMO RF, F.16-A, Op.321, D.138.
8 TsAMO RF, F.203, Op.2843, D.425, L.425.
9 TsAMO RF, F.62, Op.321, D. 16, L. 86obr.
10 TsAMO RF, F.62, Op.321, D.16, L.86.

tank battalion. Because of this, already at the end of March, the *Stavka* adopted a decision: to replenish them first and foremost.[11] In the course of April, the bulk of the armored vehicles coming out of the factories went to these two *fronts*. Thus, the rebuilding of Vatutin's armored forces proceeded at leaps and bounds. For example, only over the two weeks between 1 and 15 April, the Voronezh Front received 219 new tanks and self-propelled guns and 6,432 men for its tank corps and tank brigades.[12] As a result, if on 9 April the Voronezh Front had 276 serviceable tanks and self-propelled guns, then on 21 April it now had 540. The repair of damaged combat machines by the Front's repair services actively went on in parallel with the arrival of new equipment. In addition, on 28 April the *Stavka* officially transferred Lieutenant General M.E. Katukov's 1st Tank Army to Vatutin's Voronezh Front, which had arrived in the Kursk area from the Northwestern Front back in March, as well as several other separate tank corps and tank brigades. By 5 May, Katukov's 1st Tank Army had been almost fully brought up to strength with tanks – it now had 481 tanks and self-propelled guns, and by 5 July would receive as replenishments only an additional 61 machines.[13]

Thus at the beginning of May, the Central Front was substantially weaker than its neighbor: on 15 May the Voronezh Front had 1,380 serviceable tanks and self-propelled guns, or 76 percent of that number that it would receive by the start of the Battle of Kursk, while the Central Front had twice less. But already by the end of the month, the situation began to change and on 5 June K.K. Rokossovsky had a total of 1,216 tanks and self-propelled guns (72 percent of the amount it would have on 5 July), including 171 armored vehicles in the 13th Army (80 percent of the 5 July figure).[14]

Two notable Western scholars, David Glantz and Johnathon House, wrote: "It is an axiom of military theory and a studied product of Soviet combat analysis that the attacker should outnumber the defender, ideally by at least three to two strategically."[15] However, the German General Heinrici, the former commander of the Fourth Army that performed rather successfully as part of Army Group Center, in conversation with the British historian B. Lidell Hart asserted, "There were times when my troops held their own against odds of 12 to 1 or even 18 to 1."[16] Considering that Hitler gave primary significance to his armored forces for implementing Operation Citadel, I will cite some data regarding their size in Army Groups Center and South. For example, on 4 May 1943, there were a total of 442 tanks (Pz III, Pz IV, but not a single Pz VI Tiger) on the roster in Army Group Center, which included the Ninth Army, of which 314 (71 percent) were operational on that date, while Army Group South had 1,087 tanks, of which 728

11 *Stavka Directives:* No.46090 from 30.3.1943 about replenishing the 23rd and 2 Tank Corps and the 1st Guards Mechanized Corps, No. 46091 from 30.3.1943 about replenishing the 2nd Guards and 5th Guards Tank Corps, No.46093 from 31.3.1943 about replenishing the 3rd Guards Tank Corps; and No.46093 from 31.03.1943 about replenishing the 1st Guard "Don", 12th, 15th and 18th Tank Corps.

12 Zamulin, V.N., *Kurskii izlom: Reshaiushchaia bitva Velikoi Otechestvennoi* [*The Kursk Turning Point: The Decisive battle of the Great Patriotic War* (Moscow: Iauza, Eksmo, 2008), pp. 101-102.

13 TsAMO RF, F.203, Op.2843, D.426: the section "Boevoi sostav 6 gv., 7 gv., 40, 38 A, 1 TA za 5 maia i 5 iulia 1943" [Combat strength of the 6th Guards, 7th Guards, 40th and 38th Armies and the 1st Tank Army for 5 May and 5 July 1943].

14 TsAMO RF, F.62, Op.321, D.16, L.127, 127 obr.

15 Glantz, D. and House, D., *Kurskaia bitva: Reshaiushchii povorotnyi punkt Vtoroi mirovoi voiny* [*The Battle of Kursk: The Decisive Turning Point of the Second World War*] (Moscow: Astrel', 2006), p. 80. This is the Russian translation of Glantz and House's *The Battle of Kursk* (Lawrence: University Press of Kansas, 1999).

16 B. H. Lidell Hart, *Po drugomu storonu kholma* [*On the other side of the hill*] (Moscow: AST, 2014), p. 329. This is the Russian-language translation of Hart's *The German Generals Talk*: *Startling revelations from Hitler's high command* (W. Morrow, 1971).

(67 percent) were operational.[17] Thus already in May 1943, the correlation on the northern face of the Kursk bulge regarding this important type of armament was 1.5 to 1 in favor of the Soviet side, and 1.3 to 1 on the southern face of the salient.

A serious shortage of armor would be observed in the combat units even in mid-June. As of 16 June 1943, the four panzer divisions of the Ninth Army's XXXXVII Panzer Corps[18] would have the following number of combat tanks: 2nd Panzer Division – 59; 4th Panzer Division – 91; 9th Panzer Division – 33; and 12th Panzer Division – 61 (of which 18 were short-barreled).[19] For a general offensive, this is chicken-feed, especially when you consider that in both May and the first half of June, only some of the Tigers would arrive in Model's grouping, and none of the Ferdinand tank destroyers and Brummbär (Sturmpanzer 43] armored infantry support guns, which were used by the enemy to break through the main, most heavily-fortified line of the Soviet defenses. They would begin to arrive only in the latter half of June and beginning of July.

Moreover, the German forces on the northern side of the Kursk bulge even in June would be experiencing an acute shortage of ammunition; while the army dumps would be half-empty. On 5 June 1943 the operational headquarters of Army Group Center with Telegram No. 3398/43 would remind the Ninth Army command that "... the situation with shells for the light field howitzers [105mm], designated for Operation Citadel has deteriorated, and the creation of necessary stocks of shells remains under question. In addition, there are difficulties with the delivery of machine-gun cartridges, the expenditure of which has exceeded planned indicators in view of the high enemy activity.[20]

The situation with armor in the Fourth Panzer Army was better, but even there, the number of armored vehicles was significantly fewer than there would be before the start of the attack toward Kursk. For example, the difference in the quantity of tanks in the SS panzer grenadier divisions between 1 June and 4 July amounted to the following: in *Leibstandarte Adolf Hitler* – 26 (80 and 106 respectively); in *Das Reich* – 23 (67 and 90 respectively);[21] and in *Totenkopf* – 18 (99 and 117 respectively).[22] Thus, over June and the first few days of July, the SS Panzer Corps would receive a total of 67 tanks and self-propelled guns, or a little more than 21% of the 4 July 1943 total. Matters stood worse in the *Grossdeutschland* Panzer Grenadier Division, which by 5 July would be the most powerful Wehrmacht mobile formation in the area of the Kursk bulge. On 1 June 1943, it had a total of 92 tanks and self-propelled guns, but by 4 July this number would grow to 346 (200 in the attached 10th Panzer Brigade and 146 in its own panzer regiment).[23] Thus it is impossible not to agree with the commander of Army Group South's 7th Panzer Division *Generalmajor* von Funk, who from the outset criticized Citadel, calling it "idiotic" and who asserted that the entire "future operation violates the main principles of leadership."[24]

I cannot help but dwell on S. Newton's assertion regarding Model's supposed fundamental mistake, which he committed due to flawed intelligence when calculating the correlation of armored forces between his army and Rokossovsky's *front* at the beginning of May in a report to Hitler. The American scholar writes:

17 Archive of the IVI [Military History Institute], F.191, Op.233, D.108. Reports of General-Inspector of Armored Forces Guderian to Hitler between 3.5.1943 and 1.6.1944 (translated from the German), Part One; Military History Command of the General Staff of the USSR Armed Forces , 1947, pp. 6-7.

18 By 5 July 1943, the composition of this XXXVII Panzer Corps would be changed.

19 NARA, T.314, R.1128, F. 000410 and 000572.

20 NARA, T.312, R. 317, F. 7886113.

21 This number does not include the captured T-34 tanks, of which the *Das Reich* had 6 on 1 June, and 18 on 4 July.

22 NAR, T.313, R.368, F. 8653871.

23 Zetterling and Frankson, *Kursk 1943*, p. 186.

24 R. Cross, *Operatsiia "Tsitadel"* [*Operation Citadel*] (Smolensk: Russich, 2006), p. 133.

> Contrary to German intelligence estimates of, the Soviet Central Front had deployed only about 1,000 tanks and assault guns in late April – early May, rather than 1,500. This was a critical misinterpretation that explains much about Model's insistence on delaying the offensive. With 800 AFVs facing 1,500, the army commander had a legitimate case for arguing additional panzers, especially Panthers and Tigers, were absolutely necessary for the assault. Had Model realized that the Russian armored superiority was only about 200 vehicles, he would have been far more willing to proceed. By waiting [Author's note: May – June], Ninth Army augmented its AFV holdings by about 25 percent, but the Soviets nearly doubled theirs.

In the first place, the figures and correlation given by S. Newton are inaccurate. As the data cited above show, in early May W. Model didn't have 800 tanks. In the entire Army Group Center, there was almost half that number, while Rokossovsky's Central Front had almost 1.5 times the number of armored vehicles than the Germans had: 674 against 442.

Secondly, if we rely on the memoirs of *Feldmarschall* E. von Manstein and *Generaloberst* Guderian, who took part in the well-known conference in Munich on 4 May, where Model's letter was presented and the decision to postpone the start of the offensive from May to June was made, the demand on the delivery of more tanks put forward by the commander of the Ninth Army wasn't the main issue. Initially W. Model didn't possess a lot of armored vehicles; most of the tanks and self-propelled guns were concentrated in the south, and no one was promising to deliver large quantities of armored vehicles to him. Thus, in order to break through the Soviet defense, even back at the beginning of April, he had decided to rely on a different "instrument", than did E. von Manstein – infantry, reinforced with artillery, self-propelled guns and combat engineers. This approach remained unchanged right up to the beginning of the Battle of Kursk. Thus, in measure with the strengthening of the Central Front's defensive lines, just like the commander of the Fourth Panzer Army *Generaloberst* H. Hoth, he was mainly disturbed by the question: "Would the first echelon troops be capable of breaching the main and second belt of the Soviet forces, to that the panzers could enter operational space?" That was because in order to develop a success into the depth of the Soviet defenses, after overcoming the most strongly fortified sector of the defense, Model already had the minimum number of armored vehicles for that task by May. However, to ensure the overrunning of the lines of the Central Front, he considered it extremely necessary to give his forward units just those heavy tanks (well-armored and with a powerful main gun), which would in the first stage of the offensive, clearing the way forward for the infantry, destroy the permanent fortifications and enemy armor in case of counterattacks. As of 3 May 1943, he didn't possess a single armored vehicle like that, although back in April, the OKH command had promised to deliver Tigers to him by the end of the month. Therefore W. Model was not simply demanding more armored vehicles because the Russians already had one and a half more, but was insisting on receiving heavy fighting vehicles like the Tiger, the Panther and the Ferdinand heavy tank destroyer, which as he believed would be more effective in the first days of the operation.

In addition, as the captured documents I discovered in the US National Archives testify, for the commander of the Ninth Army, together with the acquisition of breakthrough means, the question of bringing up the infantry divisions to an acceptable strength was no less significant, because they were seriously depleted in manpower.[25] The situation with replacements was so aggravated and at the same time important, that because of the lack of a way to resolve it, the OKH on 20 April 1943 had first postponed the start date for the Kursk offensive.[26] Therefore *Generaloberst* Model had attached an aerial reconnaissance photograph to his letter, which would plainly demonstrate

25 NARA, T.312. R.317.F.7886042, 7886046.
26 NARA, T.312. R.317. F.7886050.

the scale of the work on the fortifications of the Soviet defenses, and would thereby prompt Hitler either to cancel the offensive, or to make an operational decision regarding replacements for the infantry divisions and the delivery of heavy armor.

Thus it is difficult to agree with the assertion that Model would have been ready to take part in the Kursk offensive already in May, had he known the real number of tanks in the Central Front. *Generaloberst* Model was an opponent of Operation Citadel. He was one of the few who not only understood its lack of prospects, but what was equally important, was not afraid to speak openly about this to Hitler, clearly arguing for his position.

It wouldn't be accurate to state that the restoration of the combat strength of the Central and Voronezh Fronts in the first half of May 1943 went without a hitch. All of the information in the above-cited reports from headquarters shouldn't be taken literally; if it was written that men and equipment had arrived in the Front, that doesn't mean that they had been immediately distributed to the operating formations and units. A certain amount of arms and equipment, marked as received by the *fronts*, were still only located in its supply dumps or were on their way to the railroad stations where they would be unloaded. For example, on 11 May N.F. Vatutin reported to the *Stavka*:

> The forces of the Voronezh Front are ready to carry out their defensive assignments. All of the rifle divisions of the 38th, 40th, 6th Guards and 7th Guards Armies, with very few exceptions, each have 8,000 or more men. The 69th Army has divisions numbering 6,000-7,000 men. The divisions of the 35th Guards Rifle Corps[27] are fully up to strength. The main portion of arms has arrived by railroad in the last few days. Thus the bulk of the weapons will be issued to the troops by the end of 14.5.1943.
>
> Another nine trains carrying arms are still on the way via railroad, which will be received by the troops in the period 18-20.5.1943. After this, the troops will have: 100 percent of their authorized mortars, anti-tank rifles, PPSh submachine guns and regimental artillery, 74 percent of their rifles, 57 percent of their light machine guns, 65 percent of their Maksim heavy machine guns, 71 percent of their 45mm anti-tank guns, 80 percent of their 76mm divisional artillery, and 70 percent of their 122mm howitzers.
>
> ... The divisions of the 69th Army will also be brought up to not less than 8,000 men each by 20.5.1943. The tank units and formations have almost all been brought back up to their authorized table strength.

Nevertheless, already by the middle of May, all of the forces of the Voronezh Front had been brought to a high degree of combat readiness, while its command was so confident in its own strength (not without justification) that it even presented a proposal to the *Stavka* to go on the offensive first in the area of the Kursk salient. Writes Marshal of the Soviet Union A.M. Vasilevsky:

> After the first warning [Author's note: On 8 May about the possibility of the start of the enemy offensive], when it wasn't confirmed, the Military Council of the Voronezh Front saw hesitation in this, and perhaps, even the enemy's rejection of going on the offensive, and asked the Supreme High Command to decide the question about the utility of launching a preemptive attack. I.V Stalin took very serious interest in this proposal, and it cost us – Zhukov, Antonov and me – a lot of effort to persuade him not to do this.[28]

27 The Front commander's reserve.
28 A.M. Vasilevsky, *Delo vsei zhizni, Kn. 2* [Cause of an entire life, Book 2] (Moscow: Politizdat, 1988), p. 24.

The Central Front command at a meeting with a delegation from Kazakhstan. In the center is General of the Army K.K. Rokossovsky, the Commander-in-Chief of the Central Front; April 1943 (RGAKFD)

A squad of the 13th Army's 70th Guards Rifle Division at work on building an earth and timber bunker; Central Front, 12 June 1943 (RGAKFD)

IL-2 "Sturmovik" ground attack aircraft at one of the factories in the Urals being prepared for departure to the front in the spring of 1943 (Photograph by P. Otsup, RGAKFD)

A line of new 45-mm anti-tank guns being towed toward the front; Central Front, May 1943 (RGAKFD)

Mechanics at one of the army repair shops work on an engine in field conditions; Voronezh Front, spring of 1943 (RGAKFD)

Artillerymen carrying boxes of shells from temporary field dumps; Voronezh Front, April 1943 (Author's personal archive)

SU-122 self-propelled artillery crews prepare their machines for departure to the front in the Urals city of Nizhnyi Tagil, May 1943 (Photograph by P. Otsup, RGAKFD)

Commander-in-Chief of the Voronezh Front General of the Army N.F. Vatutin on a visit to the troops. The general and his adjutant (seated in the back seat) are wearing coveralls that were specially sewn before the Battle of Kursk in order to conceal shoulder straps and other distinguishing signs of the Front's command ranks while located at the front; July 1943 (Photograph by A. Kislov, RGAKFD)

It is difficult to imagine that the Front's leadership, understanding that its forces were still not ready for combat, showed such initiative, when the *Stavka* wasn't insisting on this, and on the contrary, considered such a step premature.

Concluding the examination of the question regarding the combat readiness of the Soviet forces at the beginning of June 1943, I believe it important to emphasize once again: having taken the preliminary decision on 12 April to assume the strategic defensive, and having determined the probable axis of the enemy's main attack, the Soviet Supreme Command in the course of one month re-equipped and replenished the forces that were defending the Kursk bulge, especially those armies that were operating on the main directions. As had been planned, by 10 May the strength of Rokossovsky's and Vatutin's groupings according to two of the most important indicators – in manpower and artillery – exceeded 80 percent of the number they would have on 5 July (and respectively 40 percent and 74 percent of the armored vehicles). By 5 June, the total number of personnel of the Central and Voronezh Fronts exceeded 98 percent of the level they would have a month later, while the receipt of artillery neared 90 percent, and the quantity of tanks and self-propelled guns varied between 72 percent and 76 percent of the number on 5 July 1943.

Thus, both Fronts were essentially ready for the German Kursk offensive by mid-May. For example, by this time the Ninth Army still hadn't received that minimum number of armored vehicles that had been promised to it before Operation Citadel. Its infantry divisions and panzer formations had still not been brought back up to full strength in men and equipment and were incapable of handling the tasks of the summer campaign. But the Soviet side already in May was capable of repelling an attack by the forces available to the enemy. Thus E. von Manstein's assertion that Red Army forces opposite Army Groups Center and South were not fully combat-ready by the end of May looks far from the historical truth.[29]

Soviet strategic reserves – the Steppe Military District – played a substantial role both in the successful conclusion of the Kursk defensive operation and in the victory at Kursk as a whole. I will remind the reader that three of its five ground armies – the 5th Guards Tank, the 53rd and the 5th Guards Armies, actively participated in repulsing Army Group South's offensive in the Voronezh Front sector. Thus, for a complete analysis of the stated problem, it is extremely important to understand in what condition these troops were in the examined period. The *Stavka* of the Supreme High Command began to form these reserves in February 1943. However, because of the reversals in the course of the offensive into the Ukraine, the completion of this process, which is to say the unification of the forces into a military district, occurred only after the stabilization of the front on the southwestern direction.

On 4 April 1943, the deputy chief of the General Staff Lieutenant General A.I. Antonov sent the commander of the 41st Army an order from the USSR People's Commissariat of Defense: by 15 April to form the command of the Reserve Front (after 15 April 1943, the Steppe Military District) on the basis of the army's headquarters.[30] Two days later, though, I.V. Stalin signed a document that was addressed to the deputy commander of Southwestern Front Lieutenant General M.M. Popov, with a seal that was quite rare for that time: "Totally secret. Only personal. In your own hands". It stated:

> The *Stavka* of the Supreme High Command orders:
>
> 1. To form the Reserve Front by 30 April 1943. The dislocation of the Reserve Front's field headquarters in the Voronezh area.

29 E. Manstein, *Poteriannye pobedy*, p. 543.
30 TsAMO RF, F.240, Op.2779, D.6, L. 57.

2. To appoint Lieutenant General M.M. Popov as commander of the Reserve Front, relieving him of his post as deputy commander of the Southwestern Front. To authorize Major General F.P. Ozerov to carry out the duties as chief of staff of the Reserve Front.
3. On the list of the Reserve Front, include:
    a. Field command of the Reserve Front, deployed on the basis of the 41st Army's field command according to Table No.02/240;
    b. 2nd Reserve Army;
    c. 24th, 53rd, 66th, 47th and 46th Armies;
    d. 5th Guards Tank Army;
    e. 1st, 3rd and 4th Guards Tank Corps, and the 3rd, 10th and 18th Tank Corps;
    f. 1st and 5th Mechanized Corps
4. Report on the execution of this order.[31]

In the first stage of the *front's* (district's) formation, two main tasks stood before its command: to assemble the armies in the areas of dislocation indicated for them by the end of April and to begin building them up to table strength. Moscow was placing great hopes on its reserves in the coming summer campaign. Thus, their staffing and equipping became a high-priority matter. For this purpose, a special overseer from the State Defense Committee, Politburo member M.I. Mikoian was appointed, who had not only sweeping powers, but also high organizational skills. By the indicated time, all of the district's forces were in their designated locations and some had even begun combat training. After the resolution of the high-priority tasks, the *Stavka* demanded that the reserves be brought up to table strength in the course of May and to conduct the breaking-in of the combat units and subunits, so that by 1 June the district would be fully ready to conduct combat operations, both on the defensive and on the offensive. From 1 to 15 May, training went on at the platoon, company and reinforced battalion level, and from 16 to 31 May – exercises at the regiment level.

In addition, in the last month of spring, it was planned to change the district's composition substantially. By the end of May 1943 it was to have five armies (the 4th and 5th Guards Armies and the 27th, 47th and 53rd Armies), one tank army (the 5th Guards Tank Army) and one air army (the 5th Air Army), as well as three tank corps (3rd and 4th Guards Tank Corps and the 10th Tank Corps), three mechanized corps (the 2nd and 3rd Guards Mechanized Corps and the 1st Mechanized Corps), and three cavalry corps (the 3rd, 5th and 7th Cavalry Corps). It was with this grouping that it entered the Battle of Kursk. All of the above indicated tasks were primarily competed within the designated deadlines.

Unfortunately, information on the numerical strength of the Steppe Military District by the beginning of May still hasn't been found. As M.I. Mikoian asserted, all of its armies were to be "brought up to strength, armed and supplied with all types of allowances by the following deadlines: 2nd Reserve (63rd) Army and 24th (4th Guards) Army – by 15 April; 66th (5th Guards) Army – by 20 April; 46th and 53rd Armies – by 25 April; 27th Army – by 30 April; and 47th Army – by 10 May."[32] As already mentioned above, the procurement of the *Stavka* reserves went according to a high-priority schedule, thus their requests for men were carried out even before the requests of the Central Front and Voronezh Front commands. On 1 June 1943, the difference in the level of staffing with troops between the forces deployed around the Kursk bulge and the reserves varied between 10 and 15%. Thus it is possible to assume that the deadlines given

31 TsAMO RF, F. 240, Op. 2779, D. 285, LL. 35, 36.

32 A.I. Mikoian, *Tak byli: Razmyshlenie o minuvshem* [*As they were: Thoughts on the past*] (Moscow: Tsentpoligraf, 2014), p. 490.

by Mikoian for the main types of weapons and personnel were met. If by 10 May the numerical strength of Rokossovsky's and Vatutin's groupings according to the two most important indicators for defense – manpower and artillery – they exceeded 80% of the indicators for 5 July, whereas Popov's Steppe Military District, the 10 May indicators were between 90 and 95% of those for 5 July. Substantial problems in the district might have arisen only with armor, since the losses in armor of the acting army by the start of the muddy season were very high. In his memoirs Mikoian indicates that by 25 April, all of the Steppe Military District's 10 total tank corps were on average equipped with 60% of their men, 38% of their weaponry, and 60% of their equipment.[33] Thus I can assume that if by 10 May the tanks on the Central and Voronezh and Fronts numbered 40% and 74% respectively of their authorized numbers, then in the Steppe Military District this figure was probably somewhere between 65% to 70%. For the beginning of June 1943, extensive data has not only been found for the district as a whole, but for each of its armies as well. According to M.M. Popov's report to I.V. Stalin dated 1 July 1943, only 6,000 men were lacking to bring the troops up to their authorized number, of which it was planned to send 2,000 to the rifle divisions and 4,000 to the tank and mechanized formations.[34] Accordingly, if it is considered that by the start of the fighting the numerical strength of the Steppe Military District was 573,295 men, including 449,130 in the combat units, then it was essentially staffed with 100% of its manpower.

With artillery the situation was also normal. The overwhelming majority of its units had been brought up to table strength, but were still short:

30 45mm anti-tank guns (8 more were already en route)
37 76mm regimental cannons (47 more en route)
17 122mm howitzers (8 more en route)
71 37mm anti-aircraft guns (18 more en route)

However, for several types of artillery, the number available was already quite above table strength. For example, for 76mm Model 1942 divisional cannons, authorized strength was 1,595 cannons, but already 1,616 were present and 20 more were en route. For 50mm mortars, these figures are 2,359, 2,487 and 80 respectively; for 82mm mortars, 4,460, 4,596 and 98 respectively; and for 120mm, 1,820, 1,894 and 79 respectively.[35]

More significant, but far from critical problems at that time existed with armor, as well as with units of combat reinforcement, support and reserve. By 3 June, the district still hadn't received 433 tanks and self-propelled guns (including 233 T-34 and 196 T-70), which amounted to 25.6% of their authorized table strength.[36] The individual tank corps still hadn't received the following elements:

10th Tank Corps – its medical-sanitation platoon and tank reserve;
18th Tank Corps – its tank reserve;
3rd Guards Tank Corps – its tank reserve;
4th Guards Tank Corps – its field bakery and tank reserve;
1st Mechanized Corps – its self-propelled artillery regiment, anti-aircraft regiment and tank reserve;

33 Ibid., p. 494.
34 TsAMO RF, F.240, Op.2779, D.285, LL.49,50.
35 TsAMO RF, F.240, Op.2779; D.285, L.20.
36 TsAMO RF, F.240, Op.2779, D.285, L.13.

2nd Guards Mechanized Corps – its self-propelled artillery regiment, mortar regiment, signals battalion and tank reserve;
3rd Guards Mechanized Corps – its self-propelled artillery regiment, mortar regiment, destroyer anti-tank artillery regiment and tank reserve.[37]

However, all of these problems didn't have any large effect on the combat capability of those three armies, which would be fated to take part in foiling "Citadel" in July 1943. For example, by TO&E the rifle divisions of the 53rd and 5th Guards Armies were each to have 56,000 soldiers and officers. By 1 July 1943, they respectively numbered 55,796 (and another 1,449 had already been allocated) and 53,303 (a train carrying another 2,500 men was already on the approach to it).[38]

The 5th Guards Tank Army was also practically fully staffed and equipped, although it had certain problems. I will remind the reader that from the middle of March to 5 July 1943 inclusively, it had only two corps: the 29th Tank Corps and 5th Guards Mechanized Corps; although Moscow was promising to return his "native" 3rd Guards Kotel'nikovo Tank Corps to Rotmistrov, it was never transferred to the 5th Guards Tank Army. On 6 July, before the march to the Voronezh Front, instead of the 3rd Guards Tank Corps the 18th Separate Tank Corps was added to the tank army. Thus for the analysis of the army's condition, given below, data will be used for this formation, as well as for the 10th Tank Corps from the 5th Guards Army, which already on 7 July 1943 would be shifted to the south of the Kursk bulge (to the Prokhorovka area).

The 5th Guards Tank Army by TO&E was supposed to have 37,231 service personnel; on 1 July it had 35,302, or a shortage of 1,929 men (5% of table strength). For several types of guns (76mm divisional artillery, 122mm howitzers) and mortars (50mm and 82mm), 4 to 13 of each had yet to be received by the troops (although all of this materiel was already en route), while for certain weapons systems (120mm mortars and 45mm anti-tank guns), the 5th Guards Tank Army was already above authorized strength by anywhere from 4 to 10 tubes/barrels.[39]

Significant more armor was still lacking, but not in Rotmistrov's tank army itself, but in the Steppe Military District's separate corps, which would operate together with it on the Voronezh Front. On 3 July 1943, the shortage of tanks and self-propelled guns amounted to:

29th Tank Corps: T-34 – 4, M3A1 scout cars – 19;
5th Guards Mechanized Corps: T-34 – 2, M3A1 scout cars – 3;
Other combat units of the army: T-70 – 3;
18th Separate Tank Corps: T-34 – 35, T-70 – 7, M3A1 scout cars – 14;
10th Tank Corps: T-34 – 32, T-70 – 7, M3A1 scout cars – 8.[40]

Accordingly, if before the 5th Guards Tank Army's entry into combat on 12 July 1943, in the three corps (the 18th Separate and 29th Tank Corps and 5th Guards Mechanized), the separate motorcycle and tank regiments, Rotmistrov's tank army had a total of 690 combat machines (without self-propelled guns), then the 48 tanks missing on 3 June in the 18th, 29th Tank Corps and 5th Guards Mechanized Corps amounted to only .07% of this total, while at the same time the SS Corps on 1 June 1943 had yet to receive 21% of the tanks it had on 4 July.

37 TsAMO RF, F.240, Op.2779, D.285, L.18.
38 TsAMO RF, F.240, Op.2779, D.285, L.43
39 TsAMO RF, F.240, Op.2779, D.285, L.75
40 TsAMO RF, F.240, Op.2779, D.15, L.13.

So in conclusion I'll note that in M.M. Popov's letter to Stalin, among the most substantial problems that he cited was the large shortage of horses, 28,000, including 26,000 for the cavalry corps, and the rest for the rifle divisions. However, considering that the cavalry corps took no part in repulsing the German offensive toward Kursk, this problem has no bearing on the discussed subject.

Thus, both the entire Steppe Military District and its separate armies, which played an important role in the defensive phase of the Kursk battle, were practically fully prepared for fighting by 1 June 1943, and possessed approximately the same number of main weapons and personnel as they would have by 5 July 1943 – about which, judging from the assertions of a number of German commanders, the leadership of the Third Reich didn't even suspect. At the same time it must be acknowledged that over the subsequent month of June, the level of training of the Steppe Military District's personnel unquestionably increased, and the problems with staffing and equipping, mentioned above, were also resolved.

Now let's touch upon another important aspect of the subject under examination. It was not only the condition of our forces in the Kursk area that notably contributed to the failure of Operation Citadel, but also the skillfully constructed, deeply-echeloned defenses. Although the German general and Western scholars almost never point to this factor as the decisive one in the Wehrmacht's failure, I nevertheless consider it important to stop here and give it brief consideration. If the main efforts of both N.F. Vatutin and K.K. Rokossovsky in May-June 1943 are analyzed in detail, it is clear that they were directed toward improving the defensive lines and training the troops to use them effectively. There were also serious objective reasons for this. For example, as the inspections conducted in the first half of May by commissions sent from the General Staff testify, almost all the work on the first and second lines in the armies' main belt of defenses in the Voronezh Front's sector had been completed. As concerns the second and third belts, here the commissions found substantial, although not critical shortcomings in their construction and layout (light mine-laying in the zone between the belts, shallow trenches, poor camouflage, etc.), which had already to a significant degree been eliminated by the beginning of June. For example, prior to 5 May the 6th Guards Army had managed to deploy only 17 percent of its 90,000 anti-tank mines and 16 percent of its 64,000 anti-personnel mines, which nevertheless were all emplaced by 5 July. In the 7th Guards Army, the given indicators were also extremely low on 16 May, though higher than its neighbor's: approximately 22.4 percent of its 65,000 anti-tank mines and 16.9 percent of its 84,000 anti-infantry mines had been laid.[41] Yet by 5 June, this situation had also sharply changed: the 6th Guards Army had carried out the 50 percent of the plan regarding anti-tank mines and 62 percent of the plan regarding anti-personnel mines. The corresponding figures for the 7th Guards Army were 46.2 percent and 35.7 percent respectively.

It should be emphasized that the inadequate number of mines deployed in May is not evidence that the tank-vulnerable directions in the lines of the Central and Voronezh Fronts were open for enemy armored vehicles to exploit. By 5 May the plans for mining the area in front of and within the main army belt had been realized. Problems with laying mines remained in the zone between the belts, and well as within the second and third belts. The reasons for this are covered, firstly, by the spring thaw, which greatly hindered the work, and both the transport and the sappers, and secondly, by the inadequate supply of explosive agents. From the end of April, Moscow was tardy in deliveries, and the *front* commands were actively seeking out internal reserves, primarily relying on captured materiel – German shells and mines. However, even here there arose a lot of difficulties, including more than a few connected with subjective factors. On 18 June 1943, the Chief of

41 TsAMO RF, F.38A, Op.9022, D.5, L.21.

the Red Army's Engineering Troops Lieutenant General M. Vorob'ev issued Order No.49, which stated in part:

> On 23 May, a temporary stockpile of anti-tank mines belonging to the Voronezh Front exploded in the area of Voronezh. Representatives of the Voronezh Front had concentrated 2,700 anti-tank mines in this stockpile. ... German T-35 anti-tank mines were being transported without the actuating device, but with exposed openings in the tops and with the detonating charges positioned inside. The explosion occurred due to careless handling of the mines while unloading them. The workers hadn't been instructed, had no knowledge of the explosive mechanism or the amount of care required when handling it. The command staff didn't organize the work or direct it. With the explosion, 2,700 mines and 2 trucks were destroyed, and 7 service personnel and 15-20 civilians who were located in the vicinity of the stockpile were killed, since the chosen location of the dump was next to a main road that was carrying a lot of traffic.[42]

Nevertheless, by the beginning of summer, the readiness of the defensive system of both *fronts* was in the neighborhood of 70 percent.

For "experimental integrity" it would be helpful to compare other indicators as well, such as the Soviet troops' availability of ammunition, fuel and lubricants, etc. This is a task for future research. However, all of the information presented above, if examined in its entirety, allows one to assert with confidence that after 1 June 1943 any further postponement of the start of "Citadel" didn't have any fundamental significance for the Red Army, just as incidentally it didn't already in the beginning of May. Both German assault groupings at the base of the Kursk bulge were incapable not only of surpassing the Central and Voronezh Fronts in the numbers, I repeat, that are a necessary condition for the success of an offensive according to military theory, but even to approach their strength in manpower, armor and artillery. Even more so, in the rear, behind Rokossovsky's and Vatutin's forces, major reserves of the *Stavka* of the Supreme High Command, aggregated into the Steppe Military District, were already deployed in May.

Thus, under no condition could German count upon a victory at Kursk, not in May nor in June, and the post-war assertions of the German commanders and their supporters about the possibility of "Citadel's" success, had the attack been launched at the beginning of the summer of 1943, are only putting a brave face on a sorry business. Arguments in favor of this point of view, which are met in Western historical literature, including those that cite *Feldmarschall* von Manstein, prove unfounded given a detailed analysis of the documentary sources.

Indeed, even the *Feldmarschall* himself acknowledged that the Wehrmacht command was mistaken in its assessment of the combat capabilities of the Soviet forces at Kursk, and after the war he highly praised the work that the military-political leadership of the USSR did in the run-up to the 1943 summer fighting, including Operation Citadel. In his memoirs, he wrote that the German command hadn't expected from the Soviet side such great organizational capabilities which it demonstrated in this matter, as well as in the development of its military industry. He called the Red Army a "true hydra", which in place of one lopped-off head would grow two new ones.[43]

42 TsAMO RF, F.69A, Op.10751, L.11, Ll.37, 38.
43 Manstein, *Poteriannye pobedy* [*Lost Victories*] (Smolensk: Rusich, 2003), p. 546.

5

Did Vatutin err when planning the defense of the Voronezh Front while preparing for the Battle of Kursk?[1]

A previous version of this chapter was published as an article in the Journal of Slavic Military Studies, Vol. 28 (No. 4, 2015). This chapter updates the article with some new information obtained from the Russian Federation Ministry of Defense's Central Archive.

In the history of the Great Patriotic War, as well as in the history of the Second World War as a whole, the Battle of Kursk by rights occupies a special place. After 50 days of intense, bloody fighting, having destroyed a powerful enemy grouping, the Red Army had once and for all seized the initiative on the Eastern Front and never yielded it right up until the final victory in May 1945. The patriotism of the Soviet people, which is based upon the deep traditions of defending the Motherland that stem from the very origins of the Slavic states and their struggle with foreign aggressors for independence, was the decisive factor in this success. However, over the entire postwar history, in our country this decisive battle had never received complex, and more importantly, objective analysis. Even so, arguments regarding certain key questions have persisted for decades. One of the key questions of the history of the Battle of Kursk, around which domestic scholars have not been able to come to a unified opinion, is: "Why, despite the fact that Moscow knew of Berlin's plans to pinch off the Kursk bulge, were the Wehrmacht forces still able to make a penetration of 12-15 kilometers in the Red Army's defenses on the northern face of the salient, but in the south – a penetration of up to 35 kilometers, as a result of which there arose a threat of dispersing the Soviet strategic reserves?" In private conversations or even at official conference sessions with veteran generals of the war, this question hasn't once been raised since the latter half of the 1950s, but it was only mentioned for the first time in the open press in the book *Velikaia Otechestvennaia voina 1941-1945.Kratkaia istoriia* [*The Great Patriotic War 1941-1945. A short history*]:

> What explains the fact that even with a quantitative superiority over the foe in both men and equipment at the start of the defensive battle, the Voronezh Front was unable with its available forces to wear down and bleed white the enemy shock grouping and halt its offensive without

1 This article was prepared with the financial assistance of the Russian Humanitarian Academic Fund (RGNF), Academic Project No.15-01-00150.

> the need for additional forces? Unlike the Central Front, the Voronezh Front command was unable to determine precisely where the enemy's main blow would fall. It extended its preparations in a sector that was 164 kilometers wide, and failed to amass its strength and means on the axis of the enemy's main attack.[2]

A direct participant in those events, the former Deputy Supreme Commander and Marshal of the Soviet Union G.K. Zhukov didn't agree with this assessment. In an excerpt from his memoirs published in 1967 in the "Voenno-istoricheskii zhurnal" ["Military-history journal"], he weighed in on the matter and evaluated the results of the combat work of the Voronezh Front in the first stage of the Battle of Kursk with complete objectivity, tossing aside assertions that suggested that its commander General of the Army N.F. Vatutin made a mistake when planning the system of defense and the allocation of forces. He wrote:

> There is criticism ... that the Voronezh Front command settled upon an inaccurate calculation of the density of the [enemy's] strength and means in the specific conditions of the operational-strategic situation. ... But it mustn't be forgotten that the enemy on the first day launched his attack against the Voronezh Front's 6th and 7th Guards Armies with almost five corps (the II SS Panzer Corps, III Panzer Corps, XXXXVIII Panzer Corps, LII Army Corps and Army Detachment Raus), while at the same time against the defense of the Central Front with three corps. It is easy to grasp the difference in the strength of the attacks of the German forces from the Orel direction and out of the Belgorod area.[3]

However, already at the end of September 1967, this article drew an unexpectedly sharp reaction from the former commander of the Central Front Marshal of the Soviet Union[4] K.K. Rokossovsky – not in the open press, but in a letter sent to the chief editor of "Voenno-istoricheskii zhural" V.A. Matsulenko after the publication of Zhukov's article. You rarely encounter such an emotionally intense document that is at the same time so far from the historical truth. The arguments presented by K.K. Rokossovsky contradict the real events, which were by then already known to many:

> The enemy attack grouping activated against the Voronezh Front consisted of 14 divisions, of which 5 were infantry divisions, 8 were tank divisions, and one was a motorized division, while the attack grouping activated against the Central Front consisted of 15 divisions: 8 infantry, 6 tank and one motorized. Thus, if the enemy grouping operating against the Voronezh Front was somewhat superior in the number of tanks, his grouping operating against the Central Front was significantly superior in the amount of infantry and artillery.
>
> The more successful operations of the Central Front are explained not by the number of enemy troops, but by the more correct arrangement of the defense.[5]

This is a very debatable assertion. Probably it slipped K.K. Rokossovsky's mind that his *front* by 5 July 1943, even in the assessment of Soviet historians, had 2,740 more artillery barrels than did

2 *Velikaia Otechestvennaia voina 1941-1945. Kratkaia istoriia* [*Great Patriotic War 1941-1945. A Brief History* (Moscow: Voenizdat, 1965), p. 244.

3 Zhukov, G.K., *Vospominaniia i razmyshleniia* [*Reminiscences and Reflections*] (Moscow: Novosti, 1969), pp. 490-491.

4 At the time of the Battle of Kursk K.K. Rokossovsky held the command rank of General of the Army (awarded 28.04.43).

5 "Voenno-istoricheskii zhurnal, No. 3 (1992), p. 31.

the Voronezh Front,[6] while the German Army Group South operating against Vatutin's troops had 1.5 times more armored vehicles than did the assault grouping of the Ninth Army that attacked south of Orel. Altogether, not 14 German divisions were committed against the Voronezh Front, but 17. At the same time, the adversary hurled only 15 full-strength divisions against his Central Front.[7] Moreover, their level of manning and equipment differed: on the northern shoulder of the Kursk bulge, it was lower, whereas in the south – higher. To illustrate this I will cite only two facts. For example, the German 10th Motorized Division operating with the Ninth Army had no armor and its effective fighting strength numbered 4,322 personnel, whereas the SS Panzer Grenadier Division *Das Reich* had 7,350 men[8] and 116 tanks.[9] Opposite the Voronezh Front was also the strongest Wehrmacht formation of all those that took part in Operation Citadel, the *Grossdeutschland* Panzer Grenadier Division. On 4 July 1943 in numbered 112 tanks,[10] but it had reinforced with the 10th Panzer Brigade that had 200 Pz V Panther tanks.[11] The same situation was observable with the infantry formations as well. For example, the Ninth Army attacked on the main axis with the 6th Infantry Division and with the 73rd Assault Division on a secondary axis. On 4 July 1943, they had an effective combat strength of 3,121 and 4,545 men respectively.[12] I will note that the 73rd Assault Division was the strongest division in the entire Ninth Army with respect to effective combat personnel. Meanwhile, in the Fourth Panzer Army that attacked toward Kursk from the south along the Oboian' axis was the 167th Infantry Division (on the main axis of attack) and Army Detachment Kempf's 106th Infantry Division, which numbered respectively 6,776 and 6,577 men.[13]

The arguments of the two marshals became an interesting source of historical information for scholars, but only today, since in the 1960s they were inaccessible in their entirety for specialists and the broader community. "Competent organs" weren't interested for this argument between two highly respected commanders in the country to become known to broad society, and without looking into the essence of the matter, sought to stifle it, and all the documents, even the aforementioned letters,[14] lay under the seal "For official use only". Even so, no matter how odd it might seem, not everything was deleted from the memoirs of both Marshals of the Soviet Union. As a result a reader was given the possibility to know K.K. Rokossovsky's position, which he subsequently laid out in detail in his memoirs, whereas it is impossible to scrutinize the opinion expressed by G.K. Zhukov of those events, because he didn't dwell on them. Thus, the opinion regarding a supposed "mistake made by Vatutin" when preparing for the Battle of Kursk became entrenched in the public conscience.

Operational and account documents of both Soviet *fronts* for 1943, which have been recently declassified in the Central Archive of the Russian Federation's Ministry of Defense, allow the analysis of this problem in detail, with the use of documents that were previously known to a narrow circle of individuals at the Red Army's highest command level.

6 *Istoriia Vtoroi mirovoi voiny 1939-1945* [*History of the Second World War 1939-1945*) Volume 7 (Moscow, 1976), p. 155.
7 National Archives and Records Administration USA (NARA), t.314, r.988, f.000148-000155.
8 NARA, t.314, r.493, f.172260843.
9 N. Zetterling and A. Frankson, *Kursk 1943: a statistical analysis* (London: Frank Cass, 2000), p. 186.
10 Ibid., p. 186.
11 NARA, t.313, r.368, f.8654350
12 NARA, t.312, r.332, f.7890973 and f.7890975,
13 NARA, t.314, r.493, f.172260843.
14 K.K. Rokossovsky's letter was first published in the open press only in March 1992.

For example, when working out the concept of the Kursk defensive operation, the work on which began in the middle of April 1943, N.F. Vatutin had to resolve several important and at the same time complex tasks:

- Determine the most likely directions of the enemy's main and secondary attacks;
- Prepare a plan of actions for the Front's forces with the aim of the unconditional resolution of the task given by the *Stavka* of the Supreme High Command: To stop the enemy within the tactical belt;
- Work out a principle scheme for the concentration of strength and construction of defensive lines in order to block the enemy's offensive.

His neighbor, K.K. Rokossovsky faced all these same questions as well, but N.F. Vatutin was in a more difficult situation from the outset. In order to contain the forces of Army Group South within the tactical zone, it was necessary to create a high density of strength and means in it.[15] But it was precisely this that he lacked. In the sector of the Central Front, there were only three probable directions of attack that constituted a total of 95 kilometers (or 31% of Central Front's sector of defense), where the foe, having launched the offensive, might create a serious threat. In contrast, on the southern face of the Kursk bulge, the enemy was able to use not less than four directions that constituted 164 kilometers (or 67% of the Central Front's sector of defense). At the same time, both commanders received similar quantity of troops and heavy weapons: on 5 July 1943 the Central Front had a combat strength of 467,179 men[16] for a defensive front that extended 306 kilometers, whereas the Voronezh Front correspondingly had 417,451 men[17] to defend 245 kilometers of front. With fewer men and less certainty about where the enemy might strike, the cost of an error in Vatutin's prognoses was significantly higher than it was for Rokossovsky. This forced Vatutin to approach the planning of the defenses more exhaustively and creatively, and use every possibility in full in order to strengthen his lines of defenses.

Lacking the possibility to create a high tactical density on all the probable directions of the enemy's main attack without the use of reserves, N.F. Vatutin decided to increase the defense's resilience at the expense of raising the operational density,[18] including by the way of increasing its depth in the center and on the Front's left flank. The plan of defense devised by him was complex and multi-tiered. He had not one, but two initial tasks:

a. To stop and bleed white the enemy in the tactical zone in powerful army-level belts[19] (initially it was demanded of the troops to contain the Germans within the first two belts).
b. To prepare favorable conditions (first of all, by creating a suitable staging area) for the deployment of assault forces with the aim of going over to a counteroffensive toward Khar'kov and further on to the Dnepr.

---

15 "Tactical density – the saturation of a specific sector of the front with troops and combat equipment, as expressed by the quantity of battalions, tanks, guns and other types of combat gear per 1 kilometer of front. (*Kratkii slovar' operativno-takticheskikh i obshchevoiskovykh terminov* [*Concise dictionary of operational-tactical and multi-service terms*] (Moscow: Voenizdat, 1958).

16 TsAMO RF, f.203, op.2843, d.426, l. b/n.

17 TsAMO RF, f.62, op.321, d.138, l. b/n.

18 "Operational density – the average density of a force grouping on a specific operational direction (or within the boundaries of a strategic unit)." *Kratkii slovar' operativno-takticheskikh i obshchevoiskovykh termin.*

19 According to the *Stavka* plan, in order to hold the Kursk bulge it was planned to construct 3 army-level belts of defense, 3 *front*-level belts of defense, and one State line of defense along the Don River.

For a point of reference, General of the Army Vatutin adopted two at this moment obvious conditions. Firstly, the enemy's main aim in the first stage of the offensive should be a breakthrough to the Kursk area. In a report to I.V. Stalin dated 21 April 1943, he wrote:

> The enemy's intention is to deliver concentric blows from the Belgorod region to the northeast and from the Orel region to the southwest in order to surround our forces located west of the Belgorod, Kursk line .... Thus, opposite the Voronezh Front, the enemy will probably spearhead his main offensive from the Borisovka, Belgorod region in the direction of Staryi Oskol, with part of his forces moving on Oboian' and Kursk. Secondary attacks are to be expected along the Volchansk, Novyi Oskol and Sudzha, Oboian', Kursk axes.[20]

Thus, stemming from the Voronezh Front's battle deployment, one might expect the main blows to fall on his center and left flank, or more concretely: against the 40th Army's defenses, at the boundary between 40th Army and the 6th Guards Army, against the 6th Guards Army or its boundary with the 7th Guards Army, as well as at the boundary between the Voronezh and Southwestern Fronts.

Secondly, three areas were most suitable for the operations of the foe's mobile formations:

- along the main road running between Belgorod and Oboian' (the Oboian' highway);
- along the line: Belgorod – Iakovlevo – Prokhorovka – Mar'ino;
- the interval of ground between the Northern Donets and Razumnaia Rivers, from Belgorod in a general direction toward Korocha and further on toward the village of Skorodnoe

Resting on this assessment, the Voronezh Front commander proposed that most likely of all, the antagonist would attempt with panzer wedges supported by large aerial forces to smash the line of Lieutenant General I.M. Chistiakov's 6th Guards Army: [excl.] Trefilovka, Voskhod, southern fringe of the woods southwest of Cherkasskoe, southern outskirts of Trirechnoe, Zadel'nyi ravine, Lapin ravine, southern outskirts of Berezov, Gremuchii, Erik, Shopino, Hill 211.6, grove east of the Home of Invalids, Chernaia Poliana[21] (the main attack), and the line of Lieutenant General M.S. Shumilov's 7th Guards Army: Shishino – Staryi Gorod – Corrective Labor Colony – Bezliudovka – Volchansk [excl.][22] (secondary attack). Accordingly, the width of the sector where the main attack could be expected amounted approximately to 111 kilometers or 46.3% of the Front's defensive sector according to the layout of the forward edge.

Flowing from this, Vatutin worked out the following scheme for deploying the Front's forces. It was proposed to make the main efforts to strengthen the left flank (a sector of 164 kilometers), in order to block all possible axes of the main and auxiliary attacks. Vatutin proposed to position three combined-arms armies here in the first echelon (the 40th, 6th Guards and 7th Guards Armies). They were to occupy two of the army-level belts of fortifications. In the third belt of the 6th and 7th Guards Army (on the Prokhorovka and Korocha directions), the 69th Army was to be deployed, and behind it, in the first front-level belt (along the line Krivosheevka – Stolbishche), the reserve 35th Guards Rifle Corps.

In addition, it was planned to concentrate all of the mobile (the 2nd Guards and 5th Guards Tank Corps) and anti-tank reserves on the Front's center and left flank. As a result, of the 35 rifle

20 Glantz, D., House, J., *Kurskaia bitva: Reshaiushchii povorotnyi punkt vtoroi mirovoi voiny* (Moscow, 2006), p. 389. This is the Russian translation of their book *The Battle of Kursk* (University Press of Kansas, 1999) and the cited passage can be found on p. 365.

21 TsAMO RF, f.335, op.5113, d.235, l. 6.

22 TsAMO RF, f.203, op.2843, d.386, l. 2.

divisions that were subordinate to N.F. Vatutin, he proposed to concentrate 22 of them on the Oboian' and Korocha directions. This would result in an average of 10 kilometers of front per division along the entire front, and on the axis of the main attack – 5.2 kilometers per division. In addition, Chistiakov's and Shumilov's armies were to be given 44 of the 70 available artillery regiments of reinforcement (68%), 50% of the 6 tank brigades and 10 tank regiments dedicated to direct infantry support, and 8 of the 11 Guards mortar regiments of Katiusha rocket launchers (73%).[23]

Thus, in order to hold the most important directions, it was planned to bring forward a total of 63% of the rifle divisions, from 50% to 73% of the tank and artillery/mortar means, and to occupy four fortified belts to a depth of up to 60 kilometers (from the first line of trenches of the main army-level belt to the last line of trenches of the front-level line) with the forces of the armies of the first strategic echelon and the Front's reserves. Such a significant spacing was determined by the complex local topography. The interval between each of the army-level belts (the inter-belt zone) on different directions substantially fluctuated (as a rule, expanded). Because of this, intermediary lines were planned (and then constructed) in the center and on the right flank. They were one of the particular features of the system of field defenses on the southern face of the Kursk bulge, since Rokossovsky's front didn't have any such intermediary lines.

The Central Front would also follow the same path of force concentration, but the tactical density here was even greater. K.K. Rokossovsky would make colossal assets and means available to Lieutenant General N.P. Pukhov's 13th Army, which was defending the most probable axis of the main German attack, and would also direct his main reserves to him. Pukhov's troops would also occupy four defensive lines (three army-level belts and the first front-level line). But due to differences in the terrain, the interval between the defensive belts would be approximately half as much of that between the comparable lines on the Voronezh Front. Thus the depth of the defenses on the axis of the most likely attack here would be not 60 kilometers, but 30 kilometers. Moreover, due to the 13th Army's narrow front of defense (32 kilometers) and the enormous strength concentrated in the hands of its commander (12 divisions), it would have very high tactical density, on average just 2.7 kilometers per rifle division.

K.K. Rokossovsky writes:

> In the threatened sector, where knowing the Germans' tactics, we were expecting the enemy's main attack would fall on a front with a width of 95 kilometers, 58% of the rifle divisions, 70% of the artillery and 87% of the tanks and self-propelled guns were concentrated. ... The second echelon and the Front's reserves were also located on the axis of the main enemy grouping's likely offensive.[24]

Thus, both Front commanders used one and the same principle of arranging the defense on the likely axis of the enemy's main attack, but the means varied: K.K. Rokossovsky was creating its depth only focused on the 13th Army, while N.F. Vatutin supplemented the strength of the 6th Guards and 7th Guards Armies with Front reserves. Indeed, it could be no other way, because all of the planning went under the control of a single center – the General Staff, and all of the fundamental questions were decided there. Indeed only after its approval did the Front leadership have the right to propose its own plan of defense to the *Stavka*.

23 *Bitva pod Kurskom: Ot oborony k nastupleniiu* [*Battle of Kursk: From the defense to the offensive*] (Moscow: AST. Khranitel', 2006), p. 48.
24 "Voenno-istoricheskii zhurnal", No.3 (1992), p. 31.

A sector of the rear defensive belt of the armies of the Voronezh Front in the area of Prokhorovka Station, June 1943 (TsAMO RF)

Nevertheless, in the arguments that developed after the war regarding "Who fought better at Kursk?" K.K. Rokossovsky used precisely the difference in means with the aim of proving that he and his headquarters, having created Pukhov's "super army", with the forces of which all three probable axes of main attack were being covered, acted correctly, while N.F. Vatutin, drawing upon his reserves in order to create operational density, supposedly acted rashly, since he scattered his strength across the entire 164-kilometer sector and failed to create the necessary density there, where the enemy actually struck. However, when doing so, he kept silent about the fact that it was impossible to do this due to objective reasons. Rokossovsky insisted, "The correct determination of the most dangerous direction of an enemy offensive for the Front's forces, and accordingly the grouping of forces and the maneuvering with forces and means in the process of the battle were the main factors for the more successful operations of the Central Front, than of the Voronezh Front, where the primary, main forces of this Front were equally distributed across this entire sector."[25]

This is to say that in Rokossovsky's opinion, N.F. Vatutin should have moved up part of the strength of the 69th Army and the 35th Guards Rifle Corps from the rear *front*-level line of defense to the army-level lines, in the rear of the first-echelon armies, in order to create high tactical density. This, in his opinion, should have stopped the Germans already within 10-15 kilometers of their start line, as happened in the course of the battle on the northern shoulder of the Kursk bulge.

25 Ibid.

From a prepared trench, a battalion commander is studying the ground out in front of one of his companies' positions; Central Front, May 1943 (Photography by E. Kopyt, RGAKFD)

However, this approach was unsuitable for the situation as it existed on the Voronezh Front, since here a more powerful enemy grouping was operating than on the Central Front, and Rokossovsky had considerably more artillery than did N.F. Vatutin. It isn't understandable why, when calculating the density of defense[26] in the sector of the 13th Army, its divisions, which were covering all three directions of possible enemy attack and located in all four defensive lines (three army-level and one front-level), in K.K. Rokossovsky's opinion, should be counted, while when making the same calculations in the sector of the Voronezh Front the troops of the 69th Army and 35th Guards Rifle Corps should be excluded, even though they, like Pukhov's divisions were occupying the rear army-level belt and the first *front*-level line, covering the main axis of the enemy's attack – the Oboian' and Korocha directions.

Unquestionably, formally the commander of the Voronezh Front didn't use his reserves according to their direct designation. There existed a rule: if these were "pure" reserves, then they mustn't be tied to concrete sectors of the defense, since at any time they might be needed to localize an enemy breakthrough or to reinforce a dangerous direction. However, the war required a creative approach to the operational art, and moreover there were weighty reasons for such a decision. In the first place, the *Stavka* of the Supreme High Command assigned enormous reserves to the Voronezh Front according to the standards of those times not coincidentally, but because it had more tank-vulnerable directions in its sector than the Central Front. Secondly, it is right to assume that it was

26 Density of defense is the degree of saturation of a defense with troops and weapons. Under its definition, tactical density and operational density differ.

the Front commander's right to manage them as he saw fit, and he prudently decided that it wasn't justified to create a high tactical density with the forces of the 69th Army and 35th Guards Rifle Corps on the most critical directions, since given if the need arose in the course of the fighting, it would be impossible to remove them from there. Vatutin believed that it would be precisely more effective to use them to create operational density (meaning, I repeat, to strive for depth in the defenses). Here they might play a duel role: both to hold an occupied line in the event of an enemy breakthrough to their positions, and at the same time they could be quickly shifted to different sectors; after all, they comprised the Front's second strategic echelon, the forces of which according to the calculations shouldn't be immediately engaged in battle.

The motives behind General of the Army Vatutin's recommendations become more understandable, if you consider the important detail that at the moment when he was working out this variant, Moscow still hadn't decided whether it should attack or defend in the course of the summer campaign. Until the end of April, in addition to the 69th Army and 35th Guards Rifle Corps, N.F. Vatutin only had two mobile formations under his command, the 2nd Guards and 5th Guards Tank Corps,[27] which might be used only for flank counterattacks, but nothing more than that. Then he received a more serious force – the 1st Tank Army. However, the *Stavka* of the Supreme High Command immediately banned its use directly in the defensive fighting, other than in an extreme case, given a deep enemy penetration, since the *Stavka* was preparing to use it for an offensive into the Ukraine. In fact, it was only at the end of May 1943, when Moscow finally determined its plan for the summer campaign, that the mobile reserves would be included in the plan of defense, with the assignment of a concrete line to them. Thus if N.F. Vatutin had concentrated the 69th Army and 35th Guards Rifle Corps on vulnerable directions in order to create tactical density, as Rokossovsky had done (having subordinated his reserve 18th Guards Rifle Corps to the 13th Army),[28] he simply would have deprived himself of the greater portion of reserves – the primary lever of influence over an operational situation. On the eve of the forthcoming operation, this would have knowingly meant dooming himself to defeat – especially if the enemy undertook not one, but two powerful attacks against his defensive front, as N.F. Vatutin assumed the Germans would do. Both G.K. Zhukov and A.M. Vasilevsky, who actively participated in the development of the plan for the overall Kursk defensive operation for the Central and Voronezh Fronts, were in agreement with Vatutin's proposals regarding the allocation of forces and means.

Resting on the conception of a system of defense that has been laid out above, N.F. Vatutin proposed the following plan of actions for his troops in variants. In his opinion, when working out this document it had been absolutely necessary to resolve two key questions. First, it was necessary to prevent a deep penetration by the enemy in the Front's defense in the initial, most dangerous days of the enemy offensive, and to contain his mobile formations within the tactical zone. It should be noted that N.V. Vatutin immediately (in April) and with great accuracy calculated the size of the German panzer grouping that would be attempting to break through his Front's sector of defense: " … It should be anticipated that the enemy might create a shock grouping in strength of up to 10 panzer divisions and no less than 6 infantry divisions, altogether up to 1,500 tanks, the concentration of which should be expected in the Borisovka – Belgorod – Murom – Kazach'ia Lopan' region."[29]

On the basis of intelligence data it was assumed that these forces would be gathered together in the beginning of May, when the muddy season ended and the foe would be ready for an offensive.

27 TsAMO RF, f.203, op.2843, d.425, l. 48.
28 TsAMO RF, f.62, op.321, d.4, l. 150.
29 Zhukov, *Vospominaniia i Razmyshleniia*, Volume 3 (Moscow: APN, 1990), p. 20.

Let's recall that for the realization of "Citadel", in Operational Order No.6 from 15 April 1943, Army Group South was given 7 infantry and 9 panzer and motorized divisions,[30] and by the beginning of July 1943, Manstein's forces would include a little more than 1,500 tanks and assault guns.

Secondly, Vatutin had to wrestle with the problem of reducing the penetrating power of the German assault groups not only through the attrition of their armor and personnel by the fire of the first and second echelon, but also with the question of how to compel the enemy command to scatter the shock power of his panzer wedges across the entire front, and not concentrate them at the spearhead of the main attack.

When resolving these questions, N.F. Vatutin primarily counted upon relaying on his important "ally" – the terrain. The successful exploitation of this important factor, both when preparing for the Battle of Kursk and during the course of the summer fighting, was one of the characteristic aspects of his commander's "signature". The sole instance when he was forced to ignore the terrain characteristics in the course of the counterstroke at Prokhorovka led to tragic consequences. The highlight of his plan was the idea of splitting the combat wedge of Army Group South, directed at Kursk, by means of creating a powerful center of resistance on the joint flanks of the two shock groupings of Army Group South (the Fourth Panzer Army and Army Detachment Kempf). N.F. Vatutin assumed that Manstein's main grouping would assemble in the Tomarovka – Belgorod area and would launch the main attack to the north, in the direction of Oboian', or to the northeast, toward Prokhorovka Station (the Fourth Panzer Army), while Army Detachment Kempf would launch a secondary attack from Belgorod to the east in the direction of Korocha. A breakthrough along the Oboian' highway was the shortest path to Kursk, while at the same time here was a fine opportunity to rebuff the offensive firmly, if correct use was made of the terrain, particularly the basins of the Vorskla, Pena, Donets and Psel Rivers as natural anti-tank obstacles. However, no one could be confident that E. von Manstein would move his main forces toward Oboian'.

In order to induce the enemy to launch the main attack directly along the Oboian' highway and to mire his main grouping in the Front's defenses there, where it was most advantageous to the Soviets (and a breakthrough in the first days was practically unavoidable), N.F. Vatutin employed a military subterfuge, which to a civilian might seem most cynical. The Voronezh Front commander proposed to array the regiments of the frontline divisions of the 6th Guards Army, which was blocking the Oboian' direction, in a single echelon, while those of the 40th and 7th Guards Army, on the flanks of the 6th Guards Army would be deployed in two echelons. In other words, Vatutin was creating a greater tactical density of forces on the flanks of the 6th Guards Army, than had Chistiakov's army in the center on the Oboian' highway. At the same time, it was planned seriously to reinforce the 40th and 7th Guards Armies. The 40th Army on the right of the 6th Guards Army would be given just as much strength and means as had the 6th Guards Army, while the defense of the 7th Guards Army on the left already had a strong natural barrier – the Northern Donets River; even so the Front directed much of its mobile and anti-tank reserves to its sector. In this fashion, Vatutin was simultaneously striving to show German intelligence that the Oboian' direction was objectively the most suitable point for the main attack toward Kursk, since the operational density of the Soviet forces here wasn't as great, and at the same time he was preparing the creation of a powerful line for I.M. Chistiakov's neighbors, in case the enemy struck not toward Oboian', but toward Korocha (through the 7th Guards Army's sector) or toward Sudzha (through the 40th Army's sector). This unusual detail of the Voronezh Front's system of defense – the low tactical density of forces on the most likely axis of the enemy's main attack, and the relatively high tactical density of the 6th Guards Army's neighbors, the 40th Army and 7th Guards Army – was first observed by the Soviet military historians G.A. Koltunov and B.S. Solov'ev in their book *Kurskaia*

30 Parot'kina, I.V. [ed.], *Kurskaia bitva* [*The Battle of Kursk*] (Moscow: Nauka, 1970), pp. 520-522.

bitva [*Battle of Kursk*]. However, they didn't offer any reasons for it, but only remarked that this decision "… corresponded to the existing situation."[31]

Consequently, from the outset the Front commander was sacrificing at a minimum the two rifle divisions that were deployed at the Oboian' highway (the 52nd Guards Rifle and 375th Rifle Divisions), subjecting them to overwhelming attack of a significantly superior enemy. German reconnaissance flights and patrols could not fail to perceive the "brittleness" of Chistiakov's front-line divisions. Thus, Vatutin had to know that on the first day, even if they weren't completely destroyed, their losses would prove to be very high. However, this approach is one of the most widespread stratagems in the arsenal of military commanders. Moreover, the Front commander would do everything that depended on him to create an elaborate system of defenses for the units in this sector and to strengthen the divisions, in order to keep their losses down in the first hours of fighting.

However, "to lure" the adversary to the Oboian' direction – this was only half the matter, while the main thing was to ensure that the German forces became bogged down in this area and unable to make a further advance to the north. The analysis of documents found in the TsAMO RF reveals the following principle scheme to block the Fourth Panzer Army.

For a successful advance of the attacking forces into the depth of the Soviet defenses it was important that both of Manstein's groupings (the Fourth Panzer Army and Army Detachment Kempf) progressed at the same rate and maintained a single, unified front. This would permit the economical use of the forces, concentrating them at the spearhead of the attack, and make difficult the maneuvering of the defensive forces and means; in other words, create the conditions for the rapid overrunning of the lines of the 6th Guards and 7th Guards Armies and the expansion of the breakthrough corridor, which is extremely important in the first days of an offensive. Accordingly, it was necessary to mire the main assault grouping (the Fourth Panzer Army) within the system of the main defensive belt of Chistiakov's army, and to contain the German mobile formations within it for as long as possible, while knocking out the armor with all types of weapons. For this, the following measures were planned:

First, to assign the greatest amount of artillery and other anti-tank means of reinforcement to the 6th Guards Army, and to stuff its sector (primarily the main belt of defenses) with as many engineered obstacles as possible, thereby creating a model of the contemporary field fortification with regard for combat experience and innovative developments, so that the 6th Guards Army's forces would be able to resist the enemy for as long as possible, while inflicting losses on the attackers and gaining the time necessary to bring up the operational reserves.

Second, considering that the initial blow would be the strongest, while Chistiakov's frontline divisions were deployed "in a thread", as the Russians say, it was assumed that they might hold their positions for no longer than 24 hours. Thus it was decided to move up Lieutenant General M.E. Katukov's 1st Tank Army to the second belt of defenses of the 6th Guards Army already on the second, no later than the third day; in essence, it was to become the third echelon of Chistiakov's army. Katukov's three tank and mechanized corps were to strengthen the defense in the bend of the Pena River and like an "armored shield" block the tank-vulnerable "corridor" between the Pena and Lipovyi Donets Rivers (along the line: Syrtsevo – Izotovo woods – Iakovlevo – Bol'shie Maiachki) through which the Germans would be advancing from Belgorod to the north (toward Oboian'), and possibly to the northeast (toward Prokhorovka). Accordingly, there can be no talk about any factual weakening of the 6th Guards Army. A third echelon hadn't been planned for any of the Front's armies, much less a mechanized one, on both of the likely Oboian' and Prokhorovka axes (given the need it was proposed to shift the 5th Guards Tank Corps to this area as well).

31 Koltunov, G.A., Solov'ev, B.S., *Kurskaia bitva* [*Battle of Kursk*] (Moscow: Voenizdat, 1970), p. 55.

In addition, the commander of the 40th Army Lieutenant General K.S. Moskalenko was instructed to work out the details of several planned strong counterattacks on his left flank in the direction of the 6th Guards Army's sector. As soon as the enemy broke through the first echelon of the 6th Guards Army on the Oboian' axis, Moskalenko's forces would strike the left flank of the attacking German grouping. It was precisely for this purpose (together with the defense of the Sudzha direction) that the 40th Army commander was given significant amounts of artillery and tanks designated for direct infantry support. By their quantity, his army was in third place among all of the Voronezh Front's six armies.

Depending on how the situation developed, simultaneously with the 40th Army Lieutenant General V.D. Kruchenkin's 69th Army would prepare to launch a counterattack (from the Front's second echelon) against the right flank of the German grouping aimed toward Oboian'. In this fashion, N.F. Vatutin was proposing: On the second or third day of the fighting, Army Group South's shock grouping on the Oboian' axis should be embedded in the armored shield of the 1st Tank Army, while its flank units, squeezed by the basins of the Vorskla and Donets Rivers, would be caught in the powerful pincers created by the 40th and 69th Armies. In addition, the Germans would be still be engaged in heavy fighting with the 6th Guards Army's forces as well.

The Soviet command didn't have precise data on the forces that Army Group South would assemble for launching the main attack, and thus there remained the danger that the enemy might even be able to advance through the "corridor of fire" created by the four armies. In order to reduce this chance and to ensure that the Germans would not be able to develop the tactical success of a breakthrough in the lines of the 6th Guards Army's second echelon into an operational success, it was extremely important to contain firmly the secondary attack made by Army Detachment Raus, which in N.F. Vatutin's calculations would strike the 7th Guards Army east of Belgorod in the direction of Korocha. Given a collapse of its offensive, even the Manstein's significant forces on the Oboian' axis wouldn't be able to reach operational space within a relatively short time. Two primary factors would be affecting this: German losses in the course of the breakthrough and simultaneously the need to detach substantial forces in order to cover the flanks, which would become increasingly extended as the main attack grouping advanced.

However, all this might work only in the event that the enemy would be unable to commit major reserves once a breach had been created in the 6th Guards Army's main defensive belt. However, even this possibility was thoroughly considered, and the Voronezh Front also prepared large reserves in case it took place. Nevertheless, if simultaneously with the approach of Army Group South's significant reserves its secondary grouping hadn't been stopped by the 7th Guards Army, then naturally the Soviet's operational, and possibly its strategic reserves as well, would begin to dissipate. In such a case, the defensive operation would be following the worst-case scenario and have heavy consequences. Thus it followed that it was critically important to prevent both of the German groupings (the Oboian' and Korocha) from unifying into a single "shock" fist, and to separate them already in the first days of the offensive, in order to force Manstein to expend forces to cover not two flanks (in case Army Detachment Kempf was able to join with the Fourth Panzer Army into a unified assault grouping), but four flanks (of the two groupings on the Oboian' and Korocha directions, if kept apart).

N.F. Vatutin proposal to tackle this problem was two-fold. First, he would firmly strengthen the line of the 7th Guards Army along its entire front, in order to prevent any possibility that Army Detachment Kempf could keep pace with the advance of the German grouping on the Oboian' axis, in the event that the Germans were able to overcome the 6th Guards Army's main belt of defenses. Second, he planned to create an insurmountable obstacle on the boundary between the 6th Guards and 7th Guards Armies, and to repel the secondary attack made by Army Detachment Kempf not only with the forces of the 7th Guards Army, but also those of the 69th Army (or from its positions with the Front's reserves).

A strike at the boundary between two formations is the most widely-adopted and effective approach to create a breach when on the offensive. The Voronezh Front commander resolved to use it as well when on the defense. He took into account that behind the forward edge of the frontline divisions of the 6th and 7th Guards Armies was a relatively impassable swampy area – the confluence of the Severskii and Lipyvi Donets Rivers. Thus, it was here that he established the boundary between the 6th Guards and 7th Guards Armies, and then planned to strengthen this sector (Erik – Chernaia Poliana – Staryi gorod – Labor Corrective Colony): as already noted, the divisions here were deployed in two echelons, and they had received a lot of additional artillery. By the end of June 1943, in the two divisions on either side of the boundary between the 6th Guards and 7th Guards Armies (the 81st Guards Rifle and 375th Rifle Divisions), a density of 19-23 guns per linear kilometer had been created.[32] No other sector of the Voronezh Front had such a high concentration of artillery. In addition, as the General Staff was also demanding, their commands additionally and specially assigned impressive forces – tanks, artillery and combat engineer elements – to cover the boundary between the two armies. These units were instructed to work out in a very short period of time plans of counterattacks and cooperation between themselves in case of a German breakthrough.

However, the strengthening of this area didn't end with these measures. N.F. Vatutin was also planning to assemble the 69th Army between the basins of the two rivers in order to cover the same boundary between the 6th Guards and 7th Guards Armies. As a result, this natural obstacle – the interval between the Severskii and Lipovyi Donets Rivers, which had the form of an inverted wedge with its tip pointed at the forward edge of the Soviet defenses, would be converted through the efforts of Kriuchenkin's troops into a triangular-shaped, fortified focal point of resistance. Two echelons of rifle units, the large artillery grouping of the 81st Guards Rifle and 375th Rifle Divisions, and other assets were readied to be deployed in front of the tip of this fortified triangle. Accordingly, Vatutin assumed that if the Germans proved unable to crack the boundary between the 6th Guards and 7th Guards Armies, they would be forced to try to bypass it, which means the united front of Manstein's advancing shock grouping would split apart into two independent directions. If the adversary attempted to penetrate into the depth of the 6th Guards and 7th Guards Armies, the right flank of his main (Oboian') grouping and the left flank of his secondary (Korocha) grouping would be exposed to counterattacks by the 69th Army and Voronezh Front's mobile reserves.

Initially (in April 1943), it was being proposed to activate only the two separate tank corps (the 2nd Guards and 5th Guards Tank Corps), which Vatutin possessed at that time, for counterattacks together with Kriuchenkin's 69th Army. However, as already mentioned above, at the end of May 1943 the *Stavka* would make the decision to employ tank armies as well directly in the defense of Kursk. For this, Katukov's 1st Tank Army would go to Voronezh Front, and General of the Army Vatutin immediately issued an order to it to develop various plans for counterattacks in close cooperation with the separate tank corps within the framework of the overall plan. This step would become an important supplementary element, which would in fact give the Soviet side confidence in "Vatutin's plan" (on the main directions) and, unquestionably, increase the Voronezh Front's defensive resilience as a whole.

It was further assumed that once Army Group South had been stopped, the 6th Guards Army and 1st Tank Army, with the support of part of 69th Army, would simultaneously with the 40th Army split the German grouping on the Oboian' direction into separate pieces, while part of the Front's reserves in cooperation with the 7th Guards Army would launch a parallel attack

32 Zamulin, V.N., *Zabytoe srazhenie Ognennoi dugi* [*Forgotten battle of the Fiery bulge*] (Moscow: Iauza, 2009), p. 24.

against the German Korocha grouping. After the elimination of both of Manstein's groupings, the Voronezh Front together with the *Stavka*'s strategic reserve in the form of the Steppe Military District, which had been brought up by that time, were to launch a decisive counteroffensive through Belgorod and Tomarovka into the Ukraine.

Considering that the 7th Guards Army was defending the likely axis of the enemy's secondary offensive, as well as the fact that the Northern Donets River provided a natural barrier in front of its lines, N.F. Vatutin allocated significantly fewer artillery means to M.S. Shumilov, than he did to I.M. Chistiakov, but at the same time he gave the 7th Guards Army more infantry-support tanks (by their count, the equivalent of more than a tank corps), and directed part of his mobile (the 2nd Guards Tank Corps) and anti-tank reserve to its sector. On the whole, this army received impressive forces in order to carry out its assignment.

The forward edge of the 69th Army, which had deployed already in April behind the boundary between Shumilov's and Chistiakov's armies, ran along the line: Bogoroditskoe, Vypolzovka, Alekseevka, Nechaevka, Belyi Kolodez', Bol'she Troitskoe, Belianka, Efremovka. Three main tasks were given to it.[33] First, it was to hold its line and repel possible enemy attacks. Second, in the event of a breakthrough in the sectors of the 6th Guards and 7th Guards Armies or the retreat of their flank divisions, in cooperation with their troops and the Front reserves it was to destroy the enemy that had broken through. Third, in the event of a successful repulse of the German attack by the armies standing in front of it, the 69th Army was to be ready for an offensive and develop the success in three directions: Tomarovka – Graivoron – Aktyrka; Belgorod – Khar'kov; or Volchansk – Khar'kov.

However, there was the problem that Kriuchenkin's army initially was the weakest in the Voronezh Front. Even the reforming and replenishing of its divisions hadn't been completed by the time of the start of the Battle of Kursk. Vatutin assumed this would be the case, and back at the end of April he ordered Lieutenant General S.G. Goriachev, the commander of the 35th Guards Rifle Corps, to arrange cooperation with the 69th Army's headquarters, so that at any moment it could be operationally added to it. The 35th Guards Rifle Corps' positions were located 15-25 kilometers behind the line of the 69th Army, and thus seemingly amounted to the latter's second defensive belt. Goriachev's Guards corps had three rifle divisions. Although they had formed up only in April 1943, by the start of the fighting they had been brought up practically to table strength. In addition to the 35th Rifle Corps, already during the course of the 69th Army's combat operations, it was planned to strengthen it out of the Front's reserves.

N.F. Vatutin did everything possible in order to reinforce Kriuchenkin's army and therefore believed that the 6th Guards and 7th Guards Armies, having taken on the enemy's initial attacks, in cooperation with the 1st Tank Army would inflict serious losses to the Germans, and the 69th Army should encounter enemy divisions that had already become worn out and bled dry by the previous fighting. Thus it would be fully capable of fulfilling the tasks that had been given to it: to become a barrier at the boundary of the 6th Guards and 7th Guards Armies, and become a flank battering ram in the event of a German breakthrough of their covering flanks. However, this portion of Vatutin's plan proved to be the most weakly considered. The expectations regarding the tenacity of Kriuchenkin's and Goriachev's troops proved to be too great, including for subjective reasons. The command staff of their divisions, which had become activated in the spring of 1943, proved unable not only to carry out combat assignments, but in a number of instances even unable to execute their basic duties.

"Vatutin's plan", as it has been laid out above, until recent times was unknown to historians. The opportunity to grasp the Voronezh Front commander's conception emerged only after recently

33 TsAMO RF, f.426, op.10753, d.410, ll. 17-18.

unsealed documentary sources at the army and *front* level in the archives of the TsAMO RF had been analyzed. Possibly, therefore even today certain Russian scholars are continuing to adhere to K.K. Rokossovsky's point of view regarding N.F. Vatutin's "mistake" and even to elaborate on it. In their opinion, the 40th Army's large quantity of forces and means prior to the Battle of Kursk is confirmation of the incapability of the Voronezh Front's leadership to determine the axis of von Manstein's main attack. Thus it spread its forces thinly across all of the tank-vulnerable axes.[34] In reality, by the number of personnel and armaments, the armies of Moskalenko and Chistiakov were practically equal, but this doesn't contradict the plan of the Voronezh Front commander. After all, in a letter dated 21 April 1943, he expressed the opinion that the Germans might launch not the main attack, but a secondary attack in the sector of the 40th Army.[35] Considering that N.F. Vatutin had laid an additional task on K.S. Moskalenko to divert a portion of the enemy's strength from the sector of the 6th Guards Army, this army's substantial reinforcement was fully justified.

Nevertheless, I will stress once again that the line of the 6th Guards Army always looked like the most dangerous place, against which Army Group South might launch its main attack. Moreover, these assessments didn't remain only on paper. The point of "Vatutin's plan" about moving up all of the Front's mobile reserves – the 1st Tank Army and the 2nd Guards and 5th Guards Tank Corps – to this army's sector after the start of the fighting is evidence of this. According to the personal order from the Front's chief of staff Lieutenant General S.P. Ivanov, at the end of May their commands were to reconnoiter movement routes and conduct night-time marches of the brigades precisely into the sector of Chistiakov's army.[36] A forward command-observation post for Lieutenant General M.E. Katukov would be prepared in the sector of the 6th Guards Army's 52nd Guards Rifle Division, while the full 1st Guards Tank Brigade would be dug into the ground in the vicinity of Iakovlevo in the 6th Guards Army's second belt of fortifications in the role of a forward detachment of the 1st Tank Army's 3rd Mechanized Corps. Nothing similar was done in the 40th Army's sector.

Moskalenko's 40th Army from the beginning had an important task: together with the defense of its own sector (the possible direction of a secondary offensive), with counterattacks it was to contribute to containing the enemy grouping that had attacked against the 6th Guards Army, as well as if the need arose to detaching divisions to it to reinforce the Oboian' axis. Jumping somewhat ahead of the events, I will note that N.F. Vatutin's practical steps already in the course of the defensive operations support this conclusion. For example, between 5 and 15 July, he withdrew only 5 units and formations from the 38th Army, of which only one was a rifle division and two were tank brigades, to reinforce the 6th Guards Army's sector, but 16 from the 40th Army, including three rifle divisions, one anti-aircraft division, and eight tank and destroyer anti-tank artillery brigades.[37] In addition, even the weakened 40th Army would take part in the Soviet counterattack on 8 July 1943, conducting if only "demonstration" attacks, but nevertheless the successful counterattacks against the left flank of the Fourth Panzer Army went according to plans that had been worked out back when preparing for the battle. Incidentally, in the account of the 40th Army headquarters on the combat actions of 8 July 1943, the plan of an attack into the flank of the enemy's Oboian' grouping (in the direction of Tomarovka) with the aim of diverting German forces away from the 6th Guards Army's sector, which had previously been worked out and accepted by the Voronezh Front's leadership, and the reasons for the failure to implement it both receive mention:

34 Isaev, A.V., *1943-i: Ot Khar'kov do Kurska* [*1943: From Khar'kov to Kursk*] (Moscow: Veche, 2008), p. 193.
35 Glantz and House, *Kursk Battle*, p. 390.
36 TsAMO RF, f.203, op.2843, d.426, l. 134.
37 Parot'kina [ed.], *Kurskaia bitva*, p. 315.

> The agreed-upon question of an attack toward Tomarovka with a shock grouping of troops from the left wing of the 40th Army, after almost all of the means of reinforcement and one rifle division[38] had been removed from it, at an order from the Front headquarters on 8 July 1943 was changed to demonstration actions on this same axis with two rifle divisions. With an order from the army commander, the commander of the 52nd Rifle Corps Major General Perkhovich was directed to conduct this operation … from 10.00 8.7.1943.[39]

Finally, during an analysis of N.F. Vatutin's decisions (and, incidentally, Rokossovsky's as well) regarding key questions of preparing for the Kursk battle, two important aspects, which can help avoid mistakes in the assessments of his actions, should always be kept in mind.

First, the commander of any *front* operates with only those forces and means that the *Stavka* has given to him based on its own view of the operational situation, which unfortunately doesn't always correspond with reality. The "gulf" between two concepts: "needed for resolving assignments" and "what the *front* already has" should be bridged by the talent of the commander in organizing and conducting battle, as well as by increasing the stress on the troops. However, often the forces necessary were often beyond what the commander had available to him, and this was not recognized by higher command, while the personnel was often at their physical breaking point. K.K Rokossovsky prior to the Battle of Kursk practically had no such "gulf"; he was given everything necessary for the defense, and even more, while N.F. Vatutin's would be "off the charts", beyond all sensible margins (due to Moscow's miscalculations in determining the main axis of the enemy's attack in the area of the Kursk bulge)[40] Indeed, none of the General of the Army's or his subordinates' outstanding abilities were able to bridge this deficit. It was because of this that already on the second day of the German offensive, Moscow would be forced hastily to move entire corps and armies to the south, and not because N.F. Vatutin proved to be a short-sighted military commander, but because the troops of his Voronezh Front proved to be less stout than those of the Central Front.

Second, from 15 to 20 highly qualified (according to the measures of those times) military professionals of high rank took part in planning for the Kursk defensive operation. The Front headquarters prepared the documentation and agreed upon it with the *Stavka* representatives Marshals of the Soviet Union A.M. Vasilevsky and G.K. Zhukov, who in April-May 1943 spent more time among the *fronts* and armies in the Kursk area than it Moscow, and then the plans were thoroughly checked and analyzed in the General Staff. Only after this did the plans head to discussion in the Kremlin. Unquestionably, no one was safe from mistakes, but in such a "processing chain" the mistakes might only be very major, of a strategic nature. At the very least, the fact that that the operational density of forces in the sector of Chistiakov's army, which was defending the likely axis of the enemy's main attack, was lower than on its boundaries with its neighbors, or the fact that the 40th Army had more tanks than did the 6th Guards Army, was quite clear to those who worked out the plans. It was precisely with the availability and allocation of forces and means that the planning of any operation began. Yet if this process ended there, that means one should primarily look for motives, and not simply point to that fact and end there.

Thus, the entire plan of Vatutin was directed, from the first days of the enemy offensive, relying primarily upon the difficult local topography and the coordinated actions of all of the armies on the Front's left wing to split and attenuate the forces of the German shock groupings, and also to

38 These removals were implemented on 6 and 7 July 1943 in order to reinforce the 6th Guards Army and 1st Tank Army on the Oboian' axis.

39 TsAMO RF, f.203, op.2843, d.520, l. 220.

40 Zhukov, *Razmyshleniia i vospominaniia*, Volume 3, p. 37.

offset their qualitative superiority in armor over our forces. I will emphasize that the reliance given by the Front commander to the maximal exploitation of the terrain conditions, wound up being his sole correct decision not only when building the army-level belts of fortifications, but would cause the growing split in direction and pace that eventually developed between the Fourth Panzer Army and Army Detachment Kempf. Even though his plan wouldn't be fully realized due to the mistakes made by the *Stavka* of the Supreme High Command in determining where the main blow of the German attack toward Kursk would fall, his far-sighted vision and calculation would play a colossal role in the successful repulse of Army Group South's offensive.

6

With what forces did General W. Model begin the Battle of Kursk?

The composition of the Wehrmacht's assault grouping south of Orel prior to the start of the 1943 summer campaign

One of the least studied problems of Russian historiography regarding the Battle of Kursk is the question of the numerical strength of the German attack groupings and the combat strength of their subordinate formations prior to the Kursk offensive. This question is extremely important not only for understanding the overall intent of the Wehrmacht's summer campaign, including first of all, its key element – Operation Citadel – and determining the real capabilities of the force groupings activated to implement the operation, but also for assessing the contribution made by the armies of each of the six Soviet *fronts* that took part in thwarting the Germans' last strategic offensive in the East. There are two primary reasons that prevented our scholars from analyzing this question. Firstly, Soviet researchers from the beginning had no access to Western archives, since in the Soviet Union for ideological reasons the information they contained were considered *a priori* false. In the years 1946 to 1956, the military men who were compiling the best practices of the war with the aim of increasing the country's defensive capability were forced to use two groups of sources: captured German documents and materials of Soviet intelligence organs (the interrogation of prisoners, deserters and so forth). However, Wehrmacht documents, as a rule, did not fall into Soviet hands with any regularity, and thus were scattered and gave no overall picture of the events, while the interrogations of captured prisoners contained sparse information that was often unreliable. Meanwhile the information, for example, of the Red Army's special organs was distorted by dogmatic thinking and exaggeration of the enemy's strength. A particularly large amount of unreliable information came from the acting army's intelligence services in the war's initial stage, which forced the Soviet Supreme High Command to reorganize them twice (in the autumn of 1942 and in the spring of 1943).[1] Thus, prior to 1991, all of the Russian research on the Battle of Kursk was based upon sources in our own archives, and their reliability on questions regarding the Wehrmacht's forces was extremely low. Sometimes authors used information from publications of "ideologically close" or in the extreme case "neutral" Western authors, but they usually played only a supplementary role.

Secondly, when the possibility to work in foreign archives like, for example, the US National Archives, first appeared before Russian scholars in the 1990s, it turned out that significant time

1 See People's Commissar of Defense Order No. 0072 from 19 April 1943 (*Russkii arkhiv: Velikaia Otechestvennaia voina – Prikazy Narodnogo komissara oborony SSSR (1943-1945)* [*Russian archive: Great Patriotic War – Orders of the USSR People's Commissar of Defense (1943-1945)*] Vol. 13 (2-3) (Moscow: TERRA, 1997), pp. 127-129.

would be necessary for selecting, organizing and analyzing the large quantity of documents even on such a relatively simple question as the condition of the German forces at Kursk in the summer of 1943. Moreover, it proved problematic, first of all due to financial reasons, to obtain the all the sources necessary to conduct a comprehensive study.

Nevertheless, the first publications and monographs on this question began to appear in Russia at the beginning of the 2000s. However, these only touched upon the attacking armies of Army Group South – *Generaloberst* H. Hoth's Fourth Panzer Army and *General der Panzertruppen* W. Kempf's Army Detachment Kempf.[2] As is known, the German command planned to encircle the Central and Voronezh Fronts occupying the Kursk bulge with two meeting attacks. The southern grouping was formed north of Belgorod and after breaking through the Red Army's defense, it was to link up at Kursk with the northern grouping, attacking from the area south of Orel and consisting of *Generaloberst* W. Model's Ninth Army. Thus, in the course of the offensive all three army-sized formations played a key role.

In the summer of 1944, the German Ninth Army became trapped in a pocket at Minsk, and among the loot captured by Soviet troops was a large quantity of its combat documents, which later entered the Russian Federation's Central Archive of the Ministry of Defense. Today they comprise an impressive portion of its captured files. The rest were in part destroyed, but the bulk of them managed to be sent back to Germany by the Ninth Army's command, where they were subsequently captured by the Allies in 1945 and later sent to the US National Archives. The large batch kept in the Russian Ministry of Defense's Central Archive consists primarily of documents of an operational nature (from the headquarters' Operational and Intelligence Departments, which directly relate to combat operations), while there are practically no statistical materials or reports. Likely, this played a role in the fact that despite the availability of a large volume of sources for the Ninth Army for the year 1943, today in Russia we know about the combat potential of this Wehrmacht army both before and during the Battle of Kursk least of all.

For more than a decade I've managed to work in the US National Archives with materials of its captured files for the Second World War. In the course of this research, I've managed to uncover new, previously unpublished materials which provide the basis for this chapter.

For a more complete understanding of the question, I consider it important to make one important, in my view, clarification. During the preparations for Operation Citadel in the sector of Army Group Center, Berlin made a rather unusual decision for such a major offensive: it placed responsibility for it not on Army Group Center's commander-in-chief *Generalfeldmarschall* G. von Kluge, but on the commander of its subordinate Ninth Army W. Model, whose troops comprised the attack grouping south of Orel. The motivations for this step are not hard to discern. First was Hitler's special relationship with W. Model, who unlike most Wehrmacht generals openly displayed his Nazi convictions and his allegiance to its policies. Secondly, *Generaloberst* Model had demonstrated great tenacity and high professional qualities both when defending the Rzhev salient under difficult conditions for the Wehrmacht, and while withdrawing his army from the salient in March 1943. Thus Hitler decided that it was this general who would carry out the extremely controversial plan of Citadel, which in the spring of 1943 had divided the Reich's elite into two opposite camps. Moreover, it was important that *Generaloberst* Model had been a clear supporter of the plan from its initial phase of conception. There was one more deeply pragmatic aim. The Ninth Army commander had already been added to the list of candidates for leadership of an army

2 L.N. Lopukhovsky, *Prokhorovka bez grifa sektretnosti* [*Prokhorovka without the seal of secrecy*] (Moscow: Iauza/EKSMO, 2005); V. Zamulin, *Kurskii izlom: Reshaiushchaia bitva Otechestvennoi voiny* [Kursk turning point: Decisive battle of the Great Patriotic War] (Moscow: Iauza/EKSMO, 2007) and ibid., *Zabytoe srazhenie Ognennoi dugy* [*Forgotten clash of the Bulge of Fire*] (Moscow: Iauza/EMSMO, 2009).

group, and in the spring of 1943 Model had twice served an internship, carrying out the duties of the Commander-in-Chief of Army Group South while *Feldmarschall* E. von Manstein was convalescing in Germany. Thus, conducting such a major offensive as Citadel would be one more step in preparing him for a new, high post.

Feldmarschall von Kluge's formal removal from responsibility for preparing for the summer campaign didn't serve the German cause well. Although making Model responsible for the operation personally freed the von Kluge, who as a professional couldn't accept the operation's risks and murky prospects, from a significant portion of the problems connected with it, at the same time it wounded his pride and aggravated his already problematic relationship with the commander of the Ninth Army. All of this taken together extremely and negatively affected both the replenishment of the Ninth Army's forces after the winter fighting and the preparation of the attack grouping for the offensive toward Kursk, as well as keeping it supplied with everything necessary.

So, what was the combat and numerical strength of Model's forces on the eve of Operation Citadel? This question has been raised more than once in Russian and foreign literature, but a significant share of the data, cited in publications and monographs, differ even on basic indicators. Soviet historians as a rule used aggregate numbers either for the entire German grouping in the area of the Kursk bulge (that is to say, the Fourth Panzer Army, Ninth Army and Army Detachment Kempf), or for the entire Army Group Center, the troops of which were also defending the Orel bulge, without extracting the numbers for the Ninth Army. However, even here, there is no uniform opinion. For example, the authors of the first open Soviet work on the Battle of Kursk Colonels G.A. Koltunov and B.S. Solov'ev give an overall figure of "approximately 900,000" for the soldiers and officers of Army Groups South and Center, which were designated for Operation Citadel.[3] Meanwhile their colleagues from the Institute of Military History in the second volume of *Velikaia Otechestvennaia voina 1941-1945*, which came out in Russia in 1998, maintain that this figure was larger, "… more than 900,000",[4] while in their opinion Model possessed 22 panzer and infantry divisions under his command.[5]

At the beginning of the current century, Russian scholars continued to discuss this question fervently. In the book written by Candidate of Military Science L.N. Lopukhovsky, published in 2005, he asserts that "the northern group consisted of the Ninth Army and part of the Second Army …, altogether 26 divisions and 460,000 men."[6] But the work *Ogennaia duga* [*Bulge of fire*] by the already mentioned Institute of Military History, which came out in 2003, gives a different figure, which significantly varies from that given earlier by its colleagues – 24 infantry, 6 panzer and 1 motorized division with a total strength of 460,000 men.[7]

It should be noted that G.A. Koltunov, a veteran of the Battle of Kursk, was the only Soviet historian who for a long time persistently tried to calculate the numerical strength of Model's attack grouping – and not without success. According to his data, there were 160,000 soldiers and officers in the 10 divisions of the Ninth Army's first echelon, which went on the attack on 5 July 1943.[8] If you disregard the erroneous number of divisions that he provided and only add up the personnel of all of the Ninth Army's divisions that were actually located in the first echelon on that day, then the sum essentially dovetails with the real number, differing only by several hundred men. At the same time it must be taken into account that this estimation was made back at the

3 G.A. Koltunov and B.S. Solov'ev, *Kurskaia bitva* [*Battle of Kursk*] (Moscow: Voenizdat, 1970), p. 47.
4 *Velikaia Otechestvennaia voina 1941-1945, Tom 2: Perelom* [*Great Patriotic War 1941-1945, Volume 2: Turning Point*] (Moscow: Nauka, 1998), p. 257.
5 Ibid., pp. 254-255.
6 L.N. Lopukhovsky, *Prokhorovka bez grifa sekretnosti*, p. 27.
7 *Ognennaia duga* [*Bulge of fire*] (Moscow: Izdatel'skii dom Zvonnitsa-MG, 2003), p. 596.
8 *Voenno-istoricheskii zhurnal*, No. 6 (1968), p. 67.

beginning of the 1970s, only on the basis of captured documents from the Central Archive and Koltunov's own experience.

A number of foreign authors also took up this question, but even they haven't been able to answer it fully. For example, the well-known American specialists on the history of the Great Patriotic War D. Glantz and J. House in their book *The Battle of Kursk: The Decisive Turning Point of the Second World War* cite a practically reliable figure for Ninth Army's total strength at the start of the Battle of Kursk – 335,000 men, but it is difficult to work with this number.[9] It doesn't give a representation of either the numerical strength of the separate divisions or the combat strength of its assault divisions, and therefore it is difficult to grasp the shortages in men and equipment of both the entire army and its subordinate divisions. Thus, this figure doesn't help answer the questions: What was the actual combat strength of the forces that Model directly activated in the attack toward Kursk as a whole, and on the separate axes of attack in the course of attempting to break through Central Front's tactical zone?

The essential cause for the various figures is one and the same: the incomplete base of archival sources. Let's turn to the Ninth Army headquarters' reports to the command of Army Group Center and the German OKH [*Oberkommando des Heeres*, or Supreme Command of the Army], found in the US National Archives. Thus, on 1 July 1943, Model's army consisted of five corps – two army corps (XX and XXIII) and three panzer corps (XXXXI, XXXXVI and XXXXVII). Together, they had a total of 18 divisions [not including the two security divisions, the 203rd under the command of Lieutenant General R. Pilz and the 211th commanded by Lieutenant General H. Lendl]: 13 infantry and one Assault division (the 6th, 7th, 31st, 45th, 72nd, 86th, 102nd, 137th, 216th, 251st, 258th, 292nd, 383rd Infantry and 78th Assault Divisions) and four panzer divisions (the 2nd, 9th, 18th and 20th Panzer Divisions). In addition, as a general reserve the XXXXVI Panzer Corps received Group von Manteuffel (9th, 10th and 11th Hungarian Battalions), while the XXIII Army Corps received the 87th Infantry Regiment from the 36th Infantry Division and the 8th and 13th Hungarian Battalions. As a result, the total strength of the Ninth Army amounted to 331,131 men, including 9,316 officers, 2,638 volunteer staffers with an officer's rank, 59,296 noncommissioned officers and 259,881 enlisted men.[10] This figure does not include the 3,421 officers, volunteer staffers and enlisted men that were sick in medical units on 1 July 1943, or the personnel of the 18th Heavy Mortar Regiment and 312th Radio-Controlled Panzer Company, the headquarters of which didn't submit their reports on time. Thus, it isn't possible to determine their numerical strength on the basis of archival sources.

In addition, in order to reinforce Model's assault grouping in the event of the offensive's successful development, the commander-in-chief of Army Group Center *Feldmarschall* G. von Kluge formed a reserve consisting of one motorized division (the 10th Motorized Division, without tanks) and Group Essebeck (the 4th and 12th Panzer Divisions). However, by the start of the Battle of Kursk, these forces were directly subordinate to von Kluge and were considered his personal reserve. On 4 July 1943, there were a total of 191,755 men in all the divisions designated for Operation Citadel (excluding the 12th Panzer Division[11]) and in the two reserve formations (those of the XXIII Army Corps and Group von Manteuffel – 189,786 in the divisions and 8,312 in the reserve.

9 D. Glantz and J. House, *Kurskaia bitva: Reshaiushchii povorotnyi punkt Vtoroi mirovoi voiny* [The Battle of Kursk: The Decisive Turning Point of the Second World War] (Moscow: Astrel', 2006), p. 356. [The author is working with the Russian translation of this book, which came out in English in 1999 by the University Press of Kansas.]

10 NARA, T. 312, R. 332, F. 7890947.

11 The documentary fund for this division is sparse, and on the basis of archival sources only its effective fighting strength on 4 July 1943 has thus far been established – 4,456 men.

Thus, according to the manning table, the Ninth Army was short a total of 48,233 men on 1 July 1943, including 42,658 in the divisions and 5,575 in the units directly subordinate to corps headquarters and the army headquarters.[12] These figures include the following categories of service personnel: 23,606 enlisted men for the combat units and formations (21,583 in the divisions and 2,023 in the units directly subordinate to corps and the army), 3,007 enlisted men of the general reserve in the divisions' reserve field battalions, 15,198 Hiwi (12,564 in the divisions and 2,634 in the units directly subordinate to corps and the army), and 6,422 German soldiers serving with the Hiwi (5,504 in the divisions and 2,634 in the units).

For an army that was preparing for a general offensive, such a shortage was a genuine problem. Judging from captured documents, Model, von Kluge and the OKH realized this. However, because of the overall manpower deficit in Germany, they were unable to resolve this problem prior to the start of the offensive. Even so, it must be recognized that quite a bit was done to address it. Immediately prior to Operation Citadel, it was expected that this shortage in personnel would be reduced by 33%. On 30 June the OKH informed Ninth Army's chief of staff Colonel von Elverfeldt that 9 march battalions had been allocated for the Ninth Army (5.5 for the infantry divisions and 3.5 for the panzer divisions) with a total strength of 5,000 to 7,000 men. Their arrival in Orel was planned before "D-day" (5 July 1943). Thus, already on the night of 30 June/1 July, an order went out to the troops regarding the assignment of these personnel. According to this document, less than half of the new recruits were to be sent directly to the front:

> The arrival of replacements is anticipated in the immediate future. They should be used to replenish the shortage of personnel in the front line: 450 men for the 137th Infantry Division, 450 men for the 251st Infantry Division, 600 men for the 6th Infantry Division, 300 men for the 10th Motorized Division, 300 men for the 258th Infantry Division, 300 men for the 292nd Infantry Division, as well as for sending to the noncommissioned officer schools as the divisional reserve. In particular, 1.5 march battalions should undergo training in the technical school. A portion should form the basis of a training battalion in Loktia and the reserve of Group Weiss with direct subordination to the XX Army Corps. One march battalion is to be sent to the technical school in Briansk for training in the panzergrenadier training battalion. Give the responsibility for training the two remaining (panzergrenadier) march battalions to the Headquarters von Breitenbuch [the Ninth Army's rear structure, based on the XXXXVII Panzer Corps]. Position both battalions in the Kromy area.

However, just two days later a new message went out that the batch of replacements would arrive between 5 and 9 July, and they would begin to arrive in the troops only by the end of 9 July, which is to say, after the main combat operations in the Ninth Army's sector (within the framework of Operation Citadel) were to conclude. In particular, the XXIII Army Corps' 216th Infantry Division, which would suffer heavy casualties in the course of the offensive, would receive the 124th March Battalion on 9 July with a total strength of 963 men.[13]

There were also serious problems with the quality with the draft contingent. Heavy losses had forced the Wehrmacht to lower the standards for new recruits. Even in the SS field troops at this time, volunteers were arriving not from pure-blood Aryans or peoples close to them (according to Nazi racial theory), but from suitably healthy men from occupied countries, including those not related to the Nordic race: Poles, Czechs, Slovakians and so forth. At this same time, the major defeats at the front had serious shaken the faith in the Reich's eventual victory; an anti-military

12 NARA, T. 312, R. 322, F. 7890924.
13 NARA, T. 312, R. 689, F. 000405.

mood had grown in the occupied countries, and their people were striving by any means possible to avoid participation in the world war. Thus, relative to preceding years, the numbers of deserters and turncoats had grown in the Wehrmacht, and this was the first indication of the decline in morale among the troops and their loss of appetite for fighting.

In the documents of the German Army, the level of desertion was tracked throughout the entire war, but at different times its scale varied: prior to the start of 1943, its rate could be considered insignificant. This could be explained first of all by the powerful propaganda machine among the troops; secondly, by the military servicemen's own realization of the level of atrocities they were perpetrating in the USSR and what was waiting for them in return according to formal and human laws; and thirdly, by the still not significant number of recruits from occupied countries in the ranks of the acting army on the Eastern Front. After Stalingrad, the situation changed. The lack of confidence of the soldiers and even the noncommissioned officers in the possibility of victory in the war became widespread, and as a consequence, the desire to save their own lives grew. At the same time, replacements made up of *Volksdeutsch* [the ethnic Germans who lived outside the borders of Germany itself], Slavs and even Russians began to arrive in large numbers in the Wehrmacht, as well as recruits from such, even in the opinion of German officers, traditionally unreliable lands as Alsace and Lorraine. Moreover, the contingent called up from conquered countries, as a rule, was used to replenish the infantry divisions. Before the start of the Battle of Kursk, non-Germans comprised up to 40% of the total number of men in some of them, for example, in Army Group South's 168th Infantry Division.[14]

In certain foreign publications, it is possible to come across the assertion that by the start of Operation Citadel the defeatist moods in both German Army Groups at Kursk had dissipated. Write K. von Tippelskirch: "The period of mud, the shortening of the front lines and the periods of calm that then followed was very fortunate for the German divisions. The 'shock of Stalingrad' which had in the past been felt only in the troops of the most heavily defeated southern sector of the front, was ultimately overcome even there."[15]

Likely, the former Wehrmacht general was very much engaged in wishful thinking, which is why this passage that appeared in his book regarding the supposedly local manifestations of declining morale in the winter and early spring of 1943 is so far from reality. The documentary sources of both sides draw a different picture in all the formations of the German Army on the Eastern Front. In connection with this, an order from Army Group South on 13 April 1943 is indicative. In it, the army group command demanded, "It is necessary to follow the losses in the divisions that have arrived from the West attentively. In the event that their numerical strength has fallen to 80 men per company as a result of their first combat encounters, the threat of the loss of their combat capability arises, because their morale makes them sensitive to losses."[16] It is an interesting detail that the headquarters of the Fourth Panzer Army recalled this document several days before the Battle of Kursk and demanded that the commands of the divisions strictly follow it. It is hard to imagine that this order concerned, for example, the II SS Panzer Corps; though it had also arrived from the West, the winning mindset of its personnel was immeasurably higher than in the Wehrmacht divisions. However, one thing is clear: Even before Operation Citadel, the combat spirit of the soldiers had begun to fall everywhere, and the German command was seeking any means to put a stop to this process.

---

14 *Velikaia Otechestvennaia voina 1941-1945, Kn. 2: Perelom* [*Great Patriotic War 1941-1945, Book 2: Turning Point*] (Moscow: Nauka, 1998), p. 258.

15 K. Tippelskirch, *Istoriia Vtoroi mirovoi voiny* [*History of the Second World War*], translated from German (Saint Petersburg: Poligon, 1994), p. 23.

16 NARA, T. 312, R. 365, F. 8650576.

If for example one follows the evolution of the morale of the German troops, which were located opposite the Central Front from March to the end of June 1943, then according to Soviet intelligence data the tendency of greater discipline and combat spirit of the troops is readily discernible. However, to maintain that by the start of the Battle of Kursk, the defeatist attitudes among the troops had dissipated is a clear exaggeration. From an intelligence report of the 13th Army headquarters' Intelligence Department about the condition of the enemy troops opposite its front on 28 June 1943:

> The mood of the majority of German soldiers is rather depressed and the fatigue from the prolonged war is perceptible. The defeat suffered by the German troops in the winter of 1942-1943 undermined the soldiers' faith in the possibility of Germany's victory. Such attitudes are especially widespread among soldiers called up from the reserves (soldiers of older age) and soldiers of non-German nationality. That portion of the soldiers which still continues to believe in victory is staking all their hopes on the summer 1943 offensive. However, these soldiers don't have full confidence in a favorable outcome of the war for the Germans. For example, according to the testimony of soldier Deringer of the 20th Panzer Division's 59th Panzer Grenadier Regiment, conversations are going on among the soldiers: 'If the summer 1943 offensive fails, then in the winter the Germans will have to retreat to Poland, and the war will be lost.'
>
> The extended lull on the fronts in the USSR is acting oppressively on the soldiers. They say: 'Better to be moving to the west, than to stand pat' (from the testimony of a soldier of the 78th Assault Division Franz Jörkewitz). Among the latest replacements for the enemy's Ninth Army are a large number of soldiers of non-German nationality or Germans from territories that weren't previously part of Germany (Slovenians, Luxemburgers, Alsations), which in the majority have defeatist attitudes and don't want to fight for the Germans. A deserter from the 78th Assault Division's 215th Assault Regiment Franz Kugel declared, 'I'm not a soldier, but a Luxemburger.' Therefore he says that he has no wish to fight for Germany. These defeatist attitudes often come from the rear, in letters from families. The British bombings of the western areas of Germany continue to have a large influence on the deteriorating morale of the German soldiers.[17]

Captured sources also bear witness to the decline in morale. In them one notes a dangerous tendency for the Wermacht: an increasing number of cases of a voluntary defection to the Red Army's side among German servicemen. For example, on 17 June 1943, the Ninth Army's Operations Department reported to Army Group Center that a disturbing incident had taken place in the 78th Assault Division: six Germans, including four *Volksdeutsch*, had gone over to the Russians. There had been prior such incidents, and they were being viewed quite seriously. The army's intelligence leadership was instructed to investigate the reasons for them diligently, and rear personnel received an order to detain approximately 150 *Volksdeutsch* draftees that were about to be sent to the front. In addition, Elverfeldt's headquarters demanded a closer scrutiny of the arriving batch of replacements in the training units.[18] As evidence of the fact that this tendency was increasing is the fact that a number of Ninth Army men went over to the Red Army already during Operation Citadel itself; among them was the acting commander of the II Battalion of the 9th Panzer Division's 11th Panzer Grenadier Regiment *Oberleutnant* H. Frankenfeld, by

17 TsAMO RF, F. 361, Op. 6801, D. 53, L. 343.
18 NARA, T. 312, R. 321, F. 7886129.

nationality a German.[19] It is extremely hard to imagine that such a thing would have happened, for example, in 1942.

Even so, one should give our adversary credit: the German military machine at that time was still working properly, albeit with increasing strain. Thus Soviet army intelligence correctly pointed to the fact that "on the whole, the morale of the enemy units opposite the 13th Army remains satisfactory."[20]

Now let's examine the numerical strength of Model's assault grouping, which is to say, of those forces that were directly committed to Operation Citadel. The operation planned to use all of the army's formations, except the XX Army Corps and 102nd Infantry Division of the XXXXVI Panzer Corps, which nevertheless were still to support their attacking neighbors with fire from fixed positions. Accordingly, 18 divisions were part of the assault force: 13 of the Ninth Army (including 4 panzer divisions: the 2nd, 9th, 18th and 20th; and 9 infantry and assault divisions: the 6th, 7th, 31st, 86th, 216th, 258th, 292nd, 383rd and 78th Assault) and 3 from Army Group Center's reserve (the 10th Motorized Division and Group Essebeck's 4th and 12th Panzer Divisions). The list and combat effectives of these formations on 4 July 1943 are given in Table 1.

Incidentally, in his memoirs E. von Manstein notes that Army Group Center supposedly had subordinate to it for the offensive not one motorized division, but two.[21] The Russian scholar Colonel A.V. Lobanov even gives its numerical designation – the 20th Motorized Division, and adds that it was located in Kluge's reserve together with the 8th Panzer Division.[22] Possibly, the Field Marshal had in mind the 36th Infantry Division. It actually had been deemed a motorized division at one point, but well in advance of the Battle of Kursk. Although it was called a motorized division, this division was staffed and equipped as a normal infantry division already back in the middle of 1942, but by the beginning of June 1943, it had been re-labeled, since in the Ninth Army's captured documents for July, it and its regiments are passed off as "infantry". As for the "20th Motorized Division", in the archival sources over the period of Operation Citadel, such a formation isn't mentioned in the Orel bulge.

As is obvious from the cited information, Model formed the backbone of his assault formation according to a different principle than did his neighbor von Manstein. Unlike Army Group South, which made its panzer divisions the basis of his assault grouping, Model relied upon the infantry divisions.[23] They numbered 118,583 servicemen (including the five Hungarian battalions, their combat effectives numbered 39,212 men), which is to say 35.8% of the Ninth Army's total strength or 61.8% of the personnel involved in Operation Citadel (without including the 12th Panzer Division). The average numerical strength of one infantry division remained low and amounted to 11,853 men with 3,578 combat effectives; the average strength of one infantry battalion was 392 men. Only the 78th Assault Division,which was the largest of all the divisions in the Ninth Army stood out among all the divisions in numerical strength. On 4 July 1943 it had 15,961 servicemen with 4,545 combat effectives and an average strength of 660 men in each of its six infantry battalions. The weakest division was the 216th Infantry Division, which numbered 10,059 soldiers and officers, with 2,802 combat effectives and an average of 354 men in each of its six infantry battalions.

Nevertheless, even though the average infantry division of the Ninth Army was below establishment strength in soldiers and officers, it was still larger than their counterpart in the Central Front

19 TsAMO RF, F. 361, Op. 6081, D. 54, LL. 19-21.
20 TsAMO RF, F. 361, Op. 6081, D. 53, L. 343obr.
21 E. Manstein, *Poteriannye pobedy* [*Lost victories*] (Smolensk: Rusich, 2003), p. 522.
22 *Voenno-istoricheskii zhurnal*, No. 8 (2003), p. 10 and 12.
23 Considering that the 78th Assault Division and 10th Motorized Division had no panzer regiment, in the calculation they have been considered infantry divisions.

Table 1 Ration and combat strength of the Ninth Army's formations as of 4 July 1943

	Unit or Formation	Ration strength on 4.7.1943[a]	Combat strength on 4.7.1943[b]
		XX Army Corps	
1.	251st Infantry Division	10,385	2,736
2.	137th Infantry Division	10,396	2,826
3.	45th Infantry Division	10,770	3,747
4.	72nd Infantry Division	11,846	3,309
	Total:	**43,397**	**12,618**
		XXXXVI Panzer Corps	
5.	102nd Infantry Division	11,436	2,930
6.	258th Infantry Division	11,249	3,392
7.	7th Infantry Division	11,871	3,532
8.	31st Infantry Division	11,692	3,068
	Total:	**46,248**	**12,922**
9.	Group Manteuffel	3,765	2,025
		XXXXVII Panzer Corps	
10.	20th Panzer Division	12,154	2,831
11.	4th Panzer Division	12,932	3,549
12.	2nd Panzer Division	13,522	4,062
13.	6th Panzer Division	11,352	3,121
14.	9th Panzer Division	14,234	3,571
	Total:	**64,194**	**17,134**
		XXXXI Panzer Corps	
15.	18th Panzer Division	12,028	3,479
16.	10th Motorized Division	12,734	4,322
17.	86th Infantry Division	11,576	3,650
18.	292nd Infantry Division	10,880	3,714
	Total:	**47,218**	**15,165**
		XXIII Infantry Corps	
19.	78th Storm Division	15,961	4,545
20.	8th Jäger Battalion	1,325	722
21.	13th Jäger Battalion	1,243	685
22.	216th Infantry Division	10,059	2,802
23.	383rd Infantry Division	11,209	Of the division: 2,633 I/87 Infantry Rgt.: 482 III/87 Infantry Rgt: 519 Total: 3,634
	Total:	**39,797**	**12,388**
24.	12th Panzer Division (Army Group Center reserve)	?	4,456
	Grand Total:	**240,864 (+?)**	76,709

Notes

a NARA T.312, R. 322, F. 7890958

b NARA T.312, R. 322, F. 789073-7890875

(the rifle division) by approximately 4,000 men. However, if one considers that it was the infantry divisions that were to resolve the main task of the first, most important stage of Operation Citadel – to break through the deeply-echeloned Soviet defenses, then these figures don't seem significant, and it becomes understandable why Model throughout the course of the entire preparation for the offensive persistently appealed to von Kluge and the OKH to strengthen the army with heavy breakthrough armor and with manpower for the infantry divisions.

Moreover, the infantry divisions had a relatively modest amount of artillery. On 27 June 1943, all five corps of the Ninth Army had a total of 1,189 guns, including 620 light, 477 heavy and 92 anti-aircraft guns.[24] The bulk of them were located in the four attacking corps. The XX Army Corps had only 161 cannons and howitzers (120 and 41 respectively), or on average just 40 tubes per division.[25] This was the lowest indicator in the Ninth Army. In comparison, for example, the 8th Rifle Division, which was not even the strongest division in first echelon of the Central Front's 13th Army had 294 pieces of artillery (140 guns, 125 heavy mortars and 22 M-8 rocket launchers) according to its TO&E, but with the inclusion of reinforcements it had 407 (respectively 202, 169 and 22).[26]

The panzer divisions had a total of 64,870 men (excluding the 12th Panzer Division), which is to say 19.6% of the Ninth Army's available strength or more than 33.8% of the personnel of its assault grouping and Kluge's reserve for the Ninth Army. The mobile divisions (except the 12th Panzer Division) had more men than the infantry divisions (with the exception of the 78th Assault Division); they numbered on average 12,974 soldiers and officers with an average of 3,506 combat effectives. The strongest was the 2nd Panzer Division, which had 14,234 men on its list (and 3,571 combat effectives), while the weakest was the 18th Panzer Division, which had a total of 12,028 soldiers and officers reporting for duty (and 3,479 combat effectives). In order to conduct a major offensive operation, these were acceptable numbers, although for example the panzer divisions of Army Group South had even more manpower.

The situation with respect to the analysis of the number of tanks and self-propelled guns in the Ninth Army's units and formations before the Battle of Kursk is quite similar to the problem of determining their staffing with manpower. In the Soviet historiography, only an overall number for the armored vehicles gathered together in the two army groups for Operation Citadel has been given – 2,700, with no detailed breakdown by army or division.[27] It isn't clear where this figure was obtained, since the authors provided no footnotes. The amount of armor in Model's army before the start of the offensive was first published by Russian scholars in 1998. In the already mentioned multi-volume work by colleagues of the Institute of Military History, a figure of 746 tanks and self-propelled guns is given for the Ninth Army, including 45 Tiger tanks and 280 assault guns.[28] However, these figures also lack a reference to their sources, which unquestionably reduces the degree of confidence in them. In following years, Russian authors didn't present any new data in publications. There is also interest in this question abroad; over the last 20 years alone, N. Zetterling and A. Frankson, D. Glanz and J. House, and T. Jentz have taken it up. However, even abroad there is still no common opinion, and the majority of authors also give numbers without indicating their sources. Even given a most fleeting comparison of their data with the archival materials reveals substantial disagreements. For example, it isn't clear why the American scholars D. Glantz and J. House maintain that each of the Ninth Army's assault gun battalions, except for

24 NARA, T. 312, R. 322, F. 7891349.
25 Ibid.
26 TsAMO RF, F. 62, Op. 321, D. 139, L. 39.
27 See, for example, Koltunov and Solov'ev, *Kurskaia bitva*, p. 47.
28 *Velikaia Otechestvennaia voina 1941-1945, Book 2: Turning Point*, p. 254.

the 909th, which the authors don't even include as part of the Ninth Army, had 36 assault guns.[29] According to their TO&E at that time, they were supposed to have no more than 31. Captured sources found in the US National Archives show that this establishment strength was primarily satisfied in the units.[30] The sole exception is the 185th Assault Gun Battalion, which numbered 32 assault guns on 1 July 1943. The same sort of variety of opinions is observed as well with respect to numbers of tanks. Relying primarily on archival materials of the Ninth Army, which haven't previously entered academic circulation, as well as on the work of Zetterling and Frankson,[31] which in my view is the most reliable at the present time, I've managed to determine the number of tanks and self-propelled guns of all of Army Group Center's formations and units that were assigned to Operation Citadel. The collected data are shown in Table 2.

As of 1 July 1943, there was a total of 783 armored fighting vehicles in four of Model's corps, of which 420 were tanks (including 31 Tigers) and 363 were self-propelled guns (including the Ferdinand heavy tank destroyers). In addition, Group Essebeck had another 164 tanks. Thus, for conducting Operation Citadel, Army Group Center on 1 July 1943 had 947 combat machines (584 tanks, and 363 self-propelled guns and Ferdinands).

The Ninth Army's tanks were primarily concentrated in four panzer divisions (which had a combined 513 tanks), with another 46 in the 505th Separate Heavy Panzer Battalion and 25 in the 656th Panzerjäger Regiment. The average strength in tanks and assault guns of the divisions amounted to 87, or 81% of TO&E.[32] The most powerful was the 2nd Panzer Division, which had 118 combat machines, including 6 command tanks and 12 light tanks, the outdated Pz II, which couldn't be employed in open combat. The weakest was the 18th Panzer Division, which numbered 69 combat machines, including 5 command tanks.

Even so, I nevertheless consider it necessary to offer the reservation that even these figures might be amended in the future. In the course of work with the archival materials, two things became apparent which with high probability might contribute to this. Firstly, because of the acute lack of armor, there was a lot of redistribution of armored fighting vehicles among the units and formations of Model's assault grouping, as well as between his Ninth Army and Group Essebeck, which was subordinate to von Kluge. Moreover, each decision about transferring armor wasn't noted in all of the combat dispatches. For example, after the headquarters of Army Group Center on 21 June informed Colonel von Elverfeldt that the Ninth Army wouldn't receive the promised Panther tanks, its commander made an attempt to relieve the acute situation with armor in the first echelon with at least some half-measures. On 27 June he ordered that the "above table strength long-barreled Pz III with the L/60 cannon be again returned to the 505th Separate Heavy Panzer Battalion."[33] However, this information can only be found in the journal of combat operations; Model's order about this isn't mentioned in any of the combat dispatches. Virtually half of the combat machines of Group Essebeck's 12th Panzer Division were transferred to divisions of the Ninth Army. Of the 88 tanks numbered in it on 1 July, 12 short-barreled Pz III tanks were with the 656th Heavy Panzerjäger Regiment, 8 long-barrelled Pz IV and 1 short-barreled Pz III were with the 258th Infantry Division, 1 short-barreled Pz III was with the 102nd Infantry Division, 7 long-barreled Pz III and 1 short-barreled Pz III was with the 505th Separate Heavy Panzer Battalion, 1 short-barreled Pz IV was with the training unit in Briansk, and 4 long-barreled Pz IV

29 D. Glantz and J. House, *The Battle of Kursk* (University Press of Kansas, 1999), p. 349.
30 NARA, T. 314, R. 689, F. 000383.
31 N. Zetterling and A. Frankson, *Kursk 1943: A Statistical Analysis* (London. Portland: Frank Cass, 2000).
32 The calculation was made with the inclusion of 13 tanks of the 12th Panzer Division that had been transferred to the 656th Panzerjäger Regiment and those of the 505th Separate Heavy Panzer Battalion of Tigers, which is to say, 88 machines.
33 NARA, T. 312, R. 317, F. 788136.

Table 2 Tanks and assault guns in the units and formations of Army Group Center assigned for Operation Citadel, and in the Second Panzer Army on 1 July 1943

Unit or Formation[1] Pz. If/Pz.II		Type of Armor									
		Pz. III short[2]	Pz. III long	Pz. IV short	Pz. IV long	Pz. VI Tiger	Command tanks	Total tanks	Assault guns	Grand total	
Ninth Army											
XXIII Army Corps										63	63
185th Assault Gun Battalion										32 (27/5)[3]	32
189th Assault Gun Battalion										31[4]	31
XXXXI Panzer Corps		**/3**	**20**	**16**	**40**	**12**	**–**	**3**	**94**	**207**	**301**
18th Panzer Division[5]		–	5	9	40[6]	12	–	3	69	–	69
656th Heavy Panzerjäger Regiment	653rd Hvy Panzerjäger Battalion.(Ferdinand)									45	45
	654th Hvy Panzerjäager Battalion (Ferdinand)									45	45
	216th Assault Gun Battalion (Brummbär)									45	45
	313th and 314th Radio-controlled Goliath Companies									10	10
	Separate panzer company[7]	/3	15[8]	7[9]					25		25
177th Assault Gun Battalion										31 (22/9)[10]	31
244th Assault Gun Battalion										31 (22/9)[11]	31
XXXXVII Panzer Corps		**/21**	**18**	**80**	**14**	**144**	**31**	**18**	**326**	**62**	**388**
20th Panzer Division		/9	2	15	9	40	–	7	82	–	82
9th Panzer Division				26	4	45	–	5	80	–	80[12]

Notes
1 The allocation of the units and formation by corps was taken from the XXXXI and XXXXVII Panzer Corps orders for the offensive and the combat diaries of the XXIII AC and the XXXXVI PC: NARA, T.315 R.316, F.000845; T.314, R.988, F. 0001148; T.314, R.988, F.0001148; and T.314, R. 1086, F. 000455.
2 For this and next column, short and long refer to short-barreled and long-barreled guns.
3 Zetterling and Franksen, Kursk 1943: A statistical analysis, p. 63.
4 NARA, T.314, F.689, F.000383.
5 Information for the 18th Panzer Division taken from a report from its headquarters at 1700 on 4 July 1943 (NARA, T.315, R.718, F.001024).
6 Including one short-barreled Pz. IV located in the 2nd Co. of the 18th Panzerjäger Battalion.
7 Of the company's 25 tanks, 12 Pz. III with the short-barreled 50-mm gun and 7 Pz. III with the long-barreled 50-mm gun were operationally subordinated from the 12th Panzer Division.
8 Including 3 Pz. III tanks with the short-barreled 75-mm gun and 12 Pz. III with the short-barreled 50-mm gun from the 12th Panzer Division.
9 All 7 Pz. III tanks with the long-barreled 50-mm gun.
10 Zetterling and Franksen, Kursk 1943: A statistical analysis, p. 46.
11 This includes 22 StuG 40 (with the 75-mm gun), and 9 StuH (with the 105-mm gun); information for 3 July 1943 (NARA, T.315, R.316, F.00084.
12 Combat-capable (NARA, T.315, R.545, F.000527).

Unit or Formation Pz. If/Pz.II		Type of Armor									
		Pz. III short	Pz. III long	Pz. IV short	Pz. IV long	Pz. VI Tiger	Command tanks	Total tanks	Assault guns	Grand total	
Ninth Army (continued)											
2nd Panzer Division		/12	8	32	1	59	–	6	118	–	118
21st Separate Panzer Brigade ("Brigade Burmeister")[13]	312th Radio-controlled Goliath Company	–	–	–	–	–	–	–	–	–	–
	505th Separate Hvy Panzer Battalion		8	7	–	–	31	–	46		46
245th Assault Gun Battalion		–	–	–	–	–	–	–	–	31 (22/9)	31
904th Assault Gun Battalion		–	–	–	–	–	–	–	–	31	31
XXXXVI Panzer Corps										**31**	**31**
909th Assault Gun Battalion		–	–	–	–	–	–	–	–	31	31
Total for the Ninth Army:		***/24***	***38***	***96***	***54***	***156***	***31***	***21***	***420***	***363***	***783***
Reserve of Army Group Center planned for the Ninth Army (Group Essebeck)											
4th Panzer Division (on 30 June 1943)[14]		–	–	9	1	73[15]	–	6	89	–	89
12th Panzer Division		5/6	8[16]	15	1	36	–	4	75	–	75
Total for Group Essebeck:		***5/6***	***8***	***24***	***2***	***109***	**–**	***10***	***164***	**–**	***164***
Grand Total for Operation Citadel:		***5/30***	***46***	***120***	***56***	***265***	***3117***	***31***	***584***	***363***	***947***
Second Panzer Army											
5th Panzer Division[18]		–	–	17[19]	–	76[20]	–	9	102	–	102
8th Panzer Division (OKH Reserve, at the front from 12 July 1943)		/14	25	34	8	14	–	6	101	–	101
Total for the Second Panzer Army		***/14***	***25***	***51***	***8***	***90***	**–**	***15***	***203***	**–**	***203***

Notes

13 About the subordination of "Brigade Burmeister" to the XXXXI Panzer Corps' 6th Infantry Division and combat strength: Order No. 109 of the XXXXI Panzer Corps (NARA, T.315, R.316, F.00084.

14 NARA, T.314, R.1128, F.000147.

15 According to an entry in the 4th Panzer Division's combat diary for 4 July 1943, one long-barreled Pz. IV was detached to the Ninth Army (NARA, T.315, R.220, F.000006).

16 Another 12 short-barreled Pz. III was located in the 656th Heavy Panzerjäger Regiment and 1 short-barreled Pz. III in the 505th Separate Heavy Panzer Battalion.

17 One more Tiger company (14 tanks) arrived on 8 July 1943.

18 Information for the 5th Panzer Division comes from NARA, T.315, R.747, F.0007.

19 Of which on 1 July 1943 13 were operational, and 4 were under short-term repair of up to 3 weeks.

20 Of which on 1 July 1943 57 were operational, and 19 were under short-term repair of up to 3 weeks.

and 3 Pz I were undergoing light repairs.[34] Yet before the Battle of Kursk we find mention of this only in one of the 18th Panzer Division's reports at 1915 on 1 July 1943. Thus it can't be excluded that in the future similar transfers involving other divisions might appear that aren't known today. Secondly, a portion of the armor arrived in the army literally just several days before the start of the fighting and was recorded by various departments and offices. Thus, considering the significant quantity of documentation for both the Ninth Army and Army Group Center, it is impossible to state with confidence that new combat machines didn't arrive in one or another division just a day or two before the offensive, which haven't been discovered by us today. Moreover, a certain number of tanks might have arrived from repair shops into the combat elements between 1 July and 5 July 1943, which hasn't been indicated in combat reports. As a result, the total number of tanks and self-propelled guns might be higher, although not substantially so.

Incidentally, this supposition to a great degree also pertains to Model's neighbor, von Manstein's army group. Here, a significant amount of armor kept arriving right up to the start of combat operations. For example, if judging from a timetable of arriving equipment in the Fourth Panzer Army, which its headquarters sent to Army Group South on 1 July 1943,[35] at that moment just one of the two Panther battalions (the 51st Panzer Battalion with 104 Pz V) had arrived, while the 52nd Panzer Battalion (with 100 Pz V) was still en route and was due to arrive on approximately 3 July. Thus far there has been no success in discovering its time of arrival; it is known only that in a report from the XXXXVIII Panzer Corps at 1915 on 2 July, it still wasn't on its books.[36] If it is considered that the Panther battalion was running 7 to 15 hours behind the schedule of arrivals for a company of the 51st Heavy Panzer Battalion (at Bogodukhov Station, Novaia Bavariia and Odnorobovka), then with a great deal of confidence it can be stated that the Panther battalion might have arrived on the eve of the Battle of Kursk.

Concerning the armored vehicles that might have been transferred to the Ninth Army already during the period of the offensive between 5 and 11 July, either as separate groups or as parts of divisions, then judging from disclosed documents, they proved to be extremely few. The sole, substantial replenishment became the arrival of the already mentioned 14 Tigers of the 3rd Company of the 505th Heavy Panzer Battalion on 8 July. There was one more relatively substantial group of armored vehicles, about which the Ninth Army received a message on 8 July. This group consisted of 24 150mm sIG 33 heavy self-propelled howitzers for the 2nd and 4th Panzer Divisions, 10 Sturmpanzer IV "Brummbär" self-propelled infantry guns for the 216th Assault Gun Battalion, 2 command tanks for the 2nd Panzer Division, 12 "Hummel" self-propelled 150mm howitzers for the 12th and 18th Panzer Divisions, as well as 6 halftracks equipped with guns for the 18th Panzer Division.[37] However, their arrival was anticipated only by 9-10 July, and in the divisions a day or two later, thus all of this armor was unable to take direct part in the offensive, which means it shouldn't be counted in the assessment of the Ninth Army's condition in the course of Citadel.

In addition to the tanks, during the offensive the Ninth Army assigned a significant role to the assault guns. As the data in Table 1 show, they amounted to a little bit more than 38% of the total amount of armored vehicles of the assault force.

When planning the combat formation for the assault wedge, Model concentrated the majority of the armor, 420 tanks and 269 self-propelled guns (for a total of 689) in the XXXXVII and XXXXI Panzer Corps, which were to operate on the main Ol'khovatka axis and the secondary Ponyri axis. In so doing, 326 tanks were handed over to the XXXXVII Panzer Corps, and 207

34 Light repairs were considered any repairs that could be completed in less than 14 hours.
35 NARA, T. 313, R. 368, F. 8654240.
36 NARA, T. 313, R. 368, F. 8654350.
37 NARA, T. 312, R. 322, F. 7890982.

assault guns and Ferdinands to the XXXXI Panzer Corps. The flanking corps, the XXXXVI Panzer Corps and XXIII Army Corps received mere bits and drabs; three battalions of assault guns with a total of 91 self-propelled guns. In order to break through the main belt of defenses of Rokossovsky's Central Front (the first of three) and to repulse possible tank counterattacks, Model planned to use two strong formations equipped with the latest models of armor as an armored battering ram in his assault formations, the XXXXI and XXXXVII Panzer Corps: the 656th Panzerjäger Regiment under the command of Lieutenant Colonel E. von Jungenfeld with the XXXXI Panzer Corps and Colonel A. Burmeister's 21st Separate Panzer Brigade (which entered the documents as "Panzer Brigade Burmeister"). The regiment consisted of the Major B. Kahl's 216th Sturmpanzer Battalion, Major H. Steinwachs' 653rd Heavy Panzerjäger Battalion, Captain K. H.-Noak's 654th Heavy Panzerjäger Battalion, and a separate panzer company of the regiment's command. The I Battalion was equipped with 45 150mm Sturmpanzer IV "Brummbär", the II and III Battalions each with 45 Ferdinand heavy panzerjäger self-propelled guns, and the separate panzer company with Pz III tanks equipped with 50mm and 75mm guns. In addition, as reinforcement the regiment received 10 assault guns (in order to cover the company of remote-controlled Goliath tracked mines).

The sole armored panzer unit of the 21st Separate Panzer Brigade was the 505th Separate Heavy Panzer Battalion commanded by Major B. Sovant, which according to its TO&E was supposed to be equipped with 45 Pz VI Tiger tanks. Prior to the start of the fighting the Tigers were arriving in the units and were replacing (tank per tank) the Pz III tanks, which the battalion temporarily possessed. However, by the start of the offensive, the 505th Heavy Panzer Battalion was not up to its authorized strength in Tiger tanks. In Russian historiography on the Battle of Kursk, despite the significant number of publications, there is still no clarity on the question regarding the employment and equipping of the 505th Separate Heavy Panzer Battalion. The main reason for this is that authors have ignored archival materials, and the majority of them have used only open foreign sources, often with mistakes. In separate works one encounters plain contradictions, because of which it is even difficult to figure out what the author wanted to say. For example, in M. Bariatinsky's *Tigry v boiu* [*Tigers in battle*], on page 143 we read: "Initially the battalion was equipped according to the old table and by 20 April 1943 it numbered 20 Tigers and 25 Pz III. By 6 May the 505th Battalion was moved to the Eastern Front, to Army Group Center aboard several trains. On 10 June 1943 the Pz III tank were removed from the battalion, and in their place another 14 Tigers arrived, and the battalion had reached its authorized number of 45 heavy tanks."[38] Yet already on page 143, something completely different is given: "By 5 July 1943, there were only 31 Tiger tanks in the 505th Separate Heavy Panzer Battalion. The point is that the 3rd Company of this battalion arrived in the area of combat operations only on 8 July."[39] Obviously, it isn't clear how if the 20 Tigers were joined by another 14, they together became not 34 Tigers, but the authorized 45 Tigers. Yet at the same time the author asserts that up until 5 July, the battalion had only 31 Tigers. In the opinion of a different scholar M. Kolomiets, before the Battle of Kursk the 505th Separate Heavy Panzer Battalion "had the authorized number of Tigers according to its TO&E – 45 machines, and moreover by 5 July they were all operational."[40]

So what was the actual number of Tigers in Sovant's battalion at the moment it entered combat? In captured German documents it is noted that prior to the start of Operation Citadel, not all of the planned Pz VI tanks had yet arrived in the Ninth Army. The last batch of these machines

38 M. Bariatinsky, *"Tigry" v boiu* [*"Tigers" in battle*] (Moscow: Iauza/Eksmo, 2008), p. 143.
39 Ibid., p. 146.
40 M. Kolomiets, "'Tigry' na vostochnom fronte (ot Rostov do Kurskoi dugi)" ["'Tigers' on the eastern front (from Rostov to the Kursk bulge)", *Frontovaia illiustratsiia*, No. 6 (2005), p. 48.

was received before the battle's start between 10 and 15 June, but not 14 Tigers, only 11. All of the Pz III tanks that the battalion had at that moment were replaced by them, but then, as noted above, according to Model's personal order all of the Pz III tanks returned again to Sovant, since the arrival of the other Tigers was running behind schedule. Thus on the morning of 5 July 1943, the 505th Separate Heavy Panzer Battalion went on the attack with two types of tanks: 31 Pz VI and 15 Pz III. The other Tigers of the 3rd Company would arrive only on the fourth day of the operation.

The German command took into account the significant depth and high density of the minefields in the Soviet defense, which were covered by a powerful artillery grouping especially in the main belt. Thus, in order to reduce the losses of heavy tanks in the first stage of the offensive, three companies of remote-controlled tracked demolition vehicles consisting of 72 Sdkfz 301 "Goliaths" were attached to Jungenfeld's regiment and Burmeister's brigade; in particular, the 505th Separate Heavy Panzer Battalion[41] received the 312th Company of these demolition vehicles, and the 656th Panzerjäger Regiment received the 313th and 314th Companies.

As already mentioned above, elements of assault guns were included in the Ninth Army's assault wedge, in addition to the four panzer divisions, the 21st Separate Panzer Brigade and the 656th Heavy Panzerjäger Regiment. By 5 July Model had seven separate assault gun battalions, which had a total of 218 StuG/StuH assault guns. All of these battalions were planned to be used with the divisions of the first echelon.

This was significantly more than in the forces of Army Group South that were directed toward Kursk. Hoth and Kempf had only three assault gun battalions and one separate assault gun company, which had together 106 StuG/StuH, or 10.4% of Army Group South's armored park assigned to Operation Citadel. Because of their weak armor and small number, they could play only a limited role. Thus it was planned to use them primarily to reinforce the infantry divisions for breaking through in narrow sectors, or as a mobile anti-tank reserve of the division commanders. However, this didn't preclude the assault gun battalions' possible use to support the armored units in the course of massed panzer attacks.

If one compares the main indicators of the status of Model's and von Manstein's divisions that were directed toward Kursk, then the Ninth Army is clearly the loser. As an example let's take such an important indicator as manpower. The Fourth Panzer Army and Army Detachment Kempf comprising Army Group South's combat force (deployed on the main and secondary axes of advance), received five corps – three panzer (the III, XXXXVIII and II SS Panzer Corps) and two army (the LII Army Corps and Army Korps Raus), which consisted of 17 divisions: 8 infantry (the 57th, 106th, 167th, 168th, 198th, 255th, 320th and 332nd Infantry Divisions) and 9 panzer and panzergrenadier (the 3rd, 6th, 7th, 11th, 19th, *Grossdeutschland*, *Leibstandarte 'Adolf Hitler'*, *Das Reich* and *Totenkopf*), which numbered 297,831 men, or 106,076 more than Model had. Naturally, this substantially increased the manpower level of von Manstein's divisions. On average, Hoth's and Kempf's infantry and panzer (and panzergrenadier, which had the same TO&E as panzer) divisions had a ration strength of 16,357 and 18,522 men respectively, which exceeded that of the Ninth Army's divisions by 4,999 and 2,195 men respectively. Meanwhile the average combat effectives of an infantry division of von Manstein's assault force exceeded that of an infantry division in Model's Ninth Army by almost twice over, and amounted to approximately 6,344 men.[42]

41 On 24 June 1943, the 505th Separate Heavy Panzer Battalion had a total of 835 men, including 24 officers, 7 clerical office workers, 184 junior officers and 620 enlisted men. Its combat component consisted of 374 men, including 19 officers, 100 junior officers and 255 enlisted men.

42 S. Newton, *Kurskaia bitva: Nemetskii vzgliad* [*Kursk: The German view*] (Moscow: Iauza/Eksmo, 2006), p. 472. This is the Russian translation of Newton's book published by Da Capo Press in 2003.

There were two main reasons for such a substantial difference in the level of staffing and equipment of the divisions: first was the general deficit of manpower and equipment in Germany, and second was the differing size of the assignments that stood before the two army groups. It was planned to conduct the offensive in relatively narrow sectors, which together amounted to less than 14% of the entire Soviet-German front. Army Group South would deliver the main attack, since it was given more difficult tasks. Model's army had to cover approximately 75 kilometers to reach the designated link-up line in the Kursk area, while von Manstein's forces had to cover almost twice that distance, or 125 kilometers. In fact, each time the next spike of tension arose connected with the receipt of information about the substantial buildup in the Soviet defenses around Kursk, both Hitler and the OKH as the first order of business reinforced the southern grouping, not the northern grouping. The changes in the second half of June can serve as a plain example of this: the decision to send the 200 Panthers that had been promised to the Ninth Army to Hoth's Fourth Panzer Army instead. In addition, Army Group South, because of the fact that it had already been assigned significant forces for conducting the counterattack in the Khar'kov area, already at the end of March had significantly greater potential than its neighbor Army Group Center. Having received supplementary forces in the period of preparation for Operation Citadel, by 5 July 1943 its strength had almost doubled. Model had no such possibility to augment his own force.

In addition, the analysis of captured documents testifies to the fact that subjective factors also had a noticeable influence on the level of the Ninth Army's staffing and equipping. In April 1943, practically a month had been lost because of an indecipherable and plainly unjust decision by the OKH leadership to ignore the Ninth Army's needs; only a letter by Model addressed to Hitler himself immediately got the ball rolling.[43] The prolonged transfer of the last batch of replacements – the 9 march battalions that had been sent to Model even before 28 June – can serve as another plain example. Because of delays, it arrived in place only at the end of Operation Citadel. Yet the problem with replacements was a primary one, and all of the Wehrmacht's key actors knew about it back in spring, but no one, except for Elverfeldt's staff, even lifted a finger in order to hasten the replacements' arrival at least by the start of fighting.

There were also other factors: the lack of a working relationship between Model and von Kluge; the poor condition of the main arterial roads in the Orel bulge; partisan attacks on the railroads; numerous combat encounters in the course of May and June 1943 with Central Front's assault groups, which inflicted substantial casualties on the Ninth Army, so the army was compelled to replace them with entire march battalions (for example, in the 258th and 7th Infantry Divisions[44]); and the sluggishness of the rear echelon personnel. In the documents of the Ninth Army headquarters one encounters simply outrageous facts regarding the devil-may-care attitude of all of the structures responsible for meeting the army's needs for men and equipment, especially when it was preparing to launch a general offensive. For example, in the first days of July, its troops were confined to meager rations: there were no shells for the field artillery and anti-tank guns. From the beginning of June, Model and his headquarters had been reporting about this through every channel up the hierarchy, including to Berlin as well. During the final meeting prior to Operation Citadel, Model personally requested Hitler's help with procuring at least anti-tank shells. However, he wasn't heard. Already once the fighting was underway, *Generaloberst* Model would remind the Chief of Staff of the OKH *General der Infanterie* Zeitzler of his request, but he never in fact received them before the operation's conclusion!

43 NARA, T. 312, R. 317, F. 7886050.
44 NARA, T. 312, R. 317, F. 7886119.

It is impossible not to touch upon another such, what seems to be at first glance, "non-military" reason for the relative weakness of the Ninth Army's divisions: illness with hospitalization. In Russian historiography of the past war, the given problem, unfortunately, hasn't been shown the proper attention, even though it had a direct effect on the course of combat operations, among other things. In the historical literature, one often comes across the assertion, based on the recollections of some former frontline veterans: "Soldiers in the trenches didn't get sick; their organism quickly adapted to the extreme conditions." This is true, but only to a point. Archival documents give evidence of a different situation of affairs, and here is just one example: Between 1 and 30 June 1943, the total absence in personnel in the 6th Infantry Division of Model's army due to illness amounted to 288 soldiers and officers (or 2.5% of its total numerical strength, including 216 who'd been given leaves of absence). Almost all of the hospitalized men, 215 soldiers and officers, were from combat units, which amounted to 6.8% of the division's combat effectives given an average size of 407 men for an infantry battalion. At first glance the number is small, but if you consider that at this time the division wasn't engaged in fighting, then its significance unquestionably grows, since it plainly shows that in a rear area (virtually at rest) one division alone was deprived of 55% of an infantry battalion. After all, there were 21 such divisions in the Ninth Army. Now we'll conduct a simple arithmetic operation, 21 x 215, which yields 4,536, which is comparable to the number of combat effectives of the 78th Assault Division, Model's strongest infantry formation. Naturally, the percentage of ill men wasn't so high in all of the divisions, although in some it was even higher. For example, in the 4th Panzer Division due to an epidemic of typhus that broke out in April 1943, the number of hospitalized men noticeably increased. At this moment, the army was in the process of assembling (the first time) for launching the attack toward Kursk, but the division was forced to stop the movement of troops into their jumping-off area for more than a week. It isn't hard to imagine how events might have gone, had Operation Citadel started as originally planned on 28 April or 3 May.

The Soviet command also faced these same problems no less acutely. Here is just one example. According to an account from Voronezh Front's rear headquarters, according to incomplete data, over just two weeks of defensive fighting between 5 and 18 June 1943, 7,871 men had been hospitalized in front-zone medical facilities due to illnesses not connected with wounds on the battlefield.[45] This is equivalent to a full-strength rifle division. Moreover, the epidemic of infectious diseases wasn't yet being recorded at this time. But in the spring of 1943 the situation was even worse among all the troops in the area of the Kursk bulge. For example, in a number of frontline divisions of the Voronezh Front because of the lack of necessary fats in the rations, Red Army men, particularly the troops from Central Asia, were struck with night blindness. After sunset, the soldiers began to have difficulty seeing even nearby objects. As a result, a tense situation developed in the formations that had a lot of natives of Central Asia.[46] Their command staff was forced to send only Russians, Ukrainians and Belorussians out on night patrols, post them as sentries, or man the machine guns at nighttime, since they were less vulnerable to this illness's effect. The daily duties and nighttime watches exhausted these men, and the quality of their service fell. In frontline conditions, this matter became especially acute, and thus two of the Front's departments, the Medical and Rear Services Departments, were called upon to resolve this problem.

Typhus became a substantial threat to our troops. Because of the widespread circulation of this infectious disease throughout recently liberated territory, at first by a decision of the Central Front's Military Council on 30 March 1943, the belt of the compulsory evacuation of the civilian

45 TsAMO RF, F. 203, Op. 2843, D. 487, L. 58.

46 V. Zamulin, *Zabytoe srazhenie Ognennoi dugi* [*Forgotten battle of the Bulge of Fire*] (Moscow: Iauza/Eksmo, 2009), p. 98.

population from the front was decreased from 25 kilometers to 3 kilometers, and on 30 April, K.K. Rokossovsky was compelled for the same reason to ask I.V. Stalin personally to decrease the depth of the frontal zone for his forces from 25 kilometers to at least 15 kilometers, which was in fact done. Spotted fever was rife everywhere in March-April 1943, and an intense struggle against it was underway. The poor sanitary condition of the region and its population, as well as the extreme exhaustion of the people, was contributing to the spread of the disease. Wrote a military doctor of the medical-sanitation battalion of the Central Front's 140th Rifle Division L.M. Zhdanova (Garkavenko) in her daily journal, "I go from house to house, and I force the inhabitants to wash themselves and bake their undergarments in stoves. There are a lot of sick among the civilian population. The entire medical-sanitation unit headed by Beloborodov is sick with fever. The Germans left behind foci of spotted fever in each village and in each home. In the units there are solitary cases, but I think we won't let an epidemic break out in the division."[47]

There was another problem: incidents of suicide. In the course of preparing for the counterattack on 10 and 11 July 1943, in the units of the 5th Guards Army at Prokhorovka there was a wave of suicides among the junior officers, who had just arrived from the reserve and had never experienced combat: the commanders of companies, platoons and mortar batteries. Nervous disorders were a constant phenomenon in all of the acting armies, and grew in correlation with the intensity of the fighting. For example, when British forces first initiated combat operations in Tunis (during the Second World War) nervous disorders amounted to just 2% of all losses. However, as the situation grew more difficult, their number increased to 15% of all losses.[48] Meanwhile, in the US Army over the entire period of the Second World War, approximately 1,000,000 cases of nervous and psychiatric disorders were recorded, and for this reason approximately 525,000 military servicemen were discharged from the army.[49]

Incidents of nervous breakdowns and disorders of various degrees of severity were not few in the Red Army during the war years even among experienced, hardened military commanders. Even so, this important factor of the troops' combat life has hardly been touched upon in Russian historiography. The former Chief of the Red Army's General Staff Marshal of the Soviet Union A.M. Vasilevsky recalled:

> Stress, shock – this happened with people in the war and occurred not only back when we had just started to win, but even much later. I recall, for example, one episode back on the Mius River,[50] where the offensive had already been readied in Gerasimenko's army [the Southern Front's 28th Army, which V.F. Gerasimenko commanded between December 1942 and December 1943]. Gerasimenko's army didn't have the main role in the forthcoming offensive … but it still had offensive tasks. So one morning on the eve before the offensive, I arrived with Tolbukhin[51] at the command post. We had a talk with Gerasimenko. Everything was normal. I had spent time with him on prior occasions. He was ready for the offensive, and neither I nor Tolbukhin had any particular comments for him. In the discussion, I asked him:
>
> "Well, how are your troops, how are they feeling?"

47 *Chelovecheskie dokumenty voiny* [*Human documents of the war*] (Kursk, 1988), p. 245.

48 *Opyt sovetskoi meditsiny v Velikoi Otechestvennoi voine 1941-1945* [*The experience of Soviet medicine in the Great Patriotic War 1941-1945*], Volume 26 (Moscow: Medgiz, 1949), p. 20.

49 *Army Information Digest*, January 1957, p. 30.

50 The Donbas offensive operation, conducted between 17 July and 2 August 1943 with the aim of pinning down the Wehrmacht's forces here and not allowing them to shift reserves from the Donets Basin to the area of the Kursk bulge.

51 F.I. Tolbukhin (16 June 1894 to 17 October 1949), Marshal of the Soviet Union. From March 1943, he commanded the Southern Front (which later was renamed the 4th Ukrainian Front).

> Then suddenly, erupting into a shout, he exclaimed:
>
> "The troops, the troops", then gave a wave of his hand and said, "Nothing's going to go right for us."
>
> "What do you mean, nothing go right?"
>
> "Nothing's going to go right for us."
>
> We summoned the army's chief of staff in his presence and asked his opinion about the units' readiness for the operation. He said that everything was in order, everything was ready, and that there was confidence in success. Then I was forced to state in Tolbukhin's presence that if an army commander didn't believe in success and announces this prior to the start of the offensive, then we'll have to raise the question of his dismissal in front of the *Stavka*, because it is impossible to go on the offensive with such an attitude.
>
> Then suddenly Gerasimenko somehow went limp all over and spoke up, one can say, almost with tears in his voice, and his appearance was totally tormented:
>
> "Excuse me, I don't know what happened with me, or how all this spilled out of me. I'm exhausted. I haven't slept all night, thinking about how things would turn out and what would happen ... I'm overstrung, overwrought. ... I'm tired. I need sleep."
>
> We didn't report him to the *Stavka*, and he wasn't removed from his post. He caught up on sleep, regained his composure, and in the future carried out the task that had been allotted to his fate.[52]

All of the above listed problems in isolation played no substantial role, but taken together their influence on lowering the combat capability of the Ninth Army's forces on the threshold of the Battle of Kursk was perceptible.

Did the aforementioned problems exist in Army Group South when preparing for the Battle of Kursk? Unquestionably they did, but not on the same scale. For example, there was no such major anti-partisan operation like "Gypsy Baron", for which the entire XXXXVII Panzer Corps had been activated. Even so, a struggle with partisans at this time was also being actively conducted in the northern part of Zhitomir Oblast, where one of the major partisan areas was located, and in other places. However, these actions were substantially smaller in scale, and the main thing was that they didn't involve forces of Army Group South's assault grouping, which had been formed up for Operation Citadel.

Secondly, von Manstein didn't have the same difficult relationships with Hoth and Kempf, as Kluge had with Model. He was personally responsible for the success of Operation Citadel, and thus did all he could for them, even at the expense of the defense of other sectors of his Army Group. As an example one can cite the transfer of the 3rd Panzer Division and 198th Infantry Division from the First Panzer Army to the Fourth Panzer Army. Von Manstein believed that if the decision had been made to go on the offensive, then "everything must be done to achieve Operation Citadel's full and complete success."[53] Indeed, you have to hand it to him – throughout the entire period of preparation for the summer fighting, von Manstein firmly adhered to this principle. Yet once again I'll emphasize that all the necessary conditions for this had been created in his army group.

Finally, Army Group South's transport system and system of supply was better arranged and wasn't subjected to such powerful partisan activity, like was observed in the Orel bulge. Moreover,

52 K. Simonov, *Glazami cheloveka moego pokoleniia* [*Through the eyes of a man of my generation*] (Moscow: APN, 1988), pp. 456-457.

53 Manstein, *Poteriannye pobedy*, p. 524.

in the south there had been no need to conduct a large-scale regrouping, such as the one Model had been forced to undertake.

All of the information presented above bears witness to the fact that on 5 July 1943, Model's Ninth Army was the weaker of the two attack groupings that had been called upon to implement Operation Citadel's plan. This relates both to the total number of assault formations assigned to seize Kursk, and their numerical strength and condition. Despite the significant efforts to refit and replenish the Ninth Army's divisions and the repeated postponement of the offensive's start date, Germany's political and military leadership was unable to satisfy even the minimal needs of Model's forces, or to even bring them back up at least to establishment strength. In order to accomplish such large and extremely complex tasks, it absolutely had to receive even more means of reinforcement, especially artillery and heavy armor. However, for objective reasons, it was impossible to do this, which was one of the main reasons for the failure of the Wehrmacht's general offensive on the Eastern Front in the summer of 1943.

7

On the eve of the fundamental turning point – the role of Central Front's reconnaissance and intelligence in determining the start date for Operation Citadel

One of the most important and extremely puzzling questions in the history of the Battle of Kursk is the activity of the Soviet intelligence organs in revealing the intent of the German command during the stage of discussing and planning Operation Citadel, as well as fixing its start date. As is known, intelligence alone cannot win a battle, much less a war, but depending upon its level of organization, as a rule it offers great assistance in this. The contribution made by our special services in thwarting the 1943 summer German offensive was considerable. Nevertheless, due to objective reasons, in Soviet historiography this question has never received thorough examination. During the Soviet era, the 50-year period of the classification of documentation from the war era, which was established by law, still hadn't ended. Accordingly, there was nothing meaningful to discuss. In 1993, the process of declassifying the files for 1943 in the TsAMO RF began. A large amount of previously unknown sources began to enter academic circulation, which allowed us not only to understand the course of combat operations and to assess the plans and decisions of the command of the opposing sides, but also to discover a lot of new and key episodes that occurred during the preparations for the Battle of Kursk.

In the first place this relates to the widely known events on the night of 4-5 July 1943, when in the sector of the 13th Army a German combat engineer was captured, who revealed that the Wehrmacht offensive toward Kursk was due to begin within several hours. His name was Bruno Formella. In Russian and Western historiography, a persistent opinion has taken root that it was from this captured German that the precise date and time for the start of Operation Citadel became known to the Soviet command. This information purportedly allowed the Soviets to make the decision to initiate a planned counter-artillery preparation and to inflict heavy damage to the readied assault groupings of von Manstein and Model. Several German historians, however, consider these assertions to be a plain exaggeration. Firstly, common soldiers can't have strategic information, and secondly, the documentary evidence – the protocols of the interrogation of this prisoner – hasn't been published. Thus, it isn't clear what evidence he revealed.

In reality, not once over the entire postwar period in our country have the transcripts of B. Formella's interrogation been published, even after they were declassified in 1993. The former commander-in-chief of the Central Front Marshal of the Soviet Union K.K. Rokossovsky first wrote about this prisoner in a journal in the early 1960s, and later in his memoirs, and stated the fact that his interrogation answers were key when reaching the decision to initiate the previously-planned preemptive artillery barrage on the night of 4-5 July 1943.[1] Information with the revelation of the German engineer's name and a short review of the information he revealed was also included in the third volume of the *Istoriia Velikoi Otechestvennoi voiny Sovetskogo Soiuza 1941-1945* (Moscow: Voenizdat, 1964, p. 257) – the first official work on the history of the war.

Later, the stories of the deputy commander of the 13th Army's 15th Rifle Division Major General V.N. Dzhandzhgava and the commander of a separate reconnaissance company Major N.S. Kolesov about how this German sapper was captured were published.[2] These recollections became the main and sole source of information about those events, even though they failed to answer the main questions: What were the German engineer's exact words, and why did the Soviet command believe his information?

It is widely known when describing past events, Soviet historians took liberties with facts. Thus everything connected with B. Formella, both from Russian and Western specialists, prompts uncertainty and even caution. Did this "tongue"[3] even actually exist? Did he actually manage to say anything, or as often happened, was he killed during the capture attempt? The circumstance that two more men of the 6th Infantry Division, soldiers (grenadiers) E. Mikinj and S. Mikčič from 3./I/18th Infantry (Grenadier) Regiment came across the lines on 4 July 1943 in the sector of the very same 13th Army, and in the very same vicinity of the village of Verkhnee Tagino,[4] also clouds the situation. Naturally, they were interrogated thoroughly and in detail. However, it isn't clear why the Soviet side so highly valued the information from these deserters who voluntarily came over and from Bruno Formella, who'd been captured by force. These questions have been managed to be answered only recently, thanks to the uncovered protocols of the interrogations of the 13th Army's prisoners for July 1943 in the TsAMO RF, and captured documents of the German Ninth Army in the US National Archives.

The Soviet command was already aware that the two German groupings in the areas of Belgorod and Orel were aiming for Kursk back in the springtime of 1943. Between 29 June and 3 July 1943, from all types of intelligence the Central Front had identified the assembly of major forces of enemy armor, artillery and infantry opposite the front of the 70th, 13th and 48th Armies. However then, on 4 July, movement in the enemy rear stopped, both in the area of the Orel bulge opposite the Central Front, and south of the Kursk salient. In addition, our aerial reconnaissance spotted long columns of German troops in movement from the direction of Belgorod, but not to the north into jumping-off positions for the attack, which might have been expected, but to the south. The impression was taking shape that the German command had cancelled the offensive toward Kursk and was preparing an attack into the Donets Basin. It was only after the war, through captured documents and the memoirs of German commanders, did it become known that these were diversionary measures, designed to confuse the Soviet command regarding the immediate German plans.

At the beginning of July 1943, the enemy's unusual behavior alarmed the command of both Soviet *fronts*. Thus, the reconnaissance troops of the first-echelon armies were given the assignment to seize identification prisoners and clarify the situation. However, the strict security measures taken by the Germans over the men of the forward units and the reinforced combat outposts

1 K.K. Rokossovsky, *Soldatskii dolg* [*Soldier's duty*] (Moscow: Voenizdate, 1968), p. 267.

2 See V. N. Dzhandzhgava, *Nemerennye versty voiny: Zapiski komandira divizii* [*Unmeasured versts of the war: Notes of a division commander*] (Moscow: Izdatel'stvo DOSAAF, 1979), pp. 109-112; and Kolesov's article in *Trud* on 7 May 1985.

3 In Red Army jargon of the war years, this is what a prisoner seized behind enemy lines during a patrol was called.

4 Today an agricultural settlement situated in the southern sector of Orel Oblast.

prevented this order from being carried out. Recalled the former Chief of the General Staff Marshal of the Soviet Union A.M. Vasilevsky:

> We were well-prepared for battle. However, it was extremely necessary to ascertain the day and hour set for the fascist offensive. We were intensely seeking this secret information. Reconnaissance patrols were given the assignment to seize a "tongue" no matter what the cost. Combat reconnaissance usually carried out such operations quickly and successfully. Here, though, even the most experienced reconnaissance scouts could do nothing. ... Each night, our reconnaissance patrols, losing men, returned empty-handed. Meanwhile in our central headquarters we were waiting. We waited impatiently, I would say with feverish impatience, for the evidence so necessary for us – every day and hour. This would allow us to preempt the beginning of the enemy attack at the right moment, to bring all of our artillery and airstrikes down on the fascist soldiers just at the time when they were massed in the forward trenches. An unusual situation had emerged: the problem of capturing a "tongue" was worrying everyone, right up to the Supreme Commander-in-Chief.[5]

By this time (the first days of July), there had been successful reconnaissance probes, but the prisoners brought back so far hadn't revealed anything valuable. Before noon on 4 July 1943, A.M. Vasilevsky, who was at the Voronezh Front headquarters, got in touch with the *Stavka* representative with the Central Front Marshal of the Soviet Union G.K. Zhukov and announced that at 0600 on 4 July, a reconnaissance patrol of the 375th Rifle Division had seized a combat engineer of the 168th Infantry Division, who was lifting mines in front of our frontline trenches. Under interrogation he yielded the information that units of the 168th Infantry Division were to go on the offensive on the morning of 5 July; they had received three days of rations and were clearing paths through their own minefields and in front of our forward trenches. In addition, the prisoner had seen a lot of tanks in Belgorod.[6]

Around this same time, hope was also rising in the headquarters of the Central Front that the situation was finally changing for the better. That morning a report had come in from the 13th Army, which stated that at 0700 in the 15th Rifle Division's sector, in the area of the southern outskirts of Verkhnee Tagino, two soldiers of the 3rd Company of the 6th Infantry Division's 18th Infantry Regiment Edwin Mikinj and Stanislav Mykčič, Slovenians by nationality, had come over to our side. However, there is nothing substantial in the transcript of their preliminary interrogation, since these soldiers had only recently arrived in the division on 27 June 1943 with a batch of replacements, and thus they knew very little about the situation at the front or the short-term plans of the command, although Edwin talked in detail about everything he had experienced from the moment of his call-up in March of the current year (see Document 1). In his words, the offensive was supposed to begin within four days. However, the intelligence officers doubted this. Firstly, just several hours before a prisoner on the Voronezh Front had revealed that the offensive would probably begin on 5 July. Secondly, a briefing had arrived from the *Stavka* of the Supreme High Command on 2 July that the offensive was expected between 3 and 6 July. Thirdly, observation of the enemy's recent behavior indicated his readiness to attack. Nevertheless, in the circumstances of a paucity of information, the deserters' information was taken as evidence, and intelligence received an order: in the nearest hours, to confirm or refute their information.

---

5 Cited by V. Peskov, *Voina i liudi* [*War and people*] (Voronezh: Tsentral'no-chernozemnoe izdanie, 1989), pp. 97-98.

6 TsAMO RF, F. 23 gv. sk., Op. 1, D. 27, L. 15.

Tension was rising in the headquarters of the Central Front, and yet there was no clarity right up until the early hours of 5 July (according to Moscow time), when the commander of the 13th Army Lieutenant General N.P. Pukhov personally called K.K. Rokossovsky and reported that in the course of the latest reconnaissance patrol organized by the 15th Rifle Division's chief of reconnaissance Captain P.G. Savinov, a group headed by Lieutenant I.S. Meleshnikov[7] had seized a German combat engineer, the soldier Bruno Formella of the very same 6th Infantry Division in the area of Verkhnee Tagino. Under preliminary interrogation, which was conducted by the 13th Army's chief of intelligence Lieutenant Colonel I.I. Kryzhanovsky, the prisoner revealed that the German offensive would get underway between 0100 and 0200 on 5 July (see Document 2). If you take into account that Bruno was using Berlin time, then according to Moscow time this would be approximately at 0300. In addition, the prisoner eagerly provided many details on the composition of the 6th Infantry Division, the combat disposition of its units for the forthcoming attack, as well as its reinforcements and tasks (see Document 3). A significant amount of what the prisoner said was already known to Soviet intelligence officers. Even though the combat engineer mixed up the identity of neighboring divisions and attached units, his answers were correct and important for the Soviet side. This prompted the thought that the prisoner was speaking the truth and not concealing anything. Moreover, he wasn't a new guy in the 6th Infantry Division and might actually know that relatively large amount of information that he revealed. Accordingly, the danger of a provocation on the enemy's part or a deliberate attempt to mislead the Soviet side by the prisoner himself seemed minimal according to the preliminary evaluation. Thus, frontline reconnaissance had done its job; the decision was now in the hands of higher command and it took it. At 0220 on 5 July 1943, a thundering sound began from the depth of Central Front's defenses, and the entire sector of the enemy's Ninth Army attack grouping that was poised to attack erupted with shellfire. The counter-artillery preparation of the Soviet forces had begun, and together with it the epochal Battle of Kursk, which became the fundamental turning point in the Great Patriotic War.

Only one, but still important question remains unanswered: "Why did the deserters, who were interrogated on 4 July prior to B. Formella's capture, not know the precise start time for the offensive, or were they deliberately concealing it? The point is that according to Order No. 109 from the headquarters of the Ninth Army, which was repeated by the command of all four corps that were assigned to Operation Citadel, the order regarding the offensive and Hitler's appeal to the soldiers and officers who were to take part in the Battle of Kursk was not to be read out to the troops prior to 1900 on 4 July.[8] The document itself began to arrive directly in the divisions only at mid-day on 4 July. An assembly for listening to the gramophone record containing Hitler's appeal to the army's higher command had been organized at the command posts of the corps two days prior.[9] Accordingly, not one of the German soldiers who fell into Soviet hands prior to 1900 could know the start time of the offensive on the night of 4-5 July, while Gefreitor B. Formella was seized in the minefields at 2300 on 4 July 1943. Thus his information about the start of the offensive proved to be the most accurate of all the information that the Soviet side had managed to obtain by that time. However, his information didn't in fact correspond with the actual time set for the offensive

7 Ivan Semenovich Meleshnikov (1921-1944). Before his call-up into the Red Army in March 1941, Ivan worked as a mechanic in the locomotive depot of Riazan' Station. He fought at the fronts of the Great Patriotic War as a member of the 15th Rifle Division's reconnaissance company from 22 June 1941. By the start of the Battle of Kursk, he was a lieutenant and platoon commander of the 15th Rifle Division's 77th Separate Reconnaissance Company. During the battle, he was concussed and wounded, and awarded the Order of the Red Star and decorated with two medals "For bravery". I.S. Meleshnikov was killed near Warsaw (Poland) in 1944.

8 NARA, T. 315, R. 192, F. 000160.

9 NARA, T. 314, R. 1086, F. 000447.

– 2 –

это в основном немцы. В роте два словена. Рота состоит из
3-х взводов ; во взводе 2-3 отделения (по 5-9 солдат),
всего в роте 8 отделений. Возрастной состав роты – молод
1924 года рождения и солдаты старших возрастов от 27 до
40 лет .
Вооружение роты: 12 легких пулеметов (МГ-42), 12 автома
пистолеты и карабины. Минометов в роте не видел. На участ
отделения имеется одно ПТР. Кроме того роте придано 2 тя
пулемета. Видел также одно пех. орудие (калибр 150 мм)

Фамилии командиров роты ,батальона и полка не знает.

ВОПРОС: Задача части .

ОТВЕТ: Задача дивизии – наступать через 4 дня в направлении на
Курск. К моменту наступления для поддержки пехоты должно
сосредоточено 6 танковых дивизий. Среди солдат распростр
няли слухи, что русские якобы совсем не ожидают этого на
ления. О русских частях ,противостоящих дивизии, ничего
знает.

ВОПРОС: Хим. подготовка в роте.

ОТВЕТ: Ходят разговоры, что русские первые могут начать применят
ОВ. Противогазы у всех солдат с новыми фильтрами 1943 г.
Кроме того у всех солдат имеются бумажные накидки и лозав
Хим. занятия проводились только в Германии (Изучение ОВ)
Последнее окуривание проходили в апреле 1943 г. в Чехии.

ВОПРОС: Питание в роте.

ОТВЕТ: Дневной хлебный паек солдат – 600 гр. Кроме того солдаты
лучают раз в день горячее и черный кофэ без сахара , а та
125 гр. сыра и 50 гр. маргарина. Солдаты питанием не довол

ВОПРОС: Настроение среди солдат.

ОТВЕТ: Немцы хотя и устали от войны, но частично еще верят в по
Германии. Словены воевать не хотят. В полку были случаи са
релов. В Словении широко развертывается партизанское движен
Семьи партизан подвергаются жестоким репрессиям и расстрел

Опознавательного знака дивизии и номера полевой почты 3-е
роты 18 ПП не знает .

ДОПРОСИЛИ: ЗАМ НАЧ РО ШТАРМ 13
МАЙОР (БУХТИН

В/ПЕРЕВОДЧИК РО ШТАРМ 13
КАПИТАН А/СЛУЖБЫ (МИРОНО

Отп. в 3-х экз. 1 фр. 2 15сд. 3. дело.

Отп. В.В.

The second page of the transcript of the interrgation of E. Mekinje, a grenadier of the 6th Infantry Division in the Intelligence Department of Central Front's 13th Army on 4 July 1943. To the question, "Your unit's tasks?" he responded in the fifth paragraph from the top, "The division's task – launch an attack toward Kursk within four days …" (TsAMO RF)

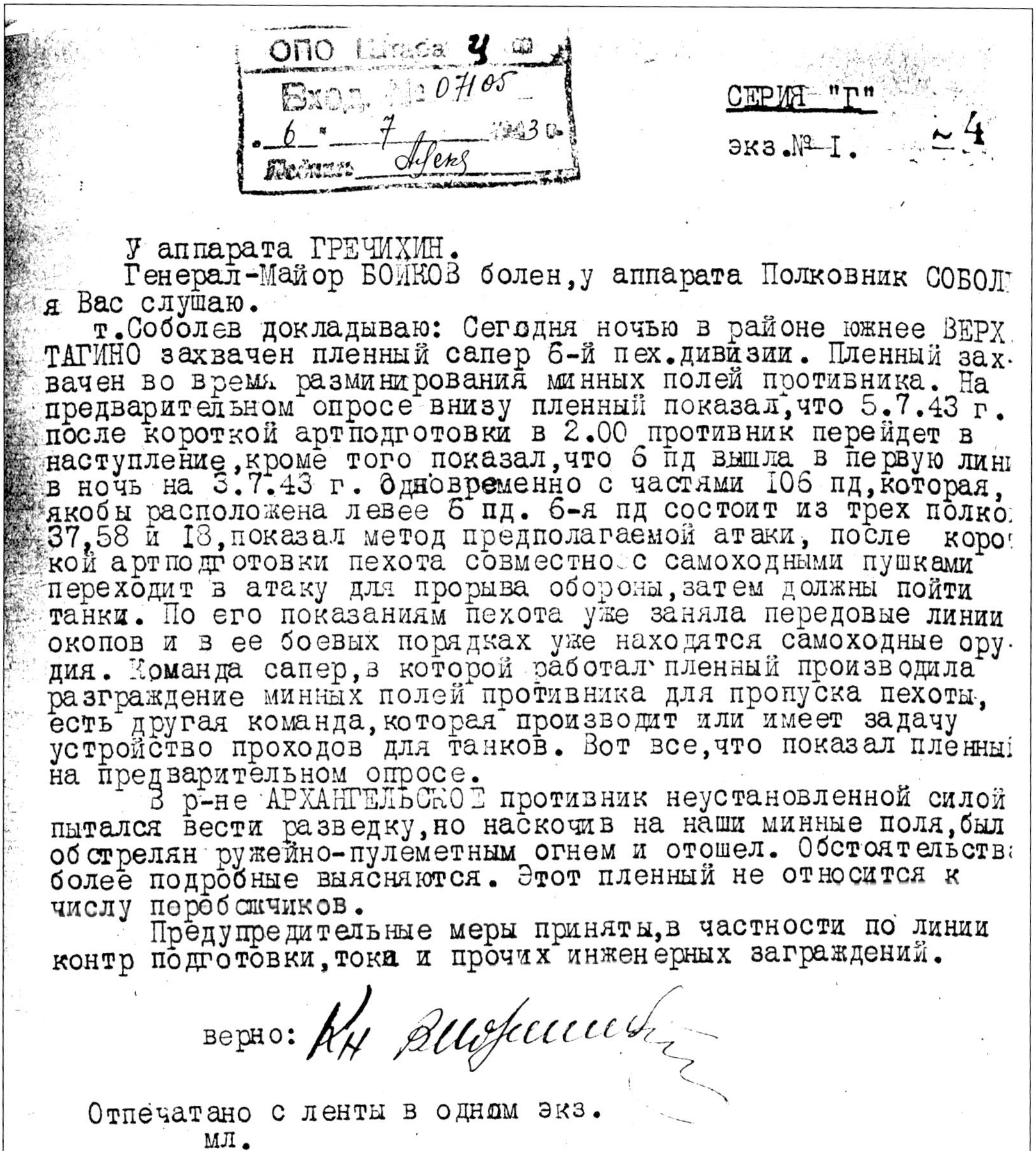

ОПО Штаба Ц Ф
Вход. № 07105
6 7 1943 г.

СЕРИЯ "Г"
экз.№ I. 4

У аппарата ГРЕЧИХИН.
Генерал-Майор БОЙКОВ болен,у аппарата Полковник СОБОЛ[ЕВ] я Вас слушаю.
т.Соболев докладываю: Сегодня ночью в районе южнее ВЕРХ. ТАГИНО захвачен пленный сапер 6-й пех.дивизии. Пленный захвачен во время разминирования минных полей противника. На предварительном опросе внизу пленный показал,что 5.7.43 г. после короткой артподготовки в 2.00 противник перейдет в наступление,кроме того показал,что 6 пд вышла в первую лини[ю] в ночь на 3.7.43 г. одновременно с частями 106 пд,которая, якобы расположена левее 6 пд. 6-я пд состоит из трех полко[в] 37,58 и 18,показал метод предполагаемой атаки, после короткой артподготовки пехота совместно с самоходными пушками переходит в атаку для прорыва обороны,затем должны пойти танки. По его показаниям пехота уже заняла передовые линии окопов и в ее боевых порядках уже находятся самоходные орудия. Команда сапер,в которой работал пленный производила разграждение минных полей противника для пропуска пехоты, есть другая команда,которая производит или имеет задачу устройство проходов для танков. Вот все,что показал пленны[й] на предварительном опросе.
В р-не АРХАНГЕЛЬСКОЕ противник неустановленной силой пытался вести разведку,но наскочив на наши минные поля,был обстрелян ружейно-пулеметным огнем и отошел. Обстоятельств[а] более подробные выясняются. Этот пленный не относится к числу перебежчиков.
Предупредительные меры приняты,в частности по линии контр подготовки,тока и прочих инженерных заграждений.

верно:

Отпечатано с ленты в одном экз.
мл.

A copy of the message sent from the headquarters of the 13th Army to the Central Front command regarding the capture of Corporal E. Formella (in the text he is identified only as a prisoner from the 6th Infantry Division) and his testimony regarding the start of an offensive. (TsAMO RF)

The intelligence chief of the 13th Army's 15th Rifle Division Captain P.G. Savinov, June 1943 (KOKM)

The commander of the 13th Army Lieutenant General N.P. Pukhov (on the right) and Military Council member Major General M.A. Kozlov; village of Arkhangel'skoe in Kursk Oblast, July 1943 (Photograph by Ia. Khalip, RGAKFD).

by all of Ninth Army's corps. This was one of the main reasons why the preemptive artillery barrage conducted by the Central Front on the night of 4-5 July proved to be not very effective. Marshal of the Soviet Union G.K. Zhukov, who was at that moment in Rokossovsky's Central Front headquarters, later recalled: "Observing the course of the battle and questioning prisoners, I came to the conclusion that both the Central and Voronezh Fronts had started it too early: the German soldiers were still crouched in the trenches, bunkers and ravines, while the tank units were concealed in their staging areas."[10]

Document One

Preliminary record of interrogation[11]

The German Army deserter soldier Edwin Mikinj, who belonged to the 3rd Company of the 6th Infantry Division's 18th Infantry Regiment, and who came over to our side in the area south of Verkhnee Tagino on 4 July 1943.

Question: Biographical information and service background before arriving at the front.
Answer: Soldier Edwin Mikinj was born on 17 June 1920 in Kühnsdorf (Klagenfurt District, Austria), a Slovenian, single, employee of an Alpine metal factory, graduate of a secondary school and trade school, no Party membership. Called up into the army in December 1942 in Weißkirchen (Moravia – Ostrava area), underwent military training in the 3rd Company of the 2nd Training Panzer Grenadier Battalion until 20 March 1943, before being transferred to Sankt-Pölten (Austria), from where as part of a march battalion (1,200 soldiers) he was sent to the USSR along the route: Vienna – Silesia – Brest – Litovsk – Minsk – Briansk – Belye Berega (28 April 1943); from this point he was sent through Briansk to the Duminichi area. The Weiss' program of combat training had been organized there.[12]

Then the battalion and its 3rd Company was sent to Kokino, where there was up to a company of tankers (he doesn't know their unit) in addition to them. In Kokino they were used as a labor battalion for constructing field works (digging narrow trenches and bunkers for ammunition stockpiles). Part of the battalion was sent to an engineer school in Briansk; more than 200 soldiers were sent through Briansk and Orel to Zmievka Station (27 June 1943). Some of the rail cars of the arriving train were sent by a different train even further, while approximately 80 soldiers remained in the Plota area, 20 kilometers west of Zmievka, where they became replacements for the 6th Infantry Division. After assignment to regiments, 6 soldiers (including Mikinj) were added to the roster of the 3rd Company of the 6th Infantry Division's 18th Infantry Regiment. On 2 July 1943 the company arrived at the front at took up a defense in the area south of Verkhnee Tagino, having replaced the units of some division (he doesn't know its identity). The weapons of the units that had been positioned there previously were left behind in the trenches, in particular MG-42 machine guns, which were positioned 50 meters apart

10 G.K. Zhukov, *Vospominaniia i razmyshleniia* [*Reminiscences and reflections*]. Vol. 3 (Moscow: Novosti), p. 46.
11 TsAMO RF, F. 361, Op. 6081, D. 64, L. 1. Original text. Machine-typed text.
12 This refers to Group Weiß, the code name for the Ninth Army prior to the Battle of Kursk.

from each other. On the way he saw a lot of new vehicles that were moving in the direction of the front (he didn't notice any insignia on them). He saw no tanks.

Question: Dislocation of the units on the front line.
Answer: His 3rd Company has a sector of 250 meters. The command post of the 3rd Company is located in a bunker 200 meters behind the front. He doesn't know the adjacent units. He also doesn't know where the headquarters are located. He saw a second line of defense (just trenches without machine gun nests) 2 kilometers behind the front line. A barbed wire obstacle (one band) extends in front of the trenches of the first line of defense. He doesn't know whether there are any minefields.

Question: Company's composition and weaponry.
Answer: The 3rd Company's strength (not including the baggage train) is 80 soldiers. They are primarily Germans. There are two Slovenians in the company. The company consists of three platoons; there are 2-3 squads (5-9 soldiers each) in a platoon, with 8 squads in his company. The company's age profile consists of young men born in 1924 and soldiers of older ages between 27 and 40.

Company's weaponry: 12 light MG-42 machine guns, 12 submachine guns, pistols and carbines; he didn't see any mortars in the company. There is one anti-tank rifle in his squad's sector. In addition, two heavy machine guns have been attached. He also saw one infantry gun (150mm caliber).

He doesn't know the names of the company and battalion commanders, nor of the regiment commander.

Question: Unit's assignment.
Answer: The division's task is to attack in the direction of Kursk within four days. Six panzer divisions should be assembled to support the infantry by the moment of attack. Rumors are circulating among the soldiers that the Russians are totally unaware of this offensive. He doesn't know anything about the Russian units opposite the division.

Question: Chemical preparation in the company.
Answer: There is talk that the Russians might be the first to use poison gas. The soldiers all have gas masks with the latest 1943 filters. In addition, all the soldiers have capes and Losantin [a skin detoxifying agent].[13] They underwent chemical training only in Germany (the study of poison gases). They had their last fumigation in April 1943 in the Czech Republic.

Question: Food in the company.
Answer: The daily bread ration for soldiers – 600 grams. In addition, they receive hot and black coffee without sugar once a day, as well as 125 grams of cheese and 50 grams of margarine. The soldiers are unhappy with the rations.

Question: Mood among the soldiers.
Answer: Although the Germans are tired of the war, some of them still believe in Germany's victory. The Slovenians don't want to fight. There were cases of self-inflicted wounds in

13 Means of defense against chemical weapons.

the regiment. In Slovenia the partisan movement is becoming extensive. The families of partisans are subjected to repressions and executions.

He doesn't know the division's insignia or the 3rd Company of the 18th Infantry Regiment's field post number.

Interrogator: Deputy Chief of the 13th Army's Intelligence Department Major (Bukhtin)
Military interpreter of the 13th Army's Intelligence Department: Captain of Administrative Service (Mironov)[14]

Document 2

Information of a preliminary interrogation[15]
Gefreitor Bruno Formella, who belongs to the 1st Company of the 6th Infantry Division's 6th Pioneer Battalion

Gefreitor Bruno Formella, a Pole by nationality, taken prisoner on the night of 4-5 July 1943 in the vicinity of Verkhnee Tagino. The prisoner stated:

> The 6th Infantry Division arrived in Orel from the area of Pochinok (near Smolensk) in the middle of July. The pioneer battalion spent 8 days in the Bulatovo area (30-35 kilometers south of Orel). On the night of 1-2 July 1943 it arrived at the front. The infantry regiments of the 6th Infantry Division arrived a day later. In the Verkhnee Tagino sector, the 6th Infantry Division replaced the 106th Infantry Division [sic],[16] which was shifted to the right (to the west). The 6th Infantry Division arrived with three infantry regiments: the 18th, 37th and 58th Infantry Regiments. The pioneer battalion was broken down into separate companies and distributed among all three infantry regiments with the task of supporting their preparation for the offensive. The 1st Pioneer Company was attached to the 37th Infantry Regiment; the 37th Infantry Regiment is occupying a sector from Verkhnee Tagino to the west. The 18th Infantry Regiment is on its left, the 58th Regiment on its right. The headquarters of the 18th Infantry Regiment is located on the Sadovod State Farm. To the west of the 58th Infantry Regiment is the 106th Infantry

14 Sergei Aleksandrovich Mironov (1910 to 1998) was a leading specialist in the field of Dutch studies and German dialectology. He received his German language training at Leningrad University. In 1940, he defended his dissertation on German dialects and was appointed Dean of the Department of Foreign Languages of Gor'kii State Pedagogical Institute. He served in the acting army from October 1941 as an interpreter of the 13th Army's Intelligence Department. In June 1943 he received a promotion and became the chief of the Intelligence Department's investigative office. On the threshold of the Battle of Kursk and during the battle itself, he personally interrogated prisoners and compiled information on their basis for the leadership of the 13th Army and the Central Front. It was he who first interrogated B. Formella of the Wehrmacht's 6th Infantry Division, who was taken prisoner on the night of 4-5 July 1943 and who revealed that the offensive would begin in the next few hours. As K.K. Rokossovsky maintained, this information was especially important before the start of the battle. For his professionalism and personal courage in the war years, Mironov was decorated with Orders of the Red Star (1943) and of the Great Patriotic War, 2nd Degree (1945), as well as with the medal "For combat merit" (1942). Between 1945 and 1953 he headed Dutch studies in the Military Institute of Foreign Languages in Moscow, but in 1955 he returned to research work in the USSR Academy of Sciences and worked in Moscow State University.

15 TsAMO RF, F. 361, Op. 6081, D. 64, L. 2. Original text. Machine-typed.

16 In reality, the 6th Infantry Division replaced the 86th Infantry Division.

Division [sic]; the prisoner heard about this from the crews of a separate battalion of assault guns.

Four tank divisions and a large amount of artillery have been assembled in the rear of the 6th Infantry Division (he learned this from conversations with soldiers and junior commanders). The 105th Assault Gun Battalion [sic] is supporting the 6th Infantry Division.[17] According to the conversations of soldiers and junior commanders, the 6th and 106th Infantry Divisions [sic] are to attack toward Kursk. At the same time, German units are to launch an offensive from the south and west with the aim of encircling the units of the Red Army located within the Kursk tongue (salient).[18] Simultaneously, demonstration attacks are to be launched in other sectors.

The start of the offensive is set between 0100 and 0200 [Berlin time, which was one hour behind Moscow time] on 5 July 1943. The assignment: the 6th Infantry Division is to penetrate 6 kilometers into the defenses, and then tanks are to exploit the success.

The group of pioneers – 3 men and 6 riflemen, equipped with a light machine gun, had the task to clear a passage in the Russian minefield for the infantry. Other groups later were to clear passages in the minefields for the assault guns.

Chief of Intelligence of the 13th Army Lieutenant Colonel Kryzhanovsky
5.7.43

Document 3

Reference No. 49. Transmitted from the 13th Army as No. 251 at 1255 6 June, received by the Front headquarters at 1330. Kaminsky[19]

Record of interrogation[20]

Prisoner-of-war *Gefreitor* Bruno Formella of the German Army, 1914 year of birth, from the village of Bolsza near the city of Neustadt, a Pole by nationality; education – 6 grades; worker in a brick factory; seized in the area of Verkhnee Tagino on the night of 4-5 July 1943, he belongs to the 6th Pioneer Battalion (1st Company) of the 6th Infantry Division,.

Question: Service background prior to arrival at the front.

Answer: He was mobilized into the German Army on 11 May 1942 in the town of Höchster (Germany), where he underwent training in the 6th Reserve Pioneer Battalion until 13 September 1942.

On 20 September 1942 he was sent to the Eastern Front from the city of Münden as part of a pioneer company (120 men), following the route: Münden – Berlin – Poznan – Warsaw – Baranovichi – Minsk – Smolensk – Viaz'ma – Rzhev (20 September 1942). Until the end of March 1943, the division was in retreat to Dorogobuzh, where it remained until May 1943. At the beginning of May, the division was moved to Smolensk,

17 In reality the 6th Infantry Division received the 904th Assault Gun Battalion as reinforcement.

18 In the jargon of the German army, the Kursk bulge was called the Kursk balcony or the Kursk tongue.

19 Aleksei Il'ich Kaminsky (1889 to 1992). Between February and August 1943, he was the Central Front's deputy chief of staff for intelligence and chief of the Intelligence Department; a colonel. For his successful completion of command assignments in the course of preparing for and conducting the Battle of Kursk, he was awarded the Order of the Patriotic War 1st Degree.

20 TsAMO RF, F. 361A, Op. 6081, D. 64, L. 3-4. Original text. Machine-typed.

and from there to the Pochinok area in the middle of May. On 15-17 June of this year, the division was sent to Orel. The pioneer battalion was positioned 30-35 kilometers south of Orel for 8 days, resting. The pioneer battalion arrived at the front on the night of 1-2 July. The infantry regiments arrived a day later. The 6th Infantry Division replaced the 106th Infantry Division [sic] in the Verkhnee Tagino sector, and the latter division was shifted to the right (westward).

Question: The disposition of the units on the front line.
Answer: The 6th Infantry Division's 37th Infantry Regiment moved into the area of Verkhnee Tagino and to the west of there; on its left (east) flank is the 6th Infantry Division's 18th Infantry Regiment; to the west of it are the 58th Infantry Regiment and the 106th Infantry Division [sic]. He doesn't know where the division headquarters is located. The headquarters of the 18th Infantry Regiment is located in a factory building on the Sadovod State Farm. A stockpile of ammunition is present in the area north of Lebedikhi. Supposedly four tank divisions and a large amount of artillery are concentrated in the 6th Infantry Division's rear. The headquarters of the pioneer battalion is located in Verkhnee Tagino. At the windmill west of Zakharovka is a new bridge across the Oka River (with a load capacity of 24 metric tons). North of Verkhnee Tagino is an old bridge across the Oka River.

Question: Composition and organization of the division and pioneer battalion.
Answer: The 6th Infantry Division consists of three regiments: the 18th Infantry Regiment, the 37th Infantry Regiment and the 58th Infantry Regiment. In addition, the division has an artillery regiment (identity unknown) and the 6th Pioneer Battalion. The infantry regiments are presumably of three-battalion composition. Four assault guns (with a caliber of approximately 75mm) of the 105th Separate Assault Gun Battalion [sic] are attached to each battalion. He doesn't have any more details on the composition of the infantry regiments.

The 6th Pioneer Battalion consists of three companies. The 1st Company has 60 pioneers, while the 2nd and 3rd Companies each have 80 pioneers. The companies are of three-platoon composition. Each platoon has three squads (with 6-7 pioneers in each squad). One company of the pioneer battalion has been attached to each infantry regiment, while each infantry battalion has been given one pioneer platoon. One squad of pioneers serves each infantry company. The 1st Company of the 6th Pioneer Battalion was attached to the 37th Infantry Regiment. The pioneers are armed with rifles and equipped with wooden probes with iron tips; they also have mine sweepers. The nationality composition of the battalion is primarily German, but there is a small percentage of Poles. Replacements for the battalion have primarily come from convalescents. There is no perceptible shortage of ammunition or equipment.

Question: Division command staff.
Answer: He doesn't know the name of the division commander.[21] *Oberst* Delmer commands the 37th Infantry Regiment.

The commander of the pioneer battalion is *Hauptman* Wellnitz.

The commander of the pioneer battalion's 1st Company is *Oberleutnant* Bim [illegible]

21 The 6th Infantry Division at this time was being commanded by *Generalleutnant* H. Großman. The division joined the Ninth Army's XXXXI Panzer Corps.

The commander of the 1st Company's 1st Platoon is *Oberfeldwebel* Stork; the pioneer battalion's adjutant is *Leutnant* Heer.

Question: The tasks of the division and sapper battalion.
Answer: The task of the 6th and 106th Infantry Divisions [sic], according to talk among the soldiers and junior commanders, is to attack toward Kursk. The Germans are to attack simultaneously from the south, north and west with the aim of encircling units of the Red Army located in the tongue. Demonstration attacks with the aim of misleading the Russians are to be launched in other sectors of the front. The offensive is supposed to begin at 0100-0200 on 5 July 1943 and tanks are supposed to support the 106th Infantry Division [sic], while the 105th Assault Gun Battalion [sic] is to support the 6th Infantry Division. The 6th Infantry Division is to penetrate 6 kilometers into the defenses, and then tanks are to exploit the success. The pioneer battalion's assignment is to clear passages through the minefields with the aim of readying the offensive.

On the night of 4-5 July 1943, a group consisting of 3 pioneers and 6 infantrymen, plus one junior officer, armed with carbines and a machine gun, received the assignment to clear one lane (1.5 to 2 meters wide) through the Russian minefield for the passage of infantry. Other groups of pioneers were later to clear wider passages for the assault guns. The mines on the forward edge of the German defense were supposedly removed by pioneers and the 106th Infantry Division [sic].

Question: Status of chemical defense preparations.
Answer: In the company there are gas masks with the latest 1943 filter (which is effective for 5 hours, not 4 hours like the old ones). The 1st Pioneer Company has 6 chemical scouts – "sniffers". They are equipped with rubber jumpsuits; the chemical scouts went through chemical warfare training in Murav'evo (near Rzhev) for three weeks. On 1 June, an order came down that the soldiers must carry gas masks on their bodies. In one pioneer company there is one portable flamethrower. The flamethrower operator is Gefreitor Lachs.

The gas officer of the pioneer battalion is Feldwebel Grode. In the pioneer companies there are also up to 100 or more smoke canisters. The last fumigation took place in Höchster (Westphalia) in August 1942. The signal for a gas alarm is a whistling rocket.

Question: Food in the company.
Answer: The soldiers daily receive 750 grams of bread, 40 grams of butter, and 40 grams of canned meat or fish. Soldiers up to 22 years-of-age receive a supplementary 500 grams of bread per day and 15 grams of meat and butter. In the morning and evening, the soldiers drink coffee. Each man is given 6 cigarettes or 2 cigars each day.

Question: Mood of the soldiers in the company.
Answer: One-quarter of the soldiers in the company believes in Germany's eventual victory. Soldiers of older age in their majority don't believe in a successful outcome of the war for Germany. The majority of the young soldiers are Hitler's Youth members – their attitudes are still rather bouyant. Discipline in the company is strict. It is maintained primarily by carping junior officers. In the rear, discussions about the situation on the fronts are conducted for the company's soldiers rather often.

Question: Circumstances of the capture.

Answer: The pioneer was taken prisoner while in the process of lifting mines from our minefields and creating passages in them at 2300 on 4 July 1943.

The emblem of the 6th Infantry Division is a dark green shield bearing a red letter "G".

The number of the field post for the 1st Company of the 6th Pioneer Battalion is 20126.

Interrogators: Chief of the 13th Army's Intelligence Department Lieutenant Colonel (Kryzhanovsky)

Interpreter of the investigative unit Captain of Administrative Service (Mironov)

8

The counter-artillery preparation – a successful decision, or a case of "firing cannons at sparrows"?

When planning the defensive operation of the Central and Voronezh Fronts, their commands worked out a number of measures intended to inflict heavy damage to the German troops even while in their jumping-off positions for the offensive toward Kursk. A preemptive artillery barrage, as anticipated, was to be the most effective. In the documents of their headquarters it is noted that the measure had as its main goal – "to disrupt the enemy attack and not allow the possibility of executing an offensive at the given moment."[1] This was a very ambitious idea; in order to implement it, both *fronts* called upon forces of artillery and mortars that were unprecedented for that time: 51 artillery and mortar regiments, 11 rocket-launching regiments, and a significant number of 82mm and 120mm mortars, while in the sector of the 6th Guards Army, it even employed the fire of tank and rifle elements.[2] Throughout the entire post-war period in official domestic historiography of the Battle of Kursk the counter-artillery preparation was seen as a highly successful strike, which went without any hitches. Most significantly, in this view, when conducting it the enemy received substantial damage, and thus it supposedly played a weighty role in thwarting Operation Citadel's plan.

This point of view originated in the three-volume fundamental work *Istoriia Velikoi Otechestvennoi voiny Sovetskogo Soiuza 1941-1945* [*History of the Great Patriotic War of the Soviet Union 1941-1945*], which came out during the "Khrushchev thaw". It states that when the Soviet artillery opened fire, "... the German command was caught by surprise. Many of the German officers and soldiers believed that the Soviet forces had preempted them and were going on the offensive themselves. This undermined the troops' confidence in the leadership, shook their faith in the operation's success, and lowered the morale of the soldiers and officers." In addition, regarding the German artillery preparation that started later "... because the enemy's network of observation and command points had been disrupted, and command and control over the artillery and aviation weakened, he [the enemy] was unable to inflict any serious losses to the Soviet troops, particularly the well-camouflaged and dispersed artillery."[3]

1 General Staff's Military-Academic Department. *Sbornik boevykh dokumentov Velikoi Otechestvennoi voiny* [*Military-academic branch. Collection of combat documents of the Great Patriotic War*], Vol. 4 (Moscow: Voenizdat, 1948), Document 21.

2 TsAMO RF, NSB.Inv. 9998, L. 24.

3 *Istoriia Velikoi Otechestvennoi voiny Sovetskogo Soiuza 1941-1945* [*History of the Great Patriotic War of the Soviet Union 1941-1945*], Vol. 3 (Moscow: Voenizdat, 1964), p. 257.

This evaluation continued to dominate even after 1964, when the political leadership of the country changed and the views of the war's events began to be re-examined. For example, Marshal of the Soviet Union A.M. Vasilevsky's memoirs, which was published in 1970, observes:

> Having consulted with Vatutin, we decided on the night of 4-5 July to conduct the planned scenario of an artillery and aviation counter-artillery preparation, which as became clear later, had an exceptional effect. ... Even without knowledge of the details of the results of the counter-artillery preparation, we were experiencing a sense of great satisfaction with its overall results. The Hitlerites, instead of launching their offensive at 0300 on 5 July, were able to begin it only three hours later.[4]

The Marshal doesn't explain from which source he obtained the information about the time of the offensive's start, but through his narrative it becomes clear: from prisoners and deserters. Let's say directly that they are a dubious source, but nevertheless this assertion passed from book to book for many long years.

Marshal of the Soviet Union K.K. Rokossovsky also believed the preemptive attack of our artillery was highly effective. In his opinion, which he gives in his memoirs, as a result of the suddenly-opened fire on the German troops that were poised to move out on the offensive, the system of command and control in the forward divisions was disrupted.[5]

However, if we turn to publications written by other commanders and military chiefs that came out in print in our country in that same period, and first of all by those who had a direct connection with the organization of the counter-artillery preparation, then far from all of them support this version of events. For example, G.K. Zhukov wrote: "No doubt, the artillery counter-preparation inflicted large losses on the enemy and disorganized control over the troops' offensive, but we were nevertheless expecting greater results from it."[6]

If to judge from information from captured documents of the headquarters of Army Group South and Army Group Center, however, all of the divisions of their assault groupings stepped-off to implement Operation Citadel right on time and according to schedule, and by the end of the offensive they had penetrated 35 kilometers into our lines in the south of the Kursk salient, and up to 15 kilometers in the north. Moreover, it was in the very first days of the Battle of Kursk that a critical situation developed. As Zhukov testifies, the enemy forces "advanced 3-6 kilometers on the very first day, despite the unprecedented density of fire from our defenses."[7] Yet this was only on the Central Front; on the Voronezh Front, the German advance was double that in the north and here they had fully breached the most heavily-fortified, main army belt of defenses by the end of the first day. Already on 5 July, N.F. Vatutin issued an order for all his reserves and the 1st Tank Army to move up to the front,[8] and on the next day Moscow was compelled to get its strategic reserves,[9] which had been designated to launch a counter-offensive to liberate Ukraine after the German offensive had been stopped, on the march to this area in order to block the German breakthrough. Thus it isn't clear: What was the "exceptional effect" of our artillery's preemptive fire, and what was its impact on the enemy offensive? After all, in Paragraph 501 of the Red

4 A.M. Vasilevsky, *Delo vsei zhizni* [*Cause of an entire life*] Vol. 2 (Moscow: Politizdat, 1988), p. 26.
5 K.K. Rokossovsky, *Soldatskii dolg* [*Soldier's duty*] (Moscow: Voenizdat, 1997), p. 267.
6 See for example G.K. Zhukov, *Vospominaniia i razmyshleniia* [*Reminiscences and reflections*] (Moscow: APN, 1971, p. 459.
7 Ibid., p. 459.
8 See G.A. Koltunov and B.S. Solov'ev, *Kurskaia bitva* [*Battle of Kursk*] (Moscow: Voenizdat, 1970), pp. 143-144.
9 Ibid., pp. 151-152.

Army's 1943 Field Manual, it is indicated that an artillery counter-preparation is the primary measure to upset an enemy offensive.[10] Thus in the documents of the Central and Voronezh Fronts it was mandatory to disrupt the offensive with preemptive fire, or at the very least put a stop to it. However, the preemptive artillery attack accomplished neither one thing nor the other.

Unfortunately, the official publications pay no attention to this contradiction between claims and results. Over the past 70-plus years, the process of planning and conducting the counter-artillery preparation has become so murky and mythologized, that even in academic works published in contemporary Russia, one still comes across the same assertion that when conducting it, " ... the German forces sufferered losses in men and equipment, their artillery fire was disorganized, and command over the troops disrupted. As a result, the offensive against the Central Front was delayed by 2.5 hours, and that against the Voronezh Front, by 3 hours."[11] However, the authors don't explain the significance of these hours either for the enemy offensive, or for the Red Army's victory in the Battle of Kursk. In fact, was there actually a delay in the start time, or did an elementary mistake creep into the reckoning of the times? Moreover, this and similar publications offer no concrete figures for the enemy losses caused by the preemptive fire, and the assertion that the Germans really did have them isn't supported by reference to archival sources. This, naturally, puts the reader on guard and reduces the value of the narrative about these events in the publications.

Documents of the TsAMO RF that were de-classified in the period between 2011 and 2014, as well as captured materials from the US National Archives, which have become accessible today for Russian scholars, allow us to investigate how the planning of the preemptive artillery barrage went and assess its real results. Therefore let's turn to these sources, although it must be said straightaway that in both archives, there are not as many documents on this subject as desired.

It is no secret that there was no element of operational surprise in Operation Citadel. Already in April 1943, the Soviet side was already well-aware of Berlin's designs to cut off the Kursk salient. Thus the planning for the preemptive artillery strike proceeded simultaneously with the planning for the Kursk defensive operation, and it was an inseparable part of it. This measure was not a new conception of the Soviet command specifically for the summer 1943 fighting, as it might seem from familiarity with military-historical literature from the Soviet era. A counter-artillery preparation had been embodied as one of the elements of Red Army defensive thought in Article 242 of Part Two of the Artillery Field Manual, adopted back in 1941. It also had a place in the 1943 Red Army Field Manual (p. 561), although with the somewhat different name "counter-preparation". However, as the artillery command of the Central Front noted in its directive for organizing it from 16 May 1943: the terms didn't change the essence of the concept; it was one and the same measure.[12] It also had certain features:

2. The counter-preparation is organized at a decision of an army commander (corps commander) with a call upon the artillery, aircraft and in certain cases even tanks.
3. The counter-artillery preparation is organized by the artillery commanders of the army (corps, division) at their own initiative or comprises the main part of the army's (corps') counter-preparation with the approval of the army commander (corps commander).

10 TsAMO RF, F. 361, Op. 6094, D. 272, L. 153.

11 *Velikaia Otechestvennaia voina: Voenno-istoricheskie ocherki* [*Great Patriotic War: Military-historical essays*] Vol. 2: *Perelom* [*Turning point*] (Moscow: Nauka, 1998), p. 261.

12 General Staff's Military-Academic Department. *Sbornik boevykh dokumentov Velikoi Otechestvennoi voiny* [*Collection of combat documents of the Great Patriotic War*] Vol. 4 (Moscow: Voenizdat, 1948), Document 21.

4. The counter-artillery preparation is organized on the basis of thorough analysis of information from all types of intelligence on the enemy and on the grouping of his manpower, tanks and artillery.
5. The counter-artillery preparation can be conducted on the scale of an army, corps or division, and in this case will carry the character of a general or partial preparation.

> … In order to conduct the counter-artillery preparation, it must include the 120mm and 82mm mortar batteries, divisional artillery and all attached artillery assets.
>
> The fire must be maximally concentrated, and the barrage – unexpected and simultaneously on all the entire depth of the targets' dispositions, subject to the effects of fire.[13]

It should be noted that the reasons that prompted Rokossovsky and Vatutin to conduct a preemptive artillery barrage were different. On the Central Front this decision was reached, if one can so express it, under the influence of a surplus of forces, whereas on the Voronezh Front, it was because of a lack of forces. Already by the end of the February-March offensive toward Briansk by Rokossovsky's forces, in addition to the authorized artillery means of the rifle divisions (separate battalions and regiments), his *front* received 20 artillery and mortar regiments from the Supreme Command Reserve, although they didn't arrive until the beginning of April, after the fighting ended. In addition, in April the process of this *front*'s refitting was underway, and in order to complete it, it was planned (and implemented) to give it significant supplementary artillery means, first in order to bring it and all of its subordinate formations and units back up to authorized strength; secondly to increase the artillery and mortars above establishment strength for the forthcoming 1943 summer counteroffensive; and finally to give it as well super-heavy rocket launching brigades (with 300mm rocket launchers). As a result it was intended that a most powerful artillery grouping would be deployed in Rokossovsky's Central Front in May 1943, with a total of up to 150 artillery regiments, brigades and separate battalions.[14]

Once again I will stress that from the beginning the Central Front received these significant artillery assets in order to repulse an enemy offensive toward Kursk, which was expected once the ground hardened after the spring thaw. Thus, here the idea of a preemptive barrage suggested itself.

Vatutin's Voronezh Front, on the contrary, after the difficult Khar'kov defensive operation, was a shadow of its former self by the end of March 1943, yet its command couldn't count upon receiving such significant artillery reinforcement as the Central Front received. In the course of April Moscow promised only to bring it up to the reduced TO&E of a *front*, because the General Staff and the *Stavka* believed that in the course of preparing for the forthcoming offensive, the foe would concentrate his main forces in the Orel salient (opposite the Central Front). In addition, parallel with the process of replenishing the forces in the Kursk salient, a process of creating a strategic reserve was underway – the Steppe Military District, which required significant resources of men and materiel. Thus simultaneously with restoring the combat capability of his formations and units, N.F. Vatutin was seeking any alternative technique or measure by which to enhance his defense and counter the enemy.[15] A preemptive artillery barrage suited this purpose like nothing else.

In order to understand the role given to the preemptive artillery barrage in the *fronts*' system of defense, as an example let's turn to the plan of Rokossovsky's headquarters for the use of the artillery grouping in the struggle with the attacking enemy. In brief it looked like this: For the first

13 Ibid.
14 G.S. Nadysev, *Na sluzhbe shtabnoi* [*At staff service*] (Moscow: Voenizdat, 1976), p. 122.
15 I'll remind the reader that at the beginning of April 1943, the Voronezh Front such an exotic means for the struggle against tanks even for those times as mine-carrying dogs.

stage – the destruction of hostile forces in the positions they occupied and immediately opposite the forward edge of our forces. In order to inflict losses to the combat groups located in their jumping-off positions 3-5 kilometers from the front before the attack, the counter-artillery fire was supposed to begin 30 to 60 minutes before the attack. After its conclusion, blocking fire from indirect firing positions was to be opened during the approach of the enemy forces to within 200-300 meters of the forward edge, in order to separate the infantry from the tanks and reduce the pace of the attack. For the second stage, it was planned to annihilate the enemy armor as it closed within direct-fire range of the anti-tank guns positioned on the forward edge of the main belt of defenses. It was expected that here the enemy would suffer his main losses, since not only the anti-tank artillery would be activated, but also mines, anti-tank rifles, grenades and Molotov cocktails. Then finally, for the third stage – in the course of a possible struggle for the main belt of defenses, it was planned to employ not only the anti-tank reserves (the destroyer anti-tank artillery regiments and brigades), but also howitzer regiments firing over open sights, mobile blocking detachments and even rocket launchers.[16] The artillerymen of the Voronezh Front were also preparing to operate according to just such a plan.

Arriving intelligence at the end of March and in April 1943, as well as the analysis of the terrain, which the troops of the Central and Voronezh Fronts were holding, allowed the Soviet side to pinpoint with a great deal of likelihood where the Wehrmacht would launch its main and secondary attacks: in the north, in the sector of the 13th Army, and possibly against its flanking neighbors on the right and left, and in the south – against the 6th Guards and 7th Guards Armies. Thus, in order to realize the intent of the counter-preparation, the leadership of the *fronts* proposed to activate the artillery forces of the five armies of the first echelon: on the Central Front, the 48th, 13th and 70th Armies; and on the Voronezh Front, the 6th and 7th Guards Armies. The General Staff approved this proposal. The plan for the preemptive artillery strike was prepared and amended over the course of three months in response to arriving information from the intelligence organs. While working it out, the headquarters of both *fronts* had to address an entire array of various types of problems, but there were three main ones: the identification of the main targets for the artillery; the determination of the amounts and types of artillery needed in order to suppress them; and finally, the most difficult – determining when to start the preemptive barrage and how long to continue it. The success of the entire measure basically depended on finding successful answers to these problems.

However, initially, in the first several weeks, these fundamental problems were shifted to a back burner by a circumstance that was unexpected even for the two *fronts*' leadership. It may seem strange, but in the first stage of planning in April and early May, the artillery command of the two *fronts* was forced first to explain to their subordinates the essence of a counter-artillery preparation and the significance of it for the future operation, and second, teach them how to work out a plan for one and prepare the documentation. In an account of the artillery headquarters of the Central Front, its commander General V.I. Kazakov wrote:

> Back in March-April 1943, the troops were given an order regarding the planning of a counter-artillery preparation. During the next inspection it turned out that the artillery headquarters of the armies didn't have a clear picture of the tasks of a counter-artillery preparation and the schedule of planning for one. Thus in the first days of May, the artillery headquarters of the Central Front had to get to work creating instructions about organizing, planning and conducting a counter-artillery preparation. The need to prepare such directives was completely urgent, since the artillery chiefs at all levels of command had differing points of view on this

16 Nadysev, *Na sluzhbe shtatnoi*, p. 112.

> matter. … A directive went out to the troops on 16 May 1943. In its wake, the Front's artillery headquarters started to take active control over its implementation at every level of command …. In order to bring the artillery headquarters to a common understanding of the main questions of a counter-artillery preparation, it wasn't enough just to issue guidance by directives; it was still necessary to work intensely among the troops and to achieve clarification of the desired result. Over May and June, the plans for the counter-artillery preparation compiled by the artillery headquarters of the armies were revised repeatedly, since they didn't meet our requirements.[17]

A similar situation emerged on the Voronezh Front as well. There are several reasons for the fact that at the end of the second year of the war the artillery chiefs on the army level didn't know how to plan procedures according to regulation. Firstly, they didn't have experience. A counter-preparation on the scale of a *front* had practically never been conducted prior to this, since in the first phase of the war the means for conducting a full-scale preemptive artillery barrage and the need for one hadn't existed. Secondly, the general professional level of the artillery commanders, even on such a level as the army, still wasn't high; the turnover in the command cadres was too rapid. Moreover, there had been few artillery headquarters. At this moment, headquarters essentially consisted of two departments: operations and intelligence. Only in March 1943 was the post of a senior assistant chief for gathering the best practices of combat operations added to the operations department. In essence, the defense of the Kursk bulge became the first strategic operation that required the command staff of the artillery of the two *fronts* to work out in practice an entire complex of problems of planning and preparing this important element of combat operations.

The hard work to reveal the enemy's system of artillery fire, his artillery firing positions, areas of possible supply stockpiles and the dispositions of the assault group began in the first days after the front stabilized. Together with aerial and ground reconnaissance, detailed and more importantly reliable information about targets for the preemptive attack came from engineer headquarters. They played a particularly important role in gathering information about the enemy in the sector of Lieutenant General M.S. Shumilov's 7th Guards Army, which was occupying a defense on the left bank of the Northern Donets River in the Belgorod area. Although the army was positioned on the axis of an assumed secondary German offensive (in the Korocha direction), in the opinion of the Voronezh Front's command, the counter-artillery preparation in its sector was an important element in the plan for the entire defensive operation. The river here played the primary role, since it dictated the location of possible crossing sites to the enemy, which meant that the assembly areas of the German assault groupings were even more predictable. The Voronezh Front's chief of engineering Major General Iu.V. Bordzilovsky reported:

> The river … has been taken under particularly close monitoring by us … as a result a concentration of enemy bridging equipment has been detected in the areas: north of Solomino, Toplinka, Andreevka (west of Toplinka). In the period of immediate preparations for the offensive by the enemy, increasing work on the construction of bridges close behind the forward edge and across the river has been revealed:
>
> 10.6 The Germans constructed a submerged bridge in the vicinity of Toplinka;
> 13.6 Repair of a bridge in the area of Pushkarnoe has been spotted;
> 13.6 The presence of a wooden, low-water truss bridge has been spotted in the Mikhailovka, Suprunovka area;

17 TsAMO RF, F. 62, Op. 321, D. 96, LL. 167-168.

20.6 Through the analysis of aerial photographs, two serviceable bridges have been identified at Mikhailovka;

20-26.6 Bridging equipment of 20 pontoons on vehicles and one pontoon section arrived in the area of Andreevka.[18]

Side by side with this, evidence was also arriving about the German preparation of sectors of terrain at the front for the passage of units, including on the the western bank of the Northern Donets River. On 15 June one of our reconnaissance groups, which penetrated into the rear of the 168th Infantry Division, established that the barbed wire and a large minefield along the railroad in the area of the village of Pokrovka (north of Belgorod) had been removed. Four days later, on the night of 19-20 June, a group of engineer scouts in the vicinity of the village of Ogurtsovo discovered flattened sections of barbed wire and a cleared minefield, which had been there previously, in front of the trenches of units of the 320th Infantry Division. On 22 June German engineers attempted to remove mines on the southeastern outskirts of Arkhangel'skoe, and two days later German engineers were spotted in the same area by an observation post, but now between Kondyrevo and the Invalid Home (left flank of the 6th Guards Army).

The information collected in bits and pieces at the front and in the enemy's tactical zone was accumulating, being compiled and supplemented by the command of both *fronts*, after which it flowed downward in the form of orders and directives. For example, in the engineer headquarters of the Voronezh Front, a special map of Army Group South's fortifications was being compiled, which was supplemented by information in the daily reports that arrived over the telephone from armies and divisions of the front line, as well as every three days by intelligence summaries that contained maps, aerial photographs, prisoner statements and information from agents behind enemy lines. Once or twice a month, 200-300 copies of this map were made and distributed through the channel of the engineers (down to the battalion engineer inclusively) and to the army commanders (down to the rifle regiment level).

As a result, by the beginning of July analysis of the collected information allowed the leadership of the Voronezh Front first to be convinced that the foe, despite the repeated postponements of the offensive's start date, still hadn't cancelled it, and was moreover sticking to the same directions that had been predicted; and second, to determine the locations in the sector of the 7th Guards Army where the enemy intended to force a crossing of the Northern Donets River. According to reports from Bordlizovsky's service, this might be the Mikhailovka staging area and the areas of Toplinka and Solomino.

Work to determine targets for the counter-artillery preparation was going much less smoothly on the most likely direction of Army Group South's main attack – in the sector of the 6th Guards Army that was holding the Oboian' direction (including the Belgorod – Oboian' highway). There were significantly more places here suitable for formations of division size or larger, including panzer divisions, to go on the attack – approximately 65% of the army's entire sector. Accordingly, in order to ensure the effectiveness of the preemptive attack, as much accurate information as possible on the likely deployment areas of the enemy's attack groupings and the firing positions of his artillery was required. Just as in the case of the neighboring 7th Guards Army, in the course of May-June 1943 all of 6th Guards Army's reconnaissance efforts, including those of engineers and aerial reconnaissance, were directed at collecting information on the possible areas of enemy concentrations. The 2nd Air Army offered substantial assistance in this work. It had under its control the 454th Bomber Aviation Regiment, which was equipped with American A-20 Havoc light bombers that were equipped with contemporary photographic equipment. Incidentally, the

18 TsAMO RF, F. 203, Op. 2845, D. 227, L. 19.

Central Front also had such means of reconnaissance. Back in April, its artillery headquarters was given the 98th Separate Artillery Spotting and Reconnaissance Aviation Regiment, which consisted of four squadrons. Both aviation regiments were actively employed to locate enemy firing positions, observation posts and major supply dumps opposite the front of the first-echelon armies. Recalled the Central Front's artillery chief of staff General G.S. Nadysev, "In the preparatory period, the pilots did enormous work to collect repeated large-scale photographic images covering the entire depth of the German defenses. By the start of the defensive fighting, all of the artillery headquarters of the armies on the main axis were furnished with detailed information on the enemy."[19] However, as subsequent events would show, reconnaissance efforts of both *fronts* were unable to reveal fully the disposition of the enemy's firing positions or the areas of deployment of his attack groupings.

There are several reasons for this. First was the weakness of our intelligence. It is no secret that the field intelligence organs of the Red Army were going through a process of reorganization and in fact were only just now beginning to stand on their own feet, while at the same time the adversary was skillfully and energetically using all of his elaborate means of camouflage while taking account of the Soviet side's technical capabilities. One of the simplest and most widespread means of revealing enemy troops concentrations is by sending a reconnaissance patrol behind enemy lines and conduct systematic visual (and audio) monitoring of the enemy's behavior. However, the penetration of reconnaissance groups into the enemy rear was an extremely difficult and rarely successful task before the offensive because of the high concentration of German troops in the tactical zone and the increased security measures that the Germans had introduced at the front at this time. Thus, intelligence possessed primarily information gleaned by observers at nighttime, when, as a rule, the most intensive movement of forces was going on. With this aim, for example, prior to the Battle of Kursk communication trenches were dug by soldiers of the Central Front that extended from our trenches across no-man's land, even under bands of barbed wire, almost up to the enemy's combat positions. In order to observe (or overhear) stealthily the enemy's immediate rear areas from these trenches, soldiers with a knowledge of the German language who also had excellent hearing, eyesight and the ability to concentrate for long periods of time while observing were selected. In the soldier's parlance, they were called *slukhachi* (listeners). From the recollections of a member of the 13th Army's Intelligence Department Colonel V.M. Doroshenko:

> The information from observation was supplemented by audio surveillance. For this purpose each night small groups of scouts would leave their trenches and crawl off into the darkness, making their way through countless minefields and barbed wire obstacles. They would silently steal their way up to the enemy's defenses and from suitable places listen to what was happening behind the enemy's lines. The information gleaned by the groups of listeners was compared with other data, and from them we in the army's Intelligence Department unmistakably determined the relief or rotation of German formations and units. For example, in the initial period we succeeded in establishing the relief of the Nazi's 20th Panzer Division on the army's left flank. The information gleaned by observation and listening in this case was confirmed by radio intelligence.[20]

Such "secret" trenches were discovered by the Germans back in May, while they were conducting a reconnaissance-in-force in the sector of the 48th and 13th Armies. At the time the Ninth Army

19 Nadysev, *Na sluzhbe shtabnoi*, p. 127.

20 *V ogne Kurskoi bitvy. Iz vospominanii uchastnikov boev* [*In the fire of the Battle of Kursk. From the recollections of participants of the fighting*] (Kursk: Kurskoe knizhnoe izdatel'stvo, 1963), p. 32.

command had mistakenly viewed them as a means for stealthily bringing up troops close to the German trenches with the aim of launching a surprise attack against the forward companies, and only ordered increased observation over the rear area of our forces, in order not to overlook the moment when the Soviet troops formed for the attack. However, in several places these trenches remained undetected, and our scouts actively used them before the start of the fighting, in order to heighten the accuracy of the collected information.

However, with each passing day it was becoming increasingly difficult to acquire the necessary information. The German side was paying close attention to camouflaging positions and deceptive measures. Directives about their active use were contained in Hitler's first Order No. 6 from 15 April 1943 about conducting Operation Citadel.[21] By the beginning of July, the system of various measures of camouflage and disinformation was in full swing. Even though a stealthy regrouping of significant forces around the Kursk bulge was impossible, the enemy often managed to keep the actual areas of assembly of separate formations and units in secrecy, and was also able to bring up heavy weapons unnoticed to the forward edge. Here is just one example. Between 1 and 4 July 1943, in the sector of Ninth Army's XXXXI Panzer Corps, which was preparing to attack the Central Front, the new Ferdinand heavy self-propelled guns began to approach the front. According to the Germans themselves, the noise of their engines was audible to an ordinary man over a distance of 30 kilometers, which was significantly greater than the operation of the engine of other tanks.[22] Moreover, the sound of this self-propelled gun's running engine was also unlike the sound of any other vehicle's engine. Model's army didn't possess any transport capable of carrying a Ferdinand, which had a combat weight of more than 65 metric tons, over the rural roads and highways. Therefore a special system of deception was devised in order to move them up to the front, namely the overflights of several aircraft over the area as the heavy tank destroyers moved up, so that their sound muffled the noise of the Ferdinand's engine. This requirement for the march of the Ferdinand battalions was especially stipulated in an order from the Ninth Army's headquarters, although it wasn't always followed. For example, on the night of 1-2 July because of bad weather the aircraft couldn't fly, so the heavy tank destroyers moved without their accompaniment. Fearing that Soviet intelligence had detected their movement, the Ninth Army command on the following day ordered the headquarters of the XXIII Army Corps to begin shifting StuG self-propelled guns to the sector of the 216th Infantry Division, through the same area where the Ferdinands had been that night. The calculation was simple: if the sound of the Ferdinands had been detected by Soviet intelligence, the movement of the StuG assault guns would create the impression that the Ferdinands were in the process of leaving this place.[23] It remains unknown whether this deception technique worked, or whether the Soviet side had been unable to detect the assembly of the heavy self-propelled guns behind the enemy's forward units opposite the center of the 13th Army's defenses. Nothing is said about self-propelled guns in the intelligence summary of the 13th Army for 2 July 1943; it is only noted that "in the course of the night, the rumble of motors was audible in the areas of Khitrova, Khitrovskii and Arkhangel'skoe.", which indicates the Ferdinands' exact area of assembly, but there is only silence in the document about what was going on there (whether equipment had approached or left the area).[24] Skipping ahead somewhat, I will note that despite the "unusual voice" of the Ferdinands, on the morning of 5 July 1943, all of the heavy tank destroyers were introduced into the fighting from their jumping-off positions without any losses caused by our preemptive artillery barrage.

21 I.V. Parot'kin (ed.), *Kurskaia bitva* [*Battle of Kursk*] (Moscow: Nauka, 1970), p. 522.
22 NARA, T. 312, R. 317, F. 7886137.
23 NARA, T. 312, R. 317, F. 7886140.
24 TsAMO RF, F. 361, Op. 6081, D. 49, L. 2.

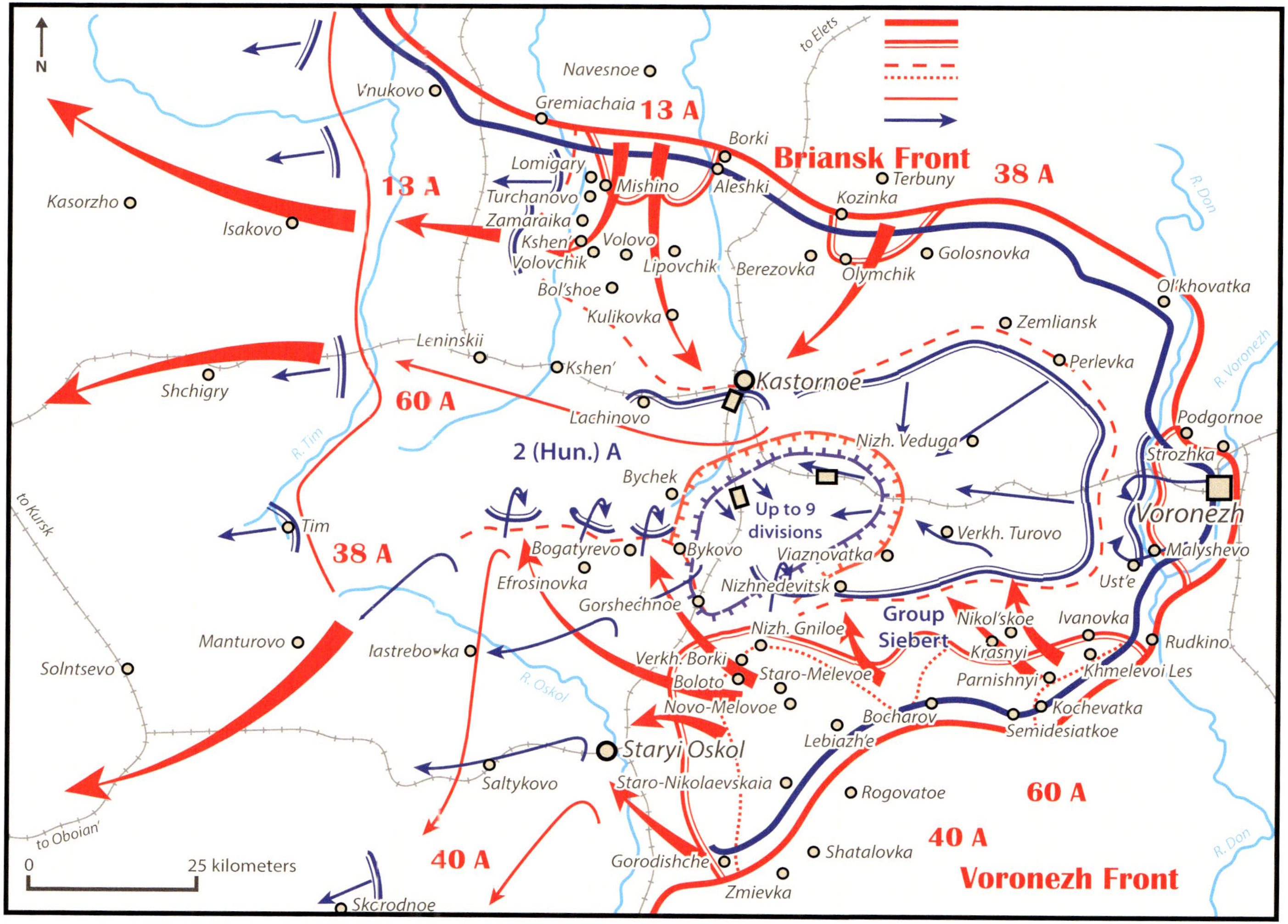

Map 1 Fighting on the Voronezh and Briansk fronts during the Voronezh-Kastornoe offensive in late January-early February 1943.

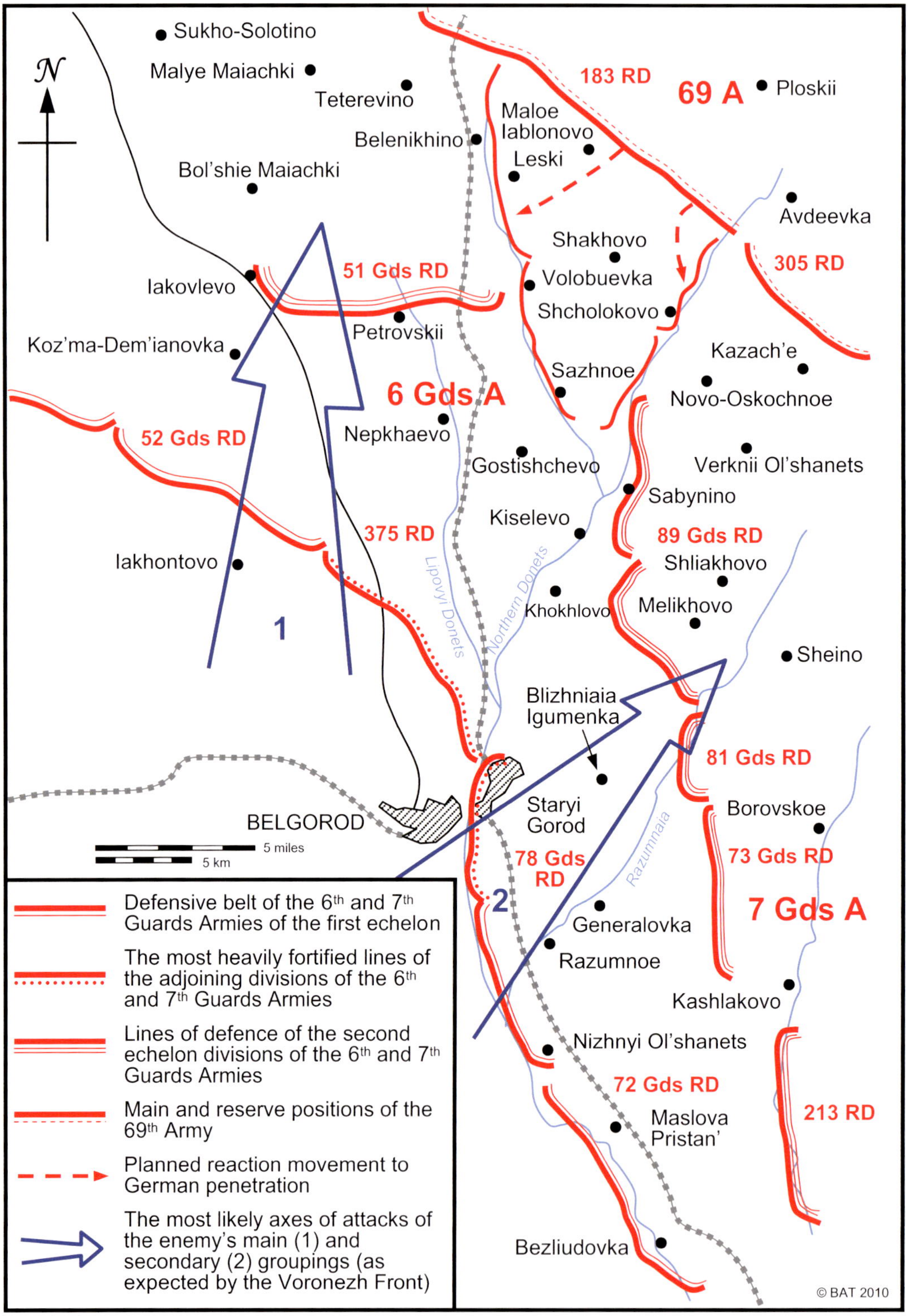

Map 2 Vatutin's Plan; Voronezh Front's system of defense and the assumed directions of enemy attack.

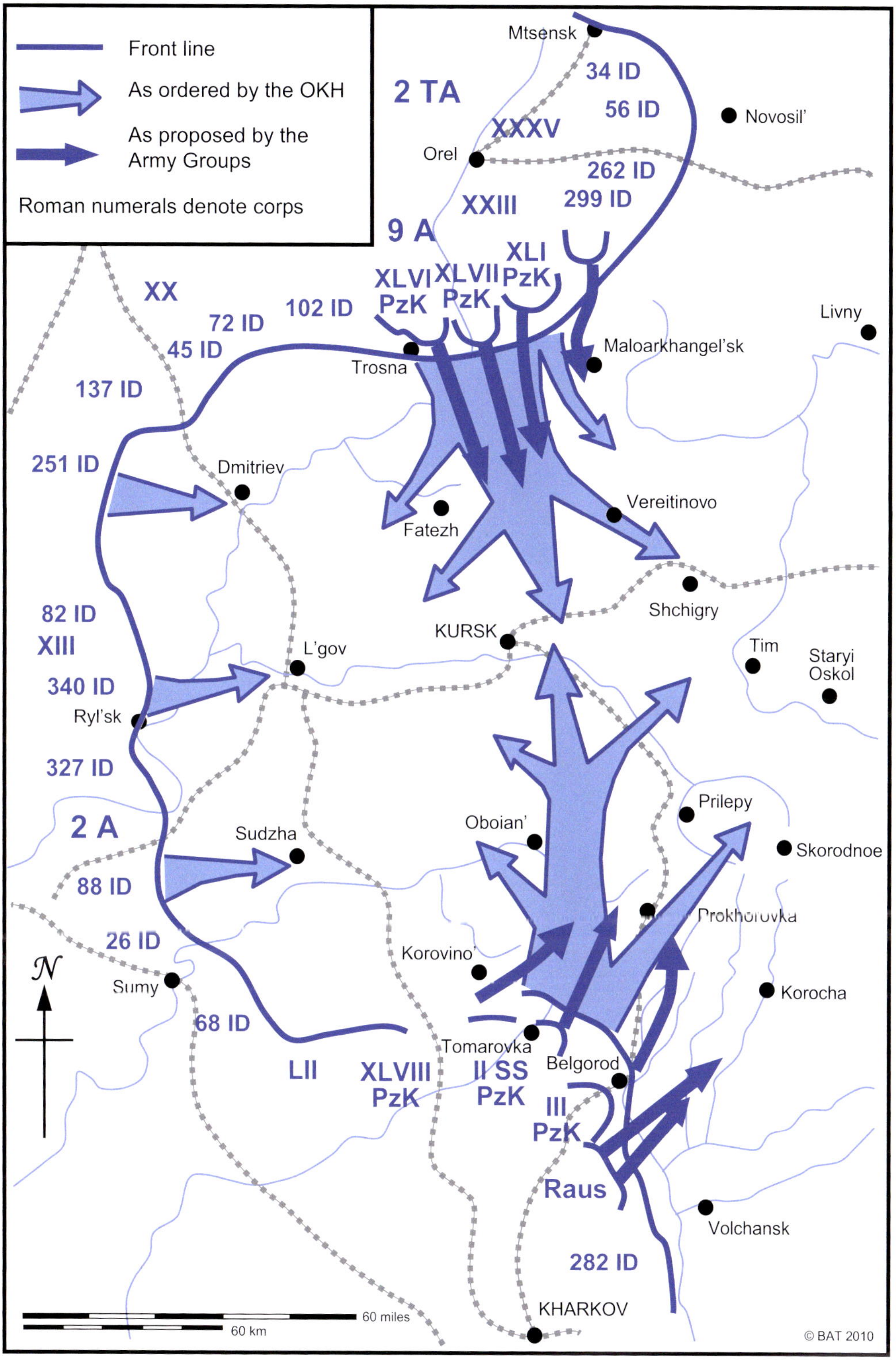

Map 3 OKH Operational Order No 6 from 15 April 1943.

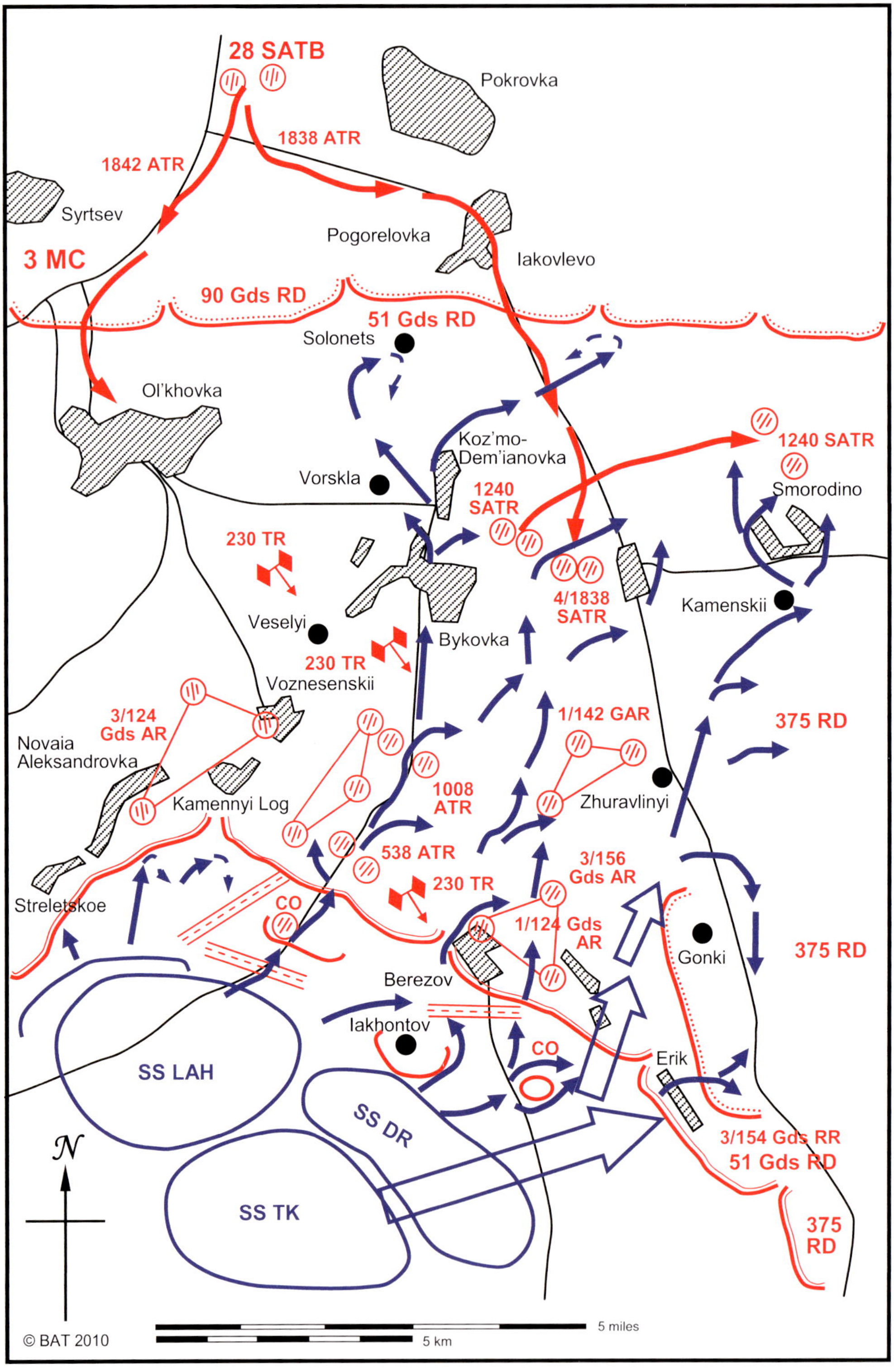

Map 4 The Penetration of the 52nd Guards Rifle Division's Defenses by Divisions of the II SS Panzer Corps, 5 July 1943.

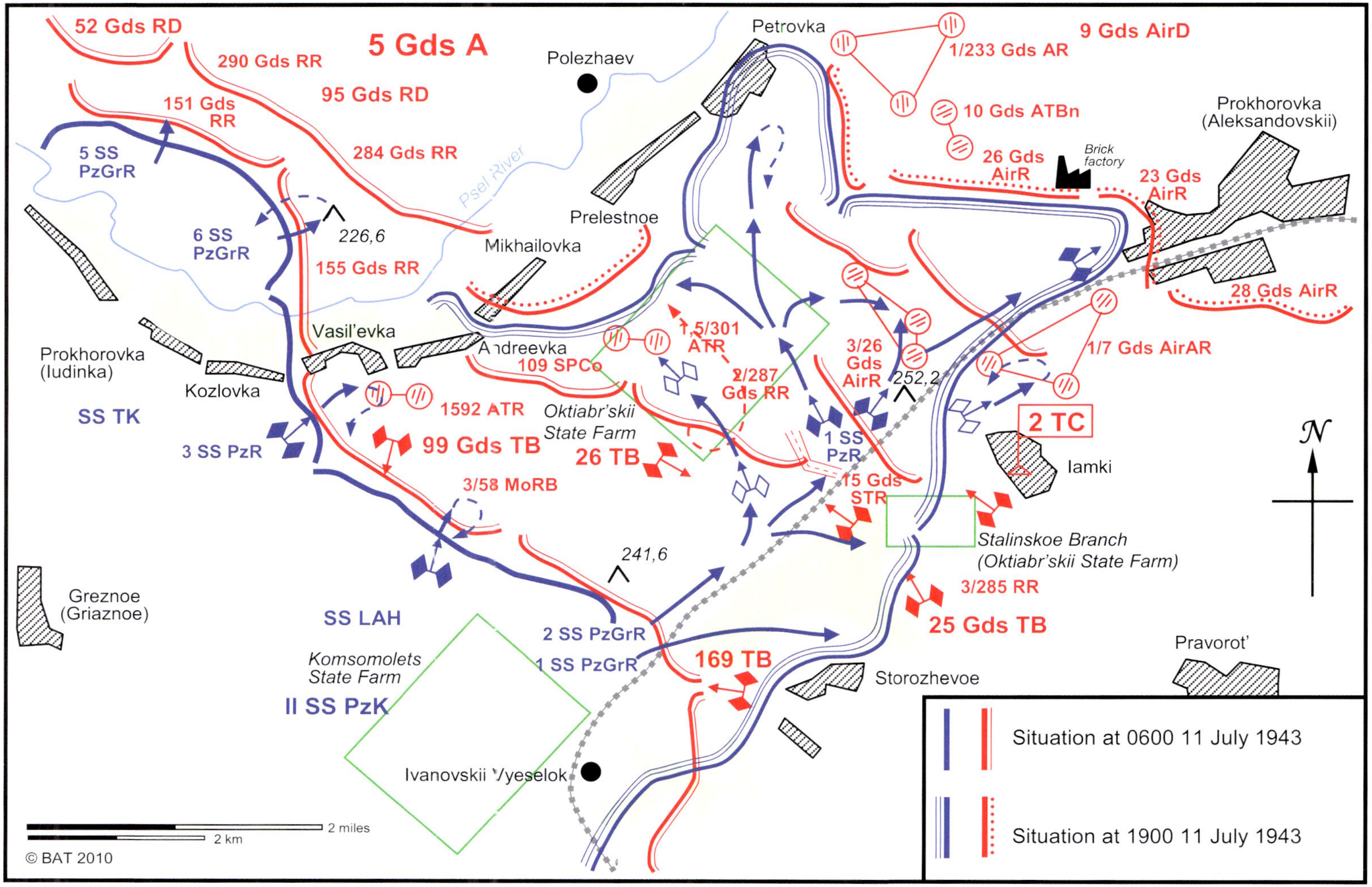

Map 5 Combat Operations Southwest of Prokhorovka on 11 July 1943.

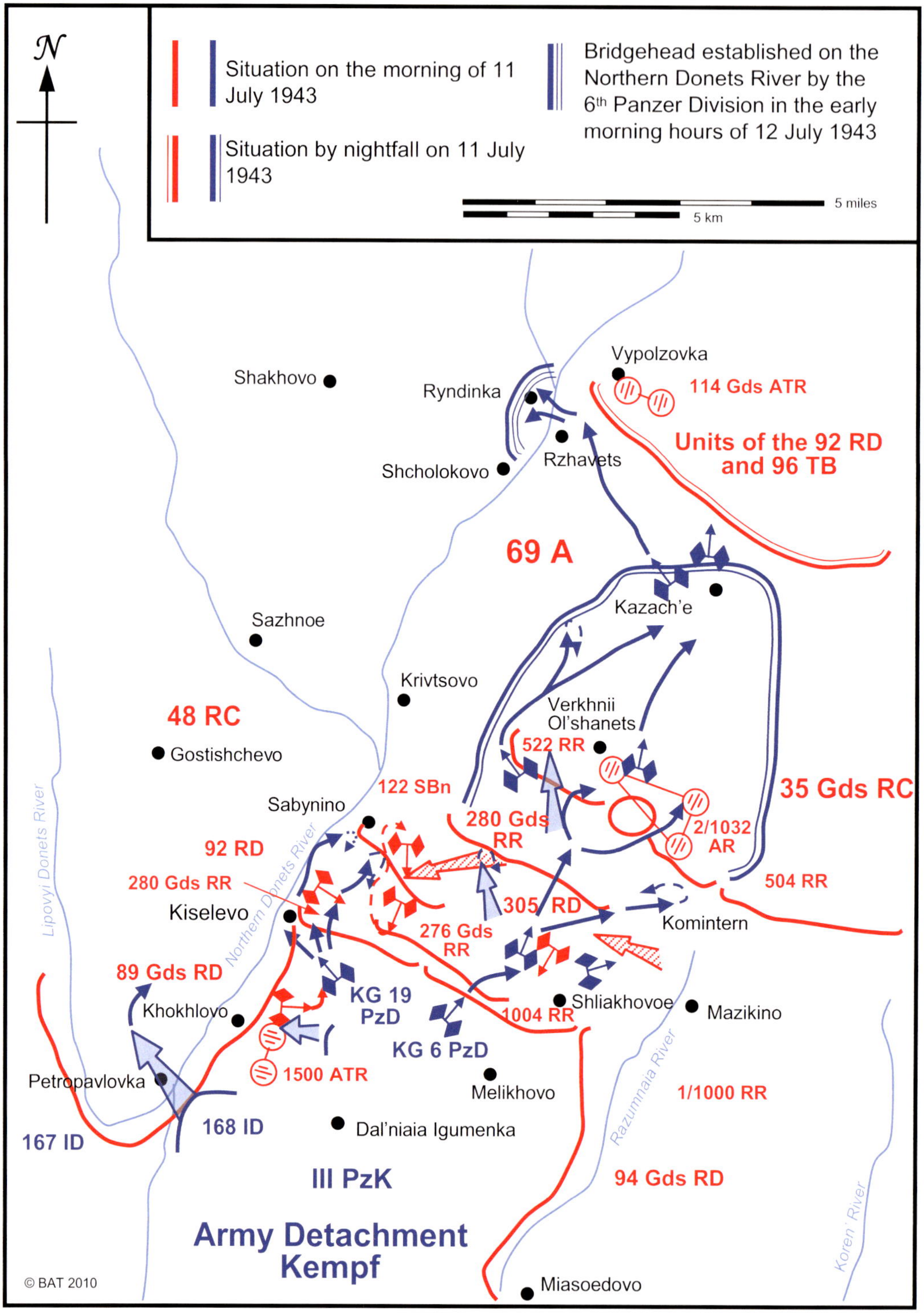

Map 6 III Panzer Corps' Breakthrough of the 69th Army's Second Army-level Line on 11 July and Pre-dawn Hours of 12 July 1943.

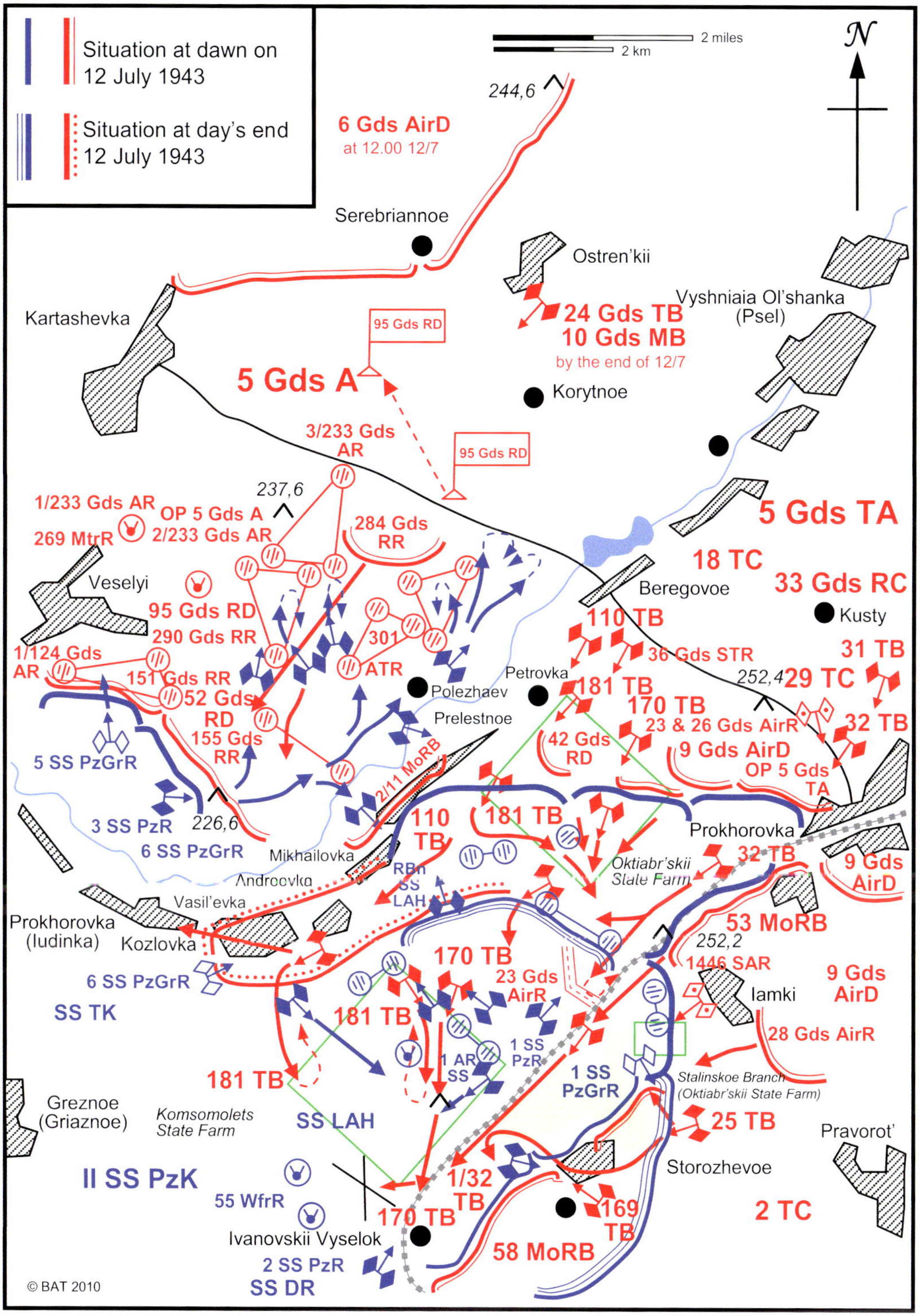

Map 7 Combat Operations in the Sector of Voronezh Front's Main Counterattack Campaign Grouping on 12 July 1943.

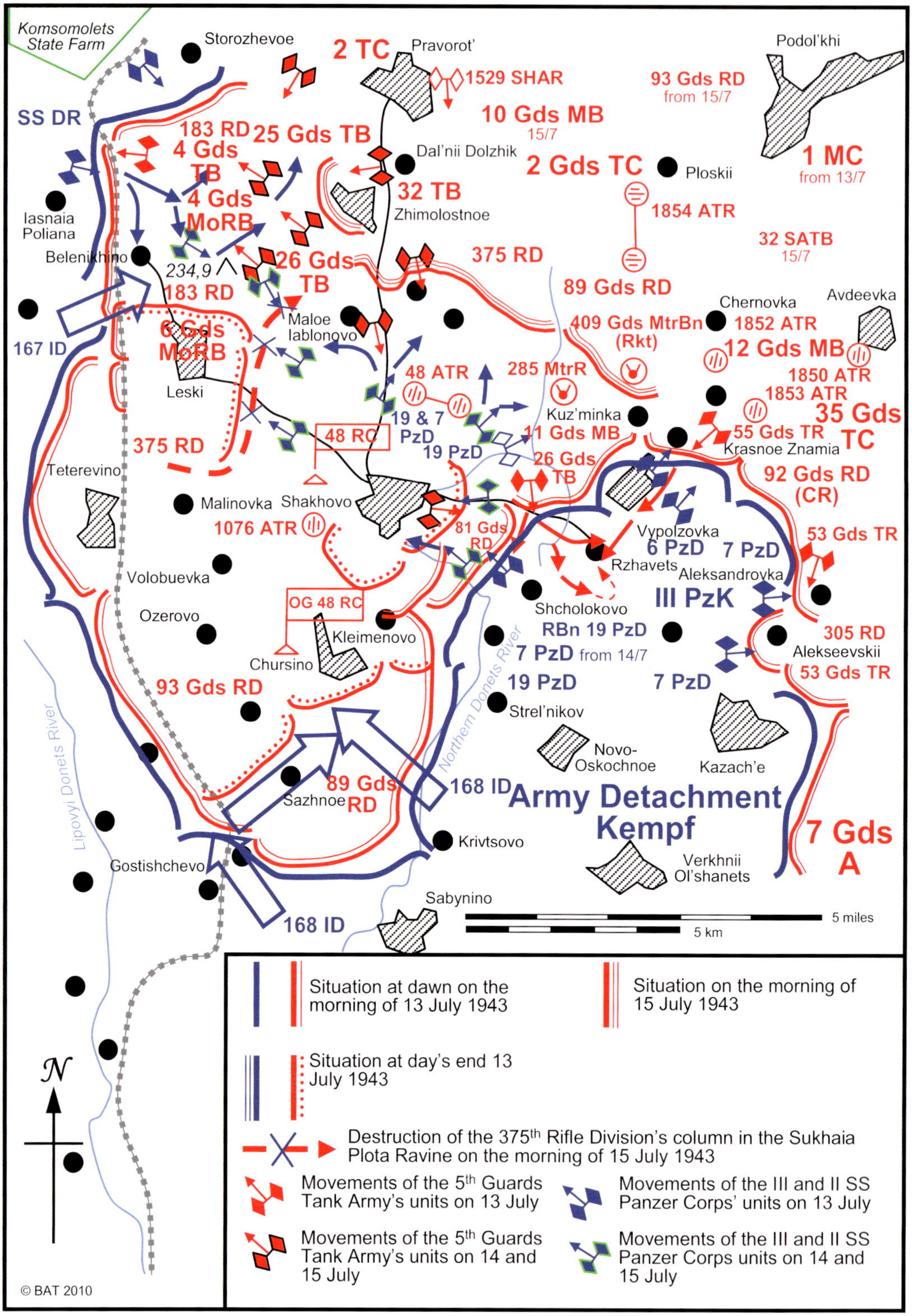

Map 8 Combat Operations between the Northern Donets and Lipovyi Donets Rivers, 13-15 July 1943.

The command of Army Group South also actively masked its preparations for the offensive. Much effort was particularly exerted in places where there was no natural concealment. For example, the terrain on the western bank of the Northern Donets River is covered by woods, but the band of woods is rather shallow, and therefore couldn't conceal the significant forces of Army Detachment Kempf as they were moving toward the forward edge. The commander of this army detachment's 7th Panzer Division *Generalmajor* H. von Funk, who in the course of Operation Citadel fought in the 7th Guards Army's sector, wrote:

> When selecting the jumping-off positions for an offensive it was necessary to reconnoiter the terrain thoroughly with the aim of revealing available pieces of cover, and also to ensure timely artificial cover from enemy observation. Troops should take position in their jumping-off positions in a dispersed manner.
>
> The terrain along both sides of the Belgorod – Brodok highway [the main road employed by the 7th Panzer Division – the author] didn't have any natural screens that would block enemy observation, particularly his aircraft. The road itself, which runs along a ridge, can be seen from the depth of the enemy's positions. Thus movement along this most important arterial road can take place only with the onset of darkness or in conditions of poor visibility.[25]

In comparison with the other armies, the deception measures used by Kempf's forces were probably the most effective, although no matter how paradoxical, they didn't save them from taking serious losses precisely in the course of the counter-artillery preparation. So, nevertheless, at 2200 on 4 July 1943, during a discussion over the Baudot machine [a teleprinter machine to send Baudot code over a telegraph line, used by the Red Army], M.S. Shumilov reported to N.F. Vatutin:

> I take the attacks by fire that the enemy is conducting as cover for the rotation of units. I've observed no large increase in infantry in this area, just the movement of small enemy groups from platoon-size to rarely company-size to and from the forward edge. Yesterday evening at 2000, we observed the chopping of trees north of Toplinka and in the Korovinskaia woods. I assume the woods are being chopped down in order to build defensive works, and not for bridges, since in the course of the present day and evening we haven't observed the lowering of fallen trees from the hill down to the river in the Arkhangel'skoe – Staritsa area. No enemy reinforcements have been detected.[26]

Thus, at the moment when Kempf's assault grouping was already in their jumping-off positions opposite the troops of the 7th Guards Army, its commander believed that there was no sign that the Germans were ready to attack.

I will cite one more illustrative example, testifying to the level of the effectiveness of another type of reconnaissance of that time – artillery reconnaissance. Immediately after the II SS Panzer Corps' offensive kicked-off, an artillery spotting/reconnaissance airplane was directed to its sector. On the basis of information from it, the 132nd Artkommando reported to the II SS Panzer Corps' headquarters that "targets spotted from the air tallied just one-third [!] of the targets already identified by artillery reconnaissance."[27] It is hard to imagine that the effectiveness of our reconnaissance at this time was superior to the German, especially since the Soviet means of revealing

25 TsAMO RF, F. 15, Op. 11600, D. 1539, L. 11.
26 TsAMO RF, F. 203, Op. 2843, D. 461, L. 17.
27 S. Stadler, *Die Offensive gegen Kursk 1943* [*The 1943 Kursk Offensive*] (Coburg, 1988), p. 44.

targets was lagging behind the analogous German means and failed to detect the presence of German forces, even when they were in movement. Even G.K. Zhukov openly acknowledged this:

> It ought to be said that by the start of the enemy's operations, our plan for the counter-preparation still hadn't been fully wrapped up in detail. Places of troop concentration in the jumping-off position and the specific disposition of targets hadn't yet been pinpointed on the night of 4-5 July. Despite the reconnaissance and intelligence means that we possessed back then, it wasn't easy to establish accurately the location of targets. … As a result, during the counter-preparation in a number of cases we had to fire not at specific targets, but at general areas.[28]

The second important factor that substantially influenced the accuracy of the information gathered by the Soviet side regarding targets for the artillery was the enemy's active use of radio interception equipment in order to determine how much information the Soviet side had on the disposition of his forces and means. For this purpose several radio interception posts had been deployed in each German corps. For example, in the Ninth Army's XXIII Army Corps alone, six such posts were operating on 4 July 1943, and two more were deployed with the start of the fighting.[29] Indeed, they were working quite effectively. Here is just one fact: On 3 July 1943, the XXXXVIII Panzer Corps' journal of combat operations observed, "In the afternoon an enemy message was intercepted by the army's means, in which the enemy was reporting on the movement of 450 of our trucks along the Graivoron – Borisovka road. In this connection, the Corps commander took supplementary measures to increase concealment."[30]

In addition, besides the specialized radio interception teams, even the enemy's regular units had the technical capability to monitor the Red Army's radio transmissions. I will mention that even before the war, the TORN.FU.g. Model 1939 radio set entered the Wehrmacht's forces and became the basic means of command and control at the regimental level. It had a frequency spectrum (between 85 and 120 Mhz), which matched the Soviet RAF, RB and RSB radio sets. Thus in combination with the accompanying TON Sb audio recorder, it was widely used for radio intelligence and misleading the Soviet side.

The Soviets were aware of these enemy capabilities. The Red Army command staffs and the SMERSH counter-intelligence departments actively struggled against gossip. For example, Voronezh Front's chief of staff, in connection with the decision to assume a defensive posture, already in the first days of April 1943 sent out a directive letter to his subordinate, in which he stated:

> Conduct a relentless struggle against gossipers; in conversations over the telephone, radio or telegraph, demand the full use of processing tables and coded maps. Change the keys to the processing tables not less than once a day. Communicate the keys only by code or special messenger.[31]

However, strict requirements and harsh measures didn't always yield the needed effect, since the manifestations of "loose lips" were numerous. Soviet officers, especially at the tactical level, frequently failed to observe discipline over the radio waves. Code tables were ignored, and

28 Zhukov, *Vospominaniia i razmyshleniia*, p. 459.
29 NARA, T. 314, R. 680, F. 000418.
30 NARA, T. 314, R. 1170, F. 000550.
31 TsAMO RF, F. 203, Op. 2843, D. 301, L. 178.

conversations often used primitive code words, only slightly similar to actual ones, which the enemy quickly figured out. For example, shells were called "cucumbers"; tanks were called "boxes"; neighboring units – "neighboring homesteads"; and so forth. Reports from the German radio interception posts are full of statements by Soviet officers that contain various types of information on the opposing enemy and their own units. When compiling the best practices of their units on the Oboian' direction in the summer of 1943, the chief of staff of the 6th Guards Army's 71st Guards Rifle Division Lieutenant Colonel Liubomudrov[32] indicated, "In reports over the telephone about the enemy's actions, the commanders are showing criminal negligence, revealing the disposition of their troops thanks to careless, open conversations, like "The enemy is attacking my left flank," "The enemy is firing at my neighbor's right flank" and so forth, which reveals the location of their flank or the boundary with the neighbor.[33]

The information from radio intelligence was attentively analyzed in the headquarters of Army Groups Center and South, which naturally took corresponding measures, including with respect to relocating artillery that had been pinpointed by the Soviet side. In the process, as a rule dummy guns and mortars were left behind in the previous spot, and the apparent presence of their crews was maintained. As an example, the journal of combat operations of the Ninth Army's 292nd Infantry Division, which was ready for the attack toward Kursk through Ponyri Station, noted on 2 July 1943: "Radio intelligence has confirmed that the enemy is attentively tracking our movements, exerting every effort for this. Thus, it is necessary to increase deception and concealment."[34] Undoubtedly, careless officers were unable to spill all the beans regarding what our intelligence had managed to establish prior to the start of fighting. However, this problem existed and affected the accuracy of the data prepared for the preemptive barrage.

In addition, when working out the scheme of the counter-preparation, the Soviet side ran into another objective factor that was impossible to overcome fully. The point is that over the months of May and June, Soviet intelligence had only been able to establish the artillery positions of the first-echelon German divisions, but it was extremely difficult to uncover where the formations that were approaching to take part in the offensive would deploy their artillery regiments, or determine their attached assets. It was unquestionably possible to surmise where some force or other might be located, depending on the terrain conditions, but for a preemptive barrage one had to know the precise starting time for the offensive, as well as the total numerical strength of the assault grouping, in order to delineate the boundaries of the territory where it might be located.

In this connection, questions of determining targets and the schedule of their suppression were paramount. At the time, there was no precise list of main and secondary targets for a counter-artillery preparation in the regulatory documents for Soviet artillery. The General Staff relegated the solution of this problem to the competence of the *fronts*. Rokossovsky and his headquarters decided that the enemy's artillery positions and observation posts were the most important targets to mark for destruction, and only later the infantry and tanks in their jumping-off positions. For example, on the 13th Army's list of targets for the artillery plan, concentrations of troops and equipment amounted to only 17% of the list. The Voronezh Front command approached this

32 Pave Ivanovich Liubomudrov (1903 -- ?), Lieutenant Colonel (1943); in the Red Army from 1920. He served on the fronts of the Great Patriotic War from 22 June 1941. Liubomudrov was a veteran of the fighting outside of Moscow and the Battle of Stalingrad. On 5 July 1943, the 71st Guards Rifle Division was located in Voronezh Front's first echelon. In the most stressful period, between 4 and 12 July 1943, he personally took part in directing the troops from the forward command posts of the division and regiments. For successes in the course of the Battle of Kursk, he was awarded the Order of the Patriotic War 2nd Degree.

33 TsAMO RF, F. 1207, Op. 1, D. 64, L. 35obr.

34 NARA, T. 315, R. 1228, F. 000158.

matter differently. It believed the artillery's main task was to destroy enemy troops that were poised to attack. In the 6th Guards Army's fire plan, such troops concentrations comprised 77% of the total number of targets designated for the preemptive barrage. Common for both *fronts* was the length of time scheduled for the counter-artillery preparation – 30 minutes – and the quantity of ammunition to expend – 0.5 of an establishment ammunition load.

Thus far no clear explanation for the reasons behind the diametrically opposed targeting decisions of the artillery commands of the *fronts* has been found in the archival documents. The first domestic scholar who not only raised this question in the open press, but also offered an answer for it, was the Soviet military historian Colonel G.T. Khoroshilov.[35] In his address to an academic conference dedicated to the 25th anniversary of the Battle of Kursk held in Moscow on 15 August 1968, he presented the following factors which in his opinion influenced the choice of Rokossovsky's headquarters:

a. The Front's possession of powerful artillery means to counter enemy artillery.
b. The availability of more reliable information on the dispositions of enemy artillery.
c. The relatively narrow sector, where the attack was expected (30-40 kilometers wide).
d. The vulnerability of the first-echelon troops to the fire of German artillery because of the high density of regiments and divisions that had been assembled in narrow sectors of the front, especially in the 13th Army.[36]

In my opinion, the first three factors (or points) if they did play a role, then it was far from the main one, and were cited as "make-weight". Only the fourth point can be considered the most legitimate, since the narrow German sector of attack and the powerful artillery strength that the Central Front possessed would on the contrary permit the inflicting of heavy damage to the Werhrmacht's infantry units in their jumping-off positions. I'll remind the reader that the amount of artillery in the Central Front exceeded the quantity possessed by the Voronezh Front by more than 2,000. As concerns the vulnerability of our first-echelon rifle units to artillery strikes due to their high density, then this factor might have been and probably was the determining factor. This is especially so after several of the *Stavka*'s warnings that the enemy was about to go on the offensive that were received in May proved not to be the case, and it became difficult to trust the intelligence information. However, this intelligence was the key for determining the time and location of the German troop's assembly in their jumping-off positions. Accordingly, K.K. Rokossovsky preferred, as the Russian saying goes, "A chickadee in hand is better than a crane in the sky". The "chickadee" in this case was the already pinpointed artillery firing positions and observation posts, while the "crane" was the areas where the troops of the Ninth Army's assault grouping might (or might not) concentrate.

It was in fact the fourth point that was the primary motive for the choice made by Rokossovsky. This is indirectly confirmed if you look at how, in Khoroshilov's opinion, the Voronezh Front

35 Georgii Trofimovich Khoroshilov (1918 -- ?), Colonel, Candidate of Military Science and associate professor. In the Red Army from August 1936 and a veteran of the Great Patriotic War. In the acting army from August 1941. Khoroshilov fought on the Leningrad, Volkhov and 1st Belorussian Fronts. He ended the war in the post of commander of the 46th Mortar Brigade's 416th Mortar Regiment and as a major. He was twice wounded and received the Orders of the Red Star, Red Banner and the Patriotic War, as well as several medals. At the time of his participation at the conference where he presented this paper, he was department chief in the USSR Ministry of Defense's Institute of Military History.

36 G.T. Khoroshilov, "Nekotorye voprosy boevogo primeneniia artilleriia v Kurskoi bitve" ["Several questions of the combat use of artillery in the Battle of Kursk"] *Kurskaia bitva* [*Battle of Kursk*] (Moscow: Nauka, 1970), p. 232.

command justified its plan of actions. In the author's opinion, the following circumstances forced N.F. Vatutin to strike the approaching tanks and infantry. First was the broad front of the possible German attack (up to 100 kilometers). Second was the heightened vulnerability of the first-echelon troops to tank attacks (given the fact that the anti-tank artillery in the Central Front's sector was 25 guns per kilometer of front, while in the 6th and 7th Guards Armies, there were only 9-10 anti-tank guns per kilometer of front). Third and finally was the smaller amount of artillery in the Voronezh Front to counter the German artillery.[37] Accordingly, in G.T. Khoroshilov's opinion, both commanders, Rokossovsky and Vatutin, despite the differing conditions in which their *fronts* were located, doubted the resilience of the first-echelon infantry. So the counter-artillery preparation was the means by which each was trying to support it, although in different ways. Unquestionably, there is logic in this.

According to the recollections of many participants in the Battle of Kursk, in the spring and early summer of 1943, one of the main problems in the Soviet troops was "tank fright". The Red Army command exerted great effort to eliminate it. Joint exercises were conducted involving the tank crews and the infantry, so that the soldiers of the rifle units could become accustomed to the clatter of tracks as the armored vehicles rolled around, which is to say the tanks and self-propelled guns would pass over the trenches in which the Red Army soldiers were crouched. Pamphlets with information about the vulnerable locations of the latest German armor were published and intensively studied. Thus, steps to support and bolster the spirits of the infantry with artillery fire on the eve of the enemy attack fully conformed to the logic of the tasks facing the *fronts.*

However, there exists another point of view regarding the main task of the counter-artillery preparation: It was meant to spoil the German offensive. For example, a veteran of the Battle of Kursk, the former commander of the Steppe Front's artillery Colonel General N.S. Fomin offered the following opinion of the differing approaches between the Voronezh and Central Fronts:

> The difference in the organization of the counter-preparation is explained, in our view, on one hand by the lack of experience, and on the other – by the presence of alternative views on the tasks of a counter-preparation. ... It seems to us that it is necessary to bring the artillery barrage down onto those forces designated for an immediate offensive. If you obliterate the tanks and infantry, no one will be able to attack even if the artillery goes untouched. In contrast, those tank and motorized rifle units and elements of the first echelon that remain intact will always go on the attack, even given significant losses in artillery. Thus, in our opinion, preference should be given to the decision of the 6th Guards Army's commander, where the artillery barrage concentrated on the enemy tanks and infantry in the jumping off area.[38]

This point of view seems more justified, especially after you become familiar with captured sources, the information of which I will present below.

From the works of domestic authors that describe the events of the night of 4-5 July 1943, the impression forms that prior to the attack, the German troops were literally huddled together on the forward edge in expectations of the attack. Thus the Soviet artillery, having initiated the implementation of the counter-artillery preparation's plan, scattered them into pieces, and the Wehrmacht command was forced to spend the next two hours gathering them together again.[39]

37 G.T. Khoroshilov, op. cit.

38 I.V. Parot'kin (ed.), *Kurskaia bitva* [*Battle of Kursk*), pp. 220-221.

39 For example, A. Domank, *Na ognevykh rubezhakh: Artilleriia v Kurskoi bitve* [*On the firing lines: Artillery in the Battle of Kursk*] (Voronezh, 1984), pp. 24-25.

In reality, everything happened quite differently. The enemy had a great respect for the capabilities of the Red Army's artillery and rightly feared it. Already a year after the start of the war, the headquarters of the combat formations on the Eastern Front were noting a substantial increase in the quality of the combat work done by the Soviet artillery units. For example, an account by the 9th Panzer Division's headquarters entitled "Experience of the recent fighting of several panzer divisions in the Crimea and in the Khar'kov area", which was issued by its Operations Department for thorough study in the subordinate units noted:

> The enemy artillery has achieved successes in directing and concentrating fire. Cases of heavily-concentrated fire are observable. In connection with this it is necessary to use dispersed combat formations (!). The skillful use of alternate positions and of ranging and "roving" guns has been noted. The camouflaging of artillery positions is excellent.[40]

The German forces both prior to this account and a year later, in the area of the Kursk salient, were taking this experience into account. Thus, as a rule, the grouping formed for the offensive was divided into a breakthrough echelon and a follow-up echelon. In turn, each echelon was also split up into assaulting combat groups and elements that were to enter the breakthrough after the capture of the first line of trenches, as well as into groups that would reinforce an emerging breach in the first line of positions, accompany the armor in order to expand the breakthrough "corridor", and so forth. All of these forces weren't intermingled; they were assigned separate holding areas and separate jumping-off areas, positioned at a rather impressive distance from each other. Their movement from position to position was set out in detail and strictly regulated by officers of the divisional level. Moreover, the enemy command, foreseeing the danger of an unexpected attack by our artillery or air force, also didn't keep the elements crowded in their positions within the echelon. Here's how *Generalmajor* H. von Funk described his panzer division's assembly for the lunge across the Northern Donets River at Belgorod:

> Radio silence was observed when taking up the jumping-off positions. Movement of infantry and vehicles along the roads in daylight hours was banned. All of the facilities of the rear services and the structures for accommodating the troops (with the exception of forward stockpiles of ammunition) were from the outset at a significant distance from the jumping-off positions. Bridging equipment, loaded onto special vehicles, stood ready in the woods.[41]

Finally, the main point, which Soviet and Russian scholars have never mentioned, and which went unnoticed in the documents of the Central Front's headquarters: Several hours before the offensive's start, all of the artillery of Model's and von Manstein's assault groupings changed their firing positions. From a telegram sent by the Ninth Army's headquarters at 1930 on 4 July 1943 to its subordinate forces [emphasis the author's]:

> In order to ensure the unexpectedness of the actions, which are forthcoming for the Russians, our offensive must be supported by concentrated, surprise artillery fire and air strikes; in connection with this, I am reminding you on the need for the division commanders to carry out the following measures on 4 July:
>
> 1. Be up close to the troops.

40 TsAMO RF, F. 203, Op. 2343, D. 124, L. 38.
41 TsAMO RF, F. 15, Op. 11600, D. 1534, L. 17.

2. Shift all the artillery and heavy weapons from reserve positions to newly-equipped main positions.
3. Do not allow premature movement of the artillery into the main positions.[42]

Thus, even if the holding positions could have theoretically been determined on a map (by identifying suitable terrain for assembling and camouflaging large forces), then the jumping-off (and main firing positions for the artillery) could be found only once the fighting was already underway. As the document cited above shows, even that information about areas of artillery concentrations, which our intelligence had managed to gather by the evening of 4 July, might have had some sort of effect only in the course of the initial stage of Voronezh Front's preemptive barrage that was conducted between 2200 and 2300. On the Central Front, the counter-artillery preparation had been planned to begin only after midnight, which is to say at a time when the enemy artillery had already moved from their reserve positions to the main ones. Accordingly, here our guns were firing on empty areas or at dummy guns. However, in order to blanket even the jumping-off positions of the enemy units accurately with fire, it was necessary to know the probable H-hour for the attack, since attacking troops normally move up into them approximately an hour to an hour and a half before the start of their own artillery preparation. This start time is understandably is a chief secret of any attacking army, and to acquire this knowledge is extremely difficult. Wrote the Central Front's former chief of artillery Colonel G.S. Nadysev:

> The most important factor that played a decisive role in the success of the artillery counter-preparation was choosing the time to conduct it. The greatest effect ... is achieved when you succeed in preempting the attacking enemy, and not by a day or two, but by several dozens of minutes or an hour, so that the artillery fire rains down on troops poised to attack. For this reason, first of all timely and accurate information on the designated time when the enemy will launch the offensive was necessary. Yet you didn't have such information very often.[43]

Unquestionably, all of this was thoroughly discussed before the start of the battle. Indeed, as we will see ahead, the Soviet command understood how difficult it would be to achieve the designated goals of such a major measure, which moreover was going to be conducted for the first time simultaneously on the scale of two *fronts*.

By the end of June the command of the armies of the Voronezh Front, which had been called upon to conduct the counter-artillery preparation, confirmed what seemed at the time to be the final plan. The 6th Guards Army's artillery was to concentrate its fire on four directions: a) Novaia Gorniaka – Iamnoe; b) Cherkasskoe; c) Iakhontov – Streletskoe; and d) Berezov – Gremuchii. For participation in it, it had been decided to use:

1. The artillery regiments of all four rifle divisions of the first echelon: the 71st Guards, 67th Guards, 52nd Guards and 375th Rifle Divisions;
2. Regimental and battalion artillery, as well as the 82mm and 120mm mortars of the 71st Guards, 67th Guards, 52nd Guards and 375th Rifle Divisions;
3. The 27th and 33rd Heavy Cannon Artillery Brigades;
4. The 628th Artillery Regiment;
5. The 295th and 263rd Guards Mortar Regiments;
6. The 5th Guards, 16th Guards, 314th Guards and 316th Guards Mortar Regiments.

42 NARA, T. 312, R. 322, F. 7891028.
43 G.S. Nadysev, *Na sluzhbe shtabnoi*, pp. 124-125.

Altogether in the above listed formations, units and elements, there were 686 pieces of artillery (244 guns, 374 mortars and 95 rocket launchers) for the attack against targets opposite the 64-kilometer sector of the armies' defenses. Thus, on average there were 11.5 guns (not including the 45mm anti-tank guns), 19 mortars and 5.3 rocket launchers per kilometer of front.[44] It was decided not to activate the artillery regiments of the anti-tank artillery strong points or the reserve artillery, in order not to disclose the system of fire at the front and the organization of the anti-tank defense. However, a report from the commander of the 1008th Destroyer Anti-tank Artillery Regiment, which was positioned in the area of the Belgorod – Oboian' highway notes that his regiment also took part in the counter-artillery preparation. This point isn't totally clear in the document, however, and one can only assume that most likely not the entire regiment was engaged, but only a reserve battery that was firing from reserve positions.[45]

The 7th Guards Army's command planned to use the following artillery of the first-echelon divisions for the preemptive attack:

1. The 81st Guards Rifle Division's artillery regiment and its attached assets: the 161st Cannon Artillery Regiment, the 256th Guards Cannon Artillery Regiment, the 114th Guards Destroyer Anti-tank Artillery Regiment, the 290th Mortar Regiment, the 97th Guards and 315th Guards Mortar Regiments, and the 153rd Guards Artillery Regiment from the 73rd Guards Rifle Division;
2. The 78th Guards Rifle Division's artillery regiment and its attached assets: the 3rd Battalion of the 671st Artillery Regiment of the 213th Rifle Division (which was positioned in the second echelon).
3. The 72nd Guards Rifle Division's artillery regiment and its attached assets: 3rd Battalion of the 109th Guards Cannon Artillery Regiment and the 1st and 2nd Battalions of the 213th Rifle Division's 671st Artillery Regiment.
4. The 36th Guards Rifle Division's artillery regiment and its attached assets: the 1st and 2nd Battalions of the 109th Guards Cannon Artillery Regiment, the 115th Guards Destroyer Anti-tank Artillery Regiment, and the 43rd Guards Artillery Regiment of the 15th Guards Rifle Division (which was positioned in the second echelon).[46]

In total, it planned to activate 328 guns, 36 mortars and 47 rocket launchers for the counter-artillery preparation.[47]

In some domestic publication one encounters the assertion that M.S. Shumilov increased the length of the preemptive fire by 10 minutes relative to that of the other armies, thus in the sector of his army it continued not for 30 minutes, but for 40 minutes.[48] However, in the 7th Guards Army's account documents, there is no confirmation of this.

Immediately prior to the start of the counter-artillery preparation, the plan for it underwent substantial changes on both *fronts*. N.F. Vatutin was forced to split his planned artillery barrage into two stages, and to conduct supplementary fire on enemy targets ahead of the designated time. It was intended as a preliminary artillery attack. The gun crews were to carry it out on the evening of 4 July. The second stage, as planned, took place later that night, in the early hours of 5 July, not long before the German attack. In essence, it was a preemptive artillery barrage in its pure form, and Vatutin was placing great hopes on it. K.K. Rokossovsky's situation was different and he didn't divide the plan into separate phases. However, the commander of the 13th Army Lieutenant

44 TsAMO RF, NSB.Inv.No. 9989, LL. 28-29.
45 TsAMO RF. F. 335, Op. 5122, D. 109, L. 280.
46 TsAMO RF, 7 gv. A., Op. 5330, D. 60, L. 140.
47 TsAMO RF, F. 203, Op. 2843, D. 426, L. (unnumbered) for the 7th Guards Army on 5 July 1943.
48 G.A. Koltunov and B.S. Solov'ev, *Kurskaia bitva*, p. 71.

Central Front's commander of artillery Lieutenant General V.I. Kazakov on an inspection trip of the 13th Army's artillery units, June 1943 (Author's personal archive)

A crew of a 152-mm howitzer of one of the Guards artillery regiments of the 6th Guards Army fires prepares to fire a shell at the enemy; Oboian' axis, July 1943 (Photography by D. Chernov, RGAKFD)

The 6th Guards Army's commander of artillery Major General D.T. Turbin; March 1943 (TsAMO RF)

Voronezh Front's commander of artillery Major General S.S. Varentsov; January 1943 (TsAMO RF)

General N.P. Pukhov on 5 July 1943 decided not to use a significant amount of artillery for the preemptive artillery barrage. His motivations for this decision still aren't clear.

What had forced the leadership of the Voronezh Front to change its plans and make a first attack before midnight on 4 July? It was the high enemy activity on its front on the afternoon and evening of 4 July 1943. At 1600, the Fourth Panzer Army attacked the combat outposts of the 71st Guards and 67th Guards Rifle Divisions on the right flank of the 6th Guards Army, with the aim of seizing high ground that was advantageous for observation and adjusting artillery fire. The combat operations unfolded on a rather broad front with the use of assault guns, and thus the Soviet side assessed them as a reconnaissance-in-force before the start of the main offensive. In essence, that is what it was. As the documents of the XXXXVIII Panzer Corps' headquarters testify, if the weather on the evening of 4 July allowed the full assembly of its attack formations, the panzer corps intended to continue the attacks on the night of 4-5 July; in other words, to transition straight into the implementation of Operation Citadel.[49] Fearing precisely this, N.F. Vatutin with the agreement of the Chief of the General Staff A.M. Vasilevsky who was present in his command post, issued an order to the commanders of the 6th and 7th Guards Army's to open fire between 2200 and 2300 at targets that had been determined for the counter-artillery preparation.

From the transcript of discussions with M.S. Shumilov:

> N.F. Vatutin: "... If you consider that the enemy over the last three days has brought up to two divisions to the Belgorod area using motorized transport and shifted tanks closer to the front, in particular the XXXXVIII Panzer Corps, then we should expect him to go over to the

49 NARA, T. 314, R. 1170, F. 000555.

Bunkers of the Ninth Army in the vicinity of Nizhnee Tagino destroyed by the Central Front's artillery supposedly during the preemptive barrage conducted on the night of 4/5 July 1943 (Photograph found in the account of Central Front's artillery headquarters, TsAMO RF)

> offensive on the Belgorod direction. Today, a deserter from the 168th Infantry Division was captured north of Belgorod, who indicated that the 168th Infantry Division was preparing for an offensive. According to the deserter, the tentative start date for the offensive is 5 July. In the assessment of the Central Front, the enemy there has also brought up forces from the depth to the forward edge, and is also intending to go on the offensive.
>
> With the aims of preempting the enemy, I am ordering:
>
> First, conduct an artillery barrage on his aggregations of mortars and batteries, and other targets that you've clearly identified, in the sector [here use the procedure table], as well as in the Toplinka, Grafovka sector with the following timetable: at 2200 4 July, a five-minute barrage, followed by a 20-minute pause, and then fire a 20-minute barrage. Make sure that the barrage is absolutely simultaneous and sudden, and in those places where you have time for this, from reserve positions. In order to conduct the attack, I'm authorizing the following expenditure of shells per gun in the above-indicated sectors: 76mm – not more than 40; 120mm – not more than 20; 152mm – not more than 10; 120mm mortar – not more than 10; 82mm mortars – not more than 20; 45mm fragmentation shells – as many as you have time to fire over 10 minutes. You can launch one salvo of rockets per battalion at enemy concentrations.[50]

In order to grasp whether the amount of shells authorized for the first phase of the counter-artillery preparation (artillery barrage) was large or small, one must imagine the effectiveness of artillery shells of various calibers. For example, the lethal radius of an explosion of a 122mm fragmentation shell is up to 40 meters, while those of shells of a smaller caliber are naturally less extensive. Moreover, while the spray of mortar fragments surrounds the explosion site and covers 360 degrees, an artillery shell doesn't strike the earth vertically, but at a sharp angle to it, so its explosion tended to project fragments only in a biased manner. Considering that in the course of the preemptive attack it was planned to use primarily cannon artillery, it was only possible to inflict substantial damage to the dispersed enemy forces by either a direct hit of a shell on a group of men or equipment, or by conducting massed, concentrated fire, which was impossible given the paucity of the allotted ammunition. Subsequently, once again the problem arises of determining the precise time for the start of the enemy offensive and the exact places of the assembly of enemy forces.

But let's return to how the Voronezh Front commander's order was carried out. Both Guards armies opened fire at 2230 on 4 July. In the 6th Guards Army, in the course of the barrage, it covered 17 assembly areas of tanks and infantry, 12 batteries, and 17 observation posts of the enemy's Fourth Panzer Army. In the opinion of officers of the General Staff, this "contributed a lot to the disruption of the German forward detachments' attack."[51] However, in the documents of the divisions of Army Group South's XXXXVIII Panzer Corps and II SS Panzer Corps, there are hardly any mentions about the initial phase of the Russians' preemptive barrage. There are two reasons for this. In the first place, at 1600 Soviet artillery was already firing on attacking troops and the concentrations of men and equipment of the XXXXVIII Panzer Corps, so the artillery fire only increased at 2300. Thus, it was practically impossible to determine where the Russians were firing to repulse the attacks on the combat outposts, and where the first phase of the counter-artillery preparation had started. Secondly, the artillery barrage itself didn't last long, and relatively insignificant forces were assigned to it. Thus the entire cannonade from the moment of the attack

50 TsAMO RF, F. 203, Op. 2843, D. 461, L. 17.

51 *Bitva pod Kurskom: Ot oborony k nastupleniiu* [*Battle of Kursk: From the defense to the offensive*] (Moscow: AST-B. Khranitel', 2006), p. 183.

against the combat outposts of the divisions of the 6th Guards Army's right flank right up until the start of the proper preemptive artillery barrage at 0330 merged into one terrible cacophony for the troops of the XXXXVIII Panzer Corps. The war diary of this panzer corps notes: "The night is passing mostly quietly. There is strong salvo fire of enemy artillery guns and mortars on the corps' entire sector."[52] The combat situation at the front is described in pretty much the same words in the documents of its divisions.

The situation on the left flank of the 6th Guards Army was unfolding differently. Here the II SS Panzer Corps set out to seize the combat outposts of the 52nd Guards and 375th Rifle Divisions only at 0230 5 July, and prior to this the situation was, just as on preceding days, relatively quiet.[53] Thus, the fire that was opened by our artillery after Vatutin's order wasn't recorded in the documents of all the SS divisions, but only in those that had begun to arrive in their jumping-off positions in the second echelon, and on firing positions on the forward edge that had been detected by reconnaissance. For example, the SS Panzer Grenadier Division *Totenkopf* reported: "From 2245 heavy artillery and mortar fire on the entire sector of the *Theodor Eicke* Regiment, as well as fire by rocket launchers against the center and on the right flank."[54]

According to information from the 7th Guards Army's artillery headquarters, the final decision about the initiation of the second phase of the counter-artillery preparation in its sector was made at midnight.[55] After a call from N.F. Vatutin, considering that the fire would be opened simultaneously on several directions, the commanders of the 6th Guards and 7th Guards Armies decided during the second phase of the counter-artillery preparation to concentrate all their fire on targets only in the sector of their own armies, and not to redirect it against targets opposite their neighbor's front, as had been stipulated previously. I.M. Chistiakov asked M.S. Shumilov to increase the fire of his 23rd Guards Rifle Corps only on the boundary between the 6th and 7th Guards Armies, employing 120mm mortars of the 1/290th Mortar Regiment against German positions opposite the right flank of his left-flank 375th Rifle Division. A number of substantial changes were made within the 7th Guards Army's artillery fire plan. Thus, whereas it had been preliminarily planned to open fire on eight directions, at the final moment the targeted directions were reduced to three, opposite the belts of defenses of not four, but only three divisions – the 81st Guards, 78th Guards and 72nd Guards Rifle Divisions, where the largest aggregation of enemy forces had been revealed. The 36th Guards Rifle Division positioned on the extreme left flank received an order to open fire on German targets in the sector of its neighbor to the right, the 72nd Guards Rifle Division, while the 265th Guards Cannon Artillery Regiment was supposed to support the 78th Guards Rifle Division standing in front of it.[56]

Precisely at 0330 on 5 July, the 7th Guards Army's artillery cannonade shattered the silence. Just like flaming arrows, salvoes of Katiusha rockets flew toward the positions of the Army Detachment Kempf's forces. In the villages and hamlets, on the fringes of woods, and along the western bank of the river rose columns of flame, smoke and dust, and an enormous gray cloud with black fringes, periodically lit up inside by additional flashes of explosions, hung above the areas of concentration of the enemy's units, which were poised to surge forward on the attack. There was an unimaginable thunder all around, and the earth shook beneath the feet.

For objective reasons, this preemptive artillery barrage was more successful in Shumilov's army than in the other armies of both *fronts*. At the moment of opening fire, the forward groups of Kempf's army detachment had already started to force a crossing of the Donets River approximately

52 NARA, T. 314, R. 1170, F. 000553.
53 TsAMO RF, F. 335, Op. 5113, D. 235, L. 20.
54 Stadler, *Die Offensive gegen Kursk 1943*, p. 40.
55 TsAMO RF, F. 7.gv.A., Op. 53330, D. 60, L. 43.
56 Ibid.

30 minutes before. Thus the shells fell not simply on possible areas of enemy troop concentrations, but just where the Germans were located. The divisions on the 7th Guards Army's right flank – the artillery of the 81st Guards Rifle (on the extreme right) and the 78th Guards Rifle – were able to carry out the assignment most successfully. From Army Detachment Kempf's journal of combat operations:

> 0325 [Moscow time]: The army detachment in accordance with the plan has started to force a crossing of the Donets with the forces of "Korps Raus" and the III Panzer Corps. The army detachment's commander is located in his observation post south of Belgorod.
>
> 0405 [Moscow time]: A call from the army detachment's commander to the chief of staff. The commander reported that at 0300 the enemy opened up with artillery fire on our positions in the Belgorod area. Particularly heavy fire fell on the bridgehead [at Mikhailovka in the sector of the 81st Guards Rifle Division – the author].[57]

Opposite the positions of the 81st Guards Rifle Division, a rare situation developed: the divisions of the III Panzer Corps had concentrated its assault groups for the crossing of the Northern Donets River precisely in those areas that were known to the Soviet side (indeed, the Germans had no other options), and the Guardsmen not only discovered these places, having a real opportunity to damage the enemy, they managed to make it happen. Here the highest density of artillery means had been created not only for an army, but for the sectors of both two *fronts*, which were subjected to the barrage on 5 July: 68.6 guns and mortars and 16 rocket launchers per kilometer of front. By comparison, the 13th Army's command on the main directions was able to create at most just 60 tubes per kilometer of front.[58] The division commander I.I. Morozov employed the reserve 97th Guards Mortar Regiment of Katiusha rocket launchers intensively and with great effectiveness. Its three battalions began striking the places of assembly of the combat groups and engineer elements of Army Detachment Kempf's 168th Infantry Division and the 6th and 19th Panzer Divisions not long before midnight and continued to fire with pauses practically until the middle of the day of 5 July. Only over the first 4.5 hours (between 2330 and 400), 424 rockets were launched at the shallow bridgehead at Mikhailovka and the outskirts of Pushkarnoe.[59] Simultaneously, 120mm mortars of the 290th Mortar Regiment (36 mortars), guns of the 161st Guards Cannon Artillery Regiment and of other artillery regiments were firing at these same areas. Naturally, in such circumstances it was hard for the enemy to avoid losses in the forward battalions, but I've not been able to find any concrete casualty figures. In the morning report from Army Detachment Kempf's III Panzer Corps, it is noted: "At night, a punishing cannonade from enemy artillery, rocket launchers and mortars on the jumping-off positions of the panzer divisions, especially within the Mikhailovka bridgehead. Thus, the bridges at Mikhailovka couldn't be constructed before the start of the offensive, as had been previously planned."[60]

However, the commander of the 81st Guards Rifle Division was unable to make full use of his available capabilities. For example, the 114th Guards Destroyer Anti-tank Artillery Regiment (equipped with ZiS-3 76mm cannons) couldn't fire, because its designated target areas were at an extreme range, and the likelihood of a hit was low. Thus it was decided not to reveal the regiment's main or alternate firing positions. For the same reason (great range to the designated target areas), the division's attached 153rd Guards Artillery Regiment from the 73rd Guards Rifle Division

57 NARA, T. 312, R. 54, F. 7569605.
58 TsAMO RF, NSB.Inv.9998, L. 32, 35.
59 Information from the regiment's Operational Summary No. 142. (TsAMO RF, F. 97 gv.mp, Op. 18715, D. 5, L. 248, 248 obr.
60 NARA, T. 314, R. 197, F. 001054.

couldn't employ all of its firepower. Its combat diary indicates, "... at 0300 on 5 July 1943, the regiment fired on revealed areas of enemy concentration, expending 306 76mm shells and 87 122mm shells."[61]

Nevertheless, the forces activated during the barrage on the crossing sites and Mikhailovka itself proved fully sufficient to prevent the 6th Panzer Division from forcing a crossing of the Northern Donets River on the first day of Operation Citadel. Thus approximately mid-day the III Panzer Corps command was forced to begin to regroup it to the area south of Mikhailovka, to roads that were already jammed with troops. This panzer division began crossing only on the following day, 6 July.

Assault groups of the 19th Panzer Division, which had started to cross the river, also came under the heavy attack of Soviet artillery. In the morning its command reported: "From 0115 [Berlin time], heavy, concentrated fire of enemy artillery and heavy weapons at the bridgehead and places of laying down bridges.... The construction of the 60-ton bridge had to be stopped because of the powerful, adjusted artillery fire."[62] In the account of its headquarters I managed to find a detailed description of what was happening in the sectors of its combat groups before crossing the river:

> The bridge for the Tigers was half-ready. At that time the Russians began a well-organized fire of artillery, mortars and flanking machine guns at the crossing sites. Despite the darkness, the fire was very accurate. Thus one of the fully-loaded inflatable boats was sunk by a direct hit. The combat engineers also suffered serious losses, because 40-60 men were clustered around each bridge abutment.[63]

Major General A.V. Skvortsov, the commander of the 78th Guards Rifle Division, concentrated all the fire of his artillery on the village of Solomino, where at that moment the forward battalions of the 7th Panzer Division were already located in their jumping-off positions. The 158th Guards Artillery Regiment, the battalion and regimental artillery of the 228th Guards and 225th Guards Rifle Regiments, and the attached 3/671st Artillery Regiment were all targeting the village. In addition, artillery of the 25th Guards Rifle Corps was also working over this area. The barrage on Solomino was quite effective, and the Germans acknowledged this.[64] As a result, in this 3-kilometer sector, a density of 8 rocket launchers and 39.6 guns and mortars was created per kilometer of front.

The preemptive artillery barrage also had a stunning effect on the troops of Army Detachment Kempf's Korps "Raus". For example as soldiers of the 106th Infantry Division, who were taken prisoner already on 5 July in the course of fighting at Toplinka Station, recalled, the nighttime strike by the Russian artillery took them completely by surprise.[65] However, in this case also I've been unable to find any casualty reports or details of the losses in the staff documents of the corps.

The 7th Guards Army's counter artillery preparation continued until 0440. On occasion I've heard the opinion of colleagues that the 7th Guards Army's command was unable to implement the plan of the counter-artillery preparation to its end – the adversary interfered with this. However, this isn't true. Although the artillery fire of the opposing sides coincided in time minute to minute, they were conducting it against different targets. As is noted in the account by the 7th Guards Army's artillery headquarters, "The enemy's artillery preparation began with a heavy barrage on the forward edge of our defense [which is to say, on the infantry's combat positions,

61 TsAMO RF, F. 153 gv.ap., Op. 1, D. 4, L. 38.
62 NARA, T. 314, R. 197, F. 001054.
63 TsAMO RF, F. 38A, Op. 9027, D. 46, L. 151, 151obr.
64 TsAMO RF, F. 15, Op. 11600, D. 1534, L. 19.
65 TsAMO RF, F. 72.gv.sd., Op. 1, D. 60, LL. 23-28.

and not the Soviet artillery], thus the enemy fire didn't have any impact on the completion of the counter-artillery preparation by our artillery."[66]

Probably for this reason, the cessation of the Soviet preemptive fire, German soldiers began to circulate the legend that due to the mastery of the German artillerymen, a significant amount of the Soviet artillery and mortars was knocked out already in the offensive's first hour. This assertion is far from reality. Just as the Germans shifted their fire into the depth of the 7th Guards Army's defenses, staff officers of the artillery headquarters began to call around all of its units, as well as the rifle divisions, to inquire about losses. As a result it turned out that not a single gun had been knocked out, though the German fire had fully obliterated a full number of dummy and alternate firing positions.[67] Judging from archival documents of the 7th Guards Army headquarters, units of the divisional artillery began to suffer its initial losses in materiel only after 0700 on 5 July 1943, when the Germans began to pinpoint the location of separate batteries. For example, in the 153rd Guards Artillery Regiment, only three guns were damaged by enemy artillery fire over the entire day, and the time that each gun was knocked out is known precisely: two 76mm Model 1939 guns at 0700 and 1000 that morning, and one howitzer a bit later.[68]

In the 6th Guards Army, the second (main) phase of the counter-artillery preparation also took place at the designated time: at 0300 on 5 July 1943. However, its results were more modest, while the exaggerations (and even simple outright lies) about it in the reports of headquarters at every level was by an order of magnitude greater. Here, the firing was conducted in the following manner: at first a 5-minute barrage from every gun, then a 15-minute methodical working over of targets, and in conclusion a 10-minute barrage on likely areas of concentration of units of the Fourth Panzer Army's assault grouping. In addition, after the first 5-minute strike, the crews of the 82mm battalion mortars shifted their fire to the German trenches, while the 120mm regimental mortars dropped their shells on the reverse slopes of hills, where presumably German soldiers were congregating. The Katiusha rocket launching battalions gave two volleys at the start and at the end of the counter-artillery preparation.[69]

Already after the war, army commander I.M. Chistiakov remembered this tense moment:

> When the guns thundered, a doubt arose in the staff officers and me: Would this counter-preparation yield the desired effect? True, we didn't say this aloud, but each one of us was thinking it. …
>
> Time dragged on agonizingly. It was now 0550 and the enemy wasn't attacking. We worried. The high-frequency radio rang. I heard the familiar calm voice of the commander-in-chief:
>
> "Ivan Mikhailovich, why isn't the enemy attacking in your sector? Soon it will be 0600 and according to the information from our intelligence, he was supposed to attack at 0500 …"
>
> I was silent. There was nothing to say. Nikolai Fedorivich continued:
>
> "Did we rain several train cars of ammunition down on an empty area? If so we'll wind up in the history of military science as an example of how not to conduct a counter-preparation."
>
> He was driving me to despair. However, at this minute I caught the distant roar of engines, and with relief I began to shout into the phone, "Comrade commander, I hear the howl of engines! Tanks! There, now the artillery has spoken up!
>
> "Well, fine, I wish you success."[70]

66 TsAMO RF, F. 7.gv.A., Op. 5330, D. 60, L. 143.
67 Ibid.
68 TsAMO RF, F. 153.gv.ap., Op. 1, D. 4, L. 38obr.
69 *Bitva pod Kurskom: Ot oborony k nastupleniiu*, p. 186.
70 I.M. Chistiakov, *Sluzhim Otechestvu* [*We serve the Fatherland*) (Moscow, 1975), pp. 144-145.

An experienced reader might wonder, "How could an army commander, located in his command post several dozens of kilometers behind the front line, catch the sound of the German tank engines, moreover prior to the start of the artillery's work; after all, the German artillery preparation preceded the general attack, didn't follow it, and it lasted almost an hour? In addition, in the first wave of the Fourth Panzer Army's attacking troops there were no panzers; they were committed as soon as the combat engineers cleared passages through the minefield." The questions are fully reasonable and not easy to answer. As in the case of the absolute majority of memoirs by top Soviet military commanders, I.M. Chistiakov didn't write his book himself. He only talked about the most memorable episodes in his combat biography, while a literary colleague consolidated them into an intact whole and prepared the original text. This writer didn't know all the details of the army's system of command and control and the work of its command staff, not to mention how the Battle of Kursk actually started. After finishing the original text, a censor began to correct the manuscript based on principles of "political expediency". To the censor, plausibility and veracity were far from the main objectives. That is how such open discrepancies and inconsistencies insinuated themselves into the text.

On the whole, the idea of a preemptive artillery barrage was interesting, and it didn't pass unnoticed by the enemy – particularly its second phase in the early morning hours of 5 July. For example, the reinforced II/2nd SS Panzer Grenadier Regiment of the SS Panzer Grenadier Division *Leibstandarte Adolf Hitler* was blanketed by heavy fire in its jumping-off positions. The I Battalion of this same division's 1st SS Panzer Grenadier Regiment also came under heavy fire. The shells and rounds primarily fell on the infantry's positions, while the 13th Heavy Panzer Company of Tiger tanks and the assault gun battalions standing behind them didn't suffer. Recalled the driver-mechanic of a Tiger tank Sturmann W. Wendt, "In the morning, Russian artillery began to fire. At this time we still weren't in the tanks; they were positioned a little ahead, just behind the infantry. We were, as we say, just beyond the range of the Russian artillery … or they simply didn't know where we were at that moment."[71]

The reports of the German units note that there were losses, but they were relatively light. At the same time, a telegraph cable was heavily damaged, so contact had to be made through couriers. At 0300 on 5 July, that is, after the units of the Voronezh Front opened fire, the chief of staff of the XXXXVIII Panzer Corps *Oberst* E. von Mellenthin began to call the headquarters of the divisions personally, in order to collect information on losses and determine whether they were still in condition to carry out Operation Citadel's plan. Of the three divisions, the command of two (the 11th Panzer Division and 167th Infantry Division) reported that they didn't have any difficulties, because their main forces had neared their jumping-off positions later than the others. Information was lacking from the third division, the Panzer Grenadier Division *Grossdeutschland*, and little could be given, because according to the information of its command, only combat groups, tied up in combat with the combat outposts of the Guards divisions, were operating at the front, while the panzer and artillery regiments were still en route. They would only arrive by morning, including the brigade of Panther tanks. There is also no information about the loss of personnel and equipment from the preemptive barrage in the divisional documents of the Fourth Panzer Army. According to the tables in the documents, the division's compiled losses only over the entire day, and the damage suffered in separate clashes is rarely given. Therefore it is virtually impossible to extract the losses suffered in the course of the counter-artillery preparation alone from the daily casualty figures.

Thus, on the basis of sources available to scholars today it is impossible to establish the precise figures for the Fourth Panzer Army's losses, as well those of Army Detachment Kempf, in the course of the preemptive barrage, though it is clear: Even though M.S. Shumilov had no inkling of the enemy's readiness to attack on the night of 4-5 July right up to the final moment, its effect

71 Author's personal archive.

in the 7th Guards Army's sector was greater than that in the 6th Guards Army's sector. There are two reasons for this. First, the main bulk of Army Detachment Kempf was strictly tied to specific locations, where it planned to build bridges, and the Soviet side had accurately identified these places. Secondly, the time to initiate the preemptive barrage was correctly chosen; our artillery fire caught the enemy massed at the crossing sites and in the places directly in front of them. The Germans also acknowledged this.[72]

The command of Army Detachment Kempf's divisions was forced to reckon with the fact that a certain amount of time would be required to force a crossing of the river. Thus their units moved into their jumping-off positions a bit before the divisions of the neighboring Fourth Panzer Army, who didn't have to build bridges and cross a river channel under fire to reach the Soviet trenches, but only had to rise and advance several hundred meters across a field.

A complex situation also developed before the start of the Battle of Kursk on the Central Front. Despite the rather accurate information collected by intelligence and the statements of the prisoner Gefreitor B. Formella of the 6th Panzer Division, who'd been captured by 13th Army scouts before midnight on 4 July, there was still no full confidence that the Germans would launch the offensive on the night of 4-5 July. In his book *Soldatskii dolg*, K.K. Rokossovsky described his thoughts at that moment:

> To believe the prisoners' statements or not? If they were speaking the truth, then we had to initiate our planned artillery counter-preparation. ... There was no time to ask the *Stavka*; the situation was forming that a delay might lead to heavy consequences. The *Stavka* representative G.K. Zhukov, who had arrived the evening before and who was present at this time, entrusted the resolution of this question to me.[73]

According to information contained in the account of the 13th Army's artillery headquarters, the initial plan for the counter-artillery preparation was compiled and distributed to the troops at the end of May 1943. For its realization, it was planned to use all of the artillery of the first-echelon divisions and formations, namely the 81st, 15th, 148th and 8th Rifle Divisions and the 4th Breakthrough Artillery Corps of the Supreme Command Reserve. In total, 29 regiments were preparing to take part in it (4 of the first-echelon rifle divisions, 2 army mortar regiments, one cannon regiment and the forces of the 4th Breakthrough Artillery Corps: 6 light artillery regiments, 8 howitzer regiments, 4 cannon regiments and 6 mortar regiments).[74] In addition, it was intended to use 30% of the 82mm and 120mm mortars of the rifle regiments of the first-echelon divisions (4 batteries of 120mm mortars and 12 companies of 82mm mortars). In total, it was planned to employ 946 tubes (507 guns and 460 mortars) for the preemptive barrage.[75] Thus, the army, which had a defensive front that extended for 32 kilometers, was planning for the preemptive barrage to create an overall density of 30.2 guns and mortars per kilometer of front, or 15.8 guns and 14.4 mortars per kilometer.

Fire would be brought down on four directions:

a) Krasnaia Slobodka – Glazunovka;
b) Glazunovka – Arkhangel'skoe;
c) Arkhangel'skoe – Verkhnee Tagino;
d) Along the entire front between Krasnaia Slobodka and Verkhnee Tagino.

72 TsAMO RF, F. 72.gv.sd., Op. 1, D. 60, L. 24.
73 K.K. Rokossovsky, *Soldatskii dolg*, p. 215.
74 TsAMO RF, NSB.Inv. 9998, L. 25.
75 Ibid.

Before the beginning of July 1943, 102 enemy artillery batteries and 49 observation posts had been spotted opposite the 13th Army's front; the counter-artillery preparation was to destroy all of them. It was also planned to strike likely aggregations of tanks and infantry.[76] The counter-preparation was to be conducted in three stages: the first, a 5-minute barrage with every participating gun and mortar; the second, a 20-minute methodical fire with 50% of the participating guns and mortars; and the last, another 5-minute barrage with the all the available artillery means.

The leadership of the 13th Army reached the final decision about the start of the counter-artillery preparation approximately 90 minutes before the first shell fired by Model's Ninth Army. With this decision, its commander Lieutenant General N.P. Pukhov decided to reduce by half the number of guns and mortars that would be engaged in it, and then also changed the timetable of fire. For the first attack he authorized the use of only two artillery regiments of the four rifle divisions that had been previously planned (the artillery regiments of the 15th and 81st Rifle Divisions), and one of the three divisions of the 4th Breakthrough Artillery Corps (the 5th Artillery Division). In absolute numbers, this meant 131 76mm guns, 126 122mm howitzers, 28 122mm cannons, 32 152mm howitzer-cannons, 183 120mm mortars and 95 82mm mortars. The fire was opened at 0215 on 5 July and continued for approximately 20 minutes; over this time, one-fourth of a standard ammunition load was expended. At 0425 it was shifted to the second phase, and this one was significantly more powerful, employing 100% of the army's previously planned artillery: 220 76mm guns, 207 122mm howitzers, 39 122mm cannons, 41 152mm howitzer-cannons, 321 120mm mortars and 139 82mm mortars. They fired on artillery positions, observation posts and sectors of probable concentrations of manpower and armor. In the course of the entire counter-artillery preparation, Pukhov's army expended 35,000 rounds of ammunition.[77]

The lack of certainty at the moment of taking the decision to open fire and the absence of reliable information about its results, which have not yet been published either in Russia or the West, to a great extent influenced the multiple and diverse assessments of historians about this important event of the war's turning stage. As already noted above, a totally unsupported point of view about the absolute success and high enemy losses reigned in Soviet and Russian historiography. It is based on the assessments contained in the accounts of the Central and Voronezh Fronts' headquarters, which were written right after the Battle of Kursk: the journals of combat operations, reports, descriptions, etc. Meanwhile, the number of veteran recollections that came out in the 1960s and 1970s under the vigilant eye of the censors and which confirmed "the adversary's enormous losses" from the surprise attack, was supposed to confirm these accounts definitively. For example, in the document "The July defensive operation conducted by the Voronezh Front in the period 4-23 July 1943 on the Belgorod – Kursk direction", the results of the counter-preparation were laid out extremely laconically, but unambiguously: "The artillery counter-preparation caught the enemy by surprise in his jumping-off positions for the offensive and, unquestionably, inflicted significant losses to him. As a result, the enemy's ensuing artillery preparation and offensive, starting at 0330 on 5 July 1943, were disorganized and started at different times."[78] It is unclear what the assertion that the enemy's artillery preparation was supposedly disorganized is based upon, because all of the documents of our armies describe it otherwise as powerful.

The detailed analysis of the entire array of archival sources accessible to us today regarding the Voronezh Front for July and August 1943 allowed the discovery of only several documents that give more or less developed assessments of the results of the preemptive fire. They all belong to the army level: in the corps and division documents, there is no mention at all of this measure. The

76 TsAMO RF, F. 316, Op. 6079, D. 233, L. 13.
77 TsAMO RF, F. 13A., Op. 6094, D. 62-63, L. 86obr.
78 TsAMO RF, F. 213, Op. 2673, D. 6, L. 49.

reason is understandable: the counter-artillery preparation was a prerogative of the army's artillery command, and thus lower-standing bodies had no direct responsibility for it and accordingly took no account of it, even though they were its direct executors. Its outcomes in the 7th Guards Army's sector were most succinctly expressed in the report by its artillery headquarters from 4 August 1943:

1. The fire of our artillery inflicted losses on the enemy before the start of the attack, which is confirmed by prisoner-of-war statements, and depressed the enemy's morale, thanks to which his offensive zeal was strongly weakened.
2. As a result of the counter-artillery preparation, the enemy completely declined to attack out of Mikhailovka, where judging by his grouping of tank divisions (the 6th and 19th Panzer Divisions) the main attack in the army's sector was designated, and he was forced to shift them to the south in pace with the development of the success in the sector of the 78th Guards Rifle Division.
3. Having opened heavy fire earlier than the enemy, our artillery thereby increased the resolve of our infantry.[79]

Of all the points listed above, it is possible to consider the first and second points to be true, and at that, only partially so. Here is why: the Mikhailovka bridgehead wasn't intended to be the direction of the main attack as the Soviet side supposed. Nevertheless, because of the heavy incoming fire and the destruction of the bridges, the III Panzer Corps command really was forced to redeploy the 6th Panzer Division to the south, behind the 7th Panzer Division's successful crossing of the river. Undoubtedly the counter-artillery preparation affected this decision, but it didn't play the key role. The order that redirected the 6th Panzer Division wasn't issued immediately after the preemptive barrage or even two or three hours later, but not until nearly mid-day on 5 July. Up to that moment, the artillery of Shumilov's army was keeping the Mikhailovka area under constant fire, and it was also being subjected to systematic air strikes by Soviet ground assault aircraft. In these conditions the Germans deemed it senseless to send an entire panzer division into the small bridgehead, since the several attempts since dawn by units of the 168th Infantry Division to penetrate the defenses of the 81st Guards Rifle Division from out of this clump of earth had led to nothing but serious losses in personnel. Therefore, as soon as the success became evident in the south, in the sector of the adjacent 78th Guards Rifle Division, the III Panzer Corps command immediately began to switch the 6th Panzer Division to this area.

As concerns the suppression of the enemy troops' morale as a result of the 30-minute artillery barrage, this assertion is debatable. Unquestionably, there were casualties in all the divisions of Army Detachment Kempf from the barrage, and naturally this didn't raise the optimism and combat spirit of the troops. However, a sharp decline in combat spirit or increase in apathy, which might have substantially reflected on the effectiveness of the troops on 5 July, was nowhere discernible. Already by the afternoon of 8 July, the entire line of the 7th Guards Army, which included two fortified belts that had been constructed according to the latest word in engineer thinking, had been breached by the soldiers of Army Detachment Kempf, and the forward units of the III Panzer Corps had already joined battle with the 69th Army. By dawn on 12 July 1943, this same panzer corps, having overcome the first defensive line of the 69th Army, reached the rear army belt of defenses, having prior to the attack on the morning of 11 July only 16-23 operational combat machines in the divisions' panzer regiments.[80] Knowing all this, it is hard to agree with the assertion of the Soviet staff officers who wrote this account.

79 TsAMO RF, F. 7.gv.A., Op.
80 N. Zetterling and A. Frankson, *Kursk: A statistical analysis*, pp. 188-189.

Conclusions in favor of the high effectiveness of the counter-artillery preparation in the 6th Guards Army, which I.M. Chistiakov cites in his book, are also not very convincing and distant from reality. The 6th Guards Army commander wrote:

> Only later, when we took the offensive, we saw thousands of birch crosses above German graves in Tomarovka, in Borovka and in other places, and the residents told us how many dead fascist soldiers and officers they had to collect after this attack. The artillery counter-preparation not only inflicted serious material damage to the fascists, it also told heavily on the morale of the troops. The Hitlerite command was convinced that a calculation regarding the element of surprise in their attack against our defenses had been mistaken. Many fascist officers and generals believed that the artillery counter-preparation signaled the start of our own offensive. However, we learned about all this later, but back then, when I was speaking, one thing troubled me: Would they go on the offensive or not? There was a second nagging thought as well: Had we struck an empty place? They might have withdrawn their troops! But I was very much hoping on the accuracy of the intelligence information ....[81]

It is interesting, but according to what signs did the local residents determine, when collecting bodies from the battlefield, whether the German soldier or officer had been killed during the counter-artillery preparation or during the course of the battle itself? This assertion seems particularly strange when coming from an army commander, if you consider the areas that were struck by the preemptive barrage were in the zone of direct combat actions for almost 72 hours, and only after it subsided could the local residents and burial teams be sent there.

We find facts that are just as dubious in the documents of his army's artillery headquarters as well. In them, they base their main conclusions in favor of the success of the counter-artillery preparation on the statements of prisoners-of-war. For example, in the account for July 1943, the artillery headquarters notes: "Prisoners of the 332nd Infantry Division's 167th Infantry Regiment [sic – the 332nd Infantry Division didn't have a regiment with this numeric designation at the time] under interrogation revealed that over the period of the artillery counter-preparation, their regiment lost up to 600 soldiers and officers and up to 25% of its materiel and weapons. From this one can draw the conclusion that the counter-artillery preparation on the whole inflicted great damage to the enemy in manpower and equipment."[82]

If we turn to the real statements of those prisoners-of-war, for example, the interrogation of Leutnant Hans Dorfel, the commander of the 1st Platoon of the 3rd Company of the 332nd Infantry Division, then we find something somewhat different: "... our regiment lost up to 600 men on 4 and 5 July from Russian artillery fire."[83] Any additional commentary in this instance is superfluous. Further we read in the artillery headquarters' account: "Destroyed: up to 4,000 soldiers and officers, 21 tanks, 3 Pz VI tanks, 2 armored cars. Suppressed: 12 artillery batteries. Set ablaze: 4 stockpiles."[84] Doubtlessly, the cited data were only estimates based upon unverified or unreliable sources, since no one could physically count the destroyed Tigers in the dispositions of the enemy's assault grouping on the night of 4-5 July, not to mention the implausible number of enemy bodies. Judging from captured documents, even after two weeks of the most bitter fighting on the Kursk bulge, the divisions of Army Group South didn't have any such irrecoverable losses in personnel, like what General I.M. Chistiakov's subordinates reported after just 30 minutes of

81 I.M. Chistiakov, *Sluzhim Otechestvu*, p. 145.
82 TsAMO RF, NSB.Inv. No 9989, L. 31 and F. 6.gv.A, Op. 5122, D. 109(l), L. 121.
83 TsAMO RF, F. 71.gv.sd., Op. 1, D. 200, L. 41.
84 TsAMO RF, F. 6.gv.A., Op. 5122, D. 109 (l), L. 121.

a barrage on "likely congested areas". Understanding this, the command of the Voronezh Front's artillery somewhat adjusted the data of the 6th Guards Army and reported that as a total for the Front, in the course of the counter-artillery preparation "not less than 2,500-3,000 soldiers and officers were killed."[85]

However, an examination of the documents from the Voronezh Front's own artillery headquarters reveals even more fantastic assertions: "It is known that the enemy intended his offensive to begin on 4 July 1943, but began it only on 5 July 1943, which is explained by the losses and disruption in command and control caused by the counter-artillery preparation."[86] From what sources did it become known to the artillery commander Major General S.S. Varentsov that the enemy intended to attack on 4 July, and why didn't he report about this to the Voronezh Front's leadership, which sincerely believed that the Germans would attack our lines at 0300 on 5 July? To this point I will add that out of all of the departments of Voronezh Front's headquarters, the documents of which I've managed to study in the TsAMO RF, the subordinates of General S.S. Varentsov are distinguished by their particular tendency to exaggerate openly their accomplishments and merits.

No less murky is the situation with the level of losses of the Ninth Army's assault grouping. In domestic publications of the Soviet era, the inaccuracy of information on the results of the preemptive fire by the Central Front is significant. For example, A. Domank asserts that in the 13th Army's sector, "the artillery counter-preparation threw the enemy ranks into disarray and inflicted losses on him. Only 8 fascist batteries [emphasis the author's] opened return fire."[87] As already noted, at the moment of the start of the preemptive barrage in the sector of Pukhov's army, 102 enemy batteries had been marked for destruction; accordingly, the enemy losses must have been colossal. According to G.T. Khoroshilov, after the conclusion of the artillery counter-preparation, only 40% of the German batteries (a little more than 40 batteries) were able to return fire.[88]

When justifying the high effectiveness of the counter-artillery preparation in the open press, the leadership of the Central Front employed those very same incorrect methods that we observed being used by the Voronezh Front's generals. For example, the former commander of the Central Front's artillery headquarters V.I. Kazakov in his memoirs wrote:

> Our artillery inflicted a powerful blow, and the fully-armed Soviet troops met the German offensive. Very interesting in this respect are the statements made by a company commander of the 9th Panzer Division: 'These 30 minutes were a genuine nightmare. We didn't understand what had happened. Senseless from fear, the officers were asking each other, "Who is intending to attack – we or the Russians?" The company lost 20 men killed and 38 wounded. Our battalion commander was killed … six tanks were knocked out without having fired a single shot."[89]

Throughout the entire operation, the 9th Panzer Division operated in the 13th Army's sector. According to its headquarters' Intelligence Department, between 4 and 25 July 1943 only one company commander of this panzer division became a prisoner-of-war. He had come over to our side on the night of 8-9 July in the area of Ponyri-2. His name was *Oberleutnant* H. Frankenfeldt, the commander of the 7 Co./II/11th Panzer Grenadier Regiment. However, neither in the transcript of his interrogation[90] nor in his appeal to the Soviet command, which was widely published

85 TsAMO RF, F. 203, Op. 2843, D. 241, L. 32.
86 Ibid.
87 A. Domank, *Na ognennykh rubezhakh: Artilleriia v Kurskoi bitve*, p. 25.
88 Parot'kin (ed.), *Kurskaia bitva*, p. 233
89 V.I. Kazakov, *Artilleriia, ogon!* [*Artillery, fire!*] (Moscow: DOSAAF, 1972), p. 128.
90 TsAMO RF, F. 361, Op. 6081, D. 54, L. 19-21.

in the Soviet press,[91] does the quote given above appear. In reality, in the record of his interrogation he mentions the death of the commander of the battalion in which he served, *Major* Frank, but this happened not on the night of 4-5 July, but in combat on 7 July. The deserter doesn't even recall the preemptive barrage fired by the artillery of the Central Front, even though the interpreters who handled his interrogation emphasized that he "had given his statements very eagerly and in detail."[92] Of all the records of interrogation of prisoners-of-war captured by the 13th Army that I've checked, only in one, that of *Gefreitor* E. Zenger of I/216th Infantry Regiment of the 86th Infantry Division, are the losses caused by the counter-artillery preparation given, though it is second-hand information: "According to the battalion doctor, as a result of the Russian artillery barrage on the night of 4-5 July 1943 prior to our offensive, I/216th Infantry Regiment suffered significant losses, 45 men killed and wounded."[93]

I think that in his senior years at the end of the 1960s, V.I. Kazakov, who incidentally was one of the leading Soviet generals of artillery, didn't himself conceive this passage, but likely was using material selected for him from the numerous accounts that his subordinates wrote after the Battle of Kursk. For the staff officers who prepared such documents, this was routine work "for the archive", since the described events had already vanished with the summer and writing about them didn't bring them anything but trouble. Therefore accuracy and veracity wasn't required of them. No one bothered to check the numbers and statements from lower-standing headquarters, which is why one often encounters both mistakes and typos in them, while the prisoners' statements, as we see, were openly distorted or even written for them to sign. However, the majority of domestic research of the Soviet period relied on the information, extracted from these same accounts and reports. This is also why extremely few documents on this matter were preserved in the TsAMO RF.

Leading Soviet specialists on the Battle of Kursk, Colonels G.A. Koltunov and B.G. Solov'ev not only confirmed the high losses of the German forces in the course of the counter-artillery preparation, they also tried to substantiate them academically. In particular, in their book *Kurskaia bitva* they present curious details, but unfortunately, without a reference to sources. They write:

> Heavy losses in manpower were inflicted on the adversary in personnel. It is sufficient, for example, to say that more than 46% of the shells exploded at a distance that ensured damage to guns or injury to personnel (the effective beaten zone). The quantity of shells that exploded at a radius of up to 20 meters from the target (the lethal radius) amounted to 21%. Five targets received a direct hit. As a result, of the 130 enemy batteries [?!] in the sector of the 13th Army that had been previously identified by our intelligence, only 58 opened fire during the artillery preparation.[94]

Unquestionably, the numbers are not only curious, but also surprising. It is hard to imagine how during a nighttime artillery barrage the Soviet side managed to measure how far each of 35,000 shells fell from its intended target. Sometime later, G.A. Koltunov, realizing that the question was extremely complex, and that a number of aspects of the official point of view didn't conform to already known facts and the opinion of a number of veterans of those events, even acknowledged that "the incomplete information on the disposition of the enemy's firing means and personnel, the somewhat premature conducting of the counter-artillery preparation, as well as the limits on

91 For example, see *Komsomol'skaia pravda, 15 July 1943, p. 3.*
92 TsAMO RF, F. 361, Op. 6081, D. 54, L. 21.
93 TsAMO RF, F. 361, Op. 6081, D. 54, L. 45.
94 G.A. Koltunov and B.G. Solov'ev, *Kurskaia bitva*, p. 104.

ammunition prevented us from obtaining the desired results."[95] It should be noted that this assessment was the most objective of all that were published in the open press in the Soviet era.

Now let's take a look at how the direct organizers of this measure on the Central Front assessed it in the combat documents. According to the material of its headquarters, the artillery of the 13th Army alone (one of the three that took part in the counter-artillery preparation) managed to suppress 90-100 enemy batteries, destroy up to 60 observation posts, blow up 10-12 dumps of ammunition and fuel, scatter or destroy up to three regiments of infantry, destroy up to 25 assault guns (according to prisoners' testimonies), and partially disrupt the enemy's pre-combat formations of the tanks and the combat formations of infantry.[96]

If to speak quite openly, for a professional these assertions are "utter nonsense". Not one of the special groups of observers were sent into the German rear and counted one-by-one the knocked-out self-propelled guns or enemy dead. Also, the clarification added in parentheses in the statement above, made by the Operation Department's staff officers with the aim of enhancing the believability of these figures, for obvious reasons don't prompt any trust. The figure "up to 25 assault guns" is particularly surprising. I've managed to familiarize myself with the transcripts of the interrogation of all the prisoners and deserters who passed through the Intelligence Department of this army between 3 and 21 July 1943, and not one of them confirms the given figure.[97] In addition, it must not be forgotten that for the Ninth Army, which was experiencing an acute deficit of artillery means, the loss of practically an entire assault gun battalion in its jumping-off positions would not be simply major damage, but a catastrophic event, which wouldn't escape the attention of higher-level headquarters. For example, in the course of the fighting on 5 July 1943, 17 assault guns in the XXIII Army Corps were knocked out of action.[98] In order to investigate the reasons for such heavy losses, according to the corps' assessment, a special commission was created, which drew up a full series of instructions, memorandums and orders, in addition to those reports and accounts that were prepared by the commission itself on the results of its work. In the case of the supposed "25 assault guns" knocked-out by the preemptive barrage, however, there is only surprising silence. The analysis of the archival files in the US National Archives shows that neither the headquarters of the Ninth Army, nor those of any of its subordinate corps and divisions reports such a major loss of armored equipment in their combat dispatches or operational summaries. I was also unable to find any documents related to an investigation of its causes. Information about it is also lacking in the journals of combat operations. All this is a reliable sign of the falsification of the data presented in the materials of the 13th Army's headquarters.

The experience of work with captured German documents gives evidence that when the enemy's headquarters reported to higher command about their losses, the information was quite accurate. Accordingly, one can assume that in this connection the documents of the Ninth Army's formations and units for July 1943 are more correct. However, unfortunately the analysis of them doesn't yield the information we need. The headquarters of the divisions recorded the counter-artillery preparation in their documents and materials, but only its first phase. All the first-echelon divisions of the XXIII Army Corps and of the XXXXI and XXXXVII Panzer Corps note the heavy fire of Soviet artillery between 0115 and 0145 (according to Berlin time). However, from these documents it is very difficult to evaluate its results, since not a single headquarters reported on the losses during the counter-artillery preparation. There is also no evidence in these sources that the incoming artillery fire disrupted the offensive, or caused it to be postponed by 2-3 hours, as

95 G.A. Koltunov, "Nekotorye osobennosti oborony na Kurskoi duge" ["Several characteristics of the defense on the Kursk bulge"] in *Kurskaia bitva* [*Battle of Kursk*] (Moscow: Nauka, 1975), p. 118.

96 TsAMO RF, F. 13A, Op. 6094, D. 62-63, L. 88.

97 TsAMO RF, F. 306, Op. 6081, D. 54, LL. 1-73obr.

98 NARA, T. 314, R. 689, F. 000383.

Russian publications maintain. On the contrary, it is noted in the journal of combat operations of the 292nd Infantry Division after midnight:

> The assembly went normally and wrapped up at 0200 [Berlin time]. Nevertheless, the Russians suspected something was up and between 0100 and 0145 opened lively artillery fire along the entire line of the front and on the immediate rear areas. However, the shells landed far from targets.[99]

In the documents of the 20th Panzer Division we find the following description of those events:

> 0115: The start of a heavy enemy barrage from all types of heavy weapons. The Russians were anticipating an offensive from our side at 0200. This is confirmed by the statements of two deserters in the 6th Infantry Division's sector. There is renewed activity of enemy aircraft during the night.
> 0200: The 112th Panzer Grenadier Regiment is occupying its jumping-off positions.
> 0340: The 21st Panzer Battalion and the 92nd Panzerjäger Battalion are also occupying their jumping-off positions.[100]

Only two mentions in the documents of the XXIIII Army Corps can be seen as evidence without any strain that its troops suffered more or less substantial damage in the course of the counter-artillery preparation itself: "At 0130 the 78th Assault Division reported a powerful artillery barrage on its right flank and on Kunach Hill. Observation posts have partially been destroyed ... At 0235 ... another message from the 78th Assault Division: there are losses from enemy artillery fire. Everything else is in order."[101]

In the messages from the Ninth Army to Army Group Center and in the operational summaries of the army group itself, for days there is not a single mention of any preemptive artillery strike by the Soviet forces. Such silence can be interpreted in various ways: it can't be excluded that the enemy was striving to prevent drawing attention to a setback. However, it is an obvious fact that the preemptive fire didn't inflict any significant damage to the German troops that were poised to attack or the German artillery, much less disrupt (or force a postponement) the start of the general offensive.

The fact that in the documents of the Ninth Army of this time there are a quite a few descriptions of tragic episodes and mistakes made by its subordinate units heightens the believability of the German information about the insignificant losses from the preemptive barrage. For example, the entry in the combat diary of the already-mentioned 292nd Infantry Division for 2 July 1943 openly acknowledges: "Thanks to numerous mistakes in the course of the march, the II/292nd Artillery Regiment was spotted by enemy observers, came under adjusted artillery fire, and suffered losses."[102] Evidence of these losses is laid out in even greater detail in a report from this artillery regiment itself.

The aforementioned facts allow Western authors to maintain that there were no substantial results from the preemptive attack of Soviet artillery and the fire was random, while the expenditure of shells was exorbitantly high.[103] Even some Russian scholars share this opinion.[104] It is

99 NARA, T. 315, R. 1928, F. 000160.
100 NARA, T. 315, R. 747, F. 000434.
101 NARA, T. 314, R. 688, F. 000722.
102 NARA, T. 315, R. 1928, F. 000158.
103 See, for example, Showalter, *Armor and Blood*, p. 78.
104 See, for example, B.G. Sokolov, *Georgii Zhukov: triumf and padenie* [*Georgii Zhukov: triumph and fall*] (no place given: AST-Press Kniga, 2003), p. 360.

impossible not to acknowledge that there are justifications for doubt in the effectiveness of this important and large-scale measure. Marshal of the Soviet Union Georgii Zhukov, who at that time was the Red Army's Deputy Supreme Commander-in-Chief, after the war recognized openly that the result of the counter-artillery preparation was far from that which both the *Stavka* and the leadership of the *fronts* had been expecting:

> It should however be pointed out that by the start of the enemy's actions, the plan for the counter-preparation hadn't yet been fully worked out (in detail) in our forces. The places of the concentrations of troops in their jumping-off positions and the disposition of targets on the night of 4-5 July still hadn't been identified precisely. It is clear that given the reconnaissance means that we had back then, it wasn't easy to determine accurately the location of targets, but it was still possible to do a lot more than the troops of the *fronts* did. As a result, our artillery during the counter-preparation had to fire primarily not at specific targets, but at general areas. This allowed the enemy to avoid massive casualties.[105]

Colonel General N.S. Fomin wrote back in 1968 in greater detail about what the "troops of the *fronts*" and their leadership didn't do:

> In general, in the Central Front's 13th Army, the moment of starting the counter-preparation was correctly chosen. However, the decision by its command to reduce by half the amount of artillery engaged in it and the time given to the first phase reduced, in our opinion, the effectiveness of the fire damage done to the enemy. It is also hard to recognize as sensible the initiation of the second phase with all the artillery, when the enemy's troops had started their own artillery preparation for the attack, as a result of which the fire of our artillery in a number of cases proved to be unwise. In the 70th Army of this Front, the counter-preparation in general terms began 10 minutes after the start of the enemy's artillery preparation. The selection of the time for implementing it wasn't one of the best. In Voronezh Front's 6th Guards Army, the counter-preparation began on the evening of 4 July, on the eve of the anticipated enemy offensive, and was restricted to a 5-minute barrage. Precisely at 0300 on the morning of 5 July the counter-preparation resumed at full volume. The artillery of the 7th Guards Army began the counter-preparation at 0300 on 5 July simultaneously according to all three options. In the process, 10 minutes before its completion, the enemy opened return fire, having started his artillery preparation. ... One can conclude that a certain lack of confidence is evidently perceptible in the armies in the selection of when the counter-preparation should start, as well as regarding its anticipated effects. Indeed this is natural, since the selection of the moment for opening fire in a counter-preparation is one of the most difficult decisions that the command must make. ... Undoubtedly ... one thing is clear: if the decision has been made, then given the absence of information and the changing situation, it must be fully implemented. The splitting of the counter-preparation into two phases only weakens the effect of the attack and the expected results. The results on both *fronts*, it must be presumed, would have been greater, if the weaknesses noted by us hadn't been present.[106]

Certain contemporary authors place responsibility for the miscalculation, in particular, in determining the moment of opening fire by the Voronezh Front's artillery on its command, but in order to justify this point of view, they draw mistaken conclusions. For example, L.N. Lopukhovsky asserts:

105 As cited in Parot'kin (ed.), *Kurskaia bitva*, p. 51.
106 Ibid., pp. 221-222.

> An interrogated prisoner in the presence of Voronezh Front's Military Council member N.S. Khrushchev announced that "the offensive would begin at 0300 with the first morning light." The prisoner wasn't lying: he, like everyone in the German army, lived and fought according to Berlin time, which is to say the start of the operation was set at 0500 (0300 Central European time) 5 July. It is hard to imagine that in the war's third year, our command (especially the interpreters) were unaware of the difference in time. More likely they were afraid to delay the opening of fire, fearing that the enemy would preempt it with the start of the artillery preparation. Moreover it had become known that the Central Front had already conducted an artillery barrage at 0220. As a result, the artillery counter-preparation began too early.[107]

Actually, the Voronezh Front leadership was in a hurry. However, not out of fear of being too late, but because of the fact that it knew the situation much better than anyone today. The point is that in the cited extract, the correct time is given according to time zones, but the Soviet Union in this period was living according to a so-called "decreed time". With the aim of a more rational use of daylight hours, the Council of People's Commissars on 16 June 1930 decreed that the time zones on the territory of our country would be shifted one hour forward. Accordingly, the difference between Berlin time and Moscow time was reduced by one hour. Indeed this change was maintained year-round, in 1943 as well, instead of semi-annual time changes. One can become easily convinced in this when the description of one and the same events in the operational documents of the German and Soviet forces are compared. Accordingly, the offensive by von Manstein's grouping in the south of the Kursk salient was supposed to begin (and did begin) not at 0500, but 0400. Its preceding artillery preparation began a half hour before H-hour, at 0330. That means Vatutin's Voronezh Front opened fire on the night of 4-5 July on time, as was planned, one hour before the enemy attack, but its relatively low effectiveness was connected with the problems that have already been laid out above.

However it was, it ought to be recognized that the large-scale measure designated by the Soviet command, which was supposed to weaken the enemy's assault groupings at the shoulders of the Kursk salient by inflicting substantial damage to them while in their jumping-off positions didn't yield the desired effect. Archival materials confirm its relatively high results only on the left flank of the Voronezh Front, in the 7th Guards Army's sector of defense. In addition to the fact that here the assault groups, assembled at the crossing sites in expectation of the signal to attack, suffered losses in manpower and to some extent in equipment, Shumilov's preemptive artillery fire contributed to the frustration of a crossing by one of the three panzer divisions of the III Panzer Corps. This unquestionably played a certain role in the fact that on the first day of the offensive, Army Detachment Kempf was unable to breach the 7th Guards Army's first belt of defenses, and its troops became tied up in heavy fighting in the Guardsmen's positions. On the northern shoulder of the Kursk bulge, the results of the counter-preparation were significantly more modest and didn't lead to any noticeable tactical results. All of the Ninth Army's divisions stepped off to carry out Operation Citadel strictly according to schedule, while the command of Ninth Army and of Army Group Center didn't take any notice at all of this measure by the Soviet side. Thus, it is impossible not to agree with General N.S. Fomin, who wrote: "It should be acknowledged that the problem of a counter-preparation in contemporary conditions requires serious study, and searches for the best ways and means of conducting it."[108]

107 See Lopukhovsky's article in *Voenno-istoricheskii arkhiv*, No. 9 (2004), p. 46.
108 Parot'kin (ed.), *Kurskaia bitva*, p. 222.

9

The Kursk turning point – What remained behind the curtain?

Revealing the real condition of the armed forces of any country is the primary goal of all intelligence services. Hundreds of agents and dozens of analytical centers, departments and services work around-the-clock compiling, comparing and analyzing a variety of information with a single goal – in order to determine the real situation of affairs in the enemy's camp. At the same time reconnaissance patrols and intelligence officers strive to obtain complete information. Not only figures regarding the number of men placed under arms and the weapons and equipment produced by factories, but also information about the level of training of the senior command staff and officers at the tactical level, and the degree of combat proficiency of replacements. In addition to this, the number of turncoats and deserters is scrupulously tracked; the ethnic composition of the opposing army is analyzed; and the systems and speed of the transmission of information and orders at various levels are studied. All this allows not only the discovery of the opposing side's materiel and technical capabilities to take part in a prolonged military conflict, but also the combat spirit of the troops, their level of discipline, and the friction among personnel due to nationality differences which can be exploited for reducing the combat capability of units, eroding the cohesion of the troops, and so forth.

No matter how paradoxical it seems, but for both sides that took part in the war, it was important to keep completely concealed accurate information on things of this nature not only from the enemy, but also from one's own people, because in the army of any country at all times there are negatives which once becoming known to broad social strata, might influence their morale: shaking the faith of the troops in their commanders, or the faith in the civilian population in the ability and desire of the state's political and military leadership to defend the country. This was as it was in the years of the Great Patriotic War as well. The propaganda of both sides actively exploited all of the failures, negatives, and crimes that took place in the troops and were often pre-planned, in order to form an image in the Soviet people of the "brutal German-fascist aggressors", and in the German people – "the faces of the subhuman races from the East". This informational repository, prepared at the time by specialists in propaganda and disinformation, and subsequently artfully inserted into the minds of millions of people, accreting over the years with new details conceived by now ordinary people, works to this very day. Indeed, an image of the Red Army distorted beyond recognition, and an image of that epochal war that is remote from reality has continued to form in the consciousness of compatriots now for almost 70 years. Meanwhile the real situation of affairs in the troops of the opposing sides and the processes that were happening in them back then were kept rigorously concealed, and thus today it is extremely difficult to understand these aspects of the war or individual battles. Documents about the "real-life war" are today concealed not so much by seals of secrecy, but primarily by the millions of pages of information that accompanied the combat actions and which flowed in a constant current up and down the ladder of command. Thus, scholars must exert a colossal effort, digging through the documentary slagheaps in the military archives, in order to uncover a description of an interesting event, or at least an echo of it.

However, there were people in the war who were supposed to know absolutely everything that was happening in the troops, and who were to take measures in order to correct negative tendencies and to prevent them from appearing. Primarily the commanders of armies and *fronts* belonged to this narrow circle of such leaders. Among them was General of the Army N.F. Vatutin, the commander-in-chief of the Voronezh Front. Dozens of messages, briefing papers and reports about the condition and actions of his subordinate troops and even individual officers and soldiers were piling up daily on his table. The majority of them were of an operational nature. This information required the taking of immediate decisions, since a delay might negatively affect the results of the Front's combat work.

In addition to this daily flow of documents, once every five days, and sometimes after 10 days, summary reports and fact sheets would arrive from various services and branches of the Front and the armies. These concerned not so much facts and events as they did the results of combat actions over a certain period and, something that was very important, touched upon revealed problems, first of all negative ones. This permitted the commander to extract immediately the most important issues from the overall informational flow and react quickly to them, if, of course, this was within his competence.

Today this material is priceless for historians. Letting drop subjective assessments and conclusions, which always are always present in documents of this nature, it is possible to assert that a familiarity with this complex array of materials actually allows one to see the real situation of affairs in the troops (although, possibly, not in every realm), in particular of the Voronezh Front. So relying on these sources, we will attempt to take a look at major problems that arose (or became more acute) in the course of repulsing Army Group South's offensive and at the situation in his armies in the first five days of the battles (which is to say, the most difficult and critical period of the Battle of Kursk).

Thus, by 9 July the first accounts that compiled the experience of the operation thus far at every level of command began to arrive at the headquarters of the Voronezh Front. Reading them, N.F. Vatutin saw that the colossal amount of work done over the three-month operational pause to refit and train the troops, and to achieve the main thing – to raise the level of preparation to the necessary level, had been unsuccessful. As is known, combat is the yardstick by which all the work of the command staff is measured. Now it had exposed all the problems in bold relief and was highlighting the mistakes made in the planning and in the practical work of the leadership of the *fronts* and armies.

In the first place, problems with command and control had begun to arise. In the Workers' and People's Red Army, despite the series of failures over the first two years of the war, the commanders had taken correct, carefully calculated, and at times simply brilliant decisions when not pressured by the political leadership; for example, the choice of the moment to launch the counteroffensive at Moscow and Stalingrad, and in choosing the points of attack against Paulus's army. To such far-sighted and well-considered decisions, with complete confidence one can also add the adoption of a premeditated defense in the spring of 1943, as well as the entire system of constructing the defenses in the area of the Kursk salient. Having familiarized yourself with the transcripts of the conversations of the Voronezh Front commander, it is impossible not to note the accuracy of his prognoses regarding the development of the operational situation and the enemy actions in the next several days. In this period the majority of N.F. Vatutin's decisions and of his headquarters regarding major questions were deliberate, far-sighted and responded in full to the emerging situation at the front. The General of the Army had fully mastered the practices of commanding the troops of a strategic formation, and no less important, in the course of combat work he was demonstrating high communication standards with his subordinates, correctness in his dealings with them, and respecting their human dignity.

The majority of the commanders at the level of the Voronezh Front's army and corps levels, thanks to their talent and combat experience also fully corresponded to their occupied posts. However, a significant portion of the officers on the operational-tactical and especially the tactical level, both of the Voronezh Front and the Red Army as a whole, were poorly prepared in a career sense. They didn't know how to assess an operational situation quickly and correctly, take adequate decisions and make them known to subordinates, organize the work of headquarters staff to assist them, or arrange cooperation with neighbors. They often became lost in combat situations, demonstrating elementary helplessness. This was one of the main reasons for the high losses in the troops subordinate to them.

A weakness of the command staff up to the corps level inclusively was the inability to organize the coordinated action of all types of troops during a battle. Speaking in a technical language, these commanders had difficulty getting the army's components working together productively and poorly handled the operations. Similar problems also existed in the German Army, but in the Wehrmacht the training of officers was more rigorous and given primary significance, as incidentally was the case with the individual training of the soldier. Thus its tactical commanders, at the very least, demonstrated an excellent level of professional skill in the course of the Battle of Kursk. This enabled the German divisions and corps to operate successfully with forces that were significantly outnumbered by the Soviet side.

Often the training for combat actions in the units and formations of the Red Army were of a schematic nature, not distinguished by specificity, and problems that might arise weren't considered in detail. Headquarters rarely worked out several alternative ways to carry out assignments, and gave little attention to "trifles", which later as a rule came back to bite them – which is to say they took no consideration of any problems that might arise during a battle. The formation commanders that took part in the operation didn't meet after the issuing of orders and didn't discuss their initial decisions and proposals regarding questions that arose in the course of planning; each commander decided them independently to his own ability.

The combat plans of lower units and formations weren't checked by higher commanders. This may seem improbable, but there were more than a few cases when during the work up of a plan for large-scale combat operations, the commands of even armies took no consideration of the actions of their neighbors along the line of defense. In documents there is only a mention of their presence, and nothing more. The combat employment of attached units was arranged with great difficulty. The organization of their cooperation with the units of the division or corps to which they'd been sent rarely went smoothly. The commands of rifle divisions and regiments had especially great difficulties when cooperating with tankers or artillerymen. The combined-arms commanders didn't know the specifics, or particularly the tactics of these types of troops, which often led to the incorrect use of the attached means of reinforcements, excessive losses and the mission's failure. Here is just one characteristic example of how the command of the rifle formations of Voronezh Front's 7th Guards Army used tank formations, as laid out by the commander of the 27th Guards Tank Brigade Colonel N.V. Nevzhinsky in a combat report from 8 July 1943:

1. At dawn on 6 July 1943, the 27th Guards Separate Tank Brigade, on the basis of a verbal order from the commander of the 24th Guards Rifle Corps was operating: Poliana State Farm (excl.), Point 192.6, Point 192.8, Point 140.1, railroad line southeast of Rzhavets. The brigade is supporting the 72nd Guards Rifle Division on the right with one tank battalion, and the 213th Guards Rifle Division on the left with one tank battalion.

   The brigade was conducting combat actions on a wide front of 12 kilometers; they were introduced in a piecemeal manner, because of which difficulties arose in commanding the brigade and organizing cooperation with different types of troops, as well as implementing evacuation and supply services.

2. The piecemeal actions of the brigade deprive it of its proper effect as a shock force and its ability to maneuver, as well as its efficient use on the most important sectors.
3. The brigade is receiving combat assignments verbally, without the confirmation of written orders. There were cases when the commanders personally gave orders to carry out a combat assignment to seize objectives without artillery support or infantry, warning "If you fail to take it, I will shoot you." Such a dialogue happened between the commander of the 1st Tank Battalion and the commander of the 72nd Guards Rifle Division (from a report by the 1st Tank Battalion commander). As a result of such use, the brigade suffers heavy losses in both materiel and men.[1]

Often, the organization of combat on the regiment or division level, and even on the corps level, was restricted to the issuing of orders alone. Senior commanders didn't look into the problems of the units and elements, made no effort to help them with words or actions, and when problems arose or the implementation of orders went tardily, they raised their voices, accusing their commanders of idleness, cowardice and foot-dragging, and threated to put them in front of a military tribunal or even a firing squad.

On the Voronezh Front, the situation was complicated by the fact that some of the regiment and division commanders had been first appointed to their posts in the weeks before the start of the Battle of Kursk, in some cases literally just a matter of days before the start of the German offensive, while at the corps level some took command of their subordinate troops already once the battle was underway. Thus even those rifle corps that had been formed up back in May-June 1943 had no time to become full-strength, efficient combat formations. A particularly large rotation of division commanders took place in the 6th Guards Army, which was positioned on the axis of Army Group South's main attack. By 5 July 1943, of the six divisions under its command, three of them had commanders who had been in place for two months, while one had been appointed just a week before the start of the fighting.[2] Moreover, three of the divisions, in which a change of command took place, were occupying the army's first echelon of defense. Since these divisions were defending prepared lines, problems and rough edges in command were primarily overcome without any particular consequences. However, the results of the fighting on the second day of the battle, 6 July, particularly in the sector of the 6th Guards Army clearly demonstrated the incapability of the corps level of command to handle their duties fully. Despite the relatively good training of a number of commanders, they were unable to achieve concerted actions by the divisions. In essence, the corps headquarters were carrying out the function of a transmission link for the flow of information and orders back and forth between the army leadership and the divisions – and doing so in a casual, offhand style.

A number of senior commanders showed no sort of initiative or resolve. There were several reasons for this, but one of the main ones was the lack of adequate time for the command staff at the corps level to familiarize themselves with their subordinate divisions. For example, the leadership of the 69th Army's 48th Rifle Corps began to take command of its divisions on 2 July, and became operational on 4 July, after just two days of familiarity with the troops. Orders to conclude the formation of the corps command in the 7th Guards Army and 40th Army were issued already after the battle began.

1 TsAMO RF, F. 3108, Op. 1, D. 7, L. 103.
2 Colonel I.P. Sivakov was appointed commander of the 71st Guards Rifle Division on 28 April 1943, Colonel V.G. Chernov assumed his post in command of the 90th Guards Rifle Division on 30 April 1943, Colonel I.M. Nekrasov took command of the 52nd Guards Rifle Division on 17 May 1943, while Colonel A.I. Baksov received command of the 67th Guards Rifle Division on 30 June 1943 (TsAMO RF, service records of the indicated officers).

The quality of the staffing of each headquarters is a separate question. Often officers who had good theoretical knowledge of their duties became lost in practice, in a dynamic, stressful combat situation. They were unable to organize the repulse of hostile attacks with their entrusted formation even on prepared lines, adequately react to an emerging situation, quickly restore lost command and control over the troops, establish and maintain robust contact with higher command or neighbors on the flank, or implement effective cooperation with them. From a briefing paper from the headquarters of the SMERSH counter-intelligence department of the Voronezh Front:

> On 8 July 1943 the commanders of the 5th Guards Tank Corps and 10th Tank Corps, having been summoned by Voronezh Front's chief of staff Lieutenant General S.P. Ivanov, received an order to attack at 0800. Upon returning to their posts, a coded message arrived that changed the start time of the attack to 0900. The 5th Guards Tank Corps carried out the order, made a 10-15 kilometer advance, but having suffered heavy losses returned by 1600 to its jumping-off line. At this time an order arrived that cancelled the day's attack order, and as it turned, the 2nd and 10th Tank Corps, having received this order in a timely manner, took no part in the offensive; as a result of this, the 5th Guards Tank Corps lacked support.[3]

It should be made clear that of these three tank corps, only the 10th Tank Corps had direct contact with the Front headquarters. However, having received the order to cancel the attack, the headquarters of the 10th Tank Corps made no effort to inform its neighbor about this, even though both tank corps had been preparing to attack together, and the problem the 5th Guards Tank Corps was having with communications was known to the 10th Tank Corps' command.

The point is that because of the rapid turnover at the end of 1942 and especially in the first half of 1943, a painful deficit of senior officers and generals who had both experience and and the capability of working in the headquarters at this level of command arose in the Red Army at the corps command level. This problem was especially acute in the Voronezh Front. The chief of staff of the 40th Army Major General A.G. Batiun' reported:

> The corps commands, formed from the reserve command staff of the People's Commissariat of Defense, in their overwhelming majority had commanders who hadn't yet participated in the Great Patriotic War. Although they had academic training, they weren't familiar with the practical responsibilities of a headquarters at this level, and their theoretical knowledge adjusted to the combat situation only slowly. This is why in the first days of the battle, the command over the troops at the corps level ran poorly, and the army headquarters entirely and totally had to cover for the work of the corps commands.[4]

However, there were also objective problems, and N.F. Vatutin was unable to influence them in a large way. Nevertheless, striving to resolve the arising difficulties with command at the corps level in the course of the operation, the command of the armies took charge of the majority of matters. This in turn complicated the work of the army headquarters: the burden on the staff officers and the means of communication increased, which in turn reduced rapid decision-making and implementation of decisions, and the quality and depth of their work diminished. The wave of tasks swamped them so heavily that there wasn't time even to monitor the execution of issued orders and instructions adequately.

3 See the *Voenno-istoricheskii zhurnal*, No. 7 (2013), pp. 26-27.

4 TsAMO RF, F. 203, Op. 2843, D. 520, L. 20.

At the same time problems of a subjective nature also became acute. A number of senior officers, appointed to high posts, demonstrated a lack of desire or inability to work toward an outcome. The situation in both of the 6th Guards Army's corps became a subject of constant attention by its commander Lieutenant General I.M. Chistiakov and subsequently by N.F. Vatutin personally. Already on 7 July, the Voronezh Front's Military Council was forced to relieve the commander of the 23rd Guards Rifle Corps Major General P.P. Vakhromeev of his duties, whose troops were holding the most tank-vulnerable axis – the Oboian' highway and the Prokhorovka axis – at first temporarily and then once and for all with the formulation "unable to handle his work". The general's lack of discipline and drunkenness became one of the main reasons for this decision.

Colonel I.P. Nagatkin, the chief of staff of the 22nd Guards Rifle Corps, was unable to get the staff work up and running effectively. All of the services and departments were working haphazardly. It was impossible to obtain clear and accurate information from the corps about the situation of affairs on the line of defense, the condition of the troops, etc. At first he received only verbal admonitions, but the situation remained unchanged. From Order No. 0125 signed by the commander of the 6th Guards Army on 25 August 1943:

> The chief of staff of the 22nd Guards Rifle Division, throughout the entire time he spent in this post, regarded the execution of his duties indifferently, gave little attention to getting the departments of the corps headquarters working properly or training the division headquarters, didn't scrutinize their daily work and combat activity, and took no control over their work.
>
> He doesn't work to improve himself, makes no effort to enhance his knowledge, doesn't study the experience of the Great Patriotic War, systematically abuses alcohol, after which he complains of stomach aches.
>
> When the corps was conducting combat operations, Guards Colonel Nagatkin showed complete inactivity in leading his staff, remained isolated from the division headquarters, lost any and all orientation, and didn't know the real situation of the troops on the battlefield, as a result of which his headquarters wasn't an organ of command and control for the corps commander in the period of fighting.[5]

Immediately after the Battle of Kursk ended, Colonel Nagatkin was relieved of his duties and placed at the disposal of the Front's Military Council.

The foe was aware of the imperfections in the Red Army's command staff in a professional sense, and naturally took advantage of this. After the war the British historian B. Lidell Hart spent many hours conversing with Wehrmacht generals, a significant number of whom fought on the Eastern Front. In their opinion, by the middle of the war the Soviet commanders had learned how to fight and their tutelage went rather quickly. One of Hart's German conversation partners put it this way: "As the war went on, the Russians developed an increasingly high standard of leadership from top to bottom. One of their greatest assets was their officers' readiness to learn, and the way they studied their job."[6] However, the quality of the Red Army's command level, in the opinion of the Germans, was perceptibly different between the north and south of the Soviet – German front. The southern sector of the front had the highest quality generals (which is to say, trained, young, rising professionals) than did the northern sector. Possibly this is due to the more active

5 TsAMO RF, F. 1207, Op. 1, D. 138, L. 150.

6 B.H. Liddell Hart, *Na druguiu storonu kholma* [*On the other side of the hill*] (Moscow: AST, 2014), pp. 338-339. This is the Russian translation of B.H. Lidell Hart's *The German Generals Talk: Startling revelations from Hitler's high command* first published in 1948. This quote is found on pages 222-223 in the 1975 paperback edition published by Harper Perennial.

and significant combat operations of both armies throughout the war in the southern sector (on the central, southwestern and southern fronts). But the military commanders who fought in the north, in the Germans' opinions, stood out in a slightly different respect, which in my view was to a certain extent characteristic of all the Red Army's commanders, including those of the Voronezh Front, if to rely upon the now de-classified materials. B.H. Lidell Hart writes:

> Broadly speaking, the run of opinion seemed to be that the top and bottom of the Russian ladder of command became the strongest sections, while the middle piece was shaky. The top rungs were filled by men who had proved themselves so able that they were allowed to exercise their own judgement, and could safely insist on doing things in their own way. The bottom rungs were filled by junior officers, who within their limited sphere, tended to develop a good tactical sense, because the incompetent soon became casualties in a field that was ruled by the hard realities of the enemy's bullets and shells. But the intermediate commanders, even more than most armies, were concerned with other factors. Their superiors' orders and judgements were more to be feared than the enemy.
>
> ...
>
> It was usually safe to encourage the Russians to attack, so long as the defence was elastically designed. The Russians were always very bull-headed in their offensive methods, repeating their attacks again and again. This was due to the way their leaders lived in fear of being considered lacking in determination if they broke off their attack.[7]

In staff language, these were called head-on attacks. The simple soldiers referred to such officers more crudely, but in a way no less accurately and concisely: "Let the fool pray to God, because his head is going to get smashed." Directives and orders issued at that time by the command of the Voronezh Front targeted just such a simplistic approach. Here is an excerpt from one such document, which was aimed at the formation commanders down to the division level, which was signed by N.F. Vatutin personally:

> The army's strength isn't being used to the full; in the flow of battle, the artillery is lagging behind the tanks and infantry. In the future, don't allow the artillery to lag behind. Crush any resistance with concentrated artillery fire and with fire in cooperation with infantry weapons. Many frontal attacks are noticeable, and there is not enough maneuvering to encircle the enemy. Quickly eliminate the shortcomings in the tactics of the troops' actions. ... Pay attention to better organization of concerted fire.[8]

In the first several days of the Battle of Kursk in the sector of von Manstein's main attack, among the troops that were defending there these problems accumulated into serious, objective difficulties connected with command and control, especially in the 6th Guards Army. The primarily reason for this was the complex configuration of the front that emerged after the breakthrough by the II SS Panzer Corps in the Prokhorovka direction on 6 July 1943, and in the course of subsequent fighting in this sector. By this time there was no continuous line of defense. The army's entire sector had been ruptured into several pieces, and thus a single center of command and control couldn't be established. Some of the divisions, which together with troops of the 1st Tank Army were covering the Oboian' direction, were being commanded by I.M. Chistiakov himself, whose main headquarters was located in a balka in the village of Kochetovka. Another group of divisions

7 Ibid., p. 340. In the 1975 English edition, p. 223.
8 TsAMO RF, F. 42.gv.sd., Op. 1, D. 76, L. 237.

that were holding a line along the Lipovyi Donets River were being led by his deputy Major General P.F. Lagutin from an auxiliary command post in the village of Sazhnoe. These two groups were split by intervening sectors of defense of formations of two others armies, the 1st Tank and 69th Armies, so the forces were intermingled. Chistiakov's groupings were operating in isolation from each other, and it was extremely difficult to coordinate their combat operations in such conditions. It was even more difficult to maintain solid communications with them and to keep them supplied. In certain cases, as with the 51st Guards Rifle Division, its units were scattered across a front of 30 kilometers.

In these conditions, the meshing and coordination in the actions of the 6th Guards and 1st Tank Army's headquarters were exceptionally important. However, unfortunately in the course of the Battle of Kursk, their headquarters were unable to achieve the necessary level of cooperation. Esssentially sharing a single combat sector, at times with their troops even sharing the same trenches, their higher headquarters were unable to arrange an effective system of interaction, neither between their own divisions and corps, nor with army headquarters. Both armies in principle fought as if the other wasn't there. Here is what a General Staff officer at the headquarters of the 6th Guards Army reported about the level of cooperation: "The 1st Tank Army was operating among the army's combat formations, but the headquarters of the two armies made no effort to achieve a continuous exchange of information, as a result of which the collaboration between the infantry and tanks was inadequate. None of the maps in the army headquarters' Operations Department showed the combat positions of the 1st Tank Army, and thus it was difficult to ensure the boundaries between neighboring formations, which at times led even to needless casualties."[9]

A similar problem, although on a lesser scale, arose at the same time within the 1st Tank Army. On its right flank and center, the regiments and brigades of the 6th Tank and 3rd Mechanized Corps, and at times even the battalions, were thoroughly intermingled, and in places mixed up with units of two divisions of the 22nd Guards Rifle Corps, as well as with troops of the 38th Army and 40th Army that had arrived as reinforcements. The tank brigades of the 6th Tank Corps that had been moved up into the sector of the 3rd Mechanized Corps had dual subordination. In order to conduct a necessary regrouping of forces or to withdraw their companies to a prepared line, the tank brigade commanders were forced in the midst of the fighting, when every minute counted, to contact both corps headquarters and request authorization from both corps commanders. Given the shortage of radios and the poor work of the means of communication, the majority of the planned decisions were doomed to failure beforehand. The corps commanders had to work according to the same scheme when issuing their orders and directives.

Tank armies of a homogenous constitution were a new formation in the Red Army, and thus a number of important considerations when creating them were either left out or were half-baked. As a result, at the order of N.F. Vatutin, when M.E. Katukov's 1st Tank Army assumed the role of a combined-arms army in order to hold the Oboian' and Prokhorovka directions, it didn't have the necessary supporting means, first of all in communications, or the establishment strength of personnel in the headquarters of all levels. It is sufficient to say, for example, that the headquarters staff for the artillery commander of a tank army was 50% smaller than that of the artillery commander of a combined-arms army, but in the course of the Battle of Kursk's defensive operation the 1st Tank Army haphazardly acquired twice as many artillery units and formations than the 6th Guards Army had prior to the start of the German offensive. The 1st Tank Army's artillery commander Colonel I.F. Frolov and his headquarters didn't receive these forces in the manner described by the book, so they were unable to arrange a system of command over them or use them effectively even though he and his subordinates were doing everything they could to achieve this.

9 TsAMO RF, F. 335, Op. 5113, D. 235, L. 53.

Remarked the artillery commander after the battle: "Throughout several days of fighting, there remained only one operational officer in the artillery headquarters; the rest of the officers were continually up with the units."[10]

Nevertheless, the artillery commander finally found out about the arrival of a number of reinforcing artillery regiments in his sector of defense when ammunition began running low in the units, and their men were arriving at the army dumps to get more shells. Understandably, in these conditions it was impossible to create centralized, effective command over the army's artillery, and the artillery means were controlled primarily by the senior commander in the combat sectors where the arriving artillery regiments deployed.

However, the absence of a single, fluid and multi-channel system of communications in the army – corps – brigade chain of command became a significantly larger problem. The point is that after the 1st Tank Army arrived within the second army-level defensive belt on the morning of 6 July with both of its forward corps (the 6th Tank and 3rd Mechanized), its headquarters quickly set up all types of communications, including a general network for the army and a communications line for the artillery headquarters. However, already after just a day of fighting, on 7 July, as a result of the German penetration into the sector of General S.M. Krivoshein's 3rd Mechanized Corps, its wire service was dismantled because of the threat of the complete destruction of the cable lines. With the arrival of Major General D.Kh. Chernienko's 31st Tank Corps on the Prokhorovka axis, as indicated in the account produced by the army headquarters, communications with it could not be fully established due to the fact that the "corps' signal chief didn't know how to organize it in the real conditions of the emerging combat situation", and because of the poor training of the signal battalion, and the high fluidity of the battle.[11] Thus, the 1st Tank Army headquarters had reliable, multiple channel signal communications only with the 6th Tank Corps, and with each passing day it became increasingly difficult to establish contact with Krivoshein's and Chernienko's corps, as well as with the commands of their subordinate brigades. Because of the Luftwaffe's aerial superiority, the army's liaison aviation regiment could be used only on occasion. Motorized transport was catastrophically deficit, yet it was these signal officers acting as couriers who proved to be the most reliable means of command and control over the troops at critical moments when delivering important orders and directives to those who were to carry them out.

The radio became the basic channel for transmitting and receiving operational information in the troops that were defending the Oboian' and Prokhorovka directions, but in the fighting some of the radios in the formations were knocked out of action or stopped working. In particular, in the vicinity of the village of Iakovlevo on 7 July, the radio-equipped tank of the commander of the 3rd Mechanized Corps was knocked out, and the radios in the headquarters of the 1st and 3rd Mechanized Brigades were damaged. Speaking before the command staff of the 1st Tank Army at a conference dedicated to the results of the Battle of Kursk, Major General S.M. Krivoshein[12] remarked:

10 TsAMO RF, F. 1.gv.TA., Op. 3072, D. 13, L. 15.

11 TsAMO RF, F. 1.gv.TA., Op. 3070, D. 4, L. 19.

12 Semen Moiseevich Krivoshein (1899-1978), Lieutenant General (1943), Hero of the Soviet Union (1945). He served in the Red Army from 1918; a veteran of the Russian Civil War and the Winter War with Finland. In March 1941 Krivoshein was appointed commander of Khar'kov Military District's 25th Mechanized Corps. From July 1941 the corps as part of the 21st Army was operating on the central sector of the Eastern Front. In October 1941 he was appointed chief of military training of the Red Army's Main Armored Command. From February 1943, Krivoshein was the commander of 3rd Mechanized Corps of the Northwestern Front's 1st Tank Army, which on 28 April 1943 was transferred to the Voronezh Front. At dawn on 6 July 1943, Krivoshein's corps took up a defense in the second defensive belt of the 6th Guards Army, which was saddling the Oboian' highway and received the simultaneous attack of two of the enemy's panzer formations, the XXXXVIII Panzer Corps and II SS Panzer Corps. Over the next

> Command in the corps was organized through command and observation posts. My operational group at the observation post included officers of the Operations and Intelligence Departments, as well as signal officers of the corps and the formations and units, representatives from the Code Department, radiomen and two radio sets. The issuing of orders and receiving of information often required the summoning of commanders to the radio sets. However, the corps' supply of RSB radio sets was unsatisfactory. The availability of one RSB radio in each brigade headquarters allows solid, robust headquarters communications [with subordinate units], but the brigade commander's lack of a second RSB radio set prevents the establishment of a command network of communications between the brigade commanders and the corps commander. The R-9 radio in the brigade commander's tank works reliably in practice at a distance of 4-5 kilometers, and therefore the corps commander and brigade commanders primarily maintained contact over the headquarters' circuit.
>
> The calculation of 2-3 users for each radio set didn't justify itself … Urgent messages from the brigade commanders arrived late … It is necessary to have no less than 8 RSB radio sets in the corps, of which two at a minimum should be mounted in tanks, while the rest should be mounted in Willys jeeps.[13]

A difficult situation also developed in the 31st Tank Corps. The 1st Tank Army headquarters was urgently forced to put together a group of Type RAF long-range radio sets and send them to the corps. To a certain extent this straightened out the situation between the army and the corps, but there was no success in getting communications within the corps up and running at the corps – brigade – battalion level, right up until the end of the operation.

The establishment number of 13 signal officers in the 1st Tank Army's Operations Department was unable to resolve the problem fully, since at especially tense moments they were sent as an operational team to the formations and units of the 38th and 40th Armies that were moving to the front. The situation with communications was especially critical on 8 and particularly 9 July. The chief of staff Major General M.A. Shalin was forced to send the entire staff of the artillery headquarters in order to meet and deploy the approaching destroyer anti-tank artillery regiments and destroyer anti-tank artillery brigades, and had to activate all of the signal officers, a portion of the Operations Department, and a full number of officers from other departments at the front in order to keep track of the operational situation and to transmit orders.

In that situation, the operational group with the army commander and his communication hub assumed a large burden. M.E. Katukov personally went in search repeatedly for the headquarters of corps and even of brigades that had shifted location, established contact with them, received a briefing on the operational situation, and issued orders on the spot. To the stated I will add that communications even with the 6th Tank Corps wasn't always stable; German airstrikes became the main reason for disruptions. The 1st Tank Army's account mentions that on average during daylight hours, up to 18 breaks were noted in the army's network between neighboring sectors,

---

10 days his brigades offered stubborn resistance to the enemy's superior forces, preventing the divisions of Army Group South from breaking into operational space. For their tenacity and courage in the fighting on the Oboian' direction, all of his brigades were awarded the Order of the Red Banner, and the mechanized corps itself was re-formed into the 8th Guards Mechanized Corps. The corps also performed successfully under Krivoshein's leadership in the course of Operation Polkovodets Rumiantsev. For his skillful command of the troops in the Battle of Kursk and the personal courage he demonstrated in the process, on 27 August 1943 he was awarded the commander's honor, the Order of Suvorov 2nd Degree. From February 1944 to the end of the war, Krivoshein commanded the 1st Mechanized Corps. In the postwar period he commanded mechanized divisions and a military district's armored and mechanized forces. He retired in 1953.

13 TsAMO, F. 8.gv.tk., Op. 1, D. 41, L. 13.

and up to 3 each night. Up to 3 kilometers of overhead cable lines between neighboring sectors had been simultaneously cut. Even before the start of the fighting because of problems with replenishments, at the order of the Front's Military Council the 1st Tank Army's command transferred elderly soldiers (50-53 years of age) to rear support and service units and elements, which noticeably reduced the smoothness of getting lines of communication up and running and their operation when in use.

As it was, the system of command and control within the 1st Tank Army, which hadn't been completely worked out, was complicated by the absence of proper teamwork between the 6th Guards Army's rifle formations and the tank and mechanized brigades. The 1st Tank Army's 90th Guards and 67th Guards Rifle Divisions were conducting operations according to instructions and orders from the 22nd Guards Rifle Corps and 6th Guards Army, and I've already discussed above how well these headquarters were working in cooperation with each other. Thus in the event of a withdrawal by any particular unit or formation from the combined front, the neighbors from the other army were as a rule the last to know about this, and were "informed" about it by the enemy's sudden emergence on the flank or rear. The foe successfully exploited such inconsistencies.

In addition to this, serious problem arose with the Voronezh Front's commanders at the tactical level. The low theoretical training and insignificant practical experience of the command cadres, especially in the regiments and battalions, also told negatively on the work of the headquarters, their efficiency, responsiveness, depth of assessing a situation and the adequacy of the decisions reached in the operational situation. The work to organize the collection and transmission of operational and intelligence information was plainly bad. There wasn't a day when the formation commanders, chiefs of staff, operations chiefs, and chiefs of other departments and branches didn't send threatening admonitions and orders to subordinates: Quit idling and get to work to collect, process and submit timely information about the actions of their own elements and those of the enemy. Not infrequently, higher-standing headquarters for days were unable to obtain a single intelligible report about the operational situation on sectors of defense that extended for many kilometers. Corps commanders and division commanders were forced to send liaison officers (the number of which, naturally, was limited) to those divisions and regiments, where the commanders, despite having every means at hand, irresponsibly neglected their direct duties, frequently ignored orders, and simply equivocated or were devious when sending objective and comprehensive information up the chain of command.

Senior officers and generals of the corps and army commands, dropping everything else, would drive up to the front in order to find out what was happening. The reports of some commanders were more akin to the work of a novelist than a combat document. This relates to both their content, which was far from reality, and their language, in which instead of precise and parsimonious phrases one encounters expressions like "fought like *bogatyrs* [ancient Russian heroic warriors, akin to the West European knights of yore]", "the enemy masses were destroyed", "the enemy took significant damage; it is impossible to ascertain his exact losses because the facsists hold the battlefield". I will cite an excerpt of a combat order from the chief of staff of the 71st Guards Rifle Division Lieutenant Colonel P.I. Liubomudrov, in which he gives an eloquent description of the work of his subordinates:

1. As a result of intense combat between 4 and 7 July 1943, units of the division demonstrated exceptional heroism to repel the enemy attacks; however, a series of the crudest shortcomings in the combat activity of the troops often leads to bad consequences, and at times puts the troops into a difficult situation for conducting the fighting. To such shortcomings I relate:
   a) The untimely reports and messages from the division's lower-standing headquarters at times contain no information at all about the situation, especially of neighboring units. For example, the 219th Guards Regiment yielded Hill 235.6 to the enemy and

didn't report this; the 213th Guards Regiment allowed two enemy battalions to reach Dmitrievka, and reported it only when the threat that the enemy would take Dmitrievka had emerged. The indicated occurrences don't give the division's command the possibility to influence the course of the fighting in a timely manner.

b) The headquarters of the regiments do not conduct reconnaissance, as a result of which they do not timely disclose the enemy's intentions and thanks to which during enemy actions they encounter quite a few surprises and unexpected events.
c) The cooperation with the means of reinforcements and supporting assets is poorly organized; the unit commanders all too often don't know who is located on the right, left or behind them; who is carrying out what sort of tasks; and thus can't properly use the combined forces to destroy the adversary.
d) The enemy's strength, as a rule, is exaggerated while our own forces are plainly understated; as a rule, wherever an enemy company is attacking, they believe battalions are attacking and request rocket artillery fire, at a time when they have fully sufficient firing means to ensure certain destruction or suppression [of the enemy].
e) The frequent shifting in location of the units' command posts and observation posts without the authorization of the division headquarters disrupts the uninterrupted communications between the regiment headquarters and the division's headquarters, and can lead to a complete loss of contact.
f) The unit commanders when committing their reserves into combat in order to offset losses don't pull them back into reserve after carrying out their missions, so the unit commanders are left without reserves, and as it happens, in critical cases don't have the means to influence the outcome of the fighting.
g) Unit commanders are not reporting the daily losses in personnel and equipment or the combat readiness and supply status of the units, which places the division command in a difficult situation when making decisions.
h) Given changes in combat positions or a shift in line, the unit commanders are not supplying a scheme of the units' dispositions, and obviously are not demanding the indicated schemes from the elements subordinate to them, and thus often they do not know where their units are located in one or another situation, which leads to the amendment of rendered decisions and the incorrect implementation of the latter in combat.[14]

A special subject is the activity of the intelligence organs at the brigade, division and corps level. In general the work of the Red Army's intelligence service at this moment still hadn't been established properly. The main problem was the supply of cadres. Even in the headquarters of armies and *fronts*, the intelligence elements weren't fully staffed with personnel. In addition, against this backdrop there was a high turnover in experienced cadres. The command was unable to create and support a stable staff of experienced intelligence officers in all the intelligence departments of the corps and armies. In addition, the very same problem existed as well in the command of the *front* headquarters. Judging from disclosed documents, a systematic approach was lacking in the work to organize intelligence and reconnaissance. In a number of cases, there was open disregard both toward the staffing of the intelligence elements with personnel and technical means, and toward the selection, education, training and retention of intelligence officers. Such an intolerable situation of affairs in the acting army disturbed the General Staff, and its leadership attempted to correct the situation. For example, on 5 January 1943, the deputy chief of the Department of

14 TsAMO RF, F. 1207, Op. 1, D. 64, L. 64.

Army Intelligence Major General L.V. Olianov sent the following letter to the chiefs of staff and intelligence commands of the departments of the *fronts* and armies:

1. Practice demonstrates that with the onset of active combat operations of our troops, the intelligence departments of the headquarters of the *fronts* and armies lose contact with each other. Instead of the timely arrival of information from combat intelligence assisting the command and the General Staff to anticipate the nature of enemy actions, it (the intelligence) becomes nearly worthless because of delays, and because of this the operational intelligence deprives the *front* and General Staff of the possibility to analyze the situation.
2. Thus far there is still the situation where the enemy's divisions aren't identified for 15-30 days despite a stable situation of the front, while during an offensive the enemy's opposing units aren't identified for 24 to 48 hours.

It is necessary:

1. To ensure the possibility of regular contact between the intelligence departments of headquarters and armies, allocate for this a regular time for the use of direct lines and telephones, no less than 3 times a day.
2. In addition, the intelligence departments of the headquarters of *fronts* and armies are to use all duplicative and supplementary means (motor vehicle and motorcycles) for communications.
3. I will remind you that the enemy operating in front of us possesses great mobility; it is necessary to check the presence of enemy divisions opposite our front no less than once every 3-5 days. In order to establish the enemy units' numerical identification on the battlefield quickly, assign a group to seize prisoners and collect documents from the dead and wounded, and support this group's constant activity.[15]

All of the problems and shortcomings recounted in the letter above were characteristic for Voronezh Front's combat intelligence. In the first place this concerned the intelligence departments of the headquarters of different types of troops. Throughout the extent of several months, they were not fully staffed, intelligence information was not collected and systematized in the necessary volume, and there was virtually no compilation of combat experience. The leadership of different types of the Front's forces wasn't giving the needed assistance to the corps and armies in getting the work of the intelligence service up and running, and demonstrated inertia and a lack of initiative. Men who were unfamiliar with this work often wound up on the analysis staff; they had neither the skills nor the capabilities to do this work. The turnover of cadres in the intelligence departments (and elements) of headquarters at every level was high. There were cases when the chiefs of intelligence organs even at the corps level changed several times a month. The chiefs of staff of a number of formations, whose duties included the collection of information on the enemy, didn't give adequate attention to the problems and needs of the intelligence officers. I will offer an extended excerpt from the manuscript of a report by the chief of intelligence at the headquarters of Voronezh Front's Armored and Mechanized Troops Lieutenant Colonel P.I. Shul'zhenko:[16]

---

15 *Russkii arkhiv: Velikaia Otechestvennaia voina*, No. 23 (12-3) (Moscow: Terra, 1999), p. 126.

16 Peter Il'ich Shul'zhenko, Lieutenant Colonel (1943). He was born in 1910 and joined the Red Army in 1932. In 1938 he completed the Orel Armored School and subsequently served in the acting army from June 1941. As the chief of staff of a separate reconnaissance battalion, the deputy commander of a tank battalion of the 130th Tank Battalion, the assistant chief of the 1st Tank Corps' Intelligence Department, the chief of the 4th Tank Corps' Intelligence Department, and the senior assistant chief for intelligence to the chief of staff of the 60th Army, Shul'zhenko took part in the fighting on the Southwestern, Briansk and Voronezh Fronts. From February 1943 he was the intelligence chief of Voronezh Front's Armored and

The People's Commissar of Defense Order No. 0072 from 19 April 1943 about measures to improve the intelligence activities of the Red Army is not being carried out in Voronezh Front's armored and mechanized forces. The reason is:

a) the irresponsibility and permissiveness on the part of the chief of staff of the Front's Armored and Mechanized Troops Colonel Mariakhin,[17] the chiefs of staff of the armies' armored and mechanized troops, separate chiefs of staff of the tank corps, mechanized corps, tank brigades and their commanders. There is a lack of desire on their part genuinely to oversee the intelligence and reconnaissance work and show fatherly concern in nurturing intelligence cadres.

b) They are not giving the intelligence chiefs (from top to bottom) the conditions and material possibilities to control the work of the subordinate intelligence departments and reconnaissance elements in a direct and timely manner. I will briefly cite several examples:

1. According to wartime rules, all the troops located in the first and second lines of defense through every possible means should try to obtain information on the enemy, study his defense, know the enemy's intentions, and report about this to higher headquarters. However, among the armored troops of our Front, the situation stands differently. For three months now, the timetable of periodic reports about the enemy has not been followed by the headquarters of the armies' armored and mechanized troops, or the headquarters of the tank brigades and of separate tank regiments An investigation has established: the headquarters of the armored and mechanized troops, the headquarters of the tank brigades and of separate tank regiments make no effort to study the foe, and do not know and do not want to know the layout of his anti-tank defenses even on likely directions. The question asks itself: What then will they report to higher headquarters? The experience of fighting with the enemy demonstrated that thanks to this disgrace, the tank forces are operating blindly and are suffering needless losses. More than once I have appealed to Colonel Mariakhin with the demand to compel lower headquarters of the tank forces and their commanders to engage genuinely in reconnaissance. All those guilty in violating People's Commissariat Order No. 0072 should be strictly punished; however, on this account responses came back: "Our main forces are located in reserve and it isn't necessary to demand from them any reconnaissance summaries," and so on. Does this mean that it isn't necessary to compel headquarters to study and know the enemy?
2. Chief of Staff Mariakhin as a rule doesn't support the taking of steps to invigorate the reconnaissance activity in the armored forces, and on the contrary directly or indirectly

Mechanized Troops. In March 1945 he enrolled in the Military Academy of the Armored and Mechanized Forces. On 29 May 1945, he became the chief of intelligence with the headquarters of the 8th Mechanized Corps' 23rd Tank Division.

17 Sergei Stepanovich Mariakhin, Colonel General (1964). He was born in 1911 and joined the Red Army in 1931. In 1941 he graduated from the Frunze Military Academy and in July 1941 became a battalion commander in the 50th Tank Division's 99th Tank Regiment. In September 1941 he became the deputy chief of staff for operations, and in January 1942, the chief of staff of the 150th Tank Brigade. On 22 April 1942, he was transferred to the headquarters of the Red Army's Armored and Mechanized Troops, before serving as Voronezh Front's chief of staff of the Armored and Mechanized Troops between 4 August 1942 and 20 November 1943. On 27 November 1943, Mariakhin became the chief of operations with the headquarters of the 4th Guards Tank Army. On 17 March 1945, he became the commander of the 4th Guards Tank Army's 93rd Separate Tank Brigade, but on 24 March, he returned to his former post as the 4th Guards Tank Army's chief of operations. On 20 June 1945, Mariakhin took command of the 10th Guards Tank Division's 81st Guards Heavy Tank Regiment.

ignores it on his part. For example, pursuant to Directive No. 1102660 from 2 May 1943 from the headquarters of the Main Command of the Red Army's Armored and Mechanized Troops, on 1 July 1943 the Headquarters of the Red Army's Armored and Mechanized Troops issued regulations regarding the intelligence service in the Red Army's armored and mechanized forces. This directive compelled all chiefs of staff of the armored forces under their personal responsibility and with their direct participation to compile basic reports, for this purpose calling upon commanders at all levels, who have rich combat experience in the Patriotic War, and to present on schedule the extrapolated and thoroughly elaborated material for this intended purpose.

Sensing the permissiveness on the part of Mariakhin, all the headquarters of the armies' armored and mechanized troops and of the tank corps submitted low-grade material to the Headquarters of the Voronezh Front's Armored and Mechanized Troops five days late. The given material was compiled "from top to bottom" only by clerks of the intelligence departments, who at times didn't have any practical experience in combat work. The armored forces of the 40th Army and their headquarters didn't take any part whatsoever in compiling the material for the indicated regulations regarding the intelligence service. The commander of the 40th Army's armored and mechanized forces Major General of Tank Troops Ivanov placed an endorsement for his chief of staff on the received directive: "Inform Mariakhin that we have no one to compile intelligence material." With this, the implementation of the directive in the army's forces came to an end. Having learned of this disgrace, I contacted Mariakhin and asked that he take the appropriate measures; however, even on this occasion he took no steps.

3. The intelligence departments and reconnaissance elements in the Front's formations and units on the part of headquarters and some commanders are not giving proper attention to the matter of the further nurturing and growth of intelligence officers. Everything is left to the conscience and initiative of the chiefs of intelligence, who because of their inexperience and insufficient training are unable to raise the intelligence service of the corps and brigades to the necessary height.

There are incidents of an impatient attitude toward intelligence chiefs. For example, in the 5th Guards "Stalingrad" Tank Corps, between 1 May and 14 July of this year alone, three chiefs of intelligence of the given corps, Lieutenant Colonel Vodeiko and Majors Povetkin and Efremov were relieved of their posts by the corps' command for their inability to cope with their duties. The point is not that Vodeiko, Povetkin and Efremov are bad intelligence officers, but that no one really led them and took any interest in their further development. For days I thoroughly inspected the conditions of work in the 5th Guards Tank Corps' Intelligence Department and established that the department's staff when given daily assistance on the part of the corps' chief of staff could cope with their duties splendidly; however, there was none of this assistance or leadership on the part of the headquarters. The Intelligence Department is the least respected department in the corps headquarters, and no preference is given to it. In order to check on the brigades' reconnaissance elements, the Intelligence Department's subordinate staff must head out on the road by catching a ride from any passing vehicles in order to reach a brigade, because, as a rule, its staff hasn't been given any vehicles for this purpose. In fact only after my interference, one motorcycle was assigned to the Intelligence Department – a single-seat motorcycle with no sidecar, which the Intelligence Department cannot operate. Such material conditions exist as well in the work of the intelligence departments of the remaining formations and units of the Front's armored forces.

Even I, as the intelligence chief with the Headquarters of the Front's Armored and Mechanized Troops conduct my work not in the best material conditions. The opportunity doesn't often arise when I can drive out to the troops in good time in order to check on and monitor the combat activity of the intelligence organs and reconnaissance elements, since with regard to the intelligence service, I'm almost never given a vehicle, and so I must rely upon only passing vehicles that are going in my direction. However the chief of staff Colonel Mariakhin, above and beyond any headquarters, personally has two vehicles and one motorcycle.

4. In his Order No. 0072, the People's Commissar of Defense Marshal of the Soviet Union Comrade Stalin categorically banned the use of intelligence officers outside of their formal duties; however, despite this, in the Voronezh Front's armored forces, thanks to the attitude toward the intelligence service and intelligence officers on the part of the above listed individuals and headquarters, the break-up of qualified intelligence cadres continues. Intelligence officers search for any means by which to leave intelligence work for other posts. For example, over the last 1.5 months alone, two qualified intelligence officers (Major Potemkin and Captain Shabalov) left for different work at a time when the Front doesn't have enough intelligence officers.

All of my attempts and demands to cease such a disgrace as the breaking up of intelligence teams led to nothing, other than the souring of relationships with the Chief of Staff Mariakhin …

Over almost the entire period of the Front's winter offensive, the department subordinated to me consisted of the chief of intelligence – myself – and translators, which were staffed up to only 40% of establishment strength. The intense combat work forced me repeatedly to place the question in front of Chief of Staff Mariakhin about staffing the Intelligence Department. However, despite all opportunities, the department remained in its former composition right up to the end of the operation. Such were the conditions of combat work that Colonel Mariakhin created for me, moreover deliberately so, and in the period of the German offensive on the Belgorod axis from 5 July 1943, one of my assistants was sent to a tank corps for a period of the fighting to serve as a liaison officer; the second assistant between 5 July and 12 July worked in a commission for checking the handling and storage of secret documents. Moreover it is characteristic to note that he worked alone in the commission, not counting the chief of the Secret Section; my senior assistant was absent until 12 July for extenuating circumstances. I appealed to Mariakhin – how can this situation be? Despite my full desire and maximal exertion of effort, I'm not really in the condition to take on the entire workload in such a stressful period. The answer came back: "You'll manage." Yes, as is obvious, Mariakhin isn't concerned with the intelligence service and all the unpleasant consequences that flow from this.

I repeat: All of my attempts and demands to cease such disgraceful behavior when it comes to the intelligence service led to nothing except souring the relationships with the chief of staff Colonel Mariakhin.

I tried more than once to report about such intolerable disgraces to the former commander of the Front's Armored and Mechanized Troops Major General Radkevich, who listened to my reports unwillingly and directed me to the chief of staff to resolve these problems, believing the fact that I couldn't reach an agreement with Mariakhin this was just a trifle.[18]

At first glance this document might seem to be slander against a chief of staff, with whom a lieutenant colonel was unable to establish a working relationship. However, the problems stated in the

18 TsAMO RF, F. 203, Op. 2851, D. 22, LL. 232-233.

report were practically repeated verbatim in a directive on the results of the summer and autumn period of fighting issued to the acting army in October 1943 by the Commander-in-Chief of the Red Army's Armored and Mechanized Troops Colonel General Ia.N. Fedorenko. Accordingly, such an attitude toward the intelligence service was characteristic not only for the Voronezh Front.

There was one more negative detail regarding Soviet combat intelligence that reduced its effectiveness: the tendency to exaggerate enemy strength. The rule went: "It is better to add than undercount," and this precept governed the intelligence service. Knowing this, some commanders didn't trust the collected intelligence information and acted at their own peril and risk. There were also quite a few of those who didn't know how to use this intelligence correctly in combat work. Here is one document that vividly demonstrates the system of work of intelligence officers of one of the main formations of Katukov's tank army – Major General Krivoshein's 3rd Mechanized Corps – in the most intense and dramatic period of the Battle of Kursk between 6 and 15 July 1943. It is a memorandum from an officer of the 1st Tank Army's Intelligence Department Major Osaumenko, who was located at this time in the 3rd Mechanized Corps' headquarters, that was sent to the chief of the 1st Section of the 1st Tank Army's Intelligence Department Lieutenant Colonel Andrianov:

1. With the start of the corps' introduction into combat against the attacking enemy, the corps' Intelligence Department had no normal communication with the brigades' headquarters, or more accurately, with the assistant chiefs of staff for intelligence and the reconnaissance elements. As a result of the absence of normal communication, the command or, more accurately, the leadership of the corps' Intelligence Department took poor account of the brigades' reconnaissance activity.

   Although the assistants of the brigades' chiefs of staff were in fact organizing reconnaissance during the battle, sending out patrols and conducting observation, and did have significant information on the enemy, his grouping and his actions in front of the brigades, this information wasn't processed and timely submitted to the corps' Intelligence Department. In the best case this information wound up in the brigade's Operations Department, and the latter presented it to the Corps' Operations Department verbally over the telephone, or in code via the radio in a general combat report. This evidence didn't wind up in the Corps' Intelligence Department. It didn't get communications up and running with the Operations Department as it should, and as a result it remained frequently uninformed about the situation on the battlefield.
2. The reconnaissance battalion of the Corps' Intelligence Department was used by the chief of intelligence depending on the situation, but the reconnaissance probes didn't produce the proper results for the Corps headquarters. Because of the poor organization of communications, reconnaissance reports and results were submitted late (or more accurately, infrequently). Mostly information on the results of a reconnaissance probe was reported after the reconnaissance patrol returned from a mission.
3. ... Despite the fact that the Corps' Intelligence Department has the authorized amount of staff, and the duties have been allocated according to the book, the department's staff doesn't strive to work according to the situation. There was no effort to organize work so as to give as much information about the enemy as possible to whomever requires it in a timely fashion, to process the information and transmit it to the 1st Tank Army's Intelligence Department.

   There were cases when seized enemy documents taken from a knocked-out tank remained either in the Operations Department or in the SMERSH Department for several hours or even days. However, even after these documents eventually reached the Corps' Intelligence Department, they were sent to the 1st Tank Army's Intelligence Department over a hotline, at a time when these documents had to be sent by a special courier.

   In view of the congested traffic on the telephone network, it is difficult for the Corps' Intelligence Department to stay in contact with the Army's Intelligence Department. The

> Corps' Intelligence Department didn't use such means of communication like a motorcycle or the motorcycle battalion.
>
> Even such a question like rest for the staff of the Corps' Intelligence Department was poorly organized. With the onset of combat operations, for two days none of the Intelligence Department's staff rested, after which there was an incident when having become totally exhausted, they all fell asleep for a certain time, without leaving an on-duty man at the telephone. Moreover, for several days the department's telephone wasn't connected, so discussions had to be held over the Operations Department's phone.[19]

I will note straight away that this wasn't any sort of investigative document, and moreover it didn't have the aim of besmirching anyone. Similar trips by staff officers to lower-standing elements were practiced in other armies as well and had the aim of improving the quality of their work. The memorandum was found in the general file of the 1st Tank Army's Intelligence Department; it is plainly of an informational nature, and was prepared for the purpose to give the army's intelligence leadership an idea of the style of work of intelligence at the corps level, and its problems and weaknesses.

Work to analyze the enemy didn't go any better in the 6th Guards Army either. More accurately, there wasn't any as such at all; the officers of the corps' intelligence departments were primarily busy with observation of the enemy and the battlefield, but there couldn't be any talk of any systematic work in the enemy rear. Thus the commander of the 22nd Guards Rifle Corps Major General N.B. Ibiansky after the conclusion of the first phase of the Battle of Kursk had to appeal to the 6th Guards Army commander I.M. Chistiakov with a request to replace his intelligence chief. In the introduction he noted that Major B.I. Dubner had demonstrated a lack of initiative and proved to be a non-energetic leader. He worked poorly to organize the service and wasn't giving the proper assistance to the corps commander. The point of the matter was that the chief of staff of this formation even during the fighting periodically hit the bottle, so there wasn't any point in hoping for any sort of effective work by the headquarters' departments.[20] This was only a small part of that enormous informational flow that N.F. Vatutin was receiving at this time.

Were steps taken to make a cardinal change to the situation that had arisen? There were attempts, and more than once; for example, that People's Commissar of Defense Order No. 0072, but unfortunately, as events demonstrated, neither prior to the start of the Battle of Kursk, nor in its immediate wake were there any fundamental changes in the matter of improving combat intelligence. In certain respects the situation even worsened despite the fact that I.V. Stalin had personally taken up this question in the spring of 1943.

Another matter that had to occupy Vatutin's attention was incidents of fratricide. Already on the third day of Army Group South's offensive, so-called ChP [extraordinary events, meaning any sort of accident, terrible blunder, misfortune or calamitous incident] became a serious problem in the troops on the front line. Because of snafus among the commands of various units and formations, mistakes, and at times because of slovenliness, irresponsibility and a negligent attitude to duties, our fighting elements began to engage in combat with each other. The tankers and pilots were particularly guilty of this. With the increase in the density of troops in the sectors of defense of the 1st Tank Army, 6th and 7th Guards Armies and the 69th Army due to the arriving regiments and brigades of the 38th Army, 40th Army and the reserve, the number of friendly fire incidents increased manifold, while strikes by our own aircraft on friendly positions accumulated with alarming rapidity.

19 TsAMO RF, F. 1 gv. TA, Op. 3109, D. 5, L. 28.
20 TsAMO RF, F. 1207, Op. 1, D. 138, L. 150.

The Commander-in-Chief of the Voronezh Front Lieutenant General N.F. Vatutin at a forward observation post; July 1943 (Photography by F. Kislov, RGAKFD)

Soviet and German tanks clash on the Oboian' axis, July 1943. On the left, a German Pz VI Tiger tank rolls past a burning T-34 tank on the right. (US NARA)

Tanks and halftracks of the Fourth Panzer Army's XXXXVIII Panzer Corps in the vicinity of the Belgorod – Oboian' highway; July 1943 (A captured German photograph, RGAKFD)

One of the battalions of the 6th Guards Army's 67th Rifle Division in the area of Novo-Cherkasskoe (Oboian direction) engaged in combat on 6 July 1943. A Maksim machine gun fires while a female combat medic bandages a wounded man. (RGAKFD)

A Red Army 45-mm anti-tank gun crew of one of the destroyer anti-tank artillery regiments in action to repel a German panzer attack on the Prokhorovka axis: the ammo handler on the left is ready to pass another discarding sabot BR-240P shell to the loader; July 1943 (RGAKFD)

The first two friendly fire incidents between the Voronezh Front's tank units took place already on 7 July 1943. In the twilight hours during a march by the 192nd Separate Tank Brigade across the bend in the Pena River (the left flank of the 1st Tank Army), a T-34 crew of the 191st Tank Battalion of the 6th Tank Corps' 200th Tank Brigade, which had taken up a defense here, destroyed a friendly M3 Stuart tank of its 417th Tank Battalion commanded by Lieutenant Fatakhov, and damaged another. The driver-mechanic and radio operator of the first machine were killed, and Fatakhov lightly wounded, while the commander of the second tank Lieutenant Matiushenko was killed. The investigation revealed that the tankers of the 200th Tank Brigade's T-34s at night confused the unfamiliar American Lend-Lease tanks with German tanks. Deciding that the Germans had broken through, they opened targeted fire, even though the 192nd Tank Brigade's column was approaching from the rear, where there could have been no enemy.[21]

The second ChP took place in the 7th Guards Army's sector. Here, fighting erupted in the daytime between units that were known to each other. According to the report by the commander of the 262nd Guards Separate Heavy Tank Regiment:

> At 2100 on 6 July 1943, because of a lack of infantry in the 81st Guards Rifle Division, tanks of the 1st Company numbering 8 KV tanks changed their line of defense and shifted

21 TsAMO RF, F. 1 gv.TA, Op. 3063, D. 20, LL. 34-35.

> to the vicinity of Bol'shaia Igumenka. At 1200 on 7 July, artillery of the 81st Guards Rifle Division opened fire at the 1st Tank Company's tanks. As a result of the concentrated anti-tank artillery fire on the enemy's part and our own artillery, 3 tanks of the 1st Tank Company were destroyed. Killed: Of the middle command staff – tank commander Lieutenant Gurov, tank commander Lieutenant Pinarsky; of the junior command staff – Senior Sergeant Kovalev, Guards Sergeant Major Diubin. Severely wounded: Lieutenant Shamarov, Sergeant Major Elin, and a junior driver-mechanic. Missing-in-action: Company commander Senior Lieutenant Belov and his tank, and company commander Senior Lieutenant Kosenov.[22]

In the following days the number of such incidents multiplied, and together with them there were casualties. For example, on the morning of 8 July, the 100th Tank Brigade engaged in battle with the very same 192nd Separate Tank Brigade, and simultaneously with elements of the 242nd Tank Brigade of its own 31st Tank Corps.[23] The reason was the same: at first the American Lend-Lease tanks were mistaken for German tanks, and then in the heat of battle, most likely, the tankers didn't realize that they were now firing at their own T-34s. On the afternoon of that same day, the 2nd Tank Corps' 99th Tank Brigade mistakenly attacked elements of the 285th Rifle Regiment of the 69th Army's 183rd Rifle Division, which were positioned in trenches of the first line, defending the nearest approaches to Prokhorovka Station (8 kilometers to the west of it).[24] Here, the count of dead and wounded ran into the dozens. From the Extraordinary Combat Report No. 05 from the commander of the 183rd Rifle Division Major General A.S. Kositsyn at 0500 on 9 July:

> 1. At 1600 on 8.07.43, the sound of engines coming from the direction of Prokhorovka Station [in the rear] and approaching Point 241.6 was heard from the command post of the 285th Rifle Regiment. Tanks were approaching, which had shaken out into a combat formation, and they opened heavy fire from their main guns at our combat positions, the anti-tank rifle company, the guns standing in firing position, and the observation post. Advancing in the direction of Vasil'evka, the tanks with their fire set ablaze several buildings and left one tank of the 10th Tank Corps (the neighbor on the right, Vasil'evka) burning. After this these same tanks poured fire on our combat positions of the 285th Rifle Regiment's 1st Rifle Battalion and began to crush soldiers in the trenches with their tracks, especially in the 3rd and 5th Rifle Companies. As a result of this at an important stage of the attack in order to regain our previous lines, our combat formations were disrupted – those of the 3rd Rifle Company, and also the 4th and 5th Rifle Companies in particular.
>
> The tanks were moving without any leadership, observing no battle-order or discipline. The 285th Rifle Regiment's command made attempts to explain the situation to the tankers; the latter, paying no attention, continued firing at our combat positions. The regiment command sent out officers toward the moving tanks with the assignment to explain their combat positions and situation – and with a demand to cease fire immediately. The tank company commanders replied that they'd been given an order: to attack in the Andreevka – Vasil'evka direction, with an additional assignment to attack toward Greznoe. They continued to fire at and attack the elements of the 285th Rifle Regiment and of the 11th Brigade [the 10th Tank Corps' 11th Motorized Rifle Brigade – the author], which was positioned in Vasil'evka.

22 TsAMO RF, F. 7 gv.A, Op. 5330, D. 60, L. 13.
23 TsAMO RF, F. 1 gv.TA, Op. 3603, D. 20, LL. 34-35.
24 TsAMO RF, F. 285 sp, Op. 46981, D. 1, LL. 132-133.

> The attacking tanks were the 2nd Tank Corps' 99th Tank Brigade. The corps commander is Major General Popov. From a report by the 99th Tank Brigade's chief of staff Captain Piniuk – the mission to attack was given to the tank brigade personally by the commander of the 2nd Tank Corps Major General Popov: "... the enemy is located in the villages of Andreevka, Vasil'evka, Kozlovka and Greznoe. So we were operating according to the given order."
>
> According to incomplete data, the regiment's companies have losses from the fire of our own tanks: 25 men killed and 37 wounded. The loss of personnel of the regiment's companies is primarily in the 3rd and 5th Rifle Companies, and was chiefly taken at the fault of the 99th Tank Brigade, the command of which was confused about the situation, failed to notify me about the pending attack, and the brigade command launched an attack against the elements of the 285th Rifle Regiment. As a result, they shot up the soldiers and crushed them in their trenches with the treads of their tanks, and blew up their own tanks in our minefields ....[25]

Yet here is how the officers of the 99th Tank Brigade's headquarters described the combat actions on 8 July:

> The 99th Tank Brigade entered combat in the direction of Point 258.2, Teterevino, and Luchki. It was attacking in the second echelon behind the 169th and 26th Tank Brigades ... in essence without any preparation, having no picture of the enemy or our own forces that were operating in front and on the flanks. When the 169th Tank Brigade operating out in front reached the line of the Komsomolets State Farm, the enemy, bringing fire to bear on the tanks with artillery, heavy mortars and Pz VI tanks that had been dug into the earth, began to conduct massed air attacks by Ju-88s and anti-tank Ju-87s ... the airstrikes increased in pace with the brigades' advance, and by approximately 1800 on 8 July 1943, these strikes turned into a relentless attack from the air. ... Our aircraft were showing no activity.
>
> The commander of the 1st Tank Battalion, attacking in the first echelon behind the 169th Tank Brigade, back at the moment of the battalion's deployment on the jumping-off line for the attack (railroad hut, 500 meters north of Ivanovskii Vyselok), took an incorrect bearing and arrived at the railroad hut 2 kilometers south of Ivanovskii Vyselok. The brigade command urgently sent the 2nd Tank Battalion to attack in the first echelon in the place of the 1st Tank Battalion. The 1st Tank Battalion was halted, and it was given the direction to attack toward the southwestern fringe of the woods on the Komsomolets State Farm. Thus, the 1st Tank Battalion wound up in the second echelon.
>
> In the vicinity of the macadam road, the commander of the 1st Tank Battalion bumped up against the column of the 26th Tank Brigade, knowing that the 26th Tank Brigade was supposed to be operating on the right. Then the commander of the 1st Tank Battalion pivoted his column and began to attack along the road side in the direction of Teterevino. On the approaches to Hill 258.2, the battalion met the fire of two Pz VI tanks. An exchange of fire erupted, and the 1st Tank Battalion, suffering losses in tanks, rolled back to the western fringe of the woods on the Komsomolets State Farm and fired from fixed positions.
>
> The 2nd Tank Battalion, moving in the wake of the 169th Tank Brigade, reached the northwestern slopes of Hill 258.2, and having run into heavy fire from Hills 224.5 and 258.2, lost two T-70 tanks before descending into the eastern portion of Iara Zaslonnyi and taking up suitable positions with 10 tanks together with the 169th Tank Brigade and the 15th Guards Separate Heavy Tank Regiment (some of the battalion's other tanks had been knocked-out

25 TsAMO RF, F. 48 sk, Op. 1, D. 44, L. 49.

> or left burning previously, while the rest had gone astray) [and were fighting with the 285th Rifle Regiment – the author].
>
> The motorized rifle battalion and anti-tank rifle company, mounted aboard the tanks of the 1st and 2nd Tank Battalions, with the start of the enemy aerial attack, dismounted from the tanks, and broken up into small, isolated groups of 6-10 men, in disorder took cover from the enemy aerial attack with infantry of other units. The commander of the motorized rifle battalion, having the mortar company with him, lost control of the battalion and together with his headquarters began to rally his men.
>
> In essence, the brigade headquarters was also busy with this …
>
> The exchange of fire by our tanks and artillery with the enemy's tanks and artillery while under fierce enemy aerial attacks continued late into the night. By this time, through the efforts of the battalion commands and the brigade headquarters, the infantry had been gathered and rallied. In the fighting the 99th Tank Brigade lost 21 T-34 tanks knocked-out or destroyed, and 2 T-70. Casualties were 21 soldiers and commanders killed, and 53 men wounded.[26]

There is no need for comment. I will add that not only the tank crews and motorized riflemen didn't know the operational situation and lacked maps of the area (!) over which they were attacking, but even General A.F. Popov himself didn't clarify either the operational situation or the layout of the 285th Rifle Regiment's companies with its commander Lieutenant Colonel A.K. Karpov, whose command post was located on the "Stalin subdivision" State Farm (practically right next to the 2nd Tank Corps' command post). These blunders and a corps commander's tardy implementation of a *front* commander-in-chief's order became the subject of an investigation by a commission of the Voronezh Front headquarters. According to the results of its work already after the conclusion of the defensive phase of the Battle of Kursk, on 30 July 1943 N.F. Vatutin signed Order No. 00212, which stated:

> On 7 July of this year at 2100 the commander of the 2nd Tank Corps Major General Popov received my order to assemble the corps in the vicinity of the Stalin State Farm, take up a jumping-off position, and be ready to attack on 8 July at 1030.
>
> Having received this order, Major General Popov didn't take the appropriate steps to organize for a meeting engagement; didn't establish contact with the commanders of the infantry units; and didn't ascertain the position of the neighbors, even though he had every possibility to do so, because he had met with the commander of the 69th Army Lieutenant General Kriuchenkin in Korocha, whose troops were occupying the area designated for the tank corps' actions.
>
> Having available 12 hours until the moment of the corps had to be ready to attack, Major General Popov didn't use this time to organize properly for the coming battle. He issued his order for the attack only at 0930 on 8 July, which was just an hour before the attack. As a result of this the brigade commanders weren't given time to conduct combat reconnaissance, didn't reconnoiter the terrain, and the forward edge of our defense wasn't established, while an attack sector was assigned to elements of the 99th Tank Brigade which was in fact occupied by our troops.
>
> As a result, the tanks of the 99th Tank Brigade passed with combat through the combat positions of the 183rd Rifle Division's 285th Rifle Regiment, and in the process 25 men were killed and 40 wounded. For such a criminal disregard of organizing for battle, the

26 TsAMO RF, F. 59 gv.tbr, Op. 1, D. 6, LL. 21-22obr.

> commander of the 2nd Tank Corps Major General Popov deserves the strictest punishment right up to be put in front of a military tribunal.
>
> Considering that in the subsequent fighting Major General Popov showed himself to be a bold, decisive commander and ensured the successful completion of the combat assignments given to him, he has atoned for his guilt.
>
> I am ordering: the announcement of a rebuke for Major General Popov for the serious violations permitted by him. I am pointing the attention of commanders at all levels to the need to pay more serious attention to coordinating their actions with neighbors.[27]

Inarguably, the guilt of the corps commander is obvious. Nevertheless, the corps' administrative officers headed by the chief of staff Colonel V.V. Koshelev, as well as the command staff of the tank brigades, should share the responsibility with him for the poorly established work of the corps headquarters in training the troops, signal officers and scouts; delivering combat documents to them; and the troops' lack of readiness for a major battle on 8 July. Uncovered documents testify that the leadership of the brigades of this tank corps didn't always promptly and precisely carry out their service duties. They not infrequently sought to avoid receiving combat assignments; shifted their duties onto the shoulders of subordinates, who by statute were not able to carry them out; and sometimes simply hit the bottle and got drunk. For this reason men often died, and performance suffered. Corps commander Popov knew the capabilities and character of his subordinates better than anyone else, and as much as he was able, sought to work with them, develop them, instruct them and make strict demands on them. When he ran out of patience, then the following orders would appear:

> To the commanders of the 15th Guards Separate Heavy Tank Regiment, the 99th, 26th and 129th Tank Brigades, and the 58th Motorized Rifle Brigade
>
> First: I'm extremely upset with the organization of radio communications in the brigades. Over the course of the current night, only with difficulty have I managed to summon the brigade commanders and chiefs of staff to a radio set for talks. The commanders and their headquarters have reached such a level of impertinence that apparently they deliberately don't want to report on the disposition of their units over the radio. Or else they can't report it, because their headquarters are located 25 kilometers from the forward combat positions (the 99th Tank Brigade). If such a state of communications will continue in the future, I will be forced to put the chiefs of staff and signal chiefs on trial.
>
> Second: I am ordering to assign constant, responsible staff officers, no lower than a deputy chief of staff, and keep them continuously at the radio. Make obligatory the constant and timely reporting on the position of your units to the corps headquarters. Radio sets must be kept in connection with the telephone, the commander and the headquarters. Whenever absolute devilry happens, they leave the radio operators alone, while all the rest go to sleep, and you can't find them anywhere.
>
> Third: The headquarters of the formations before this have become tangled up in lies; they've begun to cover their lack of knowledge about their units' positions by saying their radio sets are packed for travel – this is the greatest dishonor and shame for the headquarters.[28]

27 TsAMO RF, F. 38A, Op. 9027, D. 50, L. 375.
28 TsAMO RF, F. 8 gv.tk, Op. 1, D. 67, L. 132.

The 2nd Tank Corps wasn't a standout tank corps, but it also didn't bring up the rear. For his role in the destruction of the enemy at Kursk, A.F. Popov was awarded the Order of the Red Banner, and in September 1943 the tank corps (including the 99th Tank Brigade) was reformed into a Guards unit.[29] Thus, the organization for battle of its troops at this time differed little from the system of preparing for combat operations of the Red Army's other mobile formations. For example, on this same day, 8 July, on a different sector of the front, in the sector of Major General A.L. Getman's 6th Tank Corps, a similar event took place. Under the fire of friendly anti-tank artillery, Senior Lieutenant Kobzar', a company commander of the 6th Tank Corps' 200th Tank Brigade and one of the tank aces of Katukov's army, was killed.[30] On the single day of 8 July alone, his tank crew had knocked out or destroyed 17 enemy tanks. Prior to this he had 7 German tanks to his personal credit. From a report by the chief of the 1st Tank Army's Political Department Colonel A.G. Zhuravlev:

> It should be noted that in certain units, because of the absence of a clear understanding in the combat elements there were cases of opening fire at friendly tanks. For example, the valiant company commander Kobzar', who with his company destroyed 20 enemy tanks, on 8 July at 2100, after the fighting, began to ascend a hill in the direction of friendly units. The gun crew of one of the batteries took Kobzar's tank as an enemy tank, and opened fire at it without orders, as a result of which Kobzar' was killed.[31]

However, these incidents paled in comparison with the mistakes made by pilots of the 2nd Air Army. The first strikes by Il-2 ground attack aircraft on friendly positions were noted already on 7 July. A report from the commander of the 7th Guards Army's 148th Separate Tank Regiment indicated that at 1100, ground attack aircraft escorted by fighters bombed and strafed his company on Hill 191.8, as well as the area of the dispositions of the 2nd Guards "Tatsinskaia" Tank Corps' brigades. On the next day crews of the 1st Ground Attack Aviation Corps again stitched the combat positions of the "Tatsinskaia" Tank Corps with fire from their on-board guns, and then switched to working over the brigades of the 3rd Mechanized Corps. On 9 July, the isolated mistakes of pilots merged into a solid stream of bombing and strafing attacks on the formations of the 1st Tank Army and 6th Guards Army on the Oboian' and Prokhorovka directions. However, if the strikes on troops in the forward edge can be explained by the high dynamics of combat, which the headquarters of the air units didn't have time to follow, and the absence of a network of forward air controllers, then it is difficult to understand bombings of targets in our own rear at a distance of almost 100 kilometers from the front lines.

I will cite only several of the messages that arrived at the headquarters of the Voronezh Front on 9 July alone:

29 By People's Commissar of Defense Order No. 284 from 19 September 1943, the 2nd Tank Corps and its full complement was reformed into the 8th Guards Tank Corps.

30 Iakov Timofeevich Kobzar' (1918-1943), Senior Lieutenant (1942). Kobzar' joined the Red Army in 1938. In 1941 he completed the courses for junior lieutenants. He was at the fronts of the Great Patriotic War from June 1941. As a company commander in the 192nd Tank Battalion of the 6th Tank Corps' 200th Tank Brigade, he distinguished himself in the Operation "Mars" offensive and was awarded the Order of the Red Star. He was wounded three times. He took part in the fighting at the Kursk bulge from 6 July 1943. On 8 July in the area of Verkhopen'e (Oboian' axis), according to Soviet data, the company under his command knocked out 28 German tanks, of which 17 went to the score of his tank crew, as well as 9 assault guns. By Decree of the USSR Presidium of the Supreme Soviet on 4 October 1990, he was posthumously awarded the title "Hero of the Soviet Union".

31 From the website http://sovkub.narod.ru/kobsar.htm

0520: 8 Il-2 struck the 26th Guards Tank Brigade of the 2nd Guards Tank Corps (1 killed, 12 wounded) in the area of Ozerovo, as well as the headquarters of this corps in the village of Sazhnoe.[32]
0550: 5 Il-2 bombed and strafed with their cannons and machine guns the positions of the 2nd Guards Tatsinskaia Tank Corps' 4th Guards Tank Brigade.[33]
0845: 18 Il-2 ground attack aircraft bombed the area of Prokhorovka Station, which at this moment was serving as the 6th Guards Army's supply base.[34]
1530: 6 Il-2 bombed the area of Grushki (next to Prokhorovka Station).[35]
1832: 13 Il-2 bombed the Ol'khovskii, Peresyp' area (the 6th Guards Army's near rear area).[36]
1932: 8 Il-2 aircraft bombed the Krivtsovo railroad station in their own rear (80 kilometers behind the front lines).[37]

There were even larger-scale strikes on friendly troops, for example, those of the 69th Army. Thus, at 0258 on 9 July, its chief of staff Colonel S.M. Protas sent the following coded message simultaneously to the Voronezh Front headquarters and the commander of the 2nd Air Army:

> I request on 9.7.43 to bomb the enemy tanks and infantry:
>
> a) Prokhorovka;
> b) Belenikhino – Korocha, with a prior reconnaissance flight and a call from the army commander's command post;
> Cover the army's combat formations from the air.
> Send an operational group of the Air Force with means of communications to the army commander's command post.[38]

A second letter from the chief of staff of the 69th Army under No. 110960 addressed to the chief of staff of the Voronezh Front and the commander of the 2nd Air Army testifies to how this request was carried out:

> Between 0700 and 0900 up to 60 Il-2 bombed the combat formations of the 285th and 295th Rifle Regiments of the 183rd Rifle Division in Vasil'evka, Komsomolets State Farm, and on Hill 241.6. We are ascertaining the losses.
>
> I request that you inform me at whose request the given points were bombed.[39]

It isn't clear what prevented the headquarters of the air army from ascertaining the operational situation in the zone, where it was supposed to inflict such a heavy strike. It isn't clear why the headquarters of the 1st Ground Attack Aviation Corps ignored the letter's point about prior reconnaissance of the targets, and instead immediately issued an order to strike the areas that morning. I think the reader can easily imagine what resulted from two hours of intensive strikes upon the trench system, bunkers and minefields of the two regiments of the 183rd Rifle Division by the two regiments of the Il-2 ground attack aircraft.

32 TsAMO RF, F. 3400, Op. 1, D. 23, L. 97; D. 31, L. 40.
33 TsAMO RF, F. 4 gv.tbr, Op. 1, D. 26, L. 16.
34 TsAMO RF, F. 335, Op. 5113, D. 235, L. 33.
35 Ibid.
36 Ibid.
37 Ibid.
38 TsAMO RF, F. 426, Op. 10753, D. 65, L. 15.
39 Ibid., L. 18.

However, this is only a few of those incidents. At the start of the airstrike, the 2nd Tank Corps' 99th Tank Brigade started to move out of the Storozhevoe woods, in order to replace the 10th Tank Corps' 178th Tank Brigade in the Andreevka area. Having spotted the column, the Il-2 crews on the spot added them to the target list. The brigade had no anti-aircraft weapons, and the pilots did their best. Realizing that they were being bombed by friendly aircraft, the tankers began to maneuver and to head back into the Storozhevoe woods, but later, when a new air raid began – they fell back behind the huts of the villages in the Psel River floodplain. The main attack hit the brigade's motorized rifle battalion. Major Teptin, the chief of the 99th Tank Brigade's Political Department, wrote to the corps headquarters the following about the "ChP": "Today our own aircraft bombed the brigade's combat formation and elements on the march up to three times; as a result of the bombing attacks, up to 75% of the personnel of the 1st Company of the motorized rifle battalion were killed or wounded, and up to ten men of the [tank] crews were also wounded."[40]

I've so far been unable to discover the total losses of all the brigades during the three airstrikes against the 2nd Tank Corps; there are only scattered bits of data. Thus, in the documents of the 99th Tank Brigade's headquarters, they are given for only two locations: on Hill 258.2 and in Vasil'evka alone, 30 men were killed and wounded in the 2nd Tank Battalion and the motorized rifle battalion.

It was obligatory to report such incidents to Moscow. The "extraordinary events" in the sector of the 183rd Rifle Division and the 2nd Tank Corps in the course of 8 and 9 July were also reported. Probably at this moment, such a coincidence of events with one and the same formations and in one and the same area had never happened anywhere else along the entire Soviet-German front, so I.V. Stalin was personally informed about this – already on the next day. N.F. Vatutin received an order from the deputy chief of the General Staff Colonel General A.I. Antonov, which directed:

> The People's Commissar of Defense has ordered:
>
> 1. Immediately investigate the facts and bring the guilty parties to responsibility.
> 2. Direct the attention of the army commanders and the commanders of corps and divisions to the impermissibility of such occurrences, and demand from them a more precise organization of cooperation between different types of troops and the maintenance of constant communication with neighbors. I ask that you report on the measures taken.[41]

During fratricidal bombing attacks, the commanders of the rifle and tank units sought to give recognition signals, but this rarely helped. When, however, the aircraft of the 2nd Air Army were working over areas of the positions of friendly forces that had anti-aircraft guns, the gunners were forced to fire at the attacking aircraft. As a result of this, new casualties appeared, now among the pilots. By the end of the defensive operation, the situation had reached such a critical point that the infantry began to fear their own air force and were opening preventive fire at the 2nd Air Army's aircraft, concerned that they would bomb them. Thus, in an order from the commander of the 5th Guards Tank Army there is the statement that on 14 July 1943, motorized rifle companies of the 5th Guards Mechanized Corps' 24th Guards Tank Brigade opened heavy, but disorderly fire at Il-2 aircraft that were returning to their bases at low altitude, even though red stars were clearly visible on the sides and wings of the ground attack aircraft.[42] In documents of units of the 69th Army, which were operating south of Prokhorovka, there are acknowledgements that the

40 TsAMO RF, F. 8 gv.tk, Op. 1, D. 233, L. 13.
41 TsAMO RF, F. 48 sk, Op. 3409, D. 16, L. 511.
42 TsAMO RF, F. 3415, Op. 1, D. 48, L. 12.

commanders of some rifle battalions were afraid to set out special, regulation recognition panels in front of their forward edge because of the frequent attacks by friendly aircraft that followed on so-marked sectors.

If to compare how the opposing sides used all types of combat aircraft in the course of the defensive operation on the southern shoulder of the Kursk salient, then it must be recognized that the Germans used their air force more effectively and rationally. The enemy command understood the significant role that attack aircraft might play when breaking through deeply-echeloned lines, and thus strove not only to increase the performance characteristics of their combat aircraft, created new types of aircraft, and increased their production, but also arranged a system of cooperation between the ground and air forces, which allowed even commanders at the tactical level to use this powerful combat instrument. In the panzer and panzergrenadier divisions, there were Luftwaffe air control officers who operated on the given axis of advance. They were given armored cars with radios, thanks to which they could do their work right on the battlefield. This allowed the Germans in a rapidly-changing combat situation not only to avoid the majority of fratricidal airstrikes, but also chiefly to coordinate the attacks of the panzer wedges with precise airstrikes by dive bombers and ground attack aircraft against our centers of resistance and anti-tank regions. However, in the case of the Voronezh Front for example, not even the headquarters of the tank and mechanized corps had communication with the air formations, not to mention those of divisions.

So that it doesn't seem to the reader that I'm biased against the Soviet air forces in general and the 2nd Air Army in particular, I'll cite the airmen themselves. Let's turn to Report No. 31 "On the shortcomings in the combat work of the 2nd Air Army's fighter aircraft in the period between 4 and 9 July 1943", written by a senior officer of the General Staff with the headquarters of the 2nd Air Army Lieutenant Colonel I.A. Kuz'michev:[43]

> Starting from 4.7.43, the enemy air force regularly launched concentrated air strikes on the forward edge of our ground troops in close cooperation with armored and mechanized forces.
>
> Our fighter aircraft, struggling to gain supremacy in the sky, didn't carry out their mission. Despite having a numerical superiority in fighter aircraft in the initial stage, we didn't manage to keep the initiative in the air in our possession. The enemy drove us from the sky over their territory and shifted all of the aerial combats and battles to the territory of our forces. Although the enemy air force indeed suffered heavy losses, it carried out its assignment.
>
> In the majority of cases over the battlefield, the numerical superiority in fighter aircraft was on our side. Yet despite this, the enemy in a number of cases bombed our forces with impunity. Our fighters flew a lot of missions, burned up an immeasurable amount of fuel (on 5.7.43 alone, 907 individual combat sorties were flown by fighters), exerted large physical efforts, and individual pilots displayed genuine heroism in the struggle, yet all the same aerial superiority remained on the enemy's side. The reasons for the unsatisfactory combat performance of the fighter aircraft are the following:

43 Ivan Aleksandrovich Kuz'michev (1907-19?); in the Red Army from 1931 and a participant in the fighting at the Khal'khin-Gol River and the Winter War with Finland. Kuz'michev was awarded the Order of the Red Star (1940) and the medal "For bravery" (1939). He served on the fronts of the Great Patriotic War from May 1942. For his successful performance in the Battle of Kursk, he was worthy of the Order of the Patriotic War 2nd Degree. From the Order's commendation written by a special officer of the General Staff with the headquarters of the Voronezh Front Colonel Kostin on 30 July 1943: "In the period of the July 1943 defensive operation of the Voronezh Front, Comrade Kuz'michev demonstrated exceptionally high initiative and drive in his work. Disregarding the danger to his life and the time required, Kuz'michev timely uncovered shortcomings in the work of our air force and timely made them known to the command of the 2nd Air Army and higher headquarters; on the spot, among the troops he took decisive measures to eliminate the shortcomings and thereby enabled the pilots to launch powerful air strikes against the foe."

1. Poor ground control over the aerial combats above the battlefield. A network of radio control stations and direction over the fighters wasn't organized; the radio stations in the 6th Guards Army's sector weren't operational. The commanders of the 8th Guards Fighter Aviation Division Colonel Larushkin and of the 205th Fighter Aviation Division Colonel Nemtsevich, who drove out to the ground control radio stations on 5.7.43 in order to direct the fighters above the battlefield by radio were unable to do anything substantial. They wound up in the role of observers, not directors of their aircraft. Thus, on the day of intense aerial combats on 5.7.43, the division commanders (8th Guards Fighter Aviation Division and 205th Fighter Aviation Division) didn't command the fighter aircraft in the sky above the battlefield either from the ground, or from their headquarters, or from the air. This could not but affect the outcome of the dogfights and aerial clashes.

   The headquarters of the air army and the headquarters of the fighter aviation corps, aware of the absence of a ground control radio network to direct the aircraft over the battlefield, took no decisive steps and showed no initiative in organizing a network of radio ground control and command. Thus, at important moments of the aerial battles, the fighter aircraft were not being directed from the ground by radio. The pilots weren't hearing voices from the ground, and were bereft of the help and support of their commander in the combat.

   Even worse is the fact that command over the aerial battles took on a purely desk-bound, office character. The commanders of the fighter aviation corps and divisions or their assistants and deputies didn't fly into battle, didn't see what was happening in the sky or how our pilots were fighting. They couldn't properly react to the course of aerial combats and were not in condition to draw conclusions about the actions of our fighter aircraft.

   The control of aerial battles over the radio from the command post of the headquarters, which were separated from the battlefield by 50-60 kilometers, created unnecessary stress for the pilots when engaged in dogfights, and disoriented them about the aerial situation and the point of the missions they were flying.

   Having heard from the VNOS posts [aerial observation, alerting and communications posts] information that the enemy in large groups was bombing our forces in an area where there was none of our fighter aircraft, the command post of the division or corps headquarters would by radio redirect the fighters, which would abandon their assigned area and fly to the new area in order to repel the enemy bombers in response to the radio call. As a rule, such cases of encounters between our fighters and the enemy bombers happen rarely.

   Careening from area to area, the fighters are not carrying out their primary mission that they received prior to take-off, or the secondary mission received over the radio. The sorties turn out to be idle, aimless, fruitless, and expensive for the government.

2. The lack of preparation and lack of knowledge of the pilots to conduct group aerial combats and aerial battles.

   The 2nd Air Army on 2 July 1943 gained rich experience of large, group aerial battles in the Kursk area. This experience wasn't generalized or studied in the units and formations, and no conclusions were drawn from it. The flight staff isn't practically or theoretically prepared for the tactics of conducting large group aerial combats.

   Our fighter pilots haven't learned to use one powerful, massed, simultaneous attack against large groups of bombers with the aim of splitting them up and then destroying them. The attacks against groups of bombers are made in scattered fashion, as a rule, in elements of two fighters or more rarely flights of four.

After the initial attacks, the fighter groups scatter; cooperation between the groups is lost and cannot be re-established. Everyone flying in pairs or more rarely alone fight in the air without any team play. The leaders have poor control over their groups. They are helpless when trying to assemble a group of pilots because of poor discipline in the sky. On 5.7.43, Hero of the Soviet Union Captain Nazarenko led a group of 12 LaGG-5 fighters into a battle. They attacked the bombers as a flight of four; eight LaGG-5 fighters of the 927th Fighter Aviation Regiment provided no assistance to him in the aerial battle. They failed to respond to any of his orders, and he was forced to battle against a numerically superior enemy. The pilots in group dogfights aren't subordinate to the single will of a commander, and therefore we suffer excessively high losses, without inflicting a painful blow to the enemy. Those pilots having radios in their aircraft are not making full use of them.

3. The weak tactical training of the fighter pilots, the absence of cunning and tactical calculations when conducting aerial combat; the inadequate attacking zeal of the fighters.

   On 5.7.43 in the area of Korocha, 4 Pe-2 under the cover of 4 fighters encountered 2 German Me-109 fighters. Sensing their advantage, our pilots became lax. The Germans, choosing their moment, with a single attacking pass shot down 2 of the bombers and 1 fighter while taking no losses of their own.

   On 8.7.43, 8 Yak[44] fighters during a group sortie in the Pravarot' area encountered 2 Me-109. Without adopting a combat formation, and echeloned in altitude, the group continued the mission, paying no attention to the 2 Me-109, which were loafing about off to one side. Having caught a moment, the German element suddenly attacked the 8 Yak-1, and with two attacking passes shot down 3 Yak-1 while suffering no losses of their own.

   The technique of searching for the enemy has been poorly worked out by the fighters. Often, despite the standing air patrols by our fighters, the enemy bombers in this same area bomb our forces with impunity. On 6.7.43, 12 LaGG-5 were patrolling in the area of Iakovlevo; at this same time, 18 Ju-88 began bombing the Iakovlevo – Oboian' highway. No matter how much they tried over the radio to direct the fighters toward the bombers, they couldn't achieve a result.

   The technique of pulling fighters out of a dogfight has been worked out unsatisfactorily. Each pilot leaves the combat as soon as he thinks fit; there are no fleshed out principles of methods to exit a battle. The withdrawal from a combat is not being covered by neighbors, and for that reason we suffer large losses.

   The pairing of fighters, as before, isn't being strictly observed. Striving to score a personal victory, the wingman covering the leader attacks the enemy by himself, leaving the leader alone, and as a consequence the element, disrupted, is defenseless. It becomes a victim of enemy fighters.

   Pilot wingmen haven't been nurtured on the responsibility of covering their leader; we don't view the wingman's loss of sight of the leader as the gravest violation of combat discipline. There are no official standards of the process to become an element leader:

44 Ed. note: I've used the familiar acronym for this aircraft type rather than the Library of Congress transliteration system, which would be "Iak". However, this could be confused with the acronym of a Fighter Aviation Corps, so "Yak" in this case is preferable.

in order to deserve to be a leader, it is necessary to make 75-100 excellent sorties as a wingman to cover his leader.

Many fighters are not actively seeking combat, are not displaying the daring or the attacking zeal, which are characteristic of a fighter pilot. They are operating extremely cautiously with backward glances over their shoulders, even timidly. They are not using the technical power of their aircraft. Passivity in actions has converted the fighters into defenseless, pitiful hens. Such a manifestation has appeared because of the fact that our fighters perform above the battlefield without direction on the part of the aviation commanders and the headquarters on all levels. The commanders are not taking notice of superbly conducted aerial combats, which merit attention and respect, and haven't witnessed anemic combats either. The former and the latter are not being made into lessons for the fighter pilots of the units and formations.

4. There is operational tunnel-vision in the use of fighter aircraft and poor planning of the fighter aircraft's combat work. Our fighters are dueling with the enemy's bombers over our own territory, above our own troops. The patrol areas for the fighter aircraft rarely go beyond the boundaries of the line of combat contact. We are not sending fighter patrols deep into enemy territory with the aim of intercepting and destroying the enemy bombers over their territory before they reach the front.

   We are not implementing free hunts by fighter pilots over enemy territory with the aim of tying up and interdicting some of the enemy's fighters over his own territory, and destroying bombers that are flying alone and in small groups. Technical possibilities allow us to shift the actions of our fighters boldly over enemy territory, because our LaGG-5 fighter is superior to the Me-109F according to their flight and tactical data, and is not inferior to the FW-190.

   Having the assignment to prevent enemy bombers from bombing our own troops, the mission is being carried out in a totally elementary style (by patrolling) without operational élan and without searching for innovations in the tactics and actions of fighter aviation. The planning of the combat work of fighters is reflected in charts of patrols, and not in the forms of struggling for supremacy and superiority in the air.

5. Headquarters at all levels have disengaged from the combat work of the fighter aircraft. They poorly organize the combat work of the fighters; don't observe the aerial combat; don't monitor the carrying out of combat missions by the fighters; don't react timely to shortcomings in the combat work of fighters; don't draw operational and tactical conclusions regarding the conducted dogfights and aerial clashes. They make little study of the enemy's fighter tactics, and don't counter the enemy's tactics with their own tactics.

Conclusion: The fighter aviation of the 2nd Air Army, having numerical and qualitative superiority in fighters over the enemy fighters, as a consequence of poor command and control, the weak work of headquarters and insufficient organization cannot win supremacy and superiority in the air and have fully yielded the initative to the enemy's aircraft, and has not earned the love and respect of our ground troops with their performance.[45]

How distant these conclusions are from that empty rhetoric about the supremacy of the Soviet aircraft in the sky above the Kursk bulge, which stuffed the books and pamphlets after the war![46]

45 TsAMO RF, F. 203, Op. 2843, D. 342, LL. 181-184.

46 See, for example, S.A. Krasovsky, *Zhizn' v aviatsii* [*Life in aviation*] (Moscow: Voenizdat, 1968), p. 174;

The Commander-in-Chief of the Voronezh Front was familiar with the cited document; Vatutin read it and left his signature on it. During personal meetings and discussions over the teletype machine, N.F. Vatutin strictly demanded that the commanders establish order in the troops; alert the commanders of the defending units about the arrival of reinforcements in their sectors; before regrouping inform the command staff in detail about the operational situation in the area that is being left; give needed time to the units and formations in order to scout the routes and reconnoiter; establish contact with the units on the flanks; and establish clear communications between the aviation formations and the headquarters of the ground troops. However, unfortunately all these edicts were of little help. The poor professional training, the inadequate experience and the low discipline of many officers of the combat units and headquarters accumulated into a number of objective causes for the fratricidal aerial attacks, which unquestionably the leadership of the 2nd Air Army tried to correct, but it was unable to achieve the desired result.

For example, direct contact between the headquarters of the 2nd Guards Tatsinskaia Tank Corps and the 1st Ground Attack Aviation Corps had been established. However, despite this the latter's Il-2 ground attack aircraft struck the lines of the 2nd Guards Tank Corps at the start of the operation and continued to pound them with bombs and rockets, and later even attacked its command post.

A representative from the aviation corps also arrived in the 3rd Mechanized Corps, but he was also unable to get the proper coordination with its forces up and running. The reason why is banal – the 1st Ground Attack Aviation Corps had sent a random junior officer who had neither the experience nor the authority for such a responsible post.

Addressing a conference of the high command staff of the 1st Tank Army with an analysis of the actions of his mechanized corps in the Battle of Kursk, General S.M. Krivoshein shared the experience of establishing cooperation with the 2nd Air Army:

> Our air force was exceedingly centralized, and thus we weren't conscious of it. The cooperation between the tanks and aircraft was also unsatisfactory, especially with the ground attack aircraft, which despite recognition signals that marked our own positions, dropped bomb loads on them on several occasions and subjected the corps' forces to attacks. The fighter aviation was operating independently, failing to coordinate its actions with the ground troops. One of the main reasons for this was the absence of a proper air force representative with the corps and the lack of direct communications with the air bases.
>
> They sent me only a captain from the aviation corps, and no one listened to him. He called for aircraft, and no one paid any attention to his requests. Well, clearly, I had to send back such a representative; it was all the same to me whether he was with me or not; all the same, I wouldn't get any air support.
>
> Regarding the location of the air bases, we didn't have any of them nearby. As a rule, the bases are located 50-60 kilometers behind the forward edge of defense, and thus communication with them was bad, and it was difficult to call for aircraft from them. They usually arrived at a time when there was no longer any need for them.[47]

After each fratricidal incident on the battlefield, a commission was created that included representatives from both sides, as well as representatives from the SMERSH Department, which examined the essence of what happened and its causes in detail. On the basis of its report, measures

Kurskaia bitva: Vospominaniia, stat'I [*Battle of Kursk: Recollections and articles*], 2nd ed. (Voronezh: Tsentral'no-Chernozemnoe izdatel'stvo, 1973), p. 190.

47 TsAMO RF, F. 8 gv.mk, Op. 1, D. 41, LL. 14obr, 15obr.

would be recommended to avoid such incidents in the future, but meanwhile friendly fire incidents were continuing to happen now in other sectors.

On 11 July 1943, Voronezh Front's Military Council was forced to issue Coded Message No. 12939 to the commanders of the armies and their artillery commanders, which directed that all the incidents connected with the poor orientation of the troops on the battlefield and insufficient cooperation "resulting in cases when separate elements and groups of our forces in the course of 8-9.7 exchanged fire with each other, our aviation bombed our troops, and our anti-aircraft artillery fired at friendly aircraft"[48] would be investigated by the Front's prosecutorial office before 14 July, and corresponding conclusions would be drawn. At the same time the army commanders and artillery commanders were ordered "to aspire to more organized cooperation and communication."[49] Alas, even this threatening order helped little. On that same day, 11 July, the commander of the 69th Army Lieutenant General V.D. Kriuchenkin and his operational group in the operational rear zone were struck by Soviet aircraft. A day later, on 12 July, in the sector of defense of his army south of Prokhorovka a major friendly fire incident took place, now between rifle formations of the Voronezh Front and the 5th Guards Tank Army, which had arrived from out of the *Stavka* Reserve. Let's turn to an order from the commander of the 69th Army:

> At approximately 1700-1800 on 12.07, the 53rd Separate Tank Regiment [of the 5th Guards Tank Army – the author] initiated an attack toward Novo-Aleksandrovskii Vyselok-1. Advancing in a column toward Hill 241.5 (north of the village of Aleksandrovka), the tanks while on the move opened fire at the combat positions of the 92nd Guards Rifle Division and the tanks of the 96th Tank Brigade, which were located in the vicinity of Aleksandrovka. Combat resulted between our troops, while simultaneously ground attack aircraft were strafing the positions of the 92nd Guards Rifle Division. Only after the intervention of the senior officer of the Red Army General Staff Lieutenant Colonel Sokolov and the artillery commander of the 35th Guards Rifle Corps could this combat be halted with great difficulty.
>
> After passing through Aleksandrovka, the 53rd Tank Regiment exchanged fire with enemy tanks, but several minutes later, without carrying out its assignment, received an order to fall back. The tanks of the 53rd Tank Regiment began to retreat, carrying along with them separate groups of infantry. The anti-tank artillery that was following behind the 53rd Tank Regiment also deployed for combat, but didn't open fire at their own infantry and tanks only thanks to the intervention by the Red Army General Staff officer Lieutenant Colonel Sokolov and the artillery commander of the 35th Guards Rifle Corps. Located in the observation post on Hill 241.5, the commander of the 96th Separate Tank Brigade Major General Lebedev[50]

48 TsAMO RF, F. 203, Op. 2843, D. 489, L. 61.

49 Ibid.

50 Viktor Grigor'evich Lebedev (1901-1979), Major General of Tank Troops (1943). In the Red Army from 1919 and a veteran of the Russian Civil War and the Soviet-Finnish Winter War. From March 1941, he was the commander of the 24th Tank Regiment of Leningrad Military District's 24th Tank Division, and served in the fighting from the first month of the war. Between November 1941 and February 1942, Lebedev commanded the 107th Separate Tank Brigade with Leningrad Front's 8th Army, before taking command of the 87th Separate Tank Brigade for less than a month. From March 1942 he commanded the 96th Separate "Cheliabinsk Komsomol" Tank Brigade. In April 1942, Lebedev's brigade was transferred to Voronezh Front's 6th Guards Army. Before the Battle of Kursk, it was occupying a defense on the army's left flank, east of the Belgorod – Oboian' highway, and from the first day it was involved in the fighting against the II SS Panzer Corps in the vicinity of the Severskii Donets River. Between 5 and 8 July, it was defending the bridges in Shopino and Ternovka. In the following days, especially between 8 and 12 July, his tank brigade distinguished itself in fighting against Army Detachment Kempf's III Panzer Corps on the Korocha axis. On 11 July, covering the withdrawal of the 69th Army (between the Northern Donets

> and the commander of the 92nd Guards Rifle Division Colonel V.F. Trunin intervened too late in resolving these disgraces.
>
> The tankers were uninformed of the actual forward edge of the infantry, which in fact triggered the indicated mistakes. All of the aforementioned happened only because commanders, who've been entrusted with responsible work – the leadership of an operation – regarded it nonchalantly and negligently; they didn't think through questions of cooperation, and failed to organize reconnoitering of the terrain and reconnaissance of the enemy.[51]

On this same day ground attack aircraft of the 2nd Air Army struck the command post of the 69th Army's 48th Rifle Corps several times (at 1820 with 22 Il-2 and at 2030 with 6 Il-2), and its commander Major General Z.Z. Rogoznyi and the corps' operational group came under their fire. Because of this the corps commander was forced to shift the location of his command post hastily. On subsequent days (13 and 14 July), his headquarters and observation post in the vicinity of Leski were again pitilessly bombed by both our own air force and the Germans. And so on, and so on ….

In addition to the operational documents compiled by the command organs of the *front*'s forces, military censors prepared surveys for the *front* commander regarding the mood of the soldiers and commanders on the basis of their letters, which for some reason or another had been confiscated and didn't reach their addressees. Such surveys on the morale of the troops flowed through the channels of military counter-intelligence and up to I.V. Stalin personally. I think that the reader will be interested to find out what one Red Army private, moreover one who had gone through the First World War, was thinking about the condition of the troops of the Voronezh Front who had taken part in the Battle of Kursk. I will cite his letter; its author is E.Ia. Ignatov, a soldier in the 7th Guards Army's 270th Rifle Division:

> I'm located now in Kursk Oblast', fighting has been going on from early morning until late at night, many of my friends in the service are no longer around, wounded, and many killed. I was wounded on 22 July. The majority of non-Russians are fighting badly – the Uzbeks, Kirghiz and Kazakhs; we suffer from them, because of them the German snipers are killing or wounding the commanders, political officers and us. Under heavy fire they lie low and you can't get them to rise (into the attack), so you have to stand at full height to get them to move, and that is all the enemy needs. The Germans, in my opinion, have learned that the political officers and commanders are the first to go over the top on the attack. Of course, that's how it must be, but the German snipers catch these same leaders in their sights with the aim of beheading the element. Fierce fighting is going on. There are only (X) men left in the outfit in which I served. I will say directly that we suffer from great disorganization, for two days we've been without food and water, and this, of course, negatively affects the combat success, particularly during a relentless offensive.

---

and Razumnaia Rivers), it fell into encirclement, but broke out of the pocket. On 15 July 1943 Major General V.G. Lebedev was appointed deputy commander of the 1st Tank Army's 6th Tank Corps. He participated in Operation "Polkovodets Rumiantsev", and coordinated the actions of two of the corps' forward brigades in the fighting in the area of Khar'kov and to the south of the city. Because of conflicts with Voronezh Front's command of the Armored and Mechanized Troops, he wasn't recommended for an award for his participation in the Battle of Kursk. However, in 1949, "due to newly-revealed circumstances", he was awarded the Order of the Red Banner. In November 1943 at his own personal request, he was transferred to the 7th Tank Corps and took command of its 54th Guards Tank Brigade. After receiving a severe wound in January 1944, he served in the inspection office of the Red Army's Main Automotive Command. From November 1944 until the end of the war, Lebedev commanded the *Stavka*'s 4th Automobile Brigade. After the war he worked as a teacher. He retired in 1953.

51 TsAMO RF, F. 48 sk, Op. 1, D. 2, L. 17.

> Men have collected in our rear, who think more about themselves and their commanding officer, just as he pleases, while showing only the minimally necessary concern for the soldiers and mid-ranking commanders, who must face the enemy. Lying, subterfuges and schmoozing are blossoming with every step. Let's compare wars. When I fought in 1917-1918, the soldiers were better disciplined in comparison with the Civil War. The discipline was iron. Today "we've been democratized". No particular attention is given to the suitable mentoring of the Red Army soldier, junior commander or even senior commander, and if something is done, it is without adequate supervision. Arriving replacements haven't been trained in a military respect. As an old soldier, I know what a Red Army soldier should look like, but it must be said that the soldierly appearance of our Red Army soldier, not to mention that of the commander, isn't spic and span. When you come to the level of the present war, dissatisfaction appears, and the opinion begins to form that the commander is cruel, and so on and so forth. Laziness is as thick as blackberries. In addition to all this that I've put in a nutshell for you – I'll say that hypocrisies have demoralized us. For example, they'll tell you "The trenching tool is the soldier's friend", but then we go into battle without them. "They've been promised." We've become so sick of these promises that we don't believe them. You have to regard everyone with suspicion. Many in the headquarters are simply idiots. You see a fool, and he is occupying a post thanks to the fact that he chews the fat and tells tales. So you have to carry around a lot of grievances; there is no credibility.[52]

The author of these lines, in my view, was no ordinary man who simply rooted for a cause, but one who described the situation of affairs among our troops based only on his own life experience, great as it was. Even so, his assessment is the perspective of a man "from the inside", which means it isn't free of extreme forms of subjectivity. Once in a conversation with me, the well-known Soviet military historian and veteran of the Battle of Kursk Colonel G.A. Koltunov gave me the following piece of advice: "My own experience of combat in the Great Patriotic War taught me that for any soldier the epicenter of the battle is his own foxhole. Thus, be careful about drawing conclusions only on the basis of the statements of eyewitnesses and participants in the events, especially those of military men." Guided by this advice, let's turn to the assessment of Soviet soldiers, given by a participant in those two World Wars, including on our own territory, the German General Günther Blumentritt.[53] In a conversation with the well-known British military theoretician B. Liddell Hart, he asserted:

> The Red Army of 1941-1945 was far harder than the Czar's Army, for they were fighting fanatically for an idea. That increased their doggedness, and in turn made our own troops hard, for in the East the maxim held good: "It is either you or me." Discipline in the Red Army was far more rigorous than in the Czar's Army.[54]

---

52 *Ognennaia duga: Kurskaia bitva glazami Lubianki* [*The Bulge of Fire: The Battle of Kursk through the eyes of the Lubianka*] (Moscow: Moskovskie uchebniki i Kartolitografiia, 2003), pp. 90-91.

53 Günther Blumentritt (1892-1967), *Generalleutnant* (1944); in military service from 1911. In the years 1914-1917 Blumentritt served at the front as a lieutenant and battalion adjutant. In 1918 he rose to senior lieutenant and regiment adjutant. He was wounded. From October 1940, he was the Fourth Army's chief of staff. On the Soviet-German front from 22 June 1941. A participant of the battles in Belorussia and on the Moscow axis. For the fighting near Moscow, he was awarded the German Gold Cross. In January 1942 he was appointed deputy chief of the OKH. Between September 1942 and the end of the war, Blumentritt served on the Western Front, commanding a corps and army; his last post was commander-in-chief of Army Group Blumentritt (April-May 1945). A Knight's Cross with Oak Leaves recipient. Between 1 June 1945 and 1 January 1948, he was held in a British prison.

54 B.H. Lidell Hart, *Na drugoi storone vysoty* [*On the other side of the hill*] (Moscow: AST, 2014), p. 343. This

Possibly, it might seem to someone that the statements presented on these pages that besmirch the troops of the Voronezh Front are biased and do not objectively reflect the reality. However, there is no way around it, all this really did in fact happen, and directly and substantially affected both the results of the defensive operation and the level of combat losses. The documents cited by me were prepared by Soviet staff officers not with the aim of "besmirching" their troops, but in order to ascertain the real situation of affairs, correct mistakes, and prevent them from happening in the future.

In the course of the Battle of Kursk, the Voronezh Front with respect to the organization of cooperation of different types of forces on the battlefield and the number of ChP didn't particularly stand out. The information presented above is only a smidgen of the real life not only of the *fronts* in the area of the Kursk salient, but of the entire acting Red Army, and such problems existed in the armies of other countries as well. More than once I've happened to talk with Great Patriotic War veterans about all of these problems, and they all, from ordinary private to regiment commander have provided a similar picture: this was the reality that they encountered daily at the front. The facts of inconsistencies, friendly fire incidents, poor cooperation both on the level of neighboring battalions and the level of divisions, corps and different types of troops occurred practically every day. Given a stable front, they occurred more rarely, but during an offensive or a maneuvering defense, they happened several times a day, even in one and the same divisions. Often, the cases of this nature simply weren't put down on paper and reported up the chain of command, if there were no casualties that clearly resulted from them. The causes of them were various, from the coincidence of circumstances and the absence of communication to the elementary bungling, irresponsibility and low training of the soldiers and commanders. Indeed, no matter how strange it seems, the veterans in one voice remarked that even if one could align all of the personnel to carry out regulations by the book, which have been worked out over the decades; heed the demands of manuals and lessons; and daily monitor this with commanders at all levels, given the aggregation of a significant number of armed men crowded into a small territory, you could rarely avoid such ChP. Their number might be reduced, but it is impossible to eliminate them entirely.

So in conclusion, I will offer several personal impressions. Alas, no matter how those of us living 70 years after these events might strive to grasp the logic and actions of their participants, it isn't possible to do so fully, because it is impossible to turn back the clock, return to those times and live through their experiences. Today, an enormous amount of information about the interrelationships among the Red Army's high command staff is virtually unknown. The style of work and methods of command and control of the corps and division level of command have not been illuminated at all in the memoir literature, nor has a number of other aspects of life in our Red Army between 1941 and 1945. In addition, a number of documentary files of the *front* commands, the People's Commissariat of Defense and the *Stavka* of the Supreme High Command still remain classified. However, the work of scholars continues, and there is hope that with the passage of time, possibly an official history of the war will be written, if not in detail, then at least one that is honest and objective. There is hope that the material cited above, which has only recently been opened in the military archives, will help the reader delve more deeply into the twists and turns of those epochal events, discover new factors that affected the combat operations, and thoroughly assess the decisions and actions of key participants of that epic event in our history, such as the Battle of Kursk was.

---

is the Russian-language edition of Lidell Hart's *The German Generals Talk*, and the cited passage can be found on page 225.

10

Prokhorovka – the unknown clash of the Great Patriotic War

At the beginning of March 1943, the commander-in-chief of Army Group South *Feldmarschall* Erich von Manstein was the first to propose to cut off the Kursk salient, which had formed as a result of the Soviet counteroffensive following the disastrous German defeat at Stalingrad, by converging attacks in the direction of Kursk. He did so even before the re-capture of Belgorod by the SS Panzer Corps. However, his proposal seemed untimely: the spring thaw had begun, and the situation that Army Group Center faced was very difficult. Its Ninth Army under *Generaloberst* W. Model had just completed its withdrawal from the Rzhev salient and had re-assembled in the Orel bulge, and was unprepared for such a large-scale operation. Nevertheless, Hitler favored the idea. Berlin was forced to reject it at that time, however, and postponed its implementation to a later date, by approximately a month.

The plan of a grand offensive in the center of the Soviet-German front began to be fleshed out already at the end of March 1943, and on 12 April the prepared draft of Operation Citadel[1] arrived on Hitler's desk, and was approved by him on the same day. Three days later, on 15 April, it was embodied in the well-known operational Order No. 6, which gave both the objectives and tasks of the summer campaign in the east, and the principle scheme of actions for Army Groups South and Center. The essence of Citadel consisted of two converging attacks out of the areas of Orel in the north and Belgorod in the south in the direction of Kursk to split the defenses of two Soviet *fronts* – General of the Army N.F. Vatutin's Voronezh Front and General of the Army K.K. Rokossovsky's Central Front – and to encircle their forces. Even so, already at the time a significant portion of the Wehrmacht's generals, who took part in working out the plan for the operation, regarded this undertaking with disapproval, correctly believing that Germany lacked the strength in order to bring it to a successful conclusion.

Army Group South was to make the main effort; it faced more ambitious tasks. In order to reach the proposed line of link-up Army Group Center would have to cover approximately 75 kilometers, while Manstein's forces would have to advance nearly twice that distance, 125 kilometers. Thus a greater amount of force was planned for the breakthrough of the defenses of the Voronezh Front, which was holding the southern face of the Kursk salient. For this purpose, Army Group South received *Generaloberst* H. Hoth's Fourth Panzer Army and *General der Panzerwaffen* W. Kempf's Army Detachment Kempf, which together possessed 11 infantry and 9 panzer and panzergrenadier divisions.

The final plan was prepared after a conference between Manstein and Hoth in Bogodukhov on 11-12 May 1943. It was at this conference that the Fourth Panzer Army commander laid out his plan to destroy the Soviet mobile reserves at Prokhorovka, and this became the essence of the

1 The operation received its code name *Zitadelle* [Citadel] on 31 March 1943.

first stage of Operation Citadel. According to the testimony of Fourth Panzer Army's chief of staff General Fangohr, Hoth planned to implement "Citadel" in two stages. In the first stage, his army was given the task to break through two of the three belts of defenses held by Vatutin's forces, and to destroy the Soviet operational and strategic reserves in the area of Prokhorovka Station together with Army Detachment Kempf. Hoth believed that Moscow would release its strategic reserve, the Steppe Front, as soon as the breach had been created in the Soviet lines, and would send it to meet the attacking German over the land bridge between the Psel and Northern Donets Rivers. The *Generaloberst* wasn't confident that his forces had the strength to carry out the task of the first stage fully, so the objectives of the second stage were to be determined onlyl after the Soviet strategic reserves were defeated in the Prokhorovka Station area.

The overall offensive by the Germans' two assault groupings in the area of the Kursk bulge began on the night of 4-5 July 1943 and on the second day of the battle "Hoth's plan" began to yield its first weighty results. His panzer army, having already penetrated the second belt of defenses of the Voronezh Front, had split Lieutenant General I.M. Chistiakov's 6th Guards Army and then had attempted to throw it back to the north, toward Oboian', together with the corps of Lieutenant General M.E. Katukov's 1st Tank Army, which were approaching to bolster the 6th Guards Army and close the breach. *Kampfgruppen* of two SS panzergrenadier divisions on the right flank of the Fourth Panzer Army's attack wedge had reached the third and final army-level belt of defenses, 12 kilometers west of Prokhorovka Station.

However, although the German forces had overcome the main and a significant part of the second army belt of defenses, by the end of 6 July they'd been unable to create a continuous breakthrough front. Army Detachment Kempf's offensive on the secondary Korocha axis out of the area of Belgorod was making only slow, arduous headway against the powerful resistance offered by Lieutenant General M.S. Shumilov's 7th Guards Army that was defending here. Here, the Germans were unable to create a breach and establish contact with Hoth's panzer army on the second day, nor on the third day of the operation. As a result, the Fourth Panzer Army's right flank remained unguarded, and its command had no choice but to weaken the SS Panzer Corps' assault wedge and detach entire panzergrenadier and infantry divisions in order to cover it.

Thus, in spite of the noticeable success of the first two days of Army Group South's offensive, by the end of 6 July the Soviet side had achieved its main objective – it had forced both of the German attack groupings in the south, Army Group South and Army Detachment Kempf, to attack in diverging directions. Between their flanks, the forces of the 69th Army were stubbornly clinging to the area between the Northern Donets and Lipovyi Donets Rivers. This substantially slowed the development of Operation Citadel and was an important factor of Voronezh Front's success in the course of the defensive phase of the Battle of Kursk.

Everything wasn't going smoothly for Hoth either. Firstly, after the breakthrough on 6 July, the SS Panzergrenadier Divisions *Leibstandarte Adolf Hitler* and *Das Reich* were unable to make shoulder to shoulder contact with each other. The corps' command demanded they close the gap in the course of the next 24 hours and regroup their forces for a further drive forward, which naturally took precious time and disrupted the operation's timetable. Secondly, both these divisions reached the Prokhorovka direction in a rather narrow sector, and thus before they could push on it was extremely important that they create more elbow room. In the opposite case, it might prove easy for the Soviet side to encircle them.

On the night of 6-7 July, the Voronezh Front's Military Council placed responsibility for holding the Oboian' and Prokhorovka directions on M.E. Katukov.[2] Despite a deficit in strength and means, he quickly organized an effective system of mobile defense along the entire breakthrough

2 TsAMO RF, F. 335, Op. 5113, D. 208, L. 131.

sector, and created a powerful knot of resistance at the boundary between the XXXXVIII Panzer Corps and II SS Panzer Corps. Katukov so skillfully planned the actions of his tank and mechanized formations that right up to the start of the fighting for Prokhorovka, *General* O. von Knobelsdorff's XXXXVIII Panzer Corps of the Fourth Panzer Army, which was attacking along the Oboian' highway and covering the SS Corps' left flank, was unable in fact to emerge out of the second belt of defenses.

However, Katukov's and Chistiakov's armies were quickly melting away. The situation was worsened by the fact that already by the end of 5 July N.F. Vatutin had been forced to throw all of his reserve corps into the battle. As a result, on 8 July major villages and simultaneously strong knots of resistance on the Prokhorovka direction – Kalinin, Greznoe (Griaznoe), Kochetovka, Sukho-Solotino, and Luchki, as well as Iakovlevo, Gremuchii and Verkhopen'e on the Oboian' axis, wound up in enemy hands. However, the main danger was that the SS troops had reached the rear belt of defenses, which ran along the left bank in the bend of the Psel River and covered the only passable corridor for tanks toward Prokhorovka between the basin of the Psel River and the Belgorod – Kursk railroad. The Soviet formations that were fighting on the Oboian' highway were being subjected to colossal pressure from the Germans. In addition to the fact that the main forces of the Fourth Panzer Army's two panzer corps were operating against them (each day in a sector of approximately 40 kilometers the Germans were employing up to 500 armored combat vehicles here), the main forces of *Luftflotte* Four's VIII *Fliegerkorps* were active here.

Having no way to help Katukov with reserves, N.F. Vatutin decided on the morning of 8 July to launch a counterattack against the right flank of the Fourth Panzer Army with four tank corps, which had 530 tanks among them, including 308 T-34, supported by the rifle divisions of the 69th Army. A portion of these formations were to arrive only that morning, which is to say immediately on the day of the counterattack, from other fronts. Vatutin's aggressive measure has been evaluated by Soviet historians as unsuccessful,[3] but this label conceals not the failures of the tank corps, but more the unseemly conduct of separate generals, who'd been serving in the acting army for more than a year, but who proved unable to organize command and control over their troops. Thus, Order No. 00212 from the Commander-in-Chief of the Voronezh Front from 30 July 1943, directly points to the failure by the commander of the 2nd Tank Corps Major General A.F. Popov to carry out the order to organize the battle, despite having the possibility to do so. As a result, as we've already seen, one of his tank brigades overran the combat positions of a rifle regiment of the 183rd Rifle Division on the Prokhorovka axis and inflicted substantial losses to it.[4]

Even so, the counterstroke had a large influence on the plans of the Fourth Panzer Army's command. The appearance of large mobile formations on the Prokhorovka axis became a signal for Hoth that the battle that he had planned back in May 1943 was about to begin. On 9 July he began to pivot both panzer corps, which had been ready first to break through the third and final army belt (in the north and northeastern directions), which was still unoccupied by Voronezh Front's forces, in order to continue the grinding battles of attrition with the Soviet tank corps once more in the second belt of defenses.

Between 5 and 9 July 1943, while carrying out the scheme of Operation Citadel, Army Group South's main forces had launched their main attack against the line of Vatutin's armies along the Belgorod – Kursk highway to the north and northeast. For the Voronezh Front, this was the first, initial stage of the defensive operation. Despite all of the enemy's efforts, our troops were holding out. After five days of the heaviest, bloody fighting, it had become clear to E. von Manstein that the operation in the form that it had been planned had suffered a setback. The situation

3 G.A. Koltunov and B.G. Solov'ev, *Kurskaia bitva* [*Battle of Kursk*] (Moscow: Voenizdat, 1970), pp. 156-157.
4 TsAMO RF, F. 38A, Op. 9027, D. 50, L. 375.

before the forthcoming battle at Prokhorovka with the forces of the approaching Steppe Front had become extremely complex and far from that which Hoth had presented during the meeting in Bogodukhov. By 9 July the Fourth Panzer Army's losses in armor were very high. Of the 327 tanks that were counted as combat-ready in the XXXXVIII Panzer Corps on the morning of 5 July 1943, at 2230 (Berlin time) on 9 July there remained only 123 in that condition, or just 40%.[5] Still more catastrophic was the situation with tanks in the Panther-equipped 10th Panzer Brigade, which had been intended to play a role in the Prokhorovka clash. It was practically played out: for various reasons, more than 90% of the Pz V tanks were no longer serviceable (of the 200 Panthers that had arrived just before the Battle of Kursk, on the evening of 9 July only 16 remained operational).[6] Secondly, because of the fact that Army Detachment Kempf had thus far made little progress, H. Hoth was forced to continue to keep the SS Panzergrenadier Division *Das Reich* and the 167th Infantry Division covering the extended right flank, which didn't allow him to augment the forces on the axis of his panzer army's main attack and make a substantial advance to the north and northeast. Reconnaissance reported that lengthy columns of men and equipment were moving in the direction of Prokhorovka. Thus, the threat of powerful flank attacks out of the area of Prokhorovka Station was increasing with each passing day, while the Germans' strength was dissipating. For Hoth the destruction of our force grouping opposite the Fourth Panzer Army's right flank (in the interfluvial area between the Northern and Lipovyi Donets Rivers) and preparing to meet the Red Army's approaching tank reserves at Prokhorovka became the overriding concern for the next few days.

On 10 July, the second stage of Voronezh Front's defensive operation began. Its main events unfolded at a major center of Soviet resistance – the Prokhorovka railroad station. In this period, Vatutin's main tasks consisted in preventing a breakthrough of the third (and final) defensive belt on the Prokhorovka axis, inflicting maximal losses to the enemy, and thereby create the conditions for his destruction.

To resolve these assignments, the main role was given to the approaching 5th Guards and 5th Guards Tank Army out of the *Stavka* Reserve, as well as to the 69th Army that was defending the railroad station. The formations of the 1st Tank Army, 6th Guards Army and 7th Guards Army continued to participate in the fighting until the end of the operation, but were now no longer playing the leading role. This second stage of the battle ended on the night of 16-17 July, when the command of Army Group South, without having achieved the aims of the offensive, began to withdraw its forces, including from near Prokhorovka, back to their jumping-off positions, which meant a shift to a different operational task. Accordingly, the tasks of the Voronezh Front also changed – from a defensive posture it went in pursuit of the enemy. The third, final stage of the Kursk defensive operation for Voronezh Front was the pursuit (and in some sectors, the driving back) of the enemy, which ended on 25 July, when its armies returned to the line they were occupying prior to 5 July.

The day of 12 July 1943 became the turning point of the battle. On that day N.F. Vatutin threw practically everything that he had in his possession into the battle. In the course of the counterattack on that day, there occurred a number of tank clashes with the inclusion of artillery and infantry. The largest of them was the combat in the sector between the Psel River and the hamlet of Storozhevoe (an area which later acquired the name of the "Tank Field"), in which four Soviet tank corps (the 2nd, 18th, 29th and 2nd Guards Tank Corps of the 5th Guards Tank Army), elements of three rifle and one airborne division (the 9th Guards Airborne Division and the 183rd,

5 N. Zetterling and A. Franksen, *Kursk 1943: a statistical analysis* (London, Portland: Frank Cass, 2000), pp. 185-186.
6 NARA, T. 313, R. 368, F. 8654337.

42nd Guards and 95th Guards Rifle Divisions of the 5th Guards Army and 69th Army) took part, as well as the 11th and 6th Guards Motorized Rifle Brigades, which had been left here after the departure of the 1st Tank Army, and the 10th and 5th Guards Tank Corps. The counterstroke's main aim on this day wasn't achieved: the enemy wasn't destroyed, and the Soviet formations that took part in the counterattack took significant losses. Nevertheless, thanks to it the Fourth Panzer Army's advance was finally blunted. The fighting between the formations of the 5th Guards Tank Army and 5th Guards Army and the divisions of the II SS Panzer Corps on 12 July 1943 ended the first stage of the Prokhorovka battle.

The final, concluding stage of the battle for possession of the railroad station took place between 13 and 16 July. In this period E. von Manstein prepared to withdraw his shock grouping from the narrow salient that had formed in the course of the offensive between 5 and 12 July. In order to make the withdrawal as safe as possible, he ordered the elimination of the powerful knot of resistance on the boundary between the Fourth Panzer Army and Army Detachment Kempf, which is to say, the encirclement and destruction of the 69th Army south of Prokhorovka, in the interfluvial area between the Northern and Lipovyi Donets Rivers, by means of meeting attacks by the II SS Panzer Corps (Fourth Panzer Army) and III Panzer Corps (Army Detachment Kempf). Although the operation didn't manage to destroy the 69th Army's forces, it inflicted substantial damage to them and drove them out of the area between the rivers, thereby ensuring favorable conditions for the withdrawal for his forces.

However, let's return to the plans of the Soviet side that preceded the clash at Prokhorovka. Back on 7 July, after analyzing the situation that had arisen, N.F. Vatutin and *Stavka* representative Marshal of the Soviet Union A.M. Vasilevky, who was also Chief of the General Staff, had appealed to I.V. Stalin with a request to move up Lieutenant General A.S. Zhadov's 5th Guards Army, which was occupying a sector along the Staryi Oskol – Skorodnoe line, and Lieutenant General P.A. Rotmistrov's 5th Guards Tank Army out of the Ostrogozhsk area, to the Prokhorovka axis to reinforce it. Stalin approved the request, and by the end of 9 July Rotmistrov's tank army was assembled east of Prokhorovka, having received the assignment to reinforce the defense of the 69th Army's rifle units, while Zhadov's divisions began to arrive here a day later. Both panzer corps that were supposed to carry out the Fourth Panzer Army's main mission on 10 July were already tied up in heavy fighting. Neither Hoth nor Manstein had any available reserves, while the next, even more significant wave of Soviet mobile formations had already rolled up to Prokhorovka.

Prior to 10 July, all of the attention of Voronezh Front's command was focused on the Oboian' direction. The approach of two Guards armies not only noticeably strengthened the Front's position at the railroad station, but also allowed N.F. Vatutin to reinforce the Oboian' axis and to make a different plan for the subsequent actions. He began to prepare a major counterstroke with the aim of finally stopping the Fourth Panzer Army and to inflict heavy losses to it.

A number of factors prompted him to this decision. First, the 5th Guards Army and 5th Guards Tank Army had a combined total of more than 100,000 men and around 1,000 tanks and self-propelled guns. These enormous forces were assembled on the flank of the hostile grouping that was attacking in the general direction of Oboian'. Secondly, Front intelligence was systematically reporting that the enemy was bringing up large reserves (a corps or more), although objective information (captured documents and prisoner interrogation) wasn't confirming this. At the same time, already by 8 July information began to come from the front that on the flanks of the Fourth Panzer Army and Army Detachment Kempf, the Germans were building field works and setting up strands of barbed wire, which prompted the thought that the enemy's offensive had run out of steam, but the Germans were trying to conceal this fact. Thirdly, when releasing Rotmistrov's and Zhadov's armies from the reserve, I.V. Stalin set a condition: use them only with the *Stavka*'s authorization for a counteroffensive, while the Chief of the General Staff personally was to determine the most suitable moment to launch it, and coordinate the work to organize the introduction of the powerful, fresh reserves into combat. N.F. Vatutin understood better than anyone that prior to the Battle of Kursk, when determining the area out of which the Germans would launch their main attack, Moscow had made a mistake. The enemy's main forces had been hurled not against the Central Front, but against his own Voronezh Front. So far, however, he had been unable to persuade I.V. Stalin that in order to repel such a powerful attack, he would need significantly more strength than he possessed. The former member of Voronezh Front's Military Council N.S. Khrushchev recalled that N.F. Vatutin was daily hearing tongue-lashings and rebukes for his "inability to fight" and his poor organization of the combat work. All of this taken together was strongly suggesting the idea of conducting a powerful counterstroke (the spearhead of which was to assemble at Prokhorovka and advance in the direction of the Belgorod – Oboian' highway, into the right flank of the Fourth Panzer Army), with the aim of conclusively checking the enemy and going over to a grand counteroffensive.

Thus, the German and Soviet commands, acting according to plans unknown to the opposing side, had objectively set the conditions for a major tank clash in the II SS Panzer Corps' sector of attack. However, whereas E. von Manstein and H. Hoth had previously anticipated this, back in May 1943, and were deliberately heading toward it, N.F. Vatutin was simply improvising.

On the evening of 9 July, Vatutin requested Moscow's authorization to conduct the counterstroke. The Front command sincerely believed that the counterattack would develop into a counteroffensive, and thus in all the Soviet combat documents, reference is made to a counteroffensive.[7]

Not without hesitations, this proposal was approved by the *Stavka* and the General Staff. The divisions of the right wing of Lieutenant General V.D. Kriuchenkin's 69th Army were to keep the enemy on the distant approaches to Prokhorovka and secure the deployment of the 5th Guards Army and 5th Guards Tank Army on a line running from Greznoe (Griaznoe) to Belenikhino Station. On the morning of 12 July, passing through the positions of Kriuchenkin's troops, two tank and one mechanized corps of Rotmistrov's tank army, reinforced with Zhadov's six rifle divisions, were to split the II SS Panzer Corps apart and hurl the Germans back to the Oboian' highway, and given a favorable development of the situation, advance along the Oboian' highway toward Belgorod. The plan was fully realistic, but the main thing was that the Voronezh Front possessed the possibilities to realize it; true, only in the event that the line of deployment planned for Rotmistrov's three corps could be held.

However, *Generaloberst* Hoth was an experienced commander and realized the threatening situation, and thus made every effort in the next two days (10 and 11 July) to seize the positions in the Prokhorovka area that were suitable for the deployment of the Soviet tank corps and place the 5th Guards Tank Army in a maximally awkward position. He began to implement this mission at the very same moment that N.F. Vatutin was reporting his proposed plan to I.V. Stalin. *SS-Obergruppenführer* P. Hausser's II SS Panzer Corps was to play the main role, or more precisely, two of his divisions: *Totenkopf* and *Leibstandarte Adolf Hitler*. The former was to break through to Prokhorovka across the bend in the Psel River, along the Kliuchi – Beregovoe – Prokhorovka route of advance, while the latter was to launch a frontal assault in the direction of the southwestern outskirts of the station along the "Komsomolets" State Farm – Hill 252.2 – Prokhorovka Station direction.[8] By the morning of 10 July, the conditions were ready for the attack by the SS forces to the east and northeast.

7 For example, in the order for the 5th Guards Tank Army's 18th Tank Corps from 11 July 1943 (TsAMO RF, F. 18tk, Op. 1, D. 23, L. 9).

8 S. Stadler, *Die Offensive gegen Kursk 1943: II SS Panzerkorps als Stoskeil im Grosskampf.* NATION EUROPA Verlag GmBH COBURG, 1998; pp. 81-82.

By this time, the Soviet forces guarding the approaches to Prokhorovka had suffered significant losses. Thus, the Voronezh Front leadership sought to reinforce this area. Already by the evening of 9 July, the corps of the 5th Guards Tank Army began to take up a defense in the second echelon here. At the same time, the brigades of the 2nd Tank and 2nd Guards Tatsinskaia Tank Corps, which had in the meantime been made directly subordinate to N.F. Vatutin, were to reinforce "with fire and movement" the line of the rifle units in the first echelon. Within a couple of days, on the evening of 11 July, he would hand them over to P.A. Rotmistrov. They were supposed to create a unique "armored girding" of the rear belt of defenses on the axis of the SS Panzer Corps' main attack. However, by the start of the Prokhorovka battle, both of these tank corps had suffered painful losses. At 0800 on 10 July, in total they had 257 operational tanks of three types: T-34, T-70 and Mk IV Churchills. Of the 89 serviceable tanks in the 2nd Tank Corps, 43 were light T-70 tanks.[9]

The main natural obstacle confronting the II SS Panzer Corps' attack to the northeast was the Psel River. Its channel was relatively narrow – up to 35 meters wide. However, its broad, swampy floodplain, which extended up to 200 meters on both sides of the river, created a serious obstacle for tanks. Thus, on the night of 9-10 July, assault groups of the SS Panzergrenadier Division *Totenkopf* crossed the river and made an attempt to seize a bridgehead on the northern bank, in order to cover the work to lay down a bridge for the armor. However, this attempt was thwarted by the troops of the 6th Guards Army's 52nd Guards Rifle Division that were defending here. Even so, the lack of success didn't stop the enemy, and the SS division began to prepare a new attack.

The command of the SS Panzergrenadier Division *Leibstandarte Adolf Hitler* was focusing its main efforts along a railroad track that ran through Prokhorovka Station. At a distance of 300-400 meters from its embankment was the edge of the deep Molozhavaia balka that was impassable for tanks. These several hundred meters in fact comprised the only "corridor" that the panzers could use for the breakthrough to Prokhorovka. The Soviet forces' main knot of resistance here was the area of Ivanovskii Vyselok and the "Komsomolets" State Farm. These settlements were located on the edges of the corridor and were the key to the railroad station, and thus the main events of the first day of the battle for Prokhorovka unfolded around them.

Before sunrise a German diversionary group consisting of "Vlasovites" [Russian volunteers for the German Army] dressed in Red Army uniforms overwhelmed the combat outposts of the 183rd Rifle Division's 285th Rifle Regiment that was blocking the corridor, thereby allowing sappers of the SS Panzergrenadier Division *Leibstandarte Adolf Hitler* to clear passages through the minefields for the tanks. The morning of 10 July began with an artillery barrage. Once it ended, Tigers and assault guns went on the attack, followed by panzergrenadiers. The battalions of the 285th Rifle Regiment didn't open fire, seeing that the Germans were heading toward the minefields. Within several seconds, astonishment showed on the soldiers' faces: the mines weren't working. The German armor accelerated and surged toward our positions. After a sharp fight, the SS men took Ivanovskii Vyselok and attempted to advance further in the direction of Storozhevoe, in order to widen the gap that had been created in the defenses of the 183rd Rifle Division to the south.

The headquarters of the *Leibstandarte Adolf Hitler* division reported: "The well dug-in enemy was defending fiercely, but after taking the positions, the resistance slackened. Numerous Russians took to flight. After 1400 – intense fire of tanks from concealed positions on the slopes and from the northwest fringe of the Storozhevoe woods are preventing a further advance forward."[10] In the afternoon of 10 July, the Germans nevertheless managed to take the "Komsomolets" State Farm

9 V.N. Zamulin, *Zasekrechennaia Kurskaia bitva. Dokumenty svidetel'stvuiut* [*The Secret Battle of Kursk: Documents testify*] (Moscow, 2007), p. 61.
10 Stadler, *Die Offensive gegen Kursk*, pp. 87-88.

as well, and also to create a bridgehead across the Psel River in the bend of the river, where they hastily began to build a bridge. However, German attacks made no further headway. Attempts by combat groups of the *Leibstandarte Adolf Hitler* to launch a frontal attack along the railroad to the station were stymied by the stubborn resistance of the 69th Army's rifle units, as well as by counterattacks by the 2nd Tank Corps' tanks. Thus, on the first day of the battle for Prokhorovka, the Voronezh Front's troops prevented the SS Panzer Corps from carrying out Hoth's order to break through the third belt of defenses to their entire depth and emerge at Prokhorovka. Both SS divisions made only a 1.5 to 2.5 kilometer advance.

It should be mentioned that P. Hausser on this day was unable to employ the well-tested means of breakthrough – a powerful panzer wedge supported by Luftwaffe air strikes. In the sector of the SS Panzergrenadier Division *Leibstandarte Adolf Hitler* only Tigers and assault guns were activated for the attack because of the Soviet mines and bad weather. At the "Komsomolets" State Farm, the SS troops broke through on a rather narrow sector, where a large number of their combat machines could not deploy because of the high density of mines. Because of the bad weather, the German dive bombers made only a rare appearance. The dense mortar fire coming from the Soviet lines disrupted the work of the German sappers, and attempts to knock out the firing positions with artillery alone without Luftwaffe support, were unsuccessful. The *Totenkopf* was facing the same problems when seizing the bridgehead. With great difficulty, the SS troops drove back the battalions of the 52nd Guards Rifle Division a short distance from river basin only by evening (they took the first line of Soviet trenches here), and thus there was no success on this day in getting the armor across to the northern bank of the river. Before twilight, the place where the Germans were laying down a corduroy road through the swampy ground was hit by "Katiusha" rockets, as a result of which everything burned up and a number of the engineers killed. The building of a crossing site was renewed that night. The headquarters of the Fourth Panzer Army was forced to shift a company of an engineer battalion from the neighboring XXXXVIII Panzer Corps (from the Panzergrenadier Division *Grossdeutschland*) to the site to assist with the work.

However, the combat on 10 July once again confirmed that the troops of the Voronezh Front were dealing with a strong enemy. The capture of defensive key points on the approaches to Prokhorovka (Ivanovskii Vyselok and the "Komsomolets" State Farm), as well as the creation of the bridgehead on the northern bank of the Psel River, gave evidence that the foe wasn't wanting for professionalism.

On 11 July, the task before the SS divisions remained the same: *Leibstandarte Adolf Hitler* was to launch an attack toward Prokhorovka along the railroad; *Das Reich* was to cover its right flank and reinforce the attack in the event of a success; and *Totenkopf* was to form an assault group on the northern bank of the Psel River, which was then to attack toward the northeast. The second day of the fighting for Prokhorovka proved to be significantly harder for the Soviet side and was filled with tragic events. After noontime, the SS Corps managed to achieve almost the impossible: a *kampfgruppe* of the *Leibstandarte Adolf Hitler* with a decisive attack managed to rupture the defenses simultaneously of two armies, the 69th Army and the 5th Guards Army that had arrived in the second echelon here, and then reached a brick factory on the outskirts of Prokhorovka. Thus, the third belt of defenses was virtually breached, albeit in a narrow sector of just 900 meters.

Judging from the documents, discovered in the Russian Ministry of Defense's Central Archive, on the afternoon of 11 July the headquarters of the 69th Army was unable to handle fully the situation on its right flank. It reported to the Commander-in-Chief of the Voronezh Front about the German breakthrough only after a delay of several hours, at 1920. A combat order from N.F. Vatutin to the commander of the 69th Army states: "As a result of your carelessness and poor command and control, the enemy has broken through to Petrovka and toward Prokhorovka. I am ordering you at your personal responsibility together with Rotmistrov's and Zhadov's troops to destroy the enemy that has broken through and to reach the Vasil'evka – Belenikhino front this very day."[11]

Army commander A.S. Zhadov personally took up the matter of eliminating the German penetration by organizing better control over the troops and bringing up artillery and a regiment of "Katiusha" rocket launchers. Having come under their heavy, concentrated fire, the SS combat group fell back 2 kilometers from Prokhorovka Station to Hill 252.2, but the defending Soviets were unable to regain the planned line of departure for the counterattack. Thus, although the SS troops didn't in fact enter Prokhorovka, the German capture of the entire area southwest and west of it, where the 5th Guards Tank Army could have fully deploy its forces, had in the future tragic consequences for it and played no small role in the failure of the frontal counterstroke. The tank army's brigades, which began moving toward the jumping-off area on 11 July after the onset of darkness, had nowhere to deploy.

The breakthrough made by the combat group of the SS Panzergrenadier Division *Leibstandarte Adolf Hitler* to the brick factory resembled a bottleneck. It deeply penetrated into our defenses, while at the same time its neighbors *Das Reich* and *Totenkopf* made little progress. Accordingly, its flanks were exposed, and given a further advance, a threat of encirclement would arise for *Leibstandarte Adolf Hitler*'s combat spearhead. Division commander *SS-Brigadeführer* T. Wisch after 1700, with Hoth's agreement, was forced to issue an order to halt the offensive and go over to a temporary defense, until the neighboring formations of the SS Panzer Corps were able to draw level with Wisch's division. By midnight the bitter fighting subsided, and the Germans began to fortify the ground they had taken.

The essence of the Soviet frontal counterstroke boiled down to launching an attack with two groupings in the general direction of Iakovlevo and Pokrovka: with the 5th Guards Tank Army and 5th Guards Army out of the Prokhorovka area and the 6th Guards Army and 1st Tank Army out of the area south of Ivnia – Novoselovka – Pokrovka (in the area of the Oboian' highway). The 7th Guards Army near Belgorod was ready to launch a pinning attack, in order to deprive the enemy of the possibility of maneuvering with reserves.

Rotmistrov's tank army was given the primary role. N.F. Vatutin had decided to create a powerful wedge at Prokhorovka out of the two Guards armies, reinforced by two tank corps (the 2nd Tank Corps and 2nd Guards Tank Corps) and artillery for the Voronezh Front's further actions, which was to split Hoth's grouping and reach the Oboian' highway. The 5th Guards Tank Army and 5th Guards Army were to launch the main attack against the enemy's most active and combat-capable formation, the II SS Panzer Corps. If this scheme was crowned with success, it would sharply alter the operational situation and tip it in our favor. However, by the evening of 11 July, the operational picture had changed dramatically: some of the 5th Guards Army's divisions had already been committed into the fighting, while the 5th Guards Tank Army's designated line of deployment was now now held by the enemy, so all the preparations made by the supporting artillery units (the selection of firing positions, the stockpiling of ammunition near the guns, and the targeted areas contained in the firing plan) went down the drain.

A.S. Zhadov, the commander of the 5th Guards Army, recalled:

> Just several hours of daylight and a short summer night remained to organize the counterattack. Over this time much had to be done: decisions made, assignments issued to the troops, the necessary regrouping of the units conducted, and the army's and attached artillery allocated and placed. In the evening, mortar and howitzer artillery brigades with an extremely

11 TsAMO RF, F. 203, Op. 2777, D. 86, L. 273.

> limited amount of ammunition had arrived to reinforce the army. The army had no tanks at all.[12]

The tankers of the 5th Guards Tank Army were in no better situation. Rotmistrov had been given a very difficult assignment: with a head-on attack against the *Leibstandarte Adolf Hitler* and *Das Reich* divisions, to split the SS Panzer Corps into several pieces and to penetrate 30 kilometers into its rear, not the previously proposed 15-16 kilometers. In the process it was anticipated that the third SS division – *Totenkopf* – would be trapped between the flanks of the Guards armies.

N.F. Vatutin was staking his hopes on the tanks. He had managed to concentrate an unprecedented density of armor per kilometer of front on the axis of the main attack. At 1700 on 11 July, Rotmistrov had under his operational control 931 tanks, 42 SU-76 and SU-122, as well as 12 SU-152, including 581 T-34 (62.4%) and 314 T-70 (33.7%). Of this total of 985 tanks and self-propelled guns, there were 840 (797 tanks and 43 self-propelled guns) deployed in formation in the area of assembly of the main forces east of Prokhorovka; the rest were either being repaired or en route. By dawn on 12 July several more combat machines arrived, while others, especially self-propelled guns, developed mechanical problems, leaving the 5th Guards Tank Army with a total of 808 operational tanks and 32 SU-76 and SU-122 (for more detail, see Table 3).

The 18th and 29th Tank Corps, under the command of Generals B.S. Bakharov and I.F. Kirichenko respectively, were to lead the main attack. That morning prior to the attack, both of these corps had a combined 368 tanks and 20 self-propelled guns in formation. Initially, the density of armor per kilometer of front was supposed to reach almost 56 combat vehicles. In reality, the Soviet side was able to achieve even more – 60 tanks per kilometer of front, not including the self-propelled guns. Thus, the hopes of the Soviet command to rupture the SS Panzer Corps even in those extremely complex conditions seemed fully justified. If you also consider that more than 200 tanks of the second echelon (the 5th Mechanized Corps) and infantry were subsequently to enter the fighting, then a penetration of 30 kilometers seemed to be a fully realizable task, albeit with difficulty.

However, such important factors as the technical capabilities of the Soviet tanks and the terrain conditions hadn't been considered. Thus, of the 177 tanks and self-propelled guns located in the 18th Tank Corps on 5 July 1943, the light T-70 tank comprised 35.3%, while the rest were T-34 and Mk IV Churchill tanks.[13] The 29th Tank Corps on 9 July 1943 had a greater proportion of T-34 tanks in its complement, 38.8%.[14] The T-70 was a light tank that was not capable of fighting with a single German tank on an equal footing, nor could it stand up to the main German anti-tank guns.

Given the mission of a frontal attack, P.A. Rotmistrov recognized the high amount of risk this entailed for his army. Thus he assigned four tank brigades to the first echelon, in which the T-70 comprised only 30% of the total armor. At the same time, the brigade commanders in the first echelon each yielded a T-70 tank battalion to the second echelon, and received a T-34 tank battalion in return. In order to augment the firepower of the first-echelon tank brigades of the 29th Tank Corps, one self-propelled artillery regiment was attached to each. Thus, when planning the army's combat formation, the army commander did everything that was within his power to strengthen the tank corps that comprised the spearhead of the counterattack.

The SS Panzer Corps faced the task of withstanding the powerful blow of the Voronezh Front's counterattack grouping, delivered simultaneously by the formations of three Soviet armies. What

12 A.S. Zhadov, *Chetyre goda voiny* [*Four years of war*] (Moscow: Voenizdat, 1978), p. 91.
13 TsAMO RF, F. 18 tk, Op. 1, D. 93, L. 122.
14 TsAMO RF, F. 29 tk, Op. 1, D. 36, L. 28.

Table 3 The availability of tanks and self-propelled guns in the units and formations of the 5th Guards Tank Army on 11 July 1943

Units and Formations	T – 34			T – 70			Mk – IV							Total tanks and self-propelled guns	Armored cars		
															M3A-1	BA-64	M-2
	Operable	En route	Under repair	Operable	En route	Under repair	Operable	En route	Under repair	KV-1	SU-76	SU-122	SU-152		Operable/ Under repair	Operable/ Under repair	Operable
1st Gds Sep. MC Rgt. (by 1500 11.07. 1943)	5	2	2	–	–	–	–	–	–	–	–	–	–	10	12/1	2	5
53 Gds Sep. Tank Rgt. (by 1500 11.07.1943)	39	3	–	1	–	–	–	–	–	–	–	–	–	43	–	–	–
18th Tank Corps (by 1700 on 11 July 1943)*	63	26	5	58	5		18	2	1	–	–	–	–	183	–	31	–
Corps command (on 5.07.1943)	5	–	–	–	–	–	–	–	–	–	–	–	–	–	–	–	–
419th Sep. Signals Btn. (on 5.07. 1943)	2	–	–	–	–	–	–	–	–	–	–		–	–	–	10	–
110th Tank Brigade	22	–	2	21	–	–	–	–	–	–	–	–	–	45	–	3 (BA–20)	–
170th Tank Brigade	22	–	–	17	–	–	–	–	–	–	–	–	–	39	–	–	–
181st Tank Brigade	24	–	–	20	–	–	–	–	–	–	–	–	–	44	–	3	–
36 Gds. Sep. Heavy Tank Rgt.	–	–	–		–	–	18	2	–	–	–	–	–		–	3	–
29th Tank Corps (by 1600 on 11 July 1943)**	123	8	7	81	4	4	–	–	–	2	(10)	(11)	(12)	229(33)	(2 SU en route, in repair shop)		56/2
363rd Sep. Signals Btn. (on 9 .07.1943 г.)	3	–	–	–	–	–	–	–	–	–	–	–	–	–	–	10	–
38th Sep. Armored Car Btn.	–	–	–	7	–	–	–	–	–	–	–	–	–	–	12 (BA–10)	10	–
25th Tank Brigade***	3[illegible]	–	1	36	–	3	–	–	–	1	–	–	–	73	–	3	–
31st Tank Brigade	29	–	3	38	–	1	–	–	–	–	–	–	–	71	–	3	
32nd Tank Brigade	63	–	1	–	–	–	–	–	–	–	–	–	–	64	–	3	–
1446th SPA Rgt.	–	–	–	–	–	–	–	–	–	–	10	11	–	(21)	–	–	–
1529th SPA Rgt. (by 1800 on 10.07. 1943 г)	–	–	–	–	–	–	–	–	–	1	–	–	(11)	(12)			(1 SU under repair)
5th Gds. Mech. Corps (by 1700 11.07.1943 г.) ля 1943 года)****	120	43	1	56	4	1	–	–	–	–	(10)	(11)	–	225(21)	–	–	–
10 Gds. Mech. Brigade (by 0200 12.07. 1943 г.)	30	–	–	14	–	–	–	–	–	–	–	–	–	44	–	–	–
11 Gds. Mech. Brigade	16	–	–	15	–	–	–	–	–	–	–	–	–	31	9	8	–
12 Gds. Mech. Brigade	20	–	–	15	–	–	–	–	–	–	–	–	–	35	–	–	–
24 Gds. Tank Brigade	48	13	–	–	–	–	–	–	–	–	–	–	–	61	–	–	–
1447 SPA Rgt.	–	–	–	–	–	–	–	–	–	–	(4)	(7)	–	(21)	(10 SU en route, under repair)		

Units and Formations	T – 34			T – 70			Mk – IV							Total tanks and self-propelled guns	Armored cars		
															M3A-1	BA-64	M-2
	Operable	En route	Under repair	Operable	En route	Under repair	Operable	En route	Under repair	KV-1	SU-76	SU-122	SU-152		Operable/ Under repair	Operable/ Under repair	Operable
12 Sep. Armored Car Btn. (10.07.1943) r.)1943r._r.)	–	–	–	11	–	–	–	–	–	–	–	–	–	11			
2 Guards Tank Corps	86	–	–	52	–	–	3	–	–	–	–	–	–	141	–	–	–
4 Gds Tank Brigade	28	–	–	19	–	–	–	–	–	–	–	–	–	47	–	–	–
25 Gds Tank Brigade	28	–	–	19	–	–	–	–	–	–	–	–	–	47	–	–	–
26 Gds Tank Brigade (by 0600 12 .07. 1943)	30	–	–	14	–	–	–	–	–	–	–	–	–	44	–	–	–
47 Gds. Heavy Tank Rgt. ттпп	–	–	–	–	–	–	3	–	–	–	–	–	–	3	–	–	–
2 Tank Corps (at 1700 11 July 1943)	35	–	7	46	–	2	3	–	7	–	–	–	–	100	–	–	–
15 Gds Sep. Heavy Tank Rgt. (12 .07.1943)	–	–	–	–	–	–	3	–	7	–	–	–	–	10	–	–	–
26 Tank Brigade (at 0700 on 12 .07. 1943)	6	–	9	8	–	7	–	–	–	–	–	–	–	30	–	–	–
99 Tank Brigade (at 0700 on 12 .07. 1943)	10	–	4	10	–	–	–	–	–	–	–	–	–	24	–	–	–
169 Tank Brigade (at 0700 on 12.07. 1943)	14	–	–	4	–	–	–	–	–	–	–	–	–	18	–	–	–
894 Sep. Signals Btn. (on 10 .07. 1943)	4	–	–	–	–	–	–	–	–	–	–	–	–	4	-		
12 Sep. Armored Car Btn. (10.07.1943) r.)1943r._r.)	–	–	–	11	–	–	–	–	–	–	–	–	–	11			
Total for the 5th Guards Tank Army	477/ 580	82	22	294/ 269	13	7/11	24	2	8/7	2	(20)/ (14)	(22)	(12)/ (11)	931(54)/ 835(54)	21/1,12 (BA-10)	89/2,3 BA-20)	5

Notes: The figures for the brigades may not add up to the total for the corps due to tanks and self-propelled guns under repair, as well as the exclusion of tanks located in auxiliary units.
Source: Files for the formations and units found in the TsAMO RF.

* According to the memorandum "On the status of the 5th Guards Tank Army's materiel and supply as of 1700 on 11.07.43", which was signed by the deputy chief of staff Lieutenant Colonel Torgalo, the 18th Tank Corps had 183 tanks, of which 68 T-34 were in formation, 26 were en route and 5 were undergoing repairs; 63 were T-70, with 58 in formation and 5 en route; and 21 Mk-IV Churchills, with 18 in formation and 2 en route and 1 under repair. (TsAMO RF, F. 5 gv. TA, Op. 4948, D. 67, L. 12). In Combat Report No. 36 from the headquarters of the 18th Tank Corps on 11 July 1943 at 1600, the figure for all the tanks in the brigades was 159, including those of the 110th Tank Brigade that were undergoing repair and those of the 36th Guards Separate Heavy Tank Regiment which were still en route. (TsAMO RF, F. 3415, Op. 1, D. 26, L. 8, 8 obr.)

** According to the memorandum "On the status of the 5th Guards Tank Army's materiel and supply as of 1700 on 11.07.43", the 29th Tank Corps had 120 T-34, 81 T-70, 12 SU-122and 8 SU-76 in formation; 8 T-34, 4 T-70 and 1 SU-76 still en route, and 2 T-34 undergoing repairs. (TsAMO RF, F. 5 gv. TA, Op. 4948, D. 67, L. 12). In Combat Report No. 73 from the headquarters of the 29th Tank Corps at 1600, data for the tank brigades and the total number of all the tank of all marks equipping the tank corps were given. In both documents, it is indicated that the corps had a total of 81 T-70. However, it is impossible to establish the precise number of T-70 tanks, since the combat report gives a total number of 81 tanks, but at the same time shows 74 in formation and 4 undergoing repairs. It is unknown where the other 3 T-70 tanks were. Meanwhile the 5th Guards Tank Army's information shows 81 T-70 in formation, none undergoing repair, and 4 still en route. The table uses the figure "81" for the total number of tanks and self-propelled guns in the 29th Tank Corps.

*** The 29th Tank Corps' 25th Tank Brigade also had one captured 38 (t) Czech-manufactured tank. (TsAMO RF, F. 29 tk, Op. 1, D. 7, L. 101.

Note also that according to Operational Summary No. 110 from the headquarters of the 5th Guards Mechanized Corps at 0200 on 12 July 1943, by morning it expected the arrival of another 2 T-34, 4 T-70 and 4 SU-76 from the march. (TsAMO RF, F. 5 gv. TA, Op. 4948, D. 75, L. 10a.

did its three panzer grenadierdivisions have available at this moment? On the basis of reports from its command, N. Zetterling and A. Franksen have established the number of serviceable combat machines in their panzer regiments at 1935 on 11 July, which was just 12 hours before the start of the famous tank clash. Unquestionably, over the night the repair services managed to return a certain number of additional combat machines to service, but how many is still unknown. Thus, when laying out the course of events of the fighting, I will adhere to the data of the Western scholars.

Of the three mobile formations of Army Group South after a week of the offensive, the II SS Panzer Corps was the most combat-capable. On 11 July it had 34,118 men on its combat rosters, including 11,257 in the *Leibstandarte Adolf Hitler*, 9, 443 in *Das Reich*, 9,203 in *Totenkopf*, and another 4,215 in the corps-level units.[15] Altogether, the corps had 294 armored fighting vehicles in formation, including 236 tanks and 58 assault guns. The *Leibstandarte Adolf Hitler* had the fewest number of combat machines – 67 tanks (including 7 commander's tanks) and 10 assault guns. It was positioned in the center of the SS Panzer Corps' combat formation, and by irony of fate, it was the one that had to take on the main attack by two tank corps of the 5th Guards Tank Army and two rifle divisions of the 5th Guards Army. The right-flank *Das Reich* stood in second place in the number of available armor fighting vehicles – 68 tanks and 27 assault guns. It was to join combat with tank brigades of the 2nd Guards Tank Corps and rifle divisions of the 69th Army. Then finally, *Totenkopf* possessed the most operational combat machines – 101 tanks and 21 assault guns – which were directed to attack the center of the 5th Guards Army in the bend of the Psel River.

In terms of quality of the combat equipment, Wisch's *Leibstandarte Adolf Hitler* Division stood out; the armored fist of its panzer regiment consisted of Pz IV tanks with the long-barreled 75mm gun and Tiger tanks – 47 and 4 respectively. Its assault gun battalion had taken heavy losses and only 10 assault guns remained operational in it. In the *Totenkopf* division, more than 54 (53%) of the total number of tanks consisted of Pz III tanks, and there were only 30 Pz IV, of which only 26 had the long-barreled gun. The 10 Tiger tanks and 27 assault guns in service perceptibly enhanced the panzer regiment's combat possibilities. The *Das Reich* division's situation with armor was patchwork. As in the case of the SS *Totenkopf*, its tank park consisted of 34 Pz III and noticeably fewer Pz IV, just 18, while only 1 Tiger remained operational in its heavy panzer company. In addition to the authorized German tanks, the division still had 8 captured T-34 tanks and 27 assault guns. (The amount of the II SS Panzer Corps' armor in formation on the evening of 11 July is shown in Table 4).

One of the most discussed topics in the history of the Prokhorovka clash is whether or not the Germans knew about the preparation of such a large-scale counterstroke by the Soviet side. Those, who believe this operation was inarguably successful, refer to the memoirs of the 5th Guards Tank Army's commander, in which he clearly wrote that the operation was a surprise to the enemy. According to his view, the Germans were stunned in the first few minutes of the battle. In the opinion of P.A. Rotmistrov, this was one of the factors that helped our troops. However, there are doubts in the correctness of such a point of view, although it shouldn't be fully rejected.

When conducting any offensive operation, the attacking side gives an important place to intelligence. Without this, it is impossible to reveal the enemy's intentions, and that means it isn't possible to plan the attacking forces' further actions properly. On its part the intelligence service pays increased attention to the enemy's tank and mechanized columns, moving in the direction of the front, because of the high maneuverability and firepower of these forces.

The command of the Fourth Panzer Army and of its formations were well-aware of the fact that Soviet armored forces on the defense usually employed one of two types of combat actions: short,

15 NARA, T. 354, R. 606, F. 162, 167, 169 and 171.

Table 4 Operational tanks in the Fourth Panzer Army's II SS Panzer Corps and Army Detachment Kempf's III Panzer Corps on the evening of 11 July or morning of 12 July 1943[a]

Division	Pz II	Pz III 50/L42b	Pz III 50/L60	Pz III 75-mm	Pz IV L24	Pz IV L43, L48	Pz VI Tiger	T-34	BfWg	Total tanks	StuG	Total tanks and self-propelled guns
II SS Panzer Corps												
"Leibstandarte Adolf Hitler" (1835 on 11 July)	4	–	5	–	–	47	4	–	10	**70**	10	**80**
"Das Reich" (1835 on 11 July)	–	–	34	–	–	18	1	8	7	**68**	27	**95**
"Totenkopf" (1830 on 11 July)	–	–	54[c]	–	4	26	10	–	7	**101**	21	**122**
Total	**4**	**–**	**93**	**–**	**4**	**91**	**15**	**8**	**24**	**239**	**58**	**297**
III Panzer Corps												
6th Panzer (morning of 11 July)	2	2	11	?	–	6	–	–	2	**23(?)**	–	**23(?)**
7th Panzer (morning of 12 July)	–	–	24	2	1	9	–	–	3	**39**	–	**39**
19th Panzer (morning of 12 July)	–	–	7	4	–	3	–	–	1	**15**	–	**15**
503rd Heavy Panzer Btn. (morning of 11 July)	–	–	–	–	–	–	23	–	–	**23**	–	**23**
228th StuG Battalion	–	–	–	–	–	–	–	–	–	**–**	19	**19**
Total	**2**	**2**	**42**	**6(?)**	**1**	**18**	**23**	**–**	**6**	**100**	**19**	**119**

Notes

a Zetterling and Franksen, *Kursk 1943: A statistical analysis*, Tables A.6.4 – A.6.10.

b Caliber of the tank gun in millimeters/length of the barrel in calibers.

c In Zetterling and Franksen's book, there is a mistake; according to the reports of the SS Panzer Grenadier Division Totenkopf it had 54 Pz III 50/L60, but had no Pz III 50/L42 tanks.w sharp counterattacks with 20-40 machines and infantry support, or massive armored counter-strokes, which employed several hundred tanks and self-propelled guns simultaneously. The latter was the most dangerous, especially when an army was enmeshed in a system of strong Russian defensive lines, and when its flanks were quite exposed. Thus from the first days of "Citadel", the ground and air reconnaissance diligently searched for any sign of the movement of large tank and mechanized formations in the direction of the front from the Soviet rear area.

Judging from the available documents, this work yielded its fruits. Although only in general outlines, the command of Army Group South knew from which directions large Soviet mobile formations were being brought up and to which areas they were moving. Based on analysis of the operational situation and the nature of the terrain, it was not difficult to determine the possible places of their use in the army's sector. Until recently, the Soviet side had attempted more than once to launch attacks with strong tank groupings, primarily against the flanks of the II SS Panzer Corps. Because of this, the Fourth Panzer Army and its corps were using reconnaissance means to scan the areas east and southeast of Prokhorovka particularly carefully, and therefore the approach march of the 5th Guards Tank Army and 5th Guards Army was not a surprise for the army and corps commands. Before the end of day 12 July, the numerical designations of the armies and their formations weren't known to the Germans, or were their total strength. However, the Germans knew 2-3 fresh tank corps had assembled east of Prokhorovka. It was simply impossible for the German aerial reconnaissance flights not to notice the continuous columns of equipment, which extended for many kilometers and were moving in daylight hours toward Prokhorovka. It is impossible as well to believe that the enemy's intelligence didn't know that the formations of the 5th Guards Tank Army – the 18th Tank Corps and 5th Guards Mechanized Corps – had taken up a position on 9 July in the second echelon at Prokhorovka, and had then been replaced.

Let's turn to the documents. Thus, at 2030 on 9 July, the headquarters of the II SS Panzer Corps received information from the headquarters of the Fouth Panzer Army: "Fresh motorized formations are on the march to the west from the directions of Novyi and Staryi Oskol."

Just an hour before, P. Hausser himself had signed a combat report to Army Group South, in which he remarked: "According to information from aerial reconnaissance, the continued approach of operational tank and motorized reserves to the Prokhorovka area (railroad) is being observed. A portion of the revealed forces might be sent to counter the advancing right-hand neighbor [Army Detachment Kempf]."[16]

On the next day the II SS Panzer Corps headquarters reported: "Fresh enemy in the bend of the Psel River, presumably units of the 5th Guards Army, which before this had been located in the Ostrogozhsk area ... the enemy is bringing up operational reserves from distant sectors of the front. The appearance of 1-2 tank or motorized corps opposite the corps' attacking group should be expected."[17]

Having information on the assembly of a significant amount of Russian reserves, including tank reserves, in the area, where their appearance had been part of the plan from the beginning, the command of both panzer corps of the Fourth Panzer Army nevertheless didn't believe that the Soviet side was preparing for a major counterattack. Here's the conclusion that was drawn on 10 July on the results of a discussion of this question at a conference held by *Generaloberst* H. Guderian with the Chief of Staff of the XXXXVIII Panzer Corps F. von Mellenthin and the Chief of Staff of the II SS Panzer Corps *SS-Standartenführer* W. Ostendorff:

16 Stadler, *Die Offensive gegen Kursk*, pp. 79, 80.
17 Ibid., p. 92.

> Thus, as a consequence of the exchange of opinions with the chiefs of staff of the XXXXVIII Panzer Corps and the SS Panzer Corps, it became clear that the numerically strong, well-equipped enemy tank units opposite the front of both corps will not be brought together in a single sector in order to launch a powerful tank attack. The enemy attacks primarily with separate groups of 20-30 tanks. Possibly, the reason for this is concealed in the poor composition of the Russian infantry, which according to the words of eyewitnesses, consists of very old and very young conscripts. There are practically no soldiers of average age. Thus, the enemy is compelled to fritter away his tanks in order to strengthen the morale of the infantry.[18]

Judging from available documents, this point of view didn't change and reigned in the leadership of the II SS Panzer Corps even on the evening of 11 July. A report signed by the operations chief of the II SS Panzer Corps notes:

> General impression: the enemy's reinforcement in the Prokhorovka area is possible. The 10th Tank Corps presumably located in the bend of the Psel River is represented only by the 11th Motorized Rifle Brigade, since the other three tank brigades are situated in an area west of the Belgorod – Kursk road. Intensive traffic in the Oboian' area indicates the enemy's intention to stop the offensive of the left-hand neighbor [XXXXVIII Panzer Corps] in the area south of Oboian'. There is no sign of an attack against the corps' left flank.[19]

The presence of brigades of a fresh tank formation, the 10th Tank Corps, simultaneously in two areas was making the enemy anxious, and thus the reconnaissance of both German formations kept a close watch over their locations, trying to determine the Russians' intention regarding its use. In this situation, it is fair to assume that if the adversary by 11 July had concrete information on the presence of fresh tank or mechanized Soviet forces, located in the Prokhorovka area (for example, the 5th Guards Tank Army), or information on the enemy's intentions to launch a counterstroke, then the headquarters of the II SS Panzer Corps would not have neglected to point this out, at the very least on the evening of 11 July. However, there is no mention of this in the reports; there is only speculation and assumptions.

Likely, the point of view that dominated at the conference on 10 July and on subsequent days about the Soviet side's lack of readiness for attacks with large tank formations rested also on the experience of the previous days. After all, on 9 July there were was a grouping of more than 300 Soviet tanks opposite the II SS Panzer Corps in the Vasil'evka – Belenikhino sector, and the Fourth Panzer Army command was aware of this. However, the Voronezh Front command made no effort to launch an attack with this grouping as a unified armored wedge, although it could have done so. Instead, it started to split it up and use the pieces to strengthen the weakened sectors opposite the Fourth Panzer Army's attacking panzer wedges.

A number of recollections of German veterans of the Battle of Kursk, which have been published in the West, give evidence that the command of the SS divisions at the tactical level also didn't expect a powerful attack out of the Prokhorovka area. Prisoners captured by our scouts on 12 July also confirmed this. Thus, *Sturmann* (*Gefreitor*) K. Wucherpfennig of 6./II Battalion, Panzergrenadier Regiment 2 of the *Leibstandarte Adolf Hitler*, who was located in a combat outpost in the "Oktiabr'skii" State Farm area on the axis of the 5th Guards Tank Army's main attack on the night of 11-12 July and who was captured in the morning by soldiers of the 42nd Guards Rifle Division's 136th Guards Rifle Regiment, stated: "The company was assigned to combat security

18 NARA, T. 314, R. 1170. Kriegstagebuch 48 Pz Kps. 10.7.43, p. 48.
19 Stadler, *Die Offensive gegen Kursk*, p. 99.

and reconnaissance. It was positioned in front of our battalion. The battalion had the task to take the Russians' forward line on 12 July … We knew nothing about the Russian counteroffensive."[20] A former panzer company commander with II Panzer Battalion, SS 1st Panzer Regiment, SS 1st Panzergrenadier Division *Leibstandarte Adolf Hitler* R. Ribbentrop says just about the same thing in his memoirs.

Relying on this information, it is possible today to agree with P.A. Rotmistrov's assertion that the intention of the Soviet command to launch a counterstroke against the Fourth Panzer Army's right flank on 12 July wasn't fully detected by the enemy. At the same time, it must be considered that both H. Hoth and P. Hausser were professionals, and pragmatists with great military experience. Thus after the fact that *Leibstandarte Adolf Hitler* had become extended into a bottleneck southwest of Prokhorovka, but was unable to take the station, the SS corps commander had to foresee the possibility of a counterattack. At a conference in Luchki on 11 July with the participation of Hausser, *SS-Brigadenführer* T. Wisch had directly spoke up about the looming danger on the flanks of his division and proposed to halt the offensive until the neighboring divisions came up on either side of him. At this moment in fact, the intelligence information reached Hausser about the assembly of a large mobile grouping of Russians at Prokhorovka. After an exchange of opinions with W. Ostendorff, he agreed with the suggestion by the SS panzer division commander and issued the following order:

> The reinforced 1. Panzergrenadier-Regiment with the Panzerjäger *abteilung* is to set out at 04.50 hours [Berlin time] and to capture the Swch. Stalinsk and Jamki [Iamki]. It is to establish a positon adjacent to the I.2 [Panzergrenadier Regiment] at the road next to Hill 252.2.
>
> The reinforced 2.Panzergrenadier-Regiment, the Panzergruppe, and the reinforced *Aufklärungsabteilung* [reconnaissance battalion] are to stand ready to move in conjunction with elements of the *T*-Division [*Totenkopf*] as soon as that Division has neutralized the enemy's attacks on our flank along the Pssel [Psel] and to capture Prochorowka [Prokhorovka] and Hill 252.4.
>
> The *Artillerie-Regiment LAH* [*Leibstandarte Adolf Hitler*] is to send an Artillerie liaison Kommando to *T*-Division in order to support the attack by that Division on Hill 226.6.[21]

The adoption of a defensive posture by the main forces of the SS Panzergrenadier Division *Leibstandarte Adolf Hitler* and above cited German intelligence information for 10 and 11 July about the approach of substantial Soviet forces to Prokhorovka allowed a number of scholars to assert that the German command had nevertheless figured out the plan of the Voronezh Front command. In reality, P. Hausser only assumed that a counterattack might be in the offing on the next day. The only thing that he couldn't surmise was the fact that such a significant amount of armor would be rolling toward his corps. Thus, in order to keep the situation under control, including if the Russians would launch an attack with tanks, P. Hausser adopted a number of far-sighted steps, and the SS divisions would accurately and timely carry out the issued orders.

Wisch's SS troops didn't prepare a special line of defense in the sector where Rotmistrov's army would go on the offensive, but one can say it instead created a standard defense on a 6.5 kilometer sector of the front with the use of all of the firing means available to the division. Nevertheless, the command of *Leibstandarte Adolf Hitler* had to reckon with the fact that the division had already taken serious losses and that a counterattack in this sector by tanks was fully possible. Thus he moved up all of his artillery and anti-tank guns to the forward edge, and first of all, its main

20 TsAMO RF, F. 42.gv.sd, Op. 1, D. 79, L. 10.

21 Rudolf Lehmann, *The Leibstandarte III* (Winnipeg, Manitoba: J.J. Fedorowicz Publishing, 1990), p.

anti-tank means: the anti-tank battalion, the assault gun battalion, the panzer regiment with a company of Tigers, and the artillery regiment.

Hoth's idea for 12 July was just as ambitious: to break through at Prokhorovka toward Oboian' and with meeting attacks by the II SS Panzer Corps and the III Panzer Corps to encircle the 69th Army, as a result of which a breach should be created, into which the reserve XXIV Panzer Corps, which was assembled at Belgorod, could be introduced. In fact, his army got the jump on the Soviet side. The counterattack hadn't yet gotten underway, when at dawn on 12 July there arose the need to divert a considerable amount of strength from the axis of the 5th Guards Tank Army's main attack in order to block a breakthrough of the 69th Army's defense south of Prokhorovka by the III Panzer Corps: 161 tanks (almost a fifth of the tank army's total strength), 11 self-propelled guns, 36 armored cars, two artillery regiments and two anti-tank batteries.[22] This had a substantial effect on the 5th Guards Tank Army's subsequent counterattack. The first echelon had been weakened, and the second echelon had been reduced by half. In reserve, P. Rotmistrov was left with just two brigades with a total strength of 92 tanks.

Despite this, the Front command decided not to change the plan. At 0830 at a signal of a salvo of "Katiusha" rockets, the Guardsmen move out on the attack. The spearhead of the 5th Guards Tank Army struck a 6-kilometer sector between the hamlet of Storozhevoe and the Psel River, 1.5 kilometers southwest of Prokhorovka. The 18th and 29th Tank Corps in conjunction with the 42nd Guards Rifle and 9th Guards Airborne Divisions launched the attack. It was the resulting battle fought by these two corps against the II SS Panzer Corps' troops that subsequently became known as the meeting tank battle.

The authors of books about those events can rarely refrain from touching upon the culminating moment – the attacks by Bakharov's and Kirichenko's tank brigades toward the "Oktiabr'skii" State Farm and Hill 252.2. Sometimes in the descriptions of the start of the battle it is maintained that a steel avalanche of several hundred Soviet combat machines were moving simultaneously from Prokhorovka toward the SS men, while to meet it the enemy moved out an equally large number of his own tanks. As a result, over several minutes the combat turned into some sort of roaring, gigantic tangle of machines, fire and human bodies. The memoirs of the 5th Guards Tank Army's veterans, edited in the "needed direction", added its piece to this epic picture.

Wrote P.A. Rotmistrov:

> The intensity of the battle grew with incredible fury and force. Because of the fire, smoke and dust it became increasingly difficult to make out where our own were and where the other sides' ... Tanks were circling as if caught by a giant whirlpool. The T-34 crews, maneuvering, turning, were firing at Tigers and Panthers, but they themselves, coming under the direct fire of the enemy heavy tanks and self-propelled guns, were stopping, burning and dying.[23]

Inarguably, for a common man such a picture creates the mental image of an enormous field, more than a thousand tanks, tons of scorched, twisted metal and a sea of fire. Professionals regard such tales skeptically.

In reality, no sort of avalanche of tanks moved out from Prokhorovka on the morning of 12 July, and this proved ruinous for the Soviet side. If the 368 armored fighting vehicles of Kirichenko's and Bakharov's tank corps had really moved out in two echelons simultaneously toward the positions of Hausser's forces, then undoubtedly they would have crushed them. However, an "armored

22 V.N. Zamulin, *Prokhorovka: Neizvestnye podrobnosti ob izvestnom srazhenii* [*Prokhorovka: Unknown details about the famous battle*] (Moscow: Veche, 2013), p. 238.

23 P.A. Rotmistrov, *Stal'naia gvardia* [*Steel Guard*] (Moscow: Voenizdat, 1984), p. 187.

steamroller" didn't gather. In the ravine at the brick factory there were only somewhere around 80 armored vehicles. It was impossible to deploy a larger number of tanks here. They moved into jumping-off positions along a road, which became constricted at the brick factory and passed over the dam of a small pond. Thus, the tanks could only move in single file. However, even after having passed this place, the brigades of the 29th Tank Corps were unable to deploy into a battle line and accelerate. The places trafficable by tanks in front of the 5th Guards Army's 9th Guards Airborne Division that was defending here had been mined. There hadn't been time that morning to lift all the mines, and only narrow passages were available for the tanks to pass through them. The neighboring 18th Tank Corps was in a similar situation; its tanks had to negotiate deep balkas before the attack.

It is always important to apply maximum force to the first attack; thus it was exceptionally important at the start of the attack to achieve the simultaneous and uninterrupted introduction into combat of both the battalions and the brigades, after which with fire and the significant number of armored fighting vehicles engaged to crush the antagonist's forward positions. Here, the difficult terrain led to an increase in the interval between the introduction into combat of the brigades of the first and second echelon. The tank battalions did not move in a continuous, broad stream, like many authors maintain, but in separate pulses, the intervals between which varied from 30 minutes to an hour or more. This gave the SS troops the possibility to destroy each one in turn, as if the Soviet tanks were approaching on a conveyor belt. Subsequently analyzing the conditions, under which his tank corps went on the counterattack on 12 July, Major General B.S Bakharov[24] wrote, "The fighting of 12-14 July … once again demonstrated that the selection of good ground for tanks in the direction of attack is one of the most important questions that affects the outcome of the attack in a decisive manner."[25]

24 Boris Sergeevich Bakharov (1902-1944), Major General of Tank Troops (1942). In the Red Army from 1919. A veteran of the Russian Civil War. On 11 May 1941, he was appointed commander of the 50th Tank Division of Khar'kov Military District's 25th Mechanized Corps. With the start of the Great Patriotic War, Bakharov's division took part in the fighting on the Western, Central and Briansk Fronts. In September 1941, the division was reformed into the 150th Tank Brigade. In July 1942, he was appointed first as the chief of staff, and then on 20 July, as the commander of the 17th Tank Corps of Voronezh Front's 60th Army. On 7 September 1942, he became the commander of the 18th Tank Corps, which he would command until his tragic death. In March 1943, the tank corps was withdrawn into the *Stavka* reserve (in the Steppe Military District), where it remained until the start of the Battle of Kursk. On 6 July 1943, Bakharov's tank corps was transferred to the 5th Guards Tank Army, and having completed a 200-kilometer march, on the evening of 9 July it was assembled on the Voronezh Front, 25 kilometers east of Prokhorovka Station. On 12 July 1943, Bakharov's troops launch an attack along the Psel River (at the boundary between the SS Panzergrenadier Division *Leibstandarte "Adolf Hitler"* and the SS Panzergrenadier Division *Totenkopf*) and made a 5-kilometer advance, thereby creating a threat to *Totenkopf*'s bridges across the river and the left flank of the *Leibstandarte "Adolf Hitler"*, but it fell into semi-encirclement. B.S. Bakharov was forced to halt a further attack and issued an order to fortify the ground gained. However, the 5th Guards Tank Army command assessed this as passivity when carrying out his orders. A commission of the State Defense Committee ("Malenkov's Commision"), which arrived at the Voronezh Front in order to investigate the reasons for the 5th Guards Tank Army's heavy losses at Prokhorovka, supported this point of view, even though the corps commander's decision had been dictated by objective circumstances. On 25 July 1943 Major General Bakharov was removed from his post for "inability to cope with his command duties" and was appointed to a lower post – deputy commander of the Central Front's 9th Tank Corps. In essence, the responsibility for the failure of the counterattack on 7 July 1943 was placed on his shoulders, since only he was dismissed from his post after the Prokhorovka clash. Subsequent events showed that this decision was unjust. Already on 9 September 1943, he assumed command of the 9th Tank Corps, and on 15 September 1943 for his successful leadership of the corps, the 60th Army command awarded him the Order of the Red Banner. He was killed in action on 16 July 1944 in the area of Bobruisk during Operation Bagration.

25 TsAMO RF, F. 18tk, Op. 1, D. 27, L. 123.

At a forward observation post of the Voronezh Front in July 1943. Standing from right to left is the chief of staff Lieutenant General S.P. Ivanov, the Front Commander-in-Chief General of the Army N.F. Vatutin and an unidentified man; seated is Military Council member Lieutenant General N.S. Khrushchev (Photograph by P.G. Gapochka, RGAKFD)

The movement of strategic reserves toward the Voronezh Front; Belgorod axis, July 1943 (RGAKFD)

The commander of the 5th Guards Army Lieutenant General A.S. Zhadov (on the left) listens to a report on how the march is going; Voronezh Front, July 1943 (The family archive of V.V. Zhdanov and E.K. Simonova)

Southwest of Prokhorovka, tanks of the 5th Guards Tank Army's 29th Tank Corps wait for the signal to attack; 12 July 1943 (RGAKFD)

A ZIS-3 76-mm anti-tank gun fires a round at enemy tanks in the area of Prokhorovka Station, July 1943 (RGAKFD)

The commander of the 5th Guards Tank Army Lieutenant General P.A. Rotmistrov (in the center) dictates an order to a liaison officer (on the right). To the left is Voronezh Front Military Council member Lieutenant General N.S. Khrushchev; 12 July 1943 (author's personal archive)

A battery of a separate destroyer anti-tank artillery battalion of one of Voronezh Front's rifle divisions hastens toward the point of breakthrough by enemy tanks, July 1943 (RGAKFD)

Assault guns of Army Detachment Kempf's 7th Panzer Division in the village of Rzhavets (south of Prokhorovka Station), July 1943 (A captured German photograph, RGAKFD)

In the area of the Severskii Donets River, a mortar crew of the 167th Infantry Division placing fire on the positions of the Soviet 69th Army. In the background is a destroyed T-34 tank; July 1943 (A captured German photograph, RGAKFD)

At the observation post of the Voronezh Front's 69th Rifle Corps. From left to right: army commander Lieutenant General V.D. Kriuchenkin, the commander of the 35th Guards Rifle Corps Lieutenant General S.G. Goriachev and the deputy commander of the Voronezh Front General of the Army I.P. Apanasenko; area of the village of Rzhavets, 15 July 1943 (RGAKFD)

The commander of the 48th Rifle Corps of Voronezh Front's 69th Army Major General Z.Z. Rogoznyi; a 1943 photograph (TsAMO RF)

A group of submachine gunners of the 2nd Tank Corps fighting in the area of the Storozhevoe Woods (southwest of Prokorovka); July 1943 (author's personal archive)

Panzer grenadiers of the 6th Panzer Grenadier Division under the command of *Unter-offizier* H. Scharsch of the III Panzer Corps' 7th Panzer Division, who surrendered to troops of the 5th Guards Tank Army in the vicinity of Bol'shie Pod'iarugi on 14 July 1943. A Luftwaffe man leans in from the left. At the moment, they seem to be happy and relieved that their war is over.

The military funeral ceremony for dead soldiers and officers of the Voronezh Front, July 1943 (Author's personal archive)

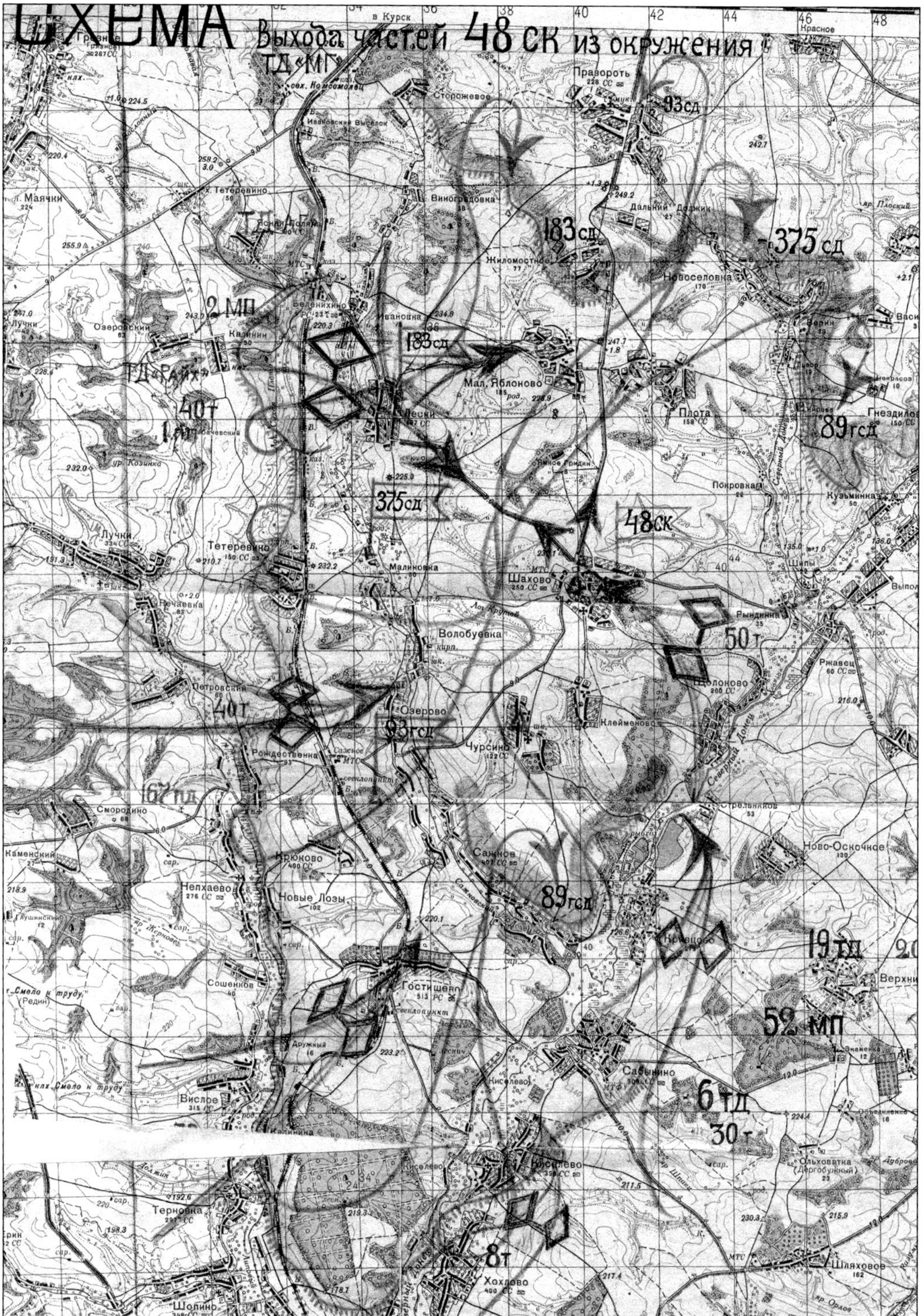

A map drawn by the Operations Department of the 48th Rifle Corps of Voronezh Front's 69th Army depicting the withdrawal of its divisions from encirclement in the interfluvial area of the Donets (south of Prokhorovka Station) on the night of 14/15 July 1943 (Author's personal archive)

In addition to the unsuccessful selection of the ground for the attack, the Front command also underestimated the strength of the enemy's anti-tank defenses in this sector. It didn't expect that the enemy could create a tenacious defense over one short summer night. When the SS troops managed to do this, and they nevertheless stopped an attack made by several hundred armored vehicles, the Front command didn't want to believe that it had miscalculated. From this there appeared a version of events, primarily in P.A. Rotmistrov's books, about the arrival of purported significant German tank reserves during the battle;[26] the decisive "repeated tank attacks";[27] and the multiple panzer "battering rams".[28]

The most intense combat actions unfolded between 0830 and 1500. In the sector of defense of the SS Panzergrenadier Division *Leibstandarte Adolf Hitler*, which extended for 6.5 kilometers, the Germans had up to 305 guns and mortars of all types, or 47 tubes per kilometer of front. At the same time only 26 of the anti-aircraft guns and the 4 Pz II tanks' main guns had a caliber of just 20mm; the rest of the artillery and the main guns of tanks had a caliber that ranged between 50mm and 150mm. The "Oktiabr'skii" State Farm was the first powerful German strong point in the path of the 18th and 29th Tank Corps. The SS troops made extensive use of our own trenches and fieldworks; over the preceding night they had dug in anti-tank artillery guns and self-propelled guns on the slopes of the State Farm and the slopes of Hill 252.2, and had mined separate sectors. In addition, they had set up ambushes with assault guns and self-propelled artillery guns in the fields of the "Stalin Branch" State Farm and on the northwestern fringes of the Storozhevoe woods. Emplaced in these areas, their guns had a field of fire that included Hill 252.2. Because of the absence of time and the bitter fighting, our scouts had been unable to reveal the enemy's system of fire, or to determine the layout of the defenses or the combat strength of the defending units. Thus, when Rotmistrov's tank corps went on the attack early that morning, the blow wasn't made at exposed enemy flanks, as had been conceived by the plan, but head-on against the defense of the SS division, which had efficiently created a strong line that was saturated with anti-tank artillery means.

When introducing major mobile formations into a breakthrough, the forces in advance of them must destroy the enemy's organized resistance, particularly the anti-tank means and artillery positioned on the forward edge. However, the reality with which the Guards tankers collided was something else. Just as the Soviet tanks had closed within direct fire range of the German positions, instantly there were flashes of flame and smoke from the guns of dozens of German tanks and self-propelled guns. The Soviet combat formation, such as it was, was thrown into disarray, the crews began maneuvering, scattering in different directions in order to get behind any fold in the ground to escape out from under the deadly fire. The tankers had to fight not only under a hail of fire, but also adapt psychologically to a positional battle, rather than the expected dash into the depth of the German defenses. A significant amount of the tanks of Colonel A.A. Linev's leading 32nd Tank Brigade were burning in less than an hour. Before noon, the attack by Colonel N.K. Volodin's 25th Tank Brigade (29th Tank Corps) ended just as tragically. Its losses were catastrophic. Over approximately four hours of time, 320 men (44 officers) became casualties, including 140 killed. No less than 55 tanks had been set ablaze or knocked out; in addition to those that had been destroyed by German fire, some had been disabled by mines,[29] and others had broken down due to mechanical problems. All eight self-propelled guns of the two attached

26 Rotmistrov, *Stal'naia gvardiia*, p. 192.

27 Ibid., p. 186.

28 E. Ivanovsky, *Ataku nachinali tankisty* [*Tankers started the attack*] (Moscow: Voenizdat), p. 131.

29 According to information that requires verification, these tanks had blundered into one of our own minefields.

batteries had also been knocked out. In the afternoon, the brigade commander was forced to merge his brigade's remnants into a single tank battalion.

After the second echelon of the 18th and 29th Tank Corps entered the battle, the number of tanks on the axis of the main attack nearly doubled; the enemy gunners and tankers physically no longer had time to fire at all of the approaching Soviet armor. This to a certain extent helped the 181st, 170th and 32nd Tank Brigades to break through to the crest of Hill 252.2 and into the "Oktiabr'skii" State Farm. Now enemy infantry directly joined battle with the Soviet armor, but unable to withstand the onslaught, the SS troops began to retreat. Exploiting a strip of woods along the railroad and the heavy battlefield smoke, 15 T-34 tanks of the 32nd Tank Brigade under the command of Major S.P. Ivanov penetrated 5 kilometers into the depth of the defenses of the SS Panzergrenadier Division *Leibstandarte Adolf Hitler* and took the "Komsomolets" State Farm.

At 1330, the enemy was finally driven from the "Oktiabr'skii" State Farm, which was situated on the boundary between Bakharov's and Kirichenko's tank corps, and began to fall back to the southwest. A distinct success was noted as well on the 29th Tank Corps' left flank. It seemed that the situation was beginning to turn in our favor. However, witnessing the signs of a Soviet breakthrough, T. Wisch summoned the Luftwaffe, and the ensuing airstrikes lasted for more than an hour. By 1430 the SS Panzergrenadier Division *Leibstandarte Adolf Hitler* with Luftwaffe support had managed to stop the advance made by the main forces of Rotmistrov's army. Despite the heroism and self-sacrifice of the Guardsmen, the attack on the direction of the main attack didn't bring the expected result, and there were no reserves left to continue the attack. The neighbor on the right – the 5th Guards Army – was also in a precarious situation. Its troops in the bend of the Psel River had been unable to attack as had been planned. The SS Panzergrenadier Division *Totenkopf* had on the night of 11-12 July managed to cross a significant portion of the panzer regiment to the northern bank of the river. Thus, the Soviet infantry that rose and went on the attack that morning were met by the dense fire of artillery and tanks, and bloody fighting in the positions of the 52nd Guards and 95th Guards Rifle Divisions ensued. No substantial success was achieved on the sectors of the 5th Guards Army's other divisions. Thus already by noon, it had become clear that the plan of the counterstroke, at least near Prokhorovka, had failed.

At 1500, making use of the confusion prompted by the retreat of our infantry and the loss of the bulk of the tanks that had attacked that morning, the SS troops switched to an active defense in the sector of the 5th Guards Army. At 1600, there was a strong airstrike against the combat positions of Zhadov's Guardsmen beyond the Psel River, followed by an artillery barrage. The columns of dust and smoke hadn't had time to disperse, when panzers and assault guns escorted by panzergrenadiers mounted on halftracks went on the attack, as well as up to 200 motorcycles crewed by submachine gunners. The German armor penetrated our positions, but the panzergrenadiers had been cut off and pinned down, and thus the panzers had to retreat. The struggle with the SS troops in the bend of the Psel River was complicated by the lack of tank support and the hastily-built combat positions that had no elaborate system of trenches. Minefields were also almost totally lacking. All this enabled the enemy not only to strike our infantry with fire, but also to crush them under the tracks of the tanks, simultaneously burying the Soviet defenders in their own trenches. Immediately after the conclusion of the Prokhorovka battle, on the evening of 17 July 1943 the 5th Guards Army's headquarters reported that over eight days of fighting, the 95th Guards Rifle Division had only 579 men left that were not among the killed or wounded.[30]

The day of 12 July didn't bring either side its desired result. N.F. Vatutin managed to hold Army Group South's formations within the fortifications of the third defensive belt. All of the Fourth Panzer Army's attempts to break through to operational space and to encircle the 69th Army

30 TsAMO RF, F. 5 gv.A, Op. 4855, D. 20, L. 4.

also had no success. With considerable effort, the Front command had also managed to bring the offensive by Army Detachment Kempf to a halt after it had broken through the 69th Army's defenses on the night of 11-12 July, and to get the situation under control south of Prokhorovka (in the Sholokovo, Rzhavets, Aleksandrovka area). However, it also can't be said that the Soviet side celebrated victory on this day. More accurately, on the contrary 12 July was a most tragic and, in essence, unsuccessful day not only in the Voronezh Front's defensive operation, but also of the Battle of Kursk as a whole. The main assignment – to destroy the enemy grouping that had penetrated into the Front's defenses and to retake the initiative – had failed. The plan of the counterattack that had been worked out by the Soviet command also proved to be unsuccessful, since by the time it started it no longer corresponded to the altered situation, nor were the troops' capabilities commensurate with the stated objectives. The shock formations of both Guards Armies were decimated over several hours, and on certain sectors they were even compelled to abandon the positions they occupied. The SS panzergrenadier divisions, having launched a counterattack that afternoon, pushed ahead up to 4 kilometers, just as on the preceding days. Moreover, all of the divisions of Fourth Panzer Army and Army Detachment Kempf had fully retained their combat capabilities. For example, the II SS Panzer Corps before the start of the counterattack had 294 tanks and assault guns, but by the evening of 13 July through the hard work to return damaged combat machines to service, still had 251 tanks and assault guns[31] (for a detailed looks at the status of the II SS Panzer Corps on 13 July 1943, see Table 5). This was aided by the fact that 13 July didn't see any heavy fighting with the use of significant amounts of armor on both sides, as had been the case the day before.

Table 5 Availability of combat-ready tanks and assault guns in the II SS Panzer Corps on the evening of 13 July 1943

Division	Pz II	Pz III 50/L42	Pz III 50/L60	Pz III 75-mm	Pz IV L-24	Pz IV L24, L48	Pz VI Tiger	T-34	StuG	Bef. Pz.III	Total tanks and self-propelled guns
"Leibstandarte Adolf Hitler"	4	–	5	–	–	31	3	–	20	7	70
"Das Reich"	–	–	43	–	–	20	1	11	24	8	107
"Totenkopf"	–	–	32	–	3	65	–	–	20	5	74
Total for II SS Panzer Corps	4	–	80	–	3	65	4	11	64	20	251

Source: NARA, T. 313, R. 366 (Panzer, Sturmgeschütz- und Paklage stand, 13 July 1943)

The main mistake made by the Soviet command when conducting the counterstroke was the decision to launch a frontal attack with two tank and two rifle corps in the area of Prokhorovka, not against the flanks, but directly into the teeth of an enemy panzergrenadier division that had adopted a hasty defensive posture. Because of this, the enemy inflicted heavy damage to them.

According to incomplete data, the Soviets lost 7,019 soldiers and officers in the two Guards Armies on 12 July. The four tank and mechanized corps, including the detachment of Rotmistrov's army that was operating in the Sholokovo – Rzhavets area south of Prokhorovka, lost 340 tanks and 19 assault guns (194 tanks were destroyed, and 146 were knocked out of action, but could have been repaired and returned to action). For more detail, see Table 6. However, a significant amount

31 Zetterling and Franksen, *Kursk 1943: A statistical analysis*, Tables A 6.4, A6.5 and A 6.6.

of disabled combat machines wound up on territory controlled by the enemy, and the Germans simply blew them up. Thus, the 5th Guards Tank Army was deprived of 53% of its tanks and self-propelled guns that took part in the counterstroke, or 47.2% of those that were in formation at the beginning of this day in all five corps. According to the tables of organization and equipment of 1943, it was possible to equip two complete tank corps with this amount of armor. The main reason for such heavy losses over less than a day was the ignoring of People's Commissar of Defense Order No. 325 from 16 October 1942, which summarized the accumulated experience in the use of armored fighting vehicles.[32] Instead of sending the tank army into an already-cleared breach in the German defenses in order to exploit a success, the army faced the task of chewing through the German defenses on its own, with no prior reconnaissance and without the necessary air and artillery support.

Now let's focus on the human losses of the 5th Guards Tank Army's tank corps that were operating west of Prokhorovka. They proved to be just as significant. Documents found in the Russian Federation Ministry of Defense's Central Archive testify that in the course of 12 July the four tank corps lost 3,139 men, of which 1,448 were either killed or missing-in-action. The 29th Tank Corps took the heaviest casualties, losing 1,991 men.[33] Behind it was the 2nd Guards Tatsinskaia Tank Corps – 550 men, including 145 killed or missing-in-action, while the 18th Tank Corps stood in third place, losing 471 men, with 271 killed or missing-in-action respectively.

The main human losses of the tank corps took place in their motorized rifle brigades. The 29th Tank Corps' 53rd Motorized Rifle Brigade led this woeful list; it lost 1,122 men (including 393 killed or mortally wounded), or more than 37% of the brigade's total manpower prior to the battle and more than 60% of its combat effectives.[34] This brigade's battalions had been caught in the epicenter of the fighting. One rifle battalion was supporting the tanks that were attacking Hill 252.2, and another accompanied the tanks attacking the "Stalin's Branch" State Farm. The 1st Battalion of the 53rd Motorized Rifle Battalion penetrated the boundary between *Leibstandarte Adolf Hitler's* 1st and 2nd SS Panzergrenadier Regiments, penetrated 7 kilometers between the railroad and the Storozhevoe woods, and took the "Komsomolets" State Farm. During the attack toward the State Farm, the rifle companies advanced along a "corridor" that was 300 meters wide between the railroad embankment and the Storozhevoe woods, where SS troops were ensconced. In the battalion's combat formation, it had no armor other than the 15 T-34 tanks of the 32nd Tank Brigade. Moreover, this cluster of tanks was moving rapidly, and the infantry couldn't keep up with them. The enemy was conducting intense fire from artillery and mortars. High explosive shell fragments shredded the crowded lines of riflemen, and when the SS troops discovered that small Russian groups had broken through to "Komsomolets" State Farm, several times they blanketed it with artillery fire. It was impossible to organize a withdrawal of the rifle battalion under the pressure of superior enemy forces. They made their way out individually, each man as he was able.

Very many soldiers were also killed in tank brigades of the 29th Tank Corps. For example, the 25th and 32nd Tank Brigades lost 320 and 230 men respectively. This noticeably exceeded the losses even of the motorized rifle brigades of the other corps (the 4th Guards Motorized Rifle Brigade of the 2nd Guards Tank Corps (272 men), the 32nd Motorized Rifle Brigade of the 18th Tank Corps (219 men), and the 58th Motorized Rifle Brigade of the 2nd Tank Corps (45 men). In the 29th Tank Corps, among the other categories of losses there was a large percentage of

32 See *Glavnoe avtobronetankovoe upravlenie: liudy, sobytiia i fakty v dokumentakh 1940-1942, Kn. 2* [*Main Armored Command: People, events and facts in documents of 1940-1942, Book 2*] (Moscow: GABTU Russian Federation Ministry of Defense, 2005), pp. 376-380.

33 TsAMO RF, F. 5 gv. TA, Op. 4948, D. 80, L. 7.

34 TsAMO RF, F. 3386, Op. 1, D. 2, L. 45.

Table Composite data on the losses of the 5th Guards Tank Army for 12 July 1943[1]

Formations and units	Personnel		Tanks and SP Guns		Losses of tanks and self-propelled guns												In service at 1300 on 13 July 1943[b]
					T–34			T–70			Mk–IV (SPG)			Total			
	Total	KIA and MIA	In service on 12.7	Took part in the fighting	Destroyed	Knocked out	Total	Destroyed	Knocked out	Total	Destroyed	Knocked	Total	Destroyed/ knocked out	Total	Percent	
Total, 18 Tank Corps	471[a]	271[a]	183	149	18	25	43	8	16	24	9	8	17	35/49	84	56	33
110 Tank Brigade	28	11	45	38 (43)?	4	4	8	1	2	3	–	–	–	5/6	11	26	–
170 Tank Brigade	49	28	39	39	5	14	19	2	8	10	–	–	–	7/22	29	74	
181 Tank Brigade	99	65	44	44	9	7	16	5	6	11	–	–	–	14/13	27	61	
32 Motor Rifle Brigade	219	147	–	–	–	–	–	–	–	–	–	–	–	–	–	–	
36 Gds Heavy Tank Regiment	25	7	19	19	–	–	–	–	–	–	9	8	17	9/8	17	89	–
Total, 29 Tank Corps[c]	1991	1033	215	199	73	36	109	30	14	44	–	–	–	103/50	153	77	51
25 Tank Brigade	320	149	73	69	13	18	31	10	14	24	–	–	–	23/32	55	80	11
31 Tank Brigade	101	62	71	67	24	–	24	20	–	20	–	–	–	44/–	44	66	28
32 Tank Brigaded	230	100	64	63	36	18	54	–	–	–	–	–	–	36/18	54	86	12
53 Motorized Rifle Brigade	1089	517	–	–	–	–	–	–	–	–	–	–	–	–	–	–	–
1446 SP Artillery Regiment	41	24	(20)	(20)	Destroyed: 6 SU–76 and 9 SU–122; 4 knocked out								(19)	(15/4)	(19)	95	(1)
Total, 2 Tank Corps	124	36	59	52	11	7	18	–	4	4	–	–	–	11/11	22	50	44
26 Tank Brigade	–	–	14	14	No detailed information available											50	7
99 Tank Brigade	–	–	24	20	–	7	7	–	1	1	–	–	–	–/8	8	42	11
169 Tank Brigade	79	36	18	18	11	–	11	–	3	3	–	–	–	11/3	14	78	11
58 Motorized Rifle Brigade	45	?	–	–	–	–	–	–	–	–	–	–	–	–	–	–	–
15 Gds Heavy Tank Regiment	–	–	3	–	Did not participate in the fighting on this day												?
Total, 2 Gds Tank Corps	550	145	140	138	20	20	40	9	5	14	–	–	–	29/25	54	39	80
4 Gds Tank Brigade	85	34	47	47	8	10	18	–	4	4	–	–	–	8/14	22	47	20
25 Gds Tank Brigade	136	61	47	47	16	4	20	9	–	9	–	–	–	25/4	29	62	14
26 Gds Tank Brigade	40	8	44	44	–	–	–	–	2	2	–	–	–	–/2	2	4	44
4 Gds Motorized Rifle Brigade	272	68	–	–	–	–	–	–	–	–	–	–	–	–	–	–	–
47 Gds Heavy Tank Regiment	–	–	2	–	Did not participate in the fighting on this day									–	–	–	2
Total, 5 Gds Mechanized Corps (at 1800)	405	?	158	66	14	4	4	–	–	–	–	–	–	5/10	15	9	158
10 Gds Mechanized Brigade	–	–	44	–	Did not participate in the fighting on this day												44

Formations and units	Personnel		Tanks and SP Guns		Losses of tanks and self-propelled guns												In service at 1300 on 13 July 1943[b]
					T-34			T-70			Mk-IV (SPG)			Total			
	Total	KIA and MIA	In service on 12.7	Took part in the fighting	Destroyed	Knocked out	Total	Destroyed	Knocked out	Total	Destroyed	Knocked	Total	Destroyed/ knocked out	Total	Percent	
11 Gds Mechanized Brigade (54 Gds Tank Regiment)	**354**	**?**	**31**	**31**	No detailed information on the losses available									**56**	**11**		**35**
12 Gds Mechanized Brigade (55 Gds Tank Regiment)	**51**	**?**	**35**	**35**	–	**4**	**4**	–	–	–	–	–	–	**/4**	**4**	**11**	**?**
24 Gds Tank Brigade	–	–	**48**	–	Did not participate in the fighting on this day; at 1800 51 tanks in service												**51**
1447 SP Artillery Regiment	–	–	**(11)**	**(10)**	No losses on this day												**?**
1 Gds Motorcycle Regiment	–	–	**10**	–	Did not participate in the fighting on this day; 8 tanks available in the morning												**8**
53 Gds Sep. Tank Regiment	**22**	**14**	**43**	**38**	**8**	**1**	**9**	**3**	–	**3**	–	–	–	**11/1**	**12**	**32**	**25**
Total for the 5th Gds Tank Army	**3563**	**1505**	**808 (32)**	**642 (30)**	**130**	**93**	**223**	**50**	**39**	**89**	**9 (14)**	**8 |(5)**	**17 (19)**	**194/146**	**340 (19)**	**53**	**399 (?)**

Notes:

1 It is important to understand that these are not summary data, but composite data, and each row must be read separately. The author is reporting what he found in the reports and combat diaries of each brigade and regiment kept in the Russian Ministry of Defense's Central Archives, and separately what each corps reported to the 5th Guards Tank Army. Thus, the brigade data when summed will not match the numbers given for the corps as a whole.

a Information on the casualties of the 18th Tank Corps were taken from TsAMO RF, F. 18 tk, Op. 1, D. 5, L. 125.

b Information on the tanks in service for the 18th, 2nd and 2nd Guards Tank Corps were taken from TsAMO RF, F. 332, Op. 4948, D. 67, L. 5, and that for the 29th Tank Corps from TsAMO RF, F. 29 tk, Op. 1, D. 6, L. 29.

c The total combat losses of the 29th Tank Corps were taken from TsAMO RF, F. 332, Op. 4948, D. 80, L. 7. The cell "KIA and MIA" for the 1446th Self-propelled Artillery Regiment gives only the KIA (TsAMO RF, F. 1446 sap, Op. 584031, D. 1, LL. 6–8.

d The report on the losses of the 32nd Tank Brigade didn't separate the destroyed tanks from the total losses; the count of 36 tanks was derived on the basis of the total number of destroyed tanks in the 29th Tank Corps.

The number of knocked-out tanks in the 25th Tank Brigades includes 7 T-34 and 4 T-70 that became immobilized on the battlefield due to mechanical problems (TsAMO RF, F. 5 gv. TA, Op. 4948, D. 70, L. 136). At midnight on 12 July 1943, just 3 tanks were counted in service; the location of the others was unknown to the command (TsAMO RF, F. 332, Op. 4948, D. 70, L. 136). In the column that gives the total personnel losses of the 58th Motorized Rifle Brigade and 12th Guards Motorized Rifle Brigade, only the number of dead and wounded is given. Altogether, the tank regiment of the 11th Guards Motorized Rifle Brigade lost 11 machines over the day of fighting (as of 1000 on 13 July). The allocation between destroyed and knocked out tanks in the row for this brigade is tentative. On 12 July 1943, while on the march 2 T-70 and 1 T-34 from the 5th Guards Mechanized Corps (presumably from the 11th Guards or 12th Guards Motorized Brigades) blew up in minefields in the Rzhavets area.

command staff (officers) – 903 men, including 184 officers and 719 of the junior command staff (sergeants and sergeant majors). Among them, 106 were killed or burned alive in their tanks and self-propelled guns, 19 went missing in action (some of whom were taken prisoner by the Germans), 40 were wounded with subsequent evacuation to a hospital, and 2 received heavy concussions.[35] Accordingly, the 29th Tank Corps' losses in command staff of all levels were comparable to the losses of the enlisted men (903 and 1,088 respectively).

There was no similar loss of personnel over a single day of fighting in any single tank or mechanized formation of the Voronezh Front throughout the entire period of the Kursk defensive operation, which I'll remind you, lasted from 5 to 23 July 1943. For example, the 1st Tank Army's 3rd Mechanized Corps over 10 days of combat operations (5-15 July 1943) on the axis of the XXXXVIII Panzer Corps' main attack (the Oboian' direction) lost a total of 5,220 men (of which 2,694 were killed or missing-in-action).[36] The loss of men in the 2nd Tank Corps between 8 and 25 July amounted to 2,767 (1,584 killed or missing-in-action), and the 2nd Guards Tatsinskaia Tank Corps lost 2,314 men between 8 and 20 July (816 killed or missing-in-action).[37] Comparing these figures, you experience the bitterness and anguish not only because so many capable men had been killed in the bloom of their lives, but also because it is hard to call these losses justified. The capture of Hill 252.2 and the advance of the front line by 1.5 kilometers essentially didn't achieve anything and didn't have any significant influence on the overall course of the defensive operation on this day. If the available forces had been used on the defense instead, the results might have been significantly better.

The losses of the 18th Tank Corps were just one-quarter of those in the 29th Tank Corps, even though both formations were operating adjacent to each other. Bakharov's troops lost 471 men, including 271 who were killed, mortally wounded or taken prisoner. Yet the loss of commanders at all levels in this tank corps turned out to be noticeably higher than those of the enlisted men; the ratio amounted to 246 to 225. The reason for such a large difference in losses between the two tank corps that were operating on the axis of 5th Guards Tank Army's main attack was the fact that all of brigades of Kirichenko's 29th Tank Corps launched several frontal attacks against two of the strongpoints in SS Panzergrenadier Division *Leibstandarte Adolf Hitler*'s sector of defense: the Hill 252.2 – Oktiabr'skii State Farm area, and the "Stalin Branch" State Farm – eastern fringe of the Storozhevoe woods area. It was in these two areas that the bulk of 29th Tank Corps' armor was knocked out and where it took the greatest casualties. If to compare the number of killed, wounded or missing-in-action in the tank brigades of the 29th and 18th Tank Corps, then it stands out that it was those of them that assaulted the SS positions on Hill 252.2 and the "Oktiabr'skii" State Farm that suffered the most. Thus, 230 men were lost in the 32nd Tank Brigade, 101 men in the 31st Tank Brigade (both of the 29th Tank Corps), 99 men in the 181st Tank Brigade, 46 men in the 170th Tank Brigade (both of the 18th Tank Corps, and 41 men in the 1446th Self-Propelled Artillery Regiment (of the 29th Tank Corps). At the same time, in the units of the 18th Tank Corps that attacked only through the villages on the left bank of the Psel River and conducted reconnaissance work in the course of the fighting, the amount of human losses proved to be substantially lower: in the 110th Tank Brigade – 28 men (of which 11 were KIAs or MIAs); in the 36th Guards Separate Heavy Tank Regiment – 25 men (of which 7 were KIA). I've already talked above about the tragedy of 29th Tank Corps' 25th Tank Brigade, which was shattered in the vicinity of the "Stalin's Branch" State Farm.

35 TsAMO RF, F. 3420, Op. 2, D. 98, LL. 79-88.
36 TsAMO RF, F. 8 gv.TK, Op. 1, D. 49, L. 26.
37 TsAMO RF, F. 5 gv.TA, Op. 4952, D. 7, L. 7.

In this connection, the losses of the SS Corps provoke great interest. Unfortunately, despite the open access to Western archives and the enormous amount of literature on the given subject by Western authors, there are still no precise data on the losses of Hausser's panzer corps. To the present day, this question has been surrounded by as many myths as the question of 5th Guards Tank Army's manpower losses. In my book *Prokhorovka – neizvestnoe srazhenie velikoi voiny* [*Prokhorovka – unknown battle of the great war*], I touched upon this topic in considerable detail. Relying on documents out of the German Bundesarchiv, with a certain amount of confidence it is possible to state that the SS Panzer Corps lost 842 men on 12 July. Of this total, *Leibstandarte Adolf Hitler* lost 279 men (39 killed, 235 wounded and 5 missing-in-action), *Das Reich* lost 243 men (41, 190 and 12 respectively), *Totenkopf* lost 316 men (69, 231 and 16 respectively, and those units directly subordinate to corps headquarters lost 4 wounded.[38]

The situation with respect to the loss of armor looks differently. A number of scholars, who have been occupied with this problem, come to the shared opinion that Hausser's II SS Panzer Corps lost 153 to 163 tanks and assault guns over the day of 12 July. As an example we can look at one of the latest Western publications on this topic. In an article that came out in 2003 for the 60th Anniversary of the battle for Prokhorovka, with a reference to the German scholar Karl-Heinz Frieser, *Generalmajor* D. Brandt asserts that in the course of the fighting on 12 July against the main forces of the 5th Guards Tank Army, the SS Panzergrenadier Divisions *Leibstandarte Adolf Hitler* and *Das Reich* lost 108 tanks and assault guns knocked out action, of which 41 required major overhauls, and 67 needed minor overhauls.[39] The analysis of data from reports of the SS Panzergrenadier Division *Totenkopf*, published by Zetterling and Franksen, testify that this division lost 46 combat machines on 12 July, including 10 Tiger heavy tanks. Thus, if we combine the cited figures, it turns out that in the three panzergrenadier divisions of the II SS Panzer Corps, of the 294 tanks and assault guns that were operational on the morning of 12 July, 154 were knocked out or 52.4% of the total. Other scholars relaying on different authors, sources and methods of computation come to pretty much the same numbers.[40]

The rifle divisions of the 5th Guards Army's 33rd Guards Rifle Corp, which was operating together with Rotmistrov's tank army, also suffered heavy casualties. They lost a total of 1,728 men, including 1,307 in the 9th Guards Airborne Division and 421 in two regiments of the 42nd Guards Rifle Division. Accordingly, if you combine the manpower losses of the 18th and 29th Tank Corps together with those of the two divisions of the 33rd Guards Rifle Corps, which were operating in their sectors, it turns out that in the epicenter of the fighting (on the front: Vasil'evka – Andreevka – Prelestnoe – "Oktiabr'skii" State Farm – "Stalin's Branch" State Farm) on 12 July 4,190 Soviet soldiers and officers were killed, wounded or went missing. This total does not include the losses for 12 July of the 183rd Guards Rifle Division, the 5th Guards Tank Corps' 6th Guards Motorized Rifle Brigade and the 158th Guards Rifle Regiment, which took part in the 2nd Guards Tank Corps' counterattack.

If you imagine that even before this day hundreds of bodies and heaps of damaged equipment were already laying on the field at Prokhorovka, which has a width of approximately 4.5 kilometers and a length of approximately 3.5 kilometers, and that on 12 July there appeared an additional 237 destroyed or knocked-out Soviet tanks and self-propelled guns alone, as well as several thousand

38 Zetterling and Franksen, *Kursk 1943: a statistical analysis*, p. 207.

39 D. Brand, *Vor 60 Jahren Prohorowka (Teil 2). Osterreichische Militerische Zeitschrift*. Ausgabe, 6/2003 (Ausfall Heeresgruppe Sud, stand 12.7.43 (Bl. 48) BA-MA:RH, zitert nach Frieser, Weltkrieg, Bd. 8 (Entwurf), p. 72.

40 For more detail, see V.N. Zamulin, *Prokhorovka – neizvestnoe srazhenie velikoi voiny* [*Prokhorovka – unknown battle of the great war*] (Moscow: EKSMO, 2005), p. 621.

more bodies of the dead from both sides, then there is no wonder that the veterans of that combat action speak in one voice that they never saw a more terrible scene in their entire lives.

Several scholars pointedly criticize N.F. Vatutin and the headquarters of the Voronezh Front, accusing them of blunders and miscalculations in the period of the defensive operation and, in particular, on 12 July at Prokhorovka.[41] This criticism isn't groundless. Obviously, the time chosen for conducting the counterstroke on 12 July was unsuccessful. The introduction of two fresh Guards armies into battle was made without prior, appropriate reconnaissance or serious preparations in the counterattack's sector. It also shouldn't have been thrown together so quickly given the high pace of combat operations.

The Soviet command underestimated the nature of the enemy's actions and the possible changes in the situation in the 48-72 hours prior to launching the counterattack, from the inception of the plan for it on 9 July. The German pivot toward Prokhorovka meant that the main attack struck the attacking enemy grouping head-on, and not in the flank as intended. Cooperation among the attacking formations and units wasn't properly implemented, which led in separate cases to fighting between our own units,[42] airstrikes against our own positions,[43] and unjustified losses.

The organization of supply for the counterattacking armies was in a bad way. The artillery was "on starvation rations". For example in the 5th Guards Tank Army the reserve of ammunition amounted to just one-half of a regulation combat load per gun instead of the 2.5 to 3 combat loads that were standard for an offensive. In his memoirs, A.S. Zhadov wrote:

> On 16 July Marshal of the Soviet Union G.K. Zhukov arrived at our command post. He was interested in how the introduction of the army for launching the counterattack on 12 July was handled. Left alone with me, he expressed his dissatisfaction with the organization of the army's introduction into the battle, and gave me a scolding for the fact that a full-strength army that was well-prepared to carry out combat assignments was committed to the fighting without tank reinforcements or an adequate amount of artillery, while being exceptionally poorly supplied with ammunition. In conclusion Georgii Konstantinovich said: "If for any reasons the Front headquarters has not managed to supply the army with everything necessary in good time, then you must request this of the Front Commander-in-Chief, or at the very least make an appeal to the *Stavka*. The army commander and the commanders of the corps and divisions are first of all responsible for the army's troops and the fulfillment of the task assigned by them." … To appeal to the *Stavka* for any sort of clarifications and assistance – such thoughts never entered my mind back then.[44]

Aleksei Semenovich Zhadov spoke more openly in a conversation with the writer K.M. Simonov on 13 August 1961 about how the Voronezh Front command and the Chief of the General Staff personally reacted to his requests before the counterattack. Noted the former commander of the 5th Guards Army:

> The army had been considerably staffed with cadres. The contingent of men was superlative, such that I deliberately didn't bring the divisions up to 9,000 men, as I might have done, but had 7,000 to 7,500 in each of them. I left approximately 9,000 men in the army's reserve,

41 For one example, see L.N. Lopukhovsky, *Prokhorovka: Bitva stal'nykh gigantov* [*Prokhorovka: The Battle of steel giants*] (Moscow, Iauza, 2005).

42 TsAMO RF, F. 48 sk, Op. 1, D. 2, L. 17.

43 TsAMO RF, F. 332 sk, Op. 4948, D. 70, L. 136; TsAMO RF, F. 95 gv. sd, Op. 1, D. 25, L. 105obr; TsAMO RF, F. 3400, Op. 1, D. 31, L. 77.

44 A.S. Zhadov, *Chetyre goda voiny*, pp. 97-98.

> in order to offset excessive losses in the very first days. The order was given to commit the army – a Guards Army, with select soldiers and officers, but no sort of reinforcement, not a single tank, not a single gun more than the authorized mix. I posed this question first to Vatutin, then to Aleksandr Mikhailovich Vasilevsky, who was there as the *Stavka* representative. Ordinarily he was a very calm man, and I'd never before seen him in a state of extreme agitation:
>
> "What, you're intending to give me an ultimatum?!" – He shouted. "An order has been given to commit the army – so commit it and don't give ultimatums. The situation demands that you introduce it as it is."
>
> So I committed the army. But my perception and feeling was such that with means of reinforcement, this army, according to its personnel, might have been a formidable force, but without means of reinforcement .... I entered the battle with a feeling of extreme bitterness on behalf of my men.[45]

The Marshal's sharp tone and irritability can be understood. This conversation took place on the afternoon of 11 July, when it had become clear that the situation had turned sharply for the worse both in the area of Prokhorovka and along Voronezh Front's entire front. Thus, the counterattack could hardly reach its objective; in its best case, it might lead only to the disruption of the enemy's offensive on this day.

According to the account by the headquarters of the 5th Guards Tank Army, between 12 and 16 July it irrecoverably lost 323 tanks and 11 self-propelled guns. Accurate losses in men still hadn't been determined. At I.V. Stalin's decision, a commission was formed to investigate the reasons for the heavy losses of the 5th Guards Tank Army suffered at Prokhorovka, headed by a State Defense Committee member and a Secretary of the Communist Party's Central Committee G.M. Malenkov. The result of its activities was an account, presented to I.V. Stalin at the end of July 1943. The conclusions were discomforting. The combat actions on 12 July were called a model for an unsuccessfully conducted operation.

Today, the transcript of the conversation that the Voronezh Front command and the Chief of the General Staff had with I.V. Stalin on the evening of 12 July is still inaccessible for study. However, judging by the decisions taken, the Supreme Commander-in-Chief of the Red Army expected greater results from the counterstroke and was extremely unhappy with the situation as it stood on southern face of the Kursk salient. In the course of the defensive operation, the *Stavka* had assigned its main reserves specifically to N.F. Vatutin. By the start of the battle his Voronezh Front had six armies, including one tank army; on 8 July he'd been given control of two more tank corps, and then of another two Guards armies. Thus, in order to look into the situation, already on 12 July I.V. Stalin contacted Marshal of the Soviet Union G.K. Zhukov, who was located at the headquarters of the Briansk Front, and directed him to the Voronezh Front as a *Stavka* representative. Simultaneously, A.M. Vasilevsky, who had been the *Stavka* representative with the Voronezh Front, was ordered to go to the Southern Front.

On the morning of 13 July G.K. Zhukov arrived at N.F. Vatutin's headquarters, where an operational meeting was held in order to examine the situation and the results of the counterattack. Recalls G.K. Zhukov: "It was decided to continue the counterattack that had been started more energetically in order to achieve better conditions for the *fronts*' counteroffensive, in order to seize

45 E. Simonova-Gudzenko and V. Zhdanov, "General A.S. Zhadov: Prokhorovka v moei sud'be" [General A.S. Zhadov: Prokhorovka was my fate"] *Patriot Otechestva,* No. 8 (2013), pp. 16-17.

Table 7 Information on the irrecoverable losses of the formations and units of the 5th Guards Tank Army from 12 to 16 July 1943[a]

	29 Tank Corps	18 Tank Corps	2 Guards Tank Corps	2 Tank Corps	5 Guards Mechanized Corps	Army units	Total
AFVs, guns and mortars							
T–34	60	32	38	10	59	23	222
T–70	31	12	24	5	14	3	89
Churchills	–	11	–	1	–	–	12
SU–122	8	–	–	–	–	–	8
SU–76	3	–	–	–	–	–	3
Total:	**102**	**53**	**62**	**16**	**73**	**26**	**334**
Vehicles	25	31	95	44	26	19	240
122mm guns	–	–	–	–	–	1	1
85mm AT guns	–	–	6	–	–	–	6
76mm guns	1	3	3	4	3	–	14
45mm guns	6	2	12	12	15	6	53
37mm A–A guns	–	–	–	1	–	5	6
122mm mortars	3	2	9	4	4	–	22
82mm mortars	5	2	9	9	4	–	29
Personnel							
Killed	656	179	807	123	1,122	53	2,940
Missing–in–action	447	163	53	425	67	2	1,157
Wounded	1,017	426	833	247	928	59	3,510
Total:	**2,120**	**768**	**1,693**	**548**	**2,117**	**114**	**7,607**

Note:
a TsAMO RF, F. 203, Op. 2851, D. 24, LL. 451-455

Table 8 Casualty report for the 5th Guards Tank Army from 12 to 18 July 1943[a]

	Killed or mortally wounded			Wounded			Sick			Missing			Other causes	Total lost				
														By category				
	Command	NCO	Enlisted	Command	NCO	Enlisted	Command	NCO	Enlisted	Command	NCO	Enlisted	Total	Command	NCO	Enlisted	Total	Including irrecoverably
2nd Tank Corps	45	125	201	112	237	501	–	1	3	64	263	727	1	221	626	1,433	2,280	1,425
2 Guards Tank Corps	85	231	363	130	421	651	2	12	24	4	7	6	1	222	671	1,044	1,937	696
18 Tank Corps	38	101	102	84	197	326	–	8	25	7	60	104	4	130	366	560	1,056	412
29 Tank Corps	63	314	362	88	342	624	1	2	3	49	210	191	–	201	868	1,180	2,249	1,189
5 Guards Mechanized Corps	49	232	409	106	419	607	–	2	1	37	164	144	2	192	818	1,162	2,172	1035
6 Anti–Aircraft Artillery Division	2	4	14	11	15	44	–	–	–	–	–	–	–	13	19	58	90	20
1 Guards Motorcycle Regiment	–	–	1	–	2	9	–	–	–	–	–	–	–	–	2	10	12	1
53 Guards Tank Regiment	9	17	–	7	15	–	–	1	–	–	2	–	–	16	35	–	51	28
689 Anti–Tank Artillery Regiment	–	2	5	1	7	12	–	–	–	–	–	–	–	1	9	17	27	7
678Howitzer Artillery Regiment.	–	1	9	1	2	32	–	–	–	–	4	5	–	1	5	46	52	17
76 Guards Mortar Regiment	3	5	3	–	–	8	–	–	–	–	–	–	–	3	5	11	19	11
Total losses	**294**	**1,032**	**1,469**	**540**	**1,657**	**2,814**	**3**	**26**	**56**	**161**	**708**	**1,177**	**8**	**1,000**	**3,424**	**5,526**	**9,945**	**4,841**
Grand total			**2,795**			**5,011**			**85**			**2,046**	**8**	–	–	–	**9,945**	**4,841**

Note
a TsAMO RF, F. 5 gv. TA, Op. 4952, D. 7, L. 3

the lines they had previously occupied in the Belgorod area on the heels of the retreating enemy."[46] However, there was still a long way to go to accomplish this.

At the same time, a meeting was taking place in the *Führer* headquarters, in which Hitler announced to the Commander-in-Chiefs of Army Group South and Army Group Center that he was halting Operation Citadel because of the impossibility of rapidly achieving its goals. However, the troops that were fighting at Kursk still didn't know about this, and the formations of the Fourth Panzer Army and Army Detachment Kempf still faced their previous assignments: to cover the left flank of the assault wedge securely and wrap-up the encirclement of the Russian forces at Prokhorovka and south of there as quickly as possible. The events of the subsequent few days remain in the shadow of the famous battle. The day of 13 July marked the last day when H. Hoth tried to close a ring of encirclement around Prokhorovka with the forces of the II SS Panzer Corps' three divisions, but thanks to the successful resistance by the Soviet forces, these calculations came to naught. After this, having abandoned his idea to take Prokhorovka Station, Hoth fully switched to preparing the encirclement of the 69th Army's 48th Rifle Corps, which was still clinging to the small piece of ground at the confluence of the Northern and Lipovyi Donets Rivers at the boundary between the Fourth Panzer Army and Army Detachment Kempf.

Initially, it had been intended to implement this plan on 12 July, but this had been disrupted by the counterattack of the 5th Guards Army and 5th Guards Tank Army. The situation began to change on 13 July, and at 1115 the commander of the II SS Panzer Corps *Obergruppenführer* P. Hausser received an order from H. Hoth to shift the panzer corps' main attack to the sector of the SS Division *Das Reich* (in the vicinity of Belenikhino Station), and at 2300 an updated order arrived:

> *Das Reich* continues the offensive in the direction of Ivanovka and Vinogradovka. The first goal is to seize Pravorot'. If possible, the division must break through further toward Prokhorovka Station and take it by surprise. The 167th Infantry Division should be oriented toward the option of an attack toward Ivanovka. … The *Leibstandarte Adolf Hitler* Division remains in its current positions and is oriented toward launching an attack with its right flank through Iamki to Prokhorovka, as soon as *Das Reich*'s offensive through Pravorot' to Prokhorovka begins.[47]

At this moment the II SS Panzer Corps was the strongest formation in Army Group South; on the evening of 13 July, it had a total of 251 tanks and assault guns.[48]

By 10 July, the start of the battle for Prokhorovka, five divisions of the 48th Rifle Corps were defending in the interfluvial area between the Northern and Lipovyi Donets Rivers (the 81st Guards, 89th Guards, 93rd Guards, 183rd and 375th Rifle Divisions), which had a total strength of 36,177 men,[49] plus units directly subordinate to corps headquarters and attached assets. In total, the grouping reached 40,000 soldiers and officers. They were holding a front that extended for approximately 32 kilometers, running from Belenikhino through Gostishchevo to Rzhavets. On average the 48th Rifle Corps' divisions numbered 8,250 men, except for the 81st Guards Rifle Division, but by the morning of 13 July they had all suffered considerable losses and had no anti-tank means, and it was precisely tanks that were the enemy's main breakthrough means. The 81st

46 Zhukov, *Vospominaniia i razmyshleniia*, p. 489.
47 Stadler, *Die offensive gegen Kursk 1943*, p. 113.
48 NARA, T. 313, R. 366, F. 597.
49 TsAMO RF, F. 69A, Op. 10757, D. 8, L. 90, 90obr

Guards Rifle Division was in essence combat-ineffective. Reported the division commander Major General I.M. Morozov:

> The men are physically exhausted, since for 2-3 days they've been fighting in the Belgorod area without food or even water. In the fighting the division has lost all of its divisional artillery and almost all of its regimental artillery. On 13.07.43 it had a total of up to 3,000 men, only a portion of which (approximately 20%) was armed, no anti-tank means (45mm anti-tank guns and anti-tank rifles), and only a few heavy and light machine guns remain.[50]

Stress and fatigue were increasing among the troops, and the incessant, bloody fighting over the last nine days and the growing threat of encirclement were making themselves felt. The massed retreat of the men from the front without any orders that had started on 12 July hadn't yet been fully stopped. For 13 July alone, 1,841 men had been detained by blocking detachments.[51] From a special communique from the SMERSH counterintelligence department on the work of blocking detachments between 12 and 17 July 1943:

> During the combat actions, there were cases of voluntary abandonment of the battlefield by entire elements on the part of military servicemen of the 92nd Guards Rifle Division, 305th Rifle Division and 290th Mortar Regiment. For example, on 14 July three elements of the 305th Rifle Division were detained by a blocking detachment in the vicinity of Novaia Slobodka: a battery of 76mm cannons, a howitzer battery and an engineer company. Three mortar batteries of the 290th Army Mortar Regiment were detained in the area of Samoilovka by a different blocking detachment. Two baggage trains of the 92nd Guards Rifle Division numbering 25 wagons and 200 men were detained by a blocking detachment in the area of Kashcheevo.[52]

The 69th Army command was taking measures to restore order, but was only able to take the situation under control on 16 July.

The divisions of the Fourth Panzer Army and Army Detachment Kempf launched the converging attacks from the north and south on the night of 13-14 July. The distance between their forward groups amounted to approximately 13 kilometers. Between 0400 and 0500, the northern grouping attacked simultaneously in three directions: the SS Panzergrenadier Division *Das Reich* (which had 90 tanks and 25 assault guns at 1800 on 14 July)[53] out of Ivanovskii Vyselok toward Vinogradovka and out of Iasnaia Poliana – Kalinin toward Belenikhino Station; and the 167th Infantry Division out of Sobachevskii toward Ivanovka and Leski. The area of Belenikhino Station was being defended by three brigades of the 5th Guards Tank Army's 2nd Guards Tank Corps, which had only 45 tanks,[54] while the 183rd and 375th Rifle Divisions were holding the area south of the station. A report from the II SS Panzer Corps stated: "The corps at 0400 with the Division *Das Reich* went on the offensive south and east of Iasnaia Poliana through Belenikhino to the east, in order to take the ridge southwest of Pravorot'. After bitter street fighting between 0700 and noon, Belenikhino fell, and the reinforced panzer regiment was able to attack at 1700 after an artillery preparation."[55]

50 TsAMO RF, F. 48 sk, Op. 1, D. 2, L. 21.
51 *Ogennaia duga. Kurskaia bitva glazami Lubianki*, p. 61.
52 Ibid.
53 Zetterling and Franksen, *Kursk 1943: a statistical analysis*, p. 187.
54 V.N. Zamulin, *Zasekrechennaia Kurskaia bitva*, p. 773.
55 Stadler, *Die offensive gegen Kursk 1943*, p. 118.

Under heavy enemy pressure the brigades of the 2nd Guards Tank Corps began to retreat from the area east of Belenikhino to Ivanovka, but badly depleted in men and equipment, they couldn't hold Ivanovka either and continued to retreat toward Hill 234.9. Having penetrated the defenses at the Belenikhino Station, the SS troops not only drove the 2nd Guards Tank Corps back in the direction of Pravorot', but also attacked the right flank of the 183rd Rifle Division, which on its left flank had been engaged in heavy fighting with the 167th Infantry Division since sunrise. Under the pressure on both flanks, the 183rd Rifle Division began gradually to fall back to the Pravorot' – Storozhevoe area. The gap on the northern (right) wing of the 48th Rifle Corps began to widen. However, the Red Army resistance was so stubborn, that the adversary, fearing unexpected attacks, was operating cautiously and was "feeling" his way forward.

The Soviet troops were also engaged in bitter fighting on this day with the southern German grouping, General Breith's III Panzer Corps (the 505th Heavy Panzer Battalion; the 6th, 7th and 19th Panzer Divisions [which at 0500 on 14 July had a combined 66 tanks];[56] and the 167th Infantry Division) in the Shakhovo, Rzhavets and Avdeevka area. Here, on the southern (left) flank of the 48th Rifle Corps, there was also a sizeable detachment from the 5th Guards Tank Army – the 5th Guards Mechanized Corps. At 2100 on 14 July, *Stavka* representative Marshal of the Soviet Union A.M. Vasilevsky reported to I.V. Stalin:

> The 5th Guards Mechanized Corps had to conduct particularly stubborn fighting on the Shchelokhovo, Vypolzovka, Avdeevka, Aleksandrovka front with three enemy tank divisions. Between 0700 and 1400 hours, up to five enemy tank attacks were driven back primarily by our artillery, and partially by our rocket artillery (firing over open sights) and tanks. ... The tankers and artillerymen of the 5th Guards Mechanized Corps are fighting splendidly; much worse – the infantry of the 92nd Guards Rifle Division, which as a rule is not holding up against tank attacks.[57]

The troops of the 5th Guards Tank Army's 53rd Guards Separate Tank Regiment were also fighting with particular skill and bravery. The regiment's journal of combat operations noted:

> Senior Lieutenant Ligman's 2nd Tank Company was positioned in ambush in Avdeevka. At 1800 a German tank appeared, and moving to within radio range of our tanks, began to conduct negotiations. The company commander sent Lieutenant Kosichenko's crew to meet the Germans. The Germans opened fire, and two more German tanks were in ambush positions. With their first shot, Kosichenko's crew knocked out the German tank, and then – a second one. However, the third German tank, camouflaged by bushes, knocked out our machine. A shell hit on the turret jammed the gun. The tank commander took the decision to advance to the forward edge of the Germans and to kill the enemy with its machine gun and treads. As a result of the extraordinary combat, the tank managed to kill up to a platoon of soldiers and to take six soldiers and one officer prisoner. Afterward the tankers returned under their own power to the unit's position.[58]

By giving *Das Reich* the assignment to break through to Pravorot' from Belenikhino Station, and further on to Prokhorovka, P. Hausser was thereby trying to secure the breakthrough's flanks and to create an outer ring of encirclement around the 48th Rifle Corps. It was planned to form

56 Zetterling and Franksen, *Kursk 1943: a statistical analysis*, pp. 189-190
57 TsAMO RF, F. 203, Op. 2777, D. 75, LL. 414-415.
58 TsAMO RF, F. 53 gv. otp, Op. 354813s, D. 1, L. 21.

the inner ring of encirclement in conjunction with the 167th Infantry Division, which launched attacks toward Leski. However, the tankers of two tank corps, the 2nd and 29th Tank Corps, were defending Pravorot', and the Germans were unable to take the village from the march. Thus after reaching the approaches to Malo-Iablonovo, at 1910 the II SS Panzer Corps received an order for 15 July, which fundamentally changed the assignment: it was to halt the attack toward Pravorot' and launch its main attack to the south, in order to link up with the III Panzer Corps.

On the evening of 14 July, the situation in the area between the Northern Donets and Lipovyi Donets Rivers became critical. The semi-encircled forces of the 48th Rifle Corps were experiencing a shortage of ammunition and anti-tank weapons. The corps' headquarters was unable to get command and control over the troops up and running smoothly, because communications were often being interrupted. Thus the 69th Army command was unable to track the situation of the divisions, and therefore couldn't organize the needed assistance to them. By 2400 up to 30 tanks and around a regiment of panzergrenadiers of the III Panzer Corps seized Shakhovo, while at around the same time 40 tanks with panzergrenadiers of the II SS Panzer Corps were digging in on Hill 234.9. By dawn on 15 July, SS troops had taken Malo-Iablonovo, and the III Panzer Corps had captured Plota. The pocket south of Prokhorovka had shut closed, but in the meantime it still wasn't solid. Four Soviet divisions with units of reinforcement wound up pocketed in an area of 126 square kilometers.

N.F. Vatutin was correctly assessing the intentions of the Army Group South command: having failed to carry out Operation Citadel, the Germans were striving to cut off the salient of Russian forces between the two rivers, in order to secure the inevitable withdrawal of its own forces. Already between 12 and 14 July, preparation was underway for a Soviet counteroffensive on the southern side of the Kursk bulge. The Steppe Front was moving in this direction, which was to go over to an offensive in the direction of Khar'kov, so the staging area in the interfluvial area would be very convenient for launching deep attacks against both the right flank of the Fourth Panzer Army's groupings at Prokhorovka (in the direction of Plota, Gostishchevo and Iakovlevo) and the left flank of Army Detachment Kempf. Thus, N.F. Vatutin was making every effort to hold the line of the 48th Rifle Corps. However, he didn't have enough strength. Because of heavy losses, the corps was holding up against the enemy attacks with difficulty. In the situation that had arisen on the evening of 14 July, there was only one option – to withdraw his forces rapidly from the pocket, because the draw string was quickly closing. Z.Z. Rogoznyi's order to his 48th Rifle Corps to withdraw to new lines has not been found, but from a preserved order of the 81st Guards Rifle Division it follows that the corps commander issued his order to the subordinate division commanders verbally.[59]

Major General V.V. Rogoznyi's sense of responsibility and composure should be noted. Over the night in the difficult circumstances of unceasing enemy tank attacks he retained his poise and, remaining within the pocket he drove repeatedly to his command post and issued orders to his division commanders to withdraw from the encirclement and take up a new defense. The 48th Rifle Corps headquarters' operational group took up the organization of the withdrawal of the troops. From 2100 on 14 July and 0200 15 July it was located in the village of Chursino, and then until 0500 its officers moved in the columns of the retreating units.[60] The withdrawal of the 48th Rifle Corps was implemented under the cover of rear guards in the following order of succession: 89th Rifle, 81st Rifle, 93rd Guards Rifle and the 375th Rifle Divisions. According to a report from the 89th Guards Rifle Division, it began moving into a new line at 0700 on 15 July.

59 TsAMO RF, F. 81 gv. sd, Op. 1, D. 5, L. 284.
60 TsAMO RF, F. 48 sk, Op. 1, D. 17, L. 36.

Unfortunately, it was impossible to bring out the troops without complications. The 375th Rifle Division was the last to come out, covering the withdrawal of the other divisions. The report of its commander Colonel P.D. Govorunenko states:

> On the approach to Kozinets, the enemy opened up artillery and mortar fire on the column in combination with a hail of machine gun and rifle fire from the east and west spurs of the Sukhaia Plota ravine. Having deployed the units and adopted a combat formation, a firefight ensued, and the division broke out in the area of Dal'nii Dolzhik with heavy losses. By 1130 the forward units were breaking through the ring of fire, losing a significant amount of men, horses and weapons. At 1200 the enemy went on the attack with newly arrived forces of infantry and tanks, blocked the Sukhaia Plota ravine (west of Malo-Iablonovo) and cut off the path of retreat for the division's remaining units. The rearguard consisting of two reinforced rifle battalions didn't come out, and together with them the commander of the 1241st Rifle Regiment Major Karklin, the commander of the 1243rd Rifle Regiment Lieutenant Colonel Frolov, the signal chief Engineer-Captain Tsukasov, two battalion commanders, and a number of lower-ranking officers went missing in action. The division's personnel – 3,526 men – upon reaching the new line of defense at Novoselovka quickly adopted a combat formation, dug in, and repulsed two attacks.[61]

The commander of a submachine-gun company of the 375th Rifle Division P.G. Zolotukhin, who came out of the pocket along a balka of the Sukhaia Plota ravine, recalled:

> The enemy set up tanks and machine guns in each side branch of the ravine and strove to block the column of retreating troops on the Malo-Iablonovo – Ivanovka line. When the Germans began an intensive barrage, panic erupted in the columns, men began to scatter, companies became intermingled, and control was lost. Commanders were trying to stop the fleeing men with difficulty. In the low ground there were jumbles of men, horses, overturned vehicles, cannons and other equipment. "Katiusha" rocket launchers that had been set ablaze were burning. When German infantry and tanks appeared right beside us and began to chop the column into pieces, the combat-experienced soldiers recollected themselves. They were acting alone and in groups. They were showing initiative and resolve. They didn't need any sort of command to fight back and kill the enemy that had appeared. Coming out toward Zhimolostnoe, we wound up under a tank duel. German tanks were firing from the woods east of Vinogradovka, while our tanks were firing from Pravorot'. The infantry was hurrying along under the trajectory of tank shells. The fire from the tanks of both sides was at close range. Moreover, the rain had stopped and German aircraft began to operate. With one platoon I somehow managed to make it to Krasnoe. Thirty men of the company gathered there. The exhausted, hungry soldiers and officers were keeping their chins up. It inspired everyone that the regiment and division remained as intact combat units, even though the only weapons left were what the men were carrying. The uniforms of the majority of them were in tatters, and their footgear was falling apart. The men collapsed onto the ground and despite the driving rain, slept directly under the open sky. Many men even rejected a dry ration. Sleep was more precious than food.[62]

61 TsAMO RF, F. 69A, Op. 107753, D. 390, LL. 32-33.

62 Author's personal archive.

One should particularly stress the fact that despite the active enemy opposition and the lack of stable communications, the command of the 48th Rifle Corps managed to bring out of the encirclement all four divisions in fairly good order. On the whole, Rogoznyi's decision to escape the pocket with his rifle corps was timely. He carried out his assignment, even though the combat losses prevented him from holding his line any longer. The withdrawal of the forces from the interfluvial area to a considerable extent proved even more advantageous to the Soviet side than to the enemy. In the first place, the front line in this sector was shortened by more than half, and because of this the 69th Army was able to make its defense more compact and solid. Secondly, the opportunity appeared to withdraw the divisions for rest and refitting; many were now no stronger than a regiment. However, the main point was that Rogoznyi's largely successful withdrawal from the pocket avoided needless losses.

Even so, those losses suffered by the 48th Rifle Corps proved to be large. Over 16 days of July, its divisions (not including the units directly subordinate to the corps) lost 18,958 soldiers and officers, of which 13,073 were KIA or MIA. Of this total, 14,022 (or 74%) were lost over the seven days between 10 and 16 July of the battle for Prokhorovka![63] (See the details in Table 7). Remember, over this same time the losses in the units of the 5th Guards Tank Army were also high. However, these data are only preliminary, taken as of the morning of 16 July, when the situation regarding the withdrawal from the pocket was still murky. How many soldiers and officers were lost between the Northern and Lipovyi Donets Rivers would become clear only by the end of the month. So far, accounts of only the 375th Rifle Division have been found. On 28 July 1943 a report from its headquarters indicated that on 20 July, 2,718 of its men were missing-in-action.[64] Considering that between 5 and 20 July, the division was only once in encirclement, and prior to 15 July its headquarters had only reported 18 men missing-in-action, there is the basis to assert that the remaining 2,700 men were either killed or captured by the enemy in the Sukhaia Plota ravine. Altogether in the middle of July in the 48th Rifle Corps, there were 10,647 MIAs.[65] This was equivalent to a full-strength Guards rifle division. Such a large number of missing men can be explained by the fact that the troops were coming out of encirclement at night under enemy fire through heavily cut terrain, and the order to withdraw came too late for the rearguard units. In addition, many of the Red Army soldiers were wounded, extremely fatigued by several days of the heaviest combat, lagging behind the rest of their units, and some simply got lost. Even as the Germans recognize: "The SS Panzer Corps closed the ring around the so-called "Belgorod Pocket" in cooperation with the III Panzer Corps, but the 69th Army that was operating south of Prokhorovka had retreated, and the majority of its forces managed to avoid encirclement."[66]

By midnight on 15 July 1943, the defense of the 69th Army's 48th Rifle Corps and the 5th Guards Tank Army south of Prokhorovka had stabilized along the line: Lutovo – Pravorot' – Novoselovka – Shipy. This was the final day when Army Group South made an advance here. A day later, it initiated the withdrawal of its forces back to the positions from which they had launched Operation Citadel on 5 July 1943. It became obvious that Citadel had ultimately failed.

When assessing the result of the combat operations in the 69th Army's sector, it is necessary to stress the following: the army carried out its assignment in the defensive operation. It had prepared a sufficiently firm line of defense, which withstood daily strong enemy attacks. In the conclusive stage of the operation, its divisions, given the absence of reserves and an adequate amount of

63 V.N. Zamulin, *Neizvestnye podrobnosti ob izvestnom srazhenii*, Table 13.

64 See http://obd-memorial.ru/html/info.htm?id=4639479 & page=1#

65 Zamulin, *Neizvestnye podrobnosti ob izveston srazhenii*, Table 31.

66 K-H. Frieser's presentation at the military history conference dedicated to the 50th Anniversary of the Battle of Kursk, 12 July 1993. Materials of the conference published by the Moscow Institute of Military History, 1993, p. 15.

Table 9 Information on the losses of the 69th Army's 48th Rifle Corps from 1 July to 16 July 1943 (according to data of the 69th Army's Operations Department on 16 July 1943)[a]

Division	Category and strength on 5.07.43	Strength on 10.07.43[b]	Strength on 16.07.43[c]	Losses						
				Killed	Missing	Wounded	Sick	Other	Total Men/%	Of which, irrecoverable Men/%
	Command			25	308	63	–	–	396	333
93 Gds Rifle	NCO			153	1,306	392	9	–	1860	1,459
	Enlisted			299	2,617	547	40	–	3,503	2,916
Total:	**9426**	**9,426**	**3,667**	**477**	**4,231**	**1,002**	**49**	–	**5,759/61**	**4,708/81.7**
	Command			57	54	75	3	78	267	111
81 Gds Rifle	NCO			329	178	272	4	293	1076	507
	Enlisted			410	730	795	4	988	2,927	1,140
Total:	**8702**	**5,725**	**4,432**	**796**	**962**[d]	**1,142**	**11**	**1,359**	**4,270/49**	**1,758/41.2**
	Command			13	95	16	3	–	127	108
89 Gds Rifle	NCO			29	784	63	2	–	878	813
	Enlisted			64	2,291 (1857)[e]	233 (1309)	5	–	2,593	2,355
Total:	**8189**	**7,979**	**4,591**	**106**	**2,736**	**1,388**	**10**		**4,240/51.8**	**3,276/77.3**
	Command			3	1	26	–	–	30	4
375 Rifle	NCO			35	8	78	4	–	125	43
	Enlisted			167	23	356	–	1	546	190
Total:	**8657**	**7,401**	**4,759**	**205**	**32 (2718)**[f]	**460**	**4**	**1**	**3,388/39.1**	**2,933/86.6**
	Command			15	–	69	–	–	84	15
183 Rifle	NCO			123	–	101	–	–	224	123
	Enlisted			260	–	732	–	–	992	260
Total:	**7981**	**7,778**	**6,681**	**398**	–	**902**	–	–	**1,301/16.3**	**3,98/30.6**
Grand Total:	**42945**	**38,152**	**24,130**	**1,982**	**10,647**	**4,894**	**74**	**1,361**	**18,958/44.1**	**13,073/69.5**

Notes

a TsAMO RF, F. 69A, Op. 10753, D. 442, L. 24; D. 8, LL. 90-91.

b TsAMO RF, F. 69A, Op. 10757, D. 8, LL. 90-91.

c Calculated by the author

d From 5 to 10 July 1943, the 81st Guards Rifle lost 815 men irrecoverably in the fighting north of Belgorod.

e On 18 July, the division clarified the number of its wounded and missing-in-action, and adjusted the numbers to 1,857 and 1,309 respectively.

f The number within the parenthesis reflects additional data from a report of the 375th Rifle Division on 28 July 1943.

weapons (particularly tanks and artillery) or ammunition, in the heaviest conditions of combat with the enemy managed to stand their ground and in good time, at an order, withdrew to a new line of defense.

At the same time one should note a number of shortcomings, which had a serious influence both on command and control of the troops and on their combat operations. This relates first of all to flaws on the organizational level. Prior to the start of July, the 69th Army had no corps commands. Just before the start of the German offensive, it received control of the 48th Rifle Corps. In the course of the fighting, there were instances when command over the formations and units became disrupted, and communications lapsed. Not coincidentally, Order No. 00194 from the Voronezh Front Commander-in-Chief on 21 July 1943 issued disciplinary rebukes regading the results of the defensive operation to a number of commanders of precisely the 69th Army's formations.

Aware of the serious losses that the Front had suffered in two weeks of fighting, and fearing a surprise from the wise and clever von Manstein, N. F. Vatutin at 1000 on 16 July 1943 issued an order to continue the defensive operation. Here is its preamble:

> The enemy has been inflicted large losses in men and materiel by the Front's stubborn defense, and the enemy's plan to seize Oboian' and Kursk has been foiled. However, the enemy is still not rejecting offensive aims and is striving with daily attacks with main forces to bypass Oboian' from the east, as well as to expand the seized staging area.
>
> With the goal of ultimately depleting the strength of the enemy's attack grouping, the armies of the Voronezh Front are to go over to a stubborn defense on occupied lines with the task to prevent an enemy breakthrough of our defense ....[67]

This document countermanded the preceding order issued before the 12 July 1943 counterattack. It conflicts with the view of certain scholars, which dominated in the Soviet historiography of the Battle of Kursk. According to their view, the counterattack that had started on 12 July came to a successful conclusion on this very day of 16 July, even though the defensive operation was continuing. However, this isn't true: the objective set before the troops of the Voronezh Front on 12 July hadn't been achieved. As has already been noted, at the meeting on 13 July with the participation of G.K. Zhukov, the decision was made to continue the counterattack, and only the form of conducting it was altered. The order on 16 July was in fact the document that officially halted the counterattack.

The day of 16 July became the conclusive one in the battle for Prokhorovka. There were no significant changes in the operational situation over the day. The normal preparations for a withdrawal were underway in the enemy's formations and units. Our forces were also putting themselves back in order and rebuilding their strength. Work was going on particularly actively in the area where the 375th Rifle Division came out of the pocket. The division command was organizing the collection of heavy weapons, transport and ammunition that had been left behind in the balkas. Even though this work went on under enemy fire, and in several places full-scale combat erupted, nevertheless in the course of several ventures out into the Sukhaia Plota ravine and its adjacent spurs, the division that had been left without artillery and vehicles managed somewhat to restore the situation.[68] In fact, this work continued on the following days.

On the night of 16-17 July the Army Group South command initiated the withdrawal of its armored units and rear service and support elements from the forward edge in the direction of

67 TsAMO RF, F. 203, Op. 2777, D. 75, L. 437.
68 TsAMO RF, F. 33, Op. 686044, Ed.khr. 2713.

Belgorod and Tomarovka. Aerial reconnaissance of the 2nd Air Army immediately detected this.[69] In the morning, under the cover of strong rear guards, the withdrawal of the enemy's main forces began. This was indisputable evidence of the fact that the Wehrmacht's offensive toward Kursk had failed. With this, the battle for Prokhorovka also came to an end.

Undoubtedly, the Prokhorovka clash was the culminating moment of the Kursk defensive operation on the southern face of the Kursk bulge, after which the intensity of the fighting sharply subsided. Unfortunately, a logical fallacy is rather widespread in many publications (either inadvertently or intentionally) – *post hoc ergo propter hoc* [A occurred, and then B occurred, so A caused B]! However, already on 11 July the Wehrmacht command, having learned of an offensive by the Western and Briansk Fronts (it took the reconnaissance-in-force, which was conducted on a broad front, as the start of the offensive), came to the conclusion: "In view of the fact that it is impossible to achieve a rapid success, now there can only be talk of inflicting the greatest damage to the enemy as possible with as few of our own losses as possible."[70]

Nevertheless this shouldn't be construed as a sign of the equivalence between the events labeled the "Battle for Prokhorovka" and the specific combat actions west of the station on 12 July 1943. The latter comprised only one part of the battle for Prokhorovka, albeit an important one.

K-H. Frieser gives an interesting assessment of these events from the German side: "... Today it is possible to assert: the meeting engagement at Prokhorovka on 12 July wasn't won by the Germans or the Soviets, since neither side was able to reach its intended objective."[71] It is hard to agree with this assertion. In reality, Voronezh Front's counterattack grouping didn't fully carry out its assignment, because it was simply unrealistic to do this given the existing correlation of forces. However, the main objective when on the defensensive is to repulse the enemy's offensive, and this our forces accomplished: they prevented a breakthrough of the third and final army-level defensive belt, retained the operational resilience of the defense, and inflicted such losses to the enemy that the Germans were forced to halt the further continuation of the offensive on the main axis of advance. After all, E. von Manstein had planned for 12 July after the regrouping of his forces to launch a decisive attack, secure a breakthrough of the Russian defenses, and reach operational space. The foe didn't accomplish this. Thus, in the final result Vatutin's troops won the battle for Prokhorovka, and then successfully concluded the defensive operation, having thereby created the conditions for a decisive counteroffensive.

After the Western and Briansk Fronts began to implement Operation "Kutuzov" on 12 July 1943, it became conclusively clear that Army Group South's offensive had reached a dead end. On 13 July Hitler made the decision to halt Operation Citadel. Manstein asserts that the Führer, having refused him the opportunity to employ the operational reserves – the XXIV Panzer Corps – at the decisive turning point of the battle, deprived him of a deserved victory.[72] However, by that time the enemy was already aware of the preparations by the Southern Front for an offensive against the First Panzer Army, which would thereby pose a serious threat to Army Group South's southern flank. Even if one allows that Manstein would have succeeded in breaking through the Soviet line at Prokhorovka (which is improbable, given the correlation of forces that existed by that time on the Prokhorovka – Kursk axis), his attack would have been "hanging in the air". Thus, after 12 July he was thinking only of conducting partial operations with limited forces: the

69 TsAMO RF, F. 203, Op. 51360, D. 5, L. 103, 105.

70 KTB/OKW Bd. 111.Hb. 11, p. 769.

71 K-H. Frieser's presentation at the military history conference dedicated to the 50th Anniversary of the Battle of Kursk, 12 July 1993. Materials of the conference published by the Moscow Institute of Military History, 1993, p. 15.

72 E. Manstein, *Poteriannye pobedy* [*Lost victories*] (Smolensk: Russich, 2003), p. 538.

encirclement of the 69th Army's 48th Rifle Corps, and then, in the future, about an attack to the northwest with the aim of unilateral envelopment and encirclement of the 40th Army.

However it went, the Soviet forces won the battle for possession of Prokhorovka. The victory in this fighting, which became the concluding stage of the combat operations on the southern face of the Kursk bulge, pre-determined the success of the Voronezh Front's defensive operation as a whole.

11

Two commanders at the Battle of Kursk (a case of biographical research)

I'm probably not mistaken if I say that the names of Marshal of Armored Forces M.E. Katukov and Chief Marshal of Armored Forces P.A. Rotmistrov have long been firmly associated in our country ever since the Battle of Kursk. Indeed it is no wonder; the contribution to the victory made by the troops under their command there is significant and indisputable. Their tank armies took part in the repulse of the offensive launched by the most powerful grouping of those that the Germans assembled at Kursk, fought several large and bloody battles successfully, and they not only withstood the attacks, but more importantly, carried out their assigned missions, though these results were achieved with enormous strain and at times, very heavy losses.

Nevertheless, for more than 70 years now, arguments continue to the present day about the individual contributions made by the two military chiefs in thwarting Operation "Citadel", or about the mistakes and miscalculations they made in the summer fighting of 1943.[1] At the same time it is impossible not to note that the main attention in these debates is focused on the battle for Prokhorovka, in the sector of the 5th Guards Tank Army, which was commanded by P.A. Rotmistrov. It wouldn't be an exaggeration to say that over the past decades, the number of publications released about the events that took place near this small railroad station rivals the number of publications about the entire Battle of Kursk. The fighting on the Oboian' axis, in which namely M.E. Katukov's 1st Tank Army played the main role, for a long time has remained in the shadows. Both historians and journalists have paid little attention to his activity as a tank army commander. Moreover, P.A. Rotmistrov and his peers made a considerable contribution to this imbalance. In the 1980s and 1990s during reunions of veterans in my village of Prokhorovka, more than once I had to hear Katukov's surviving Guardsmen critize the tankers of the 5th Guards Tank Army for their dishonorable line of approach over sharing the credits for the common victory. At the time it was impossible to write in the open press about the frictions in the veterans' community, but echoes of those disputes can be found, for example, in the book by a participant in the Battle of Kursk E.S. Katukov. Writes Ekaterina Sergeevna:

1 For example, the authors of the following books give diametrically opposed assessments of the two commanders: G.A. Koltunov and B.G. Solov'ev, *Kurskaia bitva* [*Battle of Kursk*] (Moscow: Voenizdat, 1970); A.P. Riazansky, *V ogne tankovykh srazhenii* [*In the fire of tank battles*] (Moscow: Nauka, 1975); L.N. Lopukhovsky, *Prokhorovka bez grifa sekretnosti* [*Prokhorovka without the seal of secrecy*] (Moscow: Iauza/EKSMO, 2012); and B. Sokolov, *Vse mify Vtoroi Mirovoi: "Neizvestnaia voina"* [*All the myths of the Second World war: "The Unknown war"*] (Moscow: Iauza-Press, 2013).

> On the Belgorod axis the 1st Tank Army carried out its assignment with honor. Here the enemy had a numerical advantage, but not a single unit or formation of the army withdrew a single kilometer without orders. They stood to the death and did not let the enemy pass. … Yet for some reason, the honors for the victory in the Battle of Kursk fell only to Generals P.A. Rotmistrov and A.S. Zhadov. Films, television shows, radio and literature are shamefully silent about the combat actions of M.E. Katukov's tankers, I.M. Chistiakov's Guardsmen and the acts of bravery by our pilots and aircrews. All you ever hear about is the unprecedented tank clash at Prokhorovka.[2]

Nevertheless, despite the lively and even fixed interest in this matter, relatively little is known about the combat path of both tank commanders, particularly about their difficult, ambiguous moments which never became part of the image of a general of the victorious Red Army that was carefully crafted by Soviet propaganda. I've happened to spend a lot of time working in a number of leading domestic and foreign archives. The materials found in them allow me partially to fill this gap in knowledge. The given chapter has been written on the basis of collected documents, in conjuction with the memoirs written by the commanders themselves, as well as by those who were close to them at various times of their service.

Pavel Aleksandrovich Rotmistrov and Mikhail Efimovich Katukov belonged to that small group of military commanders of the Red Army who, having entered the armored forces in the early years of their creation, thanks to their high capabilities and talent, were able to grasp the essence of the new profession within a short period of time. Later, in hard wartime conditions, they were able to acquire the necessary expertise and experience when commanding large tank formations and armies and became genuine masters of the military craft.

Their life roads and combat paths were quite similar and frequently intersected. We'll start with the fact that both of their paternal grandfathers, Egor Katukov and Matvei Rotmistrov were old warriors; at the end of the 19th Century they'd both taken part in Russia's war with Turkey, had both fought at Plevna and had been decorated for bravery. Matvei, a Cavalier with two Georgian Crosses and two medals "For bravery" was killed in Bulgaria.

Their grandsons were practically of the same age. Pavel Rotmistrov was born on 6 July 1901 in the village of Skovorovo of the Tver Guberniia to a large family. His father Aleksei Matveevich was married three times and from these three marriages he had nine sons and daughters. Mikhail Katukov appeared on the earth a bit earlier, on 17 September 1900, in the Moscow suburban village of Bol'shie Uvary in today's Ozerovskii District. The Katukov family was also large; five daughters grew up in it. In the Russian Civil War years, Mikhail's mother would die and his father re-married. From this marriage, Efim Epifanovich would have a son and a daughter.

As close friends and neighbors recall, from his early years Mikhail was an observant child who thirsted for knowledge, read a lot, and had an excellent memory. Back in childhood, when his father worked in Baron Wrangel's milk factory, the young child learned to master the Estonian language by hearing it; later, he learned to speak Polish, Belorussian and Ukrainian. At 12 years of age, Mikhail was sent to relatives in Petersburg, and for five long years he had to work as an errand boy.

Prior to 1917, Pavel Rotmistrov lived in his father's family. Only after the events of October 1917 in the capital of the Russian Empire did he travel to Moscow to see his brother Leonid, who advised him to go to Samara. According to talk around town at the time, life was easier there.

The turning point in the fate of the future military commanders was the Russian Civil War. As it happened, they both voluntarily expressed the desire to serve in the Red Army at one and

2 E.S. Katukova, *Pamiatnoe* [*Unforgettable*] (Moscow, 2000), p. 193.

the same time – at the end of March 1919. It was this hard and tragic period for our people that pre-ordained their life paths. It was in these years that they learned the difficult trade of defending the Motherland with a gun in their hands, forged their willpower and characters, and learned by experience the essence of that short but terrible word – war. As M.E. Katukov recalled in his elderly years, "Many people of my generation after the Revolution chose the soldier's profession, because war for long years had become a hard, but necessary reality. Sympathy for the poor was on the side of the new regime of workers and peasants, so I, like many of my peers, volunteered for the Red Army."[3]

Unquestionably, the cruelty, hatred and death, which stalked the Russian expanses at that time, left an indelible impression on their natures for the rest of their lives. For Pavel Rotmistrov, the three years of the civil war, while extremely hard because he lost his mother and a brother, were at the same time filled with more significant and major events than for Mikhail Katukov. At his own volition, Pavel joined the Samara workers' regiment, and already at the beginning of April 1919 he was taking part in his first battle against the forces of Admiral Kolchak at Bulgul'ma on the Eastern Front. Then in May 1919 he was sent to the Samara Soviet Engineer Courses. However, Pavel was unable to complete them; in August the course of study was abandoned in order to suppress the next insurrection, where Pavel became sick with malaria. After recovering and receiving the doctor's OK, he was assigned to the 42nd Reserve Battalion and sent to the 16th Army, which at this time was fighting on Polish territory. However, by the time of his arrival the battalion's active combat operations had ended. His participation in the Russian Civil War, though, didn't end with this. In January 1921 he became a cadet of the 3rd Western Infantry School for Red Commanders in Smolensk, and three months later the uprising in Kronstadt erupted. Almost the entire school was sent to quash it. The insurrectionists resisted bitterly. Cadet P.A. Rotmistrov had to fight for a total of ten days, between 10 and 20 March 1921, but over this short period two major events happened in his life. First, when assaulting Bastille No. 6 of the Konstadt fortress, he received his first combat wound, and subsequently also became ill. Secondly, during the battle Pavel personally destroyed a machine-gun nest. This enabled his company to make a decisive advance and ensured the attack's success. The command evaluated the cadet's feat in a complex situation as heroic, and he was awarded the Order of the Combat Red Banner. Later Rotmistrov would say that for him, this Order was not only the first, but also the most precious of all the 42 Orders and medals that he earned over the long years of his service in the country's armed forces.

Mikhail Katukov, after signing up at the Kolomenskoe enlistment center, was sent to the 54th Rifle Division's 484th Rifle Regiment.[4] He took part in the fighting in Don Oblast as part of this division, in the area of the Filonovskii and Novoannenskii railroad stations and Khoper, putting down Mironov's uprising. In the same year of 1919, just like his future command peer, he became very sick with a serious infectious disease – typhus – but his young organism fought off the ailment. In fact, just like Pavel Rotmistrov, he was again called back into the Red Army and sent to the Polish front, where he wound up in the 57th Rifle Division. Here he remained until December 1920, after which he was assigned to the 23rd Mogilev Infantry School. This was the first military educational institution that Mikhail completed. In March 1922 he was assigned to his first command post – commander of a platoon in the 235th "Nevel" Rifle Regiment of the 27th "Omsk" Red Banner Division. He served in this division for almost 10 years, and would rise to the post of chief of staff of the 80th Rifle Regiment.

3 M.E. Katukov, *Na ostrii glavnovo udara* [*At the spearhead of the main attack*] (Moscow: Voenizdat, 1974), p. 259.
4 TsAMO RF: Service record of Colonel General Mikhail Efimovich Katukov, p. 2.

During his time in the division, Mikhail Katukov became acquainted and befriended the commander of the 81st Rifle Regiment's artillery battalion, V.A. Pen'kovsky. In July 1943 they would meet again at Kursk. At that time Valentin Anatol'evich was now the chief of staff of the 6th Guards Army, while Katukov was an army commander. After the war in his recollections, M.E. Katukov spoke warmly about this man, and notes that when preparing for the Battle of Kursk, they quickly found a common language and got fruitful teamwork up and running, just like in the 1920s.

P.A. Rotmistrov's membership in the Russian Bol'shevik Communist Party, which he joined in 1919 at the age of 18, had a noticeable influence on his career as a Red Army commander. At the end of April 1921, as a Communist who had received excellent military training, he was sent to Riazan' to serve as a political instructor for a company of the 149th, and then 151st Rifle Regiments. A year and a half later, in September 1922, he was again sent to train in the 1st Unified Military School of the All-Union Executive Committee. After graduating from it in 1924, he was transferred to the Leningrad Military District to the 11th Rifle Division's 31st Rifle Regiment. He served in this regiment for four years, and on 1 October 1928 enrolled in a full-time department of the prestigious Frunze Military Academy.

The period from the end of the 1920s until the early 1930s was a very important one in Pavel Alekseevich's life. Thanks to his determination and taste for work, with the help of his wife Elena Konstantinovna, he mastered military science, which was something hard for a man who had no basic education, and laid down a solid foundation for career growth and future victories on the battlefield. Wrote P.A. Rotmistrov:

> In Leningrad I met my future wife ... She had been raised in a highly educated family, had an excellent background in general and music education, had mastered three foreign languages, and she had an exceptional influence on my cultural and general education growth, persistently inculcating in me a thirst for knowledge. We often went to theaters, films and museums together, and we read a lot. With the help of my wife, I rather quickly prepared to enter ... the academy.[5]

The knowledge he acquired at the Frunze Military Academy and in service, as well as his high capacity for work, helped the young commander form such valuable qualities of character as openness, a rapid acquisition and mastering of the new, and an unceasing desire for his own personal development.

If prior to the start of the 1930s, the life paths of the future army commanders was very similar, then later it abruptly changed. After graduating from the Frunze Academy, P.A. Rotmistrov was sent to Chita as the chief of operations with the 36th Trans-Baikal Rifle Division. It wasn't a high post, and out of the way – in the country's Far East. However, Pavel Alekseevich didn't lose his sense of spirit and devoted all of his energy to his own professional improvement. He gave six years to service in the Far East, and over this relatively short period of time he acquired excellent experience in staff work, but also demonstrated his abililty to achieve results. This was noticed by the high command. Having climbed several rungs up the service ladder, in March 1936 he became chief of the 1st (Operations) Department of the Special Red Banner Far Eastern Army. At this time, an unspoken rule existed: only experience in command of a regiment opened the path to higher posts. According to Pavel Alekseevich, he had been trying for a long time to test himself in the command arena. The army's leadership supported the healthy ambitions of the rising commander and three months later satisfied his request for a command post, appointing him to independent

5 P.A. Rotmistrov, *Stal'naia gvardiia* [*Steel guard*] (Moscow: Voenizdat, 1984), p. 17.

work as commander of the 21st Rifle Division's 36th Rifle Regiment. He worked eagerly as a regiment commander, the first positive results appeared, and within a short time he was promoted to the rank of colonel. However, an order that arrived from Moscow in the middle of autumn 1937 to come urgently to the People's Commissariat of Defense sharply changed Rotmistrov's life plans in a way that was unknowable for him.

M.E. Katukov's appointment as chief of staff of the 27th Rifle Division's 80th Rifle Regiment in December 1931 became the turning point in his career. At this time, the birth of the Soviet armored forces began. In all the districts, including in the Belorussian District in which he served, separate tank and mechanized brigades began forming. At first they were part of the rifle and cavalry divisions. Subsequently, larger armored formations appeared – the mechanized corps.

A half-year later following his appointment, the 5th Separate Mechanized Brigade began to form on the basis of the 80th Rifle Regiment, which was garrisoned in Borisov (now Barysaw) on the Berezina River. After the process of forming up concluded, in December 1932 he became its chief of intelligence, and in September of the following year the commander of its training battalion. This unit conducted the training of tankers not only for the brigade, but also for other formations of the Red Army. A significant number of them were sent as well to the Special Red Banner Far Eastern Army. Their commander studied together with the students, demonstrating in the process great success. In 1933, at the District competitions for tank gunnery, M.E. Katukov took first place and received a valuable prize for those times – a camera.

At the end of 1934, Mikhail Efremovich transferred to the Kiev Military District and was appointed to the post of chief of operations for the 45th Mechanized Corps' 134th Mechanized Brigade. The Red Army's armored forces were practically forming from scratch; the command staff was arriving primarily from rifle and cavalry divisions. It had had no knowledge of the equipment and the details of this type of force, and at first the training for the tanks was conducted in most units and formations through self-tutelage and practical group exercises with technicians and engineers. However, it was impossible to prepare competent commanders and teach them the details of armored tactics in this way. So the government made the decision to create tank schools, and subsequently the Academy of Motorization and Mechanization, before also opening retraining courses at this academy. From the middle of the 1930s, in order to increase the level of professional expertise, the entire command staff of the tank and mechanized formations went through this network of training institutions. At the beginning of June 1935, M.E. Katukov was also enrolled in the annual courses at the Red Army's Military Academy of Motorization and Mechanization.

In September 1937 he returned to his corps and at first was appointed chief of staff of the 135th Rifle – Machine-gun Brigade, and from April 1938, he was the acting chief of staff of the 45th Mechanized Corps. Mikhail Efremovich subsequently wrote: "I served the headquarters, and without bragging I knew my stuff pretty well, but I was longing for operational duties as a commander."[6] The Soviet high command accommodated this desire of the rising commander, and on 9 October 1938 Colonel M.E. Katukov took command of the 5th Light Tank Brigade of the Kiev Special Military District's 25th Tank Corps; in July 1940, he transferred to the post of commander of the 38th Light Tank Brigade.[7]

In November 1939, a reorganization of the armored forces began, which wasn't completed by the start of the war. What is more, the initial phase was based on an idea that was contrary to that which was adopted in the second phase. Initially it was considered beneficial to disband the tank

6 Katukov, *V ostrie glavnogo udara*, p. 266.

7 This information was discovered in Katukov's service record, although in his memoirs he indicates that from the post of chief of staff of the 45th Mechanized Corps he was transferred to the post of commander of the 134th Tank Brigade. His memoirs also make no mention of his short period of command of the 38th Light Tank Brigade.

corps that the Red Army had at that time, and to create in their place homogenous tank brigades of four tank battalions each with a total of 258 BT and T-26 tanks. Simultaneously the reform proposed to establish the same sort of brigades, but equipped with 156 heavy T-28 and T-35 tanks instead, as well as 15 motorized divisions, with 257 tanks in each. By the spring of 1940, four motorized divisions, 35 tank brigades of the first type, and 4 tank brigades of the second type had been formed. They could operate both jointly with the infantry and carry out independent tasks. In the opinion of several Soviet scholars, this phase had an important, positive significance for the development and improvement of the armored forces. It rested on the accumulated experience of the preceding years, including the use of this type of force structure during the Soviet Union's annexation of western Ukraine and western Belorussia. The new force structure was more mobile and easier to handle than the previous tank corps, and something that is very important, met the demands of the massed use of tanks. Doctor of History I. Krupchenko noted, "Plainly, it wasn't a coincidence that our tank and mechanized corps during the Great Patriotic War had 200-250 tanks and self-propelled guns in their inventory. The panzer divisions of the German Army of this period also included around 200 tanks."[8]

However, already in the summer of that same year (1940) there was a new, and as the events of the first weeks of the war would show, mistaken decision to create larger formations – mechanized corps, consisting of two tank and and one motorized divisions, with a total strength of more than 1,000 tanks and more than 35,000 soldiers and officers.[9] Yet their tables of organization and equipment plainly called for an inadequate amount of logistical support and means of command. In addition, the Soviet defense industry proved unable over a short period of time to produce so many tanks and self-propelled guns, and thus by the start of the Great Patriotic War, the mechanized corps were not fully equipped with them.

A considerable number of other problems also arose, which ensnared everyone, especially the trained cadres. By the end of the 1930s, the Red Army's tank forces were few, but the political repressions that swept the country eliminated thousands of trained specialists from the Red Army. They were executed or sent to labor camps and prisons based upon contrived accusations, or were simply dismissed from the armed forces because of their "political unreliability". Moreover, a significant number of service personnel could not be assigned to these same tank forces for the same reasons, even though they still had the right to continue to serve in other branches of the Red Army. Thus, the pool of senior officers and generals, from which candidates for the post of commanders and chiefs of staff of the tank divisions and mechanized corps could be chosen proved to be limited. The People's Commissar of Defense gathered them from every corner of the country to fill the command and staff positions. The selection, review and confirmation took place in Moscow in the Communist Party Central Committee. In addition, the candidate had to be a Communist Party member, and he had to meet rather strict professional requirements. After all, it was not a simple matter to command such a powerful formation.

By the middle of 1941, the Red Army managed to find men to staff for more than 100 tank divisions, and in each of them the top echelon of command was almost fully staffed. It is hard to say how many of selected commanders at this moment could fully handle their duties. The men were of varying quality. The failures of the first months of the war threw some into a state of despair, and this would have fatal consequences for them.[10] However, it was precisely in the period of 1940-1941 during the creation of the mechanized corps that the nucleus of that command staff

8 I. Krupchenko, "Razvitie tankovykh voisk mezhdu pervoi i vtoroi mirovymi voinami" ["Development of tank forces between the First and Second World Wars"] *Voenno-istoricheskii zhurnal*, No. 5 (1968), p. 44.

9 Ibid., p. 45.

10 For example, in November 1941 during the fighting for Moscow, the commander of the 58th Tank Division Major General A.A. Kotliarov committed suicide.

was formed that would later become the backbone of the Soviet armored forces in the years of the Great Patriotic War. This included men like A.G. Kravchenko, V.M. Badanov, S.I. Bogdanov, D.D. Leliushenko, and M.D. Sidenko, who subsequently commanded the homogenous tank armies, as well as men like I.D. Vasil'ev, V.G. Burkov, A.F. Popov, B.S. Bakharov and a number of others who would take command of the tank corps that took part in the Battle of Kursk. Among those who passed through the "purgatory" of the Old Square in Moscow, where the Central Committee of the Communist Party was located, was Colonel M.E. Katukov. He was given the assignment to form the 20th Tank Division in the Ukraine, which was to become part of the 9th Mechanized Corps. The People's Commissar of Defense order about appointing him as a division commander was signed on 28 November 1940, and the war found him in this post.

Those who first become familiar with P.A. Rotmistrov's service records are somewhat surprised by the fact that the first Marshal of Armored Forces in the Red Army,[11] who had served in it for its first 19 years, right up until the start of 1938 had no connection with the tank forces whatsoever. However, just three years later he would become the deputy commander of a tank division, and then the chief of staff of a mechanized corps. Such a meteoric rise is connected first of all with the political represssions that purged the Red Army's command staff in those years. The contents of a conversation that Pavel Aleksandrovich had with the chief of the Red Army's Military Academy of Mechanization and Motorization after his urgent summons from the Far East are curious. It is indicative of how the selection of specialists for posts went in that period. P.A. Rotmistrov recalled:

> In October 1937 I unexpectedly received instructions to turn the regiment over to my deputy and come urgently to Moscow at the behest of the Red Army's Main Department for Command Staff. There I was unexpectedly offered the post of a tactics instructor in the recently created Red Army Military Academy for Mechanization and Motorization. This appointment was motivated by the fact that during my time of service in the Far East, and especially in the headquarters of the Special Red Banner Far Eastern Army, I, if you will, became sufficiently familiar with the tank units and elements, saw them in action during exercises and maneuvers, and moreover had good knowledge of combined-arms tactics.
>
> Already on the next day the head of the Academy Divisional Engineer I.A. Lebedev received me.
>
> I asked Lebedev, "How will I teach tactics to tankers, when I've never been a tanker?"
>
> Ivan Andreevich replied, frowning: "None of us has ever been tankers. They've demanded that we teach tankers – so we'll instruct them and learn ourselves."
>
> "Then I ask that you give me some time to study the equipment and prepare lectures for the military students."
>
> Lebedev smiled: "That's now a different conversation."[12]

As we see, at that moment there could be no talk of basic knowledge or even elementary professional training even in the military academies, but there was no way around it; life wasn't stopping and gaps had to be filled urgently – to re-fill the growing number of vacant positions that were being created daily. Indeed, such a situation was being seen everywhere. The purges of the Red Army's command staff and the simultaneously rapid build-up of the armored forces created a mad scramble for qualified officers.

This topic became decisive during its transition to a new force structure. Classroom work was to Colonel P.A. Rotmistrov's liking. He dove into it deeply and with great enthusiasm. In order to

11 This high title was awarded to P.A. Rotmistrov and Ia.N. Fedorenko in the same order.
12 Rotmistrov, *Stal'naia gvardiia*, p. 40.

prepare for the lectures, he used not only theoretical treatises on tactics and the strategy of employing tanks, but also accounts of the recent battles in Spain and the Far East. Pavel Alekseevich planned to work in the Academy for a long time, so already in 1939 he wrote and defended his dissertation to become a Candidate of Military Science, and just a bit later he was awarded the academic title of senior lecturer. In less than two years he became firmly connected with the armored forces, and ultimately decided upon his future career path in the Red Army.

In November 1939 the Soviet-Finnish War erupted. In early 1940 at Rotmistrov's personal request, he was sent to Karelia with the aim of improving his knowledge and acquiring practical combat experience. Virtually little is known about this period of life of the future army commander. We know about it only from his memoirs, which as the collected archival documents show, do not reflect both the events that preceded his departure for the front and his time in the acting army very faithfully.

The years of service in the academy were filled not only with fruitful work to master a new field. The wave of arrests also swept through the military educational institutions. Many honest instructors were subjected to vilification, and more than a few of them disappeared into labor camps and prisons. Every day in all the academies, meetings were being held, during which Communists were branded with the disgrace of being "enemies of the people that had wormed their way into the ranks". This bitter cup didn't pass P.A. Rotmistrov either. In 1939 he was kicked out of the Party for his supposed connection with enemies of the people Pashkovsky, Valin, Derevtsov, Sangursky, Radishevsky, Rashchupkin, Dubovik and others; for his "deliberate disassociation" from his leadership work of the 2nd Branch of the 1st Department of the Headquarters of the Special Red Banner Far Eastern Army; and for the fact that he hadn't conformed to the decisions of the February Plenum of the Central Committee of the All-Union Communist Party (b).[13] An arrest was to follow after this. However, the colonel's spirits didn't sink, and disagreeing with the baseless accusations, Rotmistrov sent a letter to the Central Committee. His personal case was submitted to the Party Control Commission, and having been investigated, Rotmistrov regained his Party membership with retention of his length of service. However, the commission nevertheless gave him a strict rebuke which subsequently entered his service record. The punishment, of course, wasn't so harsh, but this episode unquestionably might have affected his fate, but soon war would break out and there would then no longer be any need for such formalities. In the meantime, though .... The review of Rotmistrov's complaint lasted for more than a half-year, and all this time the threat of arrest was hanging over him, even after the fact that the positive outcome became known. Thus it is no surprise that Pavel Alekseevich himself requested he be sent into the acting army. Possibly, more experienced comrades advised him to get away from the capital.

The Red Army didn't manage to achieve a decisive victory over the "White Finns" ["White" became the label for all the opponents to Communist power during the Russian Civil War]. Combat operations dragged on, and striving to bring the conflict to an end as quickly as possible, the leadership of the USSR changed tactics. In January 1940 a powerful grouping was formed on the basis of the Leningrad Military District – the Northwestern Front consisting of the 7th and 13th Armies. After his arrival in the acting army, Colonel P.A. Rotmistrov was offered the post of chief of operations with the 7th Army's headquarters, but he declined the offer and requested assignment to a combat tank formation, so he was sent to the 35th Light Tank Brigade. Having arrived in the brigade, due to the existing operational situation he was first given command of a

13 V.S. Mil'bakh, *Osobaia Krasnoznamennaia Dal'nevostochnaia armiia* (Krasnoznamennyi Dal'nevostochnyi okrug). *Politicheskie represii komandno-nachal'stvuiushchego sostava, 1937-1938* [*Special Red Banner Far Eastern Army* (*Red Banner Far Eastern district*). *Political repressions of the command staff, 1937-1938*] SPb. (Izdatel'stvo Sankt-Peterburgskogo universiteta, 2007), p. 99.

tank battalion, and then served as the brigade's acting chief of staff. Pavel Alekseevich took part in the fighting from February 1940 until the signing of the peace treaty in March. Over this brief period he received his first practical knowledge of command of a tank formation in his life. Unquestionably, two incomplete months were not enough for a deep study of the details of the new profession or to master it completely. After all, prior to this moment he had never before commanded an element or unit in the tank forces like M.E. Katukov had. However, within six months with just this modest "baggage" he would take command of a tank brigade, and already in the fighting on the approaches to Moscow, he would demonstrate his combat skills.

For its success in the Winter War, the 35th Light Tank Brigade would be awarded the Order of the Red Banner, and P.A. Rotmistrov would be decorated with the Order of the Red Star (14 June 1940). In 1943 in a letter to the Central Committee secretary G.M. Malenkov, he wrote about this period in his life:

> When the Soviet-Finnish war began, I asked for and was sent to participate in this war in order to study the experience of using tanks, and I was assigned to the ABTO [the Red Army's Auto-Armored Department]. However, I didn't stay in the ABTO, but voluntarily went to the 35th Tank Brigade and began to study the war's experience from the position as commander of a tank battalion, being a colonel and in the capacity of an Academy instructor.
>
> Commanding the battalion, several times I participated in tank attacks, and more than once my tank was knocked out on the battlefield, but I continued stubbornly to strive to reach my assigned objective. Later in this war I commanded a tank brigade while continuing to learn about the use of tanks on the basis of the brigade's actions.
>
> After the end of the Soviet-Finnish war, where I managed to check my theoretical understandings to a significant degree, I appeared repeatedly in the press, in particular in the *Krasnaia Zvezda* newspaper, where I openly and boldly expressed my point of view about the use of tanks. Back then, just as now, I adhered to my point of view about the use of tanks in mass on the battlefield and the boldest actions on the part of the Red Army's tank forces in order to force our will upon the enemy. Through my articles and principled posing of questions on the use of tanks, in 1940 I received a very large commissariat bonus award from the People's Commissar of Defense.[14]

However, this information is missing in his service record. Unfortunately, I've been unable to find the list of awardees, although undoubtedly there was such an award. In his service record it is indicated only "From 12 February 1940 – commander of a reserve group of the Northwest Front for special assignments."[15] Likely, this wording is taken from the documents that he was given when being sent to the Northwestern Front. Thus it can be assumed that he was assigned to all of the aforementioned posts not in the normal way, but according to the combat situation, and he carried out his duties unofficially.

March 1940 was rich with pleasant events. After concluding the peace treaty with Finland, one more piece of good news arrived: on 20 March the Main Political Command of the Red Army revoked the formal rebuke that had been given to Communist P.A. Rotmistrov. After his time at the front, he again returned to teaching work and continued to serve in the academy as a senior instructor until the end of 1940.

14 B. Sokolov, *Razvedka. Tainy Vtoroi mirovoi voiny* [*Intelligence. Secrets of the Second World War*] (Moscow: ACT-Press Kniga, 2001), pp. 332-338.

15 TsAMO RF. Service records of P.A. Rotmistrov.

At this time, intense work was continuing in order to form the first nine mechanized corps. On 9 December 1940 Rotmistrov was sent to the Baltic Special Military District to become the deputy commander of the 3rd Mechanized Corps' 5th Tank Division, which was stationed in the Lithuanian city of Alytus. However, he didn't remain long in this post; within six months, on 19 June 1941, a new order arrived appointing him to the post of chief of staff of this same mechanized corps.[16] Having turned over the command of his division to F.F. Fedorov, who had arrived from the courses for improving the command staff, he left for his new post in Kaunas, just before the German Werhmacht invaded our borders.

News about the start of the war found Colonel M.E. Katukov in Kiev, in a district hospital. The post-operation stitches still hadn't healed, but as soon as he learned about the invasion, Mikhail Efimovich persuaded the doctor that was treating him to discharge him from the hospital, and he hurried to Shepetovka, where the division headquarters was located. Indeed, already on the evening of 23 June, he reported his arrival by telephone to Major General K.K. Rokossovsky, the commander of the 9th Mechanized Corps, to which his division was still subordinate. General Rokossovsky informed him that the situation was murky and the corps had been transferred to Major General M.I. Potapov's 5th Army, which in turn was subordinate to the Southwestern Front. Rokossovsky then already issued an order to Katukov: Move the division to the area of Lutsk in order to launch a counterattack into the flank of the enemy grouping.

In his memoirs, the army commander recalled that his formation was a tank division in name only; in reality, it wasn't such. For example, at the moment of the start of the war, its two tank regiments, instead of the authorized 375 T-34 and KV tanks, had only 33 training BT light tanks, and the signal battalion had only training radio sets. All of the units that hadn't yet received their materiel had to be converted into rifle units, including specialized elements like the pontoon bridging battalion. A similar situation also existed with motorized transport: because of the shortage of trucks, the movement of troops went slowly and with great difficulty. Also, the question of raising the men's combat capabilities hadn't been fully resolved by this time. A "Report about the staffing of the 20th Tank Division with personnel for 10 March 1941", which was signed by M.E. Katukov, has been preserved. Here is an excerpt from this report:

> Command staff: According to the establishment, 1,342 are authorized; 584 are available or 43% of establishment strength. The situation stands particularly badly with staffing the headquarters at every level. Staff officers are short 85 men, including battalion adjutants – 32, regiment headquarters' clerks – 42, division headquarter's clerks – 11. The regiment headquarters, the 1st, 2nd, 3rd and 4th Departments are completely unstaffed; there is no one to plan and lead the combat training. … Of the number of command staff men to be transferred to the division headquarters by an order of the Kiev Special Military District, 52 still have not arrived. Their arrival is dubious; in response to a number of queries to the units, from which the command staff was drawn, the latter answer that the staff officers that we were to receive went instead to a completely different division at an order from the Kiev Special Military District's Department of Cadres.
>
> … Some of the command staff that the division has received is not qualified or able to handle the duties they've been given. Junior Lieutenants K. and K., who've been directed to take command of tank platoons, have extremely negative characteristics and a warning from Kiev Special Military District's Military Council about their unfitness for service in January of this year. … The designated inspector of supplies Captain D. … is sick with tuberculosis

16 This date is mentioned in his service recored, but in his memoirs P.A. Rotmistrov offers a different date – the end of May 1941.

and should be sent to the non-combatant corps, a sanitorium or a hospital. Junior Political Instructor L. … has a fourth grade education and hasn't mastered the Russian language; he isn't working in a company because he can't speak the language. Political Instructor Zh. … has been recommended for a discharge from the Red Army as an indolent and undisciplined political worker. The 32nd Tank Division re-assigned Junior Political Instructor G. to our division, who has been recommended for discharge from the Red Army due to his poor health; the same applies to the political staff that arrived from the 10th Tank Division.

Junior command staff: The division is staffed with junior commanders up to just 1% of establishment strength. It is short 1,910 men. The division has received enlisted personnel and corporals from the 10th and 15th Tank Divisions after our request to cover the shortage was passed on to higher command [the Red Army's Main Department of Cadres] by the Department of Staffing of the Kiev Special Military District. The quality of the arriving corporals is very low; the latter by both their composition and training are not fit to carry out the duties of the junior command staff. In the number of arriving corporals, 211 are of non-Russian nationality and have poor knowledge of the Russian language. Two are Germans, 1 is a Persian, 7 are illiterate and 70 are poorly-educated; 11 men have been reduced in rank to private for disciplinary reasons, 18 arrived in the army by court order or are convicts, 12 men have family members who've been repressed, and 20 men are unfit for combat service. In order to train the junior command staff, training elements have been established in the division's units and the men will be trained until September 1941; once completed, the shortage will be covered.

Enlisted men: At the present day the division has been fully supplied with enlisted men according to the establishment figure, including the 1,910 men that have been received to cover the shortage of junior command staff. … As a result, the division is above table strength in enlisted men by 127. The men have arrived from all the units of the Kiev Special Military District and even from other districts. These units, which are sending men to the division, despite orders from the Kiev Special Military District's Department of Staffing, have sent their undesirables to us. … Of the 125 men sent to us from the 164th Rifle Division, 68 (64%) are non-Russian, 22 men are of older ages (28 to 30 years of age) from the reserve of 2nd Category men; 67 men are illiterate or poorly-educated (from schools for illiterates or with only a 1st or 2nd grade education). … The majority of units are sending the men prior to the arrival of our receiving inspection staff; the 32nd Cavalry Division, bringing the men to Shepetovka [the point of intake for the arriving contingent of personnel – the author] and knowing that they were unsuitable and wouldn't be accepted (all seven were sick), brought the men to the gates of a regimental garrison camp and ordered them to enter the compound, while those accompanying them headed back to their division.

Necessary:

1. Hasten the delivery of command staff to the division, especially to staff the headquarters of the units, the tankers and the artillery supply command staff, because the absence of such slows down the planned and qualitative course of combat training, as well as the control and breaking-in of the elements.
2. Re-assign the personnel now in the division who are unfit for service in tank units and those who are simply ballast, namely: 499 men who are unfit for combat; 883 men who are illiterate or poorly-educated; and 478 men who arrived by court order or who come from repressed families; 236 men who have not masterd the Russian language; and 36 men who are not authorized to serve in a border district. Altogether send us 20,082 men

> who by their quality are fit for service in tank units, in place of the men who've been passed off on us.[17]

If you consider the subject of our discussion, this excerpt is indeed too large. However, I deliberately decided to leave it as such, so that the reader on the basis of genuine sources can form an image of the condition that our tank formations were in just three months before the war's start, and with what difficulty the process of their forming up went, one in which both future army commanders took a direct part. After all, to form a division or a corps doesn't mean simply bringing together all of their constituent parts. The main thing is to form an operable system, the nucleus of which will be a prepared (instructed, trained, educated) military collective. Only such troops will achieve success. Just a little time would pass, and in the summer of 1943, M.E. Katukov's article "Vospitanie soldata" ["A soldier's upbringing"] would appear in the *Komsomol'skaia pravda* newspaper.[18]

In it, the main thought of an experienced military commander is clearly discernible: in order to produce a soldier, hard work is required by both his commander and the larger military collective, and thus the preparation of a genuine warrior is necessary before the moment that the cannons speak up. Mikhail Efimovich emphasized, "Loads of guns and masses of men are still not an army." Yet within three months, Colonel M.E. Katukov in the summer of 1941 would join combat with an aggressor at the head of a formation that was not ready for combat – the 20th Tank Division, and, unfortunately, leading just that mass of men, who not only didn't have the guns, but also lacked the necessary combat training.

Katukov's division had its combat baptism on 24 June 1941 against units of the Wehrmacht's 13th Panzer Division at the *shtetl* of Klevan'. It turned out to be very hard: the opposing sides were unequal in strength and capabilities. Even though the enemy was temporarily checked, this success came at a costly price. The division lost all of its combat machines, one tank regiment commander was killed, and there was a lot of dead and wounded. Before the start of July, the 20th Tank Division took part in the large, but unfortunately for our side inglorious battle in the Dubno area. As a result the 5th Army managed to delay the enemy's advance to the south for several days, but this made no difference in the overall situation at the front. The foe continued to attack, not only inflicting heavy losses to the Soviet forces, but in a situation when the massed evacuation of the defense industry to the east had started. The losses were difficult to replace, first of all in heavy weapons. Wrote a participant in the fighting on the Soviet-German front, the German general H. von Manteuffel:

> In 1941, the Russians faced the same sort of problem that we faced starting in 1942. The infantry didn't have enough anti-tank weapons, and it couldn't hold a position without the aid of tanks. In other words, it was necessary to organize a flexible anti-tank defense. As a result, the tank formations were distributed among the infantry, and this weakened the tank forces themselves by scattering them.[19]

By the middle of August, a significant portion of the armor had been knocked out of action. This forced the Soviet Supreme High Command to abolish all the large formations (the tank divisions and mechanized corps), and on their basis create significantly smaller formations – brigades and separate battalions.

17 TsAMO RF, F. 131, Op. 12980, D. 3, LL. 200-205.

18 *Komsomol'skaia pravda*, 23 July 1943, p. 2.

19 E. von Manstein, *Po druguiu storonu vysoty* [*On the other side of the hill*] (Moscow: AST, 2014), p. 334,

On 18 August 1941 Colonel M.E. Katukov, who had only recently broken out of encirclement with the remnants of his division in the area of the *shtetl'* of Grental', was called back to Moscow, to the Main Auto-Armored Command. Here his former colleague, but now the Commander-in-Chief of the Red Army's Armored Forces Lieutenant General Ia.N. Fedorenko announced that Katukov would take command of the 4th Tank Brigade, then forming up in Stalingrad on the basis of the 15th Tank Division, which had already participated in the fighting. Not all of the soldiers and officers of the division were included in the brigade, but those who wound up in it, first of all, the command staff, had meritoriously passed through all of the harsh trials of the initial period of the Great Patriotic War together with M.E. Katukov.

The process of forming up went quickly; the Germans were advancing headlong toward the capital, and thus there was no time to break in the men and command staff of the new tank brigade. The brigade commander arrived in Stalingrad on 8 September, and already on 23 September the brigade was loaded aboard trains and departed for Moscow. Five days later approximately 150 of its combat machines and its small number of men were unloaded at Kubinka Station and were almost immediately directed to head south, to the Mtsensk area, where the situation was extremely precarious. Army Group Center with the forces of General Guderian's Panzergruppe 2 had torn a gap in Briansk Front's defenses, and had taken Orel on 3 October. Several formations, which were combined into the 1st Guards Rifle Corps under the command of Major General D.D. Leliushenko, were hastily sent to block the breakthrough. It had to stop the enemy and create a firm defense here. The 4th Tank Brigade was part of the 1st Guards Rifle Corps. Already on 4 October, its reconnaissance detachment was sent to the Orel area, and two days later the brigade's main forces engaged the forward units of the Panzergruppe 2's XXIV Panzer Corps.

It was in these battles that Mikhail Efimovich's abilities were first revealed as a military innovator and a creative leader who searched for new forms and methods of struggle against a numerically-superior foe. It was here that his tactic of ambushes was tested for the first time, which subsequently became widely known. M.E. Katukov recalled:

> Such a scheme emerged gradually. The motorized riflemen were positioned on the defense, having first dug real and dummy trenches. Mock-ups of cannons and machine guns were positioned in the dummy trenches. A portion of these trenches was occupied by small groups of soldiers with real machine guns. Their role was to play as "actors", feigning a forward edge of defense. The real trenches lay a short distance in their rear, while tanks were positioned further back on tank-vulnerable directions – sometimes a platoon, sometimes a single tank. In order to camouflage the tanks, whatever that was available locally for concealment was exploited: bushes, trees, haystacks and the reverse slopes of hills. Each crew prepared for itself not one position, but two or three, among which they could shift position unnoticed by the enemy. The crews beforehand determined reference objects and the distance to them. Cooperation with the infantry, artillery and sappers was arranged ahead of time, and communication was established by radio, special signals, or runners. All of the tank crews were to be positioned within each others' field of vision, ready to go to the aid of a neighboring tank.
>
> The enemy begins by conducting ground and aerial reconnaissance. The ambushes remain silent. Then only once the enemy machines approach to within 200-300 meters, the crews move into their ambush firing positions and open point-blank fire at the enemy, making hits certain. At the same time the crews of the ambush keep their neighbors within eyesight and fire at the exposed flank of enemy tanks that are breaking through. Oblique, intersecting, devastating fire is the result. The commander of the ambush moves into a firing position only in the event of extreme need. He observes the battlefield from behind a bush or from some foxhole somewhere, spots targets, gives the vector, and only after this takes a seat in a tank, and the machine bounds forward to open fire. Once the target is chosen, the gunlayer aims

> the gun at the target. Having fired three or four shots, the tank goes into reverse and backs away into cover. If you stand still too long in the same position, the tank will become the victim of targeted fire. From the concealed position the commanders again conduct observation before bounding forward once again into a firing position, but this time a different one. This process is repeated several times.
>
> Combat is an entire array of complex problems, which are often interrelated, so at times it is difficult to discern where is the cause, and where the effect. Probably it is only possible to say that success always depends on the correct resolution of many, frequently indirect questions. Success far from always accrues to the side that has force superiority. Yet almost always to the side that is superior in shaping the battlefield.[20]

This method fully justified itself and demonstrated great effectiveness not only in the fighting on the approaches to Moscow, but also in the future, including at the Battle of Kursk. Recalling the fighting at Mtsensk after the war, M.E. Katukov emphasized that "they gave a prompt to the thought of how best to use tanks in the struggle with an attacking enemy that is significantly superior in equipment and men."[21] Over seven days of combat, Katukov's tank brigade inflicted significant damage to the enemy, but the main thing was that the German advance toward Tula was stopped, and time was gained for bringing up reserves.

The Supreme High Command thought highly of the courage of the brigade's tankers and the professionalism of their commander. Already on 12 October 1941, a decree of the Presidium of the Supreme Soviet was published in all the central newspapers about honoring the tankers. Among those decorated was Colonel M.E. Katukov; he was awarded the Order of Lenin. A month later, on 10 November 1941, he acquired his first general's rank, Major General of Tank Troops, and on the following day I.V. Stalin signed People's Commissar Order No. 337 about transforming Katukov's brigade into the 1st Guards Tank Brigade. One interesting detail, which might be called a wry twist of history: The first Red Army Guardsman tanker received his highest government honor of the USSSR, the Order of Lenin, in December 1941 in field conditions in front of an assembly of his comrades from none other than the commander of the 20th Army Major General A.A. Vlasov, who in July 1942 became a prisoner and would cover himself in ignomy by cooperating with the Germans, and his name in the USSR would become the household name for treachery.

These events in the autumn of 1941 became important for M.E. Katukov's career. If his appointment to the post of tank division commander was for all that a promotion, then his acquisition of the general's rank and his receipt of a high Order at a most difficult moment for the country and its army was already a high assessment of the concrete results of his work. His skillful leadership of his tank brigade in the fighting to defend the capital city, and of course the fixed attention of I.V. Stalin personally on his brigade brought M.E. Katukov up into the first rank of the commanders that were rapidly gaining experience, who would soon take on the entire burden of leading the troops in the war against Germany. Very soon thereafter they would step into the leading role in the Red Army and not only defend the country, but also bring liberation from the Nazis to the peoples of Europe.

On 11 October the 4th Tank Brigade was pulled back into the 50th Army's reserve, and on 16 October M.E. Katukov was summoned to the 50th Army's headquarters, where over the telephone he received Stalin's personal order to shift his brigade to the area of Kubinka in order to defend the Minsk – Moscow highway. In the course of the ensuing march, the future army commander not

20 Katukov, Na ostrie glavnogo udara, pp. 22-23.
21 Ibid., p. 252.

at his own fault nearly wound up facing a tribunal for his failure to carry out an order. Katukov himself revealed what happened:

> We reached Kubinka successfully … a general arrived from the Front headquarters to meet the brigade. He'd been entrusted to lead the brigade to its assigned positions. He came by my command post, which was deployed at the time at the Tamarka railyard, and having given the Front commander's order to move my brigade to the Chismena area, he spread a map out onto the table.
>
> "Your brigade will move to Chismena along this road." His pencil drew a fat line.
>
> I objected: "Trucks can't even get through here, much less T-34s."
>
> The point was that ordinarily upon a arrival at a new place, as the first order of business we studied the condition of the roads and bridges, so in case of an order to move to a new area, we'd accurately know the routes to take. That's how it was this time. That's why with full knowledge of the real situation I objected to the general that it was impossible to move directly from Kubinka to the Chismena area, and that there was only one way to go – send the machines through Moscow along the paved roads.
>
> However, the general stood his ground. Anyone can make a mistake. No one is secure from an error. But it is always the most unpleasant thing, especially in war, when a chief persists in his mistake, persists in the name of esprit de corps, and stands on his rank and injured pride. How dearly sometimes this cost us!
>
> "Enough chit-chat! Carry out the order!" – The general ended our conversation.
>
> This was a most difficult march. The tanks, smoking heavily, strained engines howling, were clambering out of the deep ruts. … During the day, the general was still with the column, but that night he disappeared somewhere.
>
> We made our way to Istra with difficulty. But here again there was a stop. We'd run out of fuel … It isn't surprising that given such a rate of movement, we were late in getting to the assembly area. Then suddenly a telephone message from Front headquarters: For the failure to carry out a combat order, turn the brigade commander Colonel Katukov over to a trial by military tribunal. Straightaway the military prosecutor arrived, and the wheels began to turn. True, those present at my dispute with the general confirmed that the route of march had been imposed upon us from above, by force. However, the matter had nonetheless taken an unpleasant turn.
>
> My political chief Major I.G. Dereviankin retorted, "How can they do this! "Was this really our fault? It was their representative who entangled us in this story. No, I won't let this rest!"
>
> I must confess that I didn't expect such an emotional outburst from my always composed chief of the Political Department. Late that evening he climbed into a car and headed to Moscow. At 0200 Ivan Grigor'evich fought his way through to General Fedorenko. The general called Stalin, and the matter was settled.[22]

In the biographies of many Soviet generals of that time, such cases were not rare. More than once P.A. Rotmistrov also fell into such a mess. A similar experience happened with him on the Stalingrad axis in September 1942 and almost cost him his post as corps commander. However, this story lies ahead

22 Ibid., pp. 57-59.

At the end of October 1941, Mikhail Efimovich again had the opportunity to fight under Major General K.K. Rokossovsky's command, a man he regarded "with boundless respect."[23] The 4th Tank Brigade was made operationally subordinate to Rokossovsky's 16th Army and took part in the repulse of the enemy's offensive toward Moscow from the northeast. In this fighting, Katukov's tankers were supporting Panfilov's 316th Rifle Division and Major General L.M. Dovator's cavalry group. In the first half of November they took part in eliminating the so-called "Skirmanovo bridgehead", a dent the enemy had made in the defenses of the 16th Army 30 kilometers southwest of Volokolamsk. Here, on the Western Direction, the brigade commander received his first successful experience in command of a tank formation larger than a brigade, and moreover in difficult winter conditions. At the beginning of December, when the 16th Army launched a counteroffensive along with the entire Western Front, K.K. Rokossovsky created three mobile groups under the command of Generals A.P. Beloborodov, F.G. Remezov and M.E. Katukov. By their force composition, they faintly suggested a tank corps, which would begin to be formed in the Red Army in the following year. Each group included two tank brigades, a separate tank battalion, and a separate motorized rifle brigade. However, already after the initial battles, on 19 December, F.G. Remezov's group was subordinated to M.E. Katukov, and in the course of liberating Volokolamsk, he was now commanding both mobile groups.

From the end of December 1941 to the end of January 1942, his mobile group, attached to the 20th Army, was fighting to destroy the enemy's fortified lines on the Lama and Ruza Rivers. Here, Mikhail Efimovich became acquainted with the commander of a naval infantry brigade Colonel I.M. Chistiakov. The latter's brigade for a short time operated as part of Katukov's mobile group. Within a year and a half, they would happen again to fight together on the same line at the Kursk bulge, but now as army commanders.

After the 20th Army reached the territory of Smolensk Oblast at the end of January 1942, the 1st Guards Tank Brigade was transferred to General L.A. Govorov's 5th Army, and was withdrawn to Gzhatsk for refitting. Meanwhile the brigade commander was summoned to Moscow in order to receive a new, higher appointment as commander of a tank corps.

The start of the war and the first six months of it were much harder for Pavel Alekseevich Rotmistrov. At the time when division commander M.E. Katukov was fighting "on foot against tanks" in Poles'e, the chief of staff of the 3rd Mechanized Corps had to experience the bitter fate of an "encircled man" in full measure. From the first day of the Nazi's offensive, Major General A.V. Kurkin's corps wound up in an extremely difficult situation. Trying to restrain the adversary's attacking forces the 11th Army command began to throw all of its three divisions, which were still not yet fully equipped with materiel, one after another into battle without preparation. The 5th Tank Division was moved out in order to hold a bridgehead across the Nieman River west of Alytus, but its units didn't have time to take up a defense. It suffered a defeat in a meeting battle with General H. Hoth's Panzergruppe 3, and already on the night of 22-23 June 1941, having abandoned Alytus, began to retreat to Kaunas and Vilnius with its remaining 40 combat machines. Next the enemy also scattered the 84th Motorized Rifle Division.

It was planned to commit the 2nd Tank Division on the Tauragė axis in a frontal attack on 23 June against the enemy that had broken through in the sector of the 8th Army. However, the counterattack didn't come off. The division wound up encircled in the Raseiniai area, and the command of the 3rd Mechanized Corps, which by that time had been practically completely destroyed, also found itself in that situation. On 26 June enemy infantry riding on tanks that had had broken through simultaneously attacked the headquarters of the division and of the corps. The fighting was fierce and unequal; many officers were killed, among them the commander of

23 Ibid., p. 66.

the 2nd Tank Division. Communication with the 11th Army was lost. In this situation the corps commander decided to destroy all of the equipment and break out of the pocket. P.A. Rotmistrov recalled:

> Hard trials fell to our fate. For almost two months we were making our way to the east through the woods of Belorussia and the northern Briansk region, bypassing enemy-garrisoned cities, towns and villages at night, while destroying rear German elements and columns of their vehicles carrying ammunition and various supplies. Despite all the burdens and deprivations, our men didn't become dejected and kept their appearance as Soviet combatants. They came out still wearing their uniforms and carrying their personal weapons and documents, while the Communist Party members had their membership cards.
>
> After coming out of encirclement, tank crews were formed out of the tankers of General A.V. Kurkin's group and sent to factories in order to receive new equipment. The senior command staff, including myself, was ordered to go to Moscow.[24]

They came out of encirclement only by 28 August. After crossing the frontline, all of the men were subjected to strict checking by organs of the military counterintelligence. At the time this was a matter of procedure, but at the same time, a very serious test. P.A. Rotmistrov passed through it relatively quickly. The fact that the soldiers and and commanders had come out in a compact group, having kept their papers and weapons, played a key role. Possibly, Pavel Alekseevich's old friendship with the Chief of the Auto-Armored Command Lieutenant General Fedorenko played a role. At their first meeting after coming out of encirclement, Iakov Nikolaevich offered Rotmistrov the post of chief of staff of his Command, but in P.A. Rotmistrov's words, he declined the offer and asked to be given a command post in the field, but his request wasn't satisfied.[25] Thereupon he immediately sent a letter to I.V. Stalin and a day later received appointment as commander of the 8th Tank Brigade, which was forming up in Kosterevo (120 kilometers southwest of Moscow), and on 9 September 1941 he took command of it. This brigade became for the future army commander a genuine school of combat experience and command skills.

However, the first days at the front in this post almost cost him both his career and his freedom. The situation was pressing, and the staffing of the brigade went at an accelerated tempo. Already in the second half of the month, the brigade was sent to the Northwestern Front. After unloading at the Valdai Station in Novgorod Oblast, practically from the march the 8th Tank Brigade took part in the fighting in conjunction with the 11th Army. At the beginning of October the enemy took Kalinin [formerly the city of Tver'], thereby cutting the Leningrad -- Moscow highway. Thus on 14 October an order arrived from the Commander-in-Chief of the Northwestern Front about shifting Rotmistrov's tank brigade to the Torzhka area in order to reinforce the Kalinin direction. Within 48 hours, having conducted a 250-kilometer march, it arrived in the indicated area.

Here, on his native Tver' soil, in the course of the two heaviest months of fighting for Moscow, P.A. Rotmistrov was destined to defend not only the country against the aggressors, but also his own small homeland. In this period, Pavel Alekseevich had two noteworthy meetings. The first, with the man under whose direct leadership he would be fighting as an army commander in the Battle of Kursk, N.F. Vatutin, who in the future became the Commander-in-Chief of the Voronezh Front, but in the autumn of 1941 he was still the chief of staff of the Northwestern Front. Before the march to Torzhka, Rotmistrov's tank brigade was included in the Front's operational group under Vatutin's command and served as its forward detachment in the Kalinin area. The second

24 Rotmistrov, *Stal'naia gvardiia*, p. 55.
25 Ibid., p. 58.

meeting can be called a long-distance familiarity between two adversaries. Panzergruppe 3 under the leadership of General H. Hoth, the future commander of the Fourth Panzer Army, was operating on the Northwestern Front, including against the 8th Tank Brigade; in July 1943, Hoth's panzergrenadiers would collide with the Guardsmen of General P.A. Rotmistrov's tank army in savage fighting at Prokhorovka.

From the march, there was no success in driving the Germans out of Kalinin. The situation continued to deteriorate, and on 17 October the *Stavka* would assign the troops that were operating in this area an independent operational direction and create the Kalinin Front under the command of Colonel General I.S. Konev. Rotmistrov's 8th Tank Brigade, along with Vatutin's operational group, were included in the Northwestern Front. The first several days of fighting in the Kalinin area (more precisely, at the village of Mednoe), went extremely unsuccessfully for the brigade commander, just like it did at Prokhorovka in July 1943, and both occasions almost ruined his career. Twice he was accused of cowardice and the failure to carry out an order, first by N.F. Vatutin in October 1941, and second by I.S. Konev in July 1943. Neither Pavel Alekseevich himself, nor his subordinate Major General A. Egorov, who at the time in October 1941 was serving as the commander of the 8th Tank Regiment of Rotmistrov's brigade, ever even mentioned these episodes in the open press, though Egorov published an article about the 1941 battles in the *Voenno-istoricheskii zhurnal* in 1971.[26] So let's turn to recently disclosed documents. From an order sent to P.A. Rotmistrov by the commander of the operational group Lieutenant General N.F. Vatutin at 0600 on 18 October 1941:

> Your actions on 17 October 1941 are worthy of any and all condemnation and disapproval. You failed to execute my verbal order regarding the quick dispatch of tanks to the support of the 3/418th Rifle Regiment, and did this only on the morning of 17 October 1941. Formally, you approached the carrying out of my order about taking up a sector to the left of 3/418th Rifle Regiment irresponsibly and negligently. If the 46th Motorcycle Regiment hadn't been there, it would have had to have been occupied by different means. [Your] reference to fatigue and the breakdown of machines is indefensible. Apparently, the leaders and commanders fell to pieces first of all. You negligently overslept, and right under your nose an insignificant group of tanks broke into our rear, and the appropriate measures for eliminating it weren't taken. You are fully responsible for the breakthrough of the tanks and the prevention of a further enemy advance beyond the Tverets River.
>
> Immediately contact the 133rd Rifle Division and cooperate with it. The failure to carry this out might compel me to raise the question of bringing you to strict responsibility. Report to me briefly about the course of the battle 3 times a day: at 0900, 1500 and 2100.[27]

There is a note on the document: "Received at 2100 18.10.41 -- Rotmistrov".

On that same day, the brigade commander would again receive reprimands of cowardice, although the document would reach him only on the morning of 19 October. From N.F. Vatutin's order:

1. The enemy in the Kalinin area is suffering a defeat. Our troops are occupying the northwestern portion of the city of Kalinin, Malitsa and Kalinino. A small group of enemy has broken through

26 A. Egorov, "Tankovyi polk v boiiakh pod Kalininom i Klinom" ["Tank regiment in the fighting at Kalinin and Klin"] *Voenno-istoricheskii zhurnal*, No. 4 (1971), pp. 59-62.

27 TsAMO RF, F. 3 gv. tbr, Op. 1, D. 5, LL. 36-37.

to the Poddubki, Mednoe, Polustovo area, where it has been isolated by our troops. Your withdrawal is criminal.

2. I order you immediately, without wasting a single hour of time, to return to Likhoslavl', from where jointly with units of the 185th Rifle Division you are to destroy the enemy group that has broken through with an impetuous attack and to take Mednoe. In the future launch an attack toward Kalinino and enter Kalinin on 20.10.1941.
3. Comrade Luk'ianchenko's detachment is attacking along the highway from Torzhka to Mednoe. A motorized rifle brigade of the 29th Army is advancing from the south from the direction of Volyntsevo.
4. I am fully subordinating you to me. I demand the most decisive actions and complete effort. It is time to put an end to cowardice.[28]

The Commander-in-Chief of the Kalinin Front was even more categorical; on 18 October he sent an order to the operational group commander to arrest the colonel: "To Comrade Vatutin. I request the arrest of Rotmistrov for failing to carry out a combat order and his voluntary abandonment of the battlefield with his brigade, and turn him over to a military tribunal for judgement. Appoint the chief of staff to command the brigade, or a commander of your choice. Konev."[29]

Unquestionably, the situation that generated such orders was extremely tense, stressful and far from clear, even to its direct participants. It is even more difficult or perhaps even impossible for us to lay out the course of events and figure out whether the brigade commander was really guilty or not. It is possible to say only one thing: Pavel Alekseevich was lucky that at this potential turning point in his life's path, he came across namely N.F. Vatutin. I'm far from the notion of idealizing the latter, and the facts known today don't allow this to be done. Nevertheless, respect must be given to Nikolai Fedorovich's restraint and foresight. Above all else, he was able to withstand I.S. Konev's pressure and excessively emotional response, and refrained from making any hasty, harsh decisions, toward which his higher command was prompting him.

Just a relatively short time would pass, and the exact same situation would repeat itself in July 1943. At that time even higher-posted representatives from Moscow, State Defense Committee member G.M. Malenkov and his commission would demand to dismiss army commander Rotmistrov from his post and turn him over for military trial. On this occasion, Nikolai Fedorovich Vatutin was unable to help Rotmistrov. N.F. Vatutin's comrade and peer Marshal of the Soviet Union A.M. Vasilevsky would be the one to bail Rotmistrov out of the predicament then. However, such things happen in life. But as the colleagues of the Academy of Armored and Mechanized Forces, who served in it together with P.A. Rotmistrov in the 1950s, told me, he persistently blamed namely N.F. Vatutin and N.S. Khrushchev for his hard time at Prokhorovka. Yet the future army commander subsequently, especially after the war, would establish warm and to a certain respect even comradely relations with I.S. Konev.

Now let's return to the events of the autumn of 1941. Up until the start of November, Rotmistrov's tank brigade was fighting in cooperation with troops of General D.D. Leliushenko's 30th Army that were defending the approaches to the Moscow – Volga canal on the line of the Lama River (south of the Ivanovsky Reservoir). In the latter half of the month, it was made subordinate to the 16th Army's operational group under the command of General F.D. Zakharov, which was defending Klin. However, just as in the case with Kalinin, Klin couldn't be held. Incidentally, at this time Katukov's 1st Guards Tank Brigade was a neighbor of Rotmistrov's 8th Tank Brigade,

28 TsAMO RF, F. 3 gv. tbr, Op. 1, D. 5, L. 47-48.
29 TsAMO RF, F. 213, Op. 202, D. 5, L. 33.

and during the liberation of Klin Major General M.E. Katukov was Colonel P.A. Rotmistrov's immediate superior, since Katukov was heading both of the army's operational groups.

Having exhausted the enemy on the approaches to the capital, the *Stavka* issued an order for three *fronts* to launch a general counteroffensive on 5 December 1941. According to the devised plan, Western Front's 30th Army would launch the main attack in the direction of Rogachev, Spas-Korkodin and Klin. The 8th Tank Brigade was to operate in its main shock grouping. The 30th Army's counteroffensive went successfully, and already within 10 days the task was carried out. After the liberation of Klin, Rotmistrov's tank brigade was again returned to the Kalinin Front, and continued to conduct combat operations as part of it until the counteroffensive wound down.

For the bravery and tenacity demonstrated in the battle for the capital, on 11 January 1942 the 8th Tank Brigade was transformed into the 3rd Guards Tank Brigade. The merits of its commander were highly appreciated, but not as generously as in the case of brigade commander M.E. Katukov. P.A. Rotmistrov was awarded the Order of Lenin, but received no promotion. The events at Kalinin weren't the cause for this. The point was that by TO&E, only a lieutenant colonel or colonel could command a brigade, but a general could do so only by a special decision of the Supreme High Command. An exception was made for M.E. Katukov, because his brigade became the first Guards brigade in the Red Army. This step was supposed to enhance the prestige of the new form of encouraging military formations with the Guards title: "1st Guards" meant something special in everything, both in battle and in honors. This was why not only Pavel Alekseevich, but also the commander of the 9th Tank Brigade Lieutenant Colonel I.F. Kirichenko,[30] who also distinguished himself in the fighting for Moscow, was awarded the Order of Lenin, and his brigade was converted into the 2nd Guards Tank Brigade, but at the same time also kept his current rank.[31] Nevertheless, the successful command of the brigade when defending capital city gave a serious impetus to P.A. Rotmistrov's career.

The autumn and winter of 1941 were exceptionally difficult for the entire Red Army, but was twice as hard on its tank forces. While the evacuation of defense-industry factories to the east and getting production up and running in the new location place was underway, they were simply surviving, and their numerical strength fell to a minimum. By its establishment, a tank brigade had a total of 49 combat machines, and in the best case, only half were KV tanks or T-34s; the rest were light tanks. In reality at the fronts, they had fewer tanks, and even they were all patched up and far from in best condition. The presence of only two tanks brigades, sometimes reinforced with a separate tank battalion, in a combined-arms army that was defending a front of 60-90 kilometers was normal. These forces, as a rule, were used for localizing breakthroughs with brief counterattacks against the attacking German panzer wedges; to seize fortified villages, and also covering undefended sectors of the front with the method of ambushes, until reserve rifle units were brought up.

The tankers fought against a numerically superior foe in wintry conditions that were hard on the men and equipment. They had to fight without artillery or air support, having limited amounts of shells and fuel, and also in close cooperation with rifle formations, the commanders of which often had a faint notion or no understanding at all of the tactics and methods of this type of troops. In such harsh conditions, the "selection and crystallization" of the command cadres took place. The majority of those who survived the fighting and weren't placed behind bars due to fabricated

30 In February 1943, the 29th Tank Corps under the command of Major General I.F. Kirichenko would be made subordinate to Lieutenant General P.A. Rotmistrov's 5th Guards Tank Army, and with it would take part in the famous battle at Prokhorovka.

31 TsAMO RF, Service records of Lieutenant General I.F. Kirichenko, page 1.

accusations, would in the future become the core at the command level of the Red Army's tank and mechanized forces. The acquired knowledge and experience allowed them to occupy rather high posts: the commanders of companies and battalions would become brigade commanders, and the commanders of regiments and separate tank brigades would become corps commanders and army commanders.

This period was also very important for Pavel Alekseevich. In essence, this was the first time that he independently commanded a tactical tank formation for a lengthy period, for more than six months. During this time he became immersed in all the details of its combat life and everyday activities; commanded the tank companies in the course of combat actions and took daily part in their planning; and observed and to a certain extent took part in the planning of the operations of the army, to which his brigade belonged. The acquired experience added to his theoretical knowledge that was rich for those times, and became a foundation, upon which he grew as a commander of armored forces and a future leader of large troop formations and armies. However, his experience in command of a brigade should not be overestimated; it unquestionably was very important, but I stress that this was only a basis for further growth and for increasing his combat mastery, while the skills of a master, as is known, come only in the process of lengthy, daily work.

The revitalization of the tank forces began in the spring of 1942, when new equipment began to arrive from the Urals. So the *Stavka* of the Supreme High Command made the decision to begin the formation of large tank formations. At this time, with a difference of only a few weeks, both brigade commanders Katukov and Rotmistrov would receive orders appointing them in command of a tank corps: M.E. Katukov, the 1st Tank Corps, and P.A. Rotmistrov, the 7th Tank Corps.[32]

Pavel Alekseevich created his new formation in his native area, in the vicinity of Kalinin, and his Guards tank brigade became the basis for the new tank corps. A number of officers from it took posts in command of the tank corps. However, new men also arrived; among them was the commander of the 62nd Heavy Tank Brigade that became part of the tank corps, Lieutenant Colonel V.N. Baskakov. He had been commanding the 130th Tank Brigade on the Southern Front from 23 September 1941, and on 15 February 1942 he was appointed in command of the 62nd Heavy Tank Brigade. From this time, fate brought Vladimir Nikolaevich and Pavel Alekseevich together for two years of service. In the very first battle, which the 7th Tank Corps conducted on Voronezh soil, trying to sever the line of communications of the enemy that was dashing toward the Don River, it was Baskakov's tank brigade that would distinguish itself, and a short time later he became the chief of staff of the 7th Tank Corps, and on 21 March 1943, of the 5th Guards Tank Army. V.N. Baskakov's rapid rise in the ranks, from brigade commander to an army chief of staff, and the rank of major general that he received, testified to the fact that he could establish good working relationships with P.A. Rotmistrov. Analyzing the joint activity of these men, it is possible to say with confidence that their collaboration in that far from simple time was fruitful. However, for the sake of justice, it is necessary to note that it wasn't easy for Vladimir Nikolaevich to work with Rotmistrov, and moreover to keep independent views. This is not only because of the fact that Pavel Alekseevich was senior in both age and rank. Unlike M.E. Katukov or P.S. Rybalko, Rotmistrov wasn't inclined to gather experienced, up and coming commanders around him, to teach them and help them climb the service ladder (the chief of staff was an exceptional case), and thereby gradually form and expand a cohesive command team and raise the quality of its work. Personnel matters weren't his leading interest. He served together with anyone who was sent to him "from above". I never once came across any mention of how he petitioned for a combat commander or staff officer from a different formation to be transferred into his corps or army

32 M.E. Katukov was appointed tank corps commander on 31 March 1942, and the order from the People's Commissar of Defense for P.A. Rotmistrov was signed on 19 April 1942.

in a single archival document or in the memoirs of the men who served with Pavel Alekseevich. Possibly, this was my own lack of success and I can fully allow that over the lengthy years of service in the armed forces, there might have been such cases, and more than one. However, malicious tongues maintained that without open groveling, it was very hard to make a career in his tank corps, and later in his tank army; this was particularly the case after the Battle of Kursk. Indeed, as we will see below, not only his subordinates knew this well, but they were also aware of this in Moscow, although in the capital they sought to disregard this trait for a certain time.

For the sake of justice it should be also noted that M.E. Katukov as a commander didn't always make understandable decisions on cadre matters, even major ones. His conflicts with General A.L. Getman, who at first commanded the 1st Tank Army's 6th Tank Corps, including at the Battle of Kursk, before being transferred to the dependent post of deputy commander of an army, is well known. Andrei Lavrent'evich successfully commanded the tank corps; after the Battle of Kursk it became a Guards tank corps, and he personally more than once was singled out for high combat honors. There is the opinion that this transfer and the tense relations between the generals was a consequence of A.L. Getman's unworthy conduct and prickly nature.[33] However, the Getman himself maintained that "he never presented gifts to the command (to Katukov and Popel'[34] and I spoke badly of those who did."[35] It is difficult to say where the truth lies in this dispute. After the war, A.L. Getman's former subordinate, the commander of the 112th Tank Brigade, twice-Hero of the Soviet Union I.I. Gusakovsky said something wise about this: "Time will judge them. I can say only one thing: Katukov wasn't right when he removed Getman from command of the corps at the end of 1944. This was shown by the results of the subsequent fighting."[36]

However, let's return to the events of early 1942. By TO&E, the 7th Tank Corps was supposed to have 5,600 men, 168 tanks, 32 guns, 44 mortars, 20 anti-aircraft guns, and a "Katiusha" battalion (8 rocket launchers). All these forces and means were combined into three tank brigades (each with 53 tanks) and one motorized rifle brigade, as well as units directly subordinate to corps headquarters. A weakness was the presence of a significant number of light combat machines; not only T-70 light tanks, but also T-60 light tanks. The T-60 was a dated design with light armor and only a 20mm cannon. At this same time the Wehrmacht command had already by the start of the summer of 1942 updated its main tank, the Pz IV, additionally by giving it a long-barreled 75mm cannon. This perceptibly enhanced its effectiveness, although in mid-1942, naturally, not all of the machines at the front had been converted to the new standard.

Briansk Front's counterattack in the summer of 1942 on the Voronezh axis became the debut for the young tank corps commander. In the latter half of June, in connection with the enemy breakthrough to Ostrogozhsk and the emergence of the threat of the envelopment of Voronezh, the 7th Tank Corps was hastily transferred by railroad to Elets, where it joined Major General A.N. Liziukov's 5th Tank Army. The tank army received the assignment to launch an attack against the northern flank of the German Group Weichs in the direction of Zemliansk-Khokhol. The Soviet command was hoping thereby to cut the Germans' line of communications and frustrate their attempt to force a crossing of the Don River. In addition, Liziukov's troops, having penetrated into the depth of the territory of Kursk and Voronezh Oblasts that had been seized by the Germans, were to help the divisions of the Southwestern Front's 40th and 21st Armies escape the pocket that had formed in the Staryi Oskol – Chernianka – Korocha area.

33 E.S. Katukova, *Pamiatnoe* [*Unforgettable*] (Moscow, 2000), pp. 49-50.
34 Popel' was a member of the 1st Tank Army's Military Council.
35 V. Prudnikov, *Stal'noi uragan* [*Steel hurricane*] (Moscow: Iauza/EKSMO, 2008), p. 284.
36 Ibid., p. 8.

During the tank corps' unloading in Elets, P.A. Rotmistrov became acquainted with the Chief of the General Staff Colonel General A.M. Vasilevsky, who had personally arrived to pass along the order about subordinating the 7th Tank Corps to the 5th Tank Army.[37] After this, the war would often bring them back together. On the New Year's night of 1943, Aleksandr Mikhailovich would arrive to congratulate the corps command on the successful raid to Kotel'nikovo. In July 1943, he happened to have the main role in determining the fate of army commander Rotmistrov. In the words of Pavel Alekseevich himself, it was A.M. Vasilevsky who deflected the wrath of I.V. Stalin over the 5th Guards Tank Army's heavy losses at Prokhorovka.

Because of the poor organization of the 5th Tank Army's counterattack and the not always justified haste in putting it together, it failed to achieve the excpected success. Its subordinate tank corps were introduced at different times with an interval of several days, and this prevented the creation of a decisive advantage in force on the main axis of attack. A reshuffling within the command of Briansk Front also influenced the lack of success. There was not always full and complete information from the battlefield, thus at times orders arrived from the headquarters to the troops, the execution of which might and often did lead to contrary results and large losses. M.E. Katukov also took part in the fighting together with his tank corps. In one of his reports, he unambiguously commented on one such order: "To send tanks into frontal attacks against enemy anti-tank artillery is incorrect, no matter how much they berated us."[38] Incidentally, these events were studied in detail and described in the book *Taina gibeli generala Liziukova* [*Secret of the death of General Liziukov*] written by the scholar I.Iu. Sdvizhkov. In his opinion, the failure to carry out one such order in particular from Briansk Front's Commander-in-Chief K.K. Rokossovsky from 23 July 1942 possibly saved M.E. Katukov's life.[39]

Up until the end of August, the 7th Tank Corps continued to conduct stubborn fighting on Voronezh soil in the area of Zemliansk. On 25 August, after the German breakthrough to the Volga River and the formation of the semi-ring around Stalingrad, the tank corps was sent to the Stalingrad front. In this next round of fighting P.A. Rotmistrov, now a major general, not only experienced the bitterness of defeat and helplessness, but also once again felt the chill of distrust. At the beginning of September 1942, the tank corps took part in a counterattack by the 1st Guards Army with the aim of destroying the enemy that had broken through to the Volga and re-establishing contact with the 62nd Army that had been cut off in Stalingrad. The situation in the city was becoming dire, and thus it was exceptionally important operationally to divert some of the enemy force from the city. For the resolution of this task, the Deputy Supreme Commander G.K. Zhukov, Chief of the General Staff A.M. Vasilevsky and even Central Committee Secretary and member of the State Defense Committee G.M. Malenkov, who was in charge of the cadres, arrived on location here. Moscow was in a hurry, and the counterattack began without adequate preparation; the attacking troops didn't have the needed cover against air strikes, and in the 1st Guards Army itself there was not a single anti-aircraft regiment. The attackers advanced in wave after wave, suffering enormous casualties. As a result, of the 107,114 combat-effective soldiers and officers it started with, the army had lost by the end of September 53,648 men killed, wounded or missing-in-action, or 53% of the combat effectives, without having achieved its objectives.[40] Behind the backs of the troops that were pouring out their blood, Stalin's punitive system was

37 Rotmistrov, *Stal'naia gvardiia*, p. 114.

38 TsAMO RF, F. 202, Op. 5, D. 238, L. 464.

39 I.Iu. Sdvizhkov, *Taina gibeli generala Liziukova* [*Secret of General Liziukov's death*] (Moscow: Veche, 2011), p. 414. This book has been translated into English by the translator of this book, and is scheduled for publication by Helion Press under the title *Confronting Case Blue: Briansk Front's Attempt to Derail the German Drive to the Caucasus, July 1942* in April 2017.

40 TsAMO RF, F. 206, Op. 262, D. 5, L. 54.

working tirelessly, seeking "scapegoats" to blame for the failures. From a report by Stalingrad Front's Special Department, forwarded by the USSR NKVD [People's Commissariat of Internal Affairs, the forerunner of the KGB] to I.V. Stalin, V.M. Molotov and A.M. Vasilevsky:

> In the course of the last three days, the 1st Guards and 24th Armies have unsuccessfully been trying to break through the enemy's line of defense in order to link up with the Stalingrad troops, suffering heavy losses in the process. A check has established that the gap between the southern and northern groupings of our forces amounts not to 1-2 kilometers, as was indicated earlier, but up to 8 kilometers.
>
> In the last 3 days, despite the introduction of a number of orders from the Front headquarters about the offensive, and about the breakthrough of the enemy's line of defense and the link-up between both groupings, the leading staff workers don't believe in the realism of their orders and believe that the troops in their present condition will not break through the enemy's defense. For example, the deputy chief of operations with the Front headquarters Lieutenant Colonel Kramar announced, "I don't believe in the objectivity of the order."
>
> In the divisions of the 1st Guards Army, there are large losses. The 7th Tank Corps, which was introduced into the fighting on 5 September with 180 tanks, took large losses and today there are just 15 tanks in it. The materials of the investigation, which testify to the guilt of the commander of this tank corps Major General Rotmistrov, have been presented on the spot to Comrade Malenkov.[41]

The figures cited in the document, while indeed striking, don't present the entire tragedy of the situation that the 7th Tank Corps found itself in. In the TsAMO RF, I was able to discover a report by P.A. Rotmistrov, which he prepared in October 1942, on the results of this operation. In it he wrote openly that the corps was completely unprepared for introduction into combat, and the heavy consequences that resulted from it.

In the first place, the counterattack was scheduled to begin on 2 September 1942, but because of the fact that the attack grouping hadn't assembled in time, it was postponed by three days. However, the 7th Tank Corps had already moved into its jumping-off positions, so after the decision was made to postpone the attack, it had to return again to its staging area, thereby making it clear to the enemy where the Soviet offensive should be expected.

In the second place, on 5 September 1942, immediately before the attack, the tank corps didn't have 180 operational tanks, as indicated in the report by Stalingrad Front's Special Department, but 191 tanks (33 KV, 90 T-34 and 68 T-60).[42] At the same time, the 7th Motorized Rifle Brigade was far from full-strength; it had just 30% of its establishment figure.[43]

However, this was just a small part of the problems that confronted P.A. Rotmistrov back then. The mission was formulated concisely: the tank corps in conjunction with the 116th Rifle Division, launching an attack with its left flank, was to take Hill 139.7 and the railroad south of there, after which it was to link up with the units that were defending Stalingrad.[44] Now let's examine how the execution of this order was organized. Wrote Rotmistrov:

> The separate combat assignments weren't delivered to the company, platoon or individual machine. Reconnaissance was conducted only by the brigades' command staff. Cooperation

41 *Stalingradskaia epopeia* [*Stalingrad epic*] (Moscow: Zvonnitsa-MG, 2000), p. 167.
42 TsAMO RF, F. 3401, Op. 1, D. 7, L. 91.
43 Ibid., L. 90.
44 Ibid., L. 91.

> with artillery wasn't organized at all. There was no cooperation with the infantry, because the 116th Rifle Division, misdirected by staff officers of the 1st Guards Army headquarters, failed to arrive fully on its own axis, so only one rifle regiment attacked together with the 3rd Guards Heavy Tank Brigade. … There was almost no information whatsoever about the enemy; we didn't even know where his forward edge lay. Only separate points of contact with the enemy had been established by the brigade's reconnaissance platoons.[45]

In order to carry out its assignment, the 7th Tank Corps was supposed to create a "corridor" approximately 9 kilometers long through the enemy's defenses. Yet the tanks went on the offensive, as was said back then, practically "naked", which is to say with minimal infantry support, and accordingly there was no one to consolidate their success. As a result, the 7th Tank Corps' brigades came under the devastating fire of an enemy that was previously prepared to repulse their attack and were able to advance just 4 kilometers, while the German anti-tank artillery knocked out or set ablaze 156 tanks, which is to say 81.7% of those that went on the attack.[46] This entered the history of the Battle of Stalingrad as the "Combat action south of the Grachevaia Balka, but it would be more accurate to call it the "Massacre at Grachevaia Balka". Ten months later at Prokhorovka, the situation would be repeated down to the last detail, except the scale of the tragedy would be significantly larger, and the losses even higher.

The enemy also noted that Rotmistrov alone wasn't at fault in such a situation, but shared it with overwhelming majority of the Soviet command at every level who incompetently organized the combat actions, striving to resolve problems of the other types of troops with tank formations alone. Here's how the commander of the 3rd Motorized Division's 3rd Artillery Regiment *Oberst* von Hanstein assessed the actions of the Soviet troops in the course of the battles of August 1942 on the Stalingrad axis. In one of the staff documents of a promising nature, he wrote:

> The enemy's incorrect tactical actions also made it easier for us to hold the defenses. Instead of waiting for 2-4 hours, until he had that quantity of tanks here that our anti-tank artillery simply wouldn't be able to digest; instead of preparing a systematic attack, with artillery preparation, he attacked only with whatever forces he had at hand. This explains his unbelievable loss in tanks (on 2.08.42 the 3rd Motorized Division knocked out 257 tanks).
>
> The Soviet infantry is unquestionably bad. It is totally impossible to force it to advance by itself, and it needs the support of tanks. At this time the infantry is being brought up aboard tanks, and then they are unloaded from it, and the tanks turn around and head back. The large amount of alchohol [they had consumed] also helped [us] a little, just like the exhortations of the commissars that we observed, but because of a shortage of ammunition we couldn't wipe them out. …. Unquestionably … the combat tactics of the Russian tanks are adapted to their bad infantry. The Russian tanks are not penetrating into the depth of the defenses, for example, to the artillery firing positions, but try to destroy everything alive and all the weapons on the forward edge, in order to lay down a path for the infantry.
>
> It is a fact that the Russian command has concentrated all of his tanks from Moscow here and to Stalingrad. However, their output exceeds the increase in crews for them. We captured tankers who had only undergone 6-8 days of training. The tanks are also not always fully equipped.[47]

45 Ibid., LL. 94-95.
46 Ibid., L. 91.
47 TsAMO RF, F. 3401, Op. 1, D. 7, L. 87.

The lines of this survey echo the orders from the *Stavka* representatives on the Stalingrad front. For example, an order issued by G.K. Zhukov and G.M. Malenkov about the results of the fighting at Hill 154.2 by the units of the 1st Guards Army and 24th Army on 18 September 1942 testifies to the extremely irresponsible attitude toward their jobs by the senior and highest command staff of this Front.[48] Incidentally, the hill was taken and held for a certain amount of time, including by the 7th Tank Corps.

I will not hide that it is bitter to read the 3rd Motorized Division's document. It is doubly offensive that these lines, which are filled with the enemy's haughtiness over our troops, are unfortunately true. Therefore we, the ancestors of the generation of victors, shouldn't play the ostrich and try to disregard or be silent about those tragic pages in our history. There is also no need to dramatize excessively or focus the attention on the dark sides of the historical events

In September 1942, prior to being withdrawn into the reserve, the 7th Tank Corps had two more heavy combat actions on the Stalingrad front. Even though according to Pavel Alekseevich they were much better prepared and the tank corps in both cases reached its objectives, the losses were nonetheless also significant. For example, the tank corps went on the attack south of Samofalovka with a total of 87 tanks.[49] After reaching its objective, only 11 tanks were left.[50] A similar situation occurred south of Erzovka; there, of the 78 armored vehicles that took part in the fighting, the enemy knocked out or set ablaze 64.

Even the above-listed problems in the excerpt from the corps commander's report, which originated not in his headquarters alone, are fully enough to understand that the report by Stalingrad Front's Special Department as well as the documents prepared against P.A. Rotmistrov about his supposed guilt in bleeding his tank corps white were an elementary denunciation. Malenkov's commission recognized that Rotmistrov's tanks corps actually didn't carry out its assignment in the first battle and suffered heavy losses in the process. However, the NKVD agents and the representatives were sending similar documents up the ladder of command with unflattering examples from the other tank corps that were activated on this direction as well.[51] The organizational decisions that were quickly taken after such investigations were swiftly implemented with respect to almost all the corps commanders, but Pavel Alekseevich was left in his post. At the same time several generals were not only dismissed from corps command, they were shifted with a substantial reduction to take command of brigades. Judging from the available documents, the following circumstances affected the fate of the future first Marshal of Armored Forces. Firstly, the *Stavka* and the General Staff took into account the situation in which the commanders of the attacking troops found themselves in, and assumed part of the responsibility for it. Secondly, a subjective

48 Ibid., L. 79.

49 After the first disastrous combat action of the month, the corps didn't receive replacements; 52 tanks were restored to service by the recovery and repair service.

50 TsAMO RF, F. 3401, Op. 1, D. 7, L. 92.

51 For example, see "Vypisku iz doneseniia ofitsera Genshtaba RKKA pri 2tk o deistviiakh korpusa s 23 po 31.08.1942" ["Abstract from a report of the officer of the Red Army's General Staff with the 2nd Tank Corps about the corps' actions from 23 to 31.08.1942"] from 20 September 1942; "Vypisku iz doneseniia ofitsera Genshtaba pri 28 tk o deistviiakh korpusa s 5 po 9 avgusta 1942" ["Abstract from a report of a General Staff officer with the 28th Tank Corps about the corps' actions from 5 to 9 August 1942"] from 20 September 1942; and "Dokladnuiu zapisku zam. nachal'nika GABTU nachal'niku Genshtaba Krasnoi Armii o faktakh nepravil'nogo ispol'zovaniia tankovykh korpusov v boevykh deistviiakh na frontakh" ["Memorandum of the deputy chief of staff of the Main Auto-Armored Command to the Chief of the Red Army's General Staff about the facts of the incorrect use of the tank corps in combat actions at the fronts"] from 26 September 1942; as found in *Glavnoe avtobronetankovoe upravlenie: Liudy, sobytiia, fakty v dokumentakh* [*Main Auto-Armored Command: People, events, facts in documents*] (Moscow: GABTU MO RF, 2005), p. 363-368.

factor played a substantial role. In the course of the fighting, the command staff of a number of formations demonstrated their professional inadequacies, while some generals simply drank too much and made no effort to resolve the tasks standing in front of them. For example, according to the report from the General Staff officer Major Eremin from 10 September 1942, the top leadership of the 4th Tank Corps was completely dissolute.[52] Its commissar, second in command after the corps commander, systematically drank until he reached such a state that his adjutant and driver had to carry him from the staff vehicle in their arms. In addition, he began to fabricate all sorts of heroic yarns about the actions of the corps commander and to lie openly to the Deputy Supreme Commander G.K. Zhukov. The chief of staff also often "got so drunk that he couldn't stand up" and spent the days sleeping it off at the command post of one of the brigades. The corps commander himself, Lieutenant General V.A. Mishulin also "yielded to this pernicious influence." At this time, combat work in the 4th Tank Corps was practically left to its own devices. Even the personal order from the commander of the 1st Guards Army Major General K.S. Moskalenko about the evacuation of damaged equipment from the battlefields wasn't fully carried out.[53]

To one or another degree, the same thing was seen in other formations as well, but not in the 7th Tank Corps. P.A. Rotmistrov didn't tolerate such disgraces; he demonstrated his own discipline and composure, and strictly demanded the same from his subordinates. Therefore, despite the grim situation into which his brigades fell, a breakdown and collapse was not allowed: after the fighting the units and elements were rallied, the knocked-out tanks were recovered, and work to repair them went on around the clock. All of this was known to the investigators, and one must assume that this influenced the decision to leave Rotmistrov in his post, despite the fact that his corps over a short time was rendered combat-ineffective. On 6 October 1942, the 7th Tank Corps was withdrawn from the Stalingrad Front into the *Stavka* reserve, and sent by railroad to Saratov for rest and refitting.

A strong side of the character of both Pavel Alekseevich and Mikhail Efimovich was the desire to acquire the latest knowledge of the best practices in warfare, to expose the main problems that hindered more effective performance and teach the subordiates to deal with them. Analyzing the experience of using tanks corps on the Briansk and Stalingrad fronts, P.A. Rotmistrov wrote:

> The corps first entered combat north of Stalingrad, in essence from the march, not even knowing where the enemy's forward edge of defense was, not to mention the disposition of his anti-tank weapons. This led to excessive losses. However, in the subsequent fighting as well, even having information on the enemy, we suffered our main losses not when breaking through the forward edge of the enemy's defense, but when fighting in its depth, once cooperation of the tanks with the artillery and infantry became disrupted and air support was absent. The misfortune here consisted first of all of the fact that our artillerymen because of poorly-conducted reconnaissance or the shortage of heavy machine guns during the short fire preparation of the attack didn't fully suppress the Hitlerites' anti-tank weapons. Air crews

52 TsAMO RF, F. 220, Op. 220, D. 18, LL. 316-318.

53 In a telegram on 9 September 1942 to G.K. Zhukov, was was with the Stalingrad Front, I.V. Stalin wrote: "I don't consider it expedient to resurrect the 4th and 16th Tank Corps. The commanders of the tank corps Povelkin and Mishulin couldn't handle their appointment. I believe it necessary to pull these corps headquarters back to the Moscow area, but replenish the 8 tank brigades in the Saratov area and send them to the Stalingrad front. These brigades will be ready by 20 September. Do you have any objections?" (US Library of Congress, the files of General D. Volkogonov). In October 1942, Lieutenant General V.A. Mishulin "for weakening the leadership over the units" was dismissed from his post as corps commander and appointed in command of the 173rd Tank Brigade. At the same time, Major General M.I. Povelkin was dismissed from his post.

> also didn't render any assistance to them in this. Having penetrated the enemy's defense, the tanks immediately ran into the intense fire of enemy tanks and anti-tank artillery from out of the depth of his defenses, while at the same time being left isolated, since the Nazis separated the accompanying infantry with machine-gun and mortar fire, and pinned them down with constant bombing.
>
> However, it must be recognized that the lack of reliable artillery support was also partially the fault of the tankers. Preparing for battle, they were only informing the artillerymen about their tasks, and didn't agree upon cooperation according to phaselines registered by artillery fire, didn't establish signals to call for artillery fire, and didn't maintain constant communication with the command posts and observation posts for the artillery.
>
> We paid great attention in conducted training exercises to the questions of command and control over the troops in combat, and to the maintenance of constant contact between the units and elements. In the fighting near Stalingrad, radio communication between the commanders of the 87th and 62nd Tank Brigades and their subordinate battalion commanders often became disrupted. As a consequence of this, the command staff didn't always have the possibility to affect the course of the fighting in a suitable manner.[54]

In the cited excerpt, the main problem not only of the armored forces by also for the entire Red Army is accurately noted – the lack of desire on the part of commanders at all levels to get cooperation with neighbors up and running, and their inability to organize the coordinated combat work of different types of troops in the course of a battle. Even though these tasks rose before the leadership of the Red Army immediately in the war's first days, it was unable to resolve them right up until VE-Day. They became the "Achille's heel" of our armed forces. Even Pavel Alekseevich bumped up against them in various stages of his wartime service, but rarely achieved tangible results when addressing them. It must be recognized honestly that throughout the Great Patriotic War, he, like other Red Army commanders, fought with large and sometimes very large losses. Even so, I'll emphasize once again that all the problems didn't always rest solely on Rotmistrov's shoulders.

In reality, P.A. Rotmistrov's "shining hour" was the counteroffensive at Stalingrad. After the encirclement of *Feldmarschall* F. Paulus's Sixth Army and a portion of General H. Hoth's Fourth Panzer Army, the Stalingrad and Southwestern Fronts launched a decisive counteroffensive with the aim of preventing the freeing of the isolated grouping. By this time the 7th Tank Corps had already arrived from its period of rest and refitting and was made subordinate to the Stalingrad Front headquarters. In the middle of December 1942 it took part in the fighting to eliminate the German bridgehead in the area of Rychkovskii and in the liberation of the Upper Chir railroad station.

Between 12 and 30 December 1942, the forces of the Stalingrad Front conducted a successful offensive to destroy the enemy's Kotel'nikovo grouping. The tank and mechanized corps played an important role in developing the offensive to an operational depth on this axis. Hard and bloody fighting for possession of the strongly-fortified railroad station and village of Kotel'nikovo went on for 48 hours. Rotmistrov's tank corps in fact played the main role in this operation. In its conclusive stage, on 28 December, a portion of his tank corps (the 87th Tank and 7th Motorized Rifle Brigades) from the march managed to take the airfield that was located 1 kilometer from the railroad station. Their attack was so swift and strong that the Germans were not only unable to offer serious resistance; they couldn't even recover from their state of shock. German aircraft returning from missions were continuing to land on the airfield that was now occupied by Soviet

54 Rotmistrov, *Stal'naia gvardiia*, pp. 128-129.

forces.[55] On 29 December 1942, an order was issued: For the courage and heroism displayed by the 7th Tank Corps' men in this fighting, it was transformed into the 3rd Guards Tank Corps and given the honorific title "Kotel'nikovo".

Major General M.E. Katukov formed up his tank corps in the Lipetsk area. In May 1942, the Soviet command was planning to destroy the German Orel grouping. Thus the Briansk Front, which was supposed to play the main role in this operation, was reinforced with several tank formations, including the 1st Tank Corps. A promising commander, who had already demonstrated his capabilities as a brigade commander in the fighting at Moscow, Colonel A.G. Kravchenko, had been appointed chief of staff of the tank corps in March 1942. Aleksei Grigor'evich wouldn't remain in this post for very long, and in July 1942 he took command of the 2nd Tank Corps. However, a year later at the Kursk bulge their paths would again intersect. Together, the commander of the 5th Guards "Stalingrad" Tank Corps Major General A.G. Kravchenko under the command of Lieutenant General M.E. Katukov, commander of the 1st Tank Army, would defeat the enemy.

The tragic events at Khar'kov disrupted Moscow's plans. In the latter half of May 1942, the Germans encircled and destroyed the Southwestern Front; approximately 230,000 of its soldiers and officers were killed or captured alone.[56] A gap was torn into the Soviet line, and the *Stavka* was faced with the task of plugging it hastily. Thus the Briansk Front received an order to go over to a firm defense. The Wehrmacht, however, having completed the destruction of the Soviet forces that had been encircled in the Ukraine, at the end of June 1942, stepped off to implement Case "Blue", with the aim of breaking through to the Volga, blocking traffic on this important shipping artery, and seizing the Caucusus oil fields. The offensive began on 28 June, and the initial attack struck the boundary between Briansk Front's 13th and 40th Armies. The situation deteriorated with every passing hour. Already by the end of this day, M.E. Katukov received an order to move out his tank corps to the Livny area in order to launch a counterattack in conjuction with the 16th Tank Corps against the enemy that was located between the Kshen' and Tim Rivers. The resulting fighting was fierce and bloody. The Germans had aerial superiority, and the qualitative superiority of the enemy's updated Pz III and Pz IV tanks became perceptible. In addition to this, the Front command wasn't able to use its available forces properly. The Soviet mobile formations were operating piecemeal and committed into combat hastily and at different times, which allowed the Germans to smash them in turn and continue the offensive. Striving to improve command and control over the troops and thereby change the situation in its favor, the Front's Military Council on 3 July merged the 1st and 16th Tank Corps into a single group under the command of M.E. Katukov. This decision was far from spontaneous; at the time, Mikhail Efimovich stood out among the other corps commanders not only as a master of tank combat, but also by his thoughtful approach to combat matters.

The group was given the assignment to encircle the enemy and destroy him. Recalled Katukov:

> However, we didn't manage to encircle the enemy. Yet this was natural. We didn't have enough strength for such an operation, or the necessary artillery and air support. Now, when you look at the documents, it is clear that the *Stavka* was discontented with how the command of the Briansk Front was using the tank corps. At I.V. Stalin's instruction, the Chief of the General Staff Lieutenant General A.M. Vasilevsky informed the Front Commander-in-Chief: "Some of your tank corps have ceased being such, and switched to methods of infantry combat actions. For example: Katukov (1st Tank Corps) instead of the rapid destruction of the enemy

55 A.M. Samsonov, *Stalingradskaia bitva* [*Battle of Stalingrad*] (Moscow: Nauka, 1989), p. 460.

56 *Velikaia Otechestvennaia voina: Sobytiia, Liudi, Dokumenty. Kratkii istoricheskii spravochnik* [

> infantry spent a day busy with encircling two regiments, and you, apparently, were encouraging this ...."
>
> This document explains much about the situation of those days. Of course, the 1st Tank Corps encircled two infantry regiments not at its own initiative, but at an order from above. However, this was not the only matter. From this document a more important conclusion follows: the tank corps were introduced into combat disjointedly, and each of them was given narrow, limited assignments. Yet it was possible to assemble them into a powerful fist, and having reinforced it with means of air and groud support, actually launch a decisive flank attack against the Hitlerites. However, just like any experience, combat experience doesn't come right away. All these thoughts now come to us, the participants in those events, as a result of what we went through in the subsequent fighting.[57]

This was a difficult time of establishing the Red Army's large tank formations, a process that was interrupted by the war and resumed in 1942, and, in essence, a learning period for the command. However, subjective factors overlay the objective causes: the poor executive discipline, and at times, simply the laxity at every level of command. In this respect, Katukov's tank corps was no exception. From a report by the senior instructor of the Briansk Front's Political Department Senior Battalion Commissar Nikishin about the situation of affairs inside the 1st Tank Corps:

> The headquarters of the brigades (49th Tank Brigade and 1st Motorized Rifle Brigade) do not take into consideration the organization of control over the fighting, and are not organizing genuine communication. For example, in the course of 22 July the 1st Motorized Rifle Brigade had no contact with the battalions; reports arrived late and as a rule did not reflect the actual condition of the units, their losses and war booty. The shoulder to shoulder contact with neighbors was insufficient. Reconnaissance during a battle is absent, the presence of the enemy forces is not detected, and from this fulfillment of combat assignments lags. ... Information from the headquarters to the battalions isn't organized; the headquarters of battalions are not keeping higher headquarters informed and are not carrying out the orders of the brigade's command. The information supplied to higher headquarters is false. ... I've personally had a conversation on the matter of false information with the commanders of the 49th Tank Brigade and 1st Motorized Rifle Brigade; the corps' chief of staff Major General Kravchenko has given directives [on the matter].[58]

The deficit of experienced and something that is no less important, disciplined command cadres with high combat leadership skills was felt on every level of command. Even though the second year of the war was going on, the commanders of armor were in essence only learning how to organize combat and to control such large formations as a corps and an army, in the conditions of a "motorized war". M.E. Katukov was also no exception. Analyzing the available archival documents today, it is hard not to agree with V. Prudnikov, who writes, "Katukov, given all his natural quick-wittedness, having received an order had a tendency to follow them obediently and promptly, because of which many of the battles that he directed left a lot to be desired. This was particularly noticeable in the initial stage of the war when he was commanding a corps."[59] Failures not only stalked the corps commanders, but also the commanders of tank armies of mixed composition. As a former member of the Military Council of the Red Army's Armored and Mechanized Troops

57 Katukov, *Na ostrie glavnogo udara*, pp. 59-60.
58 TsAMO RF, F. 202, Op. 36, D. 132, L. 51.
59 V. Prudnikov, *Stal'nyi uragan*, p. 280.

General N.I. Biriukov testifies, I.V. Stalin, when summing up the results of the summer fighting in the south in a telephone conversation with him, advised, "Nothing came of the tank armies. There are no prepared commanders for the armies."[60]

Indeed this was actually the case; the command cadres were still maturing. In the summer of 1942 on the Voronezh axis in the role of corps commanders, a number of senior officers and generals fought that would later take part in the Battle of Kursk, including in the role of army commanders. This included not only M.E. Katukov and P.A. Rotmistrov, but also A.G. Kravchenko and A.F. Popov. Even though these battles were unsuccessful for the Soviet side, and already in the middle of August the enemy gained possession of a part of the city of Voronezh and was surging toward Stalingrad, they all absorbed from these events the main thing – the experience of handling large formations in challenging conditions. Very important also was the fact that the mid-ranking command staff of the corps began to form and undergo the trials of combat, and would later be sent to other formations.

Although the 1st Tank Corps took active part in trying to repel the attacks of the Sixth Army that was lunging toward the Volga, just like P.A. Rotmistrov, M.E. Katukov was never to take part in the Battle of Stalingrad. Up until the middle of August, his tank corps together with units of the Briansk Front's 38th Army conducted combat operations with the aim of breaking through the enemy's defenses and reaching the Don River west of Voronezh. Subsequently, the 1st Tank Corps was withdrawn into the *Stavka* Reserve near Moscow. A short time later, in September 1942, the corps commander was summoned to the Kremlin for an appointment with the Supreme Commander-in-Chief. After a lengthy discussion about the armored equipment and problems at the front, I.V Stalin said:

> "Look here, Comrade Katukov, you are being appointed commander of a mechanized corps.[61] It will be much stronger than a tank corps. You will go fight right here …" and the Supreme Commander-in-Chief showed me on a map that was lying on the table one of the areas of Kalinin Oblast. Such a decision of Stalin's was a big surprise for me. I thanked the Supreme Commander for his trust, but said:
>
> "What about keeping me with the 1st Tank Corps? I would like to bring it up to the ranks of the Guards, and only then …" Stalin only gestured with his pipe: "You, Comrade Katukov, will still be a Guardsman, but that's not the point now."
>
> I pleaded: "Comrade Stalin, it isn't so simple to prepare and teach the troops. It's a big thing for battle when the men know you well, and you know your men. The 1st Guards Tank Brigade is part of the 1st Tank Corps, and the strongest combat ties bind me with the soldiers. It isn't so easy to part with it!" Then I asked the Supreme Commander, "Include the troops of the 1st Tank Corps in the new, mechanized corps. We'll fight like the devil, not sparing lives."
>
> Stalin gave a smile and stroked his mustache: "Well, write down the numbers of the brigades of the 1st Tank Corps that you want to take."
>
> I jotted down on a piece of paper "1st Guards, 49th Tank and 1st Motorized Rifle Brigade" and handed it to Stalin.
>
> … He picked up the telephone and called the Chief of the General Staff to the phone. Having dictated the numbers to him, Stalin ordered: "Move these brigades of the 1st Tank

60 N.I. Biriukov, *Tanki – frontu! Zapiski sovetskogo generala* [*Tanks to the front! Notes of a Soviet general*] (Smolensk: Rusich, 2005), p. 204.

61 According to the information in his service records, which are kept in the TsAMO RF, M.E. Katukov was appointed to this post by People's Commissar of Defense Order No. 05943 on 18 September 1942.

> Corps to wherever Katukov is going to form the mechanized corps, and send other brigades to the 1st Tank Corps."
> Having set the telephone down on its cradle, Stalin turned to me, and with narrowed eyes asked: "So, Comrade Katukov, are you happy now?"
> I thanked the Supreme Commander and made one more request: Was it possible to transfer P.G. Dyner, my constant technical assistant, and M.T. Nikitin, my irreplaceable chief of operations to the forming mechanized corps?
> "Fine, take them with you," Stalin replied, and upon parting he wished the new mechanized corps success in the coming fighting.[62]

War is a collective business; not for nothing they say, "One man in a field isn't an army" – this in full measure relates not only to a soldier in a foxhole, but also a general at a command post. Thus each commander at his own level sought to gather a group of like-minded men around him, with whom he fought and trusted like his own self. Mikhail Efimovich understood the importance of having a command team in order to ensure effective operations, and thus he persistently asked the Supreme Commander to keep the core team of tankers together with which he had passed through the trials of the first year of the war.

In addition, those who personally knew the general and worked with him noted an important quality of his leadership. He always kept an eye on capable, budding officers; helped them climb the service ladder; arranged entry into military academies for them; and sought to resolve their everyday problems. He did all of this with one calculation: the more the intelligent and well-prepared officers in the army, to which he had dedicated his life, the stronger it would become.

Katukov's mechanized corps, which became the 3rd Mechanized Corps, was sent to the Kalinin Front and joined the 22nd Army. At that time its headquarters was headed by Major General M.A. Shalin, the future chief of staff of the 1st Tank Army. The corps' brigades fought in the Belyi – Velikie Liuki – Nelidovo area. It had to operate in difficult wooded, swampy terrain, which became roadless tracts in the winter. In these conditions, his soldiers and officers matured and gained experience; in less than a year, they were to play a very important role in the Battle of Kursk.

Now, however, in the course of a month between 25 November and 20 December 1942, Katukov's 3rd Mechanized Corps took part in the Rzhev – Sychevka offensive, code named Operation "Mars", which the Kalinin and Western Fronts jointly conducted and, as is known, ended in failure for the Soviet side. Nevertheless, even in these battles, in the opinion of the high command Katukov really rose to the occasion. Thus, already in the first month of the New Year of 1943, great changes would come in his life and career.

For P.A. Rotmistrov, the 7th Tank Corps' dash to Kotel'nikovo had brought him into the ranks of the Red Army's best-known tank commanders. On 29 December 1942, Pavel Alekseevich was promoted to the rank of lieutenant general, and just a bit later, on 9 January 1943, he received the Order of Suvorov 2nd Degree, the third one ever issued.[63] Even the subsequent setback at Bataisk in January 1943, when Stalingrad Front's mechanized group, which Rotmistrov was heading, failed to take this city and reach Rostov, in order to cut the path of retreat from the Northern Caucuses to the First Panzer Army, failed to diminish Rotmistrov in the eyes of his superiors. In February 1943 he received another promotion to take command of a newly-formed army, the 5th Guards Tank Army.

62 Katukov, *Na ostrie glavnogo udara*, p. 176.

63 At that moment, this was the highest commander's Order, which was bestowed upon the commanders of *fronts* and armies, their deputies and chiefs of staff for major combat successes.

On 27 January 1943, the State Committee of Defense had adopted Decree No. 2799 about the formation of homogenous tank armies. This document concluded the almost year-long process of creating armies that had three main qualities: powerful weapons, mobility, and the possibility to deal effectively with the enemy's anti-tank defense. By this time it had become clear that only they could resolve the ever multipying tasks of *front* operations. The first tank armies began to form back in May 1942. The stable increase in the production of tanks that was underway contributed to this. At first they were of a composite composition, having three tank corps, a separate tank brigade, two rifle divisions and specialized units under their table of organization, and were sometimes reinforced with rifle (ski) brigades. However, the first combat use demonstrated the inadequacy of such a structure. Therefore they were employed just like combined-arms armies. On the offensive, even in the event of a penetration of the defense, the relatively immobile rifle formations tied down the maneuvering of their mobile formations and didn't allow the rapid exploitation of the initial success. However, despite this unsuccessful experience, the need for large tank formations only grew. This was plainly illustrated by the counteroffensive at Stalingrad, in which the Red Army command first used tank and mechanized corps to exploit a success. Their successful application yielded a glittering result even in the hard, wintry conditions.

The process of the Wehrmacht's improvement of defenses, which began to gather momentum at the end of 1942, also prompted the *Stavka* to search for new forms of organizing the tank forces. In 1941 and 1942, the enemy constructed its lines primarily out of separate strongpoints and centers of resistance on the most important directions without a continuous line of trenches and serious field works. This allowed our infantry, reinforced by infantry support tanks, to penetrate its lines relatively easily. After Stalingrad, the German command went over to the defense along the entire Soviet-German front and until the end of the war worked on improving its defenses. The troops switched to building deeply-echeloned defenses with continuous trench lines, a large number of minefields, and elaborate field works. A new instrument was required to crack them open.

The discussion of a new structure for the tank armies went on not only in the General Staff and the Main Auto-Armored Command. The *front* commands were also extremely interested in this. The expressed opinions differed, but in the main thing they were all united: tank armies were an echelon for exploiting a *front*'s success, and thus they had to be able to operate independently and have a homogenous composition, which meant freeing them from non-motorized rifle formations, and to give their artillery units and rear units more mobility. This would allow the use of broad maneuvers and a deep penetration into the enemy rear and would improve the handling of the entire army.

At the end of January 1943, there was also a conference on this subject in the headquarters of the Southern Front, at which P.A. Rotmistrov was also present. As he recalled:

> I was invited to meet with the Southern Front Commander-in-Chief Colonel General R.Ia. Malinovsky and the Front's Military Council member Lieutenant General N.S. Khrushchev in order to discuss this question. I expressed the tankers' opinion about the need for implementing the further organizational massing of tanks, for which it was necessary to create tank armies of a homogenous composition and to re-examine the ways of employing them on the battlefield. The views I expressed received approval. At the conclusion of our discussion, N.S. Khrushchev said that he would call Stalin and ask him to listen to my proposals about creating a tank army of a new type. Soon I arrived in Moscow with a report on the matter of replenishing the 3rd Guards Tank Corps, which I was commanding at the time, with new materiel and men. In Moscow I was received by I.V. Stalin. He attentively heard me out and

> favorably regarded all of my proposals. Several days later, the decision to create the 5th Guards Tank Army was made.[64]

I.V. Stalin didn't receive Pavel Alekseevich immediately after the conference, as might seem from the cited excerpt, but only on 17 February 1943; the conversation was quite thorough, as it continued unti 0145.[65] This was his second meeting with the Supreme Commander. They met the first time in November 1942, when the corps commander had been summoned to the Kremlin for a personal discussion on the question of the employment of the tank formations in the preceding fighting. Stalin recalled the name of the commander of one of the first Guards tank brigades, which had received this title for its successes at Moscow. He had noted Rotmistov's desire to share the experience he had gained (Rotmistrov's article was published in *Pravda* on 24 June 1942). The Supreme Commander also knew the positive descripton of Rotmistrov that had been given to the tank commander by the Main Auto-Armored Command: "A well-trained commander, who firmly handles a formation, is dedicated to the Party of Lenin and Stalin, and enjoys the respect of his subordinates." Possibly, I.V. Stalin liked this short, bespectacled tanker, and he didn't really have much choice in whom to choose to command the new, homogenous tank army: the problem of prepared cadres at the army level was very acute at the moment. Thus it is no surprise that at the beginning of 1943, when the question arose about the candidates to take command of the Guards tank army of a new type, the choice fell to Rotmistrov.

The 5th Guards Tank Army's date of origin was 22 February 1943. On this day, the People's Commissar of Defense signed Directive No. 1124821 regarding the formation of two tank armies of a three-corps composition.[66] Voronezh Oblast was determined as the place where it would form. It included the 3rd Guards "Kotel'nikovo" Tank Corps, the 29th Tank Corps, and the 5th Guards "Zimovniki" Mechanized Corps, as well as an array of support units. Collective training in the new army continued until 25 March 1943. A month later, the front stabilized, and more time was available for getting ready for the summer fighting; the operational pause that had begun substantially improved the readiness of its brigades and corps. Over the course of the entire war, never would they received so much time for study and collective training, as they had in the forming-up period. By the start of the Battle of Kursk, the 5th Guards Tank Army perceptibly stood out among the other armies similar to it, including the 1st Tank Army, by its equipping and training.

A bit before P.A. Rotmistrov, in January 1943 Mikhail Efimovich Katukov had also visited the Kremlin. He received two important documents from the hands of I.V. Stalin. One of them was devoted to the subject of forming the 1st Tank Army and stated that he was to take command of it. The second announced his promotion to the rank of lieutenant general. This was a happy and at the same time worrying moment, since the level of demands on him and his responsibility as a commander would be substantially higher than they'd been as a corps commander, even of a mechanized corps. In his memoirs M.E. Katukov mistakenly gives the date of this meeting as early January 1943, and one of the papers that Stalin handed to him, the State Defense Committee Decree about forming a tank army is dated 4 January 1943. In reality, this meeting took place on 29 January 1943, on the same day when the State Defense Committee Decree No. 2791 was signed about forming the 1st Tank Army. It was to form up in the rear of the Northwestern Front on the basis of the 29th Army, but according to a composite table of organization. It was to have Mikhail Efimovich's "native" 3rd Mechanized Corps, which was now being commanded by

64 P.A. Rotmistrov, *Tankovoe srazhenie pod Prokhorovkoi* [*Tank battle at Prokhorovka*] (Moscow: Voenizdat, 1960), p. 10.

65 Ru.wikisource.org/wiki/Zhurnal_poseshchenii_Stalina/1943 [Stalin's guest book, 1943]

66 TsAMO RF, F. 48a, Op. 3409, D. 13, L. 231.

Lieutenant General S.M. Krivoshein, Major General A.L. Getman's 6th Tank Corps, as well as the 112th Tank Brigade[67] and four separate tank regiments, two rifle divisions and four ski brigades.[68] Moscow established a strict timetable for the forming up; the 1st Tank Army was to be fully ready by 8 February 1943. The hastiness was connected with the fact that it was planned to use the new tank army in the "Polar Star" offensive, the initial aim of which was the destruction of the entire Army Group North.

The tight collaboration between an army commander and his chief of staff is always the guarantee of the smooth and fruitful work of the entire command staff, especially in the forming up period and when preparing for a major offensive. It is also no secret that this relationship begins to form from the very first minutes of acquaintanceship and strengthens in the course of joint work together. The fact that the 1st Tank Army was created on the basis of a combined-arms army created quite a few difficulties. Mikhail Efimovich noted that although his appointed chief of staff Major General N.S. Dronov was a diligent and efficient man, he had no experience with tank forces. Thus his work didn't go well immediately. The army commander recalled, "The longer he worked, the more he felt like it wasn't his cup of tea."[69] So then with the support of G.K. Zhukov, the question was decided about replacing the chief of staff: Major General N.S. Dronov left for the 22nd Army, and Major General M.A. Shalin, with whom M.E. Katukov had already established a good working relationship, arrived in his place. Mikhail Alekseevich not only quickly got things running on the required level; he also became a man upon whom an army commander could rely in a difficult moment. M.E. Katukov valued the work qualities of his chief of staff, his professionalism, calm, internal composure, and ability to keep all the levers of command over the troops under constant control. The two generals not only managed to pass through the rest of the war together and greet VE-Day in vanquished Berlin, but also kept a friendly relationship until the end of their lives. M.E. Katukov, writing in his memoirs about the events at Kursk, remarked:

> I was lucky with the chief of staff Mikhail Alekseevich Shalin. Before the war he had served as the military attache in Tokyo. He was a staff officer who was unusually capable, accurate, and precise to the point of pedantism. It happened when you'd glance into the headquarters, and he was always at his desk, running his hand over his shaved head and focusing on a map or some papers. I could always rely on him: Shalin always made provisions for everything, and didn't overlook anything.[70]

Despite the significant problems, M.E. Katukov "pulled together" the army within the designated time schedule, but Moscow was forced to cancel the operation in the form in which it had originally been planned. Thus, there was no need to take part in an offensive, and on 23 February a directive arrived about hastily shifting the troops to the Kursk area. The situation in Ukraine had sharply deteriorated in connection with the start of Army Group South's counterattack, and so on 21 March the *Stavka* transferred the 1st Tank Army into G.K. Zhukov's personal reserve and directed it to the Voronezh front, where the Soviet troops were falling back from Khar'kov with heavy fighting.[71] All of Katukov's units and formations, except for the rifle divisions, arrived at Kursk by railroad, unloaded and assembled in the vicinity of Oboian' by the designated time.

67 A bit later, the 112th Tank Brigade was given to the 6th Tank Corps and in its place the 1st Tank Army received the 100th Tank Brigade.
68 *Stavka* of the Supreme High Command Directive No. 46021 from 30 January 1943 (*Russkii arkhiv: Velikaia Otechestvennaia. T. 16-5(3)*, pp. 47-48.
69 Katukov, *Na ostrie glavnogo udara*, p. 194.
70 Ibid., p. 213.
71 *Russkii arkhiv. Velikaia Otechestvennaia,* T-16-5(3), p. 101.

However, by 27 March the offensive by von Manstein's grouping was finally stopped without the need for the 1st Tank Army's commitment. A month later, on 28 April, the 1st Tank Army was transferred to the new commander-in-chief of the Voronezh Front General of the Army N.F. Vatutin and arrived to prepare for the summer campaign according to his plan.[72]

At the moment of its transfer to the Voronezh Front, the 1st Tank Army was fully equipped, if one can express it so, according to a transitional variant. It it was originally formed according to the table of an army of a composite composition, but then the rifle divisions and ski battalions were removed from it; however, no one in fact was planning to bring it up to the table of organization of a homogenous army. The Front had no way to do this, and the *Stavka* didn't have the means at hand; they had been hastily gathered into the strategic reserves. Nevertheless, M.E. Katukov like no one else was recognizing that the army would be facing such tasks as would be given to a full-strength tank army, but it wouldn't have the available forces and means to deal with them fully. The four separate tank regiments on its roster had been designated for joint operations with the ski battalions and rifle divisions, which had been removed from the army. A question now arose before the 1st Tank Army command: "How to use these tank regiment in the fighting? How best get their cooperation with the large mobile formations, the corps, up and running?" M.E. Katukov again took the initiative and G.K. Zhukov again gave him substantial assistance, even though the Marshal personally had a lukewarm attitude toward the army commander. Zhukov was irritated by Mikhail Efimovich's independence and his inclination to contradict even him, the Deputy Supreme Commander. By the end of the war, their personal relationship would totally sour. Nevertheless, wherever G.K. Zhukov was directing operations, the 1st Tank Army (subsequently the 1st Guards Tank Army) was often positioned on the axis of the main attack. This isn't surprising; professionalism and teamwork are always valued in war.

So, the 1st Tank Army's Military Council proposed to N.F. Vatutin to form one more tank corps on the basis of the separate brigades and regiments, which is to say, according to the model of a Guards army's table of organization. This tank corps, which received the designation of the 31st Tank Corps, began to form at the end of May 1943, but things didn't go smoothly, and the Front lacked the means to equip it fully. The tank army commander recalled:

> G.K. Zhukov, who was located at this time in the headquarters of the Voronezh Front, helped. I called him and briefed him on my ideas. He attentively listened to us and said, "The proposal has merit. I'm for it. Consider, though, that I can't decide everything myself. Katukov, appeal to Stalin. If he asks for my opinion, tell him that I entirely and completely support your project.
>
> On this same day, I called the Supreme Commander. Stalin asked what other forces we were planning to assign to the forming of the new corps. I reported that we had decided in place of the regular motorized rifle battalion to give each brigade of the new corps one motorized rifle company. We would be able to allocate some of the army's communication assets, but we'd have to make a request to the *Stavka* for a motorized rifle brigade, motorized rifle battalion, artillery, mortars, transport and means of communication. Stalin attentively heard me out and approved my proposal. On the next day we received a directive about forming the 31st Tank Corps. In this directive, the brigades created on the basis of the tank regiments were each given numbers (the 237th and 242nd Tank Brigades). Several days later, we received seals and stamps for the headquarters and units of the new tank corps.[73]

72 TsAMO RF, F. 16A, Op. 1720, D. 14, L. 23.
73 Katukov, *Na ostrie glavnogo udara*, pp. 204-205.

Red Commander Pavel Rotmistrov in 1922. (Archive of N. Iu. Rotmistrov)

In 1944 a column of T-34/85 tanks of Rotmistrov's army push on to the west. In the foreground are trenches and shelters abandoned by the Wehrmacht. (RGAKFD)

Company commander Pavel Rotmistrov of the 11th Rifle Division's 31st Rifle Regiment (in the center) among a batch of youth undergoing pre-conscription military training in 1928, Leningrad (Archive of N. Iu. Rotmistrov)

Colonel General M.E. Katukov (on the right) and Major General N.K. Popel' pose in a Ukrainian village, October 1943 (Photograph by G. Kapustiansky, RGAKFD)

N.K. Popel' and the chief of staff of the 1st Guards Tank Army Lieutenant General M.A. Shalin in a headquarters' tent, summer of 1944 (RGAKFD)

The Commander-in-Chief of the 1st Guards Tank Army was an avid fisherman and hunter, thus even during the war he had his hunting dog with him. In the photo M.E. Katukov during a moment of calm stands with his dog. The general is wearing a wooden holster containing a Mauser pistol, given to him as a gift in the summer of 1941 by Border Guardsmen; he never parted with this pistol until the end of the war. A summer of 1944 photograph (RGAKFD)

The army commander, after the passage of many years, probably forgot that there were three directives for the 31st Tank Corps. The first in May, about its formation, the second – on 4 June, about including the 1st Guards, 49th and 112th Tank Brigades (from the 3rd Mechanized Corps and 6th Tank Corps) in the now forming tank corps; and finally a third about creating the 31st Tank Corps on the basis of the 100th Tank Brigade and the 7th, 62nd, 63rd and 64th Tank Regiments. It was in this final document, which was dated 17 June 1943, that the numbers for the 237th and 242nd Tank Brigades were given.[74] The appearance of the third tank corps prior to the Battle of Kursk played an important positive role when defending the Oboian' and partially the Prokhorovka directions during the battle. The tank corps, which was commanded by Major General D.Kh. Chernienko, was activated already on the third day of the fighting, 7 July 1943. However, skipping ahead in the story, I'll note that the problem of logistical support for the tank corps according to its table of organization wasn't fully resolved before the start of the summer fighting, which noticeably affected its not quite successful operations. In essence, the 31st Tank Corps had to fight at half-strength against a superior adversary.

The surprising similarity of the fates of the two tank commanders on the eve of the events of Kursk once again clearly showed itself. Having simultaneously joined the newly-formed Red Army in 1919, and having traveled a difficult, at times even thorny path in its ranks for not quite 24 years, Katukov and Rotmistrov again at the same time (with a difference of a bit more than a month) became the first commanders of the Red Army's new type of tank armies.

The commanders formed their armies in different conditions. Pavel Alekseevich (and this must be recognized honestly) was in a privileged position by the war's standards. The 5th Guards Tank Army from the beginning was equipped as a Guards army (of three corps composition), and as a reserve of the *Stavka* of the Supreme High Command on the territory of the Steppe Military District. Politburo member A.I. Mikoian was personally responsible for supplying the district and the 5th Guards Tank Army. One must give credit to the energy of Anastas Ivanovich; he exerted great efforts to ensure the troops received everything they needed. Even so, the responsibility for the timely creation of a full-strength and fully-equipped tank army lay personally on the shoulders of the 42-year-old army commander and his command team. There were times when even A.I. Mikoian wasn't able to resolve problems that arose, and then Pavel Alekseevich would appeal directly to Stalin. As it happened, the 3rd Mechanized Corps was taken away from him at Khar'kov,[75] and the army didn't receive a new formation to replace it. In addition for a long time equipment failed to show up in the necessary volume, the self-propelled regiments didn't arrive, and so forth. All of these problems were resolved through common efforts, and judging from the archival documents, the 5th Guards Tank Army was one of the best in the Red Army according to its inventory of equipment and combat vehicles before the start of the summer fighting. Incidentally, even A.I. Mikoian in his memoirs especially emphasized the great contribution made by P.A. Rotmistrov in this matter.[76]

M.E. Katukov's possibilities were more modest. His army was the first to switch to the table of a homogenous tank army in frontline conditions, so it lacked much of the minimum that was required, and Mikhail Efimovich didn't have the opportunity to appeal directly to the country's political leadership, like P.A. Rotmistrov did. It should be noted, however, for the sake of justice that when such an opportunity appeared, Katukov didn't let it slip. Nevertheless, a significant amount of the equipment and personnel that had been promised by Moscow (after obtaining G.K.

74 TsAMO RF, F. 48a, Op. 3409, D. 15, LL. 63, 203.
75 TsAMO RF, F. 148a, Op. 3763, D. 143, L. 81.
76 A.I. Mikoian, *Tak bylo: Razmyshleniia o minuvshem* [*That's the way it was: Reflections on the past*] (Moscow: Tsentrpoligraf, 2014), p. 495.

Zhukov's support) didn't in fact arrive by the start of the Battle of Kursk. Thus the 1st Tank Army commander was forced to count upon only the already available forces and means; he assiduously brought up promising lower-ranked officers, and taught them how to make do with little and to rely on mutual support.

The defense of the Kursk bulge for both commanders became the first combat operation in these posts, and presented a true test. They both passed it, but historians of many countries are still arguing about how well they did so now for more than 70 years. Nevetheless, even today one can rarely hear an objective evaluation of the contribution made by both military commanders and their subordinate troops in defeating Operation Citadel. The reason for this is obvious – this argument takes place primarily on the basis of only that material that was authorized for publication in the Soviet period. In fact, no one really took up the study of the entire array of documents and a comparative analysis of the combat work of both tank armies in July 1943 even after 1993, when the archives first began to open a little.

The decision taken by the Soviet command when preparing for the Battle of Kursk about using the homogenous tank armies and separate tank corps to back up the first-echelon rifle divisions in order to hold the defensive belts in depth on a broad front was one of its most foresighted and effective steps. As M.E. Katukov later noted, "It was at the Battle of Kursk that the Soviet tank armies demonstrated that they were capable of resolving major operational and strategic tasks, both on the defense and on the offense."[77] In the defensive fighting on the Central Front, only one tank army (the 2nd Tank Army) took part, whereas on the Voronezh Front, two tank armies simultaneously fought (the 1st Tank Army and 5th Guards Tank Army). Moreover, here the 1st Tank Army operated more successfully, among other reasons thanks to the resolve and skill of its commander.

Even so, throughout the entire post-war period more than once attempts were made to downplay the 1st Tank Army's contribution to the victory at Kursk, including by P.A. Rotmistrov,[78] and to consign its commander to historical oblivion, but nevertheless, it was the 1st Tank Army, and not the 5th Guards Tank Army, that played the decisive role in tight cooperation with other of the Front's forces in foiling Army Group South's offensive on the southern face of the Kursk bulge. The analysis of de-classified documents testify that the 1st Tank Army and 6th Guards Army shouldered the main burden in blunting the armored wedge of von Manstein's grouping (*Generaloberst* H. Hoth's Fourth Panzer Army) on the main axis. Up until 9 July 1943, and in the most difficult period of fighting, when the Voronezh Front was confronting the the enemy primarily with its own forces, it was precisely the headquarters of the Voronezh Front, commanded by N.F. Vatutin, and that of M.E. Katukov's 1st Tank Army, which became the main centers for making and executing key decisions. In the most difficult circumstances they kept the situation under control and at the same time managed to accomplish the main task: to wear down and exhaust the Fourth Panzer Army's divisions and force the command of Army Group South to alter its plans fundumantally. The Voronezh Front's Military Council properly and worthily assessed the contribution made by the 1st Tank Army in successfully concluding the defensive operation. In one of its reports to the *Stavka*, it noted: "All of the army's personnel fought heroically and with tenacity; heroism in this fighting was a mass phenomenon .... The success in this fighting was the result of the soldiers', commanders' and political workers' outstanding level of training and the outcome of mass heroism displayed by the personnel of all of the army's units and formations."[79]

Without a doubt, in the course of the defensive phase of the Battle of Kursk, the commander and troops of the 1st Tank Army shouldered a far heavier burden of the fighting than did the 5th

77 Katukov, *Na ostrie glavnogo udara*, p. 240.

78 See, for example, Rotmistrov, *Tankovoe srazhenie pod Prokhorovkoi*, p. 69.

79 Katukov, *Na ostrie glavnogo udara*, p. 239.

Guards Tank Army, which was committed into the battle only on the eighth day of the operation. P.A. Rotmistrov's actions at Prokhorovka have no comparison with those of M.E. Katukov, neither in the scale of the fighting nor in the number of troops involved, both before the arrival of the reserve Guards armies and afterward.

Already on the first day of the 1st Tank Army's introduction into the fighting, on the afternoon of 6 July, its commander in essence assumed the leadership of the main forces that were holding both the Oboian' and Prokhorovka directions. Up until and including 9 July, the main forces of both of the Fourth Panzer Army's two panzer corps were operating simultaneously opposite his troops. Moreover, the XXXXVIII Panzer Corps, which had the largest amount of armor, including 200 Panthers, from the start was directed at destroying Katukov's tank army, and until the end of the operation it was located only in its sector. It should also be noted that the 1st Tank Army and 6th Guards Army from the start faced fresh enemy formations, which still hadn't suffered those significant losses like they had by 12 July. Indeed, they did so successfully. Over the first seven days of the offensive, the Fourth Panzer Army lost 10,514 men, or more than 75% of all the losses that it suffered over Operation Citadel between 5 and 16 July 1943. Even these figures aren't quite accurate, since even after 12 July the 1st Tank Army continued to bleed the Nazis white, inflicting damage to Hoth's divisions. Rotmistrov's tank army, having entered the fighting on 12 July, also engaged in combat with two hostile panzer corps, but the cited casualty figure plainly shows who broke the back of Hoth's forces, and when. Between 6 and 15 July, M.E. Katukov had operational control over 5 tank and mechanized corps, 5 rifle divisions, 3 separate tank brigades, 3 separate tank regiments, one destroyer anti-tank artillery brigade and 10 destroyer anti-tank artillery regiments. All of this enormous force was operating on a front that extended approximately 55 kilometers.

P.A. Rotmistrov introduced into the fighting at Prokhorovka a full-strength, significantly better-equipped army than the 1st Tank Army, against the II SS Panzer Corps and III Panzer Corps, which by this time had already fought their way through two defensive belts and had lost approximately 60% of their tanks and 70% of their self-propelled guns knocked-out or destroyed.[80] Even so, the German divisions were still capable of creating a strong defensive line on a narrow front, as well as still being able to break through a hastily-fortified defensive belt, as happened on 14-15 July south of Prokhorovka. Between 12 and 16 July, Rotmistrov had control over 5 tank and mechanized corps, one rifle division, one destroyer anti-tank artillery brigade and 3 destroyer anti-tank artillery regiments. His forces fought on a front of approximately 30 kilometers. In this respect it is hard not to agree with G.K. Zhukov, who wrote the following in his memoirs about P.A. Rotmistrov's myth-making:

> In his memoirs the former commander of the 5th Guards Tank Army P.A. Rotmistrov writes as if the 5th Guards Tank Army played the decisive role in defeating Army Group South's armored forces. <u>This is immodest and not quite so</u>. The forces of the 6th and 7th Guards Armies and of the 1st Tank Army, supported by the artillery of the Supreme Command Reserve and the [2nd] air army were weakening and exhausting the enemy during the bitter fighting between 4 and 12 July. The 5th Guards Tank Army encountered an extremely weakened force grouping, which had lost faith in the possibility of a successful battle with the Soviet troops.[81]

80 Zetterling and Franksen, *Kursk 1943: a statistical analysis*, pp. 188-189, Table 3.32.
81 Zhukov, *Vospominaniia i razmyshleniia*, p. 57.

Then finally, the most important thing: M.E. Katukov, despite the numerical and qualitative superiority of the enemy's panzer formations, managed to fight with fewer losses than did P.A. Rotmistrov. Let's turn to recently de-classified archival documents. According to a report from the headquarters of the 1st Tank Army, all of its inherent and attached units and formations between 5 and 20 July lost 14,363 men killed, wounded or missing-in-action (see Table 8). However, not all of these losses happened while M.E. Katukov was commanding these units. For example, the 5th Guards Tank Corps (its losses were 2,020 men) arrived in the 1st Tank Army only after it had already engaged in heavy fighting on the Prokhorovka axis. That is when it lost the bulk of its men. Moreover, the 10th Tank Corps' 11th Motorized Rifle Brigade (2,145 casualties) from 6 July was fighting on the Prokhorovka axis and wasn't subordinate to the 1st Tank Army; the 1008th Destroyer Anti-tank Regiment (188 casualties) on 5 July was under the command of the 6th Guards Army and it was at that time that it was completely destroyed, as was the 14th Destroyer Anti-tank Artillery Brigade (232 casualties). If one subtracts the losses of only the 5th Guards Tank Corps (2,020) and the 11th Motorized Rifle Brigade (2,145) from the total losses (14,363), then the 1st Tank Army's loss of manpower over 10 days of fighting (6 to 15 July) amounts approximately to 10,118 men, or 1,011.8 men each day on average.

Now let's turn to the casualty and loss reports of the 5th Guards Tank Army of only its own subordinate forces, not including its attachments, between 12 and 16 July and 12 and 18 July, which I managed to find in the files of the TsAMO RF (see Tables 9 and 10). In the first case the loss of men amounted to 7,607, and in the second, 9,945. A simple calculation yields an average daily loss of 1,521 men and 1,421 men respectively. This, I will emphasize once again, does not include the losses of the attached means of reinforcement: the rifle division and the artillery and destroyer anti-tank artillery regiments that P.A. Rotmistrov was also commanding over this period of time. The irrecoverable losses (killed, mortally wounded and missing-in-action) were also higher in the 5th Guards Tank Army. In all of the forces of the 1st Tank Army, except the 5th Guards Tank Corps and 10th Tank Corps' 11th Motorized Rifle Brigade, over 10 days of fighting 4,348 soldiers were officers were killed or went missing, or 434.8 on average each day, while in the 5th Guards Tank Army, the irrecoverable losses were 4,841 over seven days, so correspondingly the average daily irrecoverable losses amounted to 691.6. Relying on the above-cited data, it is difficult to speak about any exemplary military command skills displayed by tank army commander Rotmistrov at Prokhorovka.

Although the fighting at the Kursk bulge subsequently made Pavel Alekseevich famous, at the time, immediately after the fighting ended, it almost cost him his career. The debut of his tank army on 12 July 1943 was a complete snafu. Two of its shock formations – the 18th and 29th Tank Corps – suffering losses that were colossal even for those times, were unable to reach their objective, and with enormous efforts drove the enemy only from the single Hill 252.2 and pushed the Germans back 3.5 kilometers on the left flank. Of the total of 642 tanks and self-propelled guns of the 5th Guards Tank Army introduced into the combat on this day along the entire front in the Prokhorovka area, the enemy knocked out 53%.[82] The enormous losses suffered by the Guardsmen over 10 hours of fighting at the small railroad station provoked the wrath of the Supreme Commander-in-Chief. A State Defense Committee commission was sent to the Voronezh Front, headed by a secretary of the Central Committee G.M. Malenkov, in order to investigate what happened. After the war in a conversation with Professor F.D. Sverdlov, Pavel Alekseevich said:

82 V. Zamulin, *Gor'kaia Pravda o Prokhorovke: "Velichaishchee tankovoe srazhenie ili tankovoe poboishche"* [*Bitter Truth of Prokhorovka: "Greatest tank battle or a tank massacre"*] (Moscow: Iauza, 2013), p. 770, Table 8.

Table 10 Report on the personnel losses of the 1st Tank Army and for the formations and units attached to it from 5 July to 20 July 1943[a]

	KIA, mortally wounded			Wounded			Sick with evacuation to hospital			MIA			Other			Summary			Total
	Command	NCO	Enlisted	Command	NCO	Enlisted	Command	NCO	Enlisted	Command	NCO	Enlisted	Command	NCO	Enlisted	Command	NCO	Enlisted	
5th Guards Stalingrad Tank Corps																			
Corps command	1	-	-	1	-	1				-	1	2				2	1	3	6
20 Gds Tank Brigade	29	47	17	24	59	56				7	30	19	2	1		62	137	92	291
21 Gds Tank Brigade	21	49	41	33	31	41				8	10	79				62	90	161	313
22 Gds Tank Brigade	25	51	2	30	50	13				32	233	8				87	334	23	444
6 Gds Mortar Brigade	6	30	47	24	54	100					18	218				30	102	365	497
48 Gds Hvy Tank Regiment	8	10	2	7	10	3				3	14	6				18	34	11	63
1499 Anti-tank Artillery Regiment	3	15	25	5	6	12				5	34	51				13	55	88	156
1696 Anti-Aircraft Artillery Regiment	4	4	7	3	7	21				5	2	39				12	13	67	92
454 Mortar Regiment	-	2	4	4	7	20				-	-	-				4	9	24	37
4 Gds Signal Battalion	-	6	5	1	3	8				3	4	10				4	13	23	40
23 Separate Repair Base	1	1	2	1	7	10				1	1	2				3	9	14	26
60 Separate Engineer Battalion	-	-	-	-	-	3												3	3
80 Separate Motorcycle Battalion	-	2	3	3	7	6	1	1	1	-	1	13	-	1	2	4	12	25	41
222 Anti-Tank Artillery Regiment	-	4	1	1	3	2										1	7	3	11
Total for the corps:	98	221	156	137	244	296	1	1	1	64	348	447	2	2	2	302	816	902	2020
10th Tank Corps (7-14.7.1943)																			
Corps command	4	-	2	2	2	17										6	2	19	27
178 Tank Brigade	5	14	15	18	34	82										23	48	97	168
183 Tank Brigade	7	21	93	16	52	170										23	73	263	359
186 Tank Brigade	5	8	5	7	4	19										12	12	24	48
11 Motorized Rifle Brigade	59	178	332	135	529	892										194	707	1224	2125
30 Reconnaissance Battalion	1	-	-	3	3	-										4	3	-	7
77 Separate Motorcycle Battalion	-	-	-	-	-	2										-	-	2	2

	KIA, mortally wounded			Wounded			Sick with evacuation to hospital			MIA			Other			Summary			Total
	Command	NCO	Enlisted	Command	NCO	Enlisted	Command	NCO	Enlisted	Command	NCO	Enlisted	Command	NCO	Enlisted	Command	NCO	Enlisted	
1450 Self-propelled Artillery Rgt	2	4	-	2	4	2										4	8	2	14
727 Anti-tank Artillery Regiment	-	2	-	1	1	4										1	3	4	8
287 Mortar Regiment	2	1	11	1	7	36										3	8	47	58
1693 Anti-aircraft Regiment				-	-	2										-	-	2	2
Total for the corps:	85	228	458	185	636	1226										270	864	1684	2818
Units attached to 1st Tank Army																			
192 Tank Brigade (6-13.7)	5	21	8	10	39	27	2	1	1							17	61	36	114
203 Separate Tank Regiment (for 9.7)	2	2	–	8	5	–										10	7	–	17
29 Separate Anti-Tank Brigade (7-10.7)	4	9	18	7	10	34				1	6	23				12	25	75	112
14 Separate Anti-Tank Brigade (5-16.7)	4	16	23	9	25	66				3	24	62				16	65	151	232
4 Gds Anti-Tank Brigade (8-20.7)	–	2	–	3	14	1	–	–	1							3	16	2	21
483 Anti-Tank Regiment (10-17.7)	1	–	2	1	2	14										2	2	16	20
1244 Anti-Tank Regiment (8-14.7)	1	3	5	4	5	20	–	1	–	–	6	16				5	15	41	61
753 Anti-Tank Battalion (8-20.7)	–	1	3	3	2	5	–	–	2	–	–	7			1	3	3	18	24
756 Anti-Tank Battalion (8-20.7)	2	–	4	2	6	15	1	–	–	–	2	6				5	8	25	38
Total	202	503	677	369	988	1704	4	3	5	68	386	561	2	2	3	645	1882	2950	5477
3rd Mechanized Corps (5-19.7.1943)																			
1 Mechanized Brigade	37	106	212	75	282	514	1	2	5	17	110	318				130	500	1,049	1,679
3 Mechanized Brigade	23	121	193	43	240	329	3	1	14	–	17	84				69	379	620	1,068
10 Mechanized Brigade	34	111	193	49	216	347	–	6	18	43	260	433				126	593	1,083	1,802
1 Guards Tank Brigade	25	61	41	25	81	85	–	–	1							50	142	127	319
49 Tank Brigade	13	46	8	28	66	27	–	2	6							41	114	41	196
35 Anti-Tank Regiment	–	15	19	5	18	29	–	–	5	–	2	4				5	35	57	97
265 Separate Mortar Regiment	4	4	10	8	17	24	2	–	–	–	8	23				14	29	57	100
405 Guards Mortar Battalion	–	1	1	2	1	–	–	–	1							2	2	2	6
346 Signals Battalion				–	–	5										–	–	5	5

	KIA, mortally wounded			Wounded			Sick with evacuation to hospital			MIA			Other			Summary			Total
	Command	NCO	Enlisted	Command	NCO	Enlisted	Command	NCO	Enlisted	Command	NCO	Enlisted	Command	NCO	Enlisted	Command	NCO	Enlisted	
34 Separate Armored Car Battalion	–	1	–	1	1	–						1				1	2	1	4
58 Separate Motorcycle Battalion	–	1	1	–	3	6										–	4	7	11
27 Separate Engineer Battalion	1	–	1	–	–	9	–	–	2							1	–	12	13
Total for the corps:	137	467	7,714	236	925	1,375	6	11	52	60	307	863				439	1,800	3,061	5,300
6th Tank Corps (5-19.7.1943)																			
Corps command				1	–	–										1			1
22 Tank Brigade	14	22	30	23	66	34	–	1	5	8	57	35				45	146	104	295
112 Tank Brigade	20	65	7	32	78	40	–	–	2	17	134	68				69	277	117	463
200 Tank Brigade	14	28	22	26	69	77	2	1	5	4	18	65				46	116	169	331
6 Motorized Rifle Brigade	10	83	170	33	98	185	–	1	3	1	51	141				44	233	499	776
270 Separate Mortar Regiment	1	8	14	9	14	34				3	2	19				13	24	67	104
538 Anti-tank Artillery Regiment	2	11	18	3	6	10				2	22	33	1	–	–	8	32	61	108
351 Signals Battalion	1	–	1	–	–	2										1	–	3	4
40 Separate Armored Car Battalion	–	2	–	1	–	–	–	–	1	1	1	–				2	3	1	6
85 Engineer Battalion	1	2	9	2	4	14	–	1	1	–	3	12				3	10	36	49
85 Separate Motorcycle Battalion	1	1	1	2	7	6	–	–	5	–	–	1				3	8	13	24
Total for the corps:	64	222	272	132	342	402	2	4	22	36	288	374	1	–	–	235	856	1,070	2,161
31st Tank Corps (5-20.7.1943)																			
Corps command	–	1	–	1	–	1										1	1	1	3
100 Tank Brigade	30	48	21	33	72	57	–	1	3	8	40	27	1	–	–	72	161	108	341
237 Tank Brigade	11	24	14	20	41	44	1	–	–	9	43	83	1	–	1	42	108	142	292
242 Tank Brigade	15	33	41	41	55	68				12	26	34				68	114	143	325
31 Separate Reconnaissance Battalion	–	2	1	2	5	2	–	1	–	–	1	–				2	9	3	14
692 Signals Battalion	–	1	1	1	4	3	1	1	3	1	–	3				3	6	10	19

	KIA, mortally wounded			Wounded			Sick with evacuation to hospital			MIA			Other			Summary			Total
	Command	NCO	Enlisted	Command	NCO	Enlisted	Command	NCO	Enlisted	Command	NCO	Enlisted	Command	NCO	Enlisted	Command	NCO	Enlisted	
145 Separate Engineer Battalion				–	–	4	–	3	2							–	3	6	9
Total:	56	109	78	98	179	179	2	6	8	30	110	147	2	–	1	188	402	413	1,003
8th Anti-aircraft Battalion	3	8	19	4	27	49				–	2	14				7	37	82	126
Units subordinate to the Army headquarters																			
79 Guards Mortar Regiment	1	1	8	3	4	15										4	5	23	32
1008 Anti-tank Regiment	2	13	21	1	23	10				9	33	76				12	69	107	188
71 Separate Motorized Engineer Battalion	–	–	1	1	1	3	–	–	4							1	1	8	10
35 Motor Vehicle Regiment	–	–	1													–	–	1	1
187 Separate Service Company							–	–	1					1		–	1	1	2
146 Motorized Rifle Battalion							–	–	8							–	–	8	8
2 Separate Road Service Battalion							1	–	–				1	1	3	2	1	3	6
852 Separate Cable Line Company									1									1	1
Army's Separate Penal Company	–	2	8	1	6	21										1	8	39	48
Total:	263	822	1,189	476	1,505	2,054	11	21	96	135	830	1,474	4	2	4	889	3,180	4,817	8,886

Note

a TsAMO RF, F. 203, Op. 2851, D. 79, LL. 84-85.

Note: This is a reproduction of the original document. There are errors of addition that have not been corrected, which is not uncommon in Red Army documents. It isn't clear what the totals given in the last row of the table represent. They are not grand totals. They appear to be a summation of the figures for the 3rd Mechanized Corps, the 6th Tank Corps, the 31st Tank Corps and the units directly subordinate to army headquarters, plus the 8th Anti-aircraft Battalion, which has its own line beneath the 31st Tank Corps. The totals exclude those for the 5th Guards Stalingrad Corps and the 10th Tank Corps, plus the tank and anti-tank brigades and regiments that were subordinate to the 1st Tank Army's headquarters, which are listed after the 10th Tank Corps. However, even in this case, the numbers do not always add up.

> I.V. Stalin, when he found out about our losses, became enraged: after all, by *Stavka* plan, it was intended for the tank army to take part in the counteroffensive directed toward Khar'kov. But now it once again required significant refitting. The Supreme Commander decided to dismiss me from my post and almost turned me over to a tribunal. A.M. Vasilevsky told me this. He gave a detailed briefing to I.V. Stalin about the situation and the conclusions regarding the failure of the entire summer German offensive. I.V. Stalin calmed down somewhat and never again returned to this question.
>
> "Incidentally," Rotmistrov noted with a wry smile, "the Front commander General of the Army N.F Vatutin put me up for the Order of Suvorov 1st Degree. But I didn't receive the Order on this occasion."[83]

One can only be surprised by what skill Pavel Alekseevich and his supporters were able after the war to conver the catastrophic results of the 12 July fighting into a grandiose victory of Soviet arms. To the end of his life, he never stopped asserting that on this day his Guardsmen not only knocked out an improbable number of enemy armor, but also supposedly resolved the strategic task for the entire front. Once again let's turn to his conversation with F.D. Sverdlov:

> Back then the 5th Guards Tank Army, which I was commanding with two attached corps, defeated the entire fascist grouping that was directed toward Kursk. The Hitlerites lost approximately 350 tanks and assault guns, of which approximately 100 were heavy Tigers and Panthers, which had been designed and built especially for this operation. After this clash they were forced to abandon the further offensive and went over to a defense. Their entire strategic plan for the summer of 1943 was foiled. That's why the tank operational army carried out the strategic task(!).[84]

This is likely why, for such a "grandiose success", that I.V. Stalin almost sent the victor to face a military tribunal, if not for the intervention by A.M Vasilevsky, who judging from everything, assumed part of the blame for the disaster. Certain historians continued to regale the entire country with such fictitious history for more than a half-century, and unfortunately continue to do so today.

I also want to dwell for a moment on Pavel Alekseevich's words that N.F. Vatutin supposedly put him up for the Order of Suvorov for the successes in the first stage of the Battle of Kursk. In the first place, regarding other Soviet commanders' Orders, for example, the Order of Katuzov, which had a "defensive" nature, the Order of Suvorov was awarded strictly for successes in offensive fighting. A counterattack wasn't regarded as such, and Voronezh Front was on the defensive. Secondly, not a single Soviet armor commander was decorated in any way for the results of repelling the enemy's attack within the framework of the plan for Operation Citadel, either on the Central Front, or on the Voronezh and Steppe Fronts. The command staff was decorated for the Kursk defensive operation only up to the division-level inclusively, as well the members of Military Councils at various levels. The major Decree of the Presidium of the USSR Supreme Soviet regarding decorations for the entire period of the Battle of Kursk was signed by M.E. Kalinin only on 27 August 1943. It was in this document that both army commanders were marked as worthy of the Order of Kutuzov 1st Degree. Thus the Commander-in-Chief of the Voronezh Front would hardly have opted to put up P.A. Rotmistrov for an Order of Suvorov for such a hard, bloody operation, in the course of

83 F. D. Sverdlov, *Neizvestnoe o sovetskikh polkovodtsakh* [*Unknown about the Soviet military commanders*] (Moscow, 1995), p. 56.
84 Ibid.

which Moscow sent a special State Defense Committee commission to investigate the reasons for such high losses namely in his troops, while none of his neighbors that took part in the defensive operation suffered so many. The General of the Army didn't have the right himself to award such an honor. Thus, Rotmistrov's assertion prompts large suspicion.

In this connection, in my view, one interesting detail should be noted, which speaks to the ambiguity of a number of Rotmistrov's acts. Despite the acclamations and boastful commentary about the combat work of his troops at Prokhorovka, which he included in every one of his publications, P.A. Rotmistrov knew full-well that for specialists and his brothers-in-arms the failure of the 5th Guards Tank Army's debut on 12 July 1943 was a shock. For example, G.K. Zhukov spoke openly about this in his lifetime. At the same time, Rotmistrov couldn't help but recognize that you couldn't refute the "tale of a grandiose success" that he had started back in 1943 overnight, and that it also was disadvantageous for him personally to make his habit of exaggeration known. Nevertheless, more than once he made cautious attempts to explain the obvious fact that he wasn't guilty alone for such colossal losses and the failure. After all, from the outset it wasn't he that planned the counterattack and gave his tank army such unattainable objectives. Somewhere around the end of the 1950s and the early 1960s, in a narrow circle Pavel Alekseevich began gradually to draw open the curtain over the "inner workings" of the counterattack and to give his opinion about those who were guilty for his tank army's failures. As those who heard these monologues later told me, this wasn't an honest analysis of the past; he only "wanted to clear his name a bit from the myth, while in the process retain his status as a victor and the defender of Prokhorovka." Describing the situation as it existed at that moment on the Voronezh Front Rotmistrov asserted that for all intents and purposes, Vatutin and Khruschev had "set him up" on 12 July 1943. It was namely they who forced him to implement a plan that was not his own, the details about which he kept silent. In contrast P.A. Rotmistrov always spoke with great respect about A.M. Vasilevsky, even though he was also one of the architects of the plan for the counterattack, which means, for the failures of his tank army, since in his opinion it was namely Aleksander Mikhailovich who had saved him from an unjust fate. The conversation with Professor F.D. Sverdlov cited above, judging from everything, was one such "disclosure".

Not long before he passed away, Pavel Alekseevich decided to consolidate this point of view in his memoirs.[85] He did this quite cautiously, targeting various groups of readers. For the broad audience, in the chapter dedicated to Prokhorovka, the army commander described in detail the process of readying the 5th Guards Tank Army and A.M. Vasilevsky's participation in this, but also the "staggering" impression that the battlefield supposedly made on G.K. Zhukov when he viewed it on 13 July 1943, thereby leading the reader to the thought: "Everything was done faithfully by the army command at Prokhorovka, and both Marshals confirmed this. The overall plan for the counterattack was worked out by the Voronezh Front leadership, and thus they must shoulder the responsibility for the failure."

For professionals, a different approach was used. Talking about the events that happened already a month after Prokhorovka, during Operation "Polkovodets Rumiantsev", Pavel Alekseevich cited his conversation with Colonel General I.S. Konev, who at the time was commanding the Steppe Front, about a change in the army's tasks. I.S. Konev back then supposedly said:

> "They've decided to give you a more complex assignment. Let the infantry assault the factory [the Khar'kov Tractor Factory – the author]. Meanwhile you and your tankers are to move to the right flank of Managarov's army [the 53rd Army – the author], from where you will launch an attack toward Korotich and Liubotin with the aim of cutting the enemy's path of

85 Rotmistrov, *Stal'naia gvadiia*, p. 272.

> retreat from Khar'kov toward Poltava and to prevent the Germans from bringing up reserves from Bogodukhov."
>
> Konev's then gave a mischievous smile: "What do you think, are we weaker than Vatutin? Tanks against tanks: He moved you out against the German tank units at Prokhorovka, and I'm doing so here."[86]

For the ordinary reader, this episode testifies only to Ivan Stepanovich's determination to fight the adversary no worse than his neighbor, the Commander-in-Chief of the Voronezh Front. A professional military man, however, who passed through the war, would see significantly more in these several lines, because he had to know about the existence of Stalin's Order No. 325 from 16 October 1942 about the use of tanks in the acting army, which up until 1944 was virtually the "book" for the Red Army's armored forces. The crude violation of the demands made by this document, which categorically banned the practice of sending tanks against the German tanks, became one of the main reasons for the 5th Guards Tank Army's enormous losses on 12 July 1943. Citing I.S. Konev, the author was telling the reader: "You see, in the environment of the higher command staff of our army, orders and instructions about conducting combat actions were ignored. Even the *front* commanders were spitting on I.V. Stalin's order, in which the best practices of using armor in heavy fighting were collected. At the same time, it [the higher command staff] even considered this heroism. What could I, an ordinary army commander, change in those circumstances, if I'd been ordered to launch head-on attacks against the German tanks, which were superior to ours in quality?"

Unquestionably, there was a share of truth in this. The scheme of the counterattack was the idea of the Voronezh Front command. Indeed, the main blame for the miscalculations in the course of conducting it must rest precisely on it, as well as on the General Staff and I.V. Stalin personally. Thus, if it is possible to rebuke P.A. Rotmistrov, it is only because he, as a professional, knowing that an armored wedge couldn't be created southwest of Prokhorovka in order to split the II SS Panzer Corps because of the difficult, constricted terrain, failed to protest this decision. When employing such a large quantity of armored fighting vehicles, terrain was a primary consideration. The half-baked decisions of the Front leadership created conditions, given which the tank corps, having tanks that were inferior to the enemy's, were unable to exploit their advantage in numbers. Meanwhile the SS troops, quickly throwing up a line that was densely saturated with anti-tank weapons, were controlling the approaches to tactically important points in the defenses – Hill 252.2 and the "Oktiabr'skii" State Farm. P.A. Rotmistrov was familiar with the ground, since prior to 12 July he had been at the railroad station more than once and had reconnoitered the terrain, and thus should have foreseen the unfavorable development of the situation. Thus, he should have gotten a message across to the Front command about the looming danger, and unquestionably should have proposed a more favorable option for introducing the tank army into the battle and for resolving the given tasks.

N.F. Vatutin hadn't served in the armored forces, and thus didn't know all the conditions that would maximally reveal their combat potential, even though he more than once had successfully used tank formations in combat actions, as both a chief of staff and as a Front commander. Nevertheless, in each separate case, he needed an authoritative consultant and assistance, whose knowledge he couldn't doubt, and whose counsel he heeded. This was especially important in the summer of 1943, when the process of reorganizing the tank forces was still underway. Unfortunately, at this time the leadership of all the *fronts* still poorly understood that although tank corps and armies were a powerful means of battle, in certain circumstances they were quite

86 Ibid., p. 228.

vulnerable. A letter sent by the Commander-in-Chief of the Red Army's Armored and Mechanized Troops Colonel General Ia.N. Fedorenko to I.V. Stalin at the peak of the Kursk fighting might serve as an obvious example of this:

> According to reports from the commanders of the *fronts*' armored and mechanized forces and from the commanders I've sent to the tank and mechanized corps and tank armies, over the period of fighting between 5 and 20 July 1943 the tank forces at the fronts have suffered large tank losses. The Western, Briansk, Central and Voronezh Fronts alone between 5 and 15 July lost 3,057 tanks (38% of those in the Fronts' tank park), of which 1,912 tanks have been totally destroyed.
>
> The Western Front from the start of the operation [12 July] up to 15.7.43 lost 217 tanks, 12% of the 1,895 tanks that the Front had; the irrecoverable losses are 55 tanks – 3%.
>
> The Briansk Front from the start of the operation [12 July] up to 15.7.43 lost 360 tanks, 23% of the 1,597 tanks that the Front had; irrecoverable losses are 13%.
>
> The Central Front since the start of the operation [5 July] up to 15.7.43 lost 563 tanks, 34% of the tanks that the Front had; irrecoverable losses are 22%.
>
> The Voronezh Front since the start of the operation [5 July] up to 15.7.43 lost 1,917 tanks, 61% of the tanks that the Front had; irrecoverable losses are 41%.
>
> The tank corps suffered particularly heavy losses when using them to break through enemy defenses on their own:
>
> The Central Front's 9th Tank Corps – Corps commander Lieutenant General Bogdanov – was introduced into combat on 15.7 in the sector of the 13th Army in order to break through the enemy's defenses together with the 18th Guards Rifle Corps; having met stubborn resistance from the enemy's intact defense, the corps lost 88 tanks without achieving a success.
>
> The Southwestern Front's 23rd Tank Corps, committed to break through the enemy's defense, lost 85 tanks without achieving a success.
>
> The Southwestern Front's 1st Guards Mechanized Corps, committed into an attack against the enemy, lost 111 tanks without having any success.
>
> This [practice] is incorrect; in violation of the demands of your Order No. 325, the use of tank and mechanized corps is bringing them to their pointless annihilation .... The actions of the tank and mechanized corps are not being supported by artillery and aviation. Insufficient time is given to the organization of the corps' actions and to working out coordination with the combined-arms formations, the artillery and the air force.
>
> I request your orders to the *front* commanders regarding the inpermissibility of sending tank and mechanized corps in order to break through the enemy's defense, and supporting the actions of the corps (especially during actions in the operational depth of the enemy's defense) with artillery, aviation and other means. Compel the *front* commanders to allow adequate time for organizing the corps' actions and their coordination with other types of arms.[87]

Judging from everything, it would seem the Voronezh Front's Armored and Mechanized Troops command wasn't a capable advisor to N.F. Vatutin. Without diminishing the services of the commander of the Front's Armored and Mechanized Troops Lieutenant General A.D. Shtevnev, nevertheless, it is hard to believe that the General of the Army Vatutin would have heeded his opinion. Firstly, Andrei Dmitrievich, although he was a tanker, had never commanded

87 TsAMO RF, F. 38a, Op. 11353, D. 33, LL. 277-278.

a tank army. Secondly, he was only becoming familiarized with his duties, since he had only been appointed to this post on the eve of the Battle of Kursk.

Of course, when reaching a decision whether or not to launch a counterattack, the specifics of any types of troops didn't play a particular role for the higher command, but when preparing the plan to implement it, the influence of this factor was high. Without a doubt, the stress and nervous tension that was reigning at that time in the headquarters of the Voronezh Front because of Moscow's constant pressure didn't add to N.F. Vatutin's inner composure and contributed little to his productive work. Because of these reasons, there were cases when Voronezh Front Commander-in-Chief didn't agree with the specialists and failed to consider their points of view. Nevertheless, it is impossible to say that Nikolai Fedorovich always ignored proffered advice. For example, he agreed with a proposal from the headquarters of the 5th Guards Tank Army about altering the army's jumping-off positions from the bend of the Psel River, where it had arrived on 10 July 1943. He evaluated it as worthy and gave his approval for it.

By the middle of 1943, P.A. Rotmistrov already had authority as an experienced and knowledgeable professional tanker. I think that if he had succinctly and firmly expressed his fundamental, well-grounded position regarding a more optimal employment of the tank army, it fully might have been considered by the Front's leadership. However, those who knew Pavel Alekseevich well maintain that he wasn't that type of commander (like for example Generals A.V. Gorbatov and M.E. Katukov) who directly gave their opinion, when knowing that it differed from that of the senior commander. Judging from the memoirs of P.A Rotmistrov himself, he unconditionally supported Vatutin's plan to launch the tank army's forces like a battering ram against the II SS Panzer Corps, in terrain southwest of Prokhorovka that was difficult for tank actions.[88] When the Front Commander-in-Chief asked him how he planned to counter the qualitative superiority of the German machines over ours, the army commander colorfully depicted how his Guardsmen would join with the enemy in "hand-to-hand struggle in their tanks."[89]

Who can say that the conversation in the Front headquarters given in the army commander's memoirs *Stal'naia gvardiia* – was homage to the official point of view of the events of Prokhorovka that emerged after the war? I will fully allow that at this time, but the following facts also can't be ignored. First, not a single piece of evidence has been found of the fact that Pavel Alekseevich disagreed with the plan to commit his tank army into battle that was worked out by Voronezh Front headquarters, or expressed this to his leadership in a straightforward way or offered a different option. Secondly, there is not even any hint about this in his memoirs. In contrast, for example, M.E. Katukov, whose memoirs came out almost 10 years before P.A. Rotmistrov's in that very same "time of stagnance" [Ed. note: This is a reference to the Brezhnev years in power.], described in detail the conflicts that arose around the cancellation of the counterattack on 6 July 1943.[90]

Possibly, the observations I've made are debatable, but they involuntarily arise given familiarity with the original documents of that era. As one of our great ones once said: "Victory has many parents, but defeat is always an orphan." Likely, the only exception to this rule is the events of 12 July 1943 at Prokhorovka. However it went, the battle at the station was won by the Soviet side, although with an enormous amount of blood. Indeed, this victory was achieved only owing to the tenacity and courage of the soldiers and officers of every type of arms. It pre-ordained the success of Voronezh Front's defensive operation at Kursk as a whole.

The offensive phase of the Battle of Kursk – Operation "Polkovodets Rumiantsev", the aim of which was the destruction of the enemy's Belgorod – Khar'kov grouping – went no more smoothly

88 Rotmistrov, *Stal'naia gvardiia*, p. 180.
89 Ibid.
90 Katukov, *Na ostrie glavnogo udara*, pp. 220-221.

and no less tensely for both army commanders. This was particularly true for Pavel Alekseevich; once again he was almost dismissed from his post as army commander, this time by N.F. Vatutin personally. The offensive began on 3 August 1943. Both Katukov's and Rotmistrov's tank armies were still part of the Voronezh Front at this time, and were introduced into the breakthrough in its sector. In the first stage of the offensive they were to operate side by side. Then it was proposed to return the 5th Guards Tank Army to the Steppe Front. The first days of the offensive didn't go very smoothly, and already on 5 August N.F. Vatutin was sharply dressing down P.A. Rotmistrov. From a report of the General Staff officer at the headquarters of the Voronezh Front:

> The 5th Guards Tank Army by the end of 5 August was concentrated in the area: Baitsury, Gomzino, Novaia Orlovka, Poddubnyi. In this period of fighting, passivity was noted in the actions of the 5th Guards Tank Army – [it was] spinning its wheels in place. The 5th Guards Tank Army's slow rate of advance created a threat to the left flank of the 1st Tank Army, which at this time was advancing quickly to the south, leaving its left flank exposed. The Front Commander-in-Chief quickly reacted to this fact and was compelled to issue the strict Order No. 0011/op, with a warning to the commander of the 5th Guards Tank Army that demanded the energetic advance by the 5th Guards Tank Army, while the failure to carry out the Front's order by the 5th Guards Tank Army would indicate that the commander of the 5th Guards Tank Army should be dismissed from his occupied post and turned over to a military tribunal. This order played a positive role, since in the subsequent days of fighting the 5th Guards Tank Army operated much more energetically.[91]

A little bit later, however, the left flank of Katukov's tank army was struck by von Manstein's powerful panzer grouping in the vicinity of Bogodukhov. In the course of heavy fighting, a portion of its forces wound up encircled and suffered large losses, including significant losses among the command staff. Among those killed was the commander of the 31st Tank Corps Major General D.Kh. Chernienko, the commander of the 6th Tank Corps' 112th Tank Brigade Colonel M.T. Leonov, and a number of other commanders. Nevertheless, the enemy counterattack was ultimately stopped, and then the Germans were thrown back. Over 21 days of the offensive, the Soviet troops liberated the cities of Belgorod and Khar'kov and some of eastern Ukraine. For the results of the fighting at Kursk, both military commanders were deemed worthy of the high commander's honor, the Order of Kutuzov 1st Degree.

Judging from the archival sources accessible today to historians, on one of these days of the August fighting, Pavel Alekseevich got caught in a difficult bind and even likely suffered a light wound, though there is no mention of this episode either in the documents or his memoirs. Nevertheless, in the commendation letter for his personal driver Senior Sergeant I.G. Kazarinov, who was nominated for the Order of the Red Star (and received it[92]) it is noted:

> In the fighting for Belgorod and Khar'kov he demonstrated valor and heroism. While driving the vehicle carrying the commader to the combat formations of the units, he came under enemy machine-gun and artillery fire. Thanks to his skill of driving and maneuvering, he managed to bring the commander out and to deliver him to his appointed place. After this he came under enemy artillery fire a second time, as a result of which his car received damage.

91 TsAMO RF, F. 203, Op. 4849, D. 480, L. 65.

92 Order of the Military Council of the 5th Guards Tank Army No. 92/n from 28 November 1943 (TsAMO RF, F. 33, Op. 686044.

> Comrade Kazarinov, risking his life, under enemy fire repaired the damage and carried the wounded commander off the battlefield.[93]

As concerns M.E. Katukov, so far no documentary information has been found about any possible wounds or concussions in the war years.

In the course of Operation "Polkovodets Rumiantsev", the tank armies of homogenous composition were used according to their intended purpose for the first time: as an echelon to exploit a success by the Front Commander-in-Chief. The "new instrument" proved to be highly effective, and the Soviet side acquired a large and instructive amount of experience when using them in a major offensive. As Pavel Alekseevich properly noted, "No other formation of ground forces at this time had the capability to change the direction of our offensive so quickly and suddenly launch powerful attacks against the enemy."[94] Thus both tank armies, though badly battered, nevertheless played an important role in parrying Army Group South's counterattack and in the victorious conclusion of the entire operation.

After the Battle of Kursk, in early September the 1st and 5th Guards Tank Armies were withdrawn into the *Stavka* Reserve for rest and refitting; Katukov's to the Sumy region and Rotmistrov's – to the area northwest of Khar'kov. A month later the 5th Guards Tank Army rejoined the Steppe Front, which in October 1943 was renamed the 2nd Ukrainian Front. For the successful forcing of the Dnepr River and the defeat of the enemy's Piatikhatki grouping, P.A. Rotmistrov received a promotion to colonel general. In the first months of the new 1944, Rotmistrov's tank army again scored major successes in southern Ukraine. On 8 January his troops drove the occupiers out of the large city of Kirovograd, and in February took part in the large Korsun' – Shevchenkovskii offensive. For Pavel Alekseevich this was one of the hardest, but at the same time, most successful battles. In it he demonstrated the talent and skill, as well as the real *sang-froid* of a military chief.

According to the *Stavka*'s plan for the Korsun' – Shevchenkovskii operation, the 5th Guards Tank Army was at first supposed to cooperate with the 53rd Army with its forward corps in concluding the breakthrough of the German defenses, and then link-up with its neighbors – the 1st Ukrainian Front's 6th Tank Army – in the area of Zvenigorodka. The offensive took place in difficult winter conditions, and the enemy managed to sever the tank army's supply lines and isolate it from the the Front's main forces. This didn't rattle the tank army commander; he issued an order to the first-echelon corps to continue to carry out the main assignment – to break through to link up with Colonel General A.G. Kravchenko's 6th Tank Army. Simultaneously, having pivoted his tank army's second echelon, he threw the enemy back and thereby cleared a path for the rifle formations. As a result of the successful operations of the 1st and 2nd Ukrainian Fronts, according to Soviet data more than 70,000 men fell into encirclement.[95] However, this was just the beginning. For the next 20 days, the 5th Guards Tank Army, holding the outer ring of encirclement, repulsed fierce attacks of the enemy, which was striving to free its forces from the pocket. However, on 17 February 1944 the operation concluded, the enemy grouping was eliminated, and on 21 February P.A. Rotmistrov became the first "Marshal of Armored Forces" for his successful leadership of the army in the difficult conditions and for demonstrating military mastery in the process.[96] In addition, he was awarded the Order of Suvorov 1st Degree.

In March 1944 the 5th Guards Tank Army continued to conduct successful operations in the vanguard of the 2nd Ukrainian Front. Advancing up to 300 kilometers, its subordinate corps

93 TsAMO RF, F. 33, Op. 686044, Ed. khr. 4396.

94 Rotmistrov, *Stal'naia gvardiia*, p. 230.

95 M.M. Kozlov [ed.], *Velikaia Otechestvennaia voina 1941-1945. Entsiklopediia* [*Great Patriotic War 1941-1945. An encyclopedia* (Moscow, 1985), p. 370.

96 This rank was equivalent to General of the Army.

reached the Prut River and the USSR national border, after which it was withdrawn into the *Stavka* Reserve. In the course of the recent operations, the tankers had been forced to operate with dwindling strength; the army had taken heavy losses. Its corps wound up almost combat-ineffective, although according to *Stavka* Directive No. 30095 from 18 April 1943, Guards formations should never reach that state.[97] However, in the frontline conditions, the edicts of even very high headquarters weren't always followed. The tank army commander wrote to I.V. Stalin about the condition that his army was in at the time:

> At present the 5th Guards Tank Army has tank corps consisting of only a single tank brigade in each; at the same time, the tank brigades are equipped at no more than 50% of their establishment strength. Two tank brigades from each tank corps and the motorized rifle brigades of both tank corps have been withdrawn into the army's reserve because of their lack of materiel and personnel, and already for more than a month have taken no part in the fighting.
>
> …
>
> The 5th Guards Mechanized Corps was fully withdrawn into the army's reserve back in January because of the lack of men and equipment. In the army at the present moment there are almost no operational artillery and mortars at the army and corps levels. Because of the lack of motorized tow vehicles, part of the artillery and mortars back in January was handed over to other units of the 2nd Ukrainian Front, and in addition, the artillery and mortars have suffered heavy combat losses.
>
> There has been no motorized infantry in the army or in the tank corps or mechanized corps for more than two months now.
>
> I'm ashamed to acknowledge this, but I'm compelled to report to you that my glorious units, which have received 10 acknowlegements of personal gratitude from you in your orders over the 8 months of fighting from July 1943 to April 1944, have recently begun to perform more poorly than they did before. There is no artillery, no mortars, no motorized infantry, and very few tanks. This leads to the fact that the table organization of the units has been violated, and this never promises combat success.
>
> Comrade Stalin, don't understand from me that I'm tired and am requesting a leave; I'm ready and will fight even in one tank alone; until the foe is smashed and the war is over, I don't want anything other than to remain at war – and this isn't just talk.
>
> However, I want to request that you issue an order about re-forming my army like it had been first formed back in Ostrogozhsk [the city in Voronezh oblast, in the area the army's main forces were while forming up] in 1943.[98]

However, times had changed, and the attitude of the Supreme Commander toward both Rotimistrov and his tank army was now different. Thus Rotmistrov's request to be reinforced with a corps was turned down. Three months later Rotmistrov's tank army went to the 3rd Belorussian Front. At this time, it was preparing for Operation "Bagration", in the course of which it was planned to smash Army Group Center and liberate Belorussia and Lithuania from the occupiers. The 5th Guards Tank Army became part of the Front's mobile group.

Professor F.D. Sverdlov wrote:

97 *Russkii arkhiv: Velikaia Otechestvennaia.* Stavka *Verkhovnogo Glavnokomandivaniia: Dokumenty i materialy, 1943* [*Russian archive: Great Patriotic War.* Stavka *of the Supreme High Command: Documents and materials, 1943*] Vol. 16 (5-3), p. 122.

98 *Rodina* [*Motherland*], No. 5 (2005), p. 15.

> The offensive began on 23 June 1944. However, it didn't always and in every way go smoothly. Without going into all the details, I want to recall one episode. In the course of the tank army's offensive to the Berezina River, the Front commander-in-chief General of the Army I.D. Cherniakhovsky was dissatisfied with the insufficiently rapid progress being made by P.A. Rotmistrov's tank corps. They didn't manage to gain much separation from the following rifle formations. I.D. Cherniakhovsky reported about this to the *Stavka*, and P.A. Rotmistrov was given a reprimand. P.A. Rotmistrov's reminder that prior to the start of the operation he had made repeated requests for a third tank corps or additional mechanized corps, which might have been used to exploit a success rapidly, was disregarded.[99]

However it went back then, it was with this that Rotmistrov's direct participation in the combat operations of the Great Patriotic War as an army commander came to an end. Thus he never happened to take part in the final assault on Berlin, about which he had been undoubtedly dreaming all these years.

A different fate befell M.E. Katukov. In November 1943 his 1st Tank Army transferred to the 1st Ukrainian Front and took part in first the Zhitomir' – Berdichev, and then in the Kazatin – Berdichev offensive operations. At the end of March 1944, its formation forced a crossing of the Dnepr River in the vicinity of the city of Chernovtsy and liberated it. The day of 25 April proved to be one of his most joyful and remembered days of that terrible war. His progeny, the 1st Tank Army, became a Guards tank army.

There then followed the forcing of the Bug and San Rivers, and the liberation of the Ukrainian cities of Iaroslavl' and Peremysl'. In early August 1944 began one of the most difficult operations in the life of the tank army commander and his troops – the L'vov – Sandomir operation. In the course of this fighting the army commander once came under an intense mortar barrage and came out of it unharmed by some miracle. Mikhail Efimovich's widow, an eyewitness of the fighting, recalled:

> The most difficult days of the war, from my point of view, was the fighting for the Sandomir bridgehead. Mikhail Efimovich, M.A. Shalin and N.K. Popel' also all said this, as did all of our medics. The fighting was fierce; frequently the Guardsmen engaged in hand-to-hand combat. The tanks fired at point-blank range, and moved to ram German tanks. There were so many wounded in this fighting, so much blood … The enemy shoved us back, and Katukov personally had to rise at full height with his Mauser and repeatedly force men to return to the forward positions …. Each kilometer here is soaked with the blood of our soldiers. We paid a very dear price for it. On 18 August 1944 the enemy resistance was finally broken, and the town of Sandomir was liberated.[100]

The possession of this line and the capture of the city had important significance. From here the tank army was ready to attack in the direction of Silesia and to reach the city of Berlin from the southeast. Five days after M.E. Katukov celebrated his 44th birthday, on 23 September 1944, for successfully completing his assigned tasks to retain possession of the Sandomir bridgehead, and for his skillful leadership of the troops and the courage that he demonstrated while doing so, Katukov received his first Hero of the Soviet Union honor. He was awarded his second Gold Star on 6 April 1945 for the Eastern Pomerania offensive.[101]

99 Sverdlov, *Neizvestnoe o sovetskikh polkovodtsakh*, pp. 58-59.
100 E.S. Katukova, *Pamiatnoe*, pp. 208-209.
101 *Geroi Sovetskogo Soiuza. Kratkii biograficheskii slovar', T. 1* [*Hero of the Soviet Union. A short biographical*

The taking of Berlin was not only the last battle in the life of Mikhail Katukov, it was also probably the bloodiest. A lot has been written about the heaviest combat for the Seelowe Heights, how the Luftwaffe bombed our Guardsmen at night, including the army commander himself, and I think that there is no need to repeat it. I'll dwell only on one small episode, which however directly affected the army commander himself. Despite the fact that the 1st Guards Tank Army performed successfully in these conclusive battles, M.E. Katukov never received promotion to Marshal of Armored Forces in 1945, as did a number of his army commander peers. The reason was his independence and his inability to flatter and pander to the high command. He had a tremendous work ethic and all of his efforts were directed at achieving a result, and not to calling attention to his efforts in front of the higher command. Mikhail Efimovich always placed work matters above his own interests and wasn't distinguished by much shrewdness in his regular life. He regarded honors without awe, and believed that if he deserved them, they would come to him, and if not, that meant he wasn't worthy of one. Of course, inside he probably suffered when they undeservably bypassed him. Before the war, he'd been recommended for the Order of the Red Star three times, but for various reasons he never received it. Like any talented and successful man, those envious of him surrounded him throughout his life, but his native self-composure, bright mind and wisdom helped him endure the adversities.

His prickly relationship with G.K. Zhukov substantially affected his career, especially after the war. There were more than a few conflicts, and the army commander more than once received tongue-lashings and unflattering evaluations from the Marshal. Already in 1945 he openly put the brakes on Mikhail Efimovich. Writes E.S. Katukova:

> An argument erupted between M.E. Katukov and G.K. Zhukov about who would be first to enter Berlin. Katukov didn't submit to the Marshal's order to restrain I.S. Konev's troops and prevent him from entering Berlin first. Having sworn at M.E. Katukov, Marshal G.K. Zhukov threw his pipe. He had wanted so badly to report to the *Stavka* that his troops were first. The "failure to carry out" such an order cost Katukov a lot. G.K. Zhukov remembered this incident, never forgave Katukov for it, and later took petty revenge against him. The raising of the flag above the Reichstag made it known to the whole world that the war had reached its end. Joyful meetings and the distribution of honors began. However, M.E. Katukov didn't receive the high rank of marshal, for which he'd been put up simultaneously with P.S. Rybalko and S.I. Bogdanov. We learned about this from Ia.N. Fedorenko, who told Mikhail Efimovich that he had been first on this list and that he was considered the "No. 1 tanker". To M.E. Katukov's misfortune, it was Zhukov who was summoned to Moscow to meet with Stalin. One of his staff officers gave a list of the nominees for Georgii Konstantinovich's stamp of approval, and he crossed out Katukov's name, saying: "Let him wait on this a bit." It turned out that Marshal Zhukov bore a grudge and was vengeful. He didn't forgive Katukov for failing to carry out his order, or his independence and sense of self-worth.[102]

He had to wait a long time for this deserved honor; only on 5 October 1959, and by N.S. Khrushchev's personal order, was a Decree of the USSR Supreme Soviet signed about awarding this rank to the army commander who'd become famous in the fighting.

In my view, P.A. Rotmistrov's military service wasn't always noted for its real worth either. For example, despite the 5th Guards Tank Army's extremely successful performance in a number of operations, over the years of the war he was never awarded the highest honor of military valor – the

dictionary, Vol. 1] (Moscow: Voenizdat, 1987), p. 638.

102 E.S. Katukov, *Pamiatnoe*, p. 307.

Gold Star of Hero of the Soviet Union. He didn't even receive it during the period when N.S. Khrushchev was head of state, even though they knew each other well back in the war, and Pavel Alekseevich in his first book *Tankovoe srazhenie pod Prokhorovkoi* [*Tank battle at Prokhorovka*] was highly complimentary of Nikita Sergeevich's role in the Battle of Kursk. Only twenty years after VE-Day, on 7 May 1965, according to a summing up of all the combat merits over the entire period of the Great Patriotic War was he found worthy of this high honor.[103]

Among military men, there was a persistent opinion that from the year of 1944, the former army commander was out of favor with the country's top political leadership. Even a joke went around that initially they'd given him the rank Marshal of Armored Forces, but didn't know where to find him. In confirmation of this, malicious tongues indicated a rather strange fact for those times. During the Victory Parade on 24 June 1945, Pavel Alekseevich wasn't standing on the rostrum of the Lenin Mausoleum, where he was supposed to be according to his status as a Marshal, but only on a guest platform standing next to it. This, incidentally, can be seen in the documentary footage that was filmed at this ceremonious event.

True or not, but until the end of I.V. Stalin's life, the "largest tank battle of the Great Patriotic War", as the combat on 12 July 1943 was later called, would be very rarely mentioned in the open press, and the Marshal himself would be just one of the large cohort of military commanders of the second tier. Indeed, already in May 1948, he would swap command work in the army for the pedagogical path and become the head of the Department of Armored and Mechanized Troops of the Voroshilov Miltary-Political Academy. From this moment on, for the next 20 years until 1968, when he was transferred to the group of general inspectors (in practice, retired), he would constantly be engaged in academic work and the education of the command cadres. In the opinion of those who worked with him and of those who knew him in that period, Pavel Alekseevich exerted a lot of effort and energy in order to raise the quality of military education. A not unimportant detail that characterized him as a scholar: He never ceased to improve his knowledge actively, even having reached the pinnacle of his military career. At the age of 52 he graduated from the General Staff Military Academy, defended his doctor's dissertation, and seriously studied foreign languages. Between 1958 and 1964, he headed the Military Academy of the Armored Forces, and then served as the assistant of the USSR Minister of Defense for higher educational instituations until 1968.

After the war's conclusion, the paths of the two army commanders again were closely intertwined. They both continued service in Germany. For five years M.E. Katukov commanded the 1st Tank Army. In this period, for a period of time his chief, the Commander-in-Chief of the Armored Forces of the Group of Soviet Forces in Germany was P.A. Rotmistrov, and on 20 April 1948 Katukov replaced Rotmistrov in this post. After completing the annual highest academic courses at the Voroshilov Military Academy (the same academy where P.A. Rotmistrov was working at the time), on 17 October 1951 Mikhail Efimovich again returned to independent command, by taking leadership of the 5th Guards Mechanized Army in Belorussia – the very same army that P.A. Rotmistrov had headed in 1943 and 1944. By the mid-1950s, M.E. Katukov's health had noticeably declined. On 23 June 1955 he was appointed a general inspector of tank troops of the USSR Minstry of Defense's Main Inspectorate. Over the next eight years he occupied a number of posts in the central apparatus of the USSR Ministry of Defense, and on 21 May 1963, he was transferred into the group of general inspectors, in which he remained until his death on 8 June 1976.

103 *Geroi Sovetskogo Soiuza. Kratkii biograficheskii slovar', T. 2* [*Hero of the Soviet Union. A short biographical dictionary; Vol. 2*] (Moscow: Voenizdat, 1988), p. 374.

After the war, only P.A. Rotmistrov of the two army commanders visited the places of fighting in the area of the Kursk bulge, and at that only once, toward the end of his life. M.E. Katukov after the summer of 1943 never traveled here. In private conversations with me, veteran Guardsmen gave two main reasons for this: his poor health, which didn't allow M.E. Katukov to make long and tiring trips, and the chilly attitude that regional authorities had for him back then. However, thus far I've been unable to confirm these statements through any other sources. Pavel Alekseevich arrived in Prokhorovka on 17 February 1971 together with his wife Elena Konstantinovna. He visited Hill 254.2, where supposedly his observation post had been set up, although in 1943 there hadn't been any observation post on this hill. However, likely in order not to offend his happy hosts, he politely remained silent about this embarrassing mistake. Then there was a meeting with Young Pioneers in a school and with the public in the district Palace of Culture, where he was handed a certificate and ribbon as an "Honorable citizen of Prokhorovka" – even though I've never come across any mention of this unquestionably noteworthy event in the military-history literature, even today in the village itself no one has forgotten anything about it.

Everywhere the guest was greeted warmly, with great gusto. Thus, as he walked to the school along the village's main street, he was escorted and greeted by hundreds of residents, and in the front of the procession proudly marched Pioneer Troop "General of the Army N.F. Vatutin" to the beating of drums and the blaring of bugles. During the meeting, the Marshal was adopted as an honorable Pioneer. This, at first glance, was a somewhat naïve ceremony; nevertheless, it was sincere and came from the heart of the locals. Less than three decades had passed since the May days of 1945, and the majority of the citizens of Prokhorovka still recalled the years of terrible suffering during the war. Many had served personally in the battles of the Great Patriotic War, and for them Marshal Rotmistrov was the embodiment of the Great Victory over fascism, which the Red Army achieved through colossal efforts and at an enormous cost.

The warm, heart-felt reception of the people of Prokhorovka touched Pavel Alekseevich. As the participants of those encounters recalled, only one thing disturbed the former army commander – the bare, snow-covered field where the famous tank battle of 12 July 1943 took place, and yet there was not a single monument on it. Therefore before departing, he promised to help immortalize the achievement of the Guardsmen on the Prokhorovka soil in a worthy manner. Approximately a year later, railroad cars arrived at the station platform, first with a T-34/85 tank, and then with two ZiS-2 57mm anti-tank guns, which were intended to be part of the monument to the fallen tankers and artillerymen. In the opinion of the former leaders of the Prokhorovka District, with whom I've managed to to speak on this subject, without a doubt at that time only the Marshal could have done this, since the repeated official requests to the USSR Ministry of Defense and the Party organs had been unsuccessful. The tank arrived from a Central Asian military district. It came off the production line already after the war, and having served out its assumed lifetime, it had been dropped from combat inventory, but was still in working order. At the end of February 1973, the tank, accompanied by heavy equipment, under its own power moved to the place where it would stand forever, and drove onto the plinth on the famous Hill 252.2 southwest of Prokhorovka.[104] On 11 July 1973, the first memorial to the participants of the legendary battle was ceremoniously opened.[105] Indeed, for the next 20 years it remained as the sole monument, up until May 1995, when the white-stone monument by the Russian Federation People's Artist V.M. Klykov soared skywards next to it.

The former army commander P.A. Rotmistrov was unable to attend the ceremony, dedicated to the 30th Anniversary of the Prokhorovka battle, but a delegation from the 5th Guards Tank

104 *Kommunist*, 1 March 1973, p. 2.
105 *Kommunist*, 11 July 1973, pp. 2-3.

Army's Council of Veterans attended headed by the former member of the army's Military Council Lieutenant P.G. Grishin. Information that P.A. Rotmistrov had taken a personal hand in the construction of the first monument quickly became a legacy of the broader public. Even today they remember the army commander's "gift" not only in Prokhorovka, but also in all those who are not indifferent of the history of the Battle of Kursk.

Pavel Alekseevich outlived Mikhail Efimovich by five years; he passed away on 6 April 1981. Both were buried in the capital city, in the Novodevichii Cemetery.

Analyzing the combat path of these military commanders, it is impossible not to note their surprising dedication to their lives' main work – the tank forces. These were uncommon men, men of strong will, single-minded and talented professionals, who did much for the establishment and development of the Red Army in those years of the most difficult trials.

12

Prokhorovka – the evolution of a myth

The myth about the action at Prokhorovka being "the largest tank battle in history" is likely the most persistent of all those legends of the past war, which has become fixed in our public conscience for the last 70 years. Despite the fact that a number of fundamental studies by Russian scholars, based upon de-classified Soviet and captured documents were published in the early 2000s, which gave a well-grounded assessment of the scale and significance of the battle for the further course of the war, the myth continues to persist and permeates the mind of a new generation of Russians now in the 21st Century. Moreover, it is is being replicated not only in the articles of journalists who aren't burdened by a deep knowledge of our history, but also in books by government institutions of culture. In works of this type, the battle of four corps of the 5th Guards Tank Army with two SS panzer grenadier divisions is still called nothing other than "the largest meeting tank battle in the entire history of the Second World War"[1] and even "the most decisive battle of the Great Patriotic War."[2] In the process, the authors not without justification assert that their "their memoir-literary works originated not out of empty air, but relied upon historical events, uncovered in books by previous writers and works by literary scholars."[3]

In reality, the process of the myth's origin and shaping continued for several decades and was rooted in the summer of 1943. However, for a long time historians had no success in tracking this "assembly line". Such a possibility appeared only in 2010 and 2011, when a number of files in the TsAMO RF were de-classified.

A key point of the legend about Prokhorovka was the size of the battle. According to the point of view that persisted in Soviet historiography, two tank groupings with a total number of between 1,200 and 1,500 armored vehicles collided at the railroad station on 12 July 1943. As is the case with the majority of historical legends, its progenitors were direct participants in those events; more accurately, the commander of the 5th Guards Tank Army and his headquarters. It was namely the post-action accounts written by the Guards army's command regarding the summer 1943 fighting, and also the books and pamphlets written by Pavel Alekseevich that came out after the war, which lay at its basis. Let's turn to archival sources.

The first official document that indicated the numerical strength of the German armored vehicles that opposed the 5th Guards Tank Army at Prokhorovka (in the two areas, where its troops operated) was a report from Voronezh Front's Intelligence Department, "Information on enemy actions for 12.7.43" above the signature of the chief of its information office Lieutenant Colonel Mashkov. The evidence it presented came from the Front's intelligence officers who scrupulously

1 N.F. Naidenov, *U neznakomovo poselka* [*At an unknown village*] (Belgorod, 2006), p. 55.
2 Ibid., p. 69.
3 Ibid., p. 7.

gathered it by means of observation of the battlefield, the interrogation of prisoners, and the personal collection of information in the frontline companies. The report indicates:

> The enemy – up to three regiments of motorized infantry with the support of 250 tanks of the panzer divisions *Adolf Hitler, Das Reich* and *Totenkopf*[4] went on the offensive in the general direction of Prokhorovka from the Prelestnoe – Iamki line, and with up to two motorized regiments with a group of 100 tanks from the Krivtsovo – Kazach'e line, striving to encircle and destroy units of the 69th Army.[5]

If to compare these figures with the real data about the availability of tanks in the divisions of the II SS Panzer Corps, which operated from the Prelestnoe – Iamki line (southwest of Prokhorovka), and in the divisions of the III Panzer Corps that operated from the Krivtsovo – Kazach'e (south of Prokhorovka) line, then it should be noted that the Front's intelligence did a good job. On the evening of 11 July, the II SS Panzer Corps had 297 operational armored vehicles (239 tanks and 58 assault guns), and the three divisions and 503rd Separate Heavy Panzer Battalion of the III Panzer Corps had 119 armored vehicles operational (100 tanks and 19 assault guns).[6] Even so, it has been possible to establish through the analysis of archival sources in Russian and foreign archives that the SS Panzer Corps command activated all of the armor of the SS Panzer Grenadier Division *Leibstandarte Adolf Hitler* and *Das Reich* against the attack launched by the corps of the 5th Guards Tank Army, but not more than 30-35 tanks and assault guns of the 122 available in the SS Panzergrenadier Division *Totenkopf* (for more detail see Table 4). The rest of *Totenkopf*'s tanks and assault guns were located in the bend of the Psel River, in the sector of the neighboring 5th Guards Army.

Already after the defensive operation concluded, on 24 July 1943 the Voronezh Front's Military Council member Lieutenant General N.S. Khrushchev included the data from the Intelligence Department in his report "On the tank battle of 12 July 1943 in the area of Prokhorovka, Kursk oblast", which he addressed to I.V. Stalin personally.[7] He thereby lent credibility to the estimate.

As already discussed above, the commander of the 5th Guards Tank Army Rotmistrov committed the 18th Tank Corps (149 tanks), the 29th Tank Corps (199 tanks and 20 self-propelled guns), the 2nd Tank Corps (52 tanks) and the 2nd Guards Tank Corps (94 tanks) into the battle southwest of Prokhorovka on 12 July 1943, and committed south of there units and formations of the 2nd Guards Tank and 5th Guards Mechanized Corps (a total of 148 tanks and 10 self-propelled guns). Accordingly, 514 Soviet tanks and self-propelled guns took on 210 German tanks and assault guns on the "tank field" southwest of Prokhorovka that subsequently became famous, and south of the station 158 Soviet tanks and self-propelled guns faced 119 German tanks and assault guns. Accordingly, 1,001 armored vehicles, 672 tanks and 329 self-propelled guns, took a direct part in the combat actions throughout the day in the two areas near Prokhorovka, of the approximately 1,100 that the opposing sides had operational on the morning of 12 July.

However, it wasn't these sufficiently significant numbers that became the legacy of Soviet society and lay at the basis of the history of the Battle of Kursk and of the war as whole, but others that were provided by the command of the 5th Guards Tank Army on the basis of its commander's

4 I'll remind the reader that at this moment, these divisions were officially called panzergrenadier divisions, although they were equipped according to the table for panzer divisions, and became part of a corps that was called a panzer corps.

5 TsAMO RF, F. 203, Op. 2843, D. 452, L. 95

6 N. Zetterling and A. Franksen, *Kursk 1943: a statistical analysis* (London, Portland: Frank Cass, 2000), Tables A. 6.4 – A. 6-10.

7 RGAPSI, F. 83, Op. 1, D. 27, L. 27.

estimates and mistaken data from the intelligence service. In the "Account on the 5th Guards Tank Army's combat operations over the period from 7 to 24 July 1943" [subsequently, the "Account"] that was signed off by the army's commander P.A. Rotmistov and the first member of the Military Council Major General P.G. Grishin on 30 September 1943, it was observed that in the sector of the attack by the army's main forces (southwest of Prokhorovka), "a tank battle unfolded that was extraordinary in scale, in which more than 1,500 tanks, an enormous quantity of artillery of all types and uses, mortars and aircraft from both sides took part on a narrow sector of the front."[8]

This figure developed from the following information: In the opinion of the army's chief of staff Major General V.N. Baskakov[9] and the chief of operations Colonel M.F. Belozerov,[10] who also signed the Account, when preparing for their attack toward Prokhorovka from the southwest, the Germans assembled seven tank and four infantry divisions on this axis, as well as two tank and one motorized division on the southern axis leading to Prokhorovka, which combined had a total number of up to 1,000 tanks. At the same time, six panzer divisions that had 700-800 combat machines supposedly operated directly against the 5th Guards Tank Army.[11]

The list of the German divisions, cited in the Account, which supposedly deployed near Prokhorovka Station, is surprising. The staff officers of the 5th Guards Tank Army assigned to the group "assembled for the attack toward Prokhorovka" all of the divisions of the XXXXVIII Panzer Corps, which were attacking toward Oboian' and to the west (and were never anywhere near Prokhorovka), as well as all three divisions of General W. Nehring's XXIV Panzer Corps

8 TsAMO RF, F. 5 gv. TA, Op. 4948, D. 19, L. 8.

9 Vladimir Nikolaevich Baskakov (1909-1992), Colonel General (1968); in the Red Army from 1931. From May 1941 he commanded a tank battalion of the 15th Tank Regiment of the Kiev Special Military District's 8th Tank Division. Participated in the battles from the first day of the Great Patriotic War. In July 1941 Baskakov received a promotion and took command of the 8th Tank Division's 15th Tank Regiment. In December 1941 he became the commander of a tank battalion of the 130th Tank Brigade, and then in February 1942 – the commander of the 7th Tank Corps' 62nd Tank Brigade. In June 1942, Baskakov became the chief of staff of the 7th Tank Corps. Between 18 February and 1 March 1943, he served as the acting commander of the 3rd Guards Tank Corps. In March 1943 Baskakov became the chief of staff of the 5th Guards Tank Army. He took part in the Battle of Kursk in this post, and personally engaged in working out and implementing the plan of the army's counterattack on 12 July 1943 in the vicinity of Prokhorovka. His contribution to the victory at the Battle of Kursk was noted with the bestowing of the Order of Kutuzov 2nd Degree. From May 1944 Baskakov served as the deputy commander of the 1st Guards Mechanized Corps, and from September 1944, he was the deputy commander of the 2nd Guards Mechanized Corps. In February 1945 he transferred to the Main Command of the Red Army's Armored and Mechanized Forces. As a representative of the Commander-in-Chief of the Red Army's Armored and Mechanized Forces on the Transbaikal Front, he took part in the Soviet campaign against the Japanese forces in Manchuria. After the war Baskakov carried out staff work, before switching to teaching work. He retired in 1974.

10 Fedor Mikhailovich Belozerov (1911-1961, Lieutenant General (1961); served in the Red Army from 1930. On 15 June 1941 he was appointed as the chief of operations of the 215th Motorized Rifle Division's 133rd Tank Regiment of the Kiev Special Military District, and subsequently of the Southwestern Front, and on 20 July 1941 became its chief of staff, before taking command of this tank regiment on 15 August of the same year. On 9 October 1941 he was transferred to the post of commander of a separate tank regiment of the Southwestern Front's 132nd Tank Brigade. On 16 December 1941, Belozerov became the chief of personnel, and then of the operations department of the Southern Front's Auto-Armored Command. On 19 June 1942, he became deputy chief of staff of this same Command. On 19 October 1942 Baskakov took over the 4th Mechanized Corps' Operations Department, and on 28 March 1943 he moved to the same post in the 5th Guards Tank Army. Baskakov participated in the Battle of Kursk and the Prokhorovka tank clash. From 5 February 1944 until the end of the war, Baskakov headed the headquarters of the 18th Tank Corps. After the war, he was the chief of staff of a mechanized division, an army, and then served in the General Staff.

11 TsAMO RF, F. 5 gv. TA, Op. 4948, D. 19, L. 5.

(the 16th Motorized, 17th Panzer and SS *Wiking* Panzer Grenadier Divisions), which was in the reserve of the Commander-in-Chief of Army Group South *Feldmarshall* von Manstein and which never took part in Operation Citadel. Such substantial discrepancies are also found in the divisions assigned to the group that "operated directly against the 5th Guards Tank Army". For example, the document notes that the Panzergrenadier Division *Grossdeutschland* took part in the attack toward the station, although in reality it was operating along the Oboian' highway, which ran 35 kilometers west of Prokhorovka, and its units were never identified opposite the 69th Army or 5th Guards Tank Army.

What was this – a lack of professionalism on the part of the staff officers or a deliberate misrepresentation of the facts? As the documents I've found in the TsAMO RF show, it was both one and the other. There were always a lot of gripes about the work of the Soviet tactical and operational intelligence service. For example, one of the main reasons for the disaster ensuing from the Red Army's offensive on the southwestern axis of the Soviet-German front in February – March 1943 was the poor work of the intelligence service. It is no coincidence that already on 19 April 1943 I.V. Stalin signed a special order about strengthening the service and improving the effectiveness of its work. In the course of the summer battles of 1943, a host of substantial problems was revealed in the intelligence organs of the Voronezh Front. The main shortcomings were the low professional training of the officers; the superficial analysis and compilation of the incoming information, as well as the tendency of its leadership to play it safe and exaggerate the enemy strength. However, in comparison with the armies' intelligence services, the Front's intelligence officers worked far more effectively and accurately.

The intelligence service of the 5th Guards Tank Army was no exception. Here is just one example: according to its headquarters' information, by the end of 12 July "the enemy's 7th and 19th Panzer Divisions were operating on the southern sector [south of Prokhorovka], as well as the newly-arrived 6th Panzer Division, with a total of 400-600 tanks."[12] This information was repeated at 15.35 on 14 July by Colonel F.M. Belozerov in a report to the Front headquarters.[13] There was never such a quantity of German armor not only in the indicated area, but also in the entire Army Detachment Kempf, which was operating on the entire Korocha axis. At 0600 on 14 July, Army Detachment Kempf had just 82 tanks, not including the 505th Separate Heavy Panzer Battalion, which had between 6 and 10 Pz VI.[14] The most combat-capable division, its 7th Panzer Division (40 combat-ready tanks) wasn't even directed toward Prokhorovka; it was operating toward Korocha, while the 19th Panzer Division that was advancing toward Prokhorovka possessed only 28 operational combat machines. At noon on 13 July 1943, during discussions with P.A. Rotmistrov, General of the Army N.F. Vatutin expressed doubts in the veracity of this information: "With respect to your thoughts and assessment regarding the southern sector: the enemy could hardly have managed to concentrate such a large quantity of tanks there as you reported."[15]

Realizing that his headquarters had plainly inflated the numbers, the army commander attempted to deflect the Front Commander-in-Chief's dissatisfaction onto others. Rotmistrov responded, "In the south, two tank and one infantry division were identified through seized documents and prisoners; the total number of tanks in them I believe cannot exceed 300-400. Aircraft gave me the grouping of tanks in the villages and their number, and thus, obviously, the exaggeration of the enemy's tank forces came about from this source, if you calculate according to their

12 TsAMO RF, F. 203, Op. 2943, D. 461, L. 65.

13 Ibid.

14 N. Zetterling and A. Franksen, *Kursk 1943: a statistical analysis* (Portland, London: Frank Cass, 2000). Table A6.7, A6.8, A6.9.

15 TsAMO RF, F. 203, Op. 2843, D. 461, L. 62.

information."[16] That's how the situation stood with the reckoning of the amount of German armor in the Soviet headquarters at Prokhorovka: one thing was written in reports, and if the higher command had doubts, something totally different was given. As for the reality – no one knew. It was in this bedding, enriched with guesses, conjectures and simply outright fiction that the legend about the collision of 1,500 tanks at Prokhorovka would grow.

As veteran officers later told me, the Soviet side calculated the amount of enemy armor on any particular axis by two means. Firstly, according to the number of revealed panzer divisions (through papers, prisoners or radio interception): they would multiply their number according to their table strength – 200 tanks, and then decrease the total by 10-15 tanks per day of combat for each of those that had already participated in the fighting. However, in July 1943 it still wasn't fully known that the Germans had changed the table of organization for a panzer division's panzer regiment from a three-battalion composition (with 200 tanks) to a two-battalion composition (with 166 tanks). As has been revealed, the headquarters of the Red Army's Armored and Mechanized Forces distributed the first briefing papers on this matter to the *fronts* only in August 1943. Secondly, the headquarters of the ground troops primarily took its bearings from aerial reconnaissance, and then their own estimates were checked against this data, which were also often mistaken. From high altitude, given the battlefield smoke and the dense anti-aircraft fire, everything seemed like armored equipment: the immobilized tanks and knocked-out tanks, the transporters carrying ammunition, and self-propelled guns. There were incidents, especially when the frontlines were fluid, when Soviet reconnaissance aircraft by mistake flew over friendly territory, and together with the German counted their own armored vehicles, taking them as the enemy's. Veterans of the 2nd Air Army, who flew in the Battle of Kursk, informed me of this.

In addition, the exchange of information was not properly up and running between the intelligence departments of the armies of Voronezh Front. If the army-level commands had worked as they were supposed to do so, then the command of the 5th Guards Tank Army would have known that the 6th Panzer Division hadn't materialized out of thin air (as indicated in the report cited above), but since 6 July 1943 it had been operating opposite the 7th Guards Rifle Army, and subsequently the 69th Army, and on the morning of 14 July it had only 14 tanks.[17] At the same time it is impossible not to note one important consideration that always affected combat work: it was advantageous for our generals to exaggerate enemy strength. They wrote off the poor shaping of the battlefield, the instability of the troops, and even simply mistakes to the enemy's numerical advantage in armored equipment.

However, let's return to the calculation of the number of German tanks south of Prokhorovka. On 15 July 1943, when the main events at the railroad station had already taken place, the Soviet engineer intelligence discovered a military ruse of the Germans. The headquarters of the 69th Army reported that the enemy "… using dummies instead of real tanks, created a false concentration of tanks in the Verkhnii Ol'shanets, Raevka, Ol'khovatka area. The information was immediately reported to the Front's deputy chief of staff for intelligence."[18] Thus, the air crews of the 2nd Air Army who had reported to P.A. Rotmistrov that there were 600 German tanks south of Prokhorovka mistakenly took into account their wooden mock-ups.

Nevertheless, in the documents of the 5th Guards Tank Army for 13-16 July found in the Russian Ministry of Defense's Central Archive, the numerical strength of the enemy grouping south of Prokhorovka is set at 300 tanks, as was suggested by P.A. Rotmistrov on 13 July in his discussion with N.F. Vatutin, even though their number there was three times fewer. The army's

16 TsAMO RF, F. 203, Op. 2843, D. 461, L. 63.
17 Zetterling and Franksen, *Kursk 1943*, Table A6.7.
18 TsAMO RF, F. 426, Op. 10765, D. 13, L. 10

staff officers don't provide a clear explanation of this figure, but as has been indicated in the Account, the 16th Motorized Division, 17th Panzer Division and the SS Panzergrenadier Division *Wiking* that were supposedly attacking there from the south were to have confirmed this conjecture. In practice, a firm rule existed in the work of army headquarters: if there were no prisoners or documents, to consider the presence of one enemy formation or another opposite the front of their own forces as just a supposition. Not one of the above-listed divisions of the XXIV Panzer Corps in the period of defensive fighting was ever identified by objective means of verification opposite not only the 5th Guards Tank Army, but also any other of the Voronezh Front's armies. On 12 July the Front's radio intelligence once detected the work of a radio set of the 16th Motorized Division in the Iakovlevo area. However, this was no obvious confirmation of its presence there. In reality, an operational group of this division was active there in order to prepare for the division's introduction into combat, but the altered situation disrupted the enemy's plan. Thus, the appearance of all three enemy divisions of Nehring's XXIV Panzer Corps in the Voronezh Front's sector of defenses remained sheer conjecture. The 5th Guards Tank Army's command was aware of this, but still included them in their account of the battle at Prokhorovka in order to add them to its magnitude. This fact, as well as P.A. Rotmistrov's assertion about the activity of *Grossdeutschland* and the 11th Panzer Division opposite his army, can also be regarded with complete confidence as the army commander's deliberate myth-making.

Now, though, let's return once again to the Account, in order to find out the number of the 5th Guards Tank Army's armored fighting vehicles, which in the opinion of General V.N. Baskakov and his subordinates opposed the German armored fist of 700-800 tanks and assault guns on 12 July. They write, "Altoghether, the army with its attached corps [the 2nd and 2nd Guards Tank Corps] had 793 tanks."[19] Analysis that I conducted of the reports from the units and formations yields a different figure – 833 operational armored vehicles. However, it doesn't follow to critize the compilers of the document. Their sin in this respect is not significant and is likely connected with imperfections in the tracking of armored vehicles arriving in the troops from repair services, as well as tanks, arriving from the approach march to the area of the army's staging positions. I'll remind the reader that the march of the 5th Guards Tank Army from Voronezh Oblast to the area near Prokhorovka took place between 6 and 11 July inclusively.

Accordingly, if you add the 800 German tanks and assault guns found by Rotmistrov's headquarters (it isn't clear where) with the number of tanks and self-propelled guns of his own army (793), and subtract the approximately 100 tanks sent by it to the south on the morning of 12 July 1943 in order to parry the breakthrough made by the III Panzer Corps, then you obtain the figure of 1,500 combat machines mentioned in the Account. At the same time, one musn't forget an important detail: according to the data of Voronezh Front's Intelligence Department and N.S. Khrushchev's report, almost 1,000 tanks engaged in combat near Prokhorovka in two areas that were 18-20 kilometers apart, whereas the headquarters of the 5th Guards Tank Army brought together all 1,500 tanks in the same place, on a small field (of approximately 5x12 kilometers) southwest of Prokhorovka, which was further constricted by deep ravines that were difficult or impossible for tanks to negotiate.

Thus, two versions arose about the amount of armor that took part in the battle of 12 July 1943; we'll call them the "Front's" and the "Army's". However, if the former arose by a natural path and closely reflected the reality of the battle, the cause for the latter's appearance isn't quite clear. Why did the command of the 5th Guards Tank Army two and a half months later have the need to inflate the scale of the battle and indicate an inconceivable number of tanks and self-propelled

19 TsAMO RF, F. 5 gv. TA, Op. 4948, D. 19, L. 6.

guns there, where there couldn't possibly have been so many? In order to answer this question, we'll have to touch briefly on the situation that developed after the battle for Prokhorovka.

As already observed, the counterattack by the Voronezh Front's forces on 12 July 1943 didn't achieve their objectives, while the main shock group, Rotmistrov's tank army, over approximately 10-11 hours of constant fighting suffered very large losses – more than 50% of the tanks and self-propelled guns it committed to the battle. By the end of the defensive operation on 16 July 1943 it had been rendered virtually combat-ineffective: 323 tanks and self-propelled guns had been totally destroyed, and more than 100 of them were undergoing various amounts of repair. As already noted, Moscow sent a special commission headed by Central Committee Secretary G.S. Malenkov to investigate the reasons for the heavy losses. The investigation continued for approximately two weeks, and then its conclusions lay on Stalin's desk. It posed the question about dismissing the army commander from his post and turning him over to a trial by military tribunal. The fate of Pavel Alekseevich was hanging by a thread until the end of July, when the Chief of the General Staff Marshal of the Soviet Union A.M. Vasilevsky managed to deflect some of the Supreme Commander's wrath onto himself, and at the end of August 1943 the army commander was deemed worthy of the Order of Kutuzov 1st Degree for his participation in the Battle of Kursk. Thereby the question of how to assess the events at Prokhorovka was virtually decided: Consider the battle a victorious one, and don't pay attention to the losses. Relying upon this assessment, at the beginning of September 1943 the 5th Guards Tank Army's Military Council adopted the first letters of commendation for the soldiers and officers that distinguished themselves at Prokhorovka, nearly two months after they performed their combat exploits. Even for the standards of the war, this delay was substantial, but it once again testifies to the delicate situation in July-August 1943 that the army command found itself in and managed to survive.

At the same time, in August 1943, the 5th Guards Tank Army headquarters prepared its Account of the battle. It had two drafts, a preliminary one that was sent to the Commander-in-Chief of the Red Army's Armored and Mechanized Forces, and a final draft that was confirmed on 30 September 1943. There was no fundamental difference between the two drafts with respect to the question we are examining. The first draft was only shorter. This was a typical document for an army headquarters, which was prepared by the Operations Department after the conclusion of a certain period of fighting. Its main task was to synthesize the experience, identify new approaches and means for the struggle against the enemy, and present proposals to higher command on ways to improve the combat performance of the troops. At the same time, these accounts were a unique means that allowed the command of corps and armies, without fearing sharp criticism or moreover consequences (the information they contained could no longer directly influence the preceding combat) to put their troops (and accordingly themselves) in the best possible light before the high command and place a smokescreen over the miscalculations and mistakes that they made during the battle. Over many years of work in the TsAMO RF, I've managed to familiarize myself with several dozen such documents, and a significant portion of them are a shining model of self-conceit and elaborate fabrications.

This was also the case in the 5th Guards Tank Army's Account, but in moderation. Its command also attempted to use this document as a channel of information in order to downplay the negative impression left by the counterattack at Prokhorovka and once again stress the merits and accomplishments of the troops to the higher leadership. However, not with a simple recitation of hundreds of knocked-out German tanks and thousands of dead German soldiers, like other headquarters did, but through the creation of the image of a colossal battle, in which the army defeated an unprecedentedly strong enemy tank grouping. Thus, it is no coincidence that the Account twice mentions the number of 1,500 tanks. I cited the first mention above, and the second mention was in the "Conclusions" section, even though it was plainly out of place there. Moreover, in order to once again stress the scale of what happened at Prokhorovka, the staff officers used a vocabulary that was uncommon for military documents, and words and expressions straight out of the arsenal of propaganda organs: "On 12 July there occurred the greatest tank battle in the history of the Patriotic War; up to 1,500 tanks of both sides clashed in the meeting attack. Inflicting enormous damage to the enemy in men and equipment and having checked a further advance by the enemy, the army's units for a certain time had to conduct defensive fighting."[20] On the whole, although it is hard to call the document informative, it fully corresponds to the demands of that time, without any obvious distortions or open puffery. This is understandable too; for the compilers it was important so that the professionals of the headquarters of the Red Army's Armored and Mechanized Forces, who would become familiar with the Account, understood first of all the main point: The army suffered enormous losses not because of mistakes made by its command, but because it took part in a battle of unprecedented size – and won. For this purpose it was necessary that this key point didn't get lost in a mass of other information in the Account and stood out clearly, and ran like a red line from the beginning to the end of it.

Why then, however, was the Army's version taken as the basis by Soviet historians, and not the Front's version? It was the result of the military system of handling documents with its characteristic secrecy and the special requirements for handling documents. The reports of the Voronezh Front's Intelligence Department and N.S. Khrushchev's memorandum were documents prepared by a higher-level headquarters (than that of the 5th Guards Tank Army's Account), but were mainly of a different nature – they were operational and moreover bore the seal "Secret" and "Top Secret", and sat for a half-century in the military archive. The documentary files of the Voronezh Front in the TsAMO RF, which contained its Intelligence Department report, weren't opened until 1993, while Khruschev's letter to I.V. Stalin was first published in the open press only in 2007. In contrast, the Account from Rotmistrov's 5th Guards Tank Army arrived at the Headquarters of the of the Red Army's Armored and Mechanized Forces already in August 1943 in the Department for the Study and Use of the War's Experience. These structures had been formed in the headquarters of the Red Army in 1942 in order to compile, analyze and highlight the most successful approaches and methods for conducting battle and commanding the troops known to the command staff of the acting army. The officers who served in them were assigned to prepare analytic materials on the basis of the accounts of formations and armies for their further use in articles, published in the journals of various types of arms and in the General Staff compendia of the war's best practices, as well as in military academies for preparing lectures and seminars.

At the end of August 1943, the summer period of fighting ended and the headquarters of the Red Army's Armored and Mechanized Forces was obliged to analyze the experience of the troops' combat work quickly and publish the results in the military journals, including in the General Staff's Compendium of the War's Best Practices (henceforth, the Compendium). Thus on 10 September 1943 the chief of the Department for the Study and Use of the War's Experience in the Headquarters of the Red Army's Armored and Mechanized Forces, Colonel G. Sapozhkov[21] sent

20 TsAMO RF, F. 5 gv. TA, Op. 4948, D. 19, L. 21.

21 Grigorii Iakovlevich Sapozhkov (1903-19?), Colonel (1942), Candidate of Military Science (1953), Assistant Professor (1954); in the Red Army from 1920. He graduated from the Military Academy of Motorization and Mechanization (1937) and the Miltary Academy of the General Staff (1941). From 10 July 1941, he was the chief of staff of the Western Front's 105th Tank Division, and took part in the fighting for El'nia. On 17 October 1941 he was appointed as the chief of staff of the 146th Tank Brigade, and on 5 April 1942, Western Front's 24th Tank Brigade. From May 1942, Sapozhov was the operations chief with the headquarters of the 8th Tank Corps. In August 1942, he received a severe wound, and after recovering, on 8 January 1943, transferred to the Headquarters of the Red Army's Armored and Mechanized Forces to the post of chief of the Department for the Study and Use of the War's Experience. In November 1943, for his successful work to get the department running efficiently and for preparing the study of the Battle of Stalingrad, he was awarded the Order of the Patriotic War 1st Degree. On 26 August

two articles for publication to Major General P.P. Vechnyi,[22] the chief of a of a General Staff department with the same name, including one entitled "Iul'skaia operatsiia 5 gvardeiskoi tankovoi armii na Belgorodskom napravlenii" ["July operation of the 5th Guards Tank Army on the Belgorod axis"].[23] Major General V.N. Baskakov's Account lay at its basis, and the figure of 1,500 tanks in the article was taken from it. A bit later, on 31 October 1943, General P.P. Vechnyi sent this same material, as well as a rough draft of an article by Colonel Goncharov entitled "Tankovye voiska v sovremennoi oboronitel'noi operatsii" ["Tank troops in a contemporary defensive operation"], which also used the Account's information about the fighting for Prokhorovka, to the deputy chief of the Military Academy of Armored and Mechanized Forces, where the senior command staff of the Red Army's armored forces studied, for use in the Department of Higher Formations.[24]

All of the above mentioned works were published in 1944. It should be stressed that when preparing the publications, the editorial board of the Compendium treated the statistical data about the numerical strength of the armor in the fighting for Prokhorovka with caution. The main article of Issue 11 (March – April 1944), entitled "Tankovye voiska v oborone Kurskogo platsdarma" ["Tank troops in the defense of the Kursk staging area"] didn't contain the total number of Soviet and German tanks that took part in the fighting on 12 July, or mention the "largest tank battle". However, it was just this work that became the most important "brick" in the future myth. In it, the figure of 1,500 tanks was split into two pieces and the same cock-and-bull story from the Account about the actions of the 17th Panzer Division and 168th Infantry Divisions at Prokhorovka was repeated. In the Introduction to the "Combat actions of the 5th Guards Tank Army", it is indicated that by the morning of 12 July, the Germans had four panzer divisions and one infantry division west of Prokhorovka Station, which numbered among them more than 600 tanks, including Tigers, as well as Ferdinands that were taken from somewhere unknown, whereas the 5th Guards Tank Army posssesed 793 combat machines.[25] In doing so, the authors made it unambiguously known to the reader that on 12 July west of Prokhorovka, two opposing groupings with a total of more than 1,400 tanks and self-propelled guns collided on the tank field. With the passage of time, this figure became harmonized with the Account in the open press and was rounded up to 1,500 tanks and self-propelled guns.

1946, Sapozhkov was appointed as the 3rd Mechanized Army's chief of operations. Between 19 February 1948 and 16 May 1954, he taught in the Military Academy of Armored and Mechanized Forces, and his last post was the deputy chief of its Military History Department. He retired from active service in 1954.

22 Petr Panteleimonovich Vechnyi (1891-1957), Lieutenant General (1944), Candidate of Military Science and Assistant Professor. He participated in the First World War as a warrant officer. Vechnyi joined the Red Army in 1918. On 2 August 1941 he became the chief of the Second Department of the Red Army's Command for Combat Training. Then as a graduate of the General Staff Military Academy, he acquired the right to work in the academy for one year. On 17 August 1941, Vechnyi was chief of a General Staff operational group on the Southern Direction. On 4 September 1941, he became a deputy chief of the General Staff while remaining the chief of the Southern Direction. On 10 March 1942, he became Crimean Front's chief of staff. After this Front's destruction, he was posted on 27 June 1942 to the General Staff Department for the Study and Use of the War's Experience, and on 12 August 1942 became its chief. From December 1943, he served as the 47th Army's chief of staff. However, on 6 March 1945 Vechnyi was relieved of his duties for his inability to handle the work and was placed at the disposal of the USSR State Defense Committee's Central Deparment of Cadres. On 23 May 1945 he was appointed as chief of an academic research department of the Frunze Military Academy. From 29 October 1949 until 13 August 1955, Vechnyi served as an academic secretary of the Frunze Military Academy's Academic Council. In 1955 he was given a voluntary discharge into retirement.

23 TsAMO RF, F. 3416, Op. 1, D. 16, L. 36.

24 TsAMO RF, F. 3416, Op. 1, D. 16, L. 1.

25 Sbornik materialov po izucheniiu opyt voiny, Vypusk 11, mart-aprel' 1944 [Compendium of materials on the study of the war's experience, Issue 11, mart-aprel' 1944] (Moscow: Voenizdat NKO, 1944), p. 17.

Authors of the account by the 5th Guards Tank Army's command about the fighting at Prokhorovka, in which the number of 1,500 tanks and self-propelled guns that took part in the fighting on 12 July 1943 was given for the first time: chief of staff of the 5th Guards Tank Army Major General V.N. Baskakov (on the left) and chief of the Operations Department Colonel F.M. Belozerov, 1943 (author's personal archive)

Lieutenant General P.P. Vechnyi; a 1945 photograph (TsAMO RF)

Colonel G.Ia. Sapozhkov; a 1948 photograph (TsAMO RF)

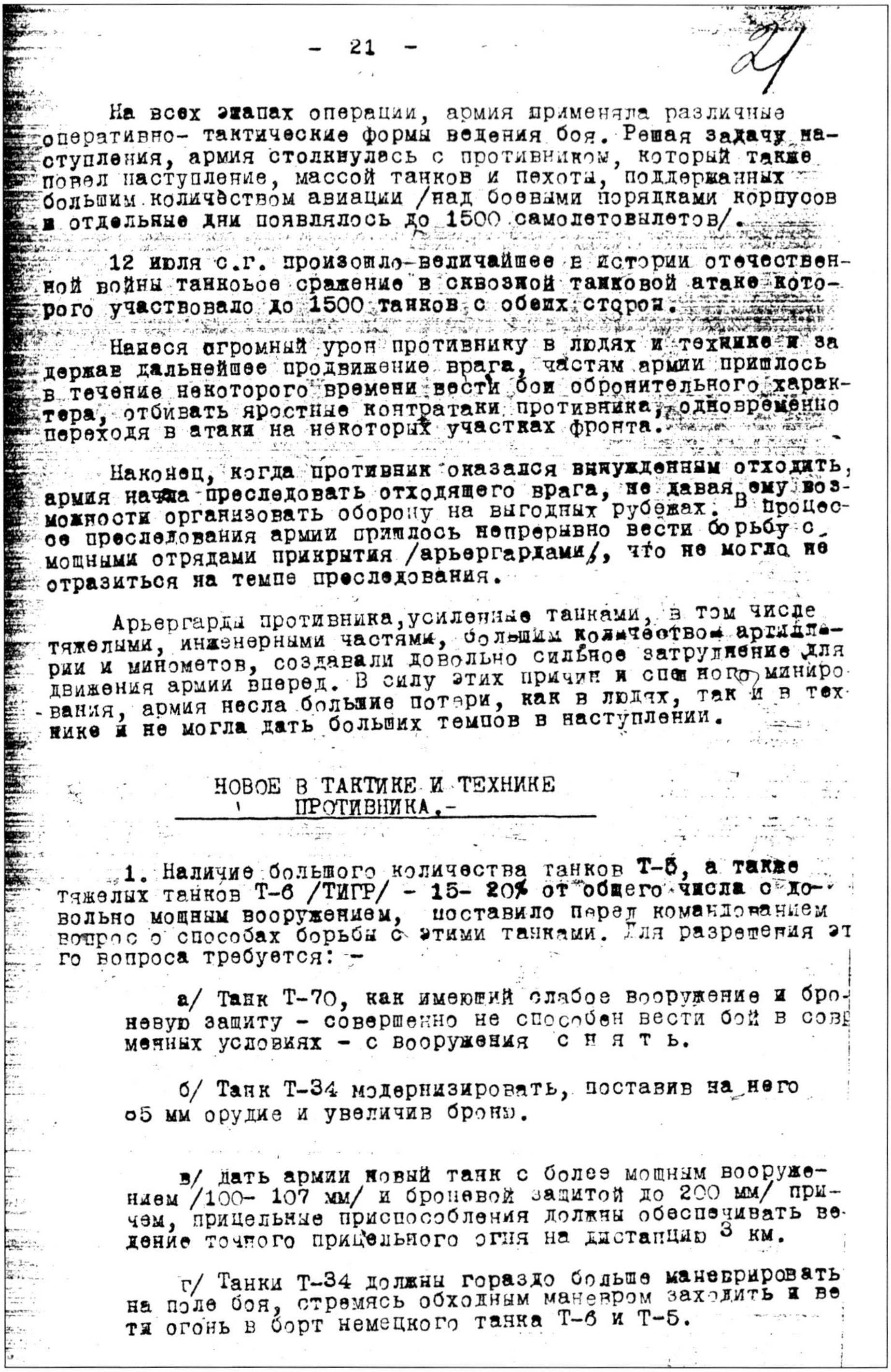

– 21 –

На всех этапах операции, армия применяла различные оперативно- тактические формы ведения боя. Решая задачу наступления, армия столкнулась с противником, который также повел наступление, массой танков и пехоты, поддержанных большим количеством авиации /над боевыми порядками корпусов в отдельные дни появлялось до 1500 самолетовылетов/.

12 июля с.г. произошло величайшее в истории отечественной войны танковое сражение в сквозной танковой атаке которого участвовало до 1500 танков с обеих сторон.

Нанеся огромный урон противнику в людях и технике и задержав дальнейшее продвижение врага, частям армии пришлось в течение некоторого времени вести бои оборонительного характера, отбивать яростные контратаки противника, одновременно переходя в атаки на некоторых участках фронта.

Наконец, когда противник оказался вынужденным отходить, армия начала преследовать отходящего врага, не давая ему возможности организовать оборону на выгодных рубежах. В процессе преследования армии пришлось непрерывно вести борьбу с мощными отрядами прикрытия /арьергардами/, что не могло не отразиться на темпе преследования.

Арьергарды противника, усиленные танками, в том числе тяжелыми, инженерными частями, большим количеством артиллерии и минометов, создавали довольно сильное затруднение для движения армии вперед. В силу этих причин и сплошного минирования, армия несла большие потери, как в людях, так и в технике и не могла дать больших темпов в наступлении.

НОВОЕ В ТАКТИКЕ И ТЕХНИКЕ ПРОТИВНИКА.-

1. Наличие большого количества танков Т-5, а также тяжелых танков Т-6 /ТИГР/ – 15- 20% от общего числа с довольно мощным вооружением, поставило перед командованием вопрос о способах борьбы с этими танками. Для разрешения этого вопроса требуется: -

а/ Танк Т-70, как имеющий слабое вооружение и броневую защиту – совершенно не способен вести бой в современных условиях – с вооружения с н я т ь.

б/ Танк Т-34 модернизировать, поставив на него 85 мм орудие и увеличив броню.

в/ Дать армии новый танк с более мощным вооружением /100- 107 мм/ и броневой защитой до 200 мм/ причем, прицельные приспособления должны обеспечивать ведение точного прицельного огня на дистанцию 3 км.

г/ Танки Т-34 должны гораздо больше маневрировать на поле боя, стремясь обходным маневром заходить и вести огонь в борт немецкого танка Т-6 и Т-5.

A copy of the first official document that put the number of tanks that supposedly took part in the fighting at Prokhorovka on 12 July 1943 at 1,500 – a page from the account produced by the 5th Guards Tank Army's headquarters. In the second paragraph it states: "On 12 July of this year there occurred the greatest tank battle in the history of this war; up to 1,500 tanks on both sides took part in the penetrating tank attack."

The cover of P.A. Rotmistrov's book *Tankovoe srazhenie pod Prokhorovkoi* [*Tank battle at Prokhorovka*], published in the Soviet Union in 1960 by the Voennoe Izdatel'stvo.

P.A. Rotmistrov at an interview with the editors of the *Izvestiia* newspaper. Seated in the center is the chief editor L.N. Tolkunov; standing behind him is the director of the Military Department V.P. Gol'tsov. This photograph was taken at the end of the 1960s (Author's personal archive).

Even though the Compendia didn't enter broad circulation and public libraries, the information that had been prepared only for the army's higher command staff became accessible to a wider audience – practically all of the senior officers and generals. Thus, the foundation for forming such a large myth about the greatest tank battle with penetrating attacks, countless tank rammings and junk heaps of knocked-out and destroyed German armor was laid, which with in postwar decades Soviet historians plied the country and the means of mass information.

Was the command of the 5th Guards Tank Army back then counting upon the fact that this figure would become so important and used so widely? I believe not; initially its task was strictly expedient, and only later, after the war, did Rotmistrov and others come to the realization of the advantages of this situation. Thus the generals, who were accessories to the creation of the legend, began to support it persistently and popularized it in their memoirs, books, articles and public addresses only beginning at the end of the 1950s.

Could officers of the General Staff and of the Headquarters of the Armored and Mechanized Forces have double-checked the information about 1,500 tanks and nipped its distribution in the bud? Yes, they could have, and without any particular effort. At this time, there was a "Group of officers of the Red Army General Staff with the headquarters of the armies and *fronts*" in the General Staff; its members monitored the execution of orders by the troops of the acting army, uncovered cases of the improper conducting of combat and use of forces, revealed negative tendencies that were beginning to take shape, and informed the leadership of the Red Army about these things through special messages and reports. These documents weren't subject to censorship and were sent directly from the composing authors to three addresses: the High Command of the Army and Navy, to which it was attached; the leadership of the group of officers of the General Staff within each *front*; and the Chief of the General Staff.

At the beginning of August 1943, just such an account arrived in Moscow from Major Chernik, a General Staff officer with the 5th Guards Tank Army's headquarters.[26] It was longer than General V.N. Baskakov's Account and significantly more informative from the point of view of synthesizing the experience of the combat actions. Its author also gives a very positive assessment of the actions of Rotmistrov's tankers and the results of the combat actions on 12 July, though makes no mention about a colossal battle involving 1,500 tanks. This account was accessible to all the members of the General Staff, including Vechnyi's own department. Colonel G.Ia. Sapozhnikov's subordinates could also have requested it. However, unfortunately the double-checking of information sent from the armies and *fronts* wasn't part of their responsibilities. The information from these documents was considered *a priori* to be true and it was immediately used in subsequent work. However other departments that were directly connected with the acting army often double-checked the contents of reports from the troops, properly assuming that in such an important matter as the collection and compilation of information, there couldn't be too much monitoring. I'll venture to assume that such an approach by the officers of Sapozhkov's department to their assigned work was connected with two considerations. First, the department wasn't busy with operational work, and thus the demands on its product weren't so rigorous. Second, as the archival sources show, all of its members were ordinary army officers, who not only had no experience in academic work, but also no experience of service in the headquarters of large bodies of troops. Commonly, officers who were considered unfit for service in the acting army, but who had combat experience, were sent to such posts. Incidentally, Colonel G.Ia. Sapozhkov had fought for more than a year at the front and was decorated for his personal courage in 1942, but after his severe wound he was assigned to staff duties.

Therefore I am far from the thought that all of the officers who used the materials of the 5th Guards Tank Army's Account knew that the information in it didn't correspond to actual fact. Nevertheless, the absence of a "filter" to screen out any type of unverified information in Colonel Sapozhkov's and General Vechnyi's departments lowered the value of their products and was one of the main reasons for the myth's transmission into the academic field (into the Academy of Armored and Mechanized Forces and then into mass media (first the military, then the civilian).

No less interesting was the process of introducing the myth to the broader public. Soviet military journalists should be considered the first historiographers of the Battle of Kursk and the battle for Prokhorovka. Already in the latter half of July 1943, after the failure of Operation Citadel, essays and articles on this subject appeared in the central newspapers, written by participants and eyewitnesses of the fighting. Their authors were primarily describing separate engagements and combat actions, the heroism of Soviet fighting men, and also attempted to extrapolate lessons from some of the experience acquired by the troops. It is especially worth dwelling on the article "Prokhorovskii platsdarm" ["The Prokhorovka staging area"] (See Appendix 1) written by the military correspondent Major K.I. Bukovsky[27] and published in *Krasnaia Zvezda* on 29 July

26 TsAMO RF, F. 5 gv. TA, Op. 4948, D. 51, LL. 1-27.

27 Konstantin Ivanovich Bukovsky, a Soviet journalist and writer; born on 5 May 1908 to a peasant family in the village of Inzhavina of the Tambov Guberniia. He worked in Moscow as an editor of factory newspapers. He joined the Red Army in March 1940 as a correspondent of the central army newspaper *Krasnaia Zvezda*. He served in the acting army from the first day of the Great Patriotic War, and was a special correspondent for *Krasnaia Zvezda* on the Western, Stalingrad, and Southwestern Fronts. For his consciencious work and personal bravery while carrying out his professional duties, Bukovsky was awarded

1943. For the first time in the open press, it told of the events that took place at a tiny, out-of-the-way railroad station in the vast expanses of the Central Black Earth zone, which later became a symbol of heroism and tragedy. His article also became one of the most important sources for the proliferation of the myth about Prokhorovka. The author didn't take a direct part in this battle; all of the information he laid out in the article came primarily from conversations with the command staff of the 5th Guards Tank Army, highly posted political workers, and staff officers of its headquarters. Thus the article's main thesis, which subsequently became the carcass of the legend about the Prokhorovka tank battle, almost precisely repeats the thoughts expressed by P.A. Rotmistrov and his service peers in their postwar books and articles. The main points were that the army assembled stealthily; the foe wasn't expecting such a powerful attack; the attack by our tankers proved to be penetrating; the fighting reached unprecedented scale and intensity, and proved "decisive in the failure of the Germans' entire July offensive on the Belgorod – Kursk axis." Just two weeks had passed since the end of combat actions at Kursk and G.T. Malenkov's commission, which was investigating the reasons for the high losses, had just wrapped up its work, and thus probably not all of the myth's aspects had been perfected. For example, Bukovsky's article doesn't present such fantastic numbers for the German tanks and assault guns that took part in the supposed head-on collision on 12 July 1943 (just around 400 in total); very modest (almost real) losses of the Germans (more than 100 combat machines) is given; and the main thing – the battle at Prokhorovka is called just "one of the largest in this war". I'll remind the reader that in the 5th Guards Tank Army's account that was sent to Moscow within a matter of days, completely different data wold be given: 700 German tanks and assault guns took part in the battle; the enemy's losses rose to 350 or 400 combat machines, and the battle on 12 July 1943 became "the greatest battle in the history of the Patriotic War".[28]

In a number of publications, as well as on Internet forums, one often comes across the assertion that the broader Soviet public learned about Prokhorovka only 10 years later from Colonel I.I. Markin's book *Kurskaia bitva* [*Battle of Kursk*], which came out in 1953.[29] However, this isn't quite so. The first work that became accessible to a civilian audience, in which the course of the Battle of Kursk, including the events at Prokhorovka, was laid out in considerable detail, was a small book (one can almost call it a pamphlet) by a group of military historians of the General Staff entitled *Bitva pod Kurskom. Kratkii ocherk* [Battle of Kursk. A brief sketch], which was published in 1945 by the same military publication house of the People's Commissar of Defense (Voenizdat) that would publish I.I. Markin's work a few years later.[30] This study had been designed for a broad

the combat Order of the Red Banner on 18 February 1943. From 1946 he worked for the journal *Ogonek*. He was the author of essays and books about village life, the peasantry and agriculture. He passed away in Moscow on 24 April 1974.

28 TsAMO RF, F. 5 gv. TA, Op. 4948, D. 19, L. 21.

29 I.I. Markin, *Kurskaia bitva* [*Battle of Kursk*] (Moscow: Voenizdat, 1953).

30 Il'ia Ivanovich Markin (1919-19?), Colonel (1952); in the Red Army from 1937. Markin was a participant in the fighting at the Khol'kin-Gol River. He served at the fronts of the Great Patriotic War from August 1941, first as the commander of a machine-gun company, then as the commander of a rifle battalion of the 152nd Rifle Division's 480th Rifle Regiment he fought on the Western Front. He was lightly wounded and concussed near Smolensk. On 17 November 1941 he enrolled in the courses at the Frunze Military Academy. He defended Moscow as part of a detachment of students. On 3 May 1942 he became the senior assistant of the chief of operations of the 9th Reserve Army, and then of the 24th Army (after 13 April 1943, the 4th Guards Army). He took part in the battles of Stalingrad and Kursk, and helped liberate Moldavia. In September 1943 he was badly wounded near Poltava. From 25 March 1944 until the end of the war, Markin was the deputy chief of operations with the 4th Guards Army's headquarters. Between 14 August 1946 and 24 April 1951, he served in the division of combat training of the Main Command of the Soviet Ground Forces. In 1948 he graduated from the Frunze Military Academy by correspondence. Between 3 May 1951 and 24 June 1954, he was an academic member of the editorial board for the journal

audience and had a rather large first printing. Even today, one can freely become familiar with its contents, not only in Russian metropolitan and specialized libraries, but in oblast public libraries as well. At its basis were all those same materials prepared by the officers of the departments for the study and use of the war's experience, including the actions of the 5th Guards Tank Army in July 1943. Thus it isn't surprising that the battle in the area of Prokhorovka was evaluated in it as "unprecedented in its scale", in which 1,500 tanks and self-propelled guns took part.[31]

I.I. Markin's book *Kurskaia bitva* published in 1953 didn't contain anything fundamentally new. Written on the sparse basis of propaganda sources, like articles from *Pravda*, I.V. Stalin's "masterwork" *O velikoi Otechestvennoi voine Sovetskogo Soiuza* [*On the Great Patriotic War of the Soviet Union*] and so forth, it almost fully repeated the work of the General Staff officers with all their same mistakes and exaggerations in the coverage of separate events. Its main feature was the fact that thanks to its appearance, the myth about the colossal tank battle at Prokhorovka reached an All-Union readership, which subsequently gave it the status of the official point of view. Nevertheless, this work became a noticeable event in the country's public life. At this time, the bibliography of the Battle of Kursk was meager and archives were closed to scholars, so the information in it received broad circulation. The information cited by the author was used in both academic and memoir literature, as well as in newspapers and journals – especially on the eve of holidays and famous dates.[32]

Scholars rarely pay attention to the second, reworked edition of I.I. Markin's book, which came out in 1958; it was a completely different book. The work was almost twice as long as the 1st Edition and it was substantially different in its contents. The 2nd Edition book's distinguishing feature and at the same time its strongest aspect was the author's use of Soviet combat and captured documents, and the use of information from German generals and field marshals when laying out the course of the combat operations in the Kursk area. For that time, this approach was a novelty. In addition, this 2nd Edition had one more important characteristic. In the mid-1950s, in the military-academic field, the supporters of a more critical approach to the official point of view regarding the battle for Prokhorovka and the total number of armored vehicles that took part in it was growing. I.I. Markin took this tendency into account and struck the passage about 1,500 tanks from his work, which clearly demonstrated that the author wasn't inclined to replicate the myth and was sincerely striving toward an academic approach when analyzing the given subject – even if there was the danger that he would provoke the wrath of veterans of the battle, who at that time were occupying high posts in the Soviet Armed Forces.

The year 1960 marked an important stage in the evolution of the myth. P.A. Rotmistrov's recollections of his participation in the fighting at Prokhorovka came out in the press, in which the information from his headquarters' Account prominently figured. The Marshal's authority was high, and thus even though his book was a pamphlet in essence, consisting of a several dozen pages, it substantially strengthened the legend about "the greatest tank battle at Prokhorovka" and gave a fresh impetus to its distribution. Rotmistrov's recollections quickly entered the Soviet propaganda system and began to be widely printed in all of the All-Union journals and the collections of recollections of Kursk veterans, which were being actively prepared for publication on the eve of the 20th Anniversary of the Battle of Kursk. In some of these publications, the "panygerics" of the fighting for Prokhorovka were repeated several times. It was called "unprecedented in scale" and "the largest in the history of the Second World War", and as a compulsory matter, they repeated

---

Voennaia mysl'. He retired from active duty in 1954.

31 N.M. Zamiatin, P.S. Boldyrev, F. D. Vorob'ev, N.F. Artem'ev and I.V. Parot'kin, *Bitva pod Kurskom. Kratkii ocherk* [*Battle of Kursk. A brief outline*] (Moscow: Voenizdat, 1945).

32 For example, see F. Selivanova, *Kurskaia bitva* [*Battle of Kursk*] (1956); and *Kurskaia bitva: Iz vospominanii uchastnikov* [*Battle of Kursk: From recollections of participants*] (Kursk: Kurskoe knizhkoe izdatel'svo, 1959).

that "more than 1,500 tanks and self-propelled guns took part in it."[33] Thus, it was no coincidence that when the question arose about covering the events of 12 July 1943 in the next volume of the *Istoriia Velikoi Otechestvennoi voiny* [*History of the Great Patriotic War*], its editorial board used the recollections of P.A. Rotmistrov alongside the materials from General P.P. Vechnyi's department and publications from the latter half of the 1940s and the 1950s. In addition, as one of the members of the authors' collective G.A. Koltunov told me, for the editorial board of the six-volume history, it was very important that the information from the three groups of sources all converged around the main point – the assessment of the battle, and that one and the same figure of 1,500 tanks figured in each of them. Back then this was considered proof of its veracity.

In this fashion, the myth created by the headquarters of the 5th Guards Tank Army, having passed through the main channels of Soviet mass information (the General Staff's Compendium of the War's Best Practices, lectures in the Academy of Armored and Mechanized Forces, the book by the group of officers of the General Staff, publications in the civilian means of mass information and in the memoir literature) was included in Volume 3 of the *Istoriia Velikoi Otechestvennoi voiny*, having been somewhat tweaked. Thereby it received the status of official information. The corrections to it were insignificant. Instead of "the greatest tank battle in the history of the war", the fighting on 12 July was given a more modest title: "one of the most grueling tank battles of the Great Patriotic War", while the figure of 1,500 tanks and self-propelled guns that took part in it remained unchanged.[34]

If up until this moment there were doubts in the accuracy of this number in the field of military historians and instructors of military academies (in unofficial get-togethers, sharp arguments were going around on this subject), then now it was useless to try to refute it and hazardous for career growth. However, by the end of the 1950s an informal group of highly-posted military men had come together, who didn't like the activity of P.A. Rotmistrov and his supporters in glorifying the role of the 5th Guards Tank Army's command in the battle for Prokhorovka by such dubious means as forcing inflated assessments and figures on the public. For example, as already mentioned above, Marshal of the Soviet Union G.K. Zhukov totally believed that on 12 July 1943, nothing particular happened at the railroad station that affected the war's outcome. He maintained that the combat actions that were only of secondary importance according to both their scope and scale were so widely known only through the efforts of P.A. Rotmistrov and called upon him to be more modest. The Marshal even included a rather sharp rebuff for the former tank army commander in his memoirs, although the censors didn't allow it. The text that was stricken back then was published in the 10th Edition of his memoirs (which was expanded according to Zhukov's own original manuscript).[35] Other generals acted more diplomatically, but weren't hiding their negative attitude toward such myth-making. These were people respected in the Soviet Army and among the people, the opinion of which was difficult to discount.

Sensing the serious dissatisfaction among his comrades-in-arms and knowing full-well that their reproaches were just, P.A. Rotmistrov already in 1963 made an attempt to amend the figure of 1,500 tanks and self-propelled guns down to 1,200. In an interview published in Issue No. 7 of the *Voenno-istoricheskii zhurnal*, he reduces the number of tanks and self-propelled guns of his own tank army that took part in the battle southwest of Prokhorovka from 800 to 500, but does so gradually, not abruptly. As before, Pavel Alekseevich maintained that the enemy introduced up to 700 tanks and assault guns in the battle southwest of Prokhorovka, while "the forces of

33 *V ogne Kurskoi bitvy: Iz vospominanii uchastnikov boev* [*In the fire of the Battle of Kursk: From the recollections of veterans of the fighting*] (Kursk: Kurskoe knizhnoe izdatel'stvo, 1963), p. 9 and 301.

34 *Istoriia Velikoi Otechestvennoi voiny, Tom 3* [*History of the Great Patriotic War, Volume 3* (Moscow: Voenizdat, 1964), p. 271.

35 G.K. Zhukov, *Vosponinaniia i razmyshleniia*, 10th Ed., Vol. 3 (Moscow: Novosti, 1990), p. 57.

the 5th Guards Tank Army's first echelon that fought directly with this grouping had in their operational inventory a little more than 500."[36] Accordingly, in this area, it wasn't 1,500 tanks and self-propelled guns that took part in the meeting tank clash, as he had maintained previously, but 1,200 combat machines. However, in the Account produced by the 5th Guards Tank Army's headquarters, it was written that both sides had a combined total of more than 1,600 armored vehicles, and the army had sent 100 of its own to the south of Prokhorovka (to the army's left flank), so where are the other 300 Soviet tanks?

In order not to renounce the already widely-circulated figure, Pavel Alekseevich begins to put forward a new legend that "the second echelon and army reserve were activated in order to liquidate the emerging threat of being enveloped by the enemy on both flanks." Accordingly, the reader was supposed to see that he could have sent these 300 combat machines either to his right flank (to the area of Ostren'kii, in the sector of the neighboring 5th Guards Army) or committed them into the fighting southwest of Prokhorovka Station. In actuality, in the course of 12 July 1943 three mechanized corps, two tank brigades and a separate tank regiment, having a combined total of 234 tanks were moved up to both of the army's flanks. However, what to make of the following facts?

Firstly, the movement of a portion of the army's strength to other directions was noted in the Account, but nevertheless, back in 1943, this in no way influenced the opinion of the Military Council (and of P.A. Rotmistrov himself), who asserted that 1,500 tanks took part in the meeting battle directly southwest of the railroad station. Secondly, in order to agree with the information given by Rotmistrov in the interview, it turns out that 300 tanks had been sent to the army's right flank. However, in its headquarters Account it is given that just two brigades – a mechanized and a tank brigade[37] – which had a combined total of 92 tanks had departed for this area (and moreover took no part in fighting on this day).[38] Where, then, are the more than 200 other combat machines? Considering that the Account and the other combat documents that we are examining were back then still classified, and the former tank army commander had to get out of an awkward situation and save face, he didn't disdain turning to any other deceptions and had no concern that anyone might point out his "juggling of the numbers". Many senior officers and generals who had occasion to be associated on close terms with the former general after the war testified to the fact that by this time Pavel Alekseevich was fully aware of both the actual state of affairs in the sector of his tank army on 12 July 1943 and of the false figures that had been sent by his headquarters to higher command. At the end of the 1990s and beginning of the 2000s, colleagues of Pavel Alekseevich at the Academy of Armored and Mechanized Forces and their students more than once visited the museum in Prokhorovka where I was working as the deputy director for academic work, and when meeting with museum staff recalled that among his circle of professionals the former tank army commander was more forthcoming and accurate in his assessments of what happened back in the July days of 1943. For example, in 2008 in a conversation with me Lieutenant General N.G. Orlov recalled a discussion that had started up in the course of an academic seminar, which was devoted to the problem of using tanks when on the defense, which was held in 1963 under P.A. Rotmistrov's leadership. On that occasion, the Marshal was asked several uncomfortable questions, including some like: "What were the reasons why the 5th Guards Tank Army, having a numerical superiority in armor, wasn't able to defeat the enemy on 12 July 1943?" and "In your memoirs you write that the enemy lost 400 tanks and self-propelled

36 "Rasskazyvaiut komandarmy" ["Army commanders relate"] *Voenno-istoricheskii zhurnal*, No. 7 (1963), p. 77.

37 TsAMO RF, F. 5 gv. TA, Op. 4948, D. 19, L. 9.

38 V.N. Zamulin, *Zasekrechennaia Kurskaia bitva* [*Classified Battle of Kursk*] (Moscow: Iauza/EKSMO, 2008), p. 770.

guns on just one day at Prokhorovka; how can this number be considered accurate, or verified by eye, if after all the Germans retained possession of the battlefield?"

To such probing questions, the Marshal gave approximately the following answer:

> We planned one thing, but in reality something different took place. Firstly, the Front's artillery in point of fact gave us no support; the Germans prevented it. The heavy self-propelled artillery regiment and the anti-tank artillery brigade that had been assigned to reinforce us, didn't show up. Secondly, two times in succession they changed the area for the deployment of the shock corps, as a result of which we were forced to deploy in a defile, while the enemy on 11 July had occupied favorable ground for a defense. Thirdly, our tanks were inferior to the German tanks; the army had a lot of light tanks. Thus we stopped the enemy, while taking large losses. The high losses are also my fault as the commander. Time was short; I didn't insist that a normal artillery preparation of the enemy's forward edge be conducted before the army launched the counterattack, that we be given the opportunity to conduct a thorough reconnaissance, and when planning, have access as well to the Front's intelligence means. After all we were told that the Germans' main forces were operating against Katukov's army, but it turned out otherwise. As a result, we didn't make an advance and didn't smash the SS corps; the intended breach was firmly protected. As concerns the German losses, then openly speaking, the figure emerged in the headquarters of our army from the reports of units. But after all on the forward edge, frequently the guns of several of our units were firing at one and the same tank, and having knocked it out, each unit claimed it as its own success. As a result, a single destroyed tank stands on the battlefield, but 3-4 are reported, and at times even a dozen.

Thus, immediately after the Battle of Kursk Rotmistrov's headquarters spun tales about Prokhorovka, in order to downplay the bitterness of the major defeat when introducing the tank army into the battle, and strove to shift the responsibility for the defeat onto other shoulders, but after the war everything followed a well-worn path. The tank army commander only now and again made slight adjustments: for open publications – a dash of more vibrant colors and a little more fancy, but for those professional military men – a little more frank and honest conversation.

At the moment when Rotmistrov's interview with *Voenno-istoricheskii zhurnal* came out, Volume 3 of the *Istoriia Velikoi Otechestvennoi voiny* had already gone to print. Thus, a murky situation emerged in 1964. Some authors, relying on P.A. Rotmistrov's latest statements, used the figure of 1,200 tanks and self-propelled guns, while the official history of the Great Patriotic War already gave a figure of 1,500 tanks and self-propelled guns. Moreover, even the direct participants of an academic conference dedicated to the 25th Anniverary of the victory at Kursk, Marshals of the Soviet Union A.M. Vasilevsky and K.S. Moskalenko submitted papers for the conference that used the new, lower figure.[39] By the end of the 1960s, it was no longer possible to ignore the situation, when two different numbers figured in official publications.

Thus, an order arrived from the Ideology Department of the CPSU Central Committee to the leadership of the USSR Ministry of Defense's Institute of Military History, which had been established in 1966: Without making any fundamental changes, in an academic publication somehow explain that both figures were essentially correct. At the same time, no additional research could be done on the question. In other words, the Institute had to update and restore harmony to the myth about Prokhorovka. Colonal G.A. Koltunov received this difficult task. In his part of the manuscript of the book about the Battle of Kursk that was written together with a colleague of the

39 Major General I.V. Parot'kin [ed.], *Kurskaia bitva* [*Battle of Kursk*] (Moscow: Nauka, 1970), p. 82, 112.

Institute of Military History Colonel B.G. Solov'ev, he attempted to find a compromise between the hardened point of view about 1,500 tanks and self-propelled guns, the new figure of 1,200 armored vehicles, and the opinion of those who were rejecting the significant scale of the battle.

In the book, he divided the enemy grouping of 700 armored vehicles, giving by P.A. Rotmistrov, into two areas. Supposedly, this was the total number of the II SS Panzer Corps that was attacking from the southwest (up to 500 tanks and assault guns) and the III Panzer Corps that was advancing toward Prokhorovka from the south (up to 200 tanks and assault guns). In addition, he plainly indicated that the SS Panzer Corps had three divisions, and discarded the assertion by the staff officers of the 5th Guards Tank Army that the 11th Panzer Division and Panzergrenadier Division *Grossdeutschland* had both participated in the fighting for Prokhorovka. As Georgii Avtonomovich told me in 1999, in his opinion this might somewhat soften the anger of those who considered both of Rotmistrov's versions sheer fantasy. At the same time, his book left the armor strength of the 5th Guards Tank Army within the boundaries of those figures cited by its headquarters in the Account: 800, while at the same time clarifying that up to 700 operated on the "tank field" southwest of Prokhorovka, while 100 became part of Trufanov's detachment that operated south of Prokhorovka. In addition, Koltunov remained silent about the brigades sent into the sector of the 5th Guards Army. This of course might prompt the dissatisfaction of the former tank army commander, but a scandal shouldn't necessarily flame up. So at the end of his explanation in the book, G.A. Koltunov concisely noted, "Thus southwest of Prokhorovka up to 1,200 tanks and self-propelled guns from both sides took part in the fighting, and south of Prokhorovka, up to 300 armored vehicles. With regard for both areas, up to 1,500 armored vehicles took part in the tank battle west and south of Prokhorovka."[40] Moreover, in order to reduce the significance of the two paragraphs, in which Koltunov's point of view was laid out, the authors placed them not in the main text, but in the form of footnotes.

All of this taken together played its role, and from that point on both figures received official approval. That's how a "revamped" version of the myth about Prokhorovka arose, which continues to one or another extent to be present in the studies and publications of Russian historians to the present day. The reasons are several. At the end of the 20th Century, the natural process began of the retirement from active work of the Soviet military historians, but their replacement by qualified specialists, capable of taking all the best from that which has been done and pushing forward, couldn't happen right away in connection with the collapse of the Soviet Union and the societal convulsions that ensued. In addition, the development of the science of history implies the search and introduction of new documentary sources into academic circulation, but to work in the archives is a costly business, very laborious and painstaking, and not everyone is up to take it on. Thus the authors of a significant portion of the publications, from which the young generation of Russians today find out about our past, travel along a well-worn path: they comment upon already published facts without adequate study of the situation at the fronts and the available materials, subordinating them to their own view of the problem. That's how new legends and myths about the Battle of Kursk are still being created today.

40 G.A. Koltunov and B.G. Solov'ev, *Kurskaia bitva* [*Battle of Kursk*] (Moscow: Voenizdat, 1970), p. 174.

Appendix I

The Prokhorovka Staging Area

The fighting in the Prokhorovka staging area played the role of a turning point in the German offensive and the counteroffensive of our forces on the Belgorod – Kursk axis. Just like the well-known fighting in the Kotel'nikovo staging area in 1942, where the German shock grouping that was advancing toward Stalingrad was defeated, here select enemy tank forces that were conducting an attack toward Kursk, were stopped in a meeting battle, then crushed and hurled back.

The area of the Prokhorovka train station not for the first time was an arena of savage fighting and a major German defeat. In the first winter campaign our troops encircled up to two enemy infantry regiments, tanks and a large quantity of artillery in Prokhorovka. Last winter our tank and motorized rifle units caught a counterattacking group of enemy mobile forces in pincers in the Prokhorovka – Belenikhino triangular area and destroyed it. In the spring, during the German counteroffensive, the final attacks by German tanks were shattered on the Prokhorovka staging area, and the enemy was shoved back to the line of the Belgorod heights. Now events once again flared up in these same places, but now on an even larger scale.

The situation by the start of the fighting in the Prokhorovka staging area came together in the following manner. The enemy, having lost hope to break through along the Belgorod – Oboian' highway, initiated a regrouping of his tank forces, shifting them to the right-hand side of the attacking wedge. The aim of the regrouping consisted of overcoming our defenses to their entire depth with an attack to the northeast in the direction of Prokhorovka and further along the railroad. By changing the axis of attack, the enemy was hoping to strike weak links of defense and achieve that which he hadn't been able to accomplish in the area of the highway – that is to say, to break through to Kursk or even east of Kursk. Meanwhile, fighting was going on southwest and southeast of Prokhorovka. In the first of these sectors, our tank units with flanking counterattacks were preventing the Germans from expanding the salient, while in the second the Germans were launching an auxiliary attack, striving to link up with its main grouping in the future.

In general, a totally unique situation had been created. Two sides of the Prokhorovka – Belenikhino triangular area were enveloped with meeting battles, while in the area of Prokhorovka itself the operation's final stage had ripened. To this place, at the base of the triangular area, concentrated strikes by German tanks were to be launched from two directions. Our tank formation moved out to this area in order to parry the enemy attacks. It received an assignment – to counterattack the main German grouping and to paralyze its activity in a decisive manner on the right flank.

A small stream [the Psel River] was separating the antagonists. At first glance it wasn't a serious obstacle, but reconnaissance showed that the wooded ground along the banks of the stream, which was cut by deep ravines, was extremely unsuitable for tank actions, and in places here and there completely inaccessible to them. To attack the enemy from this line meant to deprive ourselves of the advantages of surprise and rapidity of actions. The tanks, tightly constricted in maneuvering, might suffer losses without achieving success. The sector between the railroad and a different stream, which flowed along side this railroad, offered significantly greater advantages. The broad field with shallow balkas, gullies and patches of woods gave the tanks the necessary room and freedom of maneuver in the course of the attack.

Our tanks, which shifted to the area of Prokhorovka itself, took up jumping-off positions here. At this moment events were also taking place on the enemy's side, which determined the nature and development of the looming battle. The German side, obviously motivated by the same desire to avoid the line that was unsuitable for tanks, had moved his tank divisions to this same sector, toward Prokhorovka. The coincidence happened not only in the place of operations, but also in time. Two waves of tanks were moving simultaneously to meet each other and collided 3 kilometers outside of Prokhorovka. One of the largest tank battles this year flared up at the Komsomolets State Farm.

The appearance of our tanks on the battlefield came as a complete surprise for the enemy. Their movement concealed by the night as well as their artful regrouping with the taking up of jumping off positions had totally slipped the attention of German intelligence. The enemy, conviced that he would only have to deal with our infantry and artillery, was shocked by the sudden collision with large tank forces. From the very start of the fighting, the Germans were showing confusion and yielded the initiative to our forces.

The first echelon of attacking Soviet tanks at full speed sliced into the combat formations of the German tank column. The ranks became intermingled. The German Pz V tanks, deprived of the superiority of their main gun in close combat, were firing at our T-34s almost at point-blank range. The penetrating attack was so swift, that the forward ranks of our tanks passed through the entire enemy formation and emerged in the rear of the enemy column.

The broad field turned out to be cramped for the enormous mass of dueling tanks. Up to 400 heavy, medium and light tanks took part in this battle on the German side, accompanied by a large quantity of self-propelled artillery. These were the enemy's shock forces – divisions of the SS Panzer Corps. The fighting continued until late in the evening. The tanks that had locked horns in one gigantic clump were now unable to separate. Colliding with each other head-on, ramming each other in the flank and shooting each other up from the rear, they fought until darkness ended the battle. The heavy turrets were flying from the heavy German tanks, and shells were piercing the armor through and through. More than a hundred enemy tanks and self-propelled guns were left burning on the battlefield.

Our tankers, who had launched a meeting attack against the SS tank divisions, were victorious. The spearhead of the enemy armored wedge, which had been blunted in the area of the Oboian' highway was ultimately broken on the Prokhorovka staging area, from where the Germans had been planning to conduct a jump to Kursk. The battlefield remained in no-man's land and on it for the next several days stood the blackened carcasses of tanks that couldn't be removed from the battlefield.

To the right of the tank clash, in the neighboring sector, an infantry battle that was just as bitter went on. Here our rifle corps counterattacked the enemy and stopped him on a line of water west of Prokhorovka.

On this same day, 12 July, at the village of Rzhavets to the southeast of Prokhorovka, our units met with a different column of German tanks that was striving to link up with the main grouping. The fighting that unfolded in this sector was characterized by the successful counter-maneuver of our anti-tank and field artillery, as well as by a successful flanking counter attack by tanks.

The enemy struck the center of our defensive line, where more than 10 of our artillery batteries had been concentrated. The massed attack by enemy tanks was driven back with a powerful storm of anti-tank artillery fire, with losses for the enemy that were heavy. Having rolled back to their jumping-off positions and having restored order, the enemy no longer repeated attacks against the center, but tried to penetrate the flanks. Scouts reported that German tanks were moving to bypass the neighboring village and gathering in the ravines. All of the artillery batteries were shifted from their firing positions in the center and sent to the flank.

There was no small risk in such a counter-maneuver with the entire mass of artillery. The enemy might have detected it, and either interrupted it with an attack, or else re-directed his forces to the center again. The movement of the guns under the observation and exposure to enemy aircraft, but the calculations of our command proved correct. Having skillfully conducted the maneuver, the batteries had moved into previously prepared positions by the moment of the German attack against the flank of the defense and once again threw back the enemy. The German attempts to probe the boundaries between our units and to break through simultaneously on both flanks were also parried by the counter-maneuver of the artillery. The batteries were maneuvering with fire and were conducting rapid shifts along the front, moving up to meet the German tanks.

At a critical moment of the fighting, when the Germans managed with the help of air support to overrun one sector of our artillery positions and penetrated into the defenses with a large group of his tanks, the commander of the "N" tank regiment received an order to strike the exposed enemy flank and restore the situation. In an unequal combat the regiment suffered losses, but it stopped the advance of the enemy column and plugged the gap.

The fighting in the Prokhorovka staging area and at the village of Rzhavets was the final stage of the German offensive in the Belgorod – Kursk direction. The enemy, which had been bled white, was forced to abandon the converging attacks in the direction of Prokhorovka and went over to a defense in the sectors of the main and auxiliary attacks. However, the fighting in the Prokhorovka staging area didn't end with this. Several days later it was resumed at the initiative of our forces, which had gone over to a counteroffensive out of the Prokhorovka area and west of there.

The Germans had dug in on the line of the Prokhorovka hills and in strongpoints along both sides of the railroad. They had formed two small salients in the line of our front. Our tank units and the Guards rifle corps that was attacking on the right with flanking counterattacks cut off both salients, and having taken key positions, broke the resistance of the enemy troops.

The fighting for the hills to the southwest of Prokhorovka was marked by particular stubbornness. The Germans had time to create a system of interlocked firing positions in this area, having brought up a large quantity of artillery and mortar batteries. The enemy had mined the roads and ravines. The German infantry was using old trenches and digging new trenches for the defense, strengthening them with a system of bunkers and machine-gun nests. The Germans had deployed their batteries on the reverse slopes and crests of hills with a calculation for frontal and flanking fire.

The outcome of the battle was decided by a breakthrough by our tanks, assisted by our air force, through the combat positions of the German infantry with an emergence in the area of the artillery positions. The German anti-tank areas were to a significant extent suppressed by the fire of our artillery. In the sector west of Prokhorovka, the Guards rifle corps broke through the German defenses on the line of the stream, and energetically exploiting the success, advanced to the south. The enemy strongpoints to the left of the railroad bed were attacked by other rifle units that had gone over to a counteroffensive. As a result the German troops, boxed into a triangular area, were compelled to roll back to the south toward Belgorod with losses.

The next stage of fighting in the Prokhorovka staging area was characterized by bitter clashes between our forward units and the retreating enemy. The German troops initially offered strong opposition on intermediary lines, having organized a mobile defense with the use of villages and natural obstacles, but already on the second day the fighting of our units took on the nature of a pursuit. Our mobile groups, springing forward from the Prokhorovka trampoline, entered the breakthrough and strove to cut off the retreating enemy. Soon the Germans were thrown back to their jumping-off positions that they were occupying prior to 5 July, and the salient, which had been driven into our defenses at the cost of enormous losses, was liquidated.

In the fighting in the Prokhorovka staging area, select German tank and infantry forces suffered a major defeat. Here not only the great courage of the Soviet troops that were defending their native soil against the foe and the superb combat qualities of our army's men and equipment were on full display, but also the superiority of the Soviet tactic of maneuvering over the German tactics. This staging area will enter the history of the Patriotic War as a place of major conflicts, which determined the failure of the German offensive on the Belgorod – Kursk direction.

Major K. Bukovsky, Acting Red Army[1]

1 Bukovsky, K., "Prokhorovskii platsdarm" ["Prokhorovka staging area"], *Krasnaia Zvezda*, 29 July 1943.

Index

INDEX OF PEOPLE

INDEX OF PLACES

INDEX OF GERMAN MILITARY FORMATIONS & UNITS

INDEX OF SOVIET MILITARY FORMATIONS & UNITS

INDEX OF GENERAL & MISCELLANEOUS TERMS